"A magnificent achievement to the oral-history sources available on the American West. This collection of Ricker's interviews provides a rich resource on the Old West for the scholar and those interested in an accurate analysis of the lives of Indians, soldiers and settlers.... The strength of the volumes is in the stories told by the interviewees, with their perspectives on key historical events from the Old West, which is equally suited to the student and the academic scholar."—*American Studies*

"The interviews are a gold mine of information, and researchers will be rewarded for digging through them.... Ricker left Nebraska and the West an important source of information, and Jensen has made this more user-friendly by his organization and commentary."—*Great Plains Quarterly*

"Ricker proved himself a patient and meticulous oral interviewer, giving voice to people mostly ignored by historians of his day. His subjects document the Ghost Dance as a genuine religious movement, not as a 'craze' as described in white accounts.... Editor Richard Jensen provides a true service, for having translated Ricker's arcane handwritten notes into readable form and for his endnotes filled with biographical information."—*Kansas History*

"Priceless sources of information that offer more balanced perspectives on events than were accepted at the time.... There is no doubt that the voices and stories captured here in both books will be of significant value."—*Lincoln Journal Star*

"Anyone wishing to know more about Wounded Knee, the Little Bighorn, the history of the western frontier in general, and many other topics will certainly want to refer to Jensen's work."—*North Dakota History*

Eli S. Ricker worked for the Office of Indian Affairs in Washington DC when this portrait was taken in 1916. RG1227.PH:1-4

Voices of the American West
Volume 1

The Indian Interviews
of Eli S. Ricker, 1903-1919

Edited and with an introduction by
Richard E. Jensen

UNIVERSITY OF NEBRASKA PRESS
LINCOLN AND LONDON

© 2005 by the Board of Regents of the University of Nebraska
All rights reserved
Manufactured in the United States of America

All illustrations are courtesy of the Nebraska State Historical Society.

Set in Bulmer by Tseng Information Systems, Inc.
Designed by R. W. Boeche.

Library of Congress Cataloging-in-Publication Data
Ricker, Eli Seavey, 1843–1926.
Voices of the American West, volume 1: the Indian interviews of Eli S. Ricker, 1903–1919 /
Eli S. Ricker; edited and with an introduction by Richard E. Jensen.
p. cm.
Includes bibliographical references and index.
ISBN-13: 978-0-8032-3949-4 (hardcover: alk. paper)
ISBN-10: 0-8032-3949-1 (hardcover: alk. paper)
ISBN-13: 978-0-8032-3996-8 (paper: alk. paper)
1. Indians of North America—Historiography. 2. Indians of North America—Interviews.
3. Pioneers—United States—Interviews. 4. European Americans—Interviews. 5. Indians of North
America—History. 6. Frontier and pioneer life—United States—History. 7. Ricker, Eli Seavey,
1843–1926—Relations with Indians. I. Jensen, Richard E. II. Title.
E76.8.R53 2005
970.004'97—dc22   2005012016

ISBN-13: 978-0-8032-3967-8 [vol. 2, hardcover]
ISBN-10: 0-8032-3967-x [vol. 2, hardcover]
ISBN-13: 978-0-8032-3997-5 [vol. 2, paper]

Contents

List of Illustrations   viii
Acknowledgments   ix
Introduction   xi
Map: The West of Eli S. Ricker   xxx

Chapter One: The Garnett and Wells Interviews

1. William Garnett   1
    Biography, Treaties and Treaty Commissions, Killing of Frank Appleton, The Surround of Red Cloud and Red Leaf, Mackenzie-Dull Knife fight, Indian scouts, Crazy Horse, Sun Dances, Pine Ridge Reservation, Wounded Knee, Frank Grouard, Yellow Bear–John Richard Jr. episode, Flagpole at Red Cloud Agency

2. Philip F. Wells   121
    Biography, Sioux customs, language and religion, Little Bighorn, The Messiah/Ghost Dance, Wounded Knee, Drexel Mission fight, Agents and agency service, Sioux tribes and bands, Minnesota war

Chapter Two: The Ghost Dance and Wounded Knee

1. Short Bull. The Messiah, Ghost Dance   189

2. Joseph Horn Cloud. Wounded Knee, Wounded Knee casualties   191

3. Dewey Beard. Wounded Knee   208

4. Louis Mousseau. Wounded Knee, Pine Ridge Reservation   226

5. William Palmer. Wounded Knee   232

6. George Little Wound. Wounded Knee   232

7. Ed Janis. Wounded Knee fatalities   233

8. William Peano. Wounded Knee fatalities, Pine Ridge Reservation   233

9. Paddy Starr. Wounded Knee and burials   237

10. Frank Feather. Wounded Knee fatalities   239

11. Man Above. Wounded Knee, Indian scouts   240

12. Standing Soldier. Wounded Knee, Indian scouts, Crazy Horse   241

13. Creighton Yankton. Wounded Knee hearsay   247

14. William Denver McGaa. Pine Ridge Reservation, Wounded Knee, Indian scouts   248

15. James Garvie. Poncas, Wounded Knee, Winnebagos, Santees   251

16. John Shangrau. Reynolds's Powder River campaign, Wounded Knee, Cheyenne outbreak, Crazy Horse   256

Chapter Three: The Old West—Indians and Indian Fights

1. Chipps. Crazy Horse   273

2. American Horse. Grattan fight, Fetterman fight, Red Cloud, Biography, Crazy Horse   277

3. Charles A. Eastman. S. D. Hinman, Crazy Horse   285

4. Mrs. Richard Stirk. Biography, Crazy Horse, Saunders escape on Cache la Poudre   287

5. Louie Bordeaux. James Bordeaux, Frank Grouard, Crazy Horse, Pine Ridge Reservation   290

6. Respects Nothing. Little Bighorn   302

7. Moses Flying Hawk. Little Bighorn, Sibley Scout   307

8. Standing Bear. Little Bighorn   309

9. Nick Ruleau. Little Bighorn, Fetterman fight   311

10. Iron Hawk. Christian Indians, Little Bighorn   314

11. Frank S. Shively. Crow Indian customs,
    Little Bighorn, Indians and priests, Chief Blackfoot,
    Indian scouts at Little Bighorn   318

12. Two Moons. Battles at Tongue River,
    Rosebud, and Little Bighorn   321

13. Henry Twist. Black Hills treaty   325

14. Charles Turning Hawk. Black Hills treaty   325

15. George Sword. Biography, Crazy Horse,
    Wagon Box fight   326

16. Frank Salaway. Biography, Crazy Horse,
    Grattan fight, Ash Hollow fight, 1865 Horse
    Creek fight, Pine Ridge Reservation   330

17. Red Cloud and Clarence Three Stars. Treaties,
    Black Hills, Grattan fight, Tribal government
    and politics, Lightning Creek incident, Allotments
    in severalty   344

18. Alfred N. Coe. Dakota ministry, Two Sticks case   355

19. Jacob White Eye. Haircuts at Pine Ridge   358

20. Eagle Elk. Pine Ridge Reservation   358

21. Little Wolf. Cheyenne Indians   360

22. Peter Shangrau. Ute Indians, 1906   361

23. Maggie Palmer. Janis family   367

24. Mrs. Nicholas Janis. Nicholas Janis   367

25. Mrs. Julia Bradford. Henry C. Clifford   368

26. Nettie Elizabeth Goings.
    Goings family, Frank Grouard   369

27. William Girton. Bull Bear/Red Cloud   370

28. William Young. Henry Young   370

29. Mrs. Charles C. Clifford. Biography,
    Saunders escape on Cache la Poudre   371

30. Amos Ross. Biography, Pine Ridge ministry   373

   Appendix A. Forts   375
   Appendix B. Agencies   377
   Notes   381
   Bibliography   463
   Index   475

Illustrations
following page 272

Photographs
1. William Garnett
2. Brothers Dewey Beard, Joseph Horn Cloud, and White Lance
3. Chipps and his wife
4. Mass grave at Wounded Knee
5. Ricker's shorthand
6. American Horse and his wife

Figures
1. Phillip F. Wells's map of Wounded Knee
2. Joseph Horn Cloud's map of Wounded Knee
3. Paddy Starr's map of Wounded Knee
4. William D. McGaa's sketch of the Stronghold
5. Respects Nothing's Little Bighorn
6. Standing Bear's Little Bighorn
7. Nick Ruleau's Little Bighorn
8. Two Moons' Little Bighorn
9. Frank Salaway's Grattan fight

Acknowledgments

Due to the broad scope of the subject matter covered in the Ricker tablets, it has been necessary to elicit the expertise of several specialists. Without their contributions, the Ricker tablets might continue to languish in the recesses of the archives. Richard G. Hardorff has graciously given his permission to quote notes from two of his books, *The Surrender and Death of Crazy Horse* (Spokane: Arthur H. Clark Co., 1998) and *Lakota Recollections of the Custer Fight: New Sources of Indian-Military History* (Lincoln: University of Nebraska Press, 1997). Donald F. Danker extended the same courtesy in allowing the use of his endnotes from "The Wounded Knee Interviews of Eli S. Ricker," *Nebraska History* 62 (1981): 151–243. Eli Paul was generous enough to let me quote his biography of Sam Deon published in *Autobiography of Red Cloud: War Leader of the Oglalas* (Helena: Montana Historical Society Press, 1997). Thomas Buecker, curator, Fort Robinson Museum, answered numerous questions and recommended many sources for answers to others that had perplexed this editor. Gary H. Dunham, Native American Studies editor, and W. Clark Whitehorn, former history editor, University of Nebraska Press, offered many helpful suggestions. Mary Grindahl deserves a special thanks for the many hours she spent transcribing portions of the tablets.

Introduction

In the early 1900s Eli S. Ricker began gathering data for a book he planned to call "The Final Conflict Between the Red Men and the Palefaces." While the title would raise many an eyebrow today, Ricker's viewpoint is another matter. Unlike most of his contemporaries, he did not see the European advance across the American continent as a glorious conquest of the wilderness. Instead, Ricker recognized the terrible consequences for the Native Americans who faced this avalanche in their homeland. Ricker had been working on his book for only a few months when he wrote a brief note that summarized his views:

> When the white man landed on the shores of the New World, an eclipse, blacker than any that ever darkened the sun, blighted the hopes and happiness of the native people, races then living in tranquillity upon their own soil.[1]

In addition to chastising the whites, Ricker had the audacity to suggest that history as seen from a Native American point of view was as valid as the white man's history. In the course of his research he would interview at least fifty Native Americans about conditions and battles on the Plains in the last half of the nineteenth century.

Eli Seavey Ricker was born on September 29, 1843, the son of Bradford W. Ricker and Catherine Harmon Ricker. The family lived on a farm near the little town of Brownfield, Maine, until 1855, when they moved to a farm near Oneida in northwestern Illinois.[2]

Young Ricker planned to enter Lombard University in the fall of 1862. Then a call came for volunteers to fight in the Civil War and on August 9 he enlisted in Company I, 102d Illinois Volunteer Infantry. The regiment was stationed near Nashville, Tennessee, where it guarded railroad lines in the vicinity. Near the end of February 1864, they marched across Tennessee into the northwest corner of Georgia. During May and June the 102d was engaged in five major encounters, resulting in thirty-one fatalities. Ricker described only one close call during this campaign. His company was crossing an open field when Confederate sharpshooters opened fire from a grove of trees. Ricker admitted, "It was a miracle that none of our men got harmed." In early September his unit entered Atlanta, Georgia, and he wrote, "Atlanta has been a beautiful place [but] it is now invested with the desolation of a graveyard." A month later his company, now a part of the Twentieth Army Corps of Gen. William Tecumseh Sherman's army, continued the march through Georgia, arriving at Savannah in late December. The army then turned north and Ricker wrote, "We left a black track in South Carolina."[3]

Near the end of March 1865, Ricker was in Goldsboro, North Carolina. Two corporals in his company were killed nearby in separate skirmishes. By this time Ricker was also a corporal and the men were probably his friends. It was the only time he wrote to his mother about fatalities in the unit. The 102d continued its northward march through Raleigh, North Carolina, and Richmond, Virginia, arriving in Alexandria on May 19. On May 24, 1865, Ricker participated in the grand review of General Sherman's victorious army in Washington DC. Ricker received his discharge papers the following month.[4]

In 1864 Ricker began corresponding with Mary M. Smith, a young woman from Wyanet, Illinois. Apparently she wrote the first letter to him on the urging of her uncle. Ricker responded with extreme formality, as was typical of the times:

> Miss Smith, Esteemed Friend. It is with exquisite pleasure that I seat myself to acknowledge the receipt of your kind letter. I feel highly flattered to think you should select me for a correspondent.[5]

It took six months before Ricker felt sufficiently comfortable to use "Dear friend Mary" in the salutation. About that same time she sent him a lock of her hair. The formality in their letters disappeared as they discovered shared interests. Ricker confessed, "The subject which engages my attention is largely that of education. In me the desire for it amounts to a passion." No doubt Mary understood the feelings he expressed. She had enrolled at Lombard College in Galesburg to study art and music, but when her father died she was forced to give up her studies and take a job teaching school.

They met for the first time after Ricker came home from the army, and the correspondence continued. Eli had found work on a farm near Oneida, while

INTRODUCTION

Mary taught school in Wyanet, forty miles away. There were occasional visits and during one of them, Ricker proposed marriage. In late November 1865 Mary confessed, "I had heard of love at first sight, but I loved you before I had ever seen you." They were married on July 3, 1867, by a justice of the peace at Henderson, Knox County, Illinois.[6]

Ricker had moved to a farm in near Woodhull in November 1865, and in the spring of 1867 he borrowed $2,000 to buy a farm in the vicinity. He assured Mary the debt would not be a problem, but a lack of money would plague Ricker for most of his life. In February 1869 the couple moved to the vicinity of Loda, Iroquois County, where Ricker began raising broomcorn, apparently on a grand scale. At the end of the second season he wrote to his mother with the sad news that "broom corn is a drug this year; mine will not pay expenses at present prices If I had left it in the field I should have saved [money]." Although he was deeply in debt, Ricker later looked back on the misfortune with some pride. He had been able to overcome the obstacles and pay his debts. He admitted it took him five years to do so.[7]

In 1876 Ricker decided on a career change and enrolled in a two-year commercial course at a school in Onarga, Illinois. He also devoted a year to studies in the literary department of Grand Prairie Seminary and Commercial College. During this time he worked intermittently in the Iroquois County clerk's office at Watseka. A friend there was publishing a series of biographical sketches of pioneers and Ricker joined in the endeavor. This experience led to a position with a firm based in Chicago that published county histories. Ricker worked for more than three years compiling histories of nine counties in Illinois and Indiana.[8]

In July 1882 Ricker temporarily left his wife and five children in Galesburg, Illinois, and went to Brooklyn, Iowa, to study law under John T. Scott, a Civil War comrade. Ricker was approaching forty-two years of age when he passed the bar examination in March 1884. He continued to work for Scott, but after a year he began thinking about moving west and starting his own practice. He first considered Dakota Territory, but Mary refused to live there. Ricker then "heard of a place in the extreme northwest part of Neb. that seems to offer a good opening." He was thinking of the new town of Chadron in Dawes County, Nebraska. The Fremont, Elkhorn, and Missouri Valley Railroad was laying tracks westward in northern Nebraska and by late summer of 1885 Chadron was at the end of the line. Ricker arrived there on September 17. His family expected to follow him after he found a home for them, which took longer than expected.

In the spring of 1886 his son Leslie Ricker, then age thirteen, wrote to his father complaining, "You had disappointed me so many times I expect the next time you [write you] will say that we cant come till next spring." Leslie was nearly correct. The family did not leave for Chadron until the end of August 1886.[9]

In Chadron, Ricker formed a partnership with Fred J. Houghton. On their letterhead they offered services in law, real estate, insurance, and collections. The partnership lasted only briefly and by 1889 ads for the law firm of Ricker and Turner appeared in local papers. Now the emphasis was on loaning money if the borrower had "first class real estate" for collateral.[10]

Ricker entered politics shortly after his arrival and was elected clerk for the village of Chadron. In the spring he ran for a three-year term on the school board, but was narrowly defeated. When the county judge resigned in 1886, Ricker campaigned for the vacant position. He ran as a Democrat and won the election by fifty-nine votes out of a total of slightly more than thirteen hundred cast. At that time a county judge was authorized to probate wills, perform marriages, hear civil cases involving less than $1,000, and attend to other relatively minor legal matters.[11]

The following year he ran for judge of the Twelfth Judicial District. His opponent was Moses Kinkaid, a rising star on the political horizon, and Ricker was defeated by a margin of more than two to one. Ricker lowered his expectations in 1888 and ran for Dawes County attorney on the Democratic ticket. He was defeated again and the loss put a temporary end to Ricker's political career. Seven years later he ran for county judge and was elected in a close race. In 1897 he joined the Peoples' Independent Party, or Populists, and they won all but one of the county offices. He served his two-year term but never ran for the office again.[12]

While Ricker was practicing law he and his son Leslie were buying land along Bordeaux Creek about eleven miles southeast of Chadron. By 1904 they had acquired nearly one thousand acres of ranchland they called Gray Cliff. It seems Leslie and his mother lived on the ranch, while Ricker spent most of his time in town. Leslie recalled that his father moved to the ranch only after completing his last term as county judge, but "he did not stay on the ranch I think over two years for this kind of life did not seem congenial to him."[13]

Ricker's dissatisfaction with ranching may have been behind his decision to purchase a newspaper in Chadron. In January 1903 he and his partner, A. M. Clark, began publishing the weekly *Chadron Times*. Ricker was listed as editor and Clark as publisher. A year later Ricker offered both the newspaper and the ranch for sale. He assured readers the properties were a bargain and would be sold on easy terms. Ricker also noted jokingly, "Reason for selling—going to Cuba or someplace." The ad for the ranch ran until May 19, 1904, when it was presumably sold, and the ad offering the *Times* for sale ran until February 9, 1905. Ricker and Clark published the last issue of the paper two weeks later. That summer the Rickers moved to Grand Junction, Colorado.[14]

It is not clear why Ricker decided on this complete abandonment of his ranch and business. His eldest son, Albion, may have been living in Grand Junction at the time and the sale of the ranch and the newspaper provided a meager but sufficient income, suggesting that Ricker was contemplating retirement.

Ricker became interested in Indian history during his later years in Chadron. In what appears to be a draft for an introduction to his book, Ricker wrote, "I was somewhat past sixty years of age [ca. 1904] when I first thought of it in its present general scope." Many years later, in a letter to Addison E. Sheldon, Leslie Ricker mentioned that he thought his father's interest in the "Indian Question" arose when Eli was editor of the *Chadron Times*.[15] Ricker published somewhat more news about events at nearby Pine Ridge Reservation than could be found in other western Nebraska papers. Early in 1904 a correspondent who used the pseudonym "Sioux" began contributing articles about current politics and events on Pine Ridge, but they were brief and infrequent. In one of his early editorials Ricker urged Chadron businesses to treat Indians fairly. "Honesty and fair treatment to these customers will bring the trade. The Indian drawn by the ties of friendship is a friend to tie to. Treat him mean and cheat and rob him as has often been done by the whites and he never forgets. They like Chadron. Keep 'Honor Bright' with them."[16]

Comments in the *Chadron Times* certainly suggest Ricker was thinking about the "Indian Question." In July 1903 he mentioned a visit to the day school on Wounded Knee Creek, where the Sioux "fought to the bitter death their last battle" referring to the culmination of the Ghost Dance era and the near annihilation of Big Foot's Lakota band by the Seventh Cavalry on December 29, 1890. Ricker returned to Pine Ridge early in November, but this time he wrote about the "slaughter" at Wounded Knee and expressed his belief that it could have been avoided. This statement was a radical departure from nearly everything about Wounded Knee that had previously appeared in print. Newspaper accounts describing the "affair," as it was commonly called, tended to depict brave soldiers fighting crazed savages.[17]

The real turning point in Ricker's interest in the Indians' circumstances may have come about during the so-called Lightning Creek or Wyoming incident. He published a series of articles about it in the *Times* during the latter part of 1903. Indians from Pine Ridge Reservation had been hunting in eastern Wyoming when they were accosted by a sheriff and his deputies and accused of breaking Wyoming's hunting laws. Tempers flared and a gunfight resulted. The sheriff, a deputy, and four Indians died. Most western papers blamed the Indians because they were accused of violating the law. While Ricker's reports could not be described as pro-Indian, his view was more balanced than most. Unlike most other reporters, Ricker felt the Indians' account of the encounter should be considered as being at least as reliable as the story told by the white participants. Leslie recalled the incident years later and wrote, "Pa made a trip to the scene of trouble and got the inside facts and aspoused [sic] the Indian cause This act of justice on his part endeared him to the Indians and ever after that he was widely known by the Indians over [at] the Agency."[18]

By the end of 1903 Ricker was taking depositions from people with firsthand knowledge of the massacre at Wounded Knee and had gained a fair understanding of the tragedy. On November 30 he talked to George E. Bartlett and recorded the first of what would become known as the "Ricker interviews." Bartlett's discussion of Wounded Knee included some questionable conclusions. Ricker noted these politely with comments such as "I did not think that was so." Two weeks later he talked to Charles W. Allen, who had witnessed the massacre in 1890 when he was the editor of the *Chadron Democrat*. Ricker concluded that Allen was "a calm man not inclined to fiction, fancy or sensation but his characteristic methods are careful, accurate and truthful."[19]

Leslie Ricker recalled that his father spent two winters gathering information on the Pine Ridge Reservation, one winter traveling on foot and the other by horse and buggy.[20] Ricker's dedication to this project, and the discomforts he faced obtaining the interviews, are vividly described in a twelve-page letter to his wife in Grand Junction. The following is an excerpt:

> Monday, the 11th, I started from Louie's School No. 12, on foot, with the determination to reach Kyle either that or the following day. There was some snow and a vast amount of ice all over the ground—from the highest summit to the lowest hollow—till I ascended the divide between Wounded Knee and Porcupine creeks; from thence the ground looked quite bare, but all through the buf-

falo grass the unseen and treacherous ice was yet The 12th was balmy. Mrs. Snowden filled one of my pockets with hard tack and I started, crossing the Porcupine [Creek] on a log. Had gone but a little way when I noticed that I had lost my cotton handkerchief. Went back half a mile but did not find it. Needed it or I would not have doubled back that distance. Had left Louie's with an awful cold.[21]

About 1905 Ricker had personalized stationary printed with his name above "Ex-County Judge and Late Editor of the Chadron Times" in the upper left corner; in the upper right corner was "The Final Conflict Between the Red Men and the Pale Faces (In Preparation)."[22]

He was also was toying with an outline for his book. The emphasis was on "The Butchery at Wounded Knee" and "The Political Battle on the Little Big Horn." In addition Ricker envisioned sections on the "habits, customs, rites, imagery and oratory of the Indians" and "exploits of trappers, adventures of fur traders, and hardships of explorers."[23]

Ricker estimated the final product would consist of four octavo volumes of five to six hundred pages each. He realized, "when it comes to publishing I may be obliged to change the whole plan." Ricker realized he could not follow the lead of traditional historians of his era, who tended to write about sturdy pioneers conquering the West, while the army won glorious battles over the "savages." One of his notes clearly spells out his perspective:

> The Indians sneer at the whiteman's conventional reference to the Custer massacre and the battle of Wounded Knee. They ridicule the lack of impartiality of the whites in speaking of the two events—when the whites got the worst of it it was a massacre; when the Indians got the worst of it it was a battle.[24]

Apparently Ricker planned to write his history from the viewpoint of the people he interviewed. As a result he "found it both logical and necessary to discard the easy yet unapt [sic] word 'savages' when applied to the natives," and "to speak of the people flocking to the New World as 'foreigners.'" Ricker also was uncomfortable with the term "civilization," noting that civilized people "not infrequently inculcated acts of barbarity hardly less atrocious than the worst practiced by the 'savages.'" "As between the foreigners and the natives the former have always set up claim to superiority, and on this ground have absolved themselves from guilt for their seizure of a continent and for the endless wrongs they have inflicted and the collective wickedness they have committed upon the inferior race."

Ricker was not willing to elevate the natives too far at the expense of the foreigners. He explained that the foreigners were educated and had learned the "divinity of cleanliness and the nobility of labor" that set them above the natives. Ricker was not without prejudices, but his stance regarding native peoples placed him far ahead of most of his contemporaries and many of those who came after him.[25]

There is little in the historical record to explain Ricker's motivation for undertaking a project that was expensive, time consuming, and at times downright unpleasant. His family and friends never offered an explanation. Ricker himself begs the question in a 1907 draft of an introduction for *Final Conflict*:

> If the reader cannot see the reason for its [the book's] existence the writer . . . would not be able to assist his enlightenment But to gratify the super-curious, whose rights are to be as religiously guarded as any, he will confess that he has not written to supply a long felt want—he has not written at the urgent request of friends; for these were not numerous enough to raise the necessary insurrection—he has not done it for his bread and butter; for heaven knows it has taken these away.[26]

Ricker was sixty-seven years old and still gathering data for his *Final Conflict* when he was hired by the U.S. Office of Indian Affairs in Washington DC, beginning work on December 3, 1910. Unfortunately Ricker never bothered to explain what the job entailed or how he got it, but years later, his friend Addison E. Sheldon explained that he was a "record clerk" and that "most of his work was organizing and indexing office files."[27] It seems this would have been a menial job for the former judge and newspaperman, but it allowed Ricker the opportunity to pursue his passion for research. Ricker worked for Dr. Howard M. Hamblin, the office's assistant historian, at least part of the time, but he had little regard for the man.[28] Ricker assured his wife, "I can do any part of the work without assistance." He considered his "real director" to be Annie Heloise Abel, who taught at Johns Hopkins University, but visited the office frequently to do research. Ricker obviously admired her. His description of Abel in a letter to his wife also reveals something of Ricker:

> Like myself, she is plodding and slow, because she loves the truth; and she knows that history must be true, otherwise it is not history. Her mind, I am proud to know, is not corrupted by the dollar-lust. Who writes with his eye on shekls does not write history.

Mary joined her husband in Washington early in the summer of 1911, and they acted like tourists on vacation. They visited historical sites in the city and spent a weekend at the Bull Run battlefield. They also traveled to Maine to visit Eli's birthplace. That summer must have been one of the happiest times in the couple's lives, but the happiness did not last. In late February 1912 Ricker was notified that he had been terminated because the Indian office was running short of funds and Ricker was a victim of a last hired, first fired policy. The Rickers remained in Washington, hoping that Eli might be reinstated, but he had to wait until the next congressional appropriation. His old position was reinstated and Ricker returned to the Indian office on August 28, 1912.[29]

A more serious difficulty arose six months later when Mary suffered "several bilious attacks with sickness in her head and stomach." She was under a doctor's care in Baltimore for a time and then spent the summer in Grand Junction. Mary recovered and rejoined her husband in Washington and assisted him in his research. Years later Leslie recalled his mother's contribution:

> My mother worked at least two years writing out this historical data. For a long time she went to the [Smithsonian] Institute [sic] and did her writing there. Finally the superintendent after becoming so well acquainted with her told her she could take the books home to do her writing. This saved her much extra work. My mother contributed in many ways to my father's success in his historical research. All of which cost them thousands of dollars in labor and money."[30]

While he was in Washington Ricker occasionally hired a typist to copy archival documents he needed for his book. Mary felt paying the woman $5 a week and providing a lunch each day put an undue strain on their limited income.[31] Eli tried to explain his feelings and to justify the expense: "My thought and life and ambition are in this service. I do not want to fail to turn out something for a showing." Ricker was undoubtedly sincere in his desire to "turn out something," but he was overwhelmed by the vast historical resources available in Washington. He began to delve into diverse themes, ranging from the

Seminoles in Florida to pueblo dwellers in the Southwest, and it was his undoing. In his lust for knowledge he became sidetracked from the project and the book he originally planned.

Ricker stayed with the Indian office until July 1919. It is not clear whether he resigned, or whether the funding ceased. Whatever the cause the Rickers moved back to Grand Junction and lived in a house owned by their son, Albion.[32] There Ricker joined Leslie in a business venture. The younger man had developed the Ricker Universal Cooker, claimed to be so efficient it could cook food using only 10 percent of the fuel required by conventional methods. Prospective buyers were also assured there was no danger of explosion. After two years the Rickers admitted the undertaking was a failure and the Universal Cooker was never again mentioned in their correspondence.

Eli Ricker returned to work on his book and in 1923, told Leslie he was ready to begin the chapter on the Little Bighorn battle. He never went beyond portions of a rough draft and miscellaneous thoughts. By this time he was nearly eighty years old and his health had begun to fail.

Eli and Mary faced additional problems. He received a Civil War veteran's pension, but they had to supplement their income by renting the second floor of their house. Apparently the rental did not provide enough income because in February 1925, the Rickers decided to move into what Eli called the "garage" so they could rent the first floor as well. Ricker mentioned that the garage had a concrete floor, with shelves of books and manuscripts along two walls. The garage might have been the concrete block building that Albion built in 1921 to house his father's historical records in a nearly fireproof environment. By this time Ricker had acquired more than 2,350 books, plus voluminous copies and some original documents he obtained in Washington.[33]

On the day they moved to the garage Ricker installed a stove and started a fire. Mary stayed inside while her husband went out to chop more wood. After a short time Ricker heard screams and saw Mary running from the building. Later he would write, "My wife was near the hydrant, facing me, in a fierce wind, a pillar of fire! The flames streaming above her head." Apparently she had stood too near the stove, which ignited her clothing. The fire was quickly extinguished and a doctor and a Christian Scientist were called, but to no avail. Mary Ricker died at four o'clock the next morning, February 25, 1925.

That fall Ricker contracted the flu and never fully recovered. In the spring of 1926 he wrote Leslie, "I have been declining in physical strength very fast" and worried if it continued "I shall be lying beside your mother before the 4th of next July." He had been relying on Christian Science to prolong his life and had been taking "Science treatments" but discontinued them late in April with the concurrence of his medical attendant. His condition continued to worsen and he died in the house on Ouray Avenue on May 17, 1926. A physician was present and determined the cause of death was "myocarditis, and inflammation of the heart complicated by senility."[34]

During his long life Ricker experienced many philosophical changes. He and his wife joined the Methodist Church in 1875, but Methodism was too strict for the liberal-minded Ricker. By the late 1880s the couple were attending the Universalist Church. Mary's parents belonged to the sect so it is likely she introduced Eli to the church. Later Ricker adopted Christian Science and in 1905 wrote a long supportive editorial in the *Chadron Times*. The editorial brought a rave review from the business manager of the *Salt Lake Mining Review*, who called it a "master piece" of "rhetorical perfectness."[35]

Ricker's political ideology also moved to the left. He had been a Republican when he was a young man, but had become a Democrat by the time he came to Nebraska. In the late 1890s he embraced Populism. A few years later he moved still farther to the left when he joined the Socialist Party. In 1912 he wrote an ecstatic letter to his wife, extolling the party's platform as "the greatest public document that has appeared in this country since the Constitution."[36]

While Ricker grew more liberal in his political and religious philosophies, he became more reserved and aloof in his family relationships. His early letters to his wife and children are full of warmth, but by the time he went to work in Washington, most of the expressions of fondness were missing. Letters were occasionally signed "With Affection," but most were merely "Aff. ES Ricker." It seems Mary grew tired of his formality and apparently wrote a very personal letter, in which she must have described her love for her husband.[37]

Ricker responded with assurances "that I reciprocate everything said by you, and more especially the sentiments so deeply rooted in our hearts toward each What would I do if I were to lose my beloved companion?"

Ricker was capable of deep feelings of remorse for some of his past conduct. When he was a younger man he attended college and held a variety of jobs that kept him away from his family for extended periods. In a 1913 letter to his daughter-in-law, Margaret, he admitted, "I suffered such loss as none can ever realize by being away from my own children as much as I was in their childhood days." Three years later he expressed the same sentiment in a letter to Leslie, but this time Ricker was on the defensive. Apparently Leslie had made a disparaging remark about his long absences that Ricker interpreted as "a reflection on my course of action." Ricker went on to explain:

> The sacrifice I made—the loss I sustained—by being away from my young children when they needed me, and I needed them (had you thought of that?) can never be known nor estimated. That separation has not ceased to give me pain down to this day.

In spite of Ricker's intelligence and his obvious compassion for at least one minority he was not free of all prejudices. He clearly expressed his anti-Catholic views in a letter to his wife:

> The attitude of the Socialists toward Rome is making many friends for the party among those who are alive to the menace of Romanism. The treasonable hierarchy must be disrupted, so far as their political power and designs are concerned. The press of the country, the great publishing houses and the magazines are in subjection to-day to the Roman influence. The Protestants are simpletons for contributing as they do to the upbuilding and strengthening of the Beast of Revelation.

Ricker was a lover of the arts. In his early letters from Washington he described his numerous visits to the Corcoran Art Gallery, "but it is in the department of statuary where I go into spasms of enthusiasm." Ricker also had a passion for the Library of Congress. He took binoculars there to read the mottoes and names of people on the ceiling of the dome and described the "harmonious hues" and "fascinating beauty" of the building. He was equally excited about the books and manuscripts housed there, but "doubt that concerns me is that I may never be able to examine even a small part of all there is" in the collections.

During the waning months of his life Ricker realized he would never finish his book. He considered selling his library, and Addison E. Sheldon, superintendent of the Nebraska State Historical Society, offered to buy some of the volumes. Sheldon had settled in Chadron about the same time as Ricker and the two men became friends. Ricker declined Sheldon's offer because he wanted to keep the collection together and at a location where his descendents could use it. After Ricker died, Sheldon went to Grand Junction in June, probably in the hope he could promote a donation. He and Ricker's children discussed several options, including establishing a research library in a new facility at Albion, a little town in central Nebraska, where Ricker's daughter and her family lived.

It was only the dream of a grieving family because there was no money for such a facility. Son Albion Ricker pointed out that the family had incurred "some heavy expenses" after his father's death and thought they might have to sell what they could. Sheldon was critical of secondhand book dealers and warned, "all of them place a very low figure on things they are buying and a high one on things they are selling."[38]

In spite of Sheldon's warnings and persuasion, the family decided to sell what they could of the collection. Albion Ricker prepared a list of 2,350 books with a total asking price of $3,907 and sent it to book dealers. Sheldon selected seventy-nine books he felt would be worthwhile for the society, but by the time he was authorized to make the purchase, two-thirds had already been sold.[39]

Sheldon realized the priceless historical value of Ricker's tablets containing the interviews and told the family that the notebooks would not be "salable" and "it would require many more years on the part of a person with special training and special knowledge" to prepare a publishable manuscript. In case there was any doubt about the monetary value of such a book, Sheldon added that the writing and editing "would be largely a labor of love, for neither the sale or nor the royalties from history books of this nature are large enough to pay decent wages."[40]

Fortunately there was no market for what Albion called the "historical material" and it was donated to the Nebraska State Historical Society. This material consisted of Ricker's notebooks, and other data pertaining to his research on the Indian wars, as well as voluminous family correspondence. The manuscripts arrived at the Historical Society on November 2, 1926. In January Sheldon presented the collection to the society members at their annual meeting and asked State Senator James W. Good, who had been a friend of Ricker's, to say a few words. Good praised the Ricker family for the donation and naively added, "I find that it might take a year or two to arrange it."[41]

Ricker's Methodology

Mechanical recording devices were available when Ricker was taking the depositions but, unfortunately, they were beyond his means. He relied instead on note pads and pencils to record the interviews. Most of these tablets are the kind school children used. A few are even titled "Public School Tablet." Although they vary widely in size, most of the pads are about five by nine inches and vary in length from about one hundred to two hundred pages.

Ricker's interviewing methodology also varied considerably. In his first known interview Ricker wrote down both his questions and his informant's answers, but he used this technique briefly on only one other occasion.[42] Many of his Native American sources required an interpreter. In those instances Ricker wrote what the interpreter told him, then read it back, and the interpreter repeated it to the interviewee for his or her approval.[43] Ricker provided another clue about his methods during his interview with George Sword. Sword had described an event in his youth, which Ricker recorded. At the end of the paragraph Ricker noted, "Capt. George Sword sang several hymns in Lakota while I was busy writing down the foregoing about him."[44]

On some occasions it seems that Ricker made short notes at the time of the interview and then expanded on them in the tablets. This technique is suggested in his interview with William Rowland. Ricker wrote, "Rowland gave me the names of the guards, but I did not put them down."[45] He may have also used this method in the interviews with Philip Wells and William Garnett. In the first instance Ricker's sentences are carefully phrased in his unique style, which is not characteristic of normal conversation. If they had been written at the time of the interview, Wells would have had to wait on numerous occasions while Ricker composed his long, convoluted sentences. The exceptionally clear handwriting also suggests that Ricker was not hurried.[46] In the Garnett interview Ricker frequently writes, "Garnett said" or "Garnett described," but there are also strong hints that this version is not the first draft. When Ricker begins to describe the killing of Crazy Horse he prefaces the discussion, "But it will be for the province of this chapter to uncover some of the hidden inferences which hastened the end of this man's life."[47]

Undoubtedly Ricker chose the topics for the interviews, but there is little to suggest the extent to which he guided the discussion. There is some evidence he questioned or even challenged the interviewee on certain points. For example, William Peno said he heard the cannons firing at Wounded Knee at about sunrise. Ricker knew this was too early in the day and noted, "He will not admit, on questioning that it was much after the sun came in sight."[48]

Ricker's Writing Style and the Editor's Alterations

Ricker accumulated such a mass of information that it would not have been practical to publish the data in a single volume. It is a fortunate coincidence that the total page count for interviews of Native Americans and mixed-bloods on the one hand, and those of whites on the other, were approximately equal.

INTRODUCTION

This was the basis for the division, because there is no significant difference in the subject matter.

Eli Ricker was an educated man with an extensive vocabulary and nearly always impeccable spelling and penmanship. He did have certain stylistic idiosyncrasies that will annoy purists. For example, he preferred semicolons and em dashes over periods and commas. While these symbols may not be acceptable under the rules found in current style manuals they have been retained because they fulfill the intended purpose and also keep this printed copy somewhat closer to Ricker's original. Occasionally he put a dash after a period or a semicolon and these unnecessary dashes have been removed. He was not consistent in his use of punctuation with possessive nouns, or with abbreviations and numbers. These inconsistencies have been silently corrected.

Ricker frequently misspelled personal names, sometimes consistently (McGillicuddy instead of McGillycuddy), and sometimes only until he learned the correct spelling. Some of these mistakes were likely due to Ricker's haste in writing down what was being said. Because there is rarely a question about a person's identity, Ricker's spelling of names has been let stand. In a few instances the editor has added the correct spelling in brackets, following a name's first appearance. Ricker had his own rules for using capital letters. While his small "a" and capital "A" are similar, there is no question he intended to capitalize agency whether it is Red Cloud Agency or when speaking of the "Agency." Reservation was always capitalized, but Platte River was "Platte river" most of the time. There seemed no pressing reason to correct these inconsistencies.

On rare occasions Ricker repeated a word. Rather than use the intrusive sic, the unnecessary second word has been omitted. Ricker frequently used brackets to enclose his parenthetical thoughts, but often omitted a closing bracket. The brackets have all been changed to parentheses to avoid confusion with editorial insertions, which are in brackets. The editor added closing parentheses when needed to help define Ricker's asides.

The editor has also sometimes added quotation marks that Ricker omitted during transcription of direct discourse, and occasionally added periods and capitalized the first word of a sentence. In some instances, particularly in the Beard interview, the narrative shifts frequently from first to third person, making it difficult to distinguish Ricker's words from those of his narrator. Punctuation in this interview has been left as Ricker recorded it.

Ricker had a penchant for long, compound sentences. If the reader is attentive they do not cause a problem in understanding his meaning. Ricker allowed a somewhat wider range of subject matter to be included in his paragraphs than might be acceptable today. He usually did not bother to indent the first sentence of a new paragraph. No corrections have been made to his paragraphing because the "problem" is not significant. Ricker crossed out redundant and misspelled words and sometimes entire paragraphs. These were not included in the transcription. Occasionally words or phrases were lined though, suggesting the interviewee changed his or her mind. These have been retained. In some cases Ricker wrote a word above another word that was similar in its meaning. Although he did not cross out the original word, the editor has assumed he meant to make the substitution in his final draft and has retained the word that was written above.

Ricker usually numbered the recto side, and occasionally both sides, of each leaf. There seemed to be no reason to retain his numbers. In addition to the tablets, Ricker used an assortment of loose tablet pages, the backs of old letters, and eight-by-eleven-inch sheets, some typed and some handwritten, to record notes and interviews.

Some interviews extended over more than one tablet and the separate portions have been brought together here. Additional comments or afterthoughts by or about his informants, or the subjects being discussed, were likely to appear almost anywhere. Often Ricker indicated where these fragments were to go within the narrative, and in other instances he did not. They have been inserted as closely as possible to the related subject matter according to the editor's best judgment.

In general, the editor believes that Ricker would have addressed many minor editorial matters during subsequent work on the interviews, which clearly he did in several instances. Therefore, while the editor has tried to retain the essence of Ricker's interviewing style, he has made punctuation and format adjustments, as described above, that seemed likely to assist both the casual reader and the scholar. Those who wish to plumb every nuance of the interviews exactly as Ricker recorded them are reminded that his tablets are available on microfilm.

After the Nebraska State Historical Society acquired the collection, stickers measuring two and one-quarter by three and one-half inches were printed and affixed to the cover of each tablet. They read, "From the Historical Library of Judge E. S. Ricker formerly of Chadron, Nebraska. Part of his project for a history of the Plains Indians. Received by Nebraska State Historical Society

November 2, 1926." The Historical Society numbered the tablets, but in no particular order.

The Ricker tablets contain much more than the interviews presented here. In the early planning stages we considered making each tablet simply a long quotation, but the tablets included much material of limited historical significance. For example, Ricker's recipe for pickles has been deleted, along with reminders that someone gave him $1.50 for a year's subscription to his newspaper. Many other notes or reminders to himself, addresses, lists, and transcriptions from books and documents have also been deleted. Lengthy sections that could be described as Ricker's musings have been omitted. These may have been first drafts for his book and ranged from his views about certain historical events and the treatment of Indians to quotations he admired. This material would, however, be valuable for someone writing a full length biography of Judge Ricker, and hopefully someone will undertake that worthwhile task.

Ricker and his informants drew thirty-two maps of Wounded Knee, the Little Bighorn battlefield, and other sites, but not all of them have been reproduced in the present volumes. Some were so crudely drawn that they were meaningless. These maps are briefly described in the endnotes.

Voices of the American West, Volume 1

The West of Eli S. Ricker

1. The Garnett and Wells Interviews

[William Garnett's Interview]

Ricker wrote the following sketch of Garnett near the end of January 1907 in Tablet 22.

William Garnet lives on Cane Creek north of the White River on a ranch of his own, 8 or 10 miles south of the extension of the Milwaukee R. R. He was the son of General Garnet who was killed in the battle of Gettysburg. His father was an officer in the old army and was stationed at Fort Laramie. He had this son by a Sioux Indian woman who afterwards married a man by the name of Hunter; and hence the subject of this sketch is sometimes called Garnet and sometimes Hunter, but his true name is Garnett and this is officially recognized.[1]

Garnett is one of the best interpreters on the Reservation. He is a stirring, intelligent, able man; and while he did not have the advantages of schooling, he has absorbed much practical knowledge, and is held in high estimation for his honor, integrity and veracity. Bat says he was in the fight under Mackenzie on one of the forks of Powder River, in the mountains; the command marched from Crazy Woman [Creek] across the divide to the fork where the Cheyenne village was, and striking the village at the lower end and charged up the stream. Garnet was in this fight.

[Tablet 1]

Cane Creek, S.D. January 10, 1907

William Garnett (he had a step-father named John Hunter) He was born on the bottom below where the Sabine Creek disembogues into the Big Laramie River in April, 1855. His father was General B. Garnett who was killed on the Confederate side at the Battle of Gettysburg in the Civil War. He was a West Pointer and resigned from the old army on the breaking out of the war. He was the commanding officer at Ft. Laramie. Fort Pierre was the headquarters and detachments were sent across from Pierre to garrison Fort Laramie. This was in the early days, about 1850 and 1854 etc.²

Mr. Billy Garnet has been an Indian interpreter for 30 years and has interpreted so much about treaties and other affairs which transpired before his day that he knows their history as well as though he had lived when they occurred and had personal knowledge of them.

He remembers when the Mormons were traveling along over the trail every year.

He says that Nick Janis was a guide for Gen. Stephen W. Kearny when he went with an expedition to the Rocky Mts., the first that ever went west.³

Father De Smet baptized a great many Indians on the Laramie and Platte Rivers.⁴ He thinks Mrs. Tibbitts was baptized by De Smet. Mrs. Tibbitts' name is Emily. (Emily Janis.)⁵

The treaty made at the mouth of Horse Creek in 1851 was for the purpose of granting a right of way for the emigrant travel across the plains.⁶

Billy Garnett says that the treaty was made at the mouth of Horse Creek, 40 miles below Ft. Laramie. It was there that the first issue was made to the Indians, and they all call it "The Big Issue." The whole Sioux Nation was present but only representatives of the other tribes were there to receive the goods for their tribes. They were issued in bulk to the several tribes and by each, distributed to the members.

Mrs. Ben Tibbitts was born at the mouth of Horse Creek at the time of this issue; she was Nick's first child. Major Wham did not come out there till 1871. Garnett remembers this well. Agent Twist [Thomas S. Twiss] was there as early as 1860 or thereabout.

He says that in those days the interpreters were very poor, and he does not see how the government was able to transact any business with the natives. He has been acquainted with some of the old interpreters and knows that they were poor. He has had to interpret for Nick Janis, his own father-in-law, when he was stalled, and he was interpreter for the government a great deal.

He also had to help out Tod Randall, another interpreter.⁷

In relation to this treaty it was one object to harmonize the Indians and put an end to wars among the several tribes and to apportion the country among the tribes; but soon after it was made the Indians fell apart and continued their fighting as before. At the time of the making of this treaty the Sioux Indians elected Conquering Bear their chief.⁸ Old Man Afraid of His Horse succeeded Conquering Bear to the chieftainship of the Sioux.

When ~~Old~~ Man Afraid got very old (who died when about 90 yrs. of age) he abdicated in favor of Young Man Afraid of His Horse, who was accepted at once without controversy.⁹

This name came in this way: It is not proper to say <u>Old</u> Man Afraid, etc.; for the Indians called him Man Afraid of His Horse, because he was a very brave man and the enemy feared him and they could recognize his presence in battle by his horse, and when they saw him in the fight they were afraid, knowing his prowess. So the significance was that his enemy was Afraid of His Horse—not that he was afraid. The whites took to calling him <u>Old Man Afraid</u>, etc., but this is not right—drop the <u>Old</u>. The word Horses is not right; it was Horse, singular. <u>Young Man Afraid of His Horse</u> is right for his son, as the Indians themselves recognized the name, because he was the junior Man Afraid etc.

In 1868, shortly after the making of the 1868 treaty at Fort Laramie, the Sioux Indians moved off north and were assembled about the heads of the creeks which empty into the South Cheyenne River—one of these being Lance Creek—when the Oglalas came in to make the 1868 treaty they camped on Lance Creek, so they went back on that creek which empties into Warm Creek which empties into Cheyenne River.¹⁰

East of Lance Creek was one called Old Woman's Fork (now called by the whites, Old Woman's Creek), and into Old Woman's Fork emptied Grindstone Creek from the west. In the forks of these two creeks is the Grindstone butte which is formed of square blocks of stone of varying sizes. The Indians went there to get stones which they used for grindstones by whetting their knives and other implements on these square blocks. White people also get grindstones in the same place. These two creeks unite after passing one on either side around the butte, and flowing together thence some 8 or 10 miles empty into the Cheyenne River.

The Old Woman's Fork got its name in this way: Many years ago the small pox was virulent among the Indians, and they scattered out over the country. One old woman went to this stream and erected her lodge and lived alone. She had some dogs and they increased till there were perhaps 100—a great number. She was there a long time. Her lodge at length rotted down. An Indian trail passed close to her habitation, and her dogs were numerous and saucy and ran out and assailed passersby. The Indians being superstitious, viewed her with superstitious awe, regarding her in the nature of a witch, and were careful not to go near her but kept at a distance, avoiding her acquaintance. Her lodge disappeared; but the smoke of her fire showed that she had made her wigwam in a cave in the earth. In course of time her smoke rose no more and she was not seen. It is supposed she had been transported [?] to the hunting grounds on the other side of this life. No one knows what end the dogs came to, but hunters say that in that region there are black wolves, and it is believed that these dogs in-bred with the wolves, and though the wolves are true in size and form and feature to their species, yet they have derived their color from the old woman's dogs.

A month or two after the execution of the 1868 treaty, when these Sioux Indians were assembled on these creeks about 40 miles northwest of where Lusk, Wyoming, now is, the Sioux Indians were camped in the hereditary manner followed by these people when they are moving, viz.; In a large circle with an opening in the east or the southeast, so that it is in a general direction toward the rising sun; the several villages camp together, and generally relatives are in close proximity like neighbors. At the time in question the council house was in the center of this camp, being a large lodge comparable to a circus tent. The Indians camped this way when moving; sometimes they would remain overnight only, perhaps a day, two or three days or a week or more. At this time Mr. Garnett was a boy, 13 years old, but was apt at observation, and at an impressionable age. He saw some horsemen making the circuit of the camp on the inside and his boyish curiosity was aroused at what was going on. Other boys near his age were with him and all were likewise attracted by the novel proceedings. They saw these warriors ride round to the several villages and pick out certain young men, place them on horses and take them to the center of the camp at the council house, and the youngsters followed, led by their curiosity to know what was going on. They saw the four young men taken from their mounts and placed on robes spread in the center. The whole gathering was inside of this council house. The old men or leaders of the nations were seated at one end of the house in a half circle. In front of these and facing them were the young warriors of the tribe. On either side the Indian women were ranged, and standing back of the young warriors promiscuously were a throng of children and all others. A feast of beef, and game and dog flesh had been prepared for this important event and the women were waiting for the moment when they should address themselves to the important duty of serving the feast. An old man, probably the chief of the nation, arose and addressed the four young men seated within the circle, viz; Young Man Afraid of His Horse, American Horse, Crazy Horse and Man That Owns a Sword (the latter was a brother of George Sword, Jr. whose Indian name would be the same, but the whites have cut it down to Sword and prefixed the English Christian name of George).[11] The speaker told them that they had been selected as head warriors of their people; that their duty was to govern the people in camp and on the march; to see that order was preserved; that violence was not committed; that all families and persons had their rights, and that none imposed on the others. These men had the fullest authority and they represented in their commands and acts the entire power of the nation. To maintain peace and justice, or to secure any other end required by their system of government, they first counseled and advised, then commanded, and if their authority was not then respected, they resorted to blows, and if these failed to secure obedience to their demands, they killed the offenders without further parley, as was their legal right. Without such summary authority domestic government would have been a failure among the natives; they could not have dwelt together in peace and unity but would have broken up into thin and defenseless bands little larger than individual families. Experience has shown that human beings are selfish, passionate, and half savage at best, and when not subject to discipline and restraint, are utterly lawless and infinitely dangerous.

Next came the feast which is a function of the highest merit with the Indians and is never omitted on occasions of ceremony or celebration. Whatever doubt has been entertained in relation to whether Red Cloud signed the treaty of 1868 has been disposed of by Mr. Garnett who states that at the time of the assembly at Fort Laramie Red Cloud was not there, all statements to the contrary notwithstanding—that there is no truth in the assertion that he withdrew in sulky and angry mood—but that he was at the time off up in the Powder River country with a handful of Oglalas; that late in the fall he came in to the Fort and signed the treaty. He says that Mr. Colhoff is right when he says that the goods and cattle left for Red Cloud were removed to the Whetstone Agency, etc.[12] He further adds that numbers of the squawmen were induced to remove to this Agency and also a few of the Indians, it being thought that in this way the great body of the Indians could be drawn thither, but such influence was inadequate and the mass never went. The squawmen were given rights in the treaty of 1868 equal with the Indians for the influence of these men with the Indians to keep get the Indians on to agencies and to keep them from going to war, etc.[13] After the treaty and in [the] same year the attempt was made to get the Indians down to Whetstone Agency on the Missouri River (?) in Gregory country.

The Loafer Indians under their chief Big Mouth (father of John Farnham's wife) went down to Whetstone Agency; their camp was around Fort Laramie & from there they moved; very few of the Oglalas went, & these were relatives of squawmen who had Oglala wives; the Cutoff Indians were Oglalas and had for their chief Little Wound who was put in the place of his father named Bull Bear in 1871.

The origin of the Cutoff was in quite an early day and grew out of a drunken row in the Oglala camp. Some of Red Cloud's relatives were killed, and he and friends of his avenged themselves by killing several on the other side; Red Cloud killed Bull Bear and the Indians composing Bull Bear's band separated from the rest of the Oglalas and went off among the Cheyennes down on the Platte and the Republican. Years afterwards — in 1871 — the Cutoffs came back up to Fort Laramie and were round in that country, and the necessities of intercourse led to the resumption of amicable relations between Red Cloud and the Cutoffs.[14] A part of the Cutoffs went to the Whetstone Agency and a part did not go. Those who did not go there moved up on Lance Creek. Those who went to Whetstone moved back to Fort Laramie and vicinity in 1871 and thereabouts. The government was desirous to move the Cutoffs from the Republican and the lower Platte off from the line of overland travel, and assemble the Oglalas together; so Red Cloud was advised to make Little Wound, the son of Bull Bear, a chief of his band as a reparation for the killing of Bull Bear; and Red Cloud had been in Washington in 1870 and this scheme had been worked on him as a device agreeable both to the government and himself; so in 1871 there was a big council held near Fort Laramie, and in the transaction of business Little Wound, on the politic suggestion of Red Cloud, was made a chief to succeed Bull Bear, and from that date they had their headquarters with the rest of the Oglalas. Mr. Garnett thinks that at this council these Indians were discussing the location of the Agency and that they were permitted to designate it and that while some wanted it in a different place (up on the Rawhide Creek) the majority decided on the place where the Sod Agency was built in 1871 on the north side of the Platte, 30 miles below Fort Laramie. Spotted Tail went to Whetstone Agency from the lower Platte and the South Platte, and while he was down there, he killed Big Mouth who was half drunk and undertook first to take Spotted Tail's life and snapped his percussion revolver at him several times; but someone who knew Big Mouth well and fathomed his intentions, had unbeknown to him removed the caps, so that his revolver could not be discharged, and when he had failed in his felonious attempt Spotted Tail in self-defense shot Big Mouth and killed him.[15] Spotted Tail moved back with his Brule band to a point about six miles south of the present Pine Ridge Agency and on what was once the Nebraska extension and up in the foothills on White Clay Creek;[16] ~~next moved up just east of Crawford~~ next it was moved just ~~above~~ below the mouth of the Cottonwood where it empties into the White River below where Crawford now is, near 2 or 3 round hills on the north side of the White River; it was next moved to a point just above the mouth of the Beaver Creek, and while it was here some soldiers were encamped here and some were also first stationed at Red Cloud Agency, and from this the detachment went to mouth of the Beaver. These troops were under the command of General Smith, and were the first that came to these two agencies, and were brought here owing to the killing at Red Cloud of the chief clerk, Frank Appleton by Kicking Bear in 1874. General Smith was from Fort Laramie and he went back there after bringing over these garrisons.[17]

Continuing the subject of the Spotted Tail Agency: This was moved from the mouth of Beaver Creek to the place it finally occupied up the Beaver, on the Riekman ranch. The Agency was where I saw the location as above, and Camp Sheridan was about three-quarters of a mile below the Spotted Tail Agency.

Killing of Frank Appleton

I may as well relate here the killing of the chief clerk, Frank Appleton.[18] A party of Indians had been off south in the Platte country and in a fight with some white men ~~and~~ one of their number got killed, and in keeping with their custom of assuaging their grief by killing a white man for revenge they resolved on evening the mortuary account ~~the following night~~ by killing a white man at the Agency; but an Indian ~~belonging to the number, moved by a higher better sentiment~~ friendly to the whites came to the chief clerk and told him what was going to happen and advised him to keep his men inside the stockade that night. The clerk regarded the story as a canard, but jocosely told the people living at the Agency what he had heard, and there were some who treated the matter with more seriousness. The stockade had two main gates and there was a night-watch whose duty was to guard these and see that the enclosure was not entered by anyone. The gates were closed and fastened as usual. The carpenters had been shingling ~~some of the buildings that day next the~~ on the commissary building that day and they left their ladder standing on the outside. The agent at this time was Dr. J. J. Seville, but he was absent at Spotted Tail Agency, and the chief clerk, Frank Appleton, was acting in his stead. In the night an Indian, who, it was afterwards learned was Kicking Bear, using the ladder, came over the palisade into the enclosure and opened the front gate which was on the south side of the square stockade, and was a double gate with a small side gate for persons to enter. This main gate he left wide open after committing his foul deed which took place about 2 or 3 o'clock in the morning. He called Kicking Bear rapped on the window in an adjoining room and then knocked on the door. Appleton, after dressing, opened the door, and seeing that he was an Indian started to go for Wm. Garnett, the interpreter. Appleton had a roommate named Walters, and when Appleton opened the door he [Walters] saw the Indian with a gun in his hands and told Appleton not to go out as the Indian had a gun.[19] Disregarding the warning, he stepped outside, and as his back was turning toward the Indian, Kicking Bear threw down his gun, and Appleton seeing the motion stooped forward to escape the shot and received it in his side and back, the course of the ball being upward, leaving his body near his shoulder. The employees were aroused by the clamor made by Walters. Appleton lived a few hours, dying in the early morning. A search for the guard discovered him sitting on a chair sound asleep in a house just outside the stockade. His name was Paddy Nolan. His negligence had resulted in the tragedy. He broke down and after two days of mental anguish and crying quit his work and the place. An Indian was sent to Spotted Tail to notify the agent, and he arrived at Red Cloud just at night of the same day. This occurred in the winter of 1873–4.

When Sod Agency was Moved

Wm. Garnett says this agency was moved over to the White River in the fall of 1873, and he came over the first time that fall and the Agency was not fully moved till the next spring. At first the buildings had boards on the roof covered with tar paper, and when the mechanics were at work shingling that winter when Chief Clerk Appleton was shot they were making the buildings more permanent, and the next spring they completed moving the Agency as John Farnham stated.[20] The Red Cloud Agency was never down in the bend of the White River northeast of where Crawford now is; but the Spotted Tail Agency was there when it was moved up from the foothills on the White Clay Creek on the Nebraska Extension of the Pine Ridge Reservation.

The first Agency that the Spotted Tail Indians had was down on the Missouri, and from there it came up to the Extension. The Spotted Tail Agency was on wheels for some years. Jack Whalen always lived at that Agency and he can give full account of its changes.[21]

Red Cloud was in Washington in 1870 and again in 1872.

John Richard Jr. killed a soldier at Fort Fetterman while in a half drunken condition in the year 1869.[22] He then escaped to the Indians up north and was there from fall till the next spring. At this time he was in partnership with Jules Eccoffey and Adolph Cooney.[23] Louis Richard attended to his part of the partnership business while he was in this species of exile. He slipped in at times during his voluntary banishment, and it must have been at these times that the scheme was worked up to secure his pardon by President Grant on condition that he would induce the Indian chiefs, including Red Cloud, to go to Washington. A lot went at this time.[24] Garnett saw all these with John Richard and a lot of Indians came to Fort Laramie & saw the chiefs with Richard in the center, march up to the officer's office. They went to Washington in 1870, and Richard was pardoned for murdering the soldier.

The Surround of Red Cloud and Red Leaf

Mr. Garnett says that Red Cloud and Red Leaf were camped on Chadron Creek, four or five miles above the Price & Jenks ranch (or Half Diamond E); that Red Leaf was about a mile above Red Cloud.[25] It was just at the close of the campaign of 1876 and the evils growing out of the loose manner in which the Indians were managed which allowed them to go and come at will and to wander off to remote places from the Agency had been productive of great hardship to the country; and while the memory of this experience was fresh the commanding officer at Fort Robinson, General Mackenzie, decided to bring the Indians near the Agency so that their movements might be more easily watched.[26] Red Cloud and Red Leaf were nearly thirty miles from the fort, and it was resolved to bring them in. The interpreter, Wm. Garnett, was sent for and given orders to go to the camps of these chiefs and tell them to move up to the Agency, and that if they did not comply their rations would be taken away, and if they did not move in after that they would be brought in by force. They returned no satisfactory answer. Garnett was sent to Red Cloud solely as he was recognized as the head chief; so he went to this chief's lodge, where he found Red Cloud and Red Dog, the latter generally doing the speaking for the former.[27] Red Dog responded by saying that the troops might have the buildings of the Red Cloud Agency; that they had the Bissonette house where they were, (pointing just across the creek) to put their rations in; to tell General Mackenzie to send their rations down to them and the beef cattle; to tell this to the General, and advised the interpreter to come along to assist in the making of the issue.

Ration day came but they got no rations, and still they were obstinate and remained away. The same messenger was again called, and this time his instructions left no doubt that General Mackenzie, after trying the persuasion of hunger, was preparing to make good the promise he had delivered to the chiefs that he would use force if necessary to bring their camps to the Agency. The young man was started off about nightfall on the _____ day of October 1876, for the Clifford (Henry) ranch and stage station on the Sidney and Black Hills route.[28] He was informed that General Mackenzie would move that night at a stated hour 7 o'clock with 4 companies of the 4th Cavalry & 4 companies of the 5th Cavalry, all in charge of Major Gordon of the 5th Cavalry in the direction of the Indian camps on the Camp Sheridan trail next [to] the Pine Ridge.[29] He was given dispatches for the officer that he was informed he would meet at Clifford's on the Niobrara River. He arrived there towards midnight, delivered his messages to Major Frank North, and after taking a fresh horse, he led off at the head of 41 Pawnee scouts ~~called Pawnees, but which were an a collection of Pawnees, Otoes Winnebagoes~~ under the command of Luther H. North, and moved rapidly north into the White River Valley to join Gen. Mackenzie whom he was either to intercept or overtake.[30] (Garnett says that a way back in the 60's Major North had Indian Scouts of Pawnees, Otoe, Osages, and Winnebagos, but they went under the name of Pawnees and that was the only name recognized by these Indians. I must verify this statement before using it.) Having passed Crow butte and reached Ash Creek he was hailed by an Indian in the distance toward the hills on the right, inquiring who he was; he answered back that he had some soldiers that he was taking down to Red Cloud's camp and that he (the Indian) should go to his own camp and not follow him. The Indian shouted back that soldiers had just gone along and were only a little way ahead. The guide knew that he must be close upon Mackenzie. He had been particular to advise his interlocutor not to come near the Pawnee scouts, as a bitter enmity existed between them and the Sioux, and sight of each other was all the provocation needed to bring on a fierce clash of arms. This man belonged to Little Wound's band which was in camp up the creek toward the hills. After a few miles travel the Pawnee advance came upon Mackenzie's rear-guard which was seized with a flurry, supposing that a heavy force of Indians were at their backs, and they dashed up to the main body announcing their belief to be the fact; but their excitement was quieted when the guide who had sped in among them in the darkness asked for the commanding officer and let it be known who he was.

Prior to this movement a one-armed man named Clark had been doing duty for General Mackenzie as an emissary in the Red Cloud and Red Leaf camps and mapping in his brain the routes to be followed when the troops should be led into positions before daylight to ~~invest~~ surround the Indians. When within four miles of the Chadron Creek Gen. Mackenzie divided his force equally and also divided the Pawnees equally and taking one body himself he moved on Red Cloud's camp, and Major Gordon taking the other and being guided by Clark was to surround Red Leaf; but by some error of Clark he led Gordon's command to Red Cloud's and surrounded the camp when Gen. Mackenzie arrived as day was breaking. The general ordered Gordon to advance on Red Leaf's village, and he invested Red Cloud's. The Pawnees were ordered when the troops became occupied with the Indians that they were to stampede the horses at the camps in the usual manner. The sun was just peeping over the hills east of Chadron Creek when Major Gordon's approach on the upper village was announced by a boy who was seen at the top of a high hill just west of the camp, who cried out that the creek was full of soldiers coming up. A charge into the village was ordered and the troopers rushed forward, William Garnett, the interpreter outstripping the others and dashing in ahead to talk to the Indians and calm their fears; which he did with safety, as they all knew him; and he hurriedly counseled them not to fire on the soldiers, telling them that if they did not start a fight that they would not be harmed. Major Gordon demanded to know where Red Leaf was, and it was found that he was not there but was somewhere near the Agency with two or three lodges; then the interpreter pointed out Quick Bear who was approaching, as the chief next in rank to Red Leaf, and though he denied that the was a chief, Garnett contradicted him to his face, having been in council with him and knowing well the truth of what he affirmed; whereupon Major Gordon leveled his revolver at him and told him that he wanted his arms and horses, and the Indian instantly promised to surrender them. Just at this moment an Indian standing close to the chief aimed at Major Gordon with a six shooter, but the quick interference of Garnett and Quick Bear averted the danger. The Indians' arms were gathered in haste. The horses belonging to the Indians were brought into the camp and their owners were permitted to use them in packing and moving.

    The method was not so orderly down at the other camp, the Pawnees being allowed to take the horses of the captives about as they pleased, and some of them outfitted themselves with the best they could find. About a mile and a half on the way the two commands came together. The Indian men and women marched separately in the column, all mounted.[31] When Ash Creek was reached the women were permitted to camp for the night while the men were taken on to the fort twelve miles farther. The column was met here by a convoy of provisions which had been sent for after the capture.

After the Indians with their effects were arrived at the fort and the lodges were put up, their baggage was searched for ammunition and a considerable quantity was obtained. The same day their lodges were torn down and set up again, this time down at the Agency. The following day a council was held in the Agency stockade.

This was a commission sent out by [the] government to take the Indian chiefs down to the Indian Territory to see the country so they might decide whether they would move down there and have agencies there or whether they would move over to the Missouri & have their agencies there. Spotted Tail & Red Cloud & Young Man Afraid & others went down.[32] These did not like the territory, so the trip never amounted to anything, and [the] next year (1877) the Sioux were taken to the Missouri and the Cheyennes were moved to the Indian Territory. In a day or two after the council Garnett, Big Bat and Frank Gruard were sent to the Spotted Tail Agency to get Indians for scouts. This was the beginning of the enlistments of Indian scouts, and it was Crook's scheme and undertaking.[33]

The Red Cloud and Red Leaf Indians were released as soon as they got settled around the Red Cloud Agency. This council was one of secret cross-purposes. A man named Howard (called Major) attended this. He had at one time been agent at the Spotted Tail Agency and wanted the job again.[34] Crook told this council that he was going to enlist Indian scouts. These scouts were enlisted for periods of six months. This Howard, thinking to enlist Gen. Crook's favor and influence, said to him that he had influence among the Spotted Tail Indians and might help him to get some of those Indians. Crook said very well, help these men who are going up there. When they got to Spotted Tail Agency there was a council of the Indians held the next day and Garnett waited. Howard and Dr. Daniels, an Indian Inspector, were explaining to the Indians about the forthcoming trip to the Indian Territory.[35] A party of chiefs including Spotted Tail and others went from here at once across to Snake Creek where they were to wait for a like delegation from Red Cloud Agency consisting of Chief Red Cloud, Young Man Afraid & others, and the whole were to proceed thence to Sidney to take cars for the Territory. In this council the Agent at Spotted Tail Agency, who was an army officer, having been informed by

Garnett what the business of these men was over there, called the attention of Howard and Chief Spotted Tail to Garnett's business, and suggested that they bring the matter to the notice of the assembled Indians.[36] Howard got up and threw cold water all over the plan and disapproved it altogether. Spotted Tail expressed no opinion but left it to his men to act in the matter as suited them. Then Garnett spoke to the Indians and explained the plan and its object and the good it was expected to produce. As soon as Gruard and Bat saw themselves opposed by Howard they returned to Fort Robinson, but Garnett remained a day or two longer, and when he went back he had seven with him for scouts, though only two were of Spotted Tail's band.

Here were the two departments of government—War and Interior—working at cross-purposes.

Garnett returned to Fort Robinson and Gen. Crook had left for the east; but when Gen. Mackenzie heard of the action of Howard he said this man will never get another appointment as Indian Agent, and he caused Garnett's affidavit to be taken describing what Howard had done, and forwarded it to Crook, and Howard's appointment as Agent at Spotted Tail Agency never materialized.[37]

It should be observed here that at this council which was held at Red Cloud Agency Gen. Crook deposed Chief Red Cloud and made Spotted Tail the chief over the Indians which were enrolled and rationed at the two agencies.[38] So far as Red Cloud was interested this little affected him, much less affected the Indians who acknowledged his chieftainship which was not denied in any quarter among them. The effect of Crook's act was simply to set up another with whom the government would hold official intercourse and whom it must perforce thereafter hold responsible as the recognized head of the tribe for the good behavior of its members. If so disposed to do, Red Cloud was now freer than ever to foment trouble; for, from the new position of the ~~government~~ authorities, he could be regarded only as a private person who might be put into the guard house temporarily by arbitrary authority, or "accidentally" killed or summarily hung according to the nature of the times or the convenience of the surroundings. Here is the way the deposition was done:

The council was on the inside of the stockade. The commission had come out to take the chiefs to Indian Territory, according to the terms of the 1876 treaty which had been made there at Red Cloud Agency a few months prior to this present event. It was a new set of men from the first commission, the only one who came to both conferences was the Indian inspector, Dr. Daniel. Captain Eldon a cavalry officer, was the acting Agent at Red Cloud.³⁹ Wm. Garnett was the interpreter at the conference which made the Black Hills Treaty, and at this one. (See the Black Hills Treaty.)

Garnett was at the conference when the Commission came out in 1875. He says the meeting was under the lone tree. There were other trees along the stream, but this was a tree that stood out by itself. The commission at this time offered $7,000,000 for the Hills.⁴⁰ The Indians did not understand how much this was.

Spotted Tail was in this council and Crook told him that he was chief of both Agencies.

The Indian scouts expressed at this council their dissatisfaction with Crook's order ~~deposing Red Cloud~~ making Spotted Tail chief of the two agencies, because they had a design of their own which they were promoting with the utmost endeavor, and which had been the real motive for enlisting as scouts in 1876, when they joined the winter expedition of that year; and it was no less than to thwart the object of the 1876 treaty for getting the Indians out of their own country and settling them in Ind. Territory or on the Missouri River; hence they protested from personal motives. Red Cloud and Spotted Tail had freely signed this treaty and now were hand-tied; but Young Man Afraid (he thinks) did not sign it and it is his belief that the scouts who represented the real sentiment of the Sioux and Arapaho nations, and as a few, being chiefs only, had weakly surrendered their rights and given away the interests of their people, it was secretly determined by the younger members of the tribes to recover as much as they could of what had been lost. They were shrewd enough to calculate that if they would assist the government to reduce the hostile Indians to submission and bring them in to the agencies they would have a strong claim for recognition of their important service and would be in position to press their demand to undo the bad agreement of the chiefs and to get an Agency established in the country where they wanted to live. This secret object developed on the winter campaign of 1876, as will be related further on, when they asked for councils with Gen. Crook and succeeded in obtaining from him promises of his assistance to accomplish the design. (Crook's mind had evidently been enlightened as to Spotted Tail's real feelings by his treatment of Garnett & Gruard and Big Bat when they wanted scouts; for Spotted Tail had told Crook that he would send him scouts, & when Garnett et al. reached his camp he was lukewarm and rendered no help.)

Garnett says now that he is not sure that Red Cloud went to the Indian

Territory; but the rest of the principal chiefs went. When Garnett was getting scouts for Crook at this period, it was the first enlistment of Sioux scouts.

Crook's army, after arriving at Fort Robinson, kept sifting off to Fort Laramie to fit up. These scouts also went to Laramie in company with the 4th Cavalry and other soldiers. There were (he thinks) 68 Sioux scouts; the Arapahos, including 5 or six Cheyennes, numbered a hundred, lacking 3 or 4. These separate scouts were each in command of a sergeant. Three Bears was the sergeant in command of the Sioux and Sharp Nose was the sergeant in command of the Arapahos; but when they were all out together the Arapahos voluntarily recognized and acknowledged Three Bears as the ranking officer. Three Bears died at Pine Ridge as a sergeant of Police & is buried in the Episcopal Cemetery.[41]

This expedition started out from Laramie. These scouts drew their revolvers and Sharp's rifles.

The chief scouts on this expedition were Big Bat, Louie Richard and Louie Shangrau. The chief interpreters were Wm. Garnett and Wm. Rowland.[42] At Fort Reno on Powder River (this Fort Reno is about a mile south or up the river from old Fort Reno of 1865 & 1866) the Snake or Shoshone Indian scouts were met. These Indians were under a white leader who had a Snake wife. His name was Crosby.[43] They had an interpreter who was a mixed-blood. These scouts had their wives and children along with them. The Snake wives had their babies strapped to boards with a band fastened at one end to pass over their heads so the babes could be carried on their backs when walking; and when riding these boards and babies were hung on the horn of the saddle. After leaving the fort one of these babies hanging to the saddle was run away with by the horse. The mother dismounted to fix a pack and the horse started off. At every jump the board and baby flapped the horse and frightened him. He was surrounded and caught and the infant received no harm.

At Fort Reno Gen. Crook assembled all the Indian scouts and announced to them through the several interpreters that from that day all the Indians in the United States who remained on the reservations and were peaceable would all be as one and be as one harmonious with the white people and could visit one another no matter on what reservations they lived, and if they turned against such as were hostile and assisted the whites against them they and the whites would be as one; and that he would send out a letter or order to this effect that day. The general told them to shake hands. They did so with great rejoicing and handshaking; and some of the Indians made presents to other Indians, giving even horses in some cases. It was a most politic measure, and had an exceedingly conciliatory effect among the scouts of different tribes. Up to this time the Sioux scouts had been somewhat reserved toward the others, but after this there was the fullest freedom and warmest friendship and most cordial intercourse. (Garnett says Sheldon told him in 1903 that he had seen it, or something else about it.)[44] Garnett interpreted this speech of Crook's. Garnett says that after this speech the Pawnees who had been suspicious of the Sioux and were a little afraid to go among the Sioux were full of confidence and not afraid. The Arapahos and Sioux had formerly been friends and united in conflicts against the Snakes, and there was traditional enmity between these two & the Snakes, but now the fullest satisfaction and good will were established. It cannot be too emphatically stated that this was one of the most pacific acts that was ever performed by any agent or officer of the government. (Ask Sheldon if he ever found the order.)

Notwithstanding the Arapahos had lived up around Fort Robinson, on White River, and Deadman Creek, and a part of the time were mingled with the Sioux and had been inveterate enemies in conjunction with the Sioux against the Shoshones, in 1877 when the Sioux went down to the Missouri river, the Arapahos went off west to the Shoshone reservation.[45]

After the Indian chiefs had been to the Indian Territory and come back with their minds set against removal down there the alternative remained under the 1876 treaty of a few months before to go to the Missouri River; but removal to the latter point was a government proposition dictated by the desire to have the distributing agencies on the river on account of transportation, while to the Indians it was a sacrifice of all their desires to comply with the government's conveniences. But the Indians went reluctantly in conformity to an understanding that it would be for a year, as their rations and supplies had been sent there and the agency buildings were in course of erection. The Arapahos, however, were not required to move east, but were allowed to go in the opposite direction to the Shoshones for the year, and their supplies were to be conveyed to that Agency. They failed to return and have ever since been on that reservation. In 1877, after the death of Crazy Horse, a delegation of Indians went to Washington and had a meeting with President Hayes at the Executive Mansion,[46] and among those of the Sioux who went, he remembered the following: Young Man Afraid, Red Cloud, He Dog, a nephew of Red Cloud and one of the northern Indians and a chief—he means by the northern Indians those who had never come in to the reservation till they came in with Crazy Horse—Big Road, Little Big Man, Iron Crow all these except Red Cloud & Young Man Afraid were

Northern or Crazy Horse chiefs; and the following Red Cloud Indian chiefs who had lived on the Reservation, viz; Three Bears, Little Wound, American Horse, Yellow Bear; (Wm Garnett went as a and the following interpreters for the Sioux, viz.; Antoine Janis and Leon Palladay[47] (a relation, not a brother, but he thinks a cousin of Alfred Palladay who was killed with John Richard Sr. on Running Water);[48] on the part of the Arapahos was 1st Chief Black Cole Coal, Sharp Nose 2d chief, and Friday (so-called by white people) who was an Arapaho Indian and acted some of the time as interpreter for the Arapahos and went for this purpose; and the following Spotted Tail Indians: Spotted Tail, Sr., Spotted Tail Jr., Hollow Horn Bear, White Tail; and the following Sitting Bull Indians who were Northern Indians also, having been brought in from the north by Spotted Tail himself.[49] Red Cloud had been sent out to bring in Indians who were out up north and he passed west of the Black Hills and brought in Crazy Horse and his Indians but did not meet or see Spotted Tail who also went out going on the opposite side of the Black Hills about the same time which was in March (at any rate snow was on the ground) and he brought in these Sitting Bull Indians; Garnett says there were two villages of these Northern Indians up there and Red Cloud got one and Spotted Tail the other, and when Crazy Horse got in to Red Cloud there were 40 lodges with him that belonged to the Spotted Tail Agency and these moved on down to that agency. With the delegation that went to Washington were Garnett who was telegraphed for by Gen. Crook who was in Washington (it was on this trip that Garnett saw him dressed up in a fine broadcloth suit, plug hat, diamond studs and carrying a gold headed and gold feruled cane & G. did not know him and thought he was a Washington shark); and Lieut. Clark (sign language Clark, one of Crook's staff) who went in charge of the delegation, and Dr. Irwin, U.S. Indian Agent at Red Cloud.[50]

Garnett went as government interpreter and did all the interpreting. Boucher (who paid his own expenses) and Jo Marivaill were brought up by Spotted Tail for interpreters and they went; but they were selected by Spotted Tail as a partiality to them for their going up north with him when he went to bring in the Sitting Bull Indians.[51]

This was probably about September, 1877. All these persons composing the delegation went to the Executive Mansion accompanied by General Crook. To start in, General Crook named Lieut. Clark to President Hayes and Clark introduced each man to the President, describing each as he introduced him, giving some account of the position each held at home, and what had been the attitude of each in the complicated difficulties which had kept the northwest embroiled. The President would not allow the public and the newspapers to be represented, and he made the conference on the first day a private affair. The short-hand men it is believed belonged to the President's private corps. When the Indians went to talking to Hayes their selected interpreters became confused and unable to interpret with success, so that no progress whatever was made. After 2 or 3 hours of futile effort the conference ended with the announcement by the President that there would be another meeting the next day. This was held in the afternoon, and so was the second conference. The one on the second day turned out the same way and ended by the President announcing a third meeting the next. What had been done and taken down up to this time was thrown away as worthless. Now on the third day the meeting was opened (as he remembers) by Spotted Tail.

Garnett says some Indians on the Reservation have the printed pamphlet of all the speeches by the chiefs, by General Crook and by President Hayes and he will get one for me to be copied and returned. These Indians were working with a united purpose to obtain a change of the plan to remove them to Indian Territory & in case they decided not to go there then they were to be taken to Missouri River. They did not find the Territory agreeable—the climate did not agree with them, for the Northern Indians had fever and ague and fevers down there, and those who had settled from the north and been there some years were still dying off with too great mortality. They decided against the Territory. They did not want to go to the Missouri no more than to the Territory for another common reason, viz; there was no game in either place, and they complained that both places were dead.

Gen. Crook made a strong talk to the President detailing his councils with his Indian scouts on the expedition north from Fort Robinson and Laramie and Fetterman when Mackenzie cleaned out the Cheyennes Nov. 25, 1876, and the promises he made them that if they would help him to secure Indian scouts, & help him to cause the Northern Indians to come in to the Reservations, or in case they would not peaceably return, would aid him in forcing them in, that he would lay the case of these Indians for an agency back in their country wherever they wanted it before the President and use all his influence to obtain it for them; that they had performed their part of the agreement and were entitled to have their wants gratified.[52] The President told the Indians that their wishes were reasonable, but that as their supplies for a year had been shipped to the Missouri and it would be necessary for them to move down there for a year and consume the provisions, and then they might move back and select a location for an agency. Red Cloud got up and said he would not go down; but Young Man Afraid arose and said that Red Cloud had signed the treaty promising to go there if they did not go to the Indian Territory, and now he should go and he himself would see that he went. (Red Cloud and Spotted Tail signed the treaty, but Young Man Afraid had not done so because he was not around, but his father, Man Afraid of His Horse signed.)

As soon as these delegates came back from Washington the two agencies moved. The Spotted Tail Agency went east and crossed W. K. crossing 6 miles south of where the battleground is, and continued on east, and must have struck the Niobrara in the neighborhood of Valentine, for this band followed this River. Red Cloud followed the course of the White River. Spotted Tail took the old Ponca Reservation and drew rations there. He was a long way below Yellow Medicine.

Red Cloud stopped at the forks of the White River, and this had been agreed upon before they left Red Cloud Agency that Red Cloud should stop there and winter. This was not where the Agency was. The Yellow Medicine Agency was on the Missouri bottom and above the mouth of the Creek of the same name, and the traders' stores were between the Agency and Yellow Medicine Creek & some 300 or 400 yds. from the Agency.

The Red Cloud Indians came down from the forks of the White River to draw rations, distance 65 miles. John Deere [Dear], Tom Cogill and Major Paddock had each had main stores at the Agency and branches at the forks of the White River. The beef herd was kept up at the forks, and Ben Tibbitts was butcher and acting agent there. Ed. Stevenson was the chief herder there and Alec. Adams, Mitch Jarvis, Dan Powell and George Carson were the other herders.

I must now go back to the northern expedition of Gen. Crook when he moved troops from Robinson to Laramie and thence to Fetterman and sent Mackenzie to punish the Cheyennes on Nov. 25, 1876. While at Fetterman the Indian scouts under him asked for a council with him. Garnett was the interpreter on all these occasions. They began by saying: They told him that they wanted to talk; told him (Louie Richard and Louie Shangrau were not with the command at this time—had not yet come up—did not reach the command till it got to Sage Creek, a little creek about 15 miles out from Fort Fetterman). The first day out from Fort Fetterman the command camped on Sage Creek.

Gruard and Big Bat were present. After the command reached Fetterman Garnett made up his mind from what he saw that the scouts were in the service for an ulterior object. In the Fetterman council they informed him (Crook) as follows:

(The speakers were Keeps the Battle, a brother of Woman's Dress, and Red Shirt—who has always been a leading showman for Buffalo Bill & is out with a lot of Indians with a show company this winter of 1906-7; he has been a showman for many years—he has been Chief of the Loafer band, which is settled on Pine Ridge out north of Jack Whalen's since 1878 when he was elected to that position; and he was sergeant of scouts under Crook at this time, and has been at several times.) (Keeps the Battle and Fast Thunder were sergeants of the scouts under Crook on this winter expedition of Crook's; the former is dead, so is Feather on the Head dead; he was a sergeant also at same time under Crook; Fast Thunder is living on W. K. Creek midway between the battle ground and Manderson.)

~~Three Bears~~ Keeps the Battle was a sub-chief under Red Cloud and was one of those who were captured in the camp on Chadron Creek and stripped of horses and arms; Crook had 3 or 4 of these men of Red Cloud's as scouts on this expedition; Crook had also 2 Indians as scouts at this time, who were captured at the Slim Buttes fight, one of whom Crook made a Corporal, which act was evidently to show them that if they would submit and be really good and useful Indians to the whites that they would receive marked consideration as well as good treatment.[53]

Garnett remarks that Red Cloud Agency had a bad reputation as being troublesome and belligerent, and he believes that the young men showing wisdom beyond their years, according to the popular idea of "old men for counsel, young men for war," had resolved by wise and firm conduct to put their nation upon a better footing in the estimation of the country; and what followed with Crook was in pursuance of this sage plan.

Three Bears was not a speaker, but a very brave and reliable man. He was head sergeant of the scouts. Sharp Nose, the leading Arapaho sergeant, was a good talker, and he was backing Three Bears with his powerful aid. No other Arapaho spoke at this council, though others were present, he being the mouthpiece for his tribesmen on such occasions, and whatever he did commanded cheerful compliance from his fellows. The Arapaho nation was small in numbers, and on this expedition nearly every one of their warriors was enlisted among these scouts. Another point to be noticed was that after Crook got this force of Indian scouts the regular guides were much less needed, for the Indians all knew the country better than the official scouts; these Indians revolutionized things, brought about improved methods, showed a better way, etc. Sharp Nose led Mackenzie all through the night march before they fell on the Cheyennes. Garnett says that Sharp Nose was the best scout he ever knew; Gruard was not to be compared on a night march.

At this council Three Bears opened the speaking by telling, in a few words, Gen. Crook that his sergeants would do the talking, and whatever they said would be the sentiment of these scouts; they will tell you why we join you as scouts. To begin: He is told first about the Agencies & the recent 1876 agreement about them; they told him the greater part of the people were in the north, & only a very few Indians were at Red Cloud where the treaty was made in the summer. (This 1876 treaty was made in this way: the Commission came first to Red Cloud; a few signatures were secured; then the Com. went to Spotted Tail where a few were got; then the Com. went to the R. R. and whirled around to some other place and got a few more signers, and so on till they wound up with less than 40, and not all of these were chiefs.)[54]

These scouts told Crook that they were dissatisfied with the treaty. (Crook knew that he had a hard task before him to get the Indians in & settled and the northwest pacified; he knew that a part had gone across the border which made the settlement of the difficulties a case of indefinite postponement and duration; he understood further that the Indians were being all the time imposed on by schemers, agents & politicians and their tools and that treaties and bargains and official acts and reports and recommendations were all a part of one general scheme of injustice, the Indians being deceived by false promises and overreached; and he was also the strong arm or representative of this self-same corrupt, dishonest machine and stood between this monster with orders to execute its will, and his own uncorrupted conscience and personal honor.) They told him further: That the reason they were with him as scouts on this expedition was for the purpose of getting an Agency in their own country — they said they did not want to go to a strange place. Crook told them he was not after the Indians because there was any desire to kill them; that he did not want to kill them, but to get them in so they would mingle with the friendly Indians.

(When Red Cloud and Red Leaf were captured the Pawnee scouts took their pick of the horses taken at Red Cloud's camp — this was not allowed at Red Leaf's — and after the Indians were brought in to Red Cloud Agency from Chadron Creek all the Indian horses were taken; and here, before going out on this northern expedition Crook mounted his Indian scouts on these horses captured from Red Cloud & Red Leaf; and furthermore he took a band of them along with him to Fetterman where he turned them over to these same scouts, at this council, in his speech he gave the horses to them, and further said that all horses which they might capture on this campaign should belong to them.) He told them that his business was to get the Indians who were out, and if they would be loyal to his purpose and aid him all they could, when the object was gained he would exert his influence to get them settled down in the country of their choice with an Agency as they wanted. (This he told in Washington to President Hayes at the Indian council.)

Crook moved north and the first night camped 15 miles out on Sage Creek where Louie Shangrau and Louie Richard joined him.

It took about three days more to gain Powder River where a camp was made lasting about a week. From the time Mackenzie left Fort Robinson all through the month of November there were snow storms at short intervals, but no great depth of snow came in any single instance, until after the fight with the Cheyennes. When the troops were encamped at Fort Reno there was at least one storm. There were storms while at Fort Robinson and at Laramie; they marched from Laramie to Fetterman in the snow. It snowed the night they camped at Sage Creek just north of Fetterman.

The Snake scouts were already encamped there at the new Fort Reno (elsewhere described), about nearly 100 in number, but over one hundred with the Indian women and children (elsewhere mentioned), under their chief, Washakie.[55] In 2 or 3 days Crook asked the Sioux and Arapaho scouts to go out to look for Indians. There were 5 Sioux and 5 Arapahos, an Indian sergeant with each, Red Shirt was the Sioux sergeant and the Arapaho sergeant he cannot name.[56] The Sioux scouts besides the sergeant were Six Feather, Little Bull, White Face and Red Horse. Gen. Crook instructed them to dress as the Indians always do, and to carry their military uniforms with them, so their real character should be concealed, telling them that if they were out as an Indian party and were not suspected as belonging to Crook's army, that other Indians would not avoid but would come up to them and then these could get information desired. The Sioux and Arapahos were chosen for the special reason that the other Indians that it was hoped they would meet, knew of the old friendship of Sioux and Arapahos for each other and their habit of being and going together, and this would make the hostiles more approachable.

(Painted Horse, an Oglala, a relative of Red Cloud, was in the Custer battle; he returned to R. C. Agency and enlisted among the Oglala scouts but was not one of this little party.)

This party left Crook's camp and traveled some 40 miles northeast in the supposed direction of hostiles (Garnett was not with this party.)

(Every step from Fort Robinson to Reno Old Sitting Bull and Crazy Horse and all the hold-out Indians knew what Indians Crook had taken with him as scouts, and who the chief scouts were.)

These scouts had camped at night and picketed their horses and started a fire and cooking and around which the men were warming and singing and exchanging jokes as was usual with them when it was noticed by the others that Red Horse who was an odd Indian always passing jokes and acting the part of a clown, was uttering observations which they did not understand and which they suspected was some of his native drollery. He was craning his neck and looking toward the horses and saying: "I wonder if that fellow would take one of those horses. He is right among them now." And he kept repeating his query whether the "fellow" would take one of them, etc.

Some of the others inquired, "What are you talking about?" He said: "Don't you see that fellow out among the horses? He don't look like one of those Arapahos." The others looked. An Indian in a blanket was near the horses; he kept approaching and stopping as if in doubt and examining every object. Finally he halted at a distance and one cried out to him: "Come up! the meal is on!" and he walked up to the fire. Red Shirt was a good sign-talker, and all Arapahos were naturally expert sign-talkers while the Sioux were not as a nation. Red Shirt told him that these scouts had left the Agency to come to Sitting Bull and Crazy Horse's camps and were direct from the Agency; that there were a lot of soldiers and Pawnees and Arapahos and Sioux coming out after the hostiles, and these told that they had just left the Agency, as this Indian could see they were cooking Agency provisions as well as wild game.

This was a Cheyenne named <u>Many Beaver Dam</u>. The Arapahos and Sioux had separate fires. The Indian was put to eating at the Arapaho fire, and while he was gorging himself the Arapaho sergeant passed over to the Sioux fire to fix their plans for his capture.[57] The Arapaho told Red Shirt that the Sioux are the leaders at home and would be recognized on this scout as leaders; "You put on your sergeant's coat and I will mine; just about the time you throw your blanket off to show by your coat who you are, we will throw our guns down on him; you can tell him we are Indian soldiers & are out to look from camp for anything we can come across; and we will take your arms and take you back to camp; anybody who is good we are good to; we have a few Cheyennes as scouts, with Bill Rowland for Cheyenne and Arapaho chief interpreter." (They called him

Long Knife, he had a Cheyenne wife.) It was agreed further that they would talk more to him when he was disarmed. Red Shirt told his men to be ready. The Arapaho added that his men had been prepared since his arrival, and further that if the Cheyenne made any break while Red Shirt was disarming him that he would shoot the Indian. The capture was performed according to this agreement. Red Shirt announced to the man that he was under arrest of this party of Indian soldiers and not to put his hand on his gun; if he did he would be killed. And then his arms were taken. He had a gun and a knife and 3 cartridges. (Before his arrest he had been engaged in conversation and had told where the Indian villages were located, and given other information of value.)

After his arrest he was told that he would be taken to Three Stars (Gen. Crook) and that he must tell the general just what he had told themselves. After taking the arms from one of the scouts so that the captive could not seize them to make a fight with, he was put on behind the scout, and as one horse became weary from carrying a double load, the prisoner was transferred to another scout similarly treated as to disarming, until the party arrived in camp on the afternoon of the next day. General Crook examined the prisoner. On the following day he called a council of the Indians and told them that he was going to issue an order that, from that day they should be free to go wherever they chose to visit other Indians; that they should be friendly with one another and avoid wars among themselves; that it would be their duty to aid the government in fighting if necessary to get the hostiles in, or to assist in any way possible to do this, and to be friendly with them afterwards, and that this should apply to all the Indians, that it would promote friendship between between the whites and Indians, and that he would issue an order that day declaring these purposes; and he told them that he wanted them all to shake hands together in token of their acceptance of these new and better relations. (Elsewhere described.)

Then followed a general handshaking and universal and demonstrative rejoicing. Garnett says he never saw before or since such manifestation and acclaim of good will and genuine happiness. (Inquire of A. E. Sheldon if he ever found this order.)

The prisoner, Many Beaver Dam, had given information of the location Cheyenne village, and while this was not found where he had located it in his statement, though the troops did not go to the locality he had described, yet it had been in that place but was moved from there.

The prisoner told where Sitting Bull was camped and where Crazy Horse was camped and where the Cheyenne camp was, and also where he was camped with his friends. He said he had been watching these scouts all day, and when he discovered that they were Sioux he decided to approach their camp, and did so with the result noted.

When the Cheyenne fight came off this Indian slipped away and escaped.

After the speech by Crook aforesaid, the Pawnees and Sioux associated freely. All the way from Fort Robinson to Reno where this pacific measure was given out, the Sioux had not mingled with the Pawnees, for their ancient feud could not be forgotten, and they camped apart, Joe Bush being the only Sioux who went among them in camp; but when Crook issued this manifesto the two tribes, and all the tribes entered into the most cordial and sociable relations, and approved and cemented the conciliation by exchange of presents, some of these being valuable horses.[58]

Now came a twelve-mile move to Crazy Woman. The night the troops camped there the Sioux and the Arapahos were apprehensive of trouble, being certain that something was hovering in the vicinity, though nothing had been seen, & they watched their horses all night. The night the camp was made on Crazy Woman it snowed to the depth of three or four inches, coming from the northwest with moderate wind. At full daylight a man came over the hill northwest of the camp from the direction of old Fort C. F. Smith, bearing a white flag. When he came into camp he proved to be a Cheyenne government spy who had been in Sitting Bull's camp. Crook had two Indian spies already up among the northern Indians, and one of these remained there till Crazy Horse came in, but it is not known that they ever rendered any particular service, for the occasion for such service never came, as they had been commissioned to slip away from the Indians when Crook should approach and press them, and give him advice as to the direction in which they contemplate escaping. These two spies were Lone Bear and Iron Bear. These had been sent out by Mackenzie before the starting of the expedition. One of these, Lone Bear, came back before the other did, as some of the northern hold-outs returned in advance of C. Horse, and Lone Bear returned with one of these straggling parties.

The Cheyenne government spy who came in with a flag was named Sitting Bear; had a family back at Red Cloud Ag., and the Indians became suspicious of him, more particularly a few Cheyennes who were with the Sioux, and these denounced him as a spotter and advised that he be cast out of the camp or killed; and he, conscious that if a fragment of his tribe could so well surmise his real character that it would probably be much worse for him if he should try to pass himself off on the main camp of his tribe, he at last made up his mind to get away from them and make his way into Gen. Crook's camp. This he succeeded in doing as stated. He brought news of the present location of the Cheyenne village, a place to which they had moved from where the captured Cheyenne had said they were. The latter had not tried to deceive, but the Cheyennes had moved without his knowledge.[59]

Sitting Bear gave the information that the camp he came from, viz.; Crazy Horse's, had known from the time the expedition first started up to the day he left, every movement of the army and where it was all the while, and everything that was being done; for he had scouts out all the time passing through the country in formidable squads; and this emissary advised the scouts not to go out in twos and threes to be overcome, but always to have a strong force for protection. Sitting Bear told how the Sioux and Cheyennes were split in two and camped something like 100 miles apart.

On Sitting Bear's arrival in camp the Sioux scouts formed a plan of movement which, being carried to Crook, was executed so far as the Cheyennes were concerned, with success. Garnett knows that this was planned by the Sioux and communicated as stated, because he interpreted for the Sioux when they went to Crook with it; and he was the Sioux interpreter all through the campaign. They told the General that their plan was to go against the Cheyennes while they were so far from the Sioux, and use them up, and then to turn on the latter and finish them, thus destroying the hostiles in detail. They told him to send out some companies of soldiers two or three miles in different directions, for there were scouts of the enemy watching the movements from his camp at distances, to push these back so far that they could not see what Crook was doing — could not see movements of troops from his camp. This he did, sending them out before noon. Right after dinner the Indian Scouts under Clark, as Garnett thinks and says he knows (but, Judkins says Frank North. See Bourke), [were] followed by Mackenzie with the 4th Cavalry.[60] After camp was made that night 4 Sioux and 4 Arapahos were sent out — the Sioux were Kills A Hundred (later name Red Dog, as he took the place of his father Red Dog when the father died on Pine Ridge Reservation, and he is now — 1907 — a chief on the Reservation), Little Battle, Skunk Head, and another. All 8 were sent out to discover the Cheyenne village. A little larger force of Pawnee and Snake scouts also went forth. Next morning the command marched and at noon was in the foothills of the mountains, as the Indians opposed moving out on the open country where Mackenzie proposed to move, as they would be discovered by the enemy. Sharp Nose, the Arapaho chief who was in command of the Arapaho scouts, was the guide leading the whole command, he being in country of his acquaintance. While the column was in motion a shot was fired contrary to orders either accidentally or at some game, by a white man with the pack train, and he was not permitted to go farther with the troops but was turned right out. At noon no fires were built, as orders were issued to that effect. Mackenzie had pickets out on the hills while the column halted for dinner. Suddenly "boots and saddles" sounded from the bugles and the troops gathered their horses. A soldier was running from a hill toward the command. He gives information of the approach of Indians. Scouts go out at once to see what it was. They discover their own scouts coming with a signal; Skunk Head and the other Sioux whose name was not given, and two Arapahos were returning. The Indian scouts who had advanced to meet the returning scouts were singing and dancing some war figure. They had a blanket; they stood up a stick and hung the blanket over it and they were dancing around it, and when the scouts came in they knocked this blanket down, and one of the singers advanced to a Sioux and led him inside the circle and he was asked what he had learned. He told them that they had seen in a valley seven lodges, a lot of horses, and they thought from the great number of horses that there must be more lodges there, and the leaders other scouts, 2 Sioux and 2 Arapahos, including the leaders of this party, had remained to advance nearer to the village and make a more minute investigation of the camp, and had sent these back to report, and stated just where the other scouts would meet the command. Sharp Nose now brought his Arapahos up and these made the same report. After this the command moved and at night they found the rest of the scouts at the place where they had sent word they would be; and from these they learned that it was the main village of the Cheyennes that had been discovered; that there were 200 or more lodges and thousands of horses. Here the Indian scouts threw off all extra incumbrance and left behind the horses they had been riding, some hobbled and the rest turned loose without guard, and mounted their fast horses, as they called them, which they had been leading, as was the custom when they were on the warpath to have two and to mount the fresh one when they go into action. Sergeant Red Shirt had charge of the rear guard of the scouts, Yankton Charley being in his squad.[61] Sharp Nose was in the lead as the guide for the column, he being as familiar with every inch of the country as though it was his dooryard. Garnett was chief Sioux interpreter for Mackenzie. Lieut. Clark was in the lead at the heels of Sharp Nose. Garnett was with these all night and up to the moment when the charge was made, when he and Big Bat were ordered, on arrival at the point where the dispositions were making to charge up this branch of the Powder River, by Mackenzie to stop the Sioux scout named Scraper who was dashing ahead to reach the village. Mackenzie was back at the head of his cavalry men. Riders were passing backward and forward all night between the advance of the scouts and the Colonel.

The weather was clear and cold, no light save from the stars and it was therefore pretty dark; there was snow on the mountains and spots of ice along the line of march, all remaining from former snows, but there was no fresh snow to leave a trail but there were places where they would cross crusted snow. The scouts left their horses on a flowing stream, one of the main branches of Powder River. This stream they followed up some way that night; when they left this stream (which ran east at the point where the horses were left, they moving therefrom in a westerly direction) they crossed over to the south side and retraced their course for a little way, and then turned nearly south and passed over a high ridge a distance of nearly two miles, then descended into a dry valley, all the time going deeper and deeper into the mountains while continually ascending in elevation. Here in this valley some ears a little quicker to catch sound than others heard the first faint notes of drums in the village echoing in the night air among the hills. All the time that the column was toiling on scouts were pushing out in advance to discover all they could and were returning with whatever information they found; these accounts described scenes of revelry in the village; a while before the Cheyennes had had a fight with a hunting party of Shoshones and destroyed it, killing about 30, and the Cheyennes were celebrating their victory with dancing and singing, and the occasion was one of great joy in the scalp dance which was kept up day and night (for months usually) with the invariable accompaniment of feasting. The column picked its way along, at times being obliged to pass in single file, word being sent back along the line bearing advice of obstacles in front when these narrow passages were encountered. The distance was not so great as it seemed by reason of the obstructions which impeded the movement.

When the column emerged from this dry valley at its head it was at a pass between two mountains where it could look ~~forward and~~ down into another valley in front, very heavily timbered with cottonwood, box elder, willows and other soft woods. From this point there was a gentle descent for men on horseback for a distance of half a mile to the creek on which the village was situated farther up. From this pass or gap the eager scouts saw herds of horses to gladden the prospect before them. They were coming in from the northeast, advancing down an incline toward the southwest in a widening gap. As soon as

Mackenzie reached the center of the pass he halted the column and issued his orders to the scouts. He told them that he wanted them to take the horses belonging to the village, but not to shoot unless the Cheyennes first shot; if they do not shoot we will capture them without shooting. Meantime the Indian scouts were chafing to spring on the village as daylight was breaking and they could hear the strains of music and other sounds of merriment and knew that the village was all unconscious of the presence of any foe, and the scouts could scarce restrain themselves, so great was their desire to make the attack a perfect surprise and success. It was with the greatest difficulty that they could be held in check from breaking forward and bursting upon the village; and Three Bears, the chief sergeant of the Sioux, was kept busy in pressing the over-anxious ones back into their places in the line. One of the Sioux named Scraper had eluded the officers' notice and advanced halfway down the slope when he was discovered by Mackenzie who exclaimed: "What man is that down there?" He was told that he was a Sioux. He ordered Garnett and Baptiste Pourier to go down to bring him back. When they overtook him he had gained the bed of the creek. Garnett told him that he had been sent by Mackenzie to get him back to charge with the scouts. Just as this took place Scraper was tying his war bonnet under his chin. He answered back: "I never allow anybody to think before me in a case of this kind. You've made sergeants, even common Indians, follow me; I'm a-go-ing." Just then Sergeant Fast Thunder came up. (It should be explained that Scraper was a Wajjahje — Waz zah ze better represents the sound.

Garnett now writes it here in Oglala: Wajaje—; that is a member of Old Conquering Bear's band, and he was the only one of that band who was among these scouts; and for that reason the officers who had the appointment of non-commissioned officers did not give him an appointment, he being alone; and the seeming neglect had made him jealous and envious, while he was a very brave man and knew that he was deserving; so he did not mean to be held in restraint but intended to be in advance and in the thickest of the fight.)
[Tablet 2]
Tuesday January 15, 1907. Second Book of Interview of William Garnett. Continued from First Book [Tablet 1].

When Sergeant Fast Thunder arrived there were four in the squad. They advanced together mounted, Scraper leading; they crossed the stream in the direction of the village, being guided by the sounds of the music. Their progress was hindered by the fallen logs which lay in the way, and the inclining trees and hanging limbs, their course being through heavy timber. At length they struck the trail to the camp, and from now on they were passing among the Indians' horses which were scattered everywhere in small herds, the whole aggregating a vast number. From where the stream was crossed to the village was fully two and a half miles. The horses, some of them, had buffalo shoes to protect their feet from the rasping stones which covered that country and had made them footsore. These shoes were pieces of raw buffalo hide wrapped about the hoof and drawn up to the fetlock pastern joint and fastened by a string. The location of this village was in a park in the mountains, which was probably three miles long and a mile and a half wide, allowing liberal space for operations, as well as an ideal retreat for the Indians' winter encampment and the security of their herds. The valley was diversified with hills and depressions; in parts was dense timber, then clear spaces; the creek entered from the west not far from the southwest corner of the park, and flowing directly across to a point between the middle and the east side, abruptly bent north until facing the pass through which Mackenzie's column bore down; there it swept broadly to the west, gradually veering in a wide circle and passing the mountain north of the gap in a northeasterly course. This was its general direction, but the banks, minutely described, presented a great variety of crooks and windings, high first on one side and then on the other, according to the concavities of the channel. The village lay on both sides above the bend where the water changes flow from east to north, fixing its location near the middle of the valley east and west and not far from the southern extremity where there was a gap in the hills opposite the village. From the northwest corner of the park a crooked dry gulch extended to the village and opened into the creek. After the scouts and troopers had debauched into the valley their general movement was upward and toward the south. The borders of this park were high mountains, steep cliffs on the west side and a sloping flank on the east.

The squad of fighters consisting of Big Bat, Garnett, Scraper and Fast Thunder forged ahead four or five hundred yards when they saw the first Indian who was out looking after horses. The two Indians were in war bonnets and the scout and interpreter wore citizen's clothes. This solitary Indian gazed at these startling intruders a few seconds till he evidently realized their character, then he gave them a shot from his revolver, and turned and ran like a deer. Garnett yelled: "He fired first; now fire!" The squad fired. This was the beginning of the battle. Two of the scouts who had gone forward during the advance in the night had not returned, but in their enthusiasm and boldness to penetrate as close to the village as they could for observation had pushed themselves into such a situation that when dawn came they could not withdraw without danger of being seen and exposing the presence of the expedition in the neighborhood; so these two men secreted themselves awaiting the arrival of the troops to be released from their enforced imprisonment. These were No Neck and Last Horse, both still living on the Pine Ridge Reservation.[62] When Garnett shouted the order to fire, these scouts heard his words and recognized his voice, and they knew that the time for them to be free from their confinement was close at hand.

The scouts in this squad had listened to Mackenzie's order to the main body of the scouts regarding the capture of the horses and they understood what was necessary to give effect to his order on that part of the field where the contingencies of the morning had allotted their fighting. In pursuance of the object to get possession of these animals the squad pressed up the valley to get between them and the village and at the same time to drive back and hold in check as many of the Cheyennes as they could, giving the scouts of the main body all possible opportunity to run off the horses.

This squad kept pressing the herders back and continuing their own course now in a westerly direction till they attained a rocky ridge east of and parallel to the dry run where Lieut. McKenney was afterwards killed.[63] Scraper and Fast Thunder were now separated from the squad and fighting on their own hook somewhere else and their places were taken by the half-breed, Jim Twist and a stranger (whom Bat well knew). The Indians were increasing in number in the front of the four men, for by this time Indian scouts had passed up the stream and along the base of the hills on the east of the park and assailed the village at the southeast corner and were driving the inhabitants toward them up the main dry run; and the cavalry was advancing up the valley. The four men before taking to the top of the ridge had dismounted and hitched their horses out of the range of the enemies bullets. The approaching cavalry must have mistaken these men for Indians. On a much higher ridge at some distance opposite and on the other side of the main dry run were Cheyennes who were directing their fire at the cavalry and their shots were passing over the squad of four; but the cavalry evidently believed the bullets were coming from the ridge where the four were trying to keep back the Cheyennes who were coming up the main dry run from the village, for their shots were directed at these and made their position untenable and they changed to other places, each going his own way. But before this took place a lone Indian appeared on horseback, mistaking this squad for his own tribesmen as he came up on a canter within a few feet of them before he stopped. As he was nearing them Garnett remarked that he was a stranger, but Bat said he was one of our scouts. As he halted the four men fired on him and he instantly wheeled and rode toward the main dry run, but before he could reach it Garnett fired at his horse and brought him down. Garnett shouted to Bat that he had killed the horse. The man raised up and Garnett gave him a shot and he fell. Garnett shouted to Big Bat that he had killed the Indian.

I have gone thus much into particularity in relation to this Indian because of his notable life and subsequent celebrated career. Before he had been shot at by the four men he had received a wound from the scouts. This and the one that Garnett gave him at the last fire made six wounds for him that day. To show that this is authentic I will add that when the Cheyennes returned to Fort Robinson in March, 1877, Garnett made a feast for the chiefs and others of the tribe and this man whom he supposed he had killed, was present. In talking over this battle it was learned that this many-times wounded man was the chief of the Cheyennes, Little Wolf, who afterwards made so much history in coming up from the Indian Territory and escaping to the north by passing east of Spotted Tail Agency and Camp Sheridan.[64]

Dull Knife had two sons killed in this battle. Garnett saw one of these lying dead on the field and recognized him.

When the four men were driven from the ridge by the fire of the soldiers, Garnett dashed in the direction of the village and fell in with Three Bears, who was mounted on a bay horse which Lieut. Clark had loaned him in lieu of his own which had been shot under him. Three Bears, addressing the interpreter, said: "Go to Gen. Mackenzie with me." Riding up to the commanding officer he said to him: "Stop your paper fighting and let the soldiers fight as the Indians do. If you don't we are all going to leave you; and if we do, you will all be killed as Long Hair (Custer) was." When this was announced to him he was writing orders and three lieutenants were coming up. Immediately Mackenzie changed his tactics and sent out orders to the men to fight as they saw fit.

Between the time Garnett left the ridge and reached Mackenzie, Lieut. McKenney had made his charge with his troop over the ridge and down to the main dry run where the Cheyennes, whom the four had been standing off lower down in the run, now were, having got up in the run opposite the ridge and McKenney ran right up on to them. Here he was shot and killed. His bugler or an orderly had his horse shot at the same time and place, and the rider laid still on the ground feigning dead till a later time in the day when soldiers had taken the ground. McKenney died with sword in hand. From Fetterman to the time of his fall he had been boasting his intention, if he got in reach of an Indian on the campaign, to dispatch him with his sword. He started to redeem his promise—to assault the foe on the ultra-dry run ridge; he was unaware of the dry run—unaware of the Indians coming up this run from the village whom the four men had been resisting and checking till they themselves were driven off by the cavalry; he rushed right down on them; he was up in plain view on the bank; they were sheltered by the bank, and a bullet from their side ended all for him after the unexpected dry run had stopped his charge. When the dead were being gathered up, someone undertook to raise the soldier lying near McKenney, and the man asked if the Indians were gone and when told that they were, he announced that he was not hurt and immediately arose.

From the moment that Mackenzie's order to the soldiers to fight at will took effect, different results followed. The men protected themselves from the shots of the Indians; better success attended their exertions; and few casualties occurred afterwards. The Cheyennes scattered promiscuously westward, southwestward and northwestward; the greater number were killed along the main dry run; their dead were widely spread around; some of the tribe had started in the beginning down the stream from the village when the scouts were coming up at the outset and some of their dead lying below the village was evidence of the encounter between the two sides early in the morning. In the beginning of the action the Snakes or Shoshones were dispatched along the crown of the ridge east of the park and they proceeded along that route till they came round south of the village and to the end of the ridge where the gap is south of the village, and here they halted and remained about three hours, or until the day was well advanced; about this time Garnett, Big Bat, Louie Shangrau, Lieut. Clark, Three Bears, (Lieut. Clark was not collecting things but was present looking after his command) and two or three others had got into the village and were gathering tanned deer skins, elk skins other valuable property, and buffalo robes; the Indian scouts were also in the village at the same time picking up the best of things, and all were destroying the guns found by breaking them, etc., but no burning had yet taken place; the Garnett party needed pack animals to load with the plunder they had secured, and seeing a lot of loose horses south and southwest of the village they started for these to get some pack animals, but while getting these they were fired on by Cheyennes who had collected in some timber up the creek west of the village and some who were scattered out to the southwest and they were also fired on by the Snakes from the mountain; after the Snakes had shot at these men (~~probably~~ it was through mistake) long enough, as the latter thought, a few of these returned the fire (Garnett among them) and brought the Snakes to their senses as to what they were doing to oppose their own side. Painted Horse, (still living at the Agency & was in Custer battle) a Sioux Indian who happened to be among these, shouted to the men below who were firing up at them and said, "Hold on; these are Snakes up here; you have shot one of them;" and then the Snakes retired to the other side of the ridge or mountain they were on, out of sight; not very long afterwards Garnett was down the creek below the village some distance and here he now saw Painted Horse and numbers of the Snakes, a fact going to show that they had retraced their route of the morning and descended into the valley through the gap where the main column entered (as I understand it, they had been sent around there to encircle the village as much as possible. Bourke tells about this). It was at this time, past the middle of the forenoon, that Garnett saw the pack train under Uncle Dave Mears, in the valley;[65] ammunition was being handed out; the dead and wounded soldiers were being brought together down on the creek below the bend next [to] the village; the dead were being prepared for transportation on the pack animals by wrapping them in canvas to be laid across the animals. The battle was going on without intermission; the soldiers and the Indian scouts were pressing the foe to the west and beyond the main dry run; and some whose business it was to make some pretense of getting dinner were engaged at this. Mackenzie sent for Garnett and told him he wanted to send couriers to Gen. Crook. Sergeant Red Shirt and Charging Bear (and possibly others) were given this mission. The Indians' horses were collected down at the lower end of the valley and Garnett heard that a lot were brought in from the south through the gap and put with those which were in the park when it was invaded in the morning.

This park was a natural Indian fortress, completely surrounded by mountains rendering the place inaccessible except where the creek entered and was discharged and three other places—one where the troops came in, another on the south side, and one at the northwest corner formed by the main dry run which gashed the encircling sierra. These were all capable of easy defense, and only for the unconscious strategy of General Crook the Cheyennes would have successfully opposed him during the winter had he been able to maintain the campaign that length of time. But the Indians who were watching his movements had been completely lulled by them into a sense of perfect security. When he moved from Fort Reno his course indicated that he intended to strike Crazy Horse's camp. The Indian scouts who were with Crook on this expedition in what may be described, as it actually was, tentative service, rendered him admirable aid, not more by their numbers and scouting and fighting than by their suggestions and advice; and to this latter feature of their good work is due the signal triumph of Mackenzie in the battle now taking place. It was they, it will be remembered, who advised Gen. Crook to march companies out from his camp on Crazy Woman a few miles in various directions to cause the enemy's scouts to fall back beyond the range of knowledge before he set MacKenzie's column in motion. When the latter marched he went unobserved. The Indian scouts had done another good service in suggesting that the Cheyennes be the first ones hunted down. This was extremely fortunate, as it turned out, as they were found after a two days' march. At that season distance was a factor of no mean consideration. (Look into this fully to be exact as to whether Crook was closer to the Cheyennes than to the Sioux under C. Horse.)

The surface of the park was undulating—broken by small hills and ridges and gashed by coulees. The Cheyennes had their lodges down close to the water, so that the banks and knolls and woods screened them from observation till the last moment. When it became necessary for the defenders and their women and children to escape from their camp the protected routes by which they did so were numerous and sufficient, as was shown by the fact that the sole trophies which remained to the victors were the horses, the village and its contents, and the dead bodies which the Cheyennes were unable to carry away.

No prisoners were taken.

It should be noted that the Indian scouts had forged up the creek to the village and entered it at the lower end long before Garnett got into it, and while he was on the ridge where McKenny was killed. The fight for undisputed possession of the village lasted some time, the Cheyennes tenaciously holding on and bravely defending their homes and families and worldly possessions.

Garnett says that the Cheyennes were the most reckless, uncalculating, uncompromising and obstinate fighters of any of the northern Indians.

The son of Dull Knife that Garnett had personally known at Red Cloud Agency and saw dead on this field was lying across the stream southwest of the village on the level plateau on his back, as if he had dropped asleep undisturbed and at peace with all the world. He was a young man of noble mien and handsome face. He wore a blanket of fine cloth in two colors—one-half red, the other blue. This was doubled and suspended from his waist. Around him was a belt holding to his body a gun of the pattern then in use in the army, pointing diagonally across his body.

Garnett and Louie Shangrau were riding by in pursuit of pack animals when the former recognized this son of Dull Knife, the chief of the Cheyennes second to Little Wolf. Garnett spoke to Shangrau, suggesting that they coup the dead man after the Indian fashion, and both dismounted and struck his body with their whips. Louie Shangrau then took his gun and his moccasins, which were beaded and finely figured. Garnett says his hair was light, tinged with golden hue, unusually long, and the most beautiful he ever saw on an Indian. Thinks they were the first ones who saw him dead. Garnett afterwards heard that he had been scalped. He could not identify him exactly; that is to say, he could not determine whether he was the oldest son or the next to the oldest. He was acquainted with three sons of Chief Dull Knife. This dead son was a noble looking fellow. The three sons were all fine looking; as also Dull Knife's three daughters. The two oldest sons looked alike is the reason Garnett could not tell which it was that lay before him dead. He became acquainted with Dull Knife's family at the Sod Agency in 1872. This chief had two wives.

Garnett now got his dinner and after that went out on the firing line, but he did not stay long, for it was not necessary; the firing continued regularly all the afternoon the soldiers and scouts keeping up the battle and the Cheyennes replying doggedly. Garnett did not pay much attention after this to this part of the field, but was down in the village and at the camp made by the soldiers and the scouts just below the village, the former being next [to] the village. The arrangements for that night were as follows: The horses were herded in the southeast corner of the park, across the creek from the west half of the village; below them were the Sioux and Arapahos, and above them were the Snakes and Pawnees; the openings through the range were guarded, while the soldiers held the line west of the main dry run keeping the Cheyennes back in their positions. The fighting went on all day and continued desultorily until near midnight.

At this place I must correct the description of the sierra enclosing the park which has been given heretofore. The mountain on the east had sharp escarpments in most parts of the flank, but the west front where the Indians retreated over the range was a more gradual slope all the way from the creek increasing in grade as the climber advanced to the west. The ground on the north of the creek, after it entered the park, and on down by the village and nearly or clear down to where Mackenzie came in, was a pretty steep rise or bank, too high a pitch to go up with a loaded wagon; then when this was overcome in the ascent there were little parks, but the ground was continually rising until the mountain proper was reached, when the ascent became steeper and steeper as the summit was approached. The mountain was high.

It was on this flank where the Cheyennes held out to the last concealed behind the rocks and other objects.

The mountain on the north of the park was very high and steep and defied passage by any ordinary means. South and southwest of the village the surface of the park was low and level.

During the afternoon the work of destruction in the Cheyenne camp was carried on and completed. The scouts were allowed to take what they wanted. A lot of poles were saved from the lodges to make travois for carrying the wounded soldiers back to Crook's camp. The soldiers were working to construct these under the direction of some of the Indian scouts and chief scouts. Surgeon LeGard, who later in life served with the American army in Cuba, was the medical officer on this expedition.

One of the trophies secured in the village was the celebrated necklace of human fingers taken possession of by Big Bat and by him given to Capt. J. G. Bourke, and by him presented to the Bureau of Ethnology, and which is fully described and represented by a plate in one of the Reports; the article having been prepared by Bourke himself.[66]

The abundance of supplies in the Cheyenne camp could hardly have been improved on. There were at least 1,000 buffalo robes, but these were not yet tanned. There were all kinds of meats; dried beef done up in bundles in every lodge, and very fat and tender and juicy; pemmican in large quantities; skins of all kinds; beaver traps; dozens of bottles of arsenic to poison wolves; beaver traps in great number, some brand new.

After the village was looted, all the effects that were not destroyed by smashing, and that was not to be moved away, were thrown into piles and burned. All the skins and buffalo robes were saved and brought into camp.

When the women and children retreated from the village they were crying from alarm, mainly the children. Not many of the assailants in the park saw the escape of these people, as they went early before more than about 40 had got up in proximity to the village.

It has been mentioned before that these Cheyennes had lately met a party of Snakes and destroyed them. In this village the saddles belonging to these unfortunate Snakes were found and recognized by the Snake scouts with the expedition, and Garnett heard them crying and mourning in their customary way. The Snakes were grieving as they were scattered and moving about. There was no formal rite of mourning.

Not long after dark it commenced to snow and the storm abated little during the next two days, and when it was over the snow was a foot deep. The weather increased in severity. About seven in the morning following the battle the column withdrew and began the return march. It had been found that the Cheyennes had left.

On the morning of the second day the Pawnee and Snake scouts who had been sent out on the evening of the first day that the column moved from Crazy Woman to attack the Cheyennes, overtook the returning troops and came into camp about the time the column was to move. These had not found any Indians until after Mackenzie's fight, when they and the defeated Cheyennes came together, and the latter being too strong for them, they hastened back after a spirited encounter. It should have been said before that the troops on the first day of the return passed the place where they had left their extra horses and luggage to be in light marching order, and left it three miles in rear when they made camp that night. It was next morning that the Pawnee and Snake scouts came in.

About noon of the third day Mackenzie halted and made a distribution of the captured horses. It was done in this manner: The eight Sioux and Arapaho scouts who discovered the village were given preference of choice of the whole number, taking one apiece; next choice fell to the Sioux and Arapaho scouts who went out from Fort Reno and captured the Cheyenne Indian who came to their camp, each taking one; the third choice fell to the Snake and Pawnee scouts who had the skirmish and had returned the day before, these taking one each; Garnett was now told by Mackenzie to go in and get a horse. Garnett said to him that there were two horses in the herd which he would like to have, and they were animals which the Indians would not take; Mackenzie told him to get them and he did; these were American bred horses which had been taken from Custer; the next party to select were Red Shirt and his party who had been sent back to Crook while the battle was going on (these had come out from Crazy Woman to meet the soldiers); then one scout from each tribe was sent to take a horse; for instance a Sioux, then an Arapaho, next a Snake, then a Pawnee, and so on around these scouts till each one had a horse.

After this he began again at the head of the list and repeated the selection till the herd was reduced to about seventy head. There not being enough to go round again, and the ropes being nearly exhausted, Mackenzie told them to go and take the rest as they were minded; but only a few cared to have any more and quite a number, supposed to be upward of 40, were left; and it is understood that some camp followers picked them up.

The afternoon had been consumed with this issue, and camp was made right there. Next day by noon the command was back at Crazy Woman.

These Indian scouts were the happiest lot of people who ever performed a brilliant exploit.

It was two or three days before anything more was done.

Garnett's recollection is that the loss on the side of the army was six soldiers and Lieut. McKenney and 16 wounded. (Do not rely on this.)

The Indian loss that Garnett saw was 16 men and 1 woman dead.[67]

He is satisfied that other Indians were killed, for he was not all over the field where fighting was done. He saw a great deal of blood stains on the ground where there were no bodies and thinks that the Indians had removed them.

After a few days at Crazy Woman, Louie Richard, Louie Shangrau and some five Sioux scouts were sent by Gen. Crook back to Fort Robinson to enlist and bring up reinforcements of Sioux scouts. They raised over 500. The general told them where to meet him. He was to move back to Fort Reno and thence to head for the Belle Fourche, passing Pumpkin Buttes on the south. The point for assembling was the main crossing of the river, where the regular Indian trail from Red Cloud Agency crossed to go to the Powder River country. After their departure the army went back to Reno. Camped there on the southeast side three days and then Washakie and his Snakes departed for their homes. Crow Indians were sent for to join Crook at the camp on Belle Fourche. Crook marched to that point. It required three days to reach the first prong of the river which heads in the vicinity of Pumpkin Buttes. Here they saw the burning coal mines.

It was very cold on the morning the army left this warm place. Three citizens who were following the troops preferred to hover round these fires where the banks of earth were warm and the fires were sending up flames four and five feet high; in one place he saw the coal bed on fire covering a space of 40 feet; and there were several fires. The next camp was one day's march from the burning coal beds, at a point on the southeast branch of the Belle Fourche, a few miles just above where the Sioux Indians had made a camp of a month in 1868, from where Red Cloud and his followers marched that year to Laramie to join in the treaty of that year, and to which he returned after signing the treaty. Garnett was in this camp at the time and remained there with the other

Indians while Red Cloud and a few of his followers went down to Laramie to "make the agreement with white people," as Garnett puts it, he not knowing or hearing then anything about "signing" or what the term meant. On this trip with Crook he recognized the old camping-ground of 1868.

(In the winter of 1867–8 Garnett went with some uncles of his north from Laramie and was living a year with the Indians in the upper country, returning in the spring of 1869 to Laramie. He roamed around on the south side of the Black Hills with some band or bands of the Sioux; but Red Cloud was not with these; he was away off with a few others in the Big Horn country.

The Indians being in motion in 1868 over the treaty of that year naturally congregated on the Belle Fourche where their big camp was, and here is where Red Cloud came in and from where he with just a few went to Laramie to assent to the treaty.)

(There were Indian Agencies at this time in various places, and all the signatories did not go to Laramie, but the Commission moved about from place to place to treat with the natives. So the Missouri River Indians called this treaty the "Long Lake Treaty," from the circumstance of their meeting the Commission at a long lake; and the Republican River, Platte River and Powder River Indians called it the "Black Beard Treaty," from the circumstance that the chairman of the Commission, General Sanborn, wore a long black beard.)[68]

At Crook's camp one day's march from the coal beds in a northeast direction toward the Black Hills which they could now see from the highest points of travel, the army stopped several days. The soldiers improved the rest in getting their horses shod. A wagon with an escort was sent back to the coal beds for coal to do blacksmithing. The bodies of the three citizens who stayed by the fires when the troops marched were found where they had been attacked and killed by some of the enemy's scouts hovering on the trail of Crook and watching his movements.

It was at this camp that the Indians began the scalp dance over the victory gained against the Cheyennes. This dancing was kept up day and night—nearly all night—and the rejoicing among the Indians was a remarkable feature of life in that camp. I have noticed that the white writers who were in that camp at the time have treated this as a case of noisy demonstration as annoying to the whites as it was noisy and which was borne with patience as a concession to their customs and modes of pleasure of the Indians. Their happiness was complete. One tribe's scouts would have their scalp dance, and then another tribe's scouts would have theirs, and so on till each had had its turn or round.

These Indians who were enemies until lately, came together with great manifestations of friendship and happiness, and visited one another from camp to camp and lodge to lodge, and gave presents of value even to good horses, and thus were welded into a combination of good portent to Crook whose smiling face around the camp at what was developing among these Indians showed that while many of the white officers did not comprehend the import of these hilarious proceedings, he was happily alive to the significance of this boisterous pleasure. As when ice breaks up in a river, we know that spring has come; so in this instance Crook could see signs of bright promise in the breaking of the hostile spirit and the striking of hands with the white man in welcoming, not resisting, the day which could not be put off—inevitable, be the cost what it might in blood and money—when the final conflict for supremacy in the west between the two races should by common consent be at an end. It was the bow in the cloud. There was no mistake to those who looked below the surface of events to discern the powerful causes operating beyond the reach of common vision.

The next removal was ten or twelve miles down the creek where camp was made on the main Belle Fourche southwest of the Black Hills where Crook was to be met by Louie Richard and Louie Shangrau with such scouts as they should be able to bring back from the Red Cloud and Spotted Tail Agencies.

A short stay of about three or four days sufficed at this place; but it was a period of conference and decision of the deepest interest affecting the course of events in the near future and the policy of the more distant time.

It was now well along in December—in the dead of winter—in a northern latitude where winters are severe—already many storms had added to the snowfall till two feet of snow lay on the ground—the months of January and February—the worst of winter—were yet to come and be endured—the soldiers were less inured to these rigors than the Indians and less likely to hold out—their animals were not so hardy as the Indian ponies and would give out under the strain of work and the assaults of wind and frost and want of forage and shelter—the trains were cumbersome and burdensome—to this argument was brought forward the remarkable instance of 1865-6 (?) when the winter was so hard that the Indians suffered great misfortunes and losses, their horses died, the wild game perished, the Indians could go out and stampede animals from the bare spots into mammoth drifts where they floundered and struggled hopelessly until overtaken by their pursuers and dispatched—the soldiers in the country underwent equal hardships and even greater sufferings; and their losses of livestock were extreme; the white man's horses under such natural conditions without corn to eat could not last, his strength would fail at once—the column could not move forward or backward if the wise course should not be promptly taken now, and the expedition having probably no further likelihood of success, would be at an end so far as results were concerned. This was the reasoning of the Indian sergeants and Sharp Nose and leading Indians who were discussing the chances and probabilities and conditions, and deliberating with earnestness and far-seeing judgment in behalf of the cause to which they were bending all their faith—energies of body and mind.

Thus they thought and felt. At last it was suggested among them selves that it would be a good thing on their part to go in person to Gen. Crook and submit to him the points they had been considering. At the insistence of Three Bears and Sharp Nose and the others who had been conferring (this was confined to the Sioux and Arapahos) Garnett went to General Crook and told him that these men wanted to have a talk with him. He asked if the business was anything of importance, and being told that there were some matters on their minds that they wanted to communicate to him, he told the interpreter to fetch them to a large tent near the one he occupied, and when this was done and they were all assembled there were about twenty persons altogether inside, including Big Bat (?) Frank Gruard, Lieut. Clark, Capt. J. G. Bourke (?), Bill Rowland who was chief interpreter for the Arapahos and Cheyennes.

The speaking was begun by Three Bears, the chief noncommissioned sergeant of the Indian scouts except Sharp Nose who was second chief of the Arapahos at home, but on this expedition was their leader who sensibly and voluntarily gave the preference to Three Bears, as this latter officer was at the head of a far more numerous tribe. Three Bears arose and said: "Brother, we come to lay out our plan for this winter and the future. My men will tell you the particulars."

Three Bears was no speaker and had planned for certain of the Indians to do the talking with General Crook.

Keeps The Battle, a Sioux sergeant, was the first speaker to follow Three Bears. He spoke in substance as follows:

He explained the chances for a hard winter and spoke of the severe weather already had this winter—the deep snow—the many storms—the hardships and losses sustained on a former occasion by the troops in Gen. Connor's day (during the conference the tent kept filling up) how faint the horses would be without grain—that they would lose strength and fail—and if the winter kept up as it had begun he could not get more corn.[69] He told the General of the beneficent effect to follow if the command should break camp and go back to Red Cloud and Fort Robinson and save and keep the horses in good condition, and the men of the command also who would not be weakened by the exposures of winter service—he referred to the defeat of the Cheyennes and pointed out that they had lost all their property, including provisions and even clothing—he pictured their pitiful destitution and starvation and suffering and showed that the Cheyennes were not only defeated in battle but were reduced to such abject and hopeless extremity that they could not stay out in the hostile country if they wanted to ever so much—that they could save their lives only by coming in to the Agency; therefore this tribe was disposed of and would not have to be reckoned with as a hostile organization in the future. The plan that he would suggest to the General was that if the command should go back now the Indians would undertake by all the influences in their power to get the hostile Indians to return to the Agency this winter and the coming spring; that they would persuade the Indians on other Agencies who had members of their tribes out with Crazy Horse and Sitting Bull to send embassies to the camps of these chiefs to induce them to return to their homes on the reservations; and if possible, they would convince the chiefs themselves that it was a vain hope to stay out and perhaps could bring them in; if however they could not succeed in this latter object, they felt confident they could disaffect and draw away from these chiefs enough Indians to weaken them greatly; and then when spring should come if the army should go after the obstinate hostiles, these scouts and others that could be procured would go as a part of the army to bring them to terms. We know, he pursued, that we have reinforcements of scouts coming to join us; and we are sure that a great many more would come only on account of the horses being poor; but when we go again there will be plenty of Indians for scouts. The policy of persuasion which could be accomplishing its work in dead of winter when the army could do nothing stood a chance to render a campaign the next year unnecessary. Fast Thunder had come out on this expedition from the Spotted Tail Agency, and he spoke on behalf of that agency, following Keeps the Battle, and arguing the same propositions that his forebear had done, and promising to exert at his agency the same efforts to bring the Indians in peaceably. While these speakers were addressing General Crook the Indians kept prompting them so that they should omit nothing that had been considered among themselves. When these prompters broke in to refresh one of these speakers, the General would ask the interpreter, Garnett, what the Indian was saying when he would be told that he (the prompter) was assisting with some point that they did not wish to have forgotten in the discourse. Sharp Nose was the last to stand up and speak. He said he had no Arapaho hostiles holding out against the government to go out after as the others had, but that when the time should come for the army to move on another campaign, he and his Arapaho followers would be ready to respond.

Right here Garnett's memory fails. He cannot remember about whether Crook held a conference with his officers after this talk with the Indians, or whether Crook made his announcement this same day or the next morning. Ask Bat.

(It should have been inserted in the speech of one of the Sioux speakers that the Indians purposed to use as an argument with the hostiles when they should go out to see them, that they were working for a home Agency with General Crook assisting them to obtain it. This was another reminder to the General that they were relying on him and that they were doing their part in the agreement they had with him; and this is one more instance showing that they did not intend he should forget his obligations.)

When the time arrived for the General to announce his decision upon the propositions submitted to him by his native scouts, there was a reassembling in the same quarters and Colonel Mackenzie and Lieut. Clark were present. The General proceeded to state that he was going to abandon the expedition; that Colonel Mackenzie would conduct the Fourth Cavalry (his own reg't.) back to Forts Fetterman and Laramie and then to Fort Robinson where he would take command. Crook announced that Lieut. Clark would have his headquarters at Fort Robinson and have extensive authority in connection with the Indian scouts and direct control of them. The Pawnee scouts and Gruard and Baptiste Pourier marched with him. Wm. Garnett and Wm. Rowland, interpreters, were sent back with the Sioux and Arapaho and the very few Cheyenne scouts by a different route, viz; the regular Indian trail from the Belle Fourche to Fort Robinson. These interpreters were to carry orders to the fresh Indian scouts approaching along this route under Louie Richard and Louie Shangrau to return to Fort Robinson. The interpreters and their party marched southeast up the Box Elder Creek all day; but before noon they met Richard and Shangrau with over 500 fresh scouts and [a] large number of Indian women belonging to these fresh scouts and a few wives of the old scouts under Garnett and Rowland.

The scouts under Richard and Shangrau were obtained at both Agencies; there were about 100 from Spotted Tail, and the interpreter with them was

Charley Taggart, a quarter-blood Sioux, and White Thunder was in charge of them as their chief.[70] This party did not all get into Fort Robinson together but the hindmost with whom Garnett traveled arrived on the eighth day.

Garnett says that when he and Rowland met the scouts the latter were out of rations and the two interpreters divided what they had with them. On the second day none of them [had] anything to eat, and from that time on they all [were] famished. Garnett says they got something at the Hat Creek stage station and saloon by paying exorbitant prices, but all that the place afforded was but a mouthful for each one of nearly 700 men and the proprietor was soon eaten out. It was two or three weeks before Mackenzie and Lieut. Clark arrived from their circuitous journey at Fort Robinson. After a little while Louie Richard and Louie Shangrau were discharged by Gen. Crook with recommendations, as he had no immediate use for them.

~~At length Lieut. Clark sent Garnett to bring Red Cloud up to the Fort. The Lieutenant did not talk with him in his office where Indians and others were liable~~

About the latter part of January, 1877, Lieut. Clark dispatched George Sword and Few Tails on a mission to Crazy Horse.[71] Garnett says Sword did not have the name of Sword until some months later when he went to the Custer battlefield with Generals Sheridan and Crook (summer of 1877); that his name, as he recollects, was Hunts the Enemy.

These two men with a few leading Indians went to Crazy Horse's camp to open negotiations with him for his return, according to the Sioux custom. Packages of tobacco [were] wrapped in blue cloth and some in red cloth, a package to be given to the chief of each band in Crazy Horse's camp. If these packages were opened the act was an acceptance of the proposition which the bearers announced as the object of their business; if they were returned unopened it was rejected.

(If the packages were opened the tobacco was cut into small pieces and given around to the members of the band. If a chief had control over his band he could decide alone what to do; if he was afraid of opposition and did not wish to take the responsibility for a decision, he assembled his tribesmen and submitted the matter to them for ratification or rejection.)

These couriers were gone three or four weeks. One was the first to come back & he thinks it was Few Tails; later the other arrived, and with each there came some Indians from the hostile camp. Word was brought that the Indians would come and that some were then moving in the direction of the Reservation; that Crazy Horse would return, but that Sitting Bull had moved and was going to cross the border into Canada.

Lieut. Clark now directed the interpreter, Garnett, to bring Red Cloud to his office, but the officer did not confer with him in his public office where both Indians and white men were entering at will but he escorted him to a private room and there through this interpreter told him he had sent for him to say to him that he was going to try to help him. "You have been dismissed as chief by Gen. Crook who placed both agencies under Spotted Tail. When the General was ready to get scouts only one was obtained from the Spotted Tail Agency; there were some brought up from there, but nearly all of these belonged here and happened to be down there. They were out on the late expedition and proved themselves faithful and successful. When we called a second time for scouts your people of this Agency turned out four times as many as the Spotted Tail Agency did. The government has accused you of having your son (Jack) out in the Rosebud fight and assisting the hostile Indians, because a gun that was given to you in Washington with your name on it was taken from him in that battle and your son was seen there by some who knew him. I was the only son my father had and he wanted my name pretty well known so he got me into this position; but after I was out in this country he began to see the danger I was in, and he wanted me to resign; but I liked the service so well that I would not quit it. Red Cloud, the money that my father puts in the bank for me brings me $250 a month. I get $125 a month for this work. I am spending my official salary among you Indians as fast as I get it. This is one reason I have not married; I do not wish to leave any orphans; for a man in my place is liable to be killed any time. So I do not blame you for what your son has done. I sent for you to let you know that I am going to try to get you back where you once were, so the government will recognize you as a chief as before. Crazy Horse has agreed, as you know, to come in. (During all this speech, Red Cloud, being pleased with what was said to him, kept ejaculating, "How, how.")

"Now I want you to go out and bring Crazy Horse and all the people he claims in. Spotted Tail is going out and I think he has already started.[72] ~~I will assist you with all the rations you~~ I don't want him to get ahead of you. It was your men who studied out this scheme to get him in. Your people are striving to stay in this country and to have an Agency of their own. They are dissatisfied with Indian Territory and Missouri River. After you complete your work you people will be going to Washington to try to get an Agency. We want to have some of those northern Indians with Crazy Horse go to Washington with the delegation to let them know that they are at peace; and Gen. Crook is a friend of mine, and if you do as I tell you I'll have him to reinstate you to your place; and I will make you First Sergeant; that is as high as I can place you, for it is the highest office in the Indian scout service; I have all the other chiefs on the Agency enlisted; but I will recognize you as the highest officer among the chiefs; so that you can have control of your people. I will assist you with all the rations you think you will need."

Red Cloud was greatly pleased at the tempting offer of the officer, and instantly promised him that he would go. It took only about three days for Red Cloud to be ready to start. His party was nearly a hundred strong with a pack outfit, travois, and small tipis. After he was gone awhile couriers arrived from Red Cloud asking that provisions and beeves be sent out to meet the Indians who were coming in. Red Cloud had met many small parties drifting toward the Agency as he progressed toward the Crazy Horse camp.

Lieut. Rosecrans of the 4th Cavalry was dispatched with Garnett as interpreter, and about 50 Indian scouts under command of Chief American Horse, convoying some ten wagons loaded with rations and about 100 head of beeves going up by Soldier Creek.[73] This convoy met Red Cloud on the Laramie and Black Hills Road three miles below the Hat Creek stage station. Chief American Horse, true to his instinct as ever to help himself, posted his scouts in line in front of all the others and had them sitting down facing the Indians coming from the north. This side proceeding was not understood by the Lieutenant in command, but it was a ceremony familiar to the Indians, and when the Crazy Horse men came up they presented each Indian scout including American Horse and the Lieutenant who was surprised to get one, a pony. This Lieutenant Rosecrans shook hands with Crazy Horse and all the chiefs. It has been said that Lieut. Clark was the first army officer ever known to shake hands with Crazy Horse, but this is a mistake. They stayed at this place till the fourth day and then began the march to Fort Robinson, arriving there the third day. Before reaching the fort Lieut. Clark came out and met the procession two miles north of the Agency. The chiefs sat down in a row and they told Clark to advance and shake hands with them, using the left hand, they using the same; for, said they, the left hand is next [to] the heart, but the right hand does all manner of wickedness. Crazy Horse presented the Lieutenant a war bonnet, war shirt, pipe and beaded sack for tobacco and kinni kinnick and pipe.[74] Clark was told to put on his Indian clothing, being assisted by some of his new friends, and he made an imposing appearance.

While these Indians were camped a mile below Red Cloud Agency on the south side of the River (on that big flat) their horses were taken first and turned over to the Indian scouts. Next, the guns were taken and the census enumeration at the same time.

Before Red Cloud went out it was all explained to him how the Indians would be treated in relation to horses and arms when they should come in. So when they arrived everything went off smoothly. After they had been met at the stage station (near it) the Indian scouts were on the alert in watching for guns and counting those the Indians carried; these scouts were most active, industrious and faithful in their new capacity. After taking from the Indians in camp the guns that were brought forward there were not as many obtained by about 35 or 40 as the scouts had numbered on the stay at the station and on the way down, for these scouts were counting every day. So another effort was made to get the missing guns. The scouts knew pretty well who the men were who had kept their guns, as they were acquainted with all and knew who the fighters were; and they were very efficient in calling on them and telling each that he had a gun and to deliver it over. At length the sufficient number was found and the officers were satisfied. At this time there were a company of Cheyenne scouts for the Cheyennes had straggled into the Agency ahead of the returning Sioux. They were camped around the Agency within a few hundred, 300 or 400, yards. The snow was pretty deep when they came in, it must have been in March; Garnett saw where they had butchered horses on the snow; they were fully a week straggling in and getting settled in camp and were in a miserably forlorn condition. They were badly frosted, starving and eating horses to live, had traveled 300 miles from the north in deep snows and severe cold, for it was a hard winter; their clothing was very scant and ragged and they had little besides blankets; but they were soon provided for and made very comfortable; the Indians are a great people in such respects; their natural liberality is almost unbounded, and when examples of destitution like the case of the Cheyennes are known they are remarkably free in supplying want; this time the different bands got up dances on behalf of the Cheyennes and furnished them with clothing.

It should be said here that the Sioux themselves told afterwards that when the Cheyennes came into Crazy Horse's camp after their defeat, that the Sioux gave them all the provisions they had to spare and bestowed on them great quantities of clothing.

Scouts

The 500 scouts led by Richard and Shangrau were kept in the service after their return until the period of their enlistment had expired, which Garnett thinks was three months. After matters were settled down at the two Agencies, and shortly after Crazy Horse had come in, the organization of the Indian scouts was perfected by systematic regulation, and the number employed were 250, officered with Indian corporals and sergeants, the whole under the control of Lieut. Clark. They were formed into small companies. Of this number 80 were stationed at Camp Sheridan and the rest at Fort Robinson. All the Indian chiefs who had any influence among the Indians were made sergeants and corporals. Twenty-five of Crazy Horse's band or camp, including C. Horse, were made scouts. Crazy Horse was an officer over his scouts. Garnett kicked to Clark against making any of C. Horse's band scouts, and against making C. Horse a scout and giving him and them arms so soon after they had submitted. The scouts were armed with Sharp's carbines (for horseback use) and the six-shooting revolvers such as used in the army.

Garnett relates that on the campaign from Fort Fetterman on, Gen. Crook was impressing on his Indian scouts that if they held out faithfully to the end and were successful in getting the hostiles in, that they should have the preference around the Agencies in the service and be given authority and control over the hostiles who should be subject to them. So when Clark was making scouts from Crazy Horse's band in Crook's absence, Garnett warned him of this dangerous experiment of trusting them with arms again after having so soon disarmed them of their own arms, and Garnett reminded him of Crook's plan; but Clark, in the bigness of his heart, and to convince the late hostiles of his confidence in them (a virtue that they could not appreciate, as they could see in it only an opportunity for their advantage) declared that he was going to treat them all alike.

Crook, it is safe to believe, would not have made this mistake, one which brought any amount of trouble, and which Clark afterwards acknowledged to Garnett when he told him he was sorry he did not take Garnett's advice. Garnett says Clark had the most gratifying reputation all around, among white men and Indians, of any officer he ever knew. He was a brave, generous, and noble man and officer. When the Cheyennes had become well settled Garnett assembled the Cheyenne chiefs at his own house at Red Cloud (he had a house of 3 rooms and he took them into his kitchen); it was one Sunday and he sent

Black Bear (a Cheyenne Sergeant in the late expedition who had a Sioux wife) to invite them to his house that day for dinner. After the eating was over, a Cheyenne chief (who talked Sioux) and owned the necklace of human fingers taken from those of other tribes that had been killed (fastened together with buckskin), and who was present and acted as interpreter for Garnett, was told to tell these chiefs that he had sent for them to ask them some questions. He said the trouble was now all over and he wanted to talk about things past. Speaking of Crook's late expedition into the mountains, what did you know of us when we started out from here? They said we knew from the time you started in to enlist scouts; we knew the enlistment was going on—knew that Black Bear was enlisted; and knew from these enlistments that Crook's army was going on the warpath. They knew that the troops started for Laramie & then knew that the route would be by Fetterman, and they watched this place. They spotted Crook again when he left Fetterman. When he got to Powder River where some soldiers were stationed (Fort Reno) Crook left Powder River going in the direction of Crazy Horse's camp; when the Cheyenne scouts came back the Cheyennes said among themselves that Crook did not know where they were. Crook's scouts they said had already captured one of their Cheyennes. From that prisoner Crook learned where the Cheyennes were, they said. That man came back to us after the fight was over; we knew then that Crook had had us located. (This Cheyenne prisoner was held by the Indian scouts till the battle began when he escaped, and returned to where the troops left their horses and luggage and took a horse or two and saddle and whatever else he wanted.)

We did not know all these things that had taken place and did not know Crook was up there; we had killed 30 Snakes a little while before that; and we were having a good time dancing scalp dances. (There were two classes of dancers for night dancing and scalp dances were on at same time; both are danced at same time—during day and night—but the part danced by the young men and young women is danced at night—in scalp dances, both men and women are allowed to dance; this young peoples' dance is carried on day as well as night but is called "night dancing.")

Garnett asked: "How did you discover we were coming on you that night?" They were all talking and laughing among themselves when asked this. He said: "The women in the dance then going on were all tied to one another; one or two of the old fellows in the camp said daylight is here and it is time to cook breakfast for the dancers." At the beginning, the first they noticed, they heard a shot, then 4 or 5 shots together. As usual, the young men who were out early in the morning shooting game would do shooting in just that way. The shooting kept increasing down that way. Just then the dance came to a stop and a lot of horsemen (the Shoshones) were seen on the ridge, and the Cheyennes looking down the valley heard more firing and saw the herders running back toward the camp. The dancers then broke to run, but being tied together, they were thrown and tumbled together in wild confusion and tumult, and were tumbling and throwing one another in heaps. (It ought to be added that this tying was partly for sport and partly to keep the dancers there and from going off to their lodges.) Then the Cheyennes saw the Indian scouts coming up the creek, some in Indian war toggery and some in uniforms; it was known by this time that the village was attacked, and then there was a fearful and terrible rush and the most alarming disorder, many trying to gain the lodges, others striking for the hills.

It was in this conference that Little Wolf was present and told how the 4 men shot him, all as before related. The Indian who owned and wore the necklace of human fingers was called by the Indians "The Man Who Wears The Human Necklace," but he had also another name in which the word "Bear" occurs. He was told that Bat had the necklace; he said it was bad—good for nothing—and Bat ought not to wear it; that he wouldn't take anything for it; he knew Bat and called him his partner; Bat at this time was at Laramie where he had gone with Crook on the return from the north because his home was there; and Frank Gruard and North and his scouts all went back to Laramie. When Richard and Shangrau were stopped with their scouts they cut across to intercept Crook the day the return was begun, joined that column and went to Laramie.

These chiefs told Garnett that after leaving their stronghold in the mountains until they got into Crazy Horse's camp they had a distressing and terrible time. Few had any blankets. They had some pieces of buffalo robes, green and untanned, which were used. The cold was very severe and many of the Cheyennes froze to death on the trip to Crazy Horse's camp. The Cheyennes were helped, they said, at C. Horse's camp, but there were too many of them, and there was not much in the camp and the Sioux could not help them much; they did not get much so they started to the Agency.

Year 1877

It is understood that Crazy Horse returned in May, and some two weeks afterward and in June, General Crook came to Fort Robinson to inspect the Indians and inform himself, and the Indians of all tribes on the Red Cloud Agency were reviewed by him.[75] Lt. Clark had been drilling the scouts, and he arranged the review, all marching before the General; for two hours before the General's arrival the Lieutenant was marching the Indians around to get them in good form for the review. Only mounted men were in the review.

The general took his station on a little knoll just south of the Agency. The Indians marched in review before the General. The chiefs, in the advance of the column, wheeled out of the line when they came to Crook's position, and marching up were halted in front of him where he shook hands with all of them.

It was now arranged for a council the next day (perhaps the same day). In this council, Garnett interpreting, Agency affairs were taken up and considered. Crazy Horse and the northern Indians were in this council; also a great lot of chiefs and all the Indians. This was held, he thinks, two miles southeast of the Agency, the bulk of the Sioux being camped there. Thinks Young Man Afraid was the first to speak. He said: (Addressing Gen. Crook) "Brother: One time here there were people here who committed frauds trying to take us away from this country; some of us had been to Indian Territory; we see that that place is not good. They told us if we did not go there we might live on the Missouri River, but we don't want to go there. A lot of our people were away from this Agency now they are all back. Sitting Bull has gone over the holy road (this is what the Indians call the line between the U.S. & British possessions). Sitting Bull does not belong to us at all; he belongs to Running Antelope at Standing Rock Agency (the Oglalas recognized Running Antelope as the chief of the Unkpapas at Standing Rock Agency). We have told — sent word to — the Crazy Horse Indians that when they come in we would have an Agency in our own country. Our scouts have been with you and told when with you what we wanted. Now, this is our first meeting since those things were told to you, and we tell you again so you will not forget. If you will help us we will stay by you and do anything you want us to."

Another Indian next addressed the General.

(Crazy Horse was always inexorably silent; but Iron Hawk, Big Road, Little Hawk, He Dog and Iron Crow, chiefs under Crazy Horse were always the prominent speakers. One of these now spoke.) He shook hands with Crook as was their custom when they begin their speeches, and said:

"Brother: We were out here in our own country living on buffalo and such wild game as we generally have. We had not hunted for any trouble; but you army officers always come out to fight us. That is our country. We don't try to take any country away from you. Ever since you white people struck this county [you] have been crowding and fighting us all the time. Now I learn that you are trying to put us in a country that we do not know anything about (Ind. Territory) (Referring to the Indians on the Agency).

"You have been trying to scare our people away from this country. Our people came out and asked us to come in. They have asked us for help. Asked us to quit fighting soldiers and come in, so we could have an Agency in our own country. We have come in. These scouts told us if we came in you would help us to get an Agency in this country. Are you the same man they represented to us as Three Stars ?" (A star on his cap and one on each shoulder.)

Red Dog (the man who was always spokesman for Red Cloud) abruptly rose and said to the Indians:

"I want you Indians to hold on. One of our Agency Indians has spoken and one of Crazy Horse's Indians. We want the man to give an answer before anything more is said to him. Too much talk confuses white men."

General Crook replied:

"My friends; I am glad you are all contented with the Crazy Horse Indians and the other Indians. The government wants you to be at peace on these Agencies. We are the Great Father's soldiers. We have been ordered to bring you Indians in. That is why we went out to get you; but you don't know this; you think we came out to fight you, and you always shoot at us, which is sure to cause a fight. If you had not shot us there would have been no fight. I have had councils with your young men who first went out with me, and they had asked me for help, and I told them that I would help them if they helped me, and they suggested things to me, and I agreed with them. So far everything they told me has come true. Now there are a few stragglers out yet. When they are in we will go to Washington and there I will help you. I have to ask for help from the President, so that you will see that everything I do for you is done openly. Our president is a new man, he is not the one you Indians saw before; so he has a great many things to attend to; so we will go when he has more time."

The council ended. The Indians were satisfied. The Indians had a great feast ready. At these councils the feast is always blessed before it is eaten. Iron Hawk, a notable and learned Indian in history as handed down by tradition among his people, and who was always a prominent figure at these feasts, blessed this one in his peculiar way and ceremony in a spiritual oration lasting some ten minutes, after which the Indian soldiers (dog soldiers), as the concluding part of his ceremony, distribute the cooked viands. In passing around the eatables, General Crook, Lieut. Clark, Garnett received some dog. Clark did not wish to eat the dog, so he gave it to an Indian with a dollar to eat it for him. Crook had not eaten his dog. Clark remarked to him that if he did not want to eat his dog he would take it and dispose of it as he had his own. Crook told Clark that this was not the first time he had eaten dog, and he could eat anything the Indians could eat. He ate his dog and said it was nice. The Indians were surprised to see the General eat dog and to see his Lieutenant refuse it.

After Crook went away, Gens. Sherman (?) Sheridan and some other noted general made a trip (thinks) they went out from Laramie on a tour through the northwest. Lieut. Clark was arranging for scouts to go with Gruard to Laramie to join this party of officers. These were the scouts: Red Shirt, Little Battle, George Sword (who gained the name of Sword on this trip) Lone Bear, Charging Bear, No Neck, Little Bull, and Joe Bush.

Garnett does not know where this party of officers was going, but it was said that they were to go into the western part, to the Shoshone Agency, the Big Horn country, and to Fort Keogh. As soon as these scouts left another party of Indian scouts were sent up on Powder River under command of Big Bat. There was quite a party of Sioux and Arapahos.

For some time some white men had been looking around the Agency for Wyoming-blooded horses which had been stolen from them out there. Along about this time, say in June, a small party of Cheyennes arrived—12 men & 3 women—with 125 head of horses, the identical horses these Wyoming men had been looking for, and they took nearly all of them. The main party of Cheyennes had been gone some time with Mackenzie to the Indian Territory. This little party of Cheyennes was under White Hawk their chief, who was the son of Black Moccasin, known among the Cheyennes and Sioux as a noted chief. Wild Hawk followed to the Indian Territory behind the main body.

Sun Dances

The first sun dance in 1877 took place about 3 miles northwest of the Agency, over beyond the buttes where Red Cloud Butte is. Crazy Horse had camped over in there on a creek, and a good many other Oglalas were camped over in there. Before the sun dance was prepared the usual scouting party went out to look for the Medicine Pole to be erected in the center of the dancing amphitheater. They knew before they were sent out where it was but the going out was merely the form they always observe. They came back the same evening they went out.

Next morning they went out to cut this pole. After they went out four young men were picked out and also four girls; these four young men standing about the pole to be cut they go through the formality of each telling of his brave exploits, each when through with his recital strikes the pole one blow with his axe. These four selected girls now chop down the pole. When it falls, all the Indians who have gone out, and the whole camp is there, send up a mighty shout. A picked body of men and women, with sticks under the pole, ranged on both sides now bear it off to the place where it is to be set up. Their rule is not to stop but four times to rest. Now while all are out there they are getting boughs and foliage to enclose the back side of their dancing quarters. On this particular day Lieut. Clark was out to witness this pole-cutting. He was quick to observe and get onto anything brewing. A great many half-bloods were also out there as spectators. After they started for the camp—before the pole is brought a kind of monument is erected as much like a man as they can make it; and after the pole carriers take their last and fourth rest, the warriors from all parts of the village rush to the point where the monument stands to see which can first reach and touch it. After this is over they indulge in a sham battle.

On this occasion there came near being a real fight growing out of this sham one. This sham battle was arranged to represent the Custer fight, and the Crazy Horse Indians who had been in that were to take the side they had in that affair, and the friendly Indians were to stand for the Custer soldiers. When this fight was on, instead of striking the Custer party lightly as was usual some of the others struck their opponents with clubs and war clubs hard blows.

Garnett was on the Custer side and when he and the others got enraged they opened fire with their revolvers on the other side and drove them out of the dancing camp. Clark was on a hill observing what was going on and he rushed in and stopped the firing and prevented what might have been a serious affair.

A sun dance camp is formed by placing the lodges in a vast circle, sometimes two miles in diameter. In the center of the camp is made the dancing floor; around this is built a pavilion in exactly circular form making the amphitheater 300 or 400 feet in diameter; this pavilion is made by setting posts in the ground at some space apart, then poles are laid across and robes are spread over for shade. On the southeast side of the pavilion it is open by a space of some 40 feet; and the outside is covered with branches and leaves, but the inside facing the amphitheater is open. The sun dance continues from two to four days.

On the Medicine Pole the dancers hang their sacrifices. They cut their breasts making incisions on each side and then thrusting sharp sticks through the flesh and under the skin, between the two breasts tie a rope which is fastened above to the Medicine Pole, they dance around the center pole, leaning backwards and hanging downward, the weight of their bodies drawing on their lacerated breasts, the effect being to tear the flesh so that the sticks will be withdrawn and they will be released from the rope.

Gifts are going on all the time. Children have their ears pierced now as well as privately at other times. From one to three and sometimes four apertures are made. At the sun dance the judges determine, according to the gifts a man has made, how many incisions may be made in the ears of his children — the greater the gifts the more credit and the larger number of punctures they are entitled to. These sun dancers partake of neither food or drink for the time they have sworn themselves in.

When the sticks are inserted in the breast they are also sometimes put into the back or shoulders.

They also punish themselves by making punctures in their flesh on the arms and shoulders and cutting off pieces with knives. These sticks in the breast are by some sacrificers torn out by fastening the rope to the rider's horse and urging him to apply the violence necessary to effect the sundering of the flesh.

The sun dance is a sacrificial performance. A brave bargains with the Great Spirit; he covets a precious favor, it may involve the preservation of his life, or the success of an important enterprise, and he tells the Great Spirit that if he will protect and save him from the particular danger with which he is threatened, or will aid him to succeed in his undertaking, he will dance the sun dance, and he tells the Great Spirit sometimes just what sacrifice he will make or what species of suffering he will undergo; it being understood invariably that sacrifice on these occasions is suffering. For instance, if a warrior is confronted by enemies and he is in great danger, and in his extremity he turns to the Great Spirit for aid and says to him if he will protect him from wounds and death in the encounter that is coming and will give him victory over his assailant; or if he is going to steal horses and having come to the camp to be robbed he tells his God that if he will assist him to make the capture and to avoid the owners and to escape with his booty, he will dance the sun dance. If for any reason he cannot perform this promise, he withdraws himself from all the people and goes to a distant hill and there does penance in solitary loneliness, sleeping neither by day nor night, eating no food and drinking no drink.

Whatever the warrior promises in his appeal to the Great Spirit, that is what he does in the sun dance.

Another sun dance was held in the same year 1877 on Chadron Creek near where the crossing was near the Price and Jenks ranch built by Bob Pugh.[76]

This dance was about 10 days later than the Crazy Horse sun dance, and was held by Red Cloud and Spotted Tail Indians, the latter predominating in numbers. Garnett did not attend this but Two Strike sent a horse from Spotted Tail which Garnett had bought from him, by American Horse.[77] Another sun dance was started below Red Cloud Agency to the south of it, between the Crazy Horse dance and the one on Chadron Creek, but one man started to dance but the whole thing fell through, the camp broke on him—would not hold together, as they wanted to attend the big one coming on Chadron Creek, and it takes a good many Indians to carry through a sun dance.

There was a big sun dance in 1876 up against the hills between Ash Creek and Trunk Butte, over in the Coxville neighborhood. This dance began June 12, 1876; and lasted about three days; he remembers the date because he had a son, Charley Garnett, born on June 10. A lot of Cheyennes came up from Indian Territory on their way to join Crazy Horse and Sitting Bull in the northwest, and tarried at this dance. More description: There were always certain Indians in the tribe whose special duty was to arrange the sun dance. When the pavilion is completed the warriors ride in from all directions of the camp and hold a dance on the ground where the sun dance is to take place for the purpose of beating down the grass. An effigy of a man and a representation of a buffalo cut out of a buffalo skin hang on the Medicine Pole. The dancers who are coming to do the preliminary dancing are led by those braves who have done boastful deeds which they have done and have represented in paintings on their horses. They enter the dancing camp and shoot at the effigy with the belief that this act will bring them an advantage in fighting men and help them to overcome enemies. They shoot at the buffalo effigy under the belief that this act will assist in the chase against these food animals and give success in their destruction. Before the pole is cut there is a preliminary dancing by those who are to participate. This also is called the sun dance. There may be several parties to dance around the Medicine Pole. Each party erects a tipi out in front of his or their regular lodge and a feast is made at each place, the articles which have been selected for this only being cooked, and one kettle being used. This dancing lasts four nights, and the dancers dance the sun dance and sing sun dance songs. If they want to make the dance short they use more than one kettle on one night—they use two on one night.

In addition to sacrifices already described, they cut gashes in the back and suspend buffalo heads expecting that these will tear out the thongs by which they are held. Gashes are made in the back for six or eight buffalo heads which are fastened by long ropes to the perforated flesh, and these objects are dragged on the ground around the camp, and while they commonly tear loose, if they should fail to when the sacrificer has finished the circuit, the flesh is cut and he is released. When he is making the circuit it is not unusual for someone behind to drop on a head, causing it to be torn from him. Then some of the sacrificer's family makes a present to the person who has done this. Another thing: When the dancers are being prepared, the one who has vowed to sacrifice by sticks in his breast must procure a person who has sacrificed in the same way in a sun dance to do the gashing for him on his breast; and whatever the form of sacrifice he is to perform he must find a person who has sacrificed before him in the same manner.

These dancers believe that when they had their appeals responded to as they prayed the Great Spirit to hear and answer them, that he actually did so and that now they are merely redeeming the promise made to him.

When a sacrificer is ready to begin his performance, the Medicine Man announces to the Great Spirit that the man is about to do what he had promised him he would do, and when he is through and has succeeded the Medicine Man again tells the Great Spirit that the brave has performed as he promised, with success, and beseeches him to help him again.

[Crazy Horse]

Following these events in quick succession are the known fragments a conspiracy of circumstances to end in a much-questioned and not more than half-designed tragedy—the design not in a single mind—not personal, and impossible of particular location. The death of Crazy Horse was as spectacular as it was unexpected and momentous. It has been regarded by writers acquainted with outside facts only—and with only some of these—as a plain, unromantic affair. But it will be the province of this chapter to uncover some of the hidden influences which hastened the end of this man's life and cast over it an investiture of the tenderest and saddest pathos.[78]

After his return from the north Crazy Horse fell into a domestic trap which insensibly led him by gradual steps to his destruction. A half-blood woman, not of the best frontier variety, not lightly measuring her intentions and power by casting glances, but fixing her captivating gaze upon this man who had never known fear or a single conqueror before, in defiance of the warnings which a trustworthy advisor to whom he turned for counsel in the matter gave him, surrendered to her as her husband.[79] There cannot be the slightest question, for the evidence of circumstances points unmistakably that way, that Crazy Horse had come into the Agency with nothing but honorable intentions to accept the terms of the government and the inevitable situation of affairs. His course was induced by no misinterpretation; the influences and persuasions addressed to his mind were not initiated by the government or borne by any of its direct agents; the arguments and entreaties to which he listened fell not from any white man's lips but were uttered by tribesmen of his own blood; and he had brought his people in at a season when they all might well have stayed out.

This alliance was a misfortune which overcame this chief with ease, whereas, had it been a case of bullets, his ability to extricate himself would have been unequaled. This woman at once set about to imbue his mind with poisons.

In the course of the representations by the scouts who first went to Crazy Horse and of the later ones made by Red Cloud on his trip north to see him he was told of the contemplated mission to Washington by the Sioux Chiefs to lay before the authorities the claim of the Oglalas to be allowed to remain in their own country and to have an Agency there, notwithstanding the treaty of 1876. So on his arrival at Red Cloud [Agency] Crazy Horse was not surprised with any new proposition; nor was the journey to Washington, to be arranged for him and his fellow chiefs anything which he had not before heard of and considered. An instance will be introduced in this connection, which shows that Crazy Horse was arranging in his mind for the Washington mission, and that his frame of mind was tranquil and pacific. Three or four days after he got back Garnett, who was well acquainted with him and on account of his position as interpreter was destined to have much intercourse with him, invited him and Little Big Man and two or three others to dinner. It was on this occasion that he remarked that he would begin to learn the use of the fork at the table. He said he had got it to do. And then he began to ask Garnett questions about the traveling to Washington; how the Indians were provided for; all of which were answered to his satisfaction by this interpreter who had been there as Agency interpreter for Dr. Seville in 1875. From the moment that this insidious and evil woman came into Crazy Horse's confidence and exerted her invidious arts disaffection began to assert itself over him. She told him the trip to Washington was a trick to get him out of his country and keep him; that if he went away he would not be allowed to return. These representations might not have been insurmountable but for another conspiring circumstance which went a long way with Crazy Horse to confirm what his new (his second or double) wife had said. Black Elk who had fought in the Fetterman massacre and had a leg crushed which made him a partial cripple for life, and had always been an inveterate hater of the encroaching whites, possessed the same type of spirit as Crazy Horse to whom he would most naturally become endeared through association and sympathy, added his own vicious suggestions to those of this woman.[80] He repeated substantially the same silly falsehoods. John Provost, the son-in-law of Black Elk, one of the Indian scouts, likewise had the chief's ear into which he, too, poured the same misleading strain.[81] These latter tried to convince Crazy Horse that when once he was conveyed east he would be imprisoned; perhaps placed upon some island in the sea and indefinitely confined, or otherwise disposed of so that he would never return. The talk of the day in relation to the Modoc affair and the punishment meted out by the government was fresh on the popular tongue and did not fail of furnishing a horrible example to excite the imagination of this warrior, though he possessed as little imagination as the ordinary man possibly could.[82] The foundations of his better disposition were broken up not very long afterward. Lieutenant Clark had him and some 20 of his warriors up to his headquarters to see what could be done in his camp in getting scouts for service in the northwest against the Nez Perces.

All the scouts that had been sent out from Fort Robinson got back about August. Just about the time these got home another trouble rises in the West, and they were heading this way and entered about the same territory that Crazy Horse and Sitting Bull used to roam over. Lieut. Clark got word of the trouble; he told the scouts to get ready, that they were liable to be called on most any time to start out. Meantime he sent for Spotted Tail who came up. A wrangle came up over the pay; and there was a kind of deadlock (or something like a deadlock) about the scouts going out from his agency. Spotted Tail went back before there was an agreement. At this time Gruard & Big Bat were back and around the place. Garnett was to go this time with the scouts; they were all to be taken again. Garnett was set to work among the Red Cloud Indians letting them know there were chances for more scouts to be enlisted, and he was met with favorable responses. When returning from the Agency to the Fort he met Gruard who accosted him, saying, "Billy go back to Lieut. Clark's office; it is too hot for me." "What's the matter?" He says: "Crazy Horse is up there with his people." Garnett reached Clark's office and found some 20 northern Indians in the room when he went in. Clark directed him to ask Crazy Horse if he would not go out with the scouts and some of his men; that the Nez Perces were out & up in the country where he used to roam.[83] Crazy Horse said, "No." Garnett did not know what had taken place with Gruard but he could see that Crazy Horse was not right. Crazy Horse continued: "I told him (Lt. Clark) what I wanted to do. We are going to move; we are going out there to hunt. You are too soft; you can't fight" (speaking to Clark). Clark answered, "You can't go out there. The trouble is I don't want anybody to go out there. That is the reason I am trying to get scouts to go out there, to head them off from that country." Crazy Horse said: "If you want to fight Nez Perces, go out and fight them; we don't want to fight; we are going out to hunt." "You cannot go out there, I tell you," said Clark. That was all. Crazy Horse turned and remarked to his Indians, saying, "These people can't fight; what do they want to go out there for? Let's go home; this is enough of this," and they all obeyed him and went right out.

This passage with Crazy Horse was a revelation, though nothing was spoken out on the subject. Something was wrong, and this evident fact was soon to receive what seemed to be corroboration. Gen. Crook shortly arrived, and it was arranged to hold a council the next day out on White Clay Creek, along which the Oglalas were collected, and two miles southeast of Red Cloud. Crazy Horse had his camp at the mouth of this stream, some six miles below the Agency. Just a few Cheyennes were around the Agency. All the chiefs had been notified. Garnett and Pourier who were to be present had been told next morning to meet Crook and Clark in front of Frank Yates' store at the Agency.[84] In the meantime these two had gone to Garnett's house northeast of the Agency buildings. Woman's Dress happened to join them, and learning their business as they were going back to meet the two officers, he unraveled a tale which brought the most important affair of the day to sudden pause.[85] He recounted how Crazy Horse had planned to meet General Crook in an apparently friendly manner and intention to shake hands, and then treacherously to take his life, while his adherents would kill his attendants. At the store when all the parties met this information was imparted to the General who received it with some incredulity, yet weighed it with that consideration which a prudent man would, and had it not been for the assurances of Pourier that Woman's Dress was veracious, and the plea of his subordinate against his going farther, he would probably have proceeded to the council. After giving directions to Garnett to repair to the place of meeting, and select from the chiefs such as were known to be of the loyal brand, excluding all the northern chiefs who had lately come in, and quietly notify them to come to headquarters at the Fort [Crook returned to Fort Robinson]. In two or three hours they were all gathered at the fort in the presence of Gen. Crook and Lieut. Clark. The meeting was held in the reception room of Col. Bradley's residence.[86] There were present: Red Cloud (?),

Red Dog, Young Man Afraid Of His Horse, Little Wound, Slow Bull, American Horse, Yellow Bear, Chief Dog, Blue Horse, Three Bears, Frank Gruard, William Garnett, Baptiste Pourier (?) and possibly some others.[87]

The Woman's Dress story was repeated to the assemblage, and the chiefs learned for the first time why the council had failed. The business transacted all related to the disarming of Crazy Horse and the scouts in his camp. This was simply an undoing under the most trying and dangerous surroundings of the unhappily mistaken policies of Lieut. Clark in treating those newly-returned northern Indians in the matter of enlisting scouts on an equality with those who had been in service and tested by utmost experience. Crook put the question to the chiefs how the movement against Crazy Horse should be planned and managed. It was their opinion which was finally adopted that each chief present should pick two of his best men who should have a support of other warriors, all to go in the night to the camp of Crazy Horse and surround it and call out the chief and his scouts who had been armed for service to the government, and to require them to give up the guns and revolvers, and if he refused, they were to be taken even at the cost of Crazy Horse's life.[88] Crook told Clark to issue ammunition for this service, and the chiefs were directed to return to their camps and make due preparations for the work that night. Then the General immediately took his departure for Sidney. He had been gone but a few hours when Col. Bradley, who was in command of the Post, sent for the interpreter to learn what maneuver was about to take place. The Agent was there from Red Cloud with his interpreter (Dr. Irwin and Leon Pallady) and He Dog, one of the northern chiefs under Crazy Horse.[89] The startling undertaking had leaked out through the Indians. Bradley was desirous to find out from the interpreter what had transpired at the recent conferences, but he was reluctant to make any communication in the presence of others; so the room was cleared, and when the Colonel and the interpreter had entered a more secluded apartment the officer was told to repeat what he had heard. When he had done this Garnett confirmed what had reached his ear. Bradley said it was too bad to get after a man of the standing of Crazy Horse in this manner in the nighttime without his knowing anything about it. "They ought to do this in broad daylight. There are plenty more soldiers after we are gone. The life of Crazy Horse is just as sweet to him as my life is to me. It was a mistake in the first place to let him have pistol and gun," said Bradley.

Lieut. Clark immediately sent for Garnett and dispatched him to countermand, under directions from Bradley, the preparations which were then in progress to move that night with an armed force to Crazy Horse's camp; and to leave orders with each chief to appear at an early hour the next morning with all his warriors. These having arrived, between seven and eight o'clock, the command consisting of Indians under all the chiefs before-mentioned, several companies of Cavalry under Lt. Col. Mason, and some cannon and gatling guns which marched down the south side of the White River; and Lieut. Clark with Little Wound's Cutoff band of Oglalas, the Arapahos and a small number of Cheyennes, [began] moving down the north side of the River.[90] Specifying more fully the forces on the south side, they were in this way: Garnett went over to the Oglala camp and led the Indians along from their camp until Col. Mason was moving in their rear. When these forces were on the march couriers were passing at high speed between the camp and the advancing column on the south, keeping the camp advised of what was taking place. Garnett and a few of the best informed Indian scouts were extremely solicitous and suspicious regarding the main body of the Indians that were marching toward the camp, for among these were many Crazy Horse Indians and, besides these a large majority of the others were considered ticklish and unsafe in the extreme; so these men who had this knowledge and concern, passing word around among the trusty ones, had them gather in a body by themselves and march apart from the rest; so that in the event of a battle those who were in the procession in the guise of friends yet would be certain to assist the other side, should not have quite everything their own way by taking these wholly at disadvantage. When within half a mile of the camp Little Big Man who had been going and coming continually, now met the Indians again, bringing word this time that Crazy Horse had fled, taking with him his fullblood wife, Kicking Bear, and Shell Boy.[91] The command was halted. Something like seventy of Crazy Horse's braves had collected on a knoll on the east side of the creek about 600 yards above the River. A boy about fifteen years of age dashed down from this hill and passed through the halted Indians, men standing apart to let him through. This was pretty strong evidence that his friends had insinuated themselves among the supposedly friendly Indians. After this came a man, Black Fox, magnificently decked in war costume, who rode down from the hill on a gallop and speaking these words: "I have been looking all my life to die; I see only the clouds and the ground; I am all scarred up."[92] Drawing his knife, he placed it between his teeth. At this instant American Horse, standing with the body of selected Indians, advanced a few steps and holding in his hand a pipe, extended it toward Black Fox saying: "Think of the women and children behind you; come straight for the pipe; the pipe is yours." Black Fox ejaculated, "How." The two met and smoked. Then Black Fox spoke again: "Crazy Horse is gone. He listened to too many bad talks. I told him we came in for peace, but he would listen to them. Now he is gone and the people belong to me. I come to die, but you saved me."

His warriors were riding in a drill of the most beautiful fashion and keeping near to his person while this talking and smoking had been taking place. He now cried out to them: "All over. Go back." They returned in perfect order to the camp. American Horse told Black Fox now that they were coming to get Crazy Horse's arms, but as he was gone he supposed they would all probably have to move up to the Agency. Black Fox said they would move; and this was done the same day. (Black Fox. This chief was a surprise to Garnett who had never heard of him. He rose up without a moment's notice like a Viking. The Indians have the most laudatory accounts of him as a brave Indian. Some of them speak of him as the last of the race of brave Oglalas. The way he rode down to meet the army from the fort shows he was a man of the purest and grandest courage. He came to the front that morning unheralded, but it was seen that the warriors were under most perfect discipline. A word and a wave of the hand and the braves behind him caparisoned for conflict, boiling with passion and thirsting for blood calmed down from a tempestuous lake of fire to a quiet company of warriors who went demurely to their tents at his bidding. The Indians with Garnett knew that day that Black Fox was a prominent Indian among them. When he came forward he said that when Crazy Horse was not there he was the chief—that the people were his. He was worthy of them. He got away with others from one of the Agencies in 1877 and went north and crossed into Canada with Sitting Bull; and when he returned among the last and on the way in he was killed in a fight with some other tribe of Indians. He was remarkably cool and self-possessed, never exhibiting the slightest excitement under the most sudden surprise. His relations were all noted for their courage. His relatives are: Black Fox, his father, was a chief signing the Manaydier treaty made next year after Fauts was killed at mouth of Horse Creek, and the treaty was effected at Fort Laramie;[93] Kicking Bear, the Messiah, died about 3 years ago; Flying Hawk who lives on east side of W. K. Cr. and ¾ miles south of White River and was in the Custer battle, and can tell about the death of Lieut. Harrington, was a half-brother to Black Fox, who was in command when Crazy Horse fled; these are all the blood relations he can mention, and all related to this second Black Fox.)[94]

Lieut. Clark soon crossed over to where the main command rested. He promptly dispatched 30 Indian scouts under No Flesh in pursuit of Crazy Horse, who had just been seen at some distance. Twenty-five more were selected from the main body, placed under charge of No Water and sent forward on the same errand.[95]

All the Indians and troops now went back. All the outlying Indians were brought up close to the Agency, and when they had pitched their lodges in close order the camp covered more than a section of ground. Garnett thinks there were at least 700 Indians in line when they marched down to the camp. Garnett did not go down to Fort [Camp] Sheridan. He is now stating second hand, and will give the report of the scouts.

The scouts did not come within shooting distance of Crazy Horse that day but were in sight of him. The woman was seen in the lead & the three men behind.

Garnett explains C. Horse's own system of retreating which is always talked about by the Indians. He always ran down hill and across the level country but slowed down to a walk at the foot of a hill, and when he got to the top his horses were fresh and in this way he conserved the strength of his animals. The scouts complained that this was his tactics on this flight. While they kept about so near to him for a long time, they noticed toward the end he was lengthening the distance between them, because his way of using his steeds saved them while his pursuers racing up hill and down were wearing theirs out, when at length ten miles from Fort Sheridan they were played out. Lone Horn was a celebrated chief of the Minneconjous who resided on the Cheyenne Agency [Whetstone No. 1] which is a very old Agency, being on the River (Mo.).[96] He was the chief who in Washington when the Black Hills was raised as a question by President Grant told him that the delegation would not consider the matter there where there were only a few gathered; but that if the government wanted to treat about the Hills to come out west where all the Indians could be met and where all could take a part.

Touch the Cloud was the son of Lone Horn and succeeded his father in the chieftancy on the Cheyenne Agency (The present chief—1907—son of Touch the Cloud succeeded his father when the latter died three or four years ago; but he bears the name of his noted grand father, Lone Horn.)[97]

Touch the Cloud was in command of the Indian camp near Camp Sheridan. His father may have been and probably was living at this time. Touch the Cloud was one of the Indians who held out in the north with Crazy Horse. His people were Minneconjous; and while they did not properly belong at Spotted

Tail Agency, yet Chief Spotted Tail brought them along with him and with those who belonged to him when he came with the party that he went up north after. He did not drop or scatter these Minneconjous on the Cheyenne Reservation. The Indians composing this reservation were made up of two bands— the Minneconjous and the No Bows. Those latter were so named by the early French who passed through or occupied this country. These No Bows are the Sans Arcs (Without Bows).[98]

Red Bear was a sub-chief under Touch the Cloud.[99]

An omission from the story of Woman's Dress was made.

Crazy Horse was killed by lies and liars. Woman's Dress was a scout. He pretended that he had been keeping a brief on Crazy Horse after his return from the north. He said that Little Wolf, who stayed in that camp was learning from Crazy Horse the intentions of that chief.[100] This Little Wolf is not the Cheyenne chief by that name but a Sioux Indian who had been in the Custer battle. He was a brother to Lone Bear.[101] Woman's Dress' claim was that Little Wolf was keeping Lone Bear, his brother, advised of what he found out, and then Lone Bear told it all to Woman's Dress. Woman's Dress was magnifying his own consequence by making it appear that he was doing voluntary detective work for the benefit of the public service.

His political antecedents must be taken into account to understand him. He belonged to the Bad Face band over which was Red Cloud.[102]

Lone Bear was also a Bad Face on his mother's side, and it is barely possible that he was being actuated by precisely the same motives that Woman's Dress was, though this can be mentioned only on supposition. The Bad Faces had the reputation all over the Oglala tribe of seeking to be chiefs. They were much occupied with Indian politics, and were reputed to be tricky, an inseparable art from the actual manipulations of partisan politics without reference to the color of the actors. This slur or twit or sneer was always being thrown up in the Indian councils at or about these Bad Faces when some of them was cropping or tasseling out with schemes or ambitions in this line.

This story of a plan to kill General Crook and his attendants, as in the case of Gen. Canby and Rev. Thomas, was a fabrication. The reason for it must be sought in the secret corners and crevices of the human mind. These are alike to the understanding—identical in all men to the student of human nature. I have stated Woman's Dress' political antecedents as a fact to aid in accounting for his falsehood.

About ten years after these occurrences Little Wolf and Garnett were sitting in the guardhouse at Pine Ridge talking over old times when Little Wolf asked, reflectively: "What do you suppose caused Crazy Horse to be killed?" Quick as lightning Garnett replied, "You killed Crazy Horse!" This he said, remembering the tale that Woman's Dress had told in 1877 of Little Wolf's part in eavesdropping and reporting to Lone Bear. Garnett believed that if Little Wolf had not done that, that Crazy Horse would not have been the subject of so much gossip and the victim of misrepresentation and an innocent conspiracy of army officers to confine him and that his life, instead of being a forfeit, would have been saved.

"You killed Crazy Horse!"

Little Wolf stared as he paused to collect his senses. Had a thunderbolt shivered the roof of the building the Indian could not have been more astounded. "I killed Crazy Horse?" he inquired in a reasoning way, like one recovering from a reeling blow. "I—how can that be? I who fought with him all through the north—have always been with him—was his friend—how did I kill Crazy Horse?" Garnett coolly told him the story with which Woman's Dress had regaled Garnett, Pourier, and General Crook and Lieut. Clark in 1877. Little Wolf denounced his part of it as a base falsehood, and declared that he should see Lone Bear on the subject to find out if he ever told Woman's Dress such a story.

Afterwards—not long afterwards—Garnett was at Pine Ridge and so was Woman's Dress. The latter began a conversation betraying easily enough that Little Wolf had been calling him to account for his misrepresentations.

He was abusive to Garnett, calling him a liar for what he had said, denying that he had ever stated that Little Wolf and Lone Bear had acted such parts, and affirming now that he himself it was who overheard the secret utterances of Crazy Horse—that he had sat behind him enveloped in his blanket when the chief was unbosoming himself supposedly in secret.[103] The mischievous prevaricator had, in the course of justice which ever runs in a circuit, been overtaken and entrapped; and he had recourse to the device of cutting Little Wolf and Lone Bear out of the piece of his weaving and putting himself in; this would make him the sole master of the whole story. It was now nothing more than a game to save his reputation. But he was too late. There was one factor he could not eliminate. Baptiste Pourier had joint knowledge with Garnett of all the facts. Both men were known to speak truth—truth—truth. While Woman's Dress was arraigning Garnett with severity, Pourier unexpectedly appeared, his presence in the neighborhood not being known. Garnett applied to him and recited what Woman's Dress had said. Pourier asked Woman's Dress if that was what he said. "Yes," was the answer. "Woman's Dress, you are a liar!" exclaimed Pourier whose eyes flashed with indignation. The last story was not like the first, with which Pourier was as familiar as Garnett. Woman's Dress had caused to be spread among the officers at the post a falsehood against Crazy Horse imputing to him the basest criminal purpose. It precipitated the immediate marshaling of force against him—his flight—his pursuit—his voluntary return—the deception to get him into the guardhouse and close the doors on him before he should suspect he was a prisoner—his discovery of betrayal at the last instant—his revolt—the fierce struggle—his mortal wound—his death. Pourier was a relative of Woman's Dress (cousins by marriage); he it was who piled on the last straw to add force to Lieut. Clark's argument to prevail on Gen. Crook to abandon the council which he had called with the Indians, and which made that argument effective by declaring that Woman's Dress was one of the most credible of Indians. (Woman's Dress had credit for saving Crook's life by keeping him away from the council. Bosh.)

In 1889 when Gen. Crook was negotiating the treaty which is known by his name, this matter was discussed with him at Pine Ridge by Garnett and Pourier together, and he was informed of the deception of Woman's Dress and how his falsehood had been detected and exposed.[104] When the subject was laid before him in 1877 and the council was given over, he remarked that he did not like to start to do a thing and not finish it. In 1889 he remarked thoughtfully that he always thought that he should have gone to that council.

Crazy Horse Continues His Retreat

This same day that Crazy Horse fled from his camp below Red Cloud, he reached the camp of Touch the Cloud. His arrival threw the camp into the wildest excitement, and the warriors mounted their steeds and came out to meet the scouts.

The Touch the Cloud camp was on the Beaver Creek where Frank M. Conn now (1907) lives, about three miles below Camp Sheridan.[105]

The warriors ran the first party of scouts into Camp Sheridan. The horses belonging to the scouts were put into the quartermaster's corral, and the scouts were quartered in a building where they would be protected from the infuriated braves. As the Indians belonging to Touch the Cloud's camp were coming up to Camp Sheridan, Crazy Horse among the number, the Spotted Tail Indians who were scattered in camps, and the Indian scouts who belonged to Camp Sheridan, were all gathering at this point. Just as all these different bands got there the second party which Lieut. Clark had set off in pursuit, arrived at the camp and the Touch the Cloud Indians made a burst for them. They were armed with guns, clubs and one particular Indian had a mighty lance with which he made blood-curdling sweeps and passes at the scouts who had come from Fort Robinson. The Spotted Tail scouts by great exertions kept the Touch the Cloud Indians fended off while the assailed scouts were hurrying forward with all the speed they were able in their worried condition to make, till at length they found safety from further assault at the Agency to which place they had to be helped for accommodations.

(See Louie Bordeaux and Charles Taggart at Rosebud, the interpreters, for particulars of the negotiation at Camp Sheridan.)[106]

Next day Crazy Horse accompanied by the Indian Agent Lee, his interpreter Louie Bordeaux, and a great number of Touch The Cloud and Spotted Tail Indians, proceeded to Fort Robinson, arriving late in the day, fully two hours before sunset.

A scout flew from Red Cloud Agency bearing news to the post that Crazy Horse was coming.

Crazy Horse and the party with him rode directly up to the adjutant's office. He was under guard when he arrived. It seems that Spotted Tail and perhaps others in conjunction, had arranged for Crazy Horse to go with some of the officers at Spotted Tail and some of his own Indians to Fort Robinson, and it was further arranged for the Fort Robinson Indian scouts to follow behind, starting a long distance behind, and gradually to draw on and overtake him and go in with him surrounded by them as well as the guards with whom he started. He started from Spotted Tail under guard. The cavalcade halted in front of the adjutant's office on the south side of the parade ground. Dismounting, they entered the building, followed by some two dozen Indians.[107]

(Garnett was not in this conference and cannot give any account.)

At length they all went out, Crazy Horse between the officer of the day and Little Big Man, each of whom held him by the arm.[108] It was about fifty feet to the guardhouse, a one-story building having two apartments. In the west end was the room for the detention of prisoners. This was communicated with at this time through a door entering from the east room, and this was approached from the north side where there was a closed awning, open at the east end. A military guard was pacing his beat before this entry, with bayonet fixed and his gun on his shoulder. The officer and Little Big Man, with Crazy Horse in charge, passed in followed by Indians. Outside was a multitude of Indians trembling with anger, two sides, each with cocked revolvers in hand, bending and swaying like crouching tigers ready to spring at each other's throats. Against the adjutant's office in the space between that and the guardhouse the adherents of Crazy Horse are lined up; opposite and against the other building are the scouts forming a part of the garrison.

As they walked toward the guardhouse Little Big Man kept talking to Crazy Horse and assuring him that whenever he was taken he would go with him and stand by him.

South of these immediate buildings and toward Soldier Creek farther beyond, ~~teams, horses and Indians~~ were packed in and around that space and the commissary buildings occupying part of it, teams, horses and Indians in a seething mass.

A noise was heard in the building where Crazy Horse had entered. Indians came flying out crying "It's a guardhouse! it's a guardhouse!" There was great uproar within. Indians kept pouring out in a panic. Clanking chains could now be heard. It is but a minute and prisoners from the cell are on the scene outside with balls to their ankles. Others are coming out as if their hope is to escape. As the struggle in the building continues the tumult outside increases.

When the inner door was opened to pass Crazy Horse in, it dawned on him for the first time that he was a prisoner going into confinement. He jumped back to escape and drew his knife. Little Big Man seized him by the arms and a desperate struggle between the two ensued, the prisoner endeavoring to set himself free. At length they appeared in the open air. The two whirled into the space between the scouts and the surging Indians on the opposite side. Crazy Horse is a small man while his antagonist is short, thick, heavily built and weighs about 170 pounds. Indian scouts repeatedly raise their revolvers to fire at Crazy Horse. The officer of the day moving up and down with drawn sword forbids each successively to discharge his firearms. It sounds like a growl as Crazy Horse repeats, "Let me go! let me go! let me go!" ~~A scout leaps forward and grasps the revolver from his belt. A chorus of voices warn him not to shoot.~~ Gaining an advantage for an instant, Crazy Horse twists his wrist which holds the knife and inflicts an ugly wound in Little Big Man's forearm. ~~Swift Bear, chief of the orn Band,~~[109] ~~and one or two others spring to the assistance of the disabled combatant who~~ About this juncture the sentinel who had been gazing at the contest brought down his piece and extended his arms at full length as if making a thrust. At the precise instant that this was done, Crazy Horse swung himself around toward the soldier with great force in a desperate effort to break loose, and the bayonet pierced him in the side, passing nearly through his body and into both kidneys. ~~"Let me go; you've got me hurt now," exclaimed Crazy Horse~~ The bayonet was instantly withdrawn. "Let me go, you've got me hurt now!" exclaimed Crazy Horse. These were his last words of which there is any account. Little Big Man was still holding on to him. Some Indian, said to be an uncle of Crazy Horse, moved by this last appeal, thrust Little Big Man in the stomach with the butt of a gun, saying, "You are always in the way." The blow ~~felled him~~ sent him backwards to the ground. As his hold was released Swift Bear, chief of the Corn band, and some others caught Crazy Horse.[110] ~~In a moment he sank to the ground.~~ A scout, Yankton Charley (also called Plenty Wolf) leaps forward and grasps the revolver from Crazy Horse's belt. He holds it in the air and shouts that he has the revolver. The Indian who had knocked down Little Big Man jerked it from his hand. In a moment Crazy Horse sank to the ground. ~~About this juncture the sentinel who had been gazing at the contest brought down his piece and extended his arms at full length as if making a thrust. At the precise instant this was done Crazy Horse swung himself around toward the soldier with great force in a supreme effort to break loose and the bayonet pierced him in the side, passing almost through his body and wounding both kidneys. "Let me go! you've got me hurt now!" The bayonet was instantly withdrawn. So far as known these were his last words. He sank to the ground.~~ He had fought his last fight. The statement here made as to the bayonet performance is given without change from the personal interviews had with Chief American Horse and William Garnett both of whom saw the particular act and are confident that the killing of Crazy Horse ~~was not intentional~~ by the soldier was not intentional.[111]

(Insert footnote of death and affirmance of intention to kill by soldier who died in Washington.)[112]

Now occurred an incident showing how like wild animals human beings are sometimes swayed when under excitement. The followers of Crazy Horse were now induced by someone to withdraw along the road to the Red Cloud Agency as far as Col. Bradley's residence at the northeast corner of the quadrilateral enclosing the parade ground. The scouts and the chiefs also withdrew to Lieut. Clark's residence at the northwest corner. A short consultation was had there. Crazy Horse in the meantime was lying on the ground alone in a dying condition. At length the two crowds started back simultaneously. On the way around in rear of the soldiers barracks both went to take up their old positions. The scouts gained a few steps and were on the ground a moment in advance of the others. A strong guard several ranks deep was thrown from the southwest corner of the adjutant's office diagonally to the southwest closing the space between the two buildings to all ingress by the Crazy Horse Indians so they could not occupy front ground from the rear as before. But in front of these buildings the grounds were swarming. The study now was how to avoid a conflict over possession of the dying man's body. Chief American Horse who was always celebrated for his diplomacy (smoothness at deception) had directed the scouts when coming back to have some blankets ready to carry the wounded man on into the adjutant's office; for he was going to play the other side a trick. Then when all was ready he stood forth and addressing the crowd, said: "Maybe the man is badly hurt and maybe he is not; we will take him into the same place where they had the talk, and see how much he is hurt, and probably the Indian doctors can save him. It will not do to let him lie here." Then the blankets were spread on the ground and Crazy Horse was lifted on to them and carried into the building. When this was accomplished American Horse with the calmness and effrontery of the successful deceiver came to the door and shouted, "We have the body now and you can't have it! We've been arguing over this but we've got him in the house now! You can't have him."

The soldiers at the various barracks were in great activity getting prepared to fall into line if needed. Darkness was gathering and the crowds began to disperse. Dr. McGillicuddy, the surgeon was sent for.[113]

He said it was wonderful to observe the vitality Crazy Horse displayed in living. His age was about thirty-two.

~~The father of Crazy Horse[114] came that night to watch with his hero-son while the candle of life was burning low and fading out. Baptiste Pourier, William Garnett, Louie Bordeaux and Frank Gruard slept in the adjoining room. At daylight Crazy Horse senior shook Garnett. All he said was, "Crazy Horse is dead."~~

~~A hand shook him. He opened his eyes. A form was bending over him. It was the father of Crazy Horse. "Billy, get up." He paused, and then all he said was, "Crazy Horse is dead!"~~

Crazy Horse senior came up from the camp to watch that night with his hero-son while the light of life was fading out. He brought with him his bow and arrows and hunting knife and at Lieut. Clark's headquarters asked to be permitted to stay with him. He was told that he might, but that he must leave his arms. Then he was searched and his bow and arrows and knife were taken and put away. The elder Crazy Horse then went down to the adjutant's office where the younger Crazy Horse was lying on a pallet on the floor. Here he waited and watched till the night had ebbed away. When daylight had come he thought of his bow and arrows. He must have these. He went to Lieut. Clark's headquarters. In one of the rooms William Garnett, Baptiste Pourier, Louie Bordeaux and Frank Gruard were sleeping. ~~At Garnett's head the window was up.~~ Under Garnett's head were two big revolvers. Under Pourier's head were two more. Under Bordeaux's, one. These three were lying in a row. Gruard was sleeping on the opposite side of the room in a corner. At Garnett's head a window was up. A hand shook him. He opened his eyes. A form standing on the outside was leaning in at the window and bending over him. It was the father of Crazy Horse. "Nephew, get up; my son is dead." Then he called for his bow and quiver and knife. These were not given to him at the time, as it was not regarded as prudent to do so. When an Indian mourned for one who had fallen by a white man's hand, it was accounted among them the proper thing to kill some white ~~man~~ person. Therefore this precaution. Whatever the old man might have done at the moment of greatest grief, it is due to him to say that his later life and conduct showed him to be a good Indian.[115]

That day the body of Crazy Horse was removed in an ambulance to the camp of his people at Red Cloud. It had not been an easy thing to find two persons to perform this duty. At last two Indian scouts volunteered. It was feared that some outbreak in the camp might end in the killing of those who should bear the remains. On the way down an Indian, said to be the same uncle of Crazy Horse who had been so conspicuous in laying out Little Big Man and snatching the revolver away from Yankton Charley, leveled his gun at the driver who ~~fell over~~ involuntarily fell over into the lap of the attendant by his side.[116] The latter dissuaded the Indian from taking a shot, and the ambulance proceeded. The body was taken by the Indians to Spotted Tail Agency, wrapped in blankets and deposited according to the Indian custom. A pen was built of poles around it.[117] When the Indians were removed to the Missouri River in the fall of that year the body was placed in a cave in the butte rock three or four miles north of the Agency and about east of where Frank M. Conn lives on Beaver Creek. When the Indians were returning from the Missouri River in 1878, between the head of Wounded Knee Creek and where the beef corral is, two travois were seen moving on the road toward the east. A man was on a hill crying. It was said to be the same uncle of Crazy Horse who had been so prominent at the time of his death. Someone passing at the time told others who saw the travois and heard the lamentation, that it was the body of Crazy Horse being removed.

An Indian named Chipps, living six miles south of Kyle, claims to have superintended all the removals of the body and to have it in his possession for sale now.

Crazy Horse was about thirty-two years of age.

Before the Days of Agencies the Minneconjous and Uncpapas were Missouri River Indians just as the Oglalas and Brules were what might be called Platte River Indians. The Minneconjous and Sitting Bull Indians lived on the Missouri and adjacent country; the others clung to the line of the other river, the Republican, South Platte, etc. So when the treaty of 1851 was made the government got these widely separated tribes together for that purpose. See first book of William Garnett's Statement, [Tablet 1] which begins January 10, 1907, where the account commences of the trip of the Indian delegation to Washington, which is the next event of importance related by Mr. Garnett. In the account as given in that book there is one omission which I will supply at this point. It is to state in substance what President Hayes said in his speech to the Indians, in addition to what is given in the other book. [Not included.]

Next in the order of Mr. Garnett's statement is the removal of the Indians to the Missouri River. This began in the first book. In that book the narrative leaves the Indians after they have been taken down. Some facts of important interest belonging to that trip were omitted and they will be here supplied. (For some account of Lone Horn and Touch the Cloud, see p.87.) [Given earlier in this tablet.]

(Sitting Bull and his band belonged to the Standing Rock Reservation.)

Touch the Cloud belonged to the Cheyenne River Reservation, made up of Minneconjous and Sans Arcs.

These were Crazy Horse or Northern Indians who had come in with Spotted Tail, as heretofore explained, and had their camp at the mouth of the Beaver. They had no tribal connection with the Spotted Tail or Brule Indians, and they did not move Riverward with Spotted Tail, but when the Oglalas from Red Cloud came along down the river these Cheyenne River Agency Indians fell in with them and went along. In the course of the journey down [there were] three deflections and cleavages from the main column. When at a point where Interior, S.D. now is, a considerable body wheeled out and went north. Before the Indians turned out to leave, the Agent, Dr. Irwin, and the two companies of cavalry under Major (?) Vroom and Capt. Lawson (afterwards killed in the Apache campaign)[118] and lieut. Clark who was in charge of all the government teams and scouts, and the Chief Herder, Ed. Stevenson, went on ahead from Interior, leaving behind Ben Tibbitts, the butcher, Wm. Garnett, chief interpreter for the scouts who was also helping about the wagons which were very numerous and carrying luggage for the Indians, and Frank Yates and John Deere [Dear] the traders, and the beef herd all the government trains hauling Indians' baggage, the bull trains hauling the Agency property and Indians rations, and the train that hauled the Indians who had no conveyance. Some light trains hauling the Agent's personal supplies and the supplies for the soldiers went ahead. Paddock's store, with a man named Thompson in charge, also went ahead.

Tibbitts made a beef issue here. The column stayed here a few days. When they started the Crazy Horse Indians broke camp and wanted all the Indians to follow, but they would not, there were quite a lot of the northern Indians who would not go. Low Dog, a northern chief an upstart recently who belonged to the Lame Deer band and was a brave man, he led these Indians off.[119] Black Fox also went away. Low Dog died at Cheyenne Agency (Northern) abt. 1894. Just about half of the northern Indians left. Garnett sent a courier to notify Clark, and Clark sent a message to the Missouri River so that it could be sent by wire to intercept them with soldiers. The soldiers went after them but the Indians had crossed the Missouri River ahead of them & they got away. The Indians had begun lagging along down the river at the rate of 7 or 8 miles a day claiming that their horses were jaded and could not stand it to travel faster. They were possuming — saving their horses for a hard march after they should break away & they succeeded in their ruse. After the column got to the forks of the White River annuity goods were drawn. The scouts were paid off down at Missouri River. Clark was still there when this was done, and there he discharged a lot of them so that only about 75 remained. After While the scouts were down at the Missouri River getting pay and taking things leisurely, these northern Indians, including all the northern chiefs except Little Big Man slipped away quietly for the north and all escaped. A message was sent to Clark at the river to notify him of the departure of these Indians, and he got word to soldiers at Fort Keogh and Fort Mead, but the Indians got away. Clark was ordered back to his company — Troop K, 2d Cavalry, Capt. Egan's company; Clark was the 1st Lieut. (Ed Satterly was a member of that company.) Now in the spring of 1878 (grass was coming on) Touch the Cloud took his Minneconjous and went back to his Cheyenne River Agency. Now about all the Indians who had come down from the north had worked back in separate bodies. No Water was a northern chief. He was the one who had shot Crazy Horse through the head when Little Big Man held him.[120] These two chiefs were so unpopular on account of what they had done towards Crazy Horse that they dared not trust themselves up north. It was No Water who had command of the second detachment of scouts that Lieut. Clark sent down to Spotted Tail Agency after Crazy Horse. All the northern chiefs except Little Big Man and No Water had now gone back north.

Touch the Cloud, after his return to his reservation had his arms and horses taken from him and his hair cut off. This treatment caused him much grief and crying; for he thought that he would not be molested, though Garnett told him he would and urged him to stay down here. After Lieut. Clark left in the spring of 1878 he was succeeded by Lieut. Dodd.[121] The scouts were cut down from time to time till they numbered only 15.

Along in the summer (thinks abt. Aug.) Red Cloud took ~~the Oglalas~~ one or two lodges only besides his own and slipped back and got as far as Pass Creek when he was overtaken by Young Man Afraid with a lot of his Indian soldiers and some of the Indian scouts, and brought him and his little party back.

Conquering Bear, son of the old chief who was killed by the soldiers, acted as guide to the column down White River; he went on ahead from Interior with the advance detachments.

The Indians (he thinks) started to return from the Missouri about September, 1878. They relied on President Hayes promise to let them return in a year. They could not be held there. They had a plan to come back and were scheming to go, and secretly making preparations. Garnett at this time was in the war department service. ~~After~~ Along about the month of August Garnett worked a month for the Indian trader, Deere; then Dr. Irwin, Agent, got him appointed Agency interpreter.

A man named Haight, Commissioner of Indian Affairs, had been out to the Missouri among these Indians trying to persuade them to remain down there, but they would not hear to it.[122] So when they got the last rations to complete the year down there under the agreement with President Hayes, they acted like a whirlwind; nothing could restrain or control them. They were furious in haste and movement; they outran everything.

When these Indians started down from the Forks of White River to the mouth of the Yellow Medicine on the Missouri [it was] to get their last rations which were for a month. Before they ~~went they went to Garnett and told him to tell the Agent~~ left the Missouri to return to the Forks of White River where they always drew their beef, they told Garnett to remain down on the Missouri, and he did so for abt. 3 days, giving them time to get back to the Forks. Garnett went to the Agent abt. 4 o'clock in the afternoon and told him that the Indians were ready to move back to White Clay as soon as they had drawn their beef; that after the beef issue they were going to capture the herd and take it with them. He replied that he had no orders yet for them to move. He asked Garnett, "What are you going to do?" "I'm going with them." "If you go with those Indians I shall have to dismiss you as interpreter." Garnett said he was going anyway. Garnett told him that he and the Indians wanted the butcher, Ben Tibbitts, who was also acting agent at the Forks of the White River, and the herders to go along to make their regular issues of beef; but if they did not go the cattle would be taken anyway. Garnett now left and rode all night to reach the Forks, distance 65 miles, and arrived at daylight. The issue was made immediately. The bulk of the Indians were camped about 13 miles up Little White River. The beef issue was then on foot. The only block issues were made to the few Indians who were camped at the Forks where the traders' stores were. The Indian soldiers (who were also called White Horse soldiers for local reason) had brought down extra horses at the instance of Garnett to bear away those Indians who had no conveyance.

After the beef issue was all over, Garnett called the chiefs together, viz.; Young Man Afraid, Red Cloud, Red Dog, Slow Bull, High Wolf (an old time chief), Little Wound, Blue Horse, and a man named Day who was a Wajjaja chief, and Three Bears (who had been made a chief at the Forks of the White River through the influence of the Indian scouts who had served under him on the Crook campaign — they were partial to him and induced members of all the other bands to attach themselves to him and form a camp and he thus formed the largest band by a large number) — American Horse, Black Bear and White Bird; this was the number of bands of Indians when they left the Forks of White River. These chiefs had appointed Little Big Man the head soldier of all the Indian soldiers before the Indians went down to Yellow Medicine to draw rations. Each one of these chiefs had some Indian soldiers with a leader of his own over them, and Little B. Man was over the whole as commander.

Garnett told the assembled chiefs that he had delivered the message they gave him for the Agent, that the minute they should start to go off his own government service was ended. That he was going with them. Young Man Afraid was the first to speak to him. "Billy," he said, "your service will be with Little Big Man with the braves." So these chiefs and Little Big Man and Garnett went to Tibbitts who was now issuing the block beef. These asked him and the chief herder, who were together to come along with the herd and make their issues as they always had. They refused. The chief herder said to them that he could not turn the beeves over to them. Garnett told him that he might go along or stay, as he preferred; but that they were going to take the cattle. Little Big Man directed Garnett to tell him not to interfere with them when they took the herd, and if he did not he would not be harmed but to be sure not to interfere. He was told also that he could go along with his herders and retain control of the herd if he would. A man named Alex Adams, one of the herders, became pretty saucy when the cattle had been rounded up. Little Big Man told him he had said enough; if he did not want to get hurt, to shut up. About 20 of the Indian soldiers rode right up to the side of L. B. Man and Adams subsided. Ed Stevenson, the chief herder, rode up to Garnett and asked if it would be all safe if he and his assistant herders went along. He was told that if he went the issues would be regularly made as always before and they would be fully protected by the Indian soldiers. He told his men to get ready and follow the herd.

The Indians started off with the herd while the herders were packing up to go. The latter soon overtook the stock which was turned over to them and the Indian soldiers accompanied them the first day. They all reached the Indian camp on Little White River the first day. Four scouts had been appointed and left behind to watch Tibbitts and see what kind of a move he was going to make. They came on to the Indian camp before sundown, bringing news that Tibbitts had started to the Missouri River on horseback. Next day the Indians left Little White River and moved along camping at convenient distances till they arrived at Black Pipe Creek which is about on the line between the Rosebud and Pine Ridge Reservations. Here some Indians, about 200 including women and children, came to them from Spotted Tail's band which had already come to their Reservation, probably in the month of August. These Indians had formerly belonged to the Oglalas and were now coming back. The column next moved to Pass Creek in the eastern part of P. Ridge Reservation.

There were two or three criers whom Garnett caused to go through the camp and tell the people to bring up their beef tickets, as Tibbitts had the beef census list, so that an issue could be made; and as Garnett had some familiarity with this business and the herders had seen it done, they had no trouble to issue beef to the Indians and keep true account. After the issue, Tibbitts arrived at Pass Creek. He said he got to the Missouri and a dispatch was wired to the Commissioner of Indian Affairs telling him that the Indians had broken out and left. He got an answer and was directed to follow and issue beef and make a camp on the White Clay.

The camp lay there till next day after the beef issue, and then they moved to the head of Pass Creek. A council was held there and Little Big Man and

Garnett and 5 or 6 others were selected to go ahead to White Clay to notify the contractor there that the Agency was coming. This man was named O'Burn [O'Bierne]. He was there in a tent. No building was up yet; but some lumber which had been a part of the Red Cloud Agency was piled up in places. The Agency owned at this time quite a lot of bull teams, perhaps 30. Both agencies had just bought a lot of such teams that year. O'Burn started to building as soon as he could get workmen.

Next day after arrival of these men, a courier came from the old Spotted Tail Agency site where a camp of one company had been left when they all went down to the River under command of ~~Major Lieut. Capt.~~ Lieut. Crawford.[123]

(Omitted: When Tibbitts overtook the Indians he said some soldiers came up from Missouri River to the Forks of White River and to the Indian camp on the Little White River, and finding that the Indians were gone, returned to the Missouri.) The courier came as stated. He brought news that the Cheyennes had broken out in Indian Territory and were coming north & had crossed the North Platte River. Garnett sent Little Big Man back to the Oglalas with instructions to keep them together, not to let them scatter and to bring them in together; and told him about the Cheyennes had broken out & were coming. The Oglalas arrived. The night they got in it seems some soldiers began coming down from Fort Meade and up the White Clay Creek. The Indians got alarmed and thought the soldiers were coming to jump on them; because they themselves had gone off irregularly and without orders they thought the soldiers were after them, and would not believe the Cheyenne story. Another lot of soldiers arrived from Camp Sheridan, and it looked worse and worse to the Indians. Garnett told the soldiers not to camp near the Indians, and to quit going among them, as the Indians were scared, and the chiefs were having all they could do to hold them. These soldiers from Sheridan came up from the direction of Chadron; he does not know that they were actually from Camp Sheridan. It looked as though the troops wanted to camp by the Oglalas. Garnett got them to go up on Wolf Creek and camp above where the beef corral now is. Garnett was known by the Indians to have been in the military employ, and had been connected with the Red Cloud and Red Leaf affair and they were afraid to trust and believe Garnett.

Some more soldiers — 2 or 3 companies — came from the Porcupine direction (those who came up White Clay and down from towards Porcupine may have both been of the same original body which had come from Fort Mead and split ~~to come in on the Indian~~ so as to scatter out to look all over for Cheyennes). These from the Porcupine direction Garnett persuaded to go up on the Wolf Creek and above the later beef corral and camp there. Four nights troops came in, usually after dark, and the Indians thought they were closing all around them. Troops who had been down with Spotted Tail at his Agency were coming; also the soldiers that were down at Yellow Medicine were ordered up to concentrate at Fort Robinson; these kept coming in one after another, and it was all that Garnett and the chiefs could do to keep the Indians from attacking the soldiers. The chiefs were up at night, all night, talking and laboring with the Indians to pacify them. Those Indians who had been scouts went around with Garnett and the chiefs and argued and pleaded with them not to make any break on the soldiers. These combinations at this time barely missed breaking up this agency. The Indians were camped in great numbers along White Clay Creek where the government farm now is and above there.

On the fifth day after the arrival of the Indians at the White Clay the 15 scouts who belonged to the Agency had after arrival gone over to Camp Sheridan on government service, and while returning to White Clay one of them discovered a small party of Cheyennes—not over ten—men, women and children—Lone Bear was the one who found them—these Cheyennes had got broken off somehow from the larger party—they were in those hills southwest of the Agency; these scouts brought them in—there were perhaps two men among them—brought to Red Cloud's lodge; they told their story. Two officers got around and saw these Cheyennes. These Cheyennes settled the excitement. The Cheyennes were aiming to strike the old Red Cloud Agency. Red Cloud told the two officers that those Cheyennes had surrendered to him and he was going to keep them and was allowed to do so. The movements of the Cheyennes may be more intelligently described by explaining that a white man called Cheyenne Charley who lived among the Cheyenne Indians and during the Black Kettle disturbances was called down in the Indian Territory Little Buckshot of the Prairie (probably a translation of the name the Indians save him) had directed the course of these Indians all the way from the Indian Territory back to the north with a degree of success that has been a marvel in the eyes of white people since that day.[124] The reason for their marvelous dodgings and escapes was his being a white man and on the strength of race and color could go anywhere without being suspected by the whites, and could thus keep informed of the movements of army officers and soldiers and the knowledge he gained was communicated to the marauding Indians and their course was managed by him accordingly. They eluded all efforts to head them off and to capture them; and there would have been no Cheyenne outbreak had it not been for the waywardness of Dull Knife who would not listen to counsel. Little Wolf wanted him to stay with him. Cheyenne Charley wanted him to follow Little Wolf. But his desire was to get back among the Oglalas; so he split off from Little Wolf (probably down on the Platte) and took his course for the old Red Cloud Agency. Little Wolf bore off in a wide detour to the east, striking the head of Pass Creek, crossing White River, and making a circuit of the Black Hills, passing between them and the Missouri River and finally arriving in the northern country, the home of their choice. Cheyenne Charley had been up here in the White River Country (Garnett says he got employment here for a while and that he saw him in such service). He knew all the time how and where the troops were concentrating, and moreover, being acquainted with the locations of posts he could foresee where the soldiers would be sent and do their scouting. He quit down here and went up to Fort Keogh and told the officers there he was acquainted with the Cheyennes and could persuade them to come in and surrender. He was employed on this service and brought them in. Garnett saw him after these events had passed into history and talked with him and learned facts which he had not before known. The northern Cheyennes thus became firmly established in that country after many vicissitudes. When these went up there were a small number there who had not been away.

Speaking of the Cheyennes Garnett says that they and the Sioux in the earlier days did not have their country in the north as more latterly, but on the Plattes, the Republican, Arickaree, Cache la Poudre, in the Denver country on Cherry Creek, etc. The same of the Arapahos. By camping apart in separate bands they gradually became divided; so that there are Northern and Southern Cheyennes and Arapahos.

Garnett knows about the Dull Knife affair only from the Indians themselves, as follows:

Garnett interpreted the statement of Fire Eater to Gen. Crook as follows: He said the Dull Knife band were camped on Chadron Creek, and as they still had their arms the scouts were afraid to go in to them, so they got this Fire Eater to go and try to get them to give up. He was the only one the scouts could get to go in. He went in several times before he could get them to give up. Finally they gave up through him. Lone Bear was among the scouts at the time, and he is a policeman who lives between Pass Creek and Black Pipe.

During Agent Gallagher's incumbency this Indian Fire Eater asked for employment at the Agency during a council of the Indians when Crook was making his 1889 treaty. Fire Eater got up in the council with Crook's permission and he related his connection with this affair on Chadron Creek and said he thought he ought to get employment. Garnett did the interpreting. Gen. Crook asked in the council if anybody knew anything about this. ~~Three Bears rose~~ Lone Bear stood up and said he was present then as a scout and what Fire Eater said was true. Gen. Crook asked the Agent if he had any place he could give him, & the Agent replied that he had one as man of all work at $15 a month. This was given him and he held it some years, until (he thinks) Clapp's time when he died.[125]

The Cheyennes who were brought to the Pine Ridge Agency after the outbreak at Robinsion were given clothing and horses and provided for comfortably by the Oglalas. Garnett thinks there were from 65 to 75 of these Cheyennes.

Negotiations for Black Hills in 1875

Garnett says he went to Washington in the spring of 1875 with an Indian delegation.[126] The Indians, as near as he can give them were: Red Cloud, Little Wound, American Horse, Face, Fast Thunder, High Lance, Sitting Bull (not the old Sitting Bull, but the one who received on this trip a gold mounted gun from President Grant as a gift); Shoulder, Conquering Bear, Black Bear, Young Bad Wound and his wife; Iron Horse, White Tail. Above was Oglala delegation. Young Man Afraid would not go, though strenuous efforts were made to get him. These are all he can mention. The interpreters who went with the foregoing were: Louie Richard, Nick Janis and William Garnett. The Spotted Tail delegation was as follows, as near as he can name them: Spotted Tail, Swift Bear, Crow Dog, He Dog (this is a different He Dog from the northern chief by that name who has been mentioned before), Good Voice, Ring Thunder. Interpreter Louie Bordeaux. Garnett says he has named all the Spotted Tails. Dr. Seville, Agent at Red Cloud, was in charge of the Oglalas, and Major Howard the Spotted Tail Agent was in charge of these latter ones.

There was a delegation in Washington when these arrived from Red Cloud & from Cheyenne River Agency under charge of Agent Bingham of the latter Agency. William Feeler was interpreter for these.[127] This delegation was: Lone Horn, White Swan, Red Shirt, Long Mandan, Bull Eagle, Rattling Ribs, No Fat (who went under another name) _____ Claws. This delegation also went to Washington on the Black Hills business. These may not all have been from

Cheyenne River Agency, but they were from the Missouri River and the Agent was from Cheyenne River Agency.

(There was also a delegation at Washington same time to investigate Agent J. J. Seville. Tod Randall, a former trader at Red Cloud, and Leon Palladay as interpreter, were there. This was still going on when the Indians returned. Garnett does not know what was accomplished by this.)[128]

Garnett says that when these Indian delegations went to Washington and were on their way to Cheyenne, they met the expedition going to the Black Hills (Dodge's I think). Garnett says that there was a great body of soldiers and that the scientific man who reported on the minerals, thinks his name was Jenny, was along.[129]

These Indian delegations were in Washington a long time—fully three weeks—deliberating over the Hills questions; they were caucusing a long time among themselves at their hotel.

The government sent for these Indians and did not advise them what the business was that they were wanted for, and when they were arrived the Black Hills was sprung on them. This was why the Indians were all at sea.[130] At this same time the question was sprung on Little Wound chief of the Cutoffs, to surrender their right to hunt on the Republican River, and terms were made for $25,000.[131] (See the printed pamphlet in which this is referred to by the delegation when Red Cloud, American Horse, Clarence Three Stars and High Star went to Washington.)

President Grant raised this point in his address to these Indians, offering $12,500. Little Wound replied that he and his people knew nothing of this subject coming up, and that he could do nothing without consulting them, and that the price offered was inadequate. He advised the President to send out a delegation to see his people about it. Now coming back to the Black Hills, the chiefs Red Cloud, Spotted Tail and Lone Horn were the leaders and their decision finally was adopted by the other chiefs. Red Cloud said in their private council that we did not know anything about that this business was coming up, neither did his people know it, and he could not do anything; Spotted Tail said the same thing, and so did Lone Horn, the Minneconjou from the Cheyenne River Agency. Lone Horn said his people were starving and he wanted to get rations and beef for them. And it was at length decided by the three chiefs that they would end all consultation and go home. Lone Horn was made spokesman of the delegations to communicate their decision to President Grant. All the other chiefs assented to the agreement that the three had come to. These chiefs knew that the government had already sent an expedition into the Hills to examine the country, for they met it going. The next day after the above agreement was reached, all the Indians visited the President. Lone Horn, speaking through Louie Bordeaux, interpreter, said: "Great Father: I will give now an answer as to the decision we have all come to about the Black Hills. We did not know anything about that the Black Hills was going to come before us when we came here, and our people don't know anything about it. We have come to the conclusion that you can send your people out there among our people. I have known the Black Hills ever since I can recollect. The Black Hills have no legs and no wings and always stay in the one place. So they will be there when they come out. My people are starving. I am down here on purpose to ask you for rations and beef for them. This was all that I knew about when I left home" (when this speech was made, the room was packed with men and women & when Lone Bear [Horn] mentioned that the hills had neither legs nor wings the white folks laughed heartily). The delegations then returned to their homes. When they went to Washington they were hauled to Cheyenne in wagons; but on the return the inspector, Daniels who had been met in Washington and returned to Cheyenne bought horses for the chiefs to ride home. This was the usual way of doing, to buy horses for them to return; it was so done with Red Cloud when he returned in 1870. Garnett does not remember what was done with him on the trip in 1872. On the trip in 1875 the Commissioner of Indian Affairs gave Red Cloud a silver mounted gun as a present, valued at $250.[132] The gold mounted one [was] given at same time by President Grant to the minor Sitting Bull who was considered in those days as one of the greatest of the Indians friendly to the government.

The Crow Indians captured the Red Cloud gun from Jack Red Cloud in the Rosebud fight, June 17, 1876. The gold mounted gun, valued at $500, was captured from Sitting Bull (minor) when he was in December, 1876, driving into Fort Keogh a lot of horses, about 60, into the fort. Sitting Bull had lent this gun to a friend who went off to the hostile Indians with it, and he followed to recover it; while there he recaptured these horses which had been taken from white men, and drove them to Keogh; as he was nearly to enter the fort, some Crow Indians camped roundabout attacked and killed him and got his gun.[133]

Garnett thinks this gun afterward found its way to Washington.

Daniels had been a trader at the old Sod Agency before Whalm came.

Daniels came as a civilian and relieved Major Whalm [Wham] as Agent.

He had been an Indian agent sometime before (thinks) for the Santees. Says Whalm was an army officer.[134] Thinks when this change was made the Indians were transferred from War to Interior Dept. When Whalm came first time it was as Agent at Fort Laramie. Next time Garnett saw him come it was as a Paymaster. First time he came he issued beeves at Fort Laramie several times. While he was Agent the Red Cloud Agency was built on the River 30 miles below the Fort. It was made of sods and so got to be called the "Sod" Agency but the real name was Red Cloud. It was built in the year 1871.

Now comes next the Commission to negotiate for the Hills. The commissioners sent some of their number to the Cheyenne River and Standing Rock Agencies, taking some Indian chiefs with them — Blue Horse, Slow Bull and Red Dog — and others; Louie Bordeaux and Joe Richard, taking Indians with them went north to the camps of Crazy Horse and Sitting Bull, about a 100 in the force for safety, and they got a very few to come in to the council. This party from the East was large; Garnett thinks a lot of congressmen and other followers were out for their health and sight-seeing.[135] He cannot recall any other parties sent out; but parties of Indians were coming and going all the time; when their rations and ammunition were low they came in with a few robes to trade & they then went back, having drawn rations and exchanged robes for ammunition.

Representatives came from Spotted Tail also; and they came in great numbers from all quarters. The commissioners had quarters at Red Cloud, and they came down every day to the council at the Lone Tree. There were Indian soldiers on duty under the chief command of the minor Sitting Bull who guarded the camp, the council place. There were tents up for the officials' use, and there was a canvas pavilion or tent fly, under which the commissioners were seated, while the Indians stood outside and, generally the Indian speakers and the interpreters stood under the tree. The people out from the east were numerous; Garnett says it was the largest commission he ever saw come West. They met at the Lone Tree several days.[136] When the council was opened the commissioners stated the object of their presence on the ground, that they wanted to buy the Black Hills and offered to pay $7,000,000 in money. They did not know a million from the number of stars in the sky as was shown when Garnett talked to them. The Indians repaired to their respective camps and counseled and caucused separately on the matter.

After some days Red Dog (the usual spokesman for Red Cloud) came to the council to speak for the Oglalas. Among his remarks Garnett cannot tell what he said, only just what he wanted for the Hills. He said they did not want the $7,000,000, for the sum was not enough; but they wanted to be paid seven generations just for the tops of those Black Hills and for no other lands. Either the same or the second day after, the commissioners got a very few Oglalas to sign a document, but Garnett does not know what they were signing. It was just blank writing paper they signed. Next day some tent flies were set up down near the White River bank, probably 100 yards from the pavilion. After there had been some talking by Indians, now Spotted Tail spoke for the first time, having held out until this moment, though the pressure to get him to speak had been very great.[137]

Garnett thinks this was about the day Little Big Man [blank] A man named Wells did the interpreting for this council.[138]

Spotted Tail demanded to see the document to be signed, and also the money that was to be paid for the Hills; wanted to see it in "black and white;" he taunted them by saying that he could see nothing. The pointed remarks of Spotted Tail brought the council to a close. The commissioners could show up nothing and the conference was at a standstill. This was the last day at the Lone Tree.

Little Big Man was a Crazy Horse man, vain and troublesome. He was settled at the council by Young Man Afraid. Garnett thinks it possible that the whites were alarmed at L. B. Man's bravado.[139]

Selling the Hunting Right on the Republican River Garnett thinks that payment of the $25,000 for the surrender of this right was made in 1875. The Spotted Tail Indians (Brules) received some of this consideration, as they had always enjoyed hunting privileges down there and used them to a limited but less extent than the Cutoffs under Little Wound. This payment was made in horses, cows and wagons.

Before this Commission had come to the Lone Tree Council, a small commission came out to treat for the Hunting Right on the Republican, and the fellow Hinman was one of the number. This commission got them to sign a paper for this right sold for $25,000. The Indians insisted on having $50,000 and Hinman in his fraudulent way and manner told them to sign the paper, and "we will try to get you the other $25,000." The Indians still think that this $25,000 is due them. (See the Pamphlet containing report of speeches of Red Cloud, Am. Horse, Clarence Three Stars and High Star in Washington about 1897.) The Indian Rights Association did investigating of the work of this Hinman, and he was dispensed with. Write to this assn.)[140]

After the issue of the annuity goods, Garnett thinks Agent J. J. Seville was removed in the winter after the events detailed took place.

The Indians were continually going and coming, passing between the Agency and the camps of Crazy Horse and Sitting Bull up north. The mail service grew to be very hazardous and several carriers were killed. Indian carriers were at last employed. They traveled differently from the white men and got through all right, for they did not go by the road. Two were killed to Garnett's personal knowledge—Dave Rogers was killed on Deadman Creek; there was a man killed on White River 5 or 6 miles above Fort Robinson after the Agency had been moved over from the Platte; the one killed on Deadman was when the Agency was on the Platte; he was carrying between the Spotted Tail and Sod Agencies. One was wounded in 5 or 6 places over on Raw Hide Creek on the road from Robinson to Laramie, but he did not die; this was in the spring of 1873. The killing on White River was (he thinks) in 1876. This must have been the man Clark.[141]

Treaty of 1876

Manypenny was the Chairman of this commission, but was prevented by illness from being present, and a man named Vroom acted in his stead.[142] They came with rules regulations and a lot of writing; they brought a treaty fully cooked containing schemes for schools, children, rations, mixed bloods, etc. and they told the Indians that this treaty would be tacked to the treaty of 1868. After the document was all read through they were told that if it was made and approved by the government that they would be fed beef and rations till they should be self-supporting. They were to have (thinks) one pound and a half of dressed meat and three pounds on the hoof to each person every day, and the rations were to be provided also. This treaty provided also about the Agencies and removal to Indian Territory and the Missouri River conditionally. When the treaty had been read the minor Sitting Bull who had three knives fastened to a long handle, a revolver and a Winchester [spoke?]. He was a conspicuous friend of the whites, but the dose in this treaty infuriated him. He said they did not know anything about Indian Territory and Missouri River; that they wanted to remain in their own country; that the contents of this document were foolishness; that most all of their people were away off in the north and there were not enough there to transact such business, and in great fury he ordered the Indians out of the stockade (the Red Cloud Agency) and White Bird began talking back and taunting him with his reputation as a friend of the white man, whereupon the minor Sitting Bull struck him a blow with the back of his knives and hurried him along, at the same time telling all the Indians to "get out, get out," and he quickly cleared the premises. He brought the conference to a standstill and no further effort was made by the Commission as long as he remained, which was two or three days. Then he went off north where he was killed at Keogh. The minor Sitting Bull got his gold mounted gun from President Grant because he had been a pacific and respectable Agency Indian who had made a good name. He was conspicuous in the Flag Pole Affair in clubbing Indians who had done the cutting and narrowly escaped with his life, an Indian being prevented from shooting him. Down on the Republican he saved a lot of robes and other property belonging to hunters and ranchmen from spoilation by the Indians. During Seville's time there was considerable trouble with the Indians on account of their killing contractors' cattle before they were turned over to the government. They would meet the herds and shoot and slaughter such fat ones as they wanted. The cattle were kept in an immense herd down on the Platte, and they were brought up as needed—two or three issues all at one time. The cowboys were afraid to try to bring them up alone, and so this minor Sitting Bull made himself useful in getting together a sufficient force of Indians to bring the cattle up under guard, his business being to go with them. One contractor lost a whole herd on the Deadman.

<u>Guards at Agency</u> When the Agency was under civilian control, the chiefs provided at Red Cloud a number of Indian soldiers for guards to protect the property, numbering from 5 or 6 to something like 12, as was needed. After the minor Sitting Bull took departure for the north, the Commissioners got at it again. They read the document over again. The Indians objected to numbers of provisions distasteful to them, and whenever a clause of this kind was reached this Hinman would obligingly assure them that it would be stricken out; but Garnett says he notices that the objectionable parts were retained in the treaty. This Hinman was efficient in explanations and promises to the Indians on the point of the southern boundary of the Sioux Reservation. He was a genius at plausability and deception. He told them just where the line would run. He said that it would follow the Niobrara River from the Nebraska state line up to the 103d meridian; thence north to the Cheyenne River. The Indians were ignorant of meridians, so Hinman described the line according to Indian habit from stream to stream and peak to peak. The Indians were confused and did not understand that they were parting with the Black Hills. Red Cloud

says they did not. But few of the Indians were present. Only about 24 or 26 signed and these belonged, Garnett says it looks to him, mostly to the Cutoffs. The great bulk of the Indians were out and took no part in this partial affair and had no knowledge of it, and have not understood the swindle to this day. Those who participated were overreached and defrauded and have ever since kept up a chorus of complaint; so that those who were away have ever asked in vain for information that would be explicit and definitive. No one has ever been fair enough to tell them without equivocation. They have for years been in a ferment and agitation over the subject and debating among themselves in their councils and outside of them, and sending deputations to Washington which have been blandly received by affable officials who could not and would not help them; and lawyers have been consulted, but nothing has been accomplished and nothing can be.

(In the council at the Lone Tree some Brules were in attendance and they stated their need of an agency at the mouth of White River, as they lived there in that region. Their prayer was listened to and they got a small agency established there which is called the Lower Brule Agency, and the Agent who keeps the Crow Creek Agency attends to this.)[143] (Look this up.)

Hinman misled the Indians as to the location of the Nebraska state line, giving them the impression that it would run so as to take in a strip that would include the country where the towns on the line of the Northwestern R.R. are situated.

Hinman is represented in the Treaty of 1876 as the interpreter, but he did no interpreting. He was a figurehead and promoter and fraud operator. William Garnett did the translating for this council.

During the treaty of 1876 and the subsequent council at Spotted Tail when it was being arranged to take the chiefs to the Indian Territory & Garnett was there to obtain scouts for Crook's army for the winter campaign, Garnett was serving in the Interior Department, but as soon as he got his scouts and started to join Crook, he was transferred as interpreter in the military service.

Treaty of 1889

About 1883 Judge Shannon of S. Dakota, and Hinman, and _____ and some secretaries came to Pine Ridge first and set forth to the Indians that the government experienced inconvenience and difficulty by having six agencies on the one great Sioux Reservation; and it had been decided to cut this reservation into six, apportioning one to each Agency; and if the Indians would consent to such a change there would be given to and divided among the six Agencies 25,000 cows and 1,000 bulls.¹⁴⁴ The Indians talked the subject over. They were in considerable darkness as to the boundaries, and whether there was a scheme to cut out some of their land; at last White Bird arose in the council at the Agency where the several councils were held, and asked a question, viz; After you divide up the Reservation will the lines of the several reservations join? The one whose name is omitted answered in the affirmative.¹⁴⁵ The commissioners wanted three-fourths of the Indians' signatures but they got but few, and went to other places, first to Rosebud and to Yankton.¹⁴⁶ Before they had reached the Cheyenne River and Standing Rock Agencies a newspaper rumor got afloat saying that if this commission should succeed it would gain 11,000,000 acres of land to be opened to settlement. The Pine Ridge Indians got an eye-opener. It was stated that the St. Paul and Milwaukee RR would then build through whenever the company should pay the Indians a certain indemnity which had previously been agreed upon between the Pine Ridge and Spotted Tail Agencies and the railway company. This commission went to all the agencies where it met with cool receptions and finally retired from the field discomfited after a failure to obtain anywhere near the number of names wanted. A few months later the man Hinman came back alone to Pine Ridge. This was before there were Farmers and Districts. The Indians drew rations once a month at the Agency. The officers were the Agent, his various Agency assistants, and Day School Teachers. These latter wrote out the requests for the Indians to the Agent, and some of them did what preaching they could for the spiritual uplift of these people. The Indians prospered better in those days before the scheme of having Farmers was hatched for importunate favorites. The change to Farmers came about 1885(?).¹⁴⁷ The first batch was shaken from the political bush at Washington. Hinman started in at Medicine Root to get children's signatures, names being taken of those ranging in age from two years up. The younger children who could not sign had their tiny hands held by their parents on the pen holder while the expert Hinman swung the pen with the nonchalance of a forger. He drew into the Agency He had Captain Sword and other policemen with him to interpret and aid in explaining and persuading. He drew into the Agency, and from there he went down the White Clay accompanied by William Garnett acting as interpreter, to the flat between the Agency and the Holy Rosary Mission. It was here that William Garnett saw the little children signing. There were just forty (40) of them whose ages ran from two to eighteen years.¹⁴⁸ Next the resourceful Hinman tried his plan on the Loafer band of whom Red Shirt was the then chief. The Loafers twitted him with his smooth work in 1876 in relation to the location of the Nebraska state line. They called to his attention the misleading and false statements he had made to them, and bluntly told him that before he could hope to have them sign anything for him again he must rectify the wrong he had done on that momentous occasion. He asked how far they claimed that their line should run south of the Agency office. They replied that Red Cloud had a map showing it to be thirteen and one half miles. He told them that they could go with him that distance south and that there he would fix the line. Next day he and Agent McGillicuddy started in a buggy on which was attached an odometer. Red Shirt took about twenty of his men and a lot of the policemen also, the whole number who went out that day being about forty (40), Wm. Garnett went along also. The party went to the Nebraska state line, a mile and a quarter from his office. They went five miles farther south to the south line of the Extension. McGillycuddy told Hinman that there was the south line as stated. Thence they continued following the White Clay Creek to the forks of the stream, and thence pursued their course straight south up between the two prongs of the creek. After they had ascended to this Table and passed the pines he (Hinman) pointed out to them the place where the line between their reservation and the State of Nebraska would run. The Indians saw that his tracing gave them at that particular point, all of the Pine Ridge. Here he told them that there was going to be their line if they would sign his paper, and his work should be approved. There were at that time a lot of squatters in the territory that Hinman was so munificently giving away in opposition to all existing legal barriers, and some of them had good habitations. The Indians felicitated themselves on this tide in their fortunes, and some of them were enthusiastic enough to make their selection of the houses which they intended to occupy as their own. Agent McGillicuddy told Hinman on the spot that he could never perform the promise he was making to these uninformed men of the plains. He brazened out the lie on his lips by his insistency that he could do it. The whole party returned. Then Hinman brought forth his paper for signatures and the signing by men and babies was quickly executed. Then he left. This ended here about the spring of 1884. A while afterwards in the summer along came Herbert Welch, nephew of Herbert Welch who was a member of the Board of Indian Commissioners. This Welch was then Secy. of the Indian Rights Assn.[149] He came to find out from the census roll the ages of the Hinman signers, a list of whom he had in his possession. William Garnett was interpreting between Welch and Capt. Sword. Welch tried to learn from Sword about the ages of the signers, but Sword insisted there were none under eighteen years. Failing to discover anything from Sword, he turned to Garnett for information. Then Garnett told him all that he knew. Agent McGillicuddy advised Sword to tell Welch anything he knew, telling him that Welch represented the I. R. Assn. which was looking out for the interests of the Indians. When Garnett had made his statement to Welch in Sword's presence, Sword then stated that the signatures had been taken in the same way all over the Reservation. Sword was captain of police at this time and he had been loath probably on that account to say anything for fear that his position might be taken from him.

Having got what information he could, Welch went away. He told Garnett that it was correctly surmised that Hinman's work was fraudulent, hence the investigation that he had been making; and he furthermore advised Garnett not to be afraid to tell to any others what he had told him.

In the same summer, but somewhat later, Senators Dawes and John A. Logan and another senator came out to Pine Ridge, to investigate the work of Judge Shannon and of Hinman when he was here the second time.[150] They went back. The work of Shannon and Hinman was set aside.

Senator Dawes introduced a bill in the Senate and it was passed in 1888.[151]

Now Capt. Pratt and the Rev. Cleveland were sent under the provisions of the Dawes bill to the Standing Rock Agency.[152] The Indians over there wanted a dollar and a quarter an acre, but these men were offering less, and on this differentiation they split. These men next came to the Lower Brule Agency where delegations from Pine Ridge and Rosebud went down there where it was arranged for a delegation from all the Agencies to go to Washington. Twelve Indians and two interpreters from Pine Ridge, viz; Philip Wells and Ben Rowland went. Pratt and Cleveland met them in Washington. When the Oglala Indians came back they claimed that they asked $1.25 an acre for the land that was unoccupied and would be given up to the government after the six reservations should be set off. They also insisted on a change of the division line between the Pine Ridge and Rosebud Reservations. Pass Creek was the line, but the Oglalas wanted it from the mouth of the Black Pipe Creek south to the Nebraska state line.

Before the Crook Commission came in 1889, printed copies of the law were circulated among the Indians, giving them time to study its provisions.

The Commission was composed of Charles Foster of Ohio, Gen. [Sen.] Warner of Missouri (?) and General Crook.[153] The treaty is known as the Crook Treaty. Three Stars, as the Indians called him, was known to them; they had felt his power as a commander in the field; they had benefitted from his influence and efforts called out in their behalf; he had always spoken the truth to and for them; he had kept his promises to them; and nothing was lacking to augment their confidence in his general integrity; and therefore whatever message he brought was sure to call out their faith and lead to favorable results. These native people had been so woefully trifled with by some of the negotiators who had been among them that it must have been realized when this commission was organized that an extremity had been reached in the conduct of the government which forbade the taking of any more chances in the diplomatic intercourse with these Indians if it was considered desirable ever to have any further negotiations with them. It took all the weight of General Crook's name and his appeals to their recollections of his honorable course at all times toward them, he even instancing special occasions on which he had made good his pledged word, particularly in the case of getting their agency established according to their wishes, before any headway of consequence was made in securing signatures to this treaty.

The law provided that the assent of three-fourths of the male members of the tribe should be necessary to make it effective. The general advised the white men that they were entitled to sign, as representatives of their Indian wives who would receive allotments of land under the treaty, and these men joined in making up the required number of signatories.

Under this agreement the Sioux Reservation was partitioned into six smaller ones to be separately managed, and the 11,000,000 acres of land which was turned out as open public domain subject to settlement was to be paid for at the rate of $1.25 an acre for all that should be disposed of during the first three years, seventy-five cents an acre for all so disposed of during the next two years, and fifty cents for all, good and bad, etc. Very little of this acquisition was taken within the first two periods, so that the Indians realized scarcely more than the stipulated fifty cents an acre. Three millions of dollars were set apart for the behoof of these people, and this sum was to bear interest at three per centum one half to be annually distributed per capita, and the other half to be subject to use in maintaining schools for instruction of the young. (See the treaty itself.)

The beneficiaries under this treaty have been not a little exercised in recent years because they cannot obtain any satisfactory accounting from the government touching the funds which they calculate belong to them by virtue of its terms. The quantity of land ceded produced at the lowest figure, $5,500,000. They understand that there remains to their credit above that which is paying interest the nearly equal amount of $2,500,000. The national government is derelict in a reasonable duty in its failure to acquaint these natives fully on every point in all matters affecting their financial and administrative concerns. It should gradually relinquish its patronizing attitude, strive to escape from its self-conscious quality of "guardian" and assume toward the Indians the degree of respect and trust which a wise parent extends to a son drawing close to the earlier years of his manhood. One of the provisions of the Crook Treaty gave to the Indians 25,000 cows and 1,000 bulls. These were distributed among the several agencies with uncommonly good faith, and were distinct from the specific articles which go with each allotment.

The trip to Washington in 189_ was when Philip Wells went as interpreter.

At this time the delegation was composed of Kicking Bear, Little Wound and Thunder Bear and George Fire Thunder. When they came back Kicking Bear reported that a great many white people had had the curiosity to come and see him and Short Bull, and he could hear them speak his name, but he held no conversation with them, as Philip Wells would not interpret for him.[154]

It was during this trip that Garnett accuses Wells of quietly working some seventy-five (75) families of Santees on to the borders of the Rosebud and Pine Ridge Reservations — along the Black Pipe and Pass Creek streams — an act which none of the Indians have ever understood and the mode of which they have never found out, but which has given them universal offense and ripened for Philip much unpopularity. When the bodies of soldiers who were killed at Wounded Knee were being exhumed for removal in the summer of 1906, the superintendent of the Boarding School who was present with some of his Indian pupils took the occasion to say to them: "Look what your fathers did, causing all these to be killed."[155]

An Indian woman, Mrs. Goings, mother of Frank Goings, Agency interpreter, understanding his speech retorted: "This is no place for these soldiers to lie; they should be buried at W. K. where they got into a drunken row and killed one another." On one occasion Garnett and R. O. Pugh and Raymond Smith and Dartenberger, issue clerk were at the Wounded Knee Battle Ground, at the time taking census and issuing rations and a man whose name is something like Dorsney and who visited this Reservation at intervals from Sturgis or thereabouts, took the pains to show them over the battlefield and point out all the various positions of troops, Indians and others, and explained every feature of the action. He said that he was a Sergeant in command of one of the troops, the commissioned officer not being present with the company.[156] He was told by Col. Forsyth that at the first sound of firing to order his men at once to shoot.[157]

This Sergeant further said that when the Indian discharged his piece in the air he gave the order. He thinks all the other troop commanders must have had orders similar to his own, for instant fire rolled out simultaneously from all the other companies. When this order came from his lips he had a strange, sickening feeling as though it was something dreadful that was being done. His own men fired into the Indians and directly across into the soldiers in line beyond them. He is sure that his fire was fatal to the soldiers there. Three men (3) in his own troop were killed by the soldiers from the opposite side.

The Philip Wells Episode was explained by a brother of Looking Cloud at Manderson as follows: This brother of Looking Cloud was the one who wounded Wells, and this is his account: He was a tall young man under twenty years of age. When the butchery began he had only a knife. It will be remembered that Wells was the official military interpreter. Philip is also known to be a loquacious man. In his official capacity he had been conspicuously talking that morning, and not all of his utterances had been agreeable to the Indians as may well be conceived. How many other things which seemed officious to them he had volunteered on his own private account no Phenix from the ashes of that conflagration has volunteered to tell us; but it is known, for the young man himself has said it, that Philip's voice had made his heart bad toward him; and when the crash of many guns came as if ignited by a single electric spark, the brave raised his long knife to bury it in Philip's breast; but Philip's marvelous agility was his protector in this instance—his gun in both hands went up, and his body went down—the assailant's blow was nearly parried, the end of the long blade catching the flexible portion of his nose and severing it neatly, leaving it hanging by the skin on each side. Instantly the warrior started to seize Wells and retrieve his failure, but he stumbled on a dead body and fell close to a soldier who was on his hands and knees, likely wounded; this man he pushed to the ground, at the same time taking up his gun and rising, he ran off to that murderous angle in the ravine where a small number of the Indians did ghastly execution. His own gun that he had turned over was the same kind as the one he had taken, and the cartridges in his own belt were available in the present emergency.

The Sergeant who commanded the troop saw the Indian fall who struck at Wells; saw him push over the soldier trying to rise; saw him carry away the gun. He confirmed the Indian's story in his conversation with Garnett. The Indian that Wells killed must have been a different one from the one he thought he got.

American Horse got to be a chief in the following tricky manner: He was ~~stationed~~ staying at Fort Robinson, claiming that he needed protection, for he had just killed Sioux Jim.[158] He had a paper he was circulating for signatures among officers and others to certify his friendship and good offices, and among the Indians he got Blue Horse, the chief of the Loafer band to which American Horse belonged, to sign. He had civilians, Indians and officers recommending him for his acts testifying his friendship for the whites. He then told Mackenzie that the Loafers wanted him for chief.

Afterwards his own relations who were numerous, adhered to him. After the campaign in the north at the end of the year 1876 the scouts who had served under Three Bears made him their [leader] and influenced a great number from all the bands, to which these Indian scouts severally belonged, to join him, and this gave him by great odds the largest band among the Sioux. At a somewhat later time the Loafer band subdivided into three—one continuing with Three Bears, one with Blue Horse, and the other with American Horse. The two latter chiefs are living on Pine Ridge Res.

Some account of Sioux Jim and His
Death at the Hands of American Horse

Sioux Jim and his three sons were tough characters—thieves and robbers without honor; whenever they saw a thing they wanted they took it.

In 1873 his oldest son led a party up in the Big Horn Basin country—a murdering band, which horribly treated the women; butchered them, cut open two who were enceinte and delivered them. There was a reward for this fellow offered.

Sioux Jim belonged to the Loafer band of which Blue Horse was chief. Sioux Jim and his sons were out from the Agency and prowling around so much that it was hard to locate them.

Col. Mackenzie must have got information that they were in the camp at this time—just after the sun dance in the neighborhood of where Coxville since has been; for he took Blue Horse into his office and told him that early the next morning he was going to surround his camp (in front of Frank Yates' store at the Agency) with soldiers to try to get Jim, and that he and his people should not be alarmed as no harm was intended for them. So next morning at break of day the soldiers had encircled the camp and as the Indians began to push their heads out of lodges Blue Horse was moving around among them telling them what was the object of the situation (for Mackenzie had cautioned him to keep this secret till it transpired) and not to be worried as it meant no harm to them. Garnett went into the tent where Sioux Jim should be. It was occupied by Eagle Horse, his son-in-law who now lives with wife on Wolf Creek on Pine Ridge Reservation, and his wife; and Garnett noticed that the bed covers were raised most too high. He threw them down and pulled Eagle Horse and his wife off from Sioux Jim's youngest son, and brought the latter out. All the camp was searched without finding Sioux Jim and the two older sons. The captured son was placed in a wagon and the searching party headed for the Fort. When it was at about the place where "Arkansas John" lived, American Horse overtook them, coming from Red Cloud, shouting, "Hold on! Come back! I've got Sioux Jim! I've killed him!" The soldiers went back, and the wagon also which had been brought along originally to take Sioux Jim and his sons in to the Fort alive. It was indeed true that American Horse had ended Sioux Jim with a shot in his body, but John Bear, to make the act doubly certain, had put a bullet through his head. The body was placed in the wagon where the living younger son was lying, and again the column turned toward Fort Robinson.

This younger son became one of the famous Indian scouts that went north in the autumn of that year (1876), and he made a good record and took part in the battle against the Cheyennes Nov. 25, where, it is not doubted he fought against his two older brothers.

Garnett has heard Flying Hawk who participated in the attack on the Sibley Scouting Party say that there were only four or five, at any rate only a very few in the party which made the attack.[159] He said further that they withdrew, feeling that they were too few to whip the Sibley Scouts, and retired to their camp. Next day they returned to the place to get the body of the Cheyenne whom Gruard and Big Bat shot, not expecting to find any trace of the scouts, and there they discovered the horses that the scouts had abandoned.

Flying Hawk was in the battle of the Rosebud and in the Custer battle.
[Tablet 22]

Garnett says emphatically that the Boucher Creek is the Big Bordeaux and not the Chadron Creek. He says that Louie Bordeaux at Rosebud can tell all about the creeks. Garnett knew Mrs. Kelly.[160]

Get Crazy Horse's medicine from Garnett. He went through certain forms before going to battle invariably, all Inds. tell it; Garnett's mother had 2 painted lodges from his father etc. His father was superstitious evidently & C. H. may have inherited; C. H. had no fear etc. Crazy Horse's father's name was Crazy Horse & died on Rosebud Agency Garnett has been acq. with every Indian

Agent from Whalm down. He says Hastings, Selwyn and Royer were the failures who seemed to know nothing abt. Indians.

He ascribed the 1890 troubles to 3 causes: Crook 1889 treaty; Ghost Dance which was a sort of mesmerism; starvation induced by false glowing accounts of Farmers and Agents showing thousands of wagon loads of potatoes and vegetables when he personally knows you could have driven across the Res. with a dozen wagons and not filled them.[161]

Says Gallagher was to blame for some of the starvation.

Garnett tells of an instance of Indian cunning to avoid being tracked by an enemy in the deep snow. They march in single file all stepping in the same tracks. The two in the rear carry chopped meat which they drop in the tracks. Wolves are sure to follow for the meat, and they obliterate the Indian tracks, so that an enemy is deceived into thinking that only a pack of wolves has passed.

American Horse is a Bad Face Oglala. These were always looking to be chiefs.

Wm. Garnett tells how the Indians robbed the bodies of their dead enemies of rings, watches, money and other valuables and traded them to Boucher for guns and ammunition. Boucher has been accused of carrying on a contraband trade with the Indians, augmenting their strength for depredations and war against the whites for the profit there was in this kind of business and Garnett knows that the accusation is true; for the Indians have told him that this was done and how Boucher instructed them in the matter of collecting these gruesome trophies for their value in exchange.

Boucher once had a house on Chadron Creek and it was standing there as late as the autumn of 1876 when Red Cloud and Red Leaf were taken prisoners with their bands and disarmed and deprived of their horses; for Re This creek was called Boucher Creek by the Indians until a recent date.[162]

Garnett tells of a dispute between himself and a half-brother over the number of children in the family of Standing Bear, an old-time Oglala, who died some six years ago. The half-brother is Henry Goolay (? Fr.), who at that time had for a wife a daughter of Standing Bear. They claimed between themselves — Goolay 16 and Garnett 14. Then they referred the dispute to Goolay's wife. She answered that she knew of 36 children of her father, and he said he had others in other places, of whom she didn't know. Garnett's Indian grandfather had seven wives.

Nicholas Janis, Mr. Garnett says, had a perfect knowledge of the families of the Oglala Indians on the mothers' sides and he was the highest authority on the subject. When the government came into more intimate relations with the Indians, under the treaties, he became indispensable as an auxiliary in the distribution of rations and annuities, and numbering of the tribe; and it is information creditable to his generous impulses, for which his memory should be affectionately cherished by the race to which his wife belonged, that his Indian kinsmen by marriage were never pinched or starved or wronged by any act of his. He had also extensive similar knowledge of the Cheyennes and Arapahos; all of which was obtained as a trader among the natives, assisted by a phenomenal memory. He was particularly expert in his knowledge of mixed bloods; trappers, traders, adventurers and army officers who had temporary relations of pleasure with the native women, were ordinarily changing from place to place as the caprices or demands of their roving lives impelled them, and the subject of this sketch with his keen faculties and observation was a rich repository of this species of information.

When the new era dawned and reservations grew into prominence as the abodes of the aboriginals, Mr. Wm. Garnett proved to be the highest authority on like subjects affecting the Oglala Sioux.
[Tablet 1]

Wounded Knee Notes

William Garnett says:
Speaking of the statement of Standing Soldier concerning the bringing in of the Indians at the time of the battle of Wounded Knee, he says Standing Soldier was in command of the scouts who were out looking for bands of Indians, and he naturally wants to take the credit for everything, as officers always do.[163] But Garnett says that it was Crazy Thunder, one of Standing Soldier's scouts who actually induced those Indians to come in to the Agency. Crazy Thunder was one of those Indians who escaped from these parts when the Indians were moving to the Missouri River, and went away north and lived with Sitting Bull across the line. When the last of the Indians came in and surrendered and were concentrated at Fort Keogh (?) or Yates (?) R. O. Pugh was sent up there to bring same to this Agency at Pine Ridge. Among them was Crazy Thunder who was well known to the northern Indians — to the Standing Rocks — and when this band was found by Standing Soldier this man Crazy Thunder was an acquaintance they recognized, and he had no trouble to convince them of

the truth of statements made to them and to prevail on them to come peaceably to the Agency. Crazy Thunder should have this credit in the final account. Another incident that I do not remember that Standing Soldier mentioned: Last Horse, another of his scouts, in scouting around, whether under orders of Standing Soldier Garnett does not know, he came to Wounded Knee battle ground. (Garnett says the aim was to camp on Wounded Knee that night, but the discovery of Last Horse caused them to avoid proximity to the battlefield.) He saw the strewn field. It was after dark. He reported to Standing Soldier that it would never do to let the Indians in his charge (or under his escort) to see or know of that sanguinary field. Accordingly it was avoided. Last Horse stated that the country was covered with dead, women and children, equally with the men, victims of the slaughter. The very air, he said, was redolent (was filled with the odor) with the smell of powder. To the question what Indians they were that had been butchered he could only say that owing to the darkness he was not able to identify them.

Slaughter is too dignified a name for this killing. Butchery is a fitter word. On the soil and under the flag of a great government, with her bedizzened officers on the spot directing the carnage this crime of crimes was done in open day in face of all the world. Not Turk, nor Bedouin could have done it better. The killing of soldiers by one another proves that something was wrong. There was stupor—mental paralysis over all the proceeding. The story that the Indians began the slaughter—that they had a lot of guns concealed—that they killed the soldiers—has been studiously inculcated to bury the truth—to cover a crime. The Indians killed some soldiers, but the soldiers killed more. Most of the dead troopers lay where the fatal lines stood in the morning, crossfiring into and slaying one another. Was somebody drunk? Here is what Philip Wells tells of an officer who told the men to thrust their guns in the Indians faces.[164]

Following are traders on the Platte about the time of the Civil War, was given by William Garnett: Dripper was a trader on the Platte River (was called Old Man Dripper) had a stone trading house about 12 miles above the Sod Agency, he built the building (the Indians called him Thick Ears); his place was called Dripper's Ranch; a man named Casecellor [?] did business also in same house.[165]

Chuzon (this was the man's name) had a trading store 30 miles below Dripper's and at Scott's Bluff.

Bordeaux (Louie's father) an old time Indian trader, had his ranch abt. 8 miles above Dripper's and some 10 below Fort Laramie.[166]

Beauvais (thinks his given name was Ben) was three miles above Bordeaux.

John Tut who was succeeded by a man named Ward and he by Col. Bullock who was bookkeeper for Ward.[167]

McCormick and Collins (John S. etc) bought out Bullock.

Nine Mile Ranch (don't know who kept it, thinks the man Ward had something to do with it) stone buildings, was situated on the Platte 9 miles above Laramie.

On the Bitter Cottonwood abt. 20 miles above Laramie was a trading and mailing place and a stopping place for emigrants; log buildings here; was kept by a Frenchman whom the Indians called Bare Bad Hair. His wife was an Indian. He and his wife and an Indian who was working for him, were killed in the sixties by the Slade gang. Two or three of his children ran to escape; they found shelter in the brush and were frozen to death. It was in winter.

Thinks it was the Old Man Reynolds between Laramie and Fort Fetterman, abt. midway. This was before Fetterman was built. Laparelle Cr. is where Fetterman was.

The creeks in order as follows, going up the Platte from Horseshoe are Laparell, La Bonte, and Deer Creek.

Bissonette was on Deer Creek & a trader.

A few years later—about 1870—marked changes had taken place among these traders—new ones had taken the place of some and old ones had changed locations.

John Richard Sr. had a bridge and traders store on the Platte.

In the sixties Crazy Horse and Little Big Man were very harassing on the Platte. They carried on a lively business in horse-stealing and the killing of white people.

Horse Stealing from Indians

This pursuit was begun by white desperados in 1871, when the Red Cloud Agency was built on the Platte and it was kept up till about 1883 or 1884. Among these thieves were Lame Johnnie, Doc Middleton, Lengthy Johnson (afterwards killed in Custer City) stole from Garnett and some Indians in 1876.[168]

This same business of horse stealing was revived during the troubles of

1890. Dick Stirk had his horses stolen, but he got them back. See Stirk's statement [in Tablet 8].

English and Dakota Names of the Six Sioux Agencies.

English		Dakota	
Pine Ridge	Agency =	Oglala	Agency
Rosebud	"	Brule	"
Cheyenne River	"	Minneconjou	"
Standing Rock	"	Unkpapa	"
Lower Brulé	"	Lower Brule	"

(These split from the Spotted Tails. They are called for short the Lower Indians.)
Crow Creek Agency = Crow Creek Yanktons
These are in fact Yanktons as they speak the Yankton tongue.
Yankton Agency = Yankton Agency.
These do not belong to the great Sioux Reservation, nor the following:
Santee Sioux
Sisseton "

The Upper Yanktons in North Dakota are Sioux Indians. There are some Oglalas, Yanktons, some from Cheyenne River and Standing Rock Agencies and from other agencies scattered and wandering still in Canada so says Garnett. I have a letter from a man think in Fremont who saw some of these there two or three years ago; some were in Custer battle and afraid to mention it. He represented them to be in squalid condition.

The Cutoffs

These were separated from the main Sioux nation and had their home down on the Platte and Republican Rivers away before the treaty of 1851 was made.

School at Laramie

In the summer of 1866 a citizen who [illegible] to the soldiers at Laramie, had a class of Indian children. Was not a Catholic. Garnett went two days and ran off to Scotts Bluff where his mother was.
Ask George Colhoff for his name.
Frank Gruard's Pedigree[169]
Garnett and Big Bat were with Gruard once in the house of Louie Bor-

deaux, the interpreter at Spotted Tail Agency. David Gallino, a Missouri River half-breed whose father and family lived at the Whetstone Agency, entered the house. Gallino accosted Grouard familiarly and called him "Prazost." Gruard denied that his name was "Prazo" and said it was Gruard, adding that he was from the Sandwich Islands.

Gallino rallied him by saying to him not to talk that to him; that he himself knew Gruard and that his name was "Prazost" (Garnett pronounces it "Prazo")

Garnett thinks from many bits of evidence which he related that Gruard was an Uncapapa or Sitting Bull Indian whose father was a colored man, or a man with African blood. Prazost was spoken of to Garnett by his father-in-law, Nick Janis, as a colored man who had several wives. Janis said all men in this country at that day, as well as the natives themselves, had more than one wife. Janis, Garnett says, came here before Frank Salaway. This man Prazost ascended the Missouri and became an adjunct of this country as a steamboat cook; and he served as a cook for traders up along the river.

It is important to remember that Fort Pierre antedates Fort Laramie; that the troops kept in the early time at latter place, and the traders over there, drew their supplies from Pierre. (See also Salaway's statement [Tablet 48] and account of his trip across in three days on business in relation to getting trader's goods.)

Garnett is confident that Mrs. Goings at Pine Ridge is a sister of Gruard.[170]

Gruard came to Red Cloud in early spring of 1875 costumed in a G string. One of the Deeres who were traders at Red Cloud said he knew Gruard as a mail carrier 4 or 5 years before in the Fort Peck country. He was a strongly built, muscular man weighing over 200. He was not excessively sociable, and seemed somewhat shy at first, and it was several months before his nakedness was covered by the ordinary apparel of civilization, and the first suit of such garments was provided by the generous purse of Ben Tibbitts, probably as a gift. He had work around the Agency for a little, and when the Commission came out later in the season to begin negotiations for the Black Hills Gruard was one of the men who went as a guide. His familiarity with the country so recommended him that he had no difficulty in drifting right into the service.

Pawnee Scouts

Nick Janis told Garnett that the Pawnee name got attached to many doings in which other tribes were associated; they used to combine and go out together to hunt and fight.

Janis told Garnett says Capt. Frank North came up to Fort Laramie in the same summer that Capt. Fauts was killed at the mouth of Horse Creek, in command of 1,000 scouts, called Pawnee scouts but consisting really of Pawnees, Winnebagos, Osages, Otoes, Omahas, etc. Garnett was a boy but remembers this well.

Bill Rowland

Garnett says: The first time he ever saw him was on the Chug Water in 1870; but he had been with the Cheyennes a long time then; had a Cheyenne wife; Garnett says he was all through the events that Garnett has recounted to me. Rowland was a courageous man. Once killed a Cheyenne at Red Cloud, not wantonly but in resisting another, and the Sioux had to be called out to protect him. He was shut up in the stockade for safety.[171]

He went into the southern country with Mackenzie campaigning, and afterwards returned to the north. He was a sign talker without a superior, from [him] Clark obtained much of his knowledge for his book. He died at Lamedeer where the Rowlands are allotted, on October 6, 1906. Jones says he was one of the greatest sign talkers. Garnett says same.

The Minor Sitting Bull

Garnett ~~thinks~~ says he died either in December, 1876, or January, 1877 at Fort Keogh by the Crow Indians.

Murder of Chief Yellow Bear and Killing of John Richard[172]

Garnett who was a boy just seventeen years old was working for Baptiste Pourier. He quit to work for Jules Eccoffey, John Richard and Adolph Cooney. Pourier was on the Three-Mile Ranch (3 miles above Fort Laramie and on Laramie River) and was the post guide. The three partners had a department store at the Three-Mile Ranch and a later adjunct was a billiard hall and a saloon. Cooney and Garnett started down to Fort Laramie. When they arrived they [found] Louie Shangrau, John Richard and Peter Janis (a son of Antoine Janis Sr.) John Richard asked Garnett to go down to Sod Agency. Garnett said he had just hired to Cooney & could not. Richard spoke to Cooney & Cooney told him to go with Richard, and when he came back he would have 80 horses to bring back. Richard started out saying he must go and see the commanding officer, Gen. C. F. Smith (first man to bring troops to Camp Robinson and first man to take Red Cloud to Washington, accompanied by Col. Bullock and John

Richard when he was pardoned by Grant).[173] Cooney and Garnett and Peter Janis and Louie Shangrau went down to Jules Eccoffey's house—he lived in the east end of the Post. Just at this juncture Capt. Egan with his troop of the 2d Cavalry arrived at the fort. The Fort is up on a high table. Eccoffey's was down over the bank on a bottom at east end. When the Cavalry arrived, it lined up between the sutler's store and the bakery. Richard went to the headquarters of Gen. Smith after having a few words with Egan. Coming back from Gen. Smith's he cut across from the south to the east under the bank. Richard and Shangrau each took their Winchesters at Eccoffey's. Each also had a six-shooter on. Peter Janis had two on. They all started down to the river at the slaughter house half a mile below. Garnett had his bedding and clothes. They all got into a boat to go down to the Platte. Garnett was put into the prow, Richard took the stern and Shangrau and Janis took the oars. At the slaughter house before entering the boat Garnett received his orders. Richard told him that he had a pair of gray horses and a two-seated buggy on the other side of the Platte, and he pointed out the rig. Told him to take them on down the river, on the north side of the Platte to the village of Chief Yellow Bear, six miles above the Sod Agency (Yellow Bear's band was called the Melt Band and this same band is now at the Holy Rosary Mission) and to wait there for him and the others who would go down in the boat after crossing Garnett over.[174] They went as stated. Garnett could get sight of the boat party once in a while, and see them sometimes hooting swans. Coming to the Arapaho village, he saw a gray headed member of the tribe and asked for something to eat, and the old man took him to his lodge where his wife was frying grease bread, and had coffee and bacon. (This occurred in May, 1872.)

He went 4 or 5 miles farther and came to the large village of Man Afraid of his Horse. He went some miles farther and arrived at Yellow Bear's village. He waited there two hours for the boatmen to arrive. These men in the boat had a box of bottles containing intoxicating liquors. Garnett says that he knew that John Richard had quit drinking—had not drank for quite a long time; he thought John was all right, or would be in this respect.

They got there when the sun was a half-hour high. Garnett went down to meet them. As Richard jumped out his $250 watch fell into the water. Garnett grabbed to catch it. Richard laughed and told him it was attached to the chain around his neck, which, when let out at full length would reach to the ground—was gold—and valued at $800.

When Richard went north from Fetterman where he killed the soldier (thinks in 1869) he had an Indian wife. While out with the Indians he took another wife—a sister to the first. These two wives were sisters of Yellow Bear.

When Richard came in 1870 to go to Washington with Red Cloud, he was living with these two women (they had come in to Fetterman). These three partners were carrying on a business up there on hay and wood contracts.

In the spring of 1871 (Jan. or Feb.) Nick Janis had come up from the Whetstone Agency to which point he had removed in 1868, came back to Fort Laramie.

Richard now threw away the two Indian wives—both of whom he had bought according to Indian law and custom—and he now took Emily Janis, daughter of Nick Janis (wife of Pugh and Tibbits) and he married her, the nuptials being performed by Lieut. Cameron, Gen. Smith's adjutant general.

When the three men alighted from the boat Garnett noticed that Richard and the others staggered and that the case of liquors was gone. He spoke to Richard and remarked that he thought he (Richard) had given up drinking. Richard said his leg was asleep was what was the matter with him. He told Garnett to hitch up the team. Also pointed out to him Yellow Bear's lodge—a large one—in the east part of the village, and told Garnett to drive over there, for he was going to take the younger of the two ex-wives who were sisters of Yellow Bear, with him. Garnett began to talk to Richard and reason with him, saying that he had discarded the Indian women and had now a fine looking half-blood wife, and that he ought to let the others alone and keep the one he had and urged him to drop this scheme and to come and get into the buggy and go. Dave [Peter?] Janis was ugly in speech, abusing him, and ordered the boy to go and hitch up the team. When Garnett drove down to Yellow Bear's Peter Janis and Louie Shangrau were standing outside the tent. Yellow Bear's mother was living in a lodge a little way in rear of her son's; and the chief was coming up from her lodge and Richard was following behind with his gun lying on his arm across his breast. Four men entered the lodge. Garnett stood outside with the team. All the time after the four went in Indians kept stringing into Yellow Bear's tent until 30 or 40 had got inside. The four men had been in the lodge ten or fifteen minutes when Peter Janis (son of Antoine Janis Sr.) came out and asked Garnett to go in. Garnett objected, saying, that it was his place to stay with the team. Janis said he would watch the team and again told Garnett to go in. Garnett asked, "Why don't you bring him out?" He said he could not, and again urged Garnett to go in and bring Richard out. Garnett replied that he had had a chance to keep him away before when he was trying to persuade Richard not to go to Yellow Bear's, and that Janis had then interfered with him and caused him to abandon his persuasions, and ordered him to go and get the team. He concluded by saying that he could not get him out now. Garnett ceased his resistance and went in.

The lodge was packed with Indians. It was the ordinary lodge, circular in form, fully 20 feet in diameter. Yellow Bear had two wives. Flanking the entrance on either side were devices for couches, one for each wife; these resembled a tripod supporting a buffalo robe as a head piece while the bed was made down, foot toward the door. At the farther side and opposite the opening was a long and ample couch, probably where the youthful Yellow Bears and visitors snoozed off the long nights. When Garnett passed in Louie Shangrau was seated on this mammoth bed. Yellow Bear was on the right, opposite the center of the lodge, leaning comfortably against the robe suspended upon the tripod. John Richard sat between the Chief and Shangrau, and between Richard and Yellow Bear were two or three Indians, all seated. The beds were always piled up during the day by folding the robes and blankets and laying them down so that they afforded seats. Next [at] the tripod on the left sat Slow Bear, afterwards a son-in-law of Red Cloud (now living at the mouth of the White Clay Creek, Pine Ridge Res.) who was to be a notable actor in the scene soon to follow. Garnett went in and took a seat by this man. Another sat on Garnett's right peeling kinni kinnick. (Slow Bear was a scout afterwards on the Cheyenne expedition.) Two ranks of Indians in close order were ranged across the entrance preventing egress. A fire burned moderately in the center.

Richard held his Winchester in his lap. He was chatting nonchalantly with the assembled Indians, detailing some of his exploits and telling how he was at one time connected with a party of Indians in the killing of some soldiers in the vicinity of Fort Fetterman, members of this company of Egan's, 2d Cavalry, just arrived at the Fort.[175] He broke off the conversation to say to the chief that he had come to get that youngest wife of his. He wore a fine summer hat of some kind of vegetable fiber, with a wide black band. Garnett says it was a very fine one and must have cost $4 or $5.

Yellow Bear answered him that he could have her but that she was not there; that she was down at the Agency at the scalp dance. There had been a party out that had had a fight and killed a Ponca Indian and scalped him, and a great dance was in progress in honor of the event. Several of the Indians had just come from there and had seen the woman at the dance. They thrust in their voices declaring that they had just come from there and had seen her down there. Yellow Bear told the company that he had been telling his brother-in-law that she was at the dance, but that he would not believe him.

The conversation went on again pretty much as before. After a little while Richard reverted to the same subject, determined to be put off by no reasonable explanation. He declared that she was there in the village, but that they had hid her to keep her from him. Again the Chief assured him that she was not in the village but at the scalp dance; that she was his according to the law of the tribe—he had bought her and paid for her—and he could have her by going after her. All this time Richard was playing with the trigger of his gun. Garnett felt uneasy. These actions were symptoms of deadly trouble. He wished a hundred times that he was out of there. But the doorway was packed and he was wedged and hemmed in without possible means of escape. Had not so much as a knife to rip open the lodge if extremity should make it prudent for him to get away suddenly. Richard kept returning to the charge every few minutes.

A large number of the Indians had come up from the dance. A lot of their horses were standing around the lodge. The people of the village had attended to their horses for the night—the old mares were hobbled; these always by instinct of association held a good many of the younger animals near them during the night; others had been tethered; these precautions all showing how much the Indians were at this period on their guard; for the era of organized and systematic horse-stealing by the whites was fully inaugurated, and these were now more to be dreaded than the depredations by the Indians to whom horse-stealing was neither crime nor vice, but sanctioned by universal law and upheld as a virtue almost martial in merit, which entitled the experts of the practice to distinguished consideration.

It was now two hours since Yellow Bear and Richard had seated themselves in the lodge. Night was gathering visible objects into smaller circle. But there was a good moon.

Now Richard began to taunt this venerable chief, whose name was a sweet sound to all Indians because of his mild and just character, his peaceable disposition, his exemplary behavior, and his love for all members of his race.

He told Yellow Bear that he had given to him those horses that were grazing around his lodge and that he (Richard) ought to kill them. Yellow Bear replied that it was true he had given him some stock; that the younger animals were

~~the increase and in these he could not expect to claim interest;~~ that if it was his wish to kill those that once were his he was free to do so without objection or complaint.

(In the part where Yellow Bear describes the horses he has to Richard, it should be corrected so that he will say in addition that while some of the horses out in the camp are some that Richard gave him, and that he may do as he wishes with them; yet there are a lot that Richard did not give him, horses of his own raising, and some that he had given to his daughter, that these he would not be justified in touching. Garnett says it was in 1869 that Richard took Yellow Bear's daughters as wives, but he did not marry both at the same time.)

Richard toyed with his Winchester. Garnett heard the click when the hammer was raised. The thought rushed to his mind that perhaps Richard would go out and shoot one or two of the old horses, become satisfied with this species of revenge, and that then he would go on his journey to the Agency in peace. How many of the Indians may have thought the same thing is conjecture. Yellow Bear certainly realized his own danger and the imminence of it. Above his head hung some smoking utensils and knives and his revolver. It was noticed that he glanced upwards several times at these as if measuring the distance. They were out of reach. It would not do to get up deliberately and take down the revolver. Such an act would bring instant trouble with all the advantages against him. The only thing that he could do with any show for safety was to maintain his equanimity and trust to whatever chances might run in his favor. Richard arose, gun in hand, and took a step as if he would go out of the lodge; like a flash he swung toward the chief, presented the Winchester at his breast and fired. Yellow Bear settled backwards against the buffalo robe which had been supporting his back. There was just an effort to raise himself up, and then he was dead.

Swifter retribution for cowardly murder never came. Instantly a dozen Indians were on him to restrain him from the further deadly madness of killing. His Winchester was too long for close quarters, but somehow he had got out his revolver. Many hands held up his arm; this did not arrest his busy fingers, for he kept discharging the weapon, sending swift balls through the dry skins overhead. This was like pastime and short as it was futile. The man who had been on Garnett's right whittling kinni kinnick buried his knife in Richard's breast. Stab after stab in breast and back followed in quick succession. The men who had him by the arms were unconsciously holding him up and preventing him from falling. He was stabbed to death but perhaps not dead when Slow Bear sent a bullet crashing into his brain.

Garnett, the boy, saw all this. Who will doubt that he wanted to get away from this scene of horror, where a large crowd of excited and murderous men had scant space to turn—where two lay dead, guns were hot with use, knives were terrible (or dripping) with blood, and the air was suffocating with the fumes and smoke of powder? He essayed to lift the lower rim of the lodge back of where he had sat, but it was tied down. Then he sprang for the entrance and landed on the shoulders of the men who blocked the way. He slid down among these, and when the mass surged towards the open air he was carried along. On the outside he saw Shangrau who had forced a way out in the beginning of the melee. He saw Shangrau scuffling with some Indians who were trying to take his gun. Then there was the gleam of a knife. Shangrau let his gun go to knock the Indian down who was going to strike with the blade. Then he grabbed for his gun. Garnett had started to run. A horse lying down in his path was startled and attempted to rise just as he was bounding over it. This threw him headlong on his hands and knees. Gaining his feet he stopped to assist Shangrau who was struggling with an Indian who was holding his gun by the muzzle to keep Shangrau from shooting him. Garnett commanded the Indian to let go, telling him that the two wanted to get away. The Indian said Shangrau would shoot him. Garnett assured him that he would not and told him again to release his hold, which he did and went away. The Indians standing back watching the contest, as soon as the Indian was at a safe distance opened fire on the two, but without harm to them.

The two started to run. The boy, much more fleet than his companion, soon noticed that he was outdistancing him, and he turned back. Then they went down close to the river. The camp was in the form of a bow, the river taking the place of the string. It enclosed a large area.

They came to the water's edge. The boy was an excellent swimmer. Shangrau hurriedly asked: "What shall we do?" Garnett answered, "I am going to swim the river." The stream was then very high and icecold. Shangrau was astonished and expostulated, and begged the boy not to leave him there alone, as he could not swim.

They knew no time must be lost. Not a man of the party who came with Richard had one hope of escape if discovered. The village was in a tumult. Red rage was everywhere on horseback. The boat was thought of by Garnett, but the other said the Indians, for a certainty, were in possession of that.

The two bent their way cautiously in the direction of the Agency. East of the village was a patch of ground where there were large and high cottonwood stumps. The road which led to the Agency passed through this piece of ground. The moon, shining bright, cast heavy shadows. The two men had reached this place. Flying Indians, coming from below, were drawing nigh. The boy said, "Let us get in the shade of stumps." They did so and the riders passed between them. Then came a consultation over the route of escape. Garnett said take to the sandhills; it would be quite a circuit.

The horsemen passing all the time were Indians in search of the two men and went toward the Agency. When they got down to the water's edge they were under and shielded from view by the river bank. It was down here where Garnett suggested their trying for the boat. It was while here that Garnett asked Shangrau why he did not shoot those Indians that were giving trouble, and he said there were no cartridges in his gun; that when coming down the river in the boat he was shooting at the wild fowls and spent all his cartridges and the gun was empty. He went to reloading. Then took place the conversation about swimming the river. When it was settled that the boy would not go over alone, they deliberated on the route to be taken. Garnett said that they should bear off to the north into the hills and make a circuit, coming around to the road and river below the Agency, and then approach the Agency from the opposite direction. This, he argued, would take them three or four miles from the river and the road between the Indian village and the Agency where the Indians would be looking for them. Shangrau assented, saying it would be a good long way around and take all night, but it was the only safe course. At this point, another party of Indians was heard thundering along the road toward the Agency. Shangrau said he was going to open fire on them. Garnett forbade, saying that must be stopped, or he should plunge into the river and swim for his life; for to open fire would be to betray their present security and lead to their destruction; for the Indians were now hunting them. The two began their journey and had not passed the road more than 150 yards when other Indians came dashing out of the village, making the third party going toward the Agency after these men, supposing of course that they had gone down the road as fast as their powers of endurance would sustain them. The two laid down flat on the ground and the others went by without observing them. Then they betook themselves to the hills. It was almost morning when they arrived at the Agency. They found that Dave Janis had arrived there very early, outrunning a horse that started about the same time he did. He was a noted runner, but on this occasion outdid himself.

The boy asked the chief clerk for a bed. The clerk asked if he had seen the affair at the village; he said he had, but would not give any account till he had had rest, for he was worn out from lack of sleep previous to this exciting night, and the events he had just passed through had brought him to the point of exhaustion. Declining refreshments, he laid down to slumber. He does not know how long he slept; but the first he knew he felt someone shaking his feet. Rousing up, he saw Baptiste Pourier, who was the husband of John Richard's sister. Then he told the whole story to his old employer who listened with tears in his eyes, while the boy himself could not keep back his own tears. The clerk had stood during the narration and taken copious notes of what Garnett had said.

In closing the relation of this bloody scene it should be said that the Indians gratified their vengeance by filling Richard's body with bullets. The mixed bloods, not at first understanding that Richard was the one to blame, in their fury, mutilated the body of Yellow Bear and burned it.

Shangrau told Garnett that Dave Janis was urging Richard coming down the river to take [the] daughter of the chief. It also transpired that when Richard said at the Fort that he was going to see the commanding officer, Gen. Smith, that it was only a ruse; that he did not go near him; that when Capt. Egan spoke to him privately when the company came up, it was only to warn him to get away, as some of his soldiers either knew him or would find him out and kill him for killing some of their friends who were their comrades in Egan's company; and this is why he came round under the bank to join the other members of the party.

The Indian village was so distracted by this affair that all the people removed at once over into the White River country, it is said, in the neighborhood of the Spotted Tall Agency in the bend of the River a few miles below where Crawford now stands. A year afterwards they returned to the Platte.

Garnett did not leave the Agency enclosure for four days after these events, not being assured that his life was worth anything when he should get outside. His mother was living down there, outside of the stockade, but she could not persuade him to come to her lodge for several days. After this, he went back to work for Baptiste Pourier.

There has, ever since the 1876 treaty was made, been rivalry between two factions on Pine Ridge. The young blood of the Sioux procured the Agency. After this was accomplished the old men who had surrendered have made claims and acted as though they were entitled to the credit, and upon this assumption have ~~assumed~~ tried to make it appear that they have been and are the best counsellors of the nation and should be so respected, and be allowed to direct & control. Politics is the same among red men as white men.

McGillicuddy Stops Sun Dancing

In 1878 the sun dance was held close to the village and about thirteen (13) miles above the forks of White River, and on Little White River. Little Big Man was the leader. Every sun dance always had a leader. There were always dancers who did not have to redeem vows, and consequently did not pass through the sacrificial suffering. It was on this occasion that Little Big Man performed his vows with incredible suffering. His "carver" got the skewers too deep into the flesh and muscles, and caused him to endure prolonged and intense agony. After the Oglalas removed to Pine Ridge there were five annual sun dances — one in 1879 on Wolf Creek; in 1880 on the White Clay on the extension below Geo. Nines; in 1881 in same place; in 1882 and 1883 between Patton Creek and White Clay just east of Geo. Nines store. After this Dr. McGillicudy forbade the barbarous custom.

In 1880 & 1881 the sun dance was 2½ miles south of the Agency; in 1882 and 1883 between Patton Creek and White Clay, beginning a quarter of a mile east of the site of George Nines' store. In 1884 No Flesh, the leader for this year, came to McGillicudy and told him it was time to go around with the pipe to get ready for the annual sun dance. He was told there would be none; that the practice would have to be stopped and they might just as well begin now. No Flesh asked how he himself would get out of it. McGillicudy told him that the Indians could go out on the hills and fast and suffer and go into their sweat houses and have their "carvers" do the usual cutting of flesh as a sacrifice to their God in the sweat houses—do this as they were used to doing in times of stress or urgency when they could hold no regular dance. The agent told him that the dance took the people from their homes & caused them to neglect their gardens, their poultry and pigs and other affairs, and for this reason must be abandoned. No Flesh agreed with him but wanted to know who had told him how to avoid holding the dance, but the agent did not give Garnett away, for he it was who told him. No Flesh said no white man had told the agent how to suspend the dance. This was stopped first on Pine Ridge, and the word went speedily to all other Agencies and this ended the Sun Dance elsewhere and everywhere.[176]

Nick Janis came up to this country from St. Charles, Missouri when fifteen years of age; this he told to Garnett, except as to the place he was from.

The Flag Pole Affair

This was in 1874 when Dr. J. J. Seville was Agent.[177] The Agent in the beginning, told the chiefs that they had to have rest on Sundays, and that the employees may have their rest; told them that they, the Indians, were in the habit of bothering him every day alike, Sundays as much as any other; that white people were in habit of resting on Sunday, and so that the Indians might know the exact day of rest to the whites when they did not wish to be disturbed, he was going to raise a pole and run up the flag only on Sundays, so the Indians would not come around the Agency for business on those days of rest. The Waj-ja-ja band of which Red Leaf was chief (this was the band of old Conquering Bear killed in 1854) was a troublesome band finding fault with every little thing. These Waj-ja-jas came and objected to Seville about putting up the flag. Seville told them it did [not] make any difference, that he was going to put it up. The poles were cut and brought inside the stockade, and were not peeled. There were 2 or 3 long poles. Some of this band came in and began chopping them; they made this excuse for their action, namely, that a flag means war — that nobody has a flag but soldiers; that the Indians did not want war, and so did not want the flag on the Agency. When they commenced to do the chopping Seville tried to stop them, but they paid no attention to him and kept right on. Seville then sent an Indian named Racer (and who was an actual footracer) up to Camp Robinson with a note to the officer (thinks it was Major Jordan).[178]

(Red Leaf was not there with his men who were doing this.) There were some races going on at the Agency that day as usual, and there were 200 or 300 Indians collected there. During the summertime there was a horse race there nearly every day.

First thing those on the inside of the stockade knew, some friendly Indians began running in from the outside saying that the soldiers were coming and the Indians after them.

The Agent came forward and ordered the double gates to be thrown open. Lieut. Crawford dashed in; when all in he ordered his men to dismount & turn their mounts loose; then Crawford faced his soldiers, some 20 or 25 toward the still open gate with guns pointing toward the Indians; some of his men were so excited that they had the butts of their guns toward the Indians until Crawford struck them across the breast with his sword and told them to change ends of their pieces. Between these soldiers as they were coming up to the stockade and the pack of Indians behind them were Young Man Afraid, Spider (who was a brother of Red Cloud)[179] and Sword (a chief and brother to Capt. Sword; he went to Washington first time Red Cloud went); Three Bears with a lot of backers stood in front of the gate while it was open and held the angry and hostile Indians back and prevented their following the soldiers into the stockade. The Agent called out to the employees to close the gate. Crawford assured the Agent that he need not close it—that he could keep the Indians back, but Seville reiterated the command and the gates swung on their heavy hinges and were fastened. Now Garnett and Louie Richard passed to the outside through the side gate adjacent to the big front gate. When they got out they saw that the sub-chief, Conquering Bear (son of old Conquering Bear who was killed in 1854 & one of Red Leaf's sub-chiefs) was clubbed off his horse—saw him fall to the ground; some Indians dismounted and laid a bow across his throat and stood on the two ends of it as a punishment for his part as ring leader in the assault on Racer as he was returning to the Agency after carrying the message to Robinson; they shouted that he was the one who carried it and pounced on him and cut and beat him badly with clubs. Conquering Bear was badly beaten. It must be said that others outside—friendlies and hostiles—were clubbing and fighting one another also. Further great numbers did not understand what it all meant; as it was the Waj-ja-jas who were cutting the poles and the other Indians generally were not in [on] the secret, and did not know the cause of the presence of soldiers and the rough work going on on the outside.

Garnett and Richard were now standing outside in front of the narrow door, and Bear Brains, a brother-in-law of Red Cloud was pacing up and down in front of these men, swinging an old Remington revolver in his hand. This was a friendly Indian. The friendlies were beginning to arrive and to grasp the situation. Red Cloud and a lot of the friendly chiefs and other friendly Indians were on the inside of the stockade.

This Indian, Bear Brains, was haranguing the crowd and saying that this man who was just beaten up (Conquering Bear) was trying to make trouble just because his father Conquering Bear was killed a good many years ago. He said if the Indian had been delivered in that day there would have been no trouble, just a little inquiry would have taken place that was all; and he reasoned now that there was no ground at this time for trouble; that the flag would [do] no harm to any one, and so let it be raised; that this Conquering Bear was a troublesome fellow and did not belong here at all but he and his followers were Brules and belonged at Spotted Tail, and ought not to be allowed to make this disturbance; and much more of the same purport. Moss Apple who now lives in Rapid City came up to Garnett and Richard at this moment and asked what was the matter with all those Indians outside clubbing one another. He was a wood contractor at Camp Robinson. Garnett told him he did not realize his danger, and ordered the gate tender inside to open the little one, and Garnett shoved Apple through. Apple told Ben Tibbitts when he got in that he would [not] be in this place under such threatening circumstances for all he had in his business. Just then the minor Sitting Bull appeared on the scene with his big three knives on a sweeping handle. He was knocking men and horses right and left with the power of a giant and commanding the Indians to scatter and depart from the Agency. After this, an Indian came on a gray horse, bearing a Spencer rifle, and hailed Sitting Bull who also had the name Drum Carrier. He said "Drum Carrier: I want you to understand that you have bare flesh as well as we, and that a bullet will ~~enter you~~ go through you just as quick as any other person." He then brought his gun down to discharge at Drum Carrier, but it was seized by another Indian named Gray Eyes and held. Drum Carrier was just then driving off a crowd, and just as he was turning toward the Indian who was about to shoot, he answered back that he had had several bullets through him but he was living yet. Other Indians now crowded in between these, and the friendly Indians swelled rapidly in numbers. They soon had full control of the situation and the bad blood subsided and the Indians with bad hearts gradually dispersed and peace at length reigned.

It should not be omitted that the Indians in those times were well armed.

When the uproar was at its height the friendly Indians stationed themselves around the stockade issuing orders to one another not to let the angry ones burn the buildings.

It was arranged by the chiefs now on the inside to furnish protection to the Agency from their several bands. They said they would have done so in this case if they had known in time. Names of Indians to be used as guards were taken right down now. These chiefs did not want soldiers stationed there.

Soon afterwards the Agent distributed among the Indians who had been most conspicuous and daring in defending the Agency and had sustained the most hardship, some forty California blankets as a reward for their good faith and invaluable services. Those who rendered service afterwards as guards were given some little presents as compensation.[180]

Crazy Horse

Garnett heard Crazy Horse in 1868 tell about his "medicine." It was up in the vicinity of the Rosebud that it occurred. Whether this appeared to him in a dream or trance or when he was self-mesmerized Garnett does not know. But Crazy Horse told the story that he was near a lake. A man on horseback came out of the lake and talked with him. He told Crazy Horse not to wear a War Bonnet; not to tie up his horse's tail (The Indians invariably tie up their horses' tails in a knot.) This man from the lake told him that a horse needed his tail for use; when he jumped a stream he used his tail and at other times, and as Crazy Horse remarked in telling this, he needs his tail in summer time to brush flies. So Crazy Horse never tied his horse's tail, never wore a warbonnet. It is said he did not paint his face like other Indians. The man from the lake told him he would never be killed by a bullet, but his death would come by being held and stabbed; as it was actually. Crazy Horse was known and accounted a brave man before this vision.

Garnett says that the Indians have these presentments in dreams while fasting on the mountains; they have them when they claim they are awake &c; they claim that they actually see the tangible objects and signs, and in these latter cases he thinks they are self-hypnotized, as he calls it. In all cases they represent that, whether the knowledge or advice they receive comes admittedly in dreams, or not, they talk that they have seen it as though by ordinary sight.

Crazy Horse before going into battle observed this ceremonial, so Garnett has heard the Indians say: Taking some of the dirt thrown up by the pocket gophers, he would rub it on his horse in lines and streaks—not painting him, but passing this dirt over him in this way with his hand; and he would spat a little of the same on his own hair in a spot or two; and put in his hair also two or three straws of grass, 2 or 3 inches long. As I understand it the man from the lake told him to use the straws and the dirt as described.

Crazy Horse was good for nothing but to be a warrior or to be leading the strenuous life; stealing horses, or something of that kind. On second inquiry Garnett says that the man from the lake told him to use the dirt and the straws. He adds that Crazy Horse considered himself cut out for warfare, and he therefore would have nothing to do with affairs political or social or otherwise — like making treaties, scheming lodging [?] places, moving camp, disciplining the people and soldiers, etc.

He had no ambition to be a chief. Disdained the compliment of being great —a great leader, or anything of that sort. Spotted Tail told him to go to Washington—that he was the greatest warrior in the Sioux nation and might easily be the head chief. He depended simply and solely on himself and cared nothing for the applause of others. He [was] great in his ability to follow his own ideas and to resist the allurements of other people and their cheap homage and noise.

Crazy Horse and Custer Battle

Garnett says the Indians tell that when Reno attacked the village the Indians were almost uncontrollable, so great was their eagerness to press a counter attack, but Crazy Horse rode up and down in front of his men talking calmly to them and telling them to restrain their ardor till the right time when he should give the word; that he wanted Reno's men to get their guns hot so they would not work so well. When Crazy Horse considered the time opportune he let his men go with the result known.

Cross Purposes between Red Cloud Agency and the Military Garnett says: Hastings succeeded Seville as agent about December 1875, and was himself succeeded about July, 1876 by Eldon, a military officer.[181]

Major Jordan was in command at Robinson. Hastings never had any use for Garnett but employed him out of necessity. When he first came into office he let Garnett out, but was soon compelled to take him back because he had planned to use Hank Clifford, as he wanted to repay some personal obligation. Hank could not do the interpreting, and Hastings put him into another place and reemployed Garnett. ~~Garnett was only a boy and had not learned the virtue of silence~~ The Indians were all the time coming into the Agency from distant parts, and all the time going out to distant parts. The military were gravely concerned as to this, because it meant a great deal on the point of forces, equipment and subsistence. Major Jordan believed this system of come and go was in steady operation; but Hastings denied it. So Garnett went to Jordan and told him that he would keep a brief on what was transpiring at the Agency and bring the information to him if Jordan would note it down. This was agreed. So Garnett brought information when certain ones arrived from the disturbed country. Also when a certain Indian withdrew to the north and how many lodges went with him.

The beef herd was at this time up above the Fort, on Soldier Creek. The Indians stole the horses belonging to the herders. Hastings wanted to conceal this depredation and loss, and did so; but Garnett reported it to Jordan, and the further fact that the herders who had been set on foot had been remounted by Hastings with ponies furnished by the chiefs around the Agency, who were also were loath for it to be known that Indians had robbed the men who were guarding the cattle kept for the Indians themselves.

Finally Major Jordan came down to the Agency one day bringing Eldon with him to relieve Hastings. He showed the agent a list of charges against him. Hastings looked them over and asked who had furnished him the information. As Jordan did not say at once, Garnett who was present told him that he was the person who had done it. Hastings said to Garnett that he had done more for Garnett than any other one at the Agency. Garnett answered that he had done nothing for him because he wanted to do it for Garnett, but that whatever he had done was for his own benefit because he could not get any other to do the work; and Garnett was right. Jordan then said that the charges had been fully verified by 4 or 5 other persons, and that action had not been taken on Garnett's reports unsubstantiated.

The policy of taking the Indians from the War Dept. and placing them under the control of the Department of Interior was fraught with many evils. The Interior Department is where politicians batten on taxation in excellency of corruption. Whether the transference was inspired by the scheme to extend the list of civil appointments to gratify the politicians by giving them a larger assortment of places to pay partisan debts, or whether the change was a truly philanthropic inspiration of impractical minds, need not be examined here; but that the subdivision of authority was not a wise plan is apparent at a glance. Actual harmony was something unknown. The corrupt agents of the Interior Department were pursuing a course which estranged the nations and fostered their hostile feeling, as well as arming and feeding them after the War Dept. had been bidden to reduce them to submission and peace by force.

Seville Recants

Before the Hastings episode Garnett had been doing interpreting for the Agent Seville. Garnett was a boy without practice or training possessing a natural faculty for interpreting between whites and Indians, and without experience had not learned the virtue of silence.

At the supper table was a man who was to outside appearances acting as a sort of master of ceremonies, and in a clownish spirit and manner went the rounds of the table asking each about what he could report for the day. Garrett was taken in the trap of telling innocently enough some interesting things which he had gained knowledge of in his capacity of interpreter for Seville. There was a man always at the table who reported to the Agent. There was another who was understood to be a reporter for an eastern newspaper.

Garnett was called up by the Agent and asked if he had said certain things and he admitted that he had. He was given a fitting lecture that he had been divulging the business of the Agency which was not his own knowledge to be used as he might see fit, and he was given his discharge.

At his next report at the table he was able to say something personal to himself, and he remarked that he was now going down to Laramie where he came from. He had not fully outgrown his inexperience and innocence yet; so in the course of his talk he said he believed he would tell General Smith when he reached Laramie, about the great number of cattle scattered all over the country lying dead and decaying. They were killed by the Indians after issue and choice parts taken and the remainder left to rot. There was too much issued and the Indians could not use all of it. Garnett supposed that Gen. Smith, having military command over that country was the one affected by this waste and Garnett thought the General ought to be informed of the condition of things. He added that there were some other things he would mention to the General. Next morning Seville called him into the office and questioned him about the dead cattle, what he had said, etc., and then told him that the General had nothing to do with the Agency, etc; and hired Garnett over, giving him $50 a month instead of the $40 he had been receiving and stated that he was obligated to hire him again to prevent disclosures.

The Tall Bull Story

Garnett says: The Tall Bull fight[182] occurred about 1869 between the soldiers under Col. Carr and the Pawnee scouts of whom there were a large number, and the Sioux and the Cheyennes.[183] It was on the South Platte and Garnett has been on the ground since, but he does not know near what present place it may be. There was an adobe ranch near the place when he was there. It was in a valley something like Cane Creek. A creek ran through. The Sioux were camped on one side and the Cheyennes on the other. Little spurs of ravines ran out from the stream into the flanking plateaus which were five or six feet higher than the bed of the creek. The soldiers could not have surprised these Indians as they did had it not been for a fog, for the country was open and the Indians knew of the presence of the soldiers in the country. Tall Bull had got away safely, but learning that one of his wives was behind he went back to get her and got killed.[184]

There are a number of Indians living on Medicine Root Creek who were in this battle.

Fight Between the Sioux and Pawnees in 1873

These came together when both were out hunting, and the Sioux, greatly outnumbering the Pawnees, nearly destroyed them. A lot of the Sioux who were in this fight are living on Medicine Root Creek. It is my understanding that this was somewhere on the Republican.[185]

[Philip Wells's Interview]

Ricker wrote the following biographical sketch of Philip Wells near the end of this long interview.

[Tablet 3]
Sketch of Philip Faribault Wells. (Pronounced Faribo, Fr.)[186]

He was born in Dec. 1850 in Frontenac, Minnesota. His mother was a half-blood Sioux Indian woman who never could speak spoke English. His father was James Wells, a white American. The city of Faribault was named for the famous Alexander Faribault, his uncle.[187] The city of Faribault place was at this date wholly an Indian country, there being not a white settler there. In the territorial days of Minnesota James Wells was a noted character and once at least was a member of the legislature. At the age of two years Philip's father removed to Faribault with his family When Philip was two years old his father removed with his family to what is now Faribault, Rice County, Minn., then a wilderness swarming with Indians. The Wells family was not outranked in importance by any of the pioneers of that period, and this fact can not be better confirmed than to say that a township and a county in that state are named in honor and recognition of it. (Alex. Faribault was a half-blood; his wife and Mr. Wells' mother were sisters.) Mr. Wells' five brothers have received honorable mention for their services in Civil and Indian wars. (His youngest brother is not included, as he was too young.)

On the 18th August, 1864, Mr. James Wells who, not liking the narrow restraints of civilization and still full of fondness for the free yet perilous life of the remote frontier with which he had always been identified, accompanied by Philip, Wallace and Aaron, his sons (all of whom have since been conspicuously identified with the Indian service) and an Indian whom he had raised to manhood, and the wife of this Indian, were on their way to the Black Hills to examine the country with a view to settle there, when they ran across a party of the hostile Sioux (a relic of the recent Minnesota war), and James Wells and the woman were killed and Philip wounded. This was on a branch of the Big Sioux river called the Lone Cottonwood, in what is now South Dakota. The terrible hardships borne by this party in their endeavors to escape out of this hostile country by night marches, enduring starvation, are yet fresh themes in the recollections of the early settlers. They finally reached home in pitiable condition, being mere skeletons and scarcely recognizable. Their horses were taken by the Indians and they were on foot nearly a month, the oldest brother Wallace carrying Philip most of the time as he was ~~seriously~~ wounded. Soon after this hard experience and yet a boy of about 15, Philip left home, and during the next ten years roamed throughout the west, including Mexico south and the British possessions north. After this time he was in the Indian service almost continually; he was interpreter, farmer and acting agent for the Interior Dept.; in 1877 and 1878 he was a deputy revenue ~~collector~~ officer on the ~~northern frontier~~ Canadian line, which was merely auxiliary to his business as a fur trader among the Indians. "I occupied under the War Dept. the positions of scout, chief of scouts, and guide and interpreter. In the fall of 1876, was employed by the Rev. Mr. Fennell, missionary of the Episcopal Church under Bishop Hare, who was killed, I narrowly escaping with my life.[188] A year or two afterwards I took part in the capture of the notorious outlaw, Brave Bear, and in the killing of his brother, near Fort Totten.[189] In 1881 was employed by the War Dept. to assist in receiving the surrender of Sitting Bull and was an interpreter for seven steamboat loads of Indian prisoners of war brought from Fort Buford to Fort Yates. (This was when the final surrender of Indians took place.)[190] Served as scout, interpreter and guide with the Army on various expeditions against the Indians. Became head farmer at Standing Rock Agency (quit the War Dept. in 1882) about 1882. In 1883 took charge of Turtle Mountain Reservation as farmer and Acting Agent and remained in those positions 4 years. In spring of 1887 I was appointed Assistant Clerk at Pine Ridge Reservation, and in addition was official interpreter. In 1889 was official interpreter for the Sioux Commission which treated for a portion of the Sioux Reservation. In 1890 was appointed by Col. Gallagher, farmer in charge of Medicine Root district.

"In the fall of 1890 resigned as farmer to take position as chief of scouts under War Dept. Was in battle of Wounded Knee and affair at Drexel Mission.[191] After peace was restored, was appointed farmer of White Clay district by Capt. Brown of 11th Inf., Acting Agent." While in that capacity, the killing of the 4 cowboys by the band of the notorious Two Sticks took place; he cared for the dead and with assistance of friendly Indians saved the living that were left.[192] In 1894 he quit the public service altogether, being unable longer to harmonize with the class of men who were directing Indian affairs, he feeling that it was not intelligent supervision that was wanted, but silence and submission instead. He next established a stock ranch on the Reservation where he has made selections for allotments to himself and children of whom he has six, five sons and one daughter. Since 1886 he has been principal interpreter between the government and the Sioux tribe of Indians in the making of all the treaties between these parties, and in all the attempts at treaty making which failed.

[Tablet 5]

Interview with Philip F. Wells. His P.O. is Kadoka, S.D.

Interview with Philip F. Wells.

I arrived at his place in the N. E. corner of the Pine Ridge Reservation and on the White River in South Dakota, at 2:30 P.M. Tuesday, October 2, 1906. At Mr. Wells' home I saw the book written by Mrs. Francis Chamberlain Holley, copyrighted by her in 1890, and published in 1892 by Donohue & Hennebarry, Chicago. It is titled, "Once Their Home or Our Legacy from the Dahkotahs." Mr. Wells says it is truthful and accurate. It has some very slight inaccuracies not sufficient to detract from its general correctness and value. On the margin of page 336 he has noted a trifling correction. The author, giving an account of the arrest of Brave Bear and Isnakiyapi and the attempt of the latter to escape by springing, leaping and running, states that the soldiers pursued him firing. "Finally a ball struck him in the ankle, when he turned and faced the Sergeant with his drawn knife, like a tiger at bay; but the Sergeant instantly fired and the Indian dropped to the ground, shot through the heart. Such was the hasty surrender of The Only One?"[193] Mr. Wells had made a notation correcting the above as follows:

"Not in the ankle but in the hip, and fell floundering, and finally gained his feet and met the Sergeant. The hip wound was shot from a distance of 250 yards; the death shot was about 20 feet off. (Signed) P. F. Wells, scout at the time and then."

On Indian Customs—Law, Discipline, Government—Dog Soldiers

Mr. Philip F. Wells states: The Indian Council decrees the laws and regulations to be enforced for the control of the camp and the government of the tribe. The Dog Soldiers are the municipal or police force which executes the commands of the Council and preserves the public discipline and order. A committee appointed by the Council goes through the camp and selects the Dog Soldiers by making a black spot or mark on the face, either on cheek or chin, just so it will be in plain view, without saying a word. Each man so designated understands his duty and promptly gets his pony and makes ready for the service for which he is thus detailed.

Mr. Wells states a circumstance to illustrate this performance.

A punctilious young man who accompanied Mr. Wells on a buffalo hunt among the Indians, of spirit and honor, unacquainted with Indian customs, but full of knowledge of city life, had taken it upon himself to learn of Mr. Wells. He perceived that ~~were in a part of {6} the camp by themselves but that the women~~ the Indians were gathering together as if something of interest was attracting them and led by curiosity he went to where they were standing. The Dog soldiers came along with whips in hand and began lashing and beating ~~the women~~ them. One of the soldiers instead of dealing a severe blow to this man, merely laid the lash on him without striking. Another came up and reversing the handle of his quirt touched him with the butt ~~of his handle~~. Prior to this Mr. W. had instructed him not to resent anything which he might consider an indignity, even to a blow in the face, but to come to him to learn what he should do. The young man now came to Mr. Wells and told him what had been done to him and asked what he ought now to do.

(This was a buffalo hunt with the Indians—the last hunt ever had by these people who had ~~were at that time~~ just been released as prisoners of war at Fort Yates. It was in the fall of 1881, and Sitting Bull was in the party. Mr. Wells was sent out in charge of them by Mr. James McLaughlin, Agent. These were Indians belonging to the Standing Rock Agency.)[194]

(Fort Yates was on this Reservation.)

Mr. Wells explained to him the significance of what he had seen.

(The particular attraction in this case was some deer on the other side of the hill.) Every time the camp was pitched the Council house was put up and at night the Council met and made their orders for the next day including instructions for the next camp. The rule was made that nobody should go beyond a given line from the camp; this was to prevent scaring and stampeding the game that the party was hunting. Mr. Wells told the young man who was his guest what the rule was that had been violated, and that out of respect for him as a guest who was unfamiliar with Indian government, he had not been beaten as the others were, but had been treated with leniency. He was further told that, to be the object of the law's notice as he had been, and to receive punishment for infraction of the law in a manly spirit without complaint, sullenness or resistance was a feature of his behavior which signified possession of manly qualities, and was an honor to him, and that now to show his appreciation of such honor it would be according to Indian custom if he should invite the Indians to partake of some little refreshment. This he did. (When he went out with Mr. W. he said he would resent any insult and resist any invasion of his rights; but that his intention was to be honorable and respect the forms, and customs and civilities practiced by the Indians, but being ignorant as to what they were he would depend on the advice of his friend Mr. W.) The Dog soldiers may sometimes tear down the offender's tepee and destroy his effects; but if the penalty of disobeying the orders of the Council is something different but equally severe, and he accepts it in a way showing great self-control and cheerfulness it is looked upon as the mark of manhood, and the Indian public take pleasure in contributing to give him another start in life—one will give one thing, another something else and so on till frequently the law-breaker who has made cheerful expiation is better off in the things of which he was dispossessed than before the soldiers dealt with him. His relatives might commonly be expected to help him in any event. But if he resisted or offered any opposition, or exhibited anger or sullenness, it was regarded as evidence of lack of manhood, and instead of his punishment entitling him to honor, he is disgraced.

The authority of the Dog soldiers is supported by the universal power of the tribe, and they soldier administer such degree of punishment as they consider adequate, acting in the double capacity of judge and executioner. The Indian ordinance is as sacred as was the Greek law whose majesty was heroically affirmed by the judge when his own son was arraigned before him for an offense which called for the putting out of both eyes, he suffered the loss of one of his own instead of one of his son's, and thus the law was fulfilled requiring two eyes. No matter if it be the chief of the tribe or a member of the Council who disobeys the ordinance, the Dog soldier does his duty in vindicating the law, without abatement of the penalty or the severity of it. The law commands impartial respect and must be satisfied by corporal punishment.

On the Battle of the Little Big Horn

Mr. Wells has heard Indians variously state the time when the battle was begun by Reno at a little after sunrise, when the sun was up at about nine o'clock or a little more, and still others at about noon, but the great majority (and these were older men) agreed that it was about the middle of the forenoon.[195] He thinks there were 4,000 warriors in the battle on the Indian side.

Major Reno whom he knew quite well, was a brutal, graceless person who had no respect for a brave man.

While Mr. Wells [was] not on the Little Big Horn, he has been so much among the Indians who were in the battle and has interpreted for army officers and officers of the government, for newspaper correspondents and members of the Indian Rights Association that he knows the Indian side of the conflict by heart. There was always great conflict of statement among them except that here was unanimity that the Indians were surprised.

It is his opinion that Major Reno could not have reached Custer and that he did well to save his command.

Mr. Wells says that it is his understanding that Rain-in-the-Face was not in the Custer battle.[196] Old Rain made money out of the white man's raving over what was believed to be his inhuman killing of Custer. He sold photos in great numbers. Tenderfeet bought anything with ardor that they were told that he carried on his person in the battle when he killed Custer(!)

Mr. Wells says Faribault, Minn., is named for his uncle Alexander Faribault. Mr. Wells says his father, James Wells, commonly known all over the country as "Bully" Wells, [was] a noted character and typical frontiersman. Never met his match in muscle or daring. The family lived at Faribault until 1864 when the father becoming tired of the contact of civilization started to remove to the Black Hills. Conditions in Minnesota and northern Iowa were not safe owing to marauding bands of Indians who were remnants of the hostile forces of 1862 and 1863, and were moving across the state line forward and backward with evil intentions. Mr. Wells' father was killed on Floyd River near the line by a party of these Indians, and he himself was wounded.[197]

Sioux Indians in Minnesota were distinct from the Sioux which inhabited the country round Fort Laramie.

On the Feud between Gen. Miles and Colonel Forsythe

There was no concord of feeling between Forsythe and Miles. There were two sides among the officers on the Reservation, some favoring General Miles, and some shielding Col. Forsythe. A court of inquiry had been ordered to investigate Forsythe's conduct at Wounded Knee; but General Miles, exceeding his authority, put Forsythe under arrest.[198]

A young Second Lieutenant recently graduated from West Point and assigned to the 1st U.S. Infy. at San Francisco, on arrival at Pine Ridge Agency with his command a day or two after the battle of Wounded Knee was detailed by General Miles to go to Wounded Knee and examine the field and make a report.[199] A ~~singular~~ striking circumstance was that none of the old and competent scouts was sent out with this officer but only young Indian scouts who had no experience or knowledge. The officer himself might not be suspected of any surplus qualification. Mr. Wells does not know what kind of a report was made.

A little later Mr. Wells was in a tent where there were some officers. One of them held in his hands a paper consisting of sheets put together in the legal form.[200] An officer asked him what he thought of the report, and a paragraph was read to him in which it was averred that the soldiers were so stationed that they fired into one another. Mr. Wells denounced the statement as false. Another officer then asked if he knew whose report it was that he was criticizing. He replied that he did not; neither did he care. He was asked if he would make oath to the statement he had made, and he replied that he would not for the reason that he had used expletives which he would not repeat, but in answer to another question he said he would be qualified to such statement when couched in diplomatic language. He afterwards furnished a sworn account of the battle.

He was informed soon afterwards by some officer that there was liable to be an overhauling of what he had at first impulsively remarked; and acting on this suggestion he went among the wounded Indians and took a number of statements, ~~from among them~~ having with him to listen to what was said and to verify what was done, Rev. Charles Smith Cook; and Mr. Cook also made a sworn statement.[201] When certain of the officers learned of what Mr. Cook had done they desired to get these documents and Mr. Cook let them take them. He thinks it was these which caused General Miles to receive from the War Department a sharp reprimand. The more pointed testimonies were never recovered by him, but several he got back through General Kent either the originals or copies. I transcribe these in his possession. The first is that of Mr. Wells himself.[202]

P.O. Kadoka, S.D.

"A half-breed, P. F. Wells, being duly sworn testified as follows:

I was ~~interpreter~~ interpreting for Colonel Forsyth at the time of [the] battle on Wounded Knee, December 29, 1890. Colonel Forsyth spoke to Big Foot through me as follows: "You tell Big Foot that he tells me that his Indians had no arms, when yesterday at time of surrender they were all well armed.[203] I am sure that he is deceiving me. Tell him, Big Foot, that he need have no fear in giving up his arms, as I wish to treat you with nothing but kindness.

Have I not done enough for you to convince you that I intend nothing but kindness? Did I not put you into an ambulance and treat you kindly, and put you into a good tent, and put a stove into it to keep you warm and comfortable, and I have sent off to get provisions for your people which I expect here before long so that I can feed you well, and I have had my doctors taking care of you." Then Big Foot answered: "They have no guns only such as you have found. (Which I, the interpreter, saw was about a dozen old rifles, tied up with strings, different old-fashioned rifles, not a decent one in the lot.) I gathered up all my guns at the Cheyenne River Agency and turned them in and they were all burned up." Then General Forsyth answered: "You are lying to me in return for all my kindness to you." Big Foot answered in substance as before. At this time the soldiers were searching again. During this time a medicine man all painted up and fantastically dressed, was going on with a silent ghost dance, or rather the maneuvers of the ghost dance worship, throwing up his hands and occasionally picking up dust and throwing it towards the soldiers who were standing in ranks around; then he turned toward the young bucks who were squatted together, and said "do not be afraid and let your hearts be strong to meet what is before you; we are all well aware that there are lots of soldiers about us and that they have lots of bullets; but I have received assurance that their bullets cannot penetrate us. The prairie is large and the bullet will not go toward you but over the large prairies and if they do go towards you they will not penetrate you." (To go in Mr. Wells' Statement: This should be added to the medicine man's words after the final ones "they (the bullets) will not penetrate you:" "As you saw me throw up the dust and it floated away, so will the bullets float away harmlessly over the prairies.")[204]

Then all these young bucks answered "How" with great earnestness; this meaning that they were with him or would stand by him. I then turned to Major Whiteside and said that man is making mischief and repeated to him what he had said.[205]

He said go direct to General Forsyth and tell him about it, which I did. So he came along with me to the edge of the Indian circle of bucks and told me to tell that man to sit down and keep quiet, the man then being engaged again in silent maneuvers or incantations. But he kept on and paid no attention to the order; when General Forsyth repeated the order; and when I translated it in Indian, Big Foot's brother-in-law said, "He will sit down when he gets around the circle," and when he reached the end he squatted down. At the end of General Forsyth's conversation through me to Big Foot, the brother-in-law asked that they be allowed to take their chief, Big Foot, "who is dying," and go amongst our people, meaning to continue on the journey they had been making before the arrest. The General answered: "I can take better care of him than you can anywhere, as I have my doctor tending to him." Then General Forsyth went to one side giving instructions elsewhere. This was after I had told him that the medicine man was inciting trouble. After the medicine man sat down some sergeant of cavalry said to General Forsyth, "There goes one with a gun under his blanket." The Indian was walking around the circle. The general ordered the sergeant to take it away from the Indian and he went up and snatched the rifle away from him. Then Major Whiteside said to me, "Tell the Indians that it is necessary that they should be searched one at a time;" this while he stood to one side with five or six soldiers. The Indians, or rather the old ones assented willingly by answering "How" and the search began. Whilst the young bucks paid no attention at all, the old ones that were sitting next to us passed through (some five or six of them), and submitted to the search. Whilst this was going on I kept a watch on the medicine man for fear of a row; and then I heard some one to my left call out, "Look out!" "look out!" and that instant, as I turned my head, I brought my arms to a "port" and then saw five or six young bucks throw off their blankets and pull out their arms from under them, brandish them in the air, and immediately the older Indians that were sitting between us and the younger ones rose up so that the farther end of [the] circle, some forty feet away, was hidden from my view. I heard a shot fired from midst of them, and as I started to cock my rifle, throwing my eyes to the right to see the treacherous fellow whom I suspected; he had, or some one like him from that lot, come to within 3 or 4 feet of me with a long cheese knife ground to a sharp point raised to stab me. Then the fight between him and me prevented me from seeing anything else at the time, he stabbing me by cutting off the end of my nose, and I keeping him off till I could swing my rifle to hit him, which I finally succeeded in doing, and I then shot and killed him as soon as I had room to aim my rifle. By this time the fight between the Indians and soldiers had become general.

Up to that time the women and children in and around the tepees were not fired at until some five or six of the bucks ran amongst the women and children and began firing from there, and the fire of the soldiers was directed towards them. This was all that I saw positively, and I was bleeding profusely and was led off, my senses having almost left me. After the heavy fight was over I came back to where the dead and wounded were lying motionless, and called out: "These white people came to save you and you have brought death on yourselves. Still white people are merciful to save the wounded enemy when he is harmless; so, if some of you are alive, raise your heads; I am a man of your own blood who is talking to you." At this about a dozen heads were raised from among those that were seemingly dead; one man especially raised himself on his elbow and said: "Are you the man they call Fox?" (my Indian name). I told him I was. He says: "I want you to favor me by coming to me." I suspected him, however, and raising my gun went towards him. He says: "Who is that man lying burned there?" meaning an Indian who had run into a scout's tent, and who had from there killed three or four soldiers, until they—the soldiers—had fired a volley into the same and had finally set the tent on fire to get him out.

(Mr. Wells makes this addition to his statement about the volley fired into the tent and its destruction by fire. "After the soldiers had poured the volley into it they were ordered away and the Hotchkiss cannon trained on it and a shell thrown into it. It and the hay within caught fire and it was burned.")

I supposed he was one of the two medicine men and replied accordingly. He raised himself a little higher, raised his closed fist pointing it towards the dead Indian, shot out his fingers, which is amongst Indians a deadly insult, meaning, "I could kill you and be satisfied doing it; am sorry I could do no more to you;" and then used words trembling, but which I could not all catch, but he said this which I did hear, speaking as though to the dead man "if I could be taken to you I would stab you!" then turning to me said, "He is our murderer! Only for him inciting our other young men we would have been alive and happy!" Another old woman, whom I was conducting to a safe place, told me "the treacherous ones are of Big Foot's band; these two medicine men have been trying constantly to incite the others to trouble since we of Hump's band have been with them; some of us honestly meant peace when we raised the white flag. But in spite of that trouble has been made." Some of the women that were wounded said about the same thing. Before this, while some of the soldiers were still firing, I heard Gen. Forsyth yelling, "Quit shooting at them!" this in efforts to save women and children, and the firing towards them ceased. Some soldier replied: "That fellow," alluding to a wounded buck among the women, "is raising a gun to shoot." An instant or two before I heard a similar order given; but I heard General Forsyth's order distinctly, and the soldier's reply as though in excuse for his action in disobedience of the first orders.

A true copy.

PHILIP F. WELLS

J. Ford Kent
Lt. Col. 18th Inf.
A.I.G.

Charles Smith Cook and P. F. Wells' Statement of the [blank] Statement of He-ha-ka-wan-ya-ka-pi (Elks Saw Him) Age 38, of Hump's band. A ghost dancer. I came along with Big Foot's band as by an accident, namely: We heard that Big Foot and people were invited to come and live here with the Oglalas. I joined them, being myself an Oglala. Fifth day out we met the soldiers. We were just coming down the hills beyond Porcupine Tail Creek when we were met by four scouts. I saw only one, *Highbackbone*, the others riding back rapidly to tell the soldiers of our coming. I asked the scout the object of his coming to us. He answered: "We heard you were coming and so have come to meet you. Everything will be all right." We got into Porcupine Tail Creek and made coffee there. Then we came on, preceded by our horsemen. Presently it was said: "Soldiers are coming" I looked and saw them coming, making much dust. They came on and finally halted at a given place not far from us. We still came on toward them, preceded by our horsemen. On a little rise they placed two cannon covering us, having their other guns in readiness for firing. We came right on towards them and finally reached them, our people saying, "They are only fooling us." We finally mingled together with them, and came on with them, some of the soldiers preceding us and the rest coming on behind. We reached the Wounded Knee; we camped right by their side. Of course we were guarded. It was a lovely evening. Rations were soon given us and everything seemed friendly. There being no bad intentions on our part we didn't entertain any sense of fear. There was no suspicion on our part towards the soldiers. We were simply coming this way because of the invitation from Red Cloud, Young-Man-Afraid-of-his-Horses, and other chiefs. We did not ask for the usual passes because we knew we would be refused. At the Wounded Knee the men were not allowed to take the horses to water. The boys had charge of that. Even then I did not think that we were under suspicion. After breakfast that morning I went out and learned that all the men were wanted at a given place. I went to it, near Big Foot's tent which was near the soldiers. It was then said that all our guns were wanted. Many of the soldiers (cavalry) were arranging themselves into positions; and the infantry came on between us and the women and children. All the men were thus separated from the women. I heard an officer saying something. He must have given orders, because the soldiers began loading their guns and holding them in readiness for firing. I called out and said, "Let us give up every gun." I said this because I thought it was best to do so. Many were brought. Can not say exactly how many, but thought all had been gathered up. Every man in the Indian party did not have a gun. I gave up my Winchester which was all that I had. A man by name Hose-Yanka (a rascally fellow) was at this juncture "making medicine" but I did not hear what he was saying. Also about this time a more rigid searching of the Indians was instituted. When they came to me I gave up my cartridge belt. A soldier took it and began taking off the cartridges, apparently to return to me the belt, so I stood by him waiting for it. Just then I heard the report of a gun and saw a man throwing off his sheet covering; then followed firing from all sides. I threw myself on the ground. I then jumped up to run towards the Indian camp but was then and there shot down, being hit on my right leg, and soon after was shot again on the other leg.

When the general firing ceased I heard an interpreter calling out, saying the wounded would be kindly treated. I opened my eyes and looked about and saw the dead and wounded all around me. Five men and Mrs. Big Foot were near me alive. My wife and younger child, I hear, were not killed, but my older girl is missing. Alec. Adams, government herder here, is my brother. The young man who fired the first gun is, the one who brought all this trouble upon us.
(Signed) Charles Smith Cook
P. F. Wells
    Copied from Mr. Cook's paper by his wife.
                    Pine Ridge Agency, S.D. Jan. 7th [18]91;
                    Statement of Frog of Big Foot's Band.
I am a brother of Big Foot. We left Cheyenne River where we had been living, as Big Foot was tired of the bad treatment he had been getting at the hands of both Indians and white people; and besides, Big Foot and his band had been asked at different times during the summer by Red Cloud, Little Wound, Afraid-of-his-Horses and No Water to come to Pine Ridge Agency and join them.

(At this point Mr. Wells says that it is a matter of no little importance to know what was the secret motive of these chiefs in inviting and urging Big Foot to come to Pine Ridge and stay. Did they secretly believe that the time had come for it, and the necessity was extreme enough to require a demonstration to convince the government that to avoid serious consequences it should now put an end to the wrongs afflicting the Indians as the result of its failure to keep its treaty obligations and other promises? The leading chiefs and statesmen of the time were Red Cloud, Little Wound, Young-Man-Afraid-of-his Horses and American Horse. The latter cannot be better described than to say he was a politician. He was shrewd and sagacious, and endowed with the advantage of eloquent oratory, yet slippery in character, being wise enough to know that resistance to the government was hopeless so far as independence was concerned—that the Indians were practically a conquered race, and that if hostility was nourished into actual war this meant destruction to the last hope of the Indians to preserve even a semblance of their identity as a distinct people. American Horse won the reputation of being the friend of the white man and of the government. His course brought him consideration and favors from the conqueror. But we cannot suppress an active admiration for those truly loyal and patriotic men like Red Cloud who stood out with resolution and endurance for their people, and were ready to die with them if need be to redress and end their wrongs and promote their good, as far as there was any possibility of doing so for this despised and outraged native class. Little Wound, with perfect sincerity, had bowed his proud spirit to what he knew were inevitable conditions when the results of the fighting of 1876 were realized. He accepted as an upright man the terms of advancing civilization. He was willing that his followers should adopt the new order as taught by the white conqueror. Upon this point his heart was unmistakeably good. He placed reliance upon the good intentions of the Great Father as glowingly and emphatically pictured to him. In submitting, he acted upon the promises as though they were sacred and had been made to be kept.

Let it be pointedly stated that they were not kept, be the fault grave or otherwise without attempt specifically to locate the responsibility. How natural and politic, then, that having acquiesced in the demands of the stronger power, he should persuade those around him to act in good faith toward the conqueror, believing that his word of promise would be fulfilled. Imagine what must have been his disappointment when his people were deceived and victimized and subjected to wrongs which, from their long continuance, could not be excused or accounted for as accidental. As a dernier resort these first men whose highest duty was to secure the rights of the Indians to whom they belonged, may have planned to assemble a threatening force so that notice, and action based thereon, would be given to their demands for justice. In the interview with Mr. Wells I was informed that during the troublous situation before the tragedy occurred at Wounded Knee, he had heard leading Indians and warriors (but not any of the chiefs mentioned) say that if war should come it would not last in confidential conversations that there were good white men who wanted just treatment for the Indians but they were far away in the east and not conversant with the true state of affairs, and that if a war was to come it should be confined to the immediate regions affected by the grievances in question, and that it would acquire no great extent but be local and limited; but that it would have the effect to attract the attention of the wise and good men of the country to the abuses which were perpetrated, so that a remedy would be found and applied to satisfy the complaints of their tribe. Secret talk of this character is an index of the sentiment which generally prevailed; and it would be erroneous to say that the natives contemplated war, or even desired it except as a remote possibility to accomplish righteous ends which were impossible of attainment as an answer to appeals, earnest and supplicating as they had been.) (See account of the Rosebud Indians coming and joining the hostiles at Pine Ridge Agency; obtained from Mr. Wells.)

(Frog's Statement Continued.)

From the time we left home till we came to Pine Ridge Reservation we had not been interfered with by soldiers or any one else. When we were taken by the soldiers the day before the battle fight, they treated us with nothing but kindness and brought [us] to camp. The following morning the soldiers began blowing their bugles and they began standing around in ranks, but I thought nothing of it, as it was their natural custom to do so; and then we were told (all of us) to come out and sit down at a place near the door of Big Foot's tent, which we did. Then a lot of soldiers got in between us (men) and our camp, separating us (men) from the women and children. An officer told us then he wanted our guns and as soon as we gave them up he would give us provisions and we can go on our way. We, the older men, consented willingly and began giving them up. We had all given them up, as I thought, when I saw an Indian with a gun under his blanket, and the soldiers saw it at the same time, and they took it away from him. They (soldiers) commenced searching the Indians one at a time. The medicine man was going through the incantations of the ghost dance, stopped and began speaking to the young men. But I paid no attention to what he said, as I had not the least fear of any trouble; so I pulled my blanket over my head and didn't see anything till I heard much talking in loud voices. I uncovered my head and I saw every one had arisen on his feet; and I heard a shot coming from where the young Indians stood. Shortly after that I was shot down, and I laid there as I fell. The firing was so fast and the smoke and dust so thick I did not see much more of the fight until it was over. I heard some one saying, "Indians, all of you who are yet alive raise your heads; the white men do not wish to kill you." I raised my head and saw a man standing among the dead, and I asked him if he was the man they called Fox; and he said he was. And I said, "Will you come to me?" and he came to my side. I then asked him who is that man lying there half burnt and he said, "I understand it is the medicine man," and I threw at him (the medicine man) my bitterest hatred and contempt. I then said to Fox, "He has caused the death of all of our people."

(I copied Frog's Statement from the original in P. F. Wells' handwriting. Among Mr. Wells' papers was a typewritten copy of it, at the end of which were the following signatures:
(Signed) Charles Smith Cook, missionary of the Episcopal Church.
(Signed) P. F. Wells, A True copy
(Signed) J. Ford Kent, Lt. Col. 18th Inf. A. I. G.
Pine Ridge Agency, S.D., Jan. 7, '91

The Statement of Help Them, son of Heart Man, living on Wounded Knee

I am an Oglala. I went on a visit to Big Foot's camp on Cheyenne River, and as I was on my way home I came along with Big Foot's people.

When we were taken by the soldiers we were treated kindly by them and we were given provision to eat. The only thing that did not look friendly on the part of the soldiers was, they kept their guns in readiness for action, and when we came into camp they placed two cannons on a hill covering our camp. The men were not allowed to take the horses to water, so the watering of the horses was done by the little boys. To the best of my knowledge the Indians had no intention of fighting.

The disarming of the Indians had begun peaceably by some of the men. I had given up my gun and had left the circle and was going towards our camp where all of the women and children were.

For sometime before that the medicine man had been going through the maneuvers of the ghost dance. He stopped and turned around facing a crowd of young men who were standing together with their guns concealed under their blankets, and spoke to them. I could not hear what he said, though I heard all he spoke to answer, "How!"

Shortly after I heard a white man say something in excited tones, which I could not understand; and I looked around and I saw some of the Indians throw off their blankets and raise their guns, and one of the Indians fired a shot.

I did not recognize him. As I turned to run I heard a few shots following the first. Then the firing became so fast I could not tell what happened after that.

The medicine man had been telling the other Indians all the way that the soldiers' bullets could not reach them (the Indians), no matter how the soldiers would shoot at them.

(I copied the foregoing statement of Help Them from the original in the handwriting of P. F. Wells. This had been in the hands of General J. Ford Kent, and among the papers was a typewritten copy which ended with the following signatures.)

(Signed) Charles Smith Cook, Missionary of the Episcopal Church
(Signed) P. F. Wells
A True Copy
(Signed) J. Ford Kent, Lt. Col. 18th Inf. A. I. G.

    Headquarters Department of Dakota., Inspector General's Office.
            St. Paul, Minn. 9th Jany., 1892.
            Mr. P. F. Wells, Pine Ridge Agency,

Dear Sir:

I enclose you true copies of your own testimony & of the two Indians, all of which I made use of in the investigation of the Battle of the Wounded Knee. That of the Rev. Mr. Cook I took no copy of but appended the original statement, so cannot furnish it.

Truly yours,
J. Ford Kent
(Copy)

            United States Indian Service.
            Office of Indian Agent,
            Pine Ridge Agency, South Dakota,

October 6th, 1890.
To Whom It May Concern.

This is to certify that Philip F. Wells has several years past acted as Official Sioux Interpreter at this Agency. During this time he has proved himself reliable and efficient in the highest degree and I have no hesitation in recommending him as deserving of the confidence of any person in whose service he may engage.

H. D. Gallagher
U. S. Indian Agent.
(Copy)

United States Indian Service,
Standing Rock Agency, Fort Yates, N.D.
January 6, 1892.

P. F. Wells, Esq.
Pine Ridge Agency, S.D.
Dear Sir:

I am in receipt of your communication relative to your application for the position of Farmer at Pine Ridge Agency, and desire to state that I have known you since 1864 when you were a small boy living on your father's farm in Rice County, Minnesota, and that I have been acquainted with you since that time.

It affords me pleasure to testify to your good morals and general character as coming within my knowledge, and to your having grown to manhood on a farm, with an experience of many years amongst Indians. You were Head Farmer at this agency in 1882 and 1883 and subsequently as Farmer in charge of the Turtle Mountain Sub-Agency under ex-Agent Cramsie of Devil's Lake.[206]

I regard you as well qualified for the position of Farmer at any Indian Agency and particularly so among the Sioux whose language you have so thorough a knowledge of.

You are at liberty to use this letter if it will be of any use to you in applying for the position you seek.
With kind regards,
I am yours very respectfully,
(Signed) James McLaughlin
U. S. Indian Agent.

United States Indian Service

Devil's Lake Agency
December 18th, 1886.

To Whom It May Concern:

This is to certify, that Philip Wells has been in my employ as farmer in charge on the Turtle Mountain Reservation during the last four years. He has performed his duties faithfully & honestly, and has given entire satisfaction. Mr. Wells resigned in consequence of notice received from the Dept. that the position of farmer would be filled by a person selected by the Indian office, in pursuance of a policy adopted by the Dept. I take pleasure in recommending Mr. Wells to any one desirous of securing the services of an honest and capable man.
(Signed) John W. Cramsie
U. S. Indian Agent.

Headquarters 7th Cavalry[207]
Fort Riley, Kans. March 5, 1891.
The Adjutant General U. S. A.
Washington, D. C.
(Through Head Quarters Dept. of the Missouri)

Sir:

I have the honor to invite special attention to the conduct of Interpreter, Philip Wells, at the battle of Wounded Knee, S.D., December 29, 1890, and the engagement near Drexel Mission, S.D., December 30, 1890.

Mr. Wells accompanied Lieut. Taylor's troop of Scouts to which [he] was attached as interpreter, to Wounded Knee with my command on the evening of December 28, 1890.[208] During the council the next morning he rendered every assistance in his power to overcome the disinclination of the Indians to turn in their arms. He was within the circle of Indians when the break took place and was at once stunned by a blow from an Indian from behind. He quickly recovered himself, and turning saw the Indian in the act of striking him with a large knife. This blow he partially avoided by raising his arm, as it struck him in the face and nearly severed his nose, leaving only a small portion of flesh by which it was held to his face. Clubbing the Indian with the barrel of his gun to gain the necessary [time] to step back, he took deliberate aim and killed the buck. Hastening to the surgeon he waited only long enough to have his face partially covered with cotton to stop the flow of blood, and then returning with his gun, took an active part in the remainder of the fight—in fact, he could have rendered no better service if he had not received the wound.

He rode with the column on its return that night to the Agency, ready for any duty. Early the next morning, while waiting in the Divisional Hospital to have his wound attended to, the alarm regarding the Drexel Mission was received and the 7th Cavalry ordered out. Mr. Wells without waiting for surgical treatment attention, ran out of the hospital and jumped on the first pony he could find and accompanied the regiment during the entire day.

I consider interpreter Wells' conduct during the two days as remarkably fine and gallant, and urgently recommend him for the most substantial reward that can be given him.

Very respectfully
(Signed) James W. Forsyth
Colonel 7th Cavalry
(Briefs on the files)

Little Wound

(The following paper [See "Sketch of Little Wound" below] was written by a lady in Washington in March, 1896 when Little Wound and Philip F. Wells and Kicking Bear and George Fire Thunder—Thunder Bear went to represent the police only in police matters—were in that City as a delegation sent by the Og-la-la Indians to search for records and treaties and documents in relation to the sale of the Black Hills and which affect these Indians in any other way, as the Indians were in great confusion respecting these affairs, because of conflicting claims of the opposing parties. This lady wrote from the dictation of Mr. Wells who was familiar with the history of the chief, and the manuscript was submitted to Little Wound himself who approved it. Before I proceed to transcribe the MS it will be useful to add that this delegation, of which Little Wound was chairman, succeeded in finding much important information, among which was the extraordinary fact that the Commission which treated for the Black Hills made oral promise to the Indians which was not inserted in the written treaty, that the southern boundary should embrace a strip of country lying in Nebraska which would include the line of the Northwestern railroad with the towns of Chadron, Hay Springs, Rushville and Gordon, the real limits of which beyond those places cannot at this moment be specified. This delegation went to Washington by way of St. Paul, Minn., and at that place they obtained from General Sanborn who was one of the commissioners that negotiated the treaty, a statement in writing addressed to Little Wound as chairman, affirming this fact of the oral promise of the commissioners to the Indians. Mr. Wells gave this letter to Chief Little Wound chairman of the delegation, for preservation. At this writing (Oct. 6, 1906) Little Wound is dead, having died about 1902 or 1903, and it is not exactly known where this important document is, but it is supposed to be in the custody of some representative of the dead chief. We aim to prosecute inquiry to ascertain its whereabouts.[209]

It is fitting that in describing the make-up of this delegation I should remark that Mr. Wells stood second to Little Wound, and that Kicking Bear and George Fire Thunder ranked below him. This was a proper order of preference, as Mr. Wells had had a wider range of experience and knowledge, was a fair English scholar, a fluent conversationalist with a well-known and justly-high reputation as a Sioux interpreter, and possessed a knowledge also of the Chippewa and Crow tongues. One little circumstance regarding his credentials may well be related in this connection as showing the spirit which Agent

Clapp exhibited and how unwilling he was to do right by acting according to the facts of the case and the wishes of the Indians in this legitimate and commendable undertaking, after they had in council elected these delegates, and were supplying the funds for their expenses.

When Mr. Wells applied to Agent Clapp for his credentials the agent inserted the word "interpreter," so as to present him in that sole capacity without authority and prestige as a delegate to be heard and respected; and the agent would not alter it when Mr. Wells protested, and the delegation informed him what was Mr. Wells' true status, and requested that his letter of rank and authority be corrected. I cite this as an instance illustrative of the littleness of the ~~men who as favorites of some with influence~~ creatures of influence who held positions of great responsibility requiring ability to be just and therefore efficient, rather than the weakness which renders an officer arbitrary and offensive. In official intercourse with these natives men of broad views and large capacity were in demand, but the government by virtue of the vicious system of appointment, and the Indians by reason of their inferior status, and want of power and audience were not blessed with such officers except in rare cases. When the delegation reached Washington the subject was brought to the notice [of] Mr. Browning the Commissioner of Indian Affairs who heard the statements of the delegation and accorded Mr. Wells his rights.)[210]

Following is the Sketch of Little Wound:

Little Wound, an Ogallala Sioux Chief, is now (March, 1896) 68 years of age. In 1844, when at the age of 16, his father took him on the war path gainst the Shoshone Indians.[211] He killed his man in a singlehanded fight and was badly wounded himself. As it was customary among the Indians, when a warrior done (sic) any deeds of bravery in battle to give him a new name. He was named "Little Wound," from the fact he was small and doing such a deed of bravery. His former name being "Good Singer" when a boy.

He was engaged in numberless battles and skirmishes (with Indians) who were at war with the Sioux, and in many instances killed enemies, from which he became distinguished.

Sometime in 1860 some white people were trying to induce the Indians to live in peace with one another, and Little Wound agreed to live in peace if the other tribes would not molest him. That he would only fight in self-defense.

The Omaha warriors attacked his people, and he, with his warriors, chased them home and killed about 100 of them. He then sent word around to the neighboring tribes that he did not want to fight any more, and asked them not to force him into any more fights. But the Pawnees took advantage of his band when all the men folks were out on a buffalo chase, and took the camp where only women and children were. They killed something over 100 of his band, women, children and old men who were in camp. Shortly after that occurred, the head chief of the Pawnee Indians sent him a "Pipe of Peace." He rejected the "Pipe of Peace" and said "No, my wounds are too sore yet: the wounds that you gave me are not healed up." In reply the Pawnee chief insisted on peace, and offered to pay damages in horses. Little Wound also rejected that and in reply sent to the Pawnee chief arrows, returning the "Pipe of Peace," meaning a declaration of war, and also said, "You took advantage of me when all the men folks were away, and killed our women and children. I now notify you to make ready, and make as many arrows as you can and have them all ready, for I am coming to punish fight, for I will not sneak on and take advantage of you as you did me."

When the appointed time came he went with his warriors and attacked the Pawnee tribe, and as his were the bravest and most dreaded warriors of the Sioux tribe, after meeting in battle, they in a very short time defeated the Pawnees and killed over 200 of their number and chased the others away. He also captured from the camp a number of women and children.

It was a known practice among the Indians that Indian prisoners of war expected no mercy from their captors, but on the contrary immediate death or other inhuman treatment. Little Wound gathered all the women and children prisoners together. "I will not do as my women and children were done by your husbands: they beat my women and children and made slaves of them; but in return for that I am going to paint your faces red (a work of kindness and respect), dress you in my women's clothes, and will furnish you with good horses so that you can [go] back to your cowardly husbands," and he did as he said he would, sending Antoine Janis, a well known character in charge of them to the Pawnee tribe.[212]

The following year the Pawnees, with some of the head chiefs, came to the Ogallala camp and demanded damages, when Little Wound replied to them: "After I asked you people to let me alone, and let me live in peace, you came to my camp and murdered my women and children while my men folks were on a buffalo chase, and I never cried, or begged any one to help me get pay; but I came and punished you, captured your women and children, and when I heard them cry I took mercy on them, painted their faces red, put them on good horses and sent them back to you. So, if you want pay, get your warriors together, your bows and arrows, and take pay out of me." Nothing further was said about it. This was his last fight, and from that day to this he has lived at peace with the Indian tribes and the whites.[213]

White Flag at Wounded Knee

Mr. Wells says that Colonel Forsyth left the Agency about sundown on Dec. 28 and arrived at Wounded Knee about 11 P.M. He [Wells] was with Capt. Taylor's scouts; these did not go quite to the camp of the troops on the creek, but halted about a mile back on the hill and went into camp for the night. Next morning when he arose he noticed a white flag flying from a pole close to the ravine. This is all that he knows about it except that the battle was fought under it.

No. of Hotchkiss Cannon at Wounded Knee

Mr. Wells says there were 2 or 3 of these.

Provision Train which came to Wounded Knee Dec. 29

It arrived from the Agency in the afternoon. The sound of the battle, discharges of cannon, were heard by the Indians at the Agency and they made a hurried march to W. K., approaching the battlefield from the west over the hills overlooking the field from that direction. Some cavalry was dispatched to this quarter to receive them with a fire delivered over the summit by the men shielded behind the ridge. The Indians got up within range and a Pine Ridge Indian named Flyinghorse was killed, and two Rosebud Indians were wounded. The hostiles then retired.[214]

During the preparations the sacks of grain which had been brought by the wagons that afternoon were thrown into breastworks for defense against this threatened danger, but no necessity came for their use.

What Would Have Been the Result if There Had Been No Attempt to Disarm the Indians?

Mr. Wells says that it was due to conditions at the Agency that Big Foot's band had to be disarmed.

The Indians who had collected in the Bad Lands, north & east of the Agency, were the hostiles. Father Jutz (pronounced Utes, who was the priest who built the Drexel Mission) and Jack Red Cloud were sent out to the hostiles to persuade them to surrender. The priest made a second trip before an understanding was arranged with them, and then they came in with him and pitched their camp on the ridge north of Wolf Creek and the Agency, and they were in this position when the fight at W. K. took place.[215] The military uthorities were endeavoring to obtain the arms from the hostiles, and if Big Foot's band had been allowed to come into the Agency armed the effect on the hostiles would have been most unfavorable, especially as the general in command made it a condition of entry into the Agency that they should first deliver over their guns.

Address Father Superior, Holy Rosary Mission, Pine Ridge for the address of Father Jutz (pronounced Uts).

The Messiah Craze

(Interview of Philip F. Wells) October 6, 1906.

This rank, religious delusion gained its foothold among the Indians early in the year 1890. In the previous year Short Bull, of the Brule band of the Sioux, a Rosebud Indian, and Kicking Bear, formerly of the Minneconjou band of the Sioux of the Cheyenne River Reservation, a renegade and vagrant Indian ~~who wandered from reservation to reservation,~~ (a vagrant Indian) and a Pine Ridge Indian bearing the nickname of "Sells-the-Pistol" (Red Star, Dr. Walker has it) hearing of the so-called Messiah who was said to be living near Walker Lake, Utah (?) went there for the purpose of seeing him and bringing back word to the people of his remarkable revelations and powers.[216] They returned early in 1890. (In 1896 when the Little Wound delegation was elected to visit Washington Short Bull had some ambition to be chosen as one of the delegates, and in the council a speaker taunted him by telling him that he was the man who once went away and returned with news which had brought direful results. Short Bull replied by saying, "Why ~~taunt me with~~ speak to me of that? ~~what you all know~~ Didn't we talk of that secretly, and you chose me to go? Whatever has come of it, you are as much to blame as I." Mr. Wells was in the council and heard this and he says no refutation of Short Bull's statement was offered. It is therefore admitted by the council that these three men went with the secret approval of the Indians.)

On the return of these men in March Short Bull went to the Rosebud Reservation and set about organizing the ghost-dance among the Indians there, and Kicking Bear and "Sells-the-Pistol" began the same work on Pine Ridge Reservation.

They brought back word that the Messiah spoke miraculously the languages of all Indians who came to him. They had to approach him with certain elaborate ceremonies. He fed all his visitors. Many different versions of his teachings were given, but the one most generally circulated was that a heavy cloud would appear in the west and pass to the east, and all white men would be destroyed by it, and all Indians who did not believe and participate in the ghost dance would be destroyed along with the whites. But all Indians who believed and wore the ghost shirt and took part in the ghost dance would rise above the cloud and escape destruction. Following this cloud there would be a new earth, with all their dead relatives restored to life, and the buffalo and the game would also return. The Messiah had exhibited to ~~the three men all who saw him~~ all who went to see him, the nail-prints in his hands and feet and the spear wound in his side, of the crucified Savior, inflicted by the white man; and because the white men had crucified the Savior they would be destroyed and because the Indians had had no part in the crucifixion they would be shown mercy and be saved. The Messiah prescribed the pattern of a shirt which was called ghost shirt, which all believers should wear in the dance; and he also prescribed a song which was to be sung in the dance.

(Out of Place. The Messiah disappeared on the approach of unbelievers. Visitors to the Messiah brought him presents.)

The Ghost Dance

The converts assembled and went into camp. Prior to the dance each one performed the act of purification necessary to make himself fit for the sacred performance by passing through the sweat bath. The first step in the dance was to clasp hands and circle to the left, each jerking one another's hands forward and backward, and singing and dancing, with eyes averted to the skies.[217] The dance would proceed for hours — five or six hours — until nearly all had fallen in trance. They would begin falling within half an hour from the beginning, and by the time an hour and a half had elapsed the ground would be strewn with the prostrate forms of dancers. This was kept up until the few ~~remaining ones~~ who were ~~nearly exhausted but~~ not conquered by their frantic exertions would give up from sheer exhaustion. During the performance the dancers became wrought up to a high pitch of excitement and went through various indescribable contortions, singing meanwhile the song prescribed by the Messiah, and when going into trance uttered unearthly ~~screams, screeches and yells~~ moans and groans and all manner of utterance and noise, the most inconceivable discord and tumult smiting the ear, while they clawed the air and flung froth from their mouths, the numerous performers in the stygian concert ~~creating a veritable pandemonium~~ keeping the regular cadence of step and motion to the music, the trancers only breaking into these accents which baffle description. ~~Some who~~ Such as succumbed would lie apparently unconscious from ten minutes to three-quarters of an hour when they would rise without help. After the dance was over the leaders would call the trancers together and hold a sort of class-meeting when each would describe his vision. Some realized nothing. Others would relate how they had seen departed relatives, or buffaloes, and various game animals, or had heard or seen buffaloes or other animals passing in the air, or a buffalo or a grizzly bear had conversed with them—in short each trancer had a vision distinctly his own and unlike any others. Men, women and children engaged in the dance, and were affected without disparity on account of age or sex.

Ghost Shirts Impervious to Bullets

It should be stated in the proper place that the leaders in the ghost dance inculcated the delusion that the shirts would be impervious to bullets of the white enemy. These leaders were Short Bull, Kicking Bear and Sells-the-Pistol. They installed others to spread the work; but these were the apostles of the craze on the Pine Ridge Reservation.

The Ghost dance was inaugurated on Pine Ridge Reservation. It was done by Kicking Bear and Sells-the-Pistol. Short Bull who belonged on Rosebud Reservation went there at once and addressed himself to the planting of it there, and he stayed on his reservation till the time when the Rosebud Indians (Brules) made the break for the Bad Lands on Pine Ridge Res. and swept the Pass Creek Indians along with them.

Kicking Bear left the ghost dance work on Pine Ridge locally to Sells-the-Pistol, while he established the propaganda on Standing Rock and Cheyenne River Reservations. He it was who carried it to Sitting Bull's camp and enlisted Sitting Bull, though this wily malcontent (or chieftain) could not have required much urging. As soon as Mr. Wells learned that Kicking Bear had gone to Standing Rock he wrote to Agent McLaughlin warning him of the insidious discontent that this apostle of mischief was sure to excite, and advising him to take prompt measures to prevent or counteract his influence. Kicking Bear had the advantage of arriving in time to get his work well started and organized before Agent McLaughlin had come into possession of this information. The craze caught like a spontaneous fire on the northern reservations; it took more effort and time to make the beginnings on Pine Ridge and Rosebud; but when once the conflagration was established it swept with fury into the material that was seasoned to feed it.

The effect of this strange, weird and grotesque, not to say pathetic worship spread with rapidity and produced immediate and marked results. It affected the attendance at the Day Schools, scholars dropping out more and more as the dance progressed. The sun dance had been abolished, and the rule had become established for the Omaha and the women's society dances to be held on Friday of each week.[218] The advent of the ghost dance now so demoralized the discipline which was being enforced on the Reservation and so interfered with the new habit of dancing, that the Indians, now disregarding former restraints, plunged into the dances which were not prohibited in a manner corresponding to the excitement which possessed them. Meanwhile the agent, through his farmers and the police force, by arresting and putting in the guardhouse some of the leaders, tried to stop it. ~~Late in July~~ About the middle of July 1890, Colonel Gallagher, the agent, ~~called a council of~~ began seriously to discuss with some of the farmers and other employees at the agency ~~to obtain their views on the situation and~~ the best methods to adopt in dealing with it. Excepting Mr. Wells, all present advised the use of stern measures and even force to put a stop to the dancing. He argued that to send the police in sufficient numbers to break it up would be unwise and only aggravate the trouble.[219] The farmers were sure that they could suppress the disturbance in their several districts with force. This gathering of advisors dispersed without coming to any settled conclusion.

    Some two weeks afterwards the police had nearly all collected at the agency, and one Sunday morning, after the Indians who had been gathering from all parts of the Reservation on the White Clay ten miles below the Agency and in the neighborhood of Young-Man-Afraid's place and had been dancing several days, the Agent called a council of the agency employees to decide how to deal with the dancers so assembled. Mr. Wells advised that the agent and himself and one of the principal chiefs go alone, unarmed, as a first attempt and talk to the Indians in a friendly way, giving good counsel and trying to persuade them to abandon the mischievous practice. He was unanimously overruled by all present. It was their plan to take the police, between 20 and 30, well armed, and go with this show of force to meet the Indians, and this was what the Agent did. Mr. Wells being of the positive opinion that this was a mistaken step, was taking notice on the way down of everything that was significant in appearance. He noticed that the women and children were at the houses, but no men were in sight. As these were participants in the ghost dance equally with the men, here was something which set him to thinking. It was a sign of some extreme resolution on the part of the warriors. The Indians had had two or three days for notice of this descent by the agent and his police, which had been assembling, as it was thought, for some decisive purpose.

Arriving at the scene of the dance the dancing ground was found to be vacant. Two or three houses stood near, and as this body approached one Indian with gun in hand ran out of one of the houses to the brow of a bank above the creek bottom and dropped on one knee in position to shoot. ~~Immediately the agent~~ He was joined by another who emerged from a thicket of brush adjacent to the dancing ground. Without a moment's delay the Agent ordered the police to dismount and arrest the first man. Mr. Wells was the interpreter. He gave the order in the Indian speech. The first lieutenant, Fast Horse, repeated the order and they all dismounted. Mr. Wells instantly directed the lieutenant to halt the men, but before the lieutenant did so he turned inquiringly as if he wished to know the reason, when Mr. Wells told him that he was doing this on his own ~~responsibility and~~ suggestion and would be responsible adding that the colonel did not know, whereupon the lieutenant catching the half-expressed meaning told his men to wait. The agent ~~seeing the police hesitating,~~ started toward the Indians himself, and Mr. Wells accompanying him a little ahead and crowding in front of him, he presently stopped, as though the danger of the situation was at that moment apprehended. By this time several Indian heads were discovered peering above the bank behind the two who had advanced ~~to the level bottom~~ toward the party. Gallagher said: "What do you mean when I come as your agent to talk to you and you draw guns on me?" Mr. Wells added to this to make it thoroughly affective: "Father I want you to obey me; put that gun down and come here." The son of this Indian had been especially friendly to Mr. Wells and according to Indian custom, Mr. W. addressed him as "father." It was the same custom for the Indian to answer by calling Mr. Wells "son"; and so he answered, at the same time laying down his gun and advancing. "Yes my son, I will obey you." Addressing the agent he said: "If you have come to me to talk as my father, why bring so many with guns?" The agent explained that it was the duty of the police to carry their arms wherever they went, and told him not to take offence. The situation was becoming satisfactory when an Indian came up from behind the bank with gun in hand and called out: "Where is Thunder Bear; why don't he stand in sight?" This was equivalent to a challenge. Thunder Bear was a Sergeant of the police against whom the Indian bore some grudge. Thunder Bear stepped out into view replying: "Here I am in sight; if you cannot see me I will come closer to you;" this being an acceptance of the other's challenge. At that instant several other Indians came up into view above the bank with their guns threateningly poised, and the police drew their own arms in readiness for use. At this juncture Chief Young-Man-

Afraid of His Horses arrived on the scene and set about to restore an amicable understanding and prevent bloodshed. This was soon done and the party returned to the agency.[220]

The writer inquired of Mr. Wells generally concerning Col. Gallagher as an agent. His reply was that he regarded Colonel Gallagher as a fearless man, a perfect gentleman, having good capacity for his position, was a useful and honest agent, and, had he not been handicapped by the appointing power would have become notable in the service. His subordinates, ~~were of such inferior~~ whom be did not select and whom he could not remove, were of such inferior quality as to thwart much of his good purpose. During the summer settlers living near the Reservation on the south and west were several times seized with alarm at false reports, given out of an Indian uprising and collected in assemblies for flight or protection and Col. Gallagher and Mr. Wells went out to assure them that their fears were groundless and to advise them to remain at their homes. That part of the prophecy of the Messiah which the Indians believed, to the effect that when the great cloud, which was to traverse the firmament from west to east should sweep athwart the heavens the white race would be destroyed, was not understood by the settlers who heard of it and interpreted it as meaning that the Indians would take to the warpath to accomplish the destruction; and this kept them in a state of nervous excitement ~~and later making demands for military protection~~ and afterwards led to appeals (or urgency or demands) for military protection.

Going back now to the reign of Agent V. T. McGillicuddy it is necessary to follow the mutations of political power and ambition and of religious bigotry in control of the reservation to understand the causes which led to the difficulties and disasters of 1890-1.[221]

When the Democratic party assumed the reins of government under Mr. Cleveland in 1885, McGillicudy, a courageous man but rank partisan whose native disposition was to rule arbitrarily and vigorously, was the agent. The Democratic press could not say enough against him as being corrupt, dishonest and tyrannical, and the Republican press was just as alert and devoted to his praise and defense as the other was strenuous and unscrupulous in efforts for his removal. He was a man, as I am told by Mr. Wells who has kindly stated his opinion in answer to my direct inquiry, who accomplished a great amount of good by having the Indians well started at making homes and engaging in stock raising, although he had taken them in their native and wild condition fresh from war, defeated, discontented, untrained, intractable and sullenly hostile, while thousands of their friends were beyond the line in Canada, unsubdued and full of hatred for the United States. Mr. Wells was not here during any part of McGillicuddy's administration; for he was at Turtle Mountain in charge of that Reservation when McGillicudy was removed and succeeded by ~~Capt. Charles G. Penny~~ Captain Bell of the 7th U.S. Cavalry; and what he says of McGillicuddy's work is his conclusion from the results which he subsequently had good opportunity to view and consider. Like the majority of Indian Agents, he was accused of being dishonest and making his own personal interests paramount to all other objects, notwithstanding it was confessed that he was achieving great success in benefits for the Indians. He was strong and independent and too firmly poised to become the weak tool of the army of rascals, scoundrels and thieves who infested the frontier service and had powerful friends entrenched in high places to care for their private and perhaps mutual interests. If McGillicuddy was a rascal, his gains were his exclusive profit never subjected to division with accomplices. He was the man who left the framework of whatever progress the Indians have made from the beginning of his labors on Pine Ridge Reservation. Replying to another question from me on the subject covered by his answer, Mr. Wells estimates that his was the only constructive work that has ever been done for these Indians; that he ~~cleared the ground~~ blazed the way through a maze of dangers and difficulties, made the opening and cleared the ground, laid at enduring depth the foundations of security and advancement and reared the framework of that fabric which civilization compels. Major Bell's service was of brief duration, so that he could not leave distinctive marks of a like or differing individuality. Colonel Gallagher's personal excellence was beyond dispute; but he was so hampered by those above him in authority that the best he could do was to hold together and maintain what had been built up before him. His term of four years was nearly equally divided between the administrations of Cleveland and Harrison. Not until about the end of Cleveland's term was the agent given any choice in the selection of his subordinates. So Gallagher found no great occasion to introduce reforms, to elevate the service and extend improvements. McGillicudy had been removed for recalcitrancy when the Bureau had appointed a chief clerk to take the place of the one he had _____ [Donald] Brown (?) and he refused to accept him. Under Harrison, Gallagher found himself meanly assailed for two artificial defects—his politics and his religion. Commissioner Morgan was a narrow partisan and still narrower sectarian.[222] He was Republican and Protestant. Gallagher was Democrat and Catholic. This ought to have caused no friction and would not if the Commissioner had been capable of statesmanlike views. Gallagher being of an opposite political faith, Morgan had no desire to allow him to make ~~a noticeable~~ much reputation, and he being a Catholic, Morgan was careful not to encourage that church in its aspirations, if he was not hopeful to thwart them altogether. Therefore the agent was remarkably successful when he was able to hold his own. ~~Captain Charles G. Penny came after Agent Dr. Royer (of Woonsocket, S.D.) came after him~~

The Commissioner cut down the rations and the allowance of beef which had been promised by the Commissioners who negotiated the treaty of 1889, should be continued as under the earlier treaty. These arbitrary and demoralizing acts fomented the disturbances which harassed Gallagher's closing months of duty, for the reason that it put the Indians on a starvation basis. Suffering from hunger created wide spread discontent.[223] This state of unavoidable feeling was the soil in which the Messiah Craze took root. It enabled the leaders with designs and wrongs urging them, to harangue and influence the others and to work up a formidable cohesion and organization, and finally to upset all order and bring civil government to an end. Dr. Royer (of Woonsocket, S.D.) came after him, and with him a change of policy also; this latter, however, wrought no effect in the mental attitude of the Indians, or gave hope of a solution of the

Philip F. Wells interview continued from Tablet No. [5].

[Tablet 4]

grave problem which the government began to feel that its shortsighted policy had engendered.[224] The Indians were not to be appeased with tardy justice coming in the form of beefsteaks; for now they were beginning to satisfy the cravings of hunger by slaughtering the cattle found at large on the Reservation, and the new remedy was wanting in efficacy. The evil had been put in motion by faithless administrative orders, creating a whirlwind now beyond control, and it was growing apparent that the sower must reap what he had sown. It is not denied that the Commissioner could find some justification for his course based on the reports of farmers on the Reservation who gave glowing accounts of successful Indian husbandry. The changing of farmers frequently was deleterious; few of these had any qualifications or could boast of so much as common interest in the welfare of the helpless natives on whose behalf they were employed. Every succeeding one realized the urgency and helpfulness to himself of making it appear in his showing that the improvement he had made over his predecessor was considerable; and so it was in the aggregate that the Commissioner discovered no little encouragement to do the unwise things which precipitated disaffection tumult and war. When Mr. Wells was appointed farmer at Medicine Root district, by Agent Gallagher, in August, 1890, he found not more than half of the agricultural progress which the reports pretended to describe. Truck patches and gardens varying in area from one-fourth of an acre to a full acre were about the extent of what had been accomplished. These were often on high ground where no crop would grow productively. The larger part of all that had been done was only evidence that these farmers were such only in official designation; that both knowledge and inclination were wanting to make them fit for the places to which they had been assigned.

The unsettled division between the Pine Ridge and the Rosebud Reservations requires some notice before proceeding farther. These two reservations were established at the time of the return from the Missouri River in 1878. The divisional line was in a general way recognized accepted as ~~along Bear Creek~~ somewhere between Bear Creek and Eagle Nest Butte. In 1888 Capt. Pratt of the Carlisle school headed a commission which came out for the purpose of obtaining a treaty ceding the country between the Big White River and the Missouri River. In the bill passed by Congress creating this commission it was provided that the boundary between the two reservations should be on Pass Creek, some 12 miles east of the Bear Creek division. The Pratt commission failed to obtain the consent of the Indians to the proposed treaty.[225] In the fall of the same year a delegation consisting of the Agents of Pine Ridge, Rosebud, Crow Creek, Cheyenne Agency and Standing Rock and their interpreters and a lot of Indian delegates, including Mr. Wells, all comprising about 80 persons, went to Washington and held conferences with the Secretary of the Interior.[226] On the application of Mr. Wells and Fast Thunder it was agreed that the line between Pine Ridge and Rosebud should be moved still farther east along the Black Pipe Creek where it was established by the next bill passed by Congress for the appointment of the Sioux Commission of 1889. The treaty was accepted by the Sioux and ratified by the government.[227] While the commission was at the Rosebud Agency the Pass Creek Indians refused to sign the treaty for fear they would be obliged to give up their homes and move eastwardly to establish themselves within the limits of the Rosebud Reservation, as they were enrolled therein. The commission promised them that if they would consent to the treaty they should be transferred to the rolls of the Pine Ridge Reservation and with this understanding they gave their signatures. The treaty was ratified in March, and soon after, the Indians began to ask to be enrolled at Pine Ridge. The Agent assured them that they would be transferred, while the Agent at Rosebud as positively affirmed that they would not; and thus they were kept in unrest by these diverse statements alternately acting on their fears for their homes.[228] This continued during the summer and fall, and along about the forepart of December they decided to go in a body to Pine Ridge Agency in the hope that they might now secure their enrollment there, thinking that the Agent would do this for them as an inducement to hold them at that place through the ~~disturbed~~ turbulence which was at its height. (Mr. Wells says this was the scheme of the Indians.) Information had gone out that the U.S. troops were going to concentrate at Pine Ridge Agency. Agent Royer had called for military assistance, and the forces were arriving.[229] This acted as a spur to drive the Indians into [a] defensive attitude. When the Indians on the Rosebud reservation learned what these Pass Creek Indians were about to do, ~~they gathered~~ the ghost-dancing element gathered together and marched over to Pine Ridge Reservation and took these, as Dog Soldiers would have done, along with them, and sending couriers in advance to announce their coming to the various settlements of Indians on Pine Ridge, a general movement took place as they moved away all together when these from Rosebud came among them. The Indians in the western part of Pine Ridge Reservation moved toward those advancing, and a meeting took place in the Wounded Knee region. The united bodies agreed to take up a position in the bad lands [called The Stronghold] and they at once moved to it. It was upon ~~a mesa~~ an elevation difficult of access, which in the southwest would be called a mesa. The main part of this table was some 4 miles long and 2 miles wide, and it could be ascended only at the eastern and western extremities; at the latter the passage-way was much broader in extent and easier grade, while the other was of trifling width and more difficult ascent. This place occupied by the Indians is sometimes erroneously called Sheep Mountain. Sheep Mountain is a tall peak near the mesa. On the north side and near the east end there was a spur of this mesa containing about 1,000 acres, and at the point where it connected with the main table it narrowed to a small neck, 5 or 6 rods across. From the elevated position they had taken they kept a vigilant watch to guard against approach and surprise. They had taken their families with them, and also a herd of cattle for their subsistence. They climbed up the east passage-way. This mesa was surrounded by a perpendicular wall of Bad Land rock, except at the points mentioned. When Gen. Brooke arrived at the Agency he began to send out Indian messengers to these Indians to establish communication with them in the interest of peace, but these were driven off by threats and refusal to receive them, until Father Jutz (pronounced Uts) (He was a Jesuit priest at Holy Rosary Mission) and Jack Red Cloud, son of the noted chief Red Cloud, were sent out by General Brooke.[230] The Indians received Father Jutz kindly and agreed to surrender if the terms proposed should be satisfactory, and it is understood that they proposed some conditions which they would insist on. Father Jutz returned to the Agency and later made another trip into the Bad Lands, and obtained their surrender. They returned with him and went into camp on White Clay below the Mission. (It was now that Prof. Bailey called at the Mission and was hospitably entertained by Father Jutz overnight and given every information in his power to assist him in his writings, and granted his request to go out next day with Father Jutz to the Indian camp and ride by his side at the head of the column while coming into the Agency; and afterwards he assailed the Catholics and Father Jutz and accused them with responsibility for the war, and falsely told how the priests received the confessions of the Indians and made charges and took payment in furs and bead work for forgiveness of their sins, etc.)[231] (Get Father Jutz's address from the Father Superior, Holy Rosary Mission, Pine Ridge.)

The next morning they moved in and pitched camp on the ridge north of Wolf Creek and the Agency. Provisions had been sent out to them from the Agency to their camp below the Mission. Sitting Bull had been killed on or about December 15 and the authorities were desirous to secure the surrender of the hostiles and get their arms before the latter could be informed by couriers that fighting had begun and the old chief was dead.[232] After Sitting Bull's death a party consisting of about 100 Indians left Standing Rock Agency. These were relatives and followers of Sitting Bull. An Indian scout named Standing Soldier, belonging to Capt. Taylor's Scouts, was sent out with a squad by Mr. Wells who was the chief of scouts with instructions to go near the head of Medicine Root Creek and get on the east divide and follow north thereon to the Big White River, thence back to the Agency, for the purpose of ascertaining the whereabouts of Big Foot and his band. This band of 100 from Standing Rock, it is understood, were seeking to join the hostiles in the Bad Lands, and having discovered the U.S. soldiers stationed by General Carr, they made a wide detour to the east expecting to pass around their flank and rear and affect a junction with their friends in spite of the obstacle they had found in their way.[233]

Standing Soldier met these Indians on the divide and persuaded them to believe that the soldiers had surrounded the hostile position in the Bad Lands, and that the best thing for them to do would be to go into the Agency where all the friendly Indians were camped. He sent a courier forward to ~~advise General Brooke~~ inform Captain Taylor that he was coming with this party, when the latter came in sight of the battle of Wounded Knee, but swiftly returned to let Standing ~~Bear~~ Soldier know of what had occurred directly in his path. Standing Soldier was obliged to deceive the Indians by telling them that there were troops in their way and that it would be necessary to move into the sand hills ~~south toward~~ in a wide circuit and come into the Agency from the south. Standing Soldier arrived with his prisoners at the Agency sometime in the night of the 30th. These Indians had slipped away from Standing Rock unknown to the Agent, James McLaughlin, or to General Sumner. They camped south of the Agency with the friendly Indians.

There were a few Indians who were acting as neutrals who were camped on the ridge north of Wolf Creek before the hostiles were brought there. The very friendly Indians were south of the Agency and near the military.

(I omit an account of Carr's and Sumner's forces over north, as Mr. Wells knows about these only from hearsay. See Gus Craven who was a scout for Carr.)[234]

Big Foot slipped away from ~~Standing Rock~~ Cheyenne River Reservation and from General ~~Carr~~ Sumner. He came down through the Bad Lands, descending into the White River valley through the Big Foot pass which took its name from him, and crossed the White River a little above Interior, S.D. and near the mouth of Medicine Root Creek, and moved southward to Porcupine Butte, from which place he was proceeding northwest when he was intercepted by the scouts.

(Capt. Taylor had two troops of scouts; Mr. W. thinks there were 100 of the Sioux Troop, and 50 of the Troop of Cheyennes. The Northern Cheyennes were settled at Pine Ridge Agency as a part of the Pine Ridge Indians; but after the troubles of the year they were at their request allowed to remove to and settle on Tongue River. There were two other troops of scouts consisting of young Indians and boys who were ~~enlisted~~ organized after the battle in the hope of enlisting them in the U.S. service, but the plan failed, and they never did anything. There were also a body of headquarters scouts—7 or 8 in number, among whom were Big Bat, Little Bat, Frank Gruard, Louis Shangrau, John Shangrau, No Neck, Woman's Dress.)

On the 28th the scouts located Big Foot at Porcupine Butte. A courier was sent to Major Whiteside at Wounded Knee, who had been out there two or three days. Whiteside marched with the cavalry to Big Foot and found his men drawn up in line, but after a parley it was agreed that they should come in with the soldiers and camp at W.K.

The Battle

Mr. Wells spent the night before the battle about half a mile down the road leading to the Agency, with a troop of Capt. Taylor's scouts. These came out the night before with Col. Forsyth and arrived about 11 P.M. In the morning after taking breakfast where they had camped that night, he could see that the soldiers were drawn up between the Indians and the Wounded Knee Creek. The positions were about as follows. [Figure 1]

(The fragments following are intended to supplement in detail the written statement made by Mr. Wells and copied in Tablet [5].)

Mr. Wells adds to his written statement at this place the following details:

Colonel Forsyth turned away while Mr. Wells was watching and listening to the medicine man on the west side of the circle, who was facing to the west and holding up his hands and praying for protection. The Colonel asked Mr. W. what the man was saying. "It is nothing but a harmless prayer that he is saying, Colonel; but don't disturb me, for I must pay very close attention to catch all he means; however, I will let you know just as soon as he says anything you should know." "All right," answered the Colonel, and he walked away. Then the medicine man stopped praying, and stooping down took some dirt and rose up facing the west, raised his two hands, and still facing the west cast the dirt with a circular motion of his hand toward the soldiers in rear. Then he walked round the circle, and when he got back to the starting point on the west side he stopped and uttered exclamations which in Sioux signify regret, and that he has decided on a desperate course; for instance if he has submitted to abuse, insult or wrong with patience and fortitude but has made up his mind to retaliate or take revenge upon the offender, he exclaims: "Haha! Haha! I have lived long enough" (which means in Sioux that he is ready to give his life for this purpose). ~~Now Continue with the written statement from the top of page 30. 7th line from the bottom on page 30, viz. "then he turned toward the young bucks etc"~~

Then he turned toward the young ~~bucks~~ men who were standing together and said: "Do not be afraid and let your hearts be strong to meet what is before you; we are all well aware that there are lots of soldiers about us and that they have lots of bullets; but I have received assurance that their bullets cannot penetrate us. The prairie is large and the bullet will not go toward you but over the large prairies, and if they do go towards you they will not penetrate you. As you saw me throw up the dust and it floated away, so will the bullets float away harmlessly over the prairies." (Mr. W. does not want the word "buck" used. He did not and never does use it.)

Mr. Wells then stepped to Big Foot's brother-in-law to talk with him and get him to try to quiet and pacify the Indians. This brother-in-law impressed Mr. Wells by his better dress and his generally intelligent appearance as a man of more than average parts—as a rather superior Indian. Just then Colonel Forsyth called out to him saying that he better get out of there, for it was beginning to look dangerous. Mr. Wells answered, "In a minute, Colonel; I want to see if I cannot get this fellow to quiet them." Then he addressed the Indian and said: "Friend, go in among the young men and quiet them, and talk to them as a man of your age should." This was said to him in a low ~~whisper~~ tone so that the others should not hear. He replied, very loud so that all the Indians could hear his words: "Why, friend, your heart seems to beat. Why, who is talking of trouble or fighting?" "Yes, friend, my heart beats when I see so many helpless women and children if anything should happen," replied Mr. Wells. "Friend, it is unnecessary that your heart should beat," again said in a loud voice by the Indian. After the Indian's first reply to Wells a ~~young and~~ powerfully built young man stepped out of the circle and came around to where these two were standing and talking. He kept taking steps slowly as though he intended to get behind Mr. Wells without his observing what he was doing. But Mr. Wells suspected his purpose and was watching him, and as the young Indian moved around, he ~~himself~~ kept turning his own body so that he did not get in rear of him; at the same time, seeing that he could not persuade the older Indian, he ~~was talking~~ continued to talk attempting to change the subject. He held his rifle with both hands at the muzzle, the butt resting on the ground. The young Indian had no gun under his blanket, but Mr. Wells could not tell but he had a revolver or a knife concealed, and he was reflecting on the different modes of attack which this Indian might be contemplating—whether he would grapple ~~him~~ and try to overpower him—whether he would strike him with a club or knife—whether he would shoot with a revolver—or whatever else he would attempt to do to dispose of Mr. Wells and get his gun; for one of his main objects was to obtain that, as Mr. Wells saw from the way he was eyeing it. He dared not turn his back on the Indian, but began to move backwards with the intention that when he got far enough from him to walk away with safety he would ~~walk~~ get out of the circle. By this time Mr. Wells was convinced that a clash was coming. On that instant he heard the cry to his rear and left, coming from the direction of the soldiers, "Look out! Look out!" Wells threw his gun into position of "port" and turned his head quickly to the left and rear for a look at the Indians standing in a circle; one Indian near the center of the circle stood facing the soldiers with his gun pointing at an upward angle — in the last position in which a hunter holds his piece before placing it to his shoulder to fire; still holding his gun so, it was discharged, the contents going into the air, over the soldiers' heads, as the smoke indicated. At that instant 5 or 6 young warriors behind him threw off their blankets and drew their guns. Mr. Wells says that when this first shot was fired and the Indians dropped their blankets and drew their guns, he heard the command which sounded like Colonel Forsyth's voice: "Fire! Fire on them!" Mr. Wells states that the soldiers were the next to fire after the first gun went off. Mr. Wells having the Indian near him in his thought, turned toward him, both movements occupying but only an instant of time; the Indian was already upon him with an upraised long butcher knife ground to a sharp point, in the act of dealing a deadly blow. A man of surprising agility, Mr. Wells dropped on one knee, at the same time throwing up his gun with both hands as a guard, and ducking his head to avoid a blow in his face, the Indian's wrist struck the gun, but the knife was long enough to reach his nose which was nearly severed, and hung down over his mouth, held by the skin. Before Mr. Wells could rise, the Indian renewed the attack, standing over him with the savage knife uplifted and trying to grasp his gun with his left hand. It was a desperate play between life and death and lasted but a moment. Mr. Wells, holding the gun above his head kept it in swift motion as a guard against the knife; the Indian now summoned all his strength to break down the guard with a furious blow and the weight of his body, and raising his blade higher in the air for the mighty stroke he opened his own guard and Wells gave him a blow on the ear with the muzzle of his gun which staggered stunned him. This gave Wells time to regain his feet. The Indian staggered back a step or two. Wells sprang backwards. Now they are three paces apart. Wells leveled his piece at his breast; the Indian was glaring into his eyes; to escape the shot that he thought could not be withheld he turned a quarter round and dropped on his hands and knees; Wells had saved his fire; like a flash the muzzle of the gun went down and the bullet entered the Indian's side below the arm; he pitched forward on his face dead. Then a corporal rushed up to the prostrate body, placed the muzzle of his own gun between the shoulders and fired. About the same instant a bullet struck him inflicting a mortal wound from which he died in a day or two in the hospital at the Agency. Having vanquished his foe Wells started for shelter behind the wagon close by in which some of the guns taken from the Indians had been placed. While running he slipped on the grass and nearly fell; a young brave who it was afterwards learned, was following him, dealt a blow with his knife from behind, intending to stab between neck and shoulder, overreached and left a cut in the front of Wells' coat.

(This wagon is the one of which McFarland speaks as being almost overturned by the mules swinging round. Mr. Wells describes the incident. As he was running towards it a bullet hit one of the leaders and the animals plunged and swung round, upset the wagon, and mules and wagon were tangled up. Some of the men disengaged them.)

Mr. Wells remained in the action until the main part was over; when he was taking aim with his gun the piece of his nose suspended by the skin was in the way and once he tried to pull it off but could not, and it is well that for him that it would not yield, for it was replaced by the surgeon and he has had many years' use of it since and it has performed its offices functions, including that of good appearance, down to the present time. Lieut. Preston saw him in the fight covered with blood, and came up and asked if he was badly hurt, and seeing his condition led him away to the surgeon. Preston was the second in command of the Taylor scouts.

Killing of Capt. Wallace

Capt. Wallace was killed in rear of his troop K.[235] He was struck by a bullet in the upper part of his forehead and it tore through the top of his skull. Mr. Wells saw him carried on a stretcher and saw his wound and was told by good authority that he bore no other wound. Mr. Wells confirms what McFarland has said about the Indians falling back up the ravine and whenever the place where one was concealed hidden was discovered, a Hotchkiss shell was thrown there, etc.

The first dispatch from the battlefield to the Agency announcing what had taken place was borne by Lieut. Guy Preston accompanied by a soldier of the 7th Cavalry.

I asked Mr. Wells his opinion as to the intention of Big Foot as to giving the whites battle, and he said:

"I do not believe they had any intention of fighting, and for these reasons, first: when Major Whiteside met Big Foot at Porcupine Butte Big Foot was drawn up in battle array and was perhaps equal to Whiteside in numbers, or nearly so.

"Second, the ground was in his favor, being adapted to the Indian style of fighting; whereas, the soldiers would have had, for awhile at least, to operate on the open plain.

"Third, after the Indians knew they were discovered and the troops were coming, the Indians had ample time for defensive preparations and did not improve the opportunity to make themselves more impregnable. "When Whiteside met them he formed his troops in line of battle. While in these positions a long parley took place. If the Indians had not been willing to yield they could have retreated safely with the landscape favoring their movements and their rear guard fighting.

"Fourth, but the Indians surrendered. This was where the actual surrender was. When they came to Wounded Knee they were prisoners in possession of their arms. The battle there was over the question of giving up the guns. Big Foot admitted the principle which Forsyth contended for, namely, that the Indians should surrender their weapons, but used evasion to avoid doing so. The Indians had delivered before the action only some inferior pieces." See Mr. W.'s written statement.

Mr. Wells believes the Indians put up a bluff, but it got away from their control, it was carried too far, till the young warriors plunged over the danger line and precipitated the tragedy. He relates the following circumstance:

After the action he stood by the dead body of Big Foot's brother-in-law, and after Indian custom addressed the dead man "Haha!" the Indian exclamation of regret. "Friend, I tried to save you but you would not obey me, and now you have destroyed yourself." At that the wounded Indians lying within hearing uttered their approval of what he said, by the usual "How." They had heard him in conversation with this man before the battle and knew from the Indian's answers that Wells was pleading with him to pacify the people.

Correction. Mr. Wells wishes to correct his statement about what occurred in the Club room at the Agency. He does not intend to intimate that certain officers were for or against either Miles or Forsyth. But he has been informed on what he considers good authority that he offended General Miles by his statements at the time bearing on the action at W. K. After the battle his pay was raised from $75 to $100 a month and he was informed through the regular channel that as long as he continued in the service he would receive the latter compensation; this was in consideration of former valuable services as well as for present worth. But he was kept in the field till all the positions were filled and no place remained for him. General Miles was in command of this Dept. The fact is Wells was frozen out. He wants the Club room incident dropped.

In the battle Father Francis M. J. Croft was wounded. Read the account on the back of the picture lent me by Mr. Wells. The latter says the Rev. Father Croft was the bravest of the brave, most earnest, enthusiastic and sincere in his duty.[236]

I like to hold up examples of heroism. The Catholic missionaries stood their ground to a man. The sisters or nuns did likewise, while the Protestant missionaries removed with their families to the railroad.

Mr. Wells says that when the main part of the action was over at W. K. he sent a scout to the by Lieut. Preston, who went with his dispatch from Forsyth to the Agency about 9 A.M., for protection to be furnished for his wife and children. Preston found that they were safe. A little later Wells sent an Indian scout, one of Taylor's named White Deer, and on his way to the Agency he met some Indian friends relatives who told him that the Indian women had removed them to the Mission, and he returned to W. K.

Engagement Near Drexel Mission
(properly Holy Rosary Mission) Dec. 30, 1890

When Mr. Wells reached the Agency the night of the battle about 10 or 11 o'clock P.M. he went to the hospital inside the Agency enclosure, in hospital tents and saw 30 or 40 wounded soldiers and the surgeons were very busy. He stepped in and was shown by a doctor a place in another tent where he could lie down, there being plenty of robes. He rested there till daylight. Word came that the Holy Rosary Mission was on fire, all its occupants having been killed. His wife was teaching a Day School on the hill south of the Mission and on the south side of the big ravine just south of the Mission. She had two young children which she kept with her. This Day Sch. had been built before the Mission. The latter was begun to be built in the summer of 1887, the same season Mr. Wells came from the north.

Mr. Wells heard the report and alarm given outside; he jumped up and buckled on his revolver and grabbed his rifle. The first thought in his mind was that his family was killed, and as he came out he saw several cavalry horses saddled and cow ponies with cowboy saddles; from these not knowing to whom any of them belonged, he selected what looked to be the best cow pony and mounted and started for the Mission. He flew half-crazed and heedlessly for a mile. Then, recovering his equilibrium, he began to reason. Until now, contemplating revenge for the death of his family, he asked himself, "Am I likely to get revenge by this wild chase when I may dash into an ambush and be killed?" A second thought was quickly in his mind, and that was to exonerate the Indians and to wreak his vengeance on the authors of these horrible scenes and bereavements; and these were instantly depicted in his mind, standing out as the responsible monsters who should pay swift penalty for this crime. He seized the instant resolve to take their lives upon sight, and if the consequences be to ~~close to~~ follow his murdered family, that he would do so as his free choice and cheerfully. He would first make affectionate disposition of their remains. He dashed onward now taking precautions against surprise and ambuscade. Smoke was rising in dense volume in the direction of the Mission. He was now convinced that the news was correct and that the worst could be expected. Riding a mile and a half farther, to his great joy he discovered that the conflagration was at the Day School where he had been living; a little farther on he saw the spire of the Mission church standing unharmed; and then his thoughts and feelings were changed to thanksgiving and gratitude, and the war within himself was over. Mrs. Wells was at the Day School in the forenoon on the 29th of Dec., 1890. About 11 A.M. she noticed that there was commotion among the young Indians, at first the children, and then it spread to older ones, the parents gathering at the school and talking to the children, the meaning not being apprehended by Mrs. Wells; about noon or a little after she noticed that the young men were stripping to a war footing; that is, were naked except the breech clout, and they were bestirring themselves and getting their ponies. An Indian woman came and asked Mrs. Wells, who guessed from her signs, to go to the Mission; Mrs. W. tried to put her off for a little while till she could finish clearing away her dinner table; but the woman was persistent, and as Mrs. Wells seemed in no hurry to go, she caught the younger child, Alma, in her arms and started off on the run ~~with her in her arms~~ (the child was nearly 3 years old) to the Mission. Mrs. Wells did not understand what it all meant, but she had a secret fear that the woman was kidnapping the little girl; so she grasped the boy Tommy who was between 5 and 6 years old, and ran after her as hard as she could. They reached the Mission nearly together; but when Mrs. Wells saw the woman directing her course to the Mission she felt relieved, ~~though~~ but she could not conjecture what the trouble was all about, though she realized that some danger was impending. Mrs. Wells went to Father Jutz, the Father Superior, and inquired the cause of so much commotion, but he did not know. He said he was just starting to the Agency to learn the cause. He was not gone more than half an hour when he returned and said that he had been stopped by the Indians who would not let him pass, but they told him that there was fighting going on and to go back and stay at the Mission. He advised Mrs. Wells to remain there also, and she stayed. That ~~night~~ afternoon and night people kept coming and going, and about 20 persons from the neighborhood were there all the time. Some sat up and spent the slow hours of suspense in conversation; others retired, but there was no sleep at the Holy Rosary Mission that night.

It should be observed that from the beginning of the difficulties the Indians had told Father Jutz to keep within the enclosure around the Mission and he would be safe; that those precincts would be treated as sacred, and that all that was therein would receive protection and be exempt from danger. When it became apparent to the hostile Indians that there was probability of fighting, the full bloods had quietly notified their half-blood relations that, if it came, they had better go to the Mission, for they would be safe in that place, as it was agreed among all of them that the enclosed premises of the institution should not be invaded. Father Jutz had been specified as the only friend the Indians had among the whites on the Reservation.

(I should have stated farther back that when Mrs. Wells went to the Mission she found it practically emptied; there were not more than a dozen children remaining; the others had run away; and the Father Superior was in the dark as to what was causing the exodus.)

Mrs. Wells states that on the morning of the 30th many straggling Indians who were passing the Mission from the direction of the Agency towards their rendezvous north of there, stopped at the gate and were fed by the Sisters of St. Francis, Mrs. Wells herself assisting. Later the soldiers came along, as they had been ordered out in that direction to reconnoiter and extend succor to any who were in peril. These, hearing that the Mission was on fire, left the Agency without breakfast, and as they passed along were also fed as the Indians had been. Mrs. Wells says that the Indians had been refreshed in the same manner on the 29th. This was done by carving bread and meat and carrying these out on trays and large vessels.

Returning to Mr. Wells, he states that he reached the Mission and found everything all right. ~~The 7th Cavalry followed down~~

On the 29th these Indians about the Mission and north of the Agency gathered, apart on the ridge north of Wolf Creek and fired into the Agency. See other accounts for description of this. A part of these hostiles moved to W. K. and were driven off by the cavalry as elsewhere stated by Mr. Wells. On the night of the 29th the fighting Indians at the Agency fell back to a position about 12 miles north of the Agency and about 4 miles east of the White Clay, in the hills, a good position, well protected, a very broken, hilly country. The Indians who had marched to Wounded Knee retired from there and joined these in the new position in the hills.

On the morning of the 30th, about daylight, the 7th Cavalry was ordered out and moved down past the Mission, and were regaled there with a piece of bread and meat which each took from the baskets of the donors as he passed. They went about two miles below the Mission, where they were fired on from the hill tops near the rear of the column. The firing came from one side. The troops formed, facing the danger, though no Indians could be seen. Then came a hostile volley from the opposite side of the column. A disposition of some of the soldiers was made to meet the fire from this quarter. Then a fresh fire came into the column from the front. Then some more troops were wheeled into position to repel this attack. It looked as though the enemy had closed in on all sides, and the concern was that they had established themselves in the rear as well as elsewhere. This situation lasted an hour or more until the 9th Cavalry appeared. The situation was felt to be critical because the Indians kept out of sight and it was impossible to tell whether they were all around the troops, nor could their numbers be conjectured. Not more than three or four could be seen at any one time. Lieut. Mann of the 7th Cavalry was wounded and afterwards died.[237] A soldier of the 7th Cavalry was killed. Three Indians were wounded. One of these died afterwards.

As was afterwards learned these shots came from 30 or 40 young Indians who were without experience, some of whom had returned from eastern schools. They fired from one side, then ran to another place and fired, then repeated this in another place. The 9th Cavalry made one charge, the boys scattered and hid, and the affair was done. Mr. Wells considered at the time that the troops were in a dangerous situation and that was the universal feeling.

About a month after this affair Mr. Wells was ordered to investigate this, and he did so. He found that this force of young men had been directed by the Indians at the rendezvous not to engage the troops that might come in sight, but to get what information they could and retire before them and report, so that the main body might be put in readiness for battle. End of Wounded Knee Battle and the affair at the mission.

Various Topics on Which Mr. Wells Gives Views

He has done more or less interpreting in court for 20 years, and he says not a case has come within his knowledge which was between a white man and an

Indian in which the latter did not lose. Mr. Wells was satisfied of the impartiality of the judge. Juries, he thinks, are taken from the inferior intelligence of the community. They are often packed. There is prejudice against the Indian also. And then prosecuting attorneys and other attorneys who are reputed to be working for the Indian are not always reliable.

Question: "Mr. Wells, will you state why, after holding important positions in the Indian service, and being one of the best of interpreters, and ~~having by a variety of employments by~~ having an extensive acquaintance with Indian character and habits, and qualified yourself by a variety of employments, that you are not holding a position in the government service?"

Answer: "The qualifications of which you speak are such a personal detriment to one who aspires to serve in government employ that he is barred therefrom. I always loved to work among the Indians; and at a time when I saw some men holding positions because of merit, I had beautiful dreams of what I would do in the future when I should have qualified myself for usefulness; but when I had fitted myself to be of benefit to my people I discovered that qualifications are not ~~required~~ wanted but that something else is; that instead of these being a recommendation they are a drawback. Those dreams of promise have turned to realities which are revelations. If I had known then what I now know as the result of experience, I should not have spent the better part of my life for ~~acquisitions~~ a special knowledge which is of little financial benefit to me and cannot be put to service for my unhappy kindred who need ~~their practical~~ it for their improvement. I therefore yield to the inevitable, feeling at the same time that a man may have an honorable ambition to do good to his fellows, and thus have a source of large personal happiness apart from all merely sordid considerations."

Question: "Have you no expectation of employment in the Indian service?"

Answer: "None at all, unless the Indians shall first be emancipated from the evils of our partisan system which places them under the immediate supervision of men who are in most cases inferior in acquirements and incompetent to instruct, assist and civilize the Indian."

Question: "In your opinion would it have been more beneficial for the Indians to be under the War Department than under the Interior Department?"

Answer: "Yes. ~~The War Dept would have~~ Under the War department the Indians would have escaped the ravages of politics to a great extent."

Question: "Did not the appointment of army officers as agents since the

Indians passed under the control of the Interior department obviate your objections?"

Answer: "No. I can speak only concerning Pine Ridge Reservation with which I have been familiar since the year 1887. The detail of army officers as agents began at Pine Ridge in 1891. I think the system a mistaken one. It brings from the army the class of men least desirable in character. Those who are 'good riddances' are most likely to be selected for this special duty. If the Indians were in charge of the War department which would be responsible before the country for their successful treatment the better class of officers would be placed over them, and a higher rate of progress would be the result."

Question: "Have you had acquaintance with the service when the Indians were under the War Dept?"

Answer: "No. But I have seen the Indians held as prisoners of war by the army at different times. My observation was that the officers in charge were invariably men of high character, scrupulous as to the truth, and as painstaking in treatment of the lowliest Indian, and as ~~regardful~~ careful to tell him the truth as they would be with any other man. They regarded the Indian as a man. It was not always so when the agents on reservations were detailed from the army."

Question: "Mr. Wells, you have allowed me to interview you at your house on the subject of the Indians for ten consecutive days. May I ask you if you have ever before given an interview for publication either wholly or partly?"

Answer: "At different times I have consented to be interviewed for publication. Before I went far I discovered the object was a special or sensational one; and then I cut them short, because I ~~am opposed to such things~~ object to making a statement for either purpose."

Question: "Mr. Wells, can you state any facts which illustrate the degree of efficiency in the service on any of the reservations?"

Answer: "I refer only to Pine Ridge Reservation on which I live. I have made a study of ~~20 years~~ certain methods pursued during a residence here of 20 years. I have noticed that a given policy adopted to attain a desirable end defeats its own intention by producing an opposite result, and in the face of this effect the policy is adhered to without change. I will speak first of the denial of privileges. Take as a specimen illustration of how the business is generally done, the case of ~~wood on the reservation~~ timber, wood, and hay. There is a large quantity of timber in many parts; a great deal of this falls annually and enters into decay and becomes waste. ~~Reason would~~ Common sense ought to teach that ~~this waste~~ it would be better if this waste was prevented and turned to the little profit which could be derived from the wood when it is cut and sold. The effect of allowing, and more, encouraging the Indians to work up and save such fuel and get a little income would be educative and improving, by inviting industry, teaching economy and helping the natives to understand more of their ability to provide for themselves, and to give more practice in buying and selling. Settlers living off the reservation would like to buy the wood and pay good prices. Perhaps only a few of the Indians would give much attention to this kind of work. But these would become an example to others who could see how much labor properly directed was doing for the few. If not many were by these attracted to the same kind of work, they would to some extent be stimulated to labor in other ways. The object of helping them to think and devise would lead them gradually into higher attempts along the white man's way. Instead of such an intelligent policy, when an Indian wants a permit to save wood that is wasting and to earn something from his labor, he is forbidden to exercise the privilege and thus to ~~exercise~~ develop his powers. One source of good is cut off and a source of evil opened. This restriction, when multiplied by other equally indefensible ones, produces a situation which is discouraging and repressive. The road for him which should be a thoroughfare of opportunities is unwisely narrowed and hedged in until he is driven to day labor for others. Day labor is the first pleasing condition in the gamut of resources above starvation. The government, with benign intent, has reluctantly undertaken to instill enlightenment into darkened minds, as they have been called, and to civilize for their own and the nation's good, our native population. Would it not be well to turn all means for improvement to practical account in the course of the instruction proposed? Why not make the instruction active and real rather than passive and stagnant? So long as there is the pretense of making out of the Indian a new creature, a citizen and useful member of society, and making generous expenditure to realize this purpose, should there not be faithful endeavor along the whole line and at every point upon it? Else of what use to the country is the keeping of such an enormous establishment as the Indian Bureau and the pay of salaries to thousands of employees? Is the service mainly for the doling out of bread and butter to these? Intelligent thinkers should ponder this question.

"On Pine Ridge thousands of dollars have been paid for the making of roads and of irrigating ditches. It is not a delightful task to speak against such popular and generally useful improvements. They look admirable upon paper and stunningly plausible in reports — and are irresistible in public prints. But it cannot be gainsaid that money may be wondrously lavished upon works of beneficial character and at the same time partially and even totally wasted. Some have been irreverent enough to venture the sacrilegious hint that possibly something like this has been the result at Pine Ridge. Indians do the work. It is a school for day labor. It has not stirred a creative or resourceful thought in one Indian. It is affirmed that the road making has been carried much beyond any need of it, and that the ditching has not made a single Indian family one cent better off in Pass Creek district.

"Another feature of the evil mentioned is that legitimate avenues are closed to the Indian who aspires. Still another feature is that the Indian whose aspirations run about an even race with indifference, sees an opening for gain by cutting the valuable cedars growing on the hills and in the valleys and ~~marketing these~~ making them into fence posts and marketing them to stockmen. It may be said that this is unlawful. But then, by denying a legitimate income, the Indian is pinched till he resorts to the less legitimate and the openly dishonest and lawless. His education has tendency downward, not upward. Swelling pretensions impress him unfavorably. Civilization has its farcical sides. The Indian laughs while he is idle under its banners and its deceptions and its platitudes. Farming, notwithstanding all the ditching for irrigation uses, has actually retrograded. Where once farms and homes were fairly thriving, now only patches of weeds, and the decaying evidences of a tolerable Indian agriculture and prosperity mark the locations."

At this point Eagle Elk entered and I asked him to tell me how the management had affected the Indians in Pass Creek district. [Eagle Elk's interview appears in Chapter 3.]

Returning now to Mr. Wells' statement and continuing it, he says that when an Indian asked permission to cut hay and sell it off the Reservation he was forbidden to do so; neither was he permitted to take live stock to his premises to feed, though a vast abundance and surplus of grass was wasting all round him, and he was lacking in stock of his own to consume it. Nevertheless unscrupulous Indians and other residents violated these unreasonable restrictions with impunity and without penalty; and thus was a premium put on disobedience which was natural and could hardly be called wrongful.

"Objections can be urged against what is here advocated, and it may be asked what might be the effect if these permits were granted.

"These permits, and others besides, should be allowed if the primary object of reservations ~~is not subjected~~ the elevation of the aboriginals—is not subverted. If the Indian is ever to have a chance to develop into the white man's status, he should be advanced toward freedom, be made answerable before the law as a man, and conducted in such a way as to establish his habits and his intercourse with all men upon the firm foundation of self-reliance. The hand of power must be relaxed. The props need not all be taken away; for the red man will have to be steadied a while longer till he can fence a little better against the cunning and the fraud and the falsehood which are the artful weapons of his paleface Christianizer. But if the Indians are to be hand-tied and kept at a standstill, continue this infant-control; if you are determined that he shall never walk take care that he shall never stand upon his feet; do all these things and there will be an eternity of the Indian Bureau—there will be scheming and applauding employees forever—and a train of expectants waiting for the doors of the Civil Service ~~Commission~~ to swing in exciting harmony on their worn hinges to let in those whose hearts flutter for salaries.

"To show how much improvement has come since school employees have been chosen from Civil Service examinations, I will say that those who occupied positions in the Boarding School and were appointed by political influence were not comparable to those who have come into the service through the Commission. Among those teachers who owed their places to politics there was drunkenness, and loose morals, and as a specimen of impropriety in speech which was not rare, I once heard a lady teacher tell the superintendent to go to a place which I hope to avoid hereafter. ~~She was entrenched because~~ I was sometimes sent by the Agent to the school as a mediator to calm differences which arose, and had good occasion to observe conditions and make comparisons. The schools upon Pine Ridge Reservation since Civil Service examinations have been served by a competent and valuable corps of teachers and managers. I wish I could give like testimony of the farmers. There are farmers without any farming. These are commonly called 'Boss Farmers,' but officially 'additional farmers.' Qualifications of the ordinary white farmer do not fit a man for this responsible position. The first requirement is that he shall have a good knowledge of Indian character. He should, after that is ascertained, be able to prove that he is a competent natural mechanic. He should not be lacking in force or decision. He should be patient and industrious. If he has the tactful quality combined with executive talent he will be all the more successful. He ~~ought to be a farmer and~~ should be a practical farmer and stock raiser. ~~actually raised~~

~~to the business~~ Last of all he should ~~be crowned with~~ have sympathy for the Indians—a love for the work to which he is appointed; and sufficient integrity to prevent him from making merchandise of his office.

"It is doubtful whether the Civil Service examiners are, themselves qualified to make selection of these farmers."

Question: "Have you met in actual experience men who had practical knowledge and held official position in the Indian service as a result of their personal merit?"

Answer: "Yes; I have known two cases, namely, Colonel James McLaughlin, now U.S. Indian Inspector, and John W. Cramsie of St. Paul, Minnesota. I have been intimately acquainted with McLaughlin from my childhood. In about 1868 he was appointed blacksmith at Devil's Lake, N.D., under Major Wm. Forbes, Agent. Be it said to Major Forbes' credit that he saw and acknowledged McLaughlin's great worth. The Minnesota Massacre was fresh in the memory of the Indians and it was as much as a man's life was worth to go among them ~~at that date~~ for they were a bad lot that time. Major Forbes put McLaughlin right into the harness with full discretion to organize and manage them and this while he was only the Agency blacksmith. He displayed at once great practical talent and a familiarity with details, and it was not long before his wards were prosperous and self-supporting, and they had schools well established. About three years after the schools were started Major Forbes died. At that early day the Indians had not become ~~prey of a system~~ the legitimate (!) prey of partisanship. So McLaughlin was appointed to succeed Major Forbes. He continued to improve the condition of the Indians until 1881.[238]

"For several years prior to 1881 the Standing Rock Agency had been in almost constant ~~turmoil~~ strife with Fort Yates adjoining, each fighting for supremacy, one representing the War and the other the Interior department, and both ambitious to control the Indians. The situation was more tense than ever before, owing to the fact that Sitting Bull had surrendered that summer and was already there, so that Standing Rock was on a powder magazine, so to speak; and the department was under the necessity of finding and appointing an able man, and as McLaughlin answered the several requirements the position was tendered him. He accepted with the understanding that he should select his successor at Devil's Lake. His choice fell upon John W. Cramsie, of St. Paul, Minn., who had had wide experience on the frontier and in Indian warfare, and had been blacksmith at Fort Totten adjoining Devil's Lake Agency.[239] Major

Cramsie continued the creditable work which McLaughlin had begun and greatly advanced. Cramsie was not the diplomat that McLaughlin was, but was bold, fearless, and honest, and he struck at everything which was crooked or showed signs of becoming so. The local and opposition press assailed him ~~fearlessly~~ fiercely, charging him with despotic rule, but some papers defended him. ~~from motives of honesty.~~

"I was never an employee under either one of the agents McLaughlin or Cramsie, on Devil's Lake Agency. I was a scout stationed at Fort Totten adjoining Devil's Lake Agency, and I had opportunity to observe closely the work of both these men.

"Since the time of Gallagher on the P. Ridge Reservation the government has been undoing the good work which had been accomplished."

Death of Lieutenant Casey

This took place while the Indians were in their strong position about 12 miles north of the agency.[240] Lieutenant Casey had command of the Cheyenne Scouts and was posted on White River between the mouth of the White Clay and the west line of the Reservation.[241] He started from his camp accompanied by some of his scouts to go to the hostile camp. The scouts advised him to refrain from the attempt, but he was determined. He crossed White Clay when he was met by Jack Red Cloud, Broken Arm, Sleeping Bear and Peter Reichart (pronounced Reshaw).

(Mr. Wells was the interpreter on the trial of Plenty Horses who was tried at Sioux Falls.)

Jack Red Cloud et al. urged him to go back, advising that there was high feeling among the young hostiles, because they had lost relatives killed at W. K. and had others who were lying wounded at the agency, and they were hot headed and it would be hard work to do anything with them, and no one could tell what they would do. He held out that he would go, and while they were arguing about it, Plenty Horses, who was a Carlisle graduate, rode up, and as Casey turned to go back, having decided to give up his rash purpose, Plenty Horses placed his gun to the back of his head and shot him. Mr. Wells translated the testimony on the trial and he is good authority. On the first trial 11 jurors stood for a life sentence in the penitentiary, and one for the death penalty, and as the jury disagreed there was [a] second trial. On this the army officers testified that a state of war existed; it was so held by the court who instructed the jury to acquit.[242]

Owls and Eagles

Mr. Wells says that people sometimes suppose that the Indians worship owls and eagles, but it is a misconception. Owls are more easily imitated by the human voice than anything else in animated nature, unless it be the wolf. So the Indians have resorted to the cry of the owl to communicate with their fellows when they wish to conceal themselves and give to their enemies the impression that it is in fact an owl instead of a person that is hooting. They use the simple, familiar sound made by the owl when they have discovered the camp, or village of the enemy to impart intelligence of the fact to their companions or friends or to give notice to companions where they are, etc. The number of hoots have a meaning, and a given number of hoots and a number of pauses have a certain meaning, etc. etc., and these signals vary in a great many ways, and the system or code may very correctly be compared to the system of telegraphy as marked by sounds or dashes.

The eagle is to the Indian as it is to the American people, an emblem, because it is the king of birds. He is the emblem of war. In the days of war an Indian, to be entitled to wear an eagle feather with respect, must have done a deed of prowess. There was no law preventing him from donning the feather without such act, but if he had been so mean or silly as to do it he was ridiculed and scoffed at. When he had fairly earned the right to wear it without exciting contempt, he was always invested with it at a council or society of warriors, and so there was no occasion for him to put it on himself. He might wear more than one feather according to the degree of his merit as determined by his deeds, and the council or society would decide that and decorate him. The way in which these feathers leaned had a signification.

Society of Warriors

What is called the Omaha dance was this society. Only those who had been on the warpath were entitled to take part in that and be a member of the society. A very little boy had the right to dance in the society dance if his father had invested him with a feather. The squaws did not usually dance in this dance, but if her husband, father or brother who had the right to wear a feather had adorned her with a feather she could go into the dance.

I forgot to say that an eagle's feathers to be of value to the Indian should be young; while they are white with black color on the tips; after about two years old they become wholly black and are worthless.

The Coup

An Indian who shoots and kills an enemy gets no credit unless he touches him in some way. The reason for this is that he may kill him at a distance and this would be no sign of bravery; but if he is near enough to touch his body it is evident that he was in proximity to exposure and danger, and so this is honorable and confers a warrior's prestige, and he is rewarded accordingly. So the Indian who did not shoot at him at all, but was the first to touch him, says "I killed him first;" the one who did not shoot at all but can truthfully say, "I killed him second," comes next in rank of honor, and this preference is carried to the third person or warrior. If this last be the man who actually shot him, he will be obliged to say, "I killed him third," and take the last degree.

The Owl Again

The habit of imitating the owl has produced marked characteristics. The Indian was so used to pause with caution and circumspection in the old days when he heard the voice of this bird, and listen to determine if he could whether it was indeed an owl or an imitation of an enemy signaling. The sound would instantly cause a pause among the Indians to listen. Just lately—last winter—Mr. W. and Eagle Elk were walking out towards the stable at night, and an owl hooted. Eagle Elk stopped and said: "There is an owl; I don't like to go there." Wells said: "You know that won't hurt you." "I know it," he replied but I am afraid." This was force of habit—his old training—education. It is not now so with the younger generation.

Copy of Parts of a Letter by Philip F. Wells to Commissioner of Indian Affairs, Francis E. Leupp. (Not yet—Oct. 1906—finished and sent.)[243]

It has always been a mystery to me what is meant by the common saying, Indian Problem. The only problem I have been able to find is, How can the Indian be emancipated from the evil practice of "to the victor belongs the spoils" in politics, and how can the merit system be applied to the Indian service. The following are my reasons for so believing. The tendency has been, though very strongly denied by interested parties, to place a penalty on the honest endeavor to uplift the Indian from his degraded condition. I use the words "degraded condition". Twelve or fifteen years ago the Indians of Pass Creek settlements were industrious and prosperous, having well established homes, cultivating patches of ground varying in size from one to four or five acres, well cultivated, that enabled them to live through the winter very comfortably on their own industry; each family had chickens and hogs, so that one could buy eggs or chickens; but now the conditions are all changed; the fields have all gone back to sod; the homes all destroyed, and neither pigs nor chickens to be found, and all that made home attractive gone, while very few, if any, have increased their cattle, and the majority have less now than they had then, and the very men that worked faithfully to establish the aforesaid conditions were dismissed from the service to be replaced by men who recognize the fact, though they speak of it in a whimpering way, "It does not pay to be any ways fresh about solving the Indian problem." These men were appointed to office through political influence only and not because of any previous knowledge or fitness to fill the position to which they were appointed.

Now, I will speak of my own personal experience, though I can cite many other cases similar to my own. These show there is a penalty on the honest endeavor to aid the Indian in progress, and at the same time showing there is no Indian problem, and how readily the Indians can adapt themselves to conditions that they have come face to face with, if they were only aided by faithful and competent employees. In 1889 I was assistant clerk at Pine Ridge Agency, and at the same time acting in the capacity of interpreter. On days of issuing rations, which were drawn by the women only, it was done in the most disgraceful inhuman manner imaginable. There would be hundreds of women crowding into the issue house like sardines packed in a can, trampling over one another and very frequently you could see some woman dragged out who had fainted and policemen would go in there and beat them over their heads with their clubs like so many cattle in a beef pen and blood would be streaming from the blows.

When I drew the Agent's attention to it he asked me if I knew of any man that could remedy that evil. I told him yes, I could do it. And he said you take hold and do it and I will back you, which he did as an honest, conscientious man. In less than two weeks I succeeded in establishing perfect order, so that such disgraceful scenes were never seen afterwards.

I will quote your words: "Whatever you do for him in the line of improvement, you have as a rule to press upon him by endless patience and tact and by a multitude of persuasive devices." That is just what I did by taking the Indian as I know him and putting to good use his characteristics.

In 1890 I was Farmer in charge of Medicine Root District when the never-to-be-forgotten ghost dance craze among the Indians was in full progress. Here again, by putting in practice the methods you recommend for dealing with the

Indians, gathering together all the Indians I had strong control over, and with the aid of the Rev. Mr. Ross, an Episcopal clergyman, who is a mixed blood Indian, and his following, I succeeded in freeing my district of the disturbing ghost dance. I was the only farmer in Pine Ridge Reservation who kept the Indians of his district under full control and kept them from participating in the dance. I could tell many other similar instances of the acts of others, but as these two particular cases I could prove by the whole Pine Ridge Reservation, if need be; so I will let this suffice. Don't understand me to mean that my fellow employees were not good men; on the contrary, I believe them to be faithful to do their duty as they understood it. But what I do mean is that they were inexperienced and incompetent to get the best out of the Indian. that was in him. Here let me draw your attention to the evil effects of appointment to the Indian service through political influence and not by any previous experience of Indian character.

Of the four different farmers, each in charge of a district, I was the only one appointed on my own merits, and not by any political influence; while the three others were appointed through such influence. They had never probably never seen an Indian till they came to Pine Ridge. I am perfectly satisfied, had my fellow employees had any previous experience of Indian character they could have controled the Indians of their own district as well as I controled mine. And the frightful loss of life at Wounded Knee and Drexel Mission in 1890–1 would never have occurred.

The Civil Service Commission, like all other bodies of men, has its limits of efficiency. The good and practical work they are doing is confined to the school service, as through their determination of fitness of its employees, in my opinion, there could be no more efficient and commendable department than the teachers of this Reservation as compared with those of the past when they were appointed merely through political influence.

Though I seem to condemn the present agent and his farmers and the administration of this Reservation generally, let me draw your attention to the following facts:

It would be worse than folly to expect the subordinates to be more efficient than the influence to which they owe their choice. Look through the Indian service as I will, from the Commissioner of Indian Affairs to the humblest employee on the Reservation, I cannot pick out any particular official that I could charge with responsibility for the very inferior class of work being done among these Indians. As the Commissioner of Indian Affairs had to rely on the congressmen for the recommendation of employees, they in turn had to rely on political friends who probably never saw an Indian at the Indian's own home, and knew nothing of his characteristics. And the board of examination determining fitness of the applicant had no previous knowledge of him, nor the particular Indians amongst whom he is to labor, when it is to be understood that the different tribes vary widely in different stages of progress to civilization than the American people generally. Then the board of examination can only do their work in the manner of a lottery; so the agent and his farmers have been in the habit of considering the only duty they have to perform is to keep their papers straight, and attend strictly to their political pull. Under these conditions could an Indian Agent and his farmers be blamed for the insufficient work they do.

In my opinion another mistake, let the blame rest on whom it may, is the placing [of] such a small force in the field to allot lands to the Indians, as experience shows us that some of these will have to wait 8 or 10 years for their allotment. This delay, after the Indian has become animated over a roseate prospect of doing something for himself, chills his enthusiasm with ~~disappointment~~ discouragement and he settles back into his old ways.

[Tablet 3]

Mr. Philip F. Wells tells me that Og-la-la is the correct form of the word, representing, as it does, the correct sounds.

Mr. Wells says: The word "Enemy" (toka) has two significations in the Sioux language, namely;

1. An actually hostile person or body.

2. Any person or body whose relation or identity is that of a ~~stranger or~~ member of another tribe of Indians. The Sioux do not speak of the whites as enemies, and therefore do not scalp them, as a rule, for the reason that it is no honor, and a white man's scalp is never exhibited at a council of warriors, or Omaha dance. In old Indian times only warriors could participate with freedom in the Omaha, but since there are no longer any warriors any Indian is now admitted without distinction. Formerly, if an impostor or person who had made no reputation by killing an enemy (man or woman), he was not excluded but went into the dance; however, if he attempted to speak and declaim about his exploits of courage, immediately a confusion followed of beating the drums and renewal of the dance, no one listening to him and no respect being shown him. Allowing that he has killed an enemy, if he was known to be untruthful

and devoid of respect he would be treated to this form of disrespect and insult which announced the purpose of the warriors not to hear him.

They did not speak of a white man as an enemy; he was regarded as embracing all men besides the Indians. The white race was not presented to them or to their contemplation in the same way that the Indians were, in divisions into nations, tribes, and bands. To them the whites all formed one grand division; whereas, the Indians comprised many nations and subdivisions, and therefore an Indian or a tribe could have many enemies. Indians would kill whites for personal spite or on account of the aggression or oppression of many of them or of their government.

Final Round-Up of Buffaloes

(Interview of Philip F. Wells)

This took place in the summer of 1882. Mr. Wells was at this time ~~employed~~ out of the employment of the War Dept. and was a civilian employee of the Interior Dept. and was chief of Indian police under James McLaughlin.[244]

After the campaigning of 1876 had broken the power of the Indians and thousands of them with Sitting Bull and other chiefs had crossed the international boundary on the north, white people rushed into the great territory now practically freed of the Indians' presence, and the slaughter of wild game, and especially the buffaloes, assumed wholesale proportions. The government through the Interior Dept. was patroling parts of this vast domain but could not cover the whole. Mr. Wells was on duty at Standing Rock Agency. Beginning at the mouth of the Cannon Ball above Fort Yates on the Mo. River and following south to what was then called in Indian "Pretty Stone Buttes," thence east to the headwaters of Grand River, thence nearly to the mouth of it, thence west back to Standing Rock.[245] This was the general route of Mr. Wells and his force. Patroling parties also went out from Cheyenne River Agency and up to Grand River and circled around and arrested trespassing white men, confiscated their animals and wagons, and arms and outfits & carried the captured men back ~~for trial or rather to allow them to escape to get rid of a troublesome matter.~~ to be turned over to the U.S. Marshal. Mr. Wells took his prisoners to Fargo and Bismarck. The offenders recovered their horses which were taken from them. In some cases light fines were awarded them.

In the summer of 1882 Mr. Wells with 2,800 men under his orders rounded up between the Grand and Cannon Ball Rivers the last of the buffaloes and slaughtered about 3,500. He had every robe counted. This was the hunt when Mr. W's guest accompanied him and the Dog Soldiers punished him.

(The following pages relate to the Black Hills)

Mr. Wells went out as guide for different parties entering the Black Hills in 1875, starting from Covington opposite Sioux City. The last trip he made that year the whole party was arrested and taken back to Fort Randall where they were allowed nearly full liberty, and they all scattered except the leaders who were put into the guardhouse.[246] Nothing was ever done with any of the men. When Mr. W. got ready he went his way as a free man. He corrects his statement by adding that before this last trip for 1875 he had piloted two parties. He was not employed by the last party; that started out from Covington ahead of himself and a small party he was with, but he & his party overtook the advance party & were proceeding with them when the whole were arrested. He was not locked up at all.

In the early spring of 1877, Mr. Wells states, it was reported among the people on the frontier that the president had given permission for miners to enter the Hills upon their own responsibility, taking their own chances as to their lives and property, and after this no more persons were apprehended or interfered with.[247]

(See Vol. of Treaties; also Executive Orders of President Grant and Pres. Hays to find out whether any such orders can be found.)

If the Executive did such a thing what other meaning can be attached to it than this: That proceedings having been commenced in 1875 on Chadron Creek for a cession of the Black Hills, and the attempt having failed to obtain the consent of the Indians, were the Indians to have an object lesson to discourage them so that they would decide to yield to the pressure of the government and give up this coveted ground? Such a thing may have been a part of a plan to get the Hills. The treaty for cession was made in the fall of 1876. The treaty of 1868 (?) guaranteed to the Indians that the land secured to them by it should not be taken from them unless ¾ of the Indians consented. Only some 200 Indians signed in 1876. To show what a glaring fraud was perpetrated Mr. Wells suggests that the remotest and the latest census statistics be obtained from Pine Ridge, Rosebud, Ponca, Santee, Flandreau, Crow Creek (S.D. just above Chamberlain) Lower Brule, Cheyenne River, Standing Rock Agencies, and from the Northern Cheyenne Agency on Tongue River, Montana, so as to show how many thousands there were entitled to a voice in the surrendering of the lands, and after all how few were whose consent was obtained. No treaty, only a pretext for injustice and war, was secured. Indians 18 years old had a right to be heard and to sign or refuse.

Further Interview with Mr. Wells

In relation to the Sioux Indians of Minnesota and the Sioux farther West.

The Santee (E-san, meaning knife; ah-tee meaning, "live at") the whole meaning being "Live at the knife." Santee is formed by a part of each Indian word. The first white men that the Sioux Indians came in contact with were American soldiers, and because they carried sabres which the Indians call "big knives," they named the American white men "Big Knives."[248] But they called the white race as a whole Wah-she-tschun (nasal n) which is God in the character of intercessor (not in the character of Father or of Holy Ghost). Later Indians—this generation—have lost sight of the original meaning of Wah-she-tschun and apply the word to any white man. The statement here given of this word is of the original signification. The reason why the white man was honored with this appellation of an intercessory God was because of the marvelous weapons he bore, giving him such wonderful power and command over opposition and obstacles, and other implements equally marvelous in their use; they therefore looked upon the whole race as supernatural. They called the French Wah she tschunik cha, adding ik-cha (meaning common) to wah-she-tschun, making the full signification, "Common Intercessory God." They had first made the acquaintance of the French who came in a more common character as voyageurs (not superior in power by reason of superior implements); so they had to re-name the French after becoming acquainted with the Americans, and this was done by adding to the word which designated the whole white race, the word ik-cha, making it mean the common white man.

Now returning to the Santee Sioux. They got this name from the other Indians (not from the whites at all) by reason of their location bringing them in contact with the "Big Knives." They formed the name by combining a part from the name they had given the whites, "Knife," and a part of the name they had given those particular Indians in contact with such whites, "Live at;" hence these western Indians applied to these eastern Indians "Santee." This account is wholly Indian history; it is not derived from any white. From this same history it is known there were three distinct bands of the Sioux tribe. The Santee, we will for convenience, call the first band. The second would be the Teton band which comprises by reservations Pine Ridge, Rosebud, Lower Brule,

Cheyenne River Agency, and Standing Rock Agency. The word "teton" is abbreviated from the words Ten-tah (nasal n) and Ahtunwan (both nasal n's). Ten-tah means "prairie," and Ah-tunwan means "dwellers at;" the derivation "teton" meaning "the dwellers of the prairie;" hence the ~~Indians~~ western Indians who dwelled on the prairie, received this name. From whom did they get it; that is, by whom was it applied? By the Santees. The third band were the Yanktons ~~and Yanktonnais,~~ comprising Yanktons of South Dakota and the Crow Creek of South Dakota, and the Yanktonnais of the Poplar River Reservation of Montana, and scattering ones on other reservations before mentioned.

The word "Yankton" is formed as follows: Ehanka-ah-tunwan. Ehanka means "the end;" Ah-tunwan, ~~"dwellers at"~~ means "to live in a big camp or community or settlement in form of a village." In the word Yankton the Y is an English prefix or addition or corruption. Auk-tun, is a derivation from Ehanka-Ah-tunwan. The reason for the Yanktons having this name applied to themselves by both of the two other bands was that their range of country lay between that occupied by the Santees and that occupied by the Tetons; that is, they were "the dwellers of the end" because they were on the end (at the west) of the Santee, and were on the end of the Tetons (at the east). In each band both mentioned them by the same name.

Each of these three bands was subdivided into small bands too numerous for description, and these also have been subdivided until there seems to be no end to division; but we will portray some of the most prominent and interesting.

~~Taking Santees first~~ Take first for purpose of elucidation, the relationship of marriage. A mother-in-law and a son-in-law were not, as a mark of respect and honor, to speak to the other. This rule applied with some relaxation to the father-in-law and the daughter-in-law, but the relaxation was in favor of the father-in-law only. If these parties wished to communicate together it was done through their intermediary, that is, the mother-in-law and the son-in-law communicated through the wife of the latter, and the father-in-law and daughter-in-law through the husband of the latter. In the case of the father-in-law and the son-in-law they can address each other but this must be done in the strictest reserve and respect. In the case of the mother-in-law and the daughter-in-law, these too, may address each other, but it must be with the same reserve and respect. As to brothers-in-law and sisters-in-law there was no restriction; on the contrary, it seemed as though they had uncommon license to nag, tease, joke with and annoy one another, a liberty which was enjoyed to the utmost; and, in a general way this was regarded as a good way to try a brother-in-law's heart.

Of the Santees. There was one principal band called Wahpa-kuta which means "Shoot the leaf." Out of this spirit of nagging grew this name. Upon a time some brothers-in-law (and for the sake of this sport described, the cousins of the one tormented were allowed to be considered in the relation of brothers-in-law to help on the revelry) having in mind to "April-fool" a certain brother-in-law, made a figure of a man out of leaves, etc., and set it up to lead him to suppose it was an enemy. The instant he saw it he seized his bow and arrow and shot this dummy. Those who were watching got their fun and dubbed him and his brothers and cousins "Shoot-the-Leaf."

Wahpa-tunwan. This band obtained its name because they inhabited the thick timber of the forests of Minnesota. Wahpa means "leaf," tunwan means dwellers—hence "dwellers under the leaf." The city of Wahpeton got its name from this band, as they lived near where it stands. (It should be noted here that the word ah-tee—ah is a word meaning "at" and tee is another word meaning live—and ah-tee is more properly applied to an individual "dweller," whereas tunwan is more properly applied to a community of dwellers in form of a village.)

Hay-minne-choka-ha, meaning "the bluff standing in the midst of water" (Hay means bluff," minne means "water," choka means "in the midst," and ha means "stand" and it is applied to inanimate form—something in inanimate form). This is a bluff standing in Lake Pippin on whose shores now stands the city of Redwing. The band of Indians took its name from that bluff, and the city was named for a chief of the band who was called Redwing.

Of the Tetons: Og-la-la means for a person to pour something that he is connected with and which is in pulverized form—pour it in to that which is his own or he is connected with.

The origin was as follows: Two brothers in council fell to disputing. For brothers to dispute or quarrel is disgraceful. So one asked the other if he was strong and the latter replied that he was. The first then caught up a handful of ashes from the fire and threw them into the other's face and exclaimed: "Take that if you are strong of heart." It was taken without dodging or anger. Then this one rose and taking a handful of ashes threw them back into the other brother's face saying, "Take that if you are strong!" This one was not angry at this but calm like the other, and they both ended their disputation in peace, having shown their hearts were strong. From this circumstance these brothers and their kindred were called Og-la-las. These names are generally first given as nicknames, but they stick, and those so denominated increase in numbers until they have the importance and rank of a tribe. This is the Og-la-la history of the origin of this tribe.

Og-la-la comprises all the Indians on Pine Ridge Reservation. The Og-la-las are subdivided into numerous small bands.

Key-yah-k'csar means "bites in two." The band got this name from a young warrior chief of considerable following at the time, who had violated a pledge. He was sentenced by his followers to bite a live snake in two, which he did, and they all went by this name, growing into a prominent band.[249] This was the band of which Little Wound was a noted chief in his day. This is the most prominent among the Og-la-las. The Red Cloud band was equally prominent.

Among the other bands there may be mentioned the

Don't Eat the Badger band
Soreback "
Flatfoot "
Flatbottle "

This last is of recent origin, after the members of it came into frequent contact with white men. These bands like all others of small beginning and few in number are offshoots which live in separate settlements and are properly called clans. Mr. Wells now thinks of the Loafer band which got this designation because they were the first to settle and live around agencies and in proximity to soldiers, and those Indians who kept out on the warpath and followed the chase gave them this to express the contempt which they felt for them.[250] The Loafers were not a vagabond class, but they were the first friendly Indians. They were one of the three distinct bands of the Og-la-las. These three distinct bands of "Red Cloud's Band," the "Key-yah-k'csar Band" and the "Loafer Band," together with a number of clans, each of which is generally composed of members who are relations, compose the Og-la-la tribe.

The Extravagance band is a clan.

On Rosebud Reservation is the "Brulé Band" comprising all on this Reservation. The Brulé band of the Sioux have in the Sioux tongue this name: Sechan-gu, meaning "burnt thigh" which, being translated into French by their early French visitors, they were called On ofés brulé and the English abbreviated it to Brulé. Mr. W. says ofes means "thigh" in French, and brulé is "burnt"—burnt thigh. This name originated in another brother-in-law escapade but Mr. W. has forgotten the details.

This band also has its sub-bands, and these have numerous clans.

On the Cheyenne River Agency we have mainly the Minneconjou Band of the Sioux. This word is ~~formed~~ an abbreviation of Minne (water) kanyala — (close by) — wojou (plant) = "Plant close by the water."

On this same agency are three distinct bands, viz., the "Minneconjous," the "Sans Arcs" and the "Two Kettle Band" as officially known.

Sans Arc (Fr.) in Sioux is Etahzepah-cho which is abbreviated from Etahzepah-Choka-la, meaning "without a bow. The French translated this into Sans (without) Arc (bow ?).

Two Kettle Band obtained its name from this circumstance. These Indians were starving, and a woman came up to where the cooking was going on, and said, "Give me the two cookings," meaning a certain part of the buffalo which was called among them "the two cookings" for the reason that it was a piece of the animal which ordinarily made two meals for a lodge. This is the product of the nagging spirit again; for a man took up what she said in jollity and said, "What a selfish woman! She wants two cookings of that meat when any of us are glad to get a mouthful." The [illegible] word was "two cookings;" through poor interpreters it got translated into "two kettles," and by this name the band became prominent and known. All foregoing have sub-bands and they have their clans.

On Standing Rock Agency the principal band is Uncpapa or Unkpapa, [which] is abbreviated from Ho-inkpa-payah-tee, meaning "Lives towards the end of the circle" of the camp. Ho-inkpa means such a circle as is formed by a wagon corral such as freighters on the plains made when at one end of the oblong circle they left an opening; there were then two ends of the circle. Ho-inkpa means these two ends. <u>Payah</u> means "towards;" <u>tee</u> means "to live." An old band; tradition of the origin of name is lost.

In what Mr. Wells says about the language terms following is the product of his study — his own deduction. There are words which are in use by both whites and Sioux Indians under misconception. The Sioux Indians use them believing that they are English words, while the white man uses the same words believing that they are ~~Indian~~ <u>Sioux</u> words; for instance the words, <u>Pappoose</u> for a child. Pocachee for to go, to leave, to depart; (This is both noun and verb.) A command to go or depart; or that he is going, or has gone; expresses also departure, as an Indian says he is going, or another says one has gone.

Swop — trade or traffic

~~Neppo~~ <u>Nepo</u> meaning dead, death, etc., used as a noun and a verb in all senses.

Squaw for woman. The Sioux understand this to be an English word, while the English suppose the word is of Indian origin. The Indians are dropping its use now that they are coming to understand that it is a term of degradation. Its use should be avoided by the whites. The Indians innocently used this word thinking the white person would understand what was meant, as he supposed it was a white man's word. Self-respect of white people should forbid them to use this word and its counterpart (which Mr. Wells says is of quite recent origin) buck. They are low terms. The Indians should be addressed with equal civility with white persons, should be treated without rudeness and with respect, for this is not only a sign of the gentleman and the lady, but it has a certain civilizing or uplifting effect. It must be known sooner or later that the Indian in the truest sense a man and that the Indian woman is in the noblest sense a woman.

If the origin of "buck" as applied to the Indian was innocent in comparing him to the deer as being wild of untamed nature, fleet of foot and tireless, alert and daring and whose instincts were of freedom, it was unobjectionable in past days when the Indian was roaming the mountains and plains; but now the deer is passing and the old Indian is passed, and the occasion for the use of the word is no more, and common sense and self-respect demand a discontinuance of its use.

Mr. Wells says so far as he can discover from his experience, the Platte River is the dividing line between the Spanish and French influences on Indian speech. All tribes that he has come in contact with north of this river clear to the British Northwest Territory, and including that, have the same name for "hog." It is Ku-ku-cha, pronounced Koo-Koo-shay. This, he says, is corrupted from French word which he sounds Koshon (nasal n). He explains that this is Kanuck or Canadian French and may not be Parisian French, since I may have trouble to find the word.

Potato is Potack in Canadian French; in Parisian French it is Pum de terre (apple of the ground). Mr. Wells says that while the several tribes he has met vary the sound of the word in use among them for "potato" in all of them one can recognize the sound of the last word "potack." This shows that these Indians took the name for this vegetable which is indigenous to America—which was first learned of from the Indians themselves—from the French who swept up the St. Lawrence and across the lakes and bore the term spreading it among all the northern tribes.

The "hog" is known among the southern Indians as "Long Nosed dog," the "Rooter" and "Ground Rooter," and the "Sharp-back." He does not know the Indian words, but has given their meaning.

Turtle Mountain Country Again

The Red River half-breeds of the north and the band of the Chippeway tribe of Indians, known as the Little Shell Band, claimed the portion of country lying about 15 or 20 miles west of Devil's Lake, extending to the Pembina River on the north, which is the Canadian boundary line, taking in the Turtle Mountains on the west, which these Indians and half-breeds had been contending for before settlement began in that country. About the beginning of 1880 the government set off a number of townships from this territory as a reservation for these Indians, including that portion of the half-breeds recognized as U.S. Indians.

These Indians and half-breeds began settling on this reservation, ~~when it was cut down to two townships while settlers came also, but owing to the uncertainty of~~ and white settlers came on to it also as invaders, and as the attitude of the government was hesitating and vacillating—spiritless and indifferent—and the Indians did not dig up the tomahawk but suffered the outrage, conditions ripened into almost open disturbance. Finally the government took away all of the reservation from the Indians and half-breeds except two townships.

Mr. Wells says he is confused as to this history, and asks me to write to John W. Cramsie, St. Paul, Minn., [for] full history, as he was agent at Devil's Lake at the time. Mr. W. was farmer under him and in charge on Turtle Mountain Reservation.

Now comes in the Riel Rebellion.[251] The Chippeway Indians and the Red River half-breeds were each divided by the international boundary line, some being British Indians and others under the U.S. Many of Riel's emissaries were crossing to this side to get arms and munitions and to secure personal assistance from the Indians, inviting them to cross and bear arms. Mr. Wells was directed to keep close watch and to prevent fillibustering. He replied that his force was not sufficient to do this effectually, and the government sent Troop I, 7th Cavalry, commanded by Capt. Nolan; and with this aid he captured the Riel emissaries and prevented international complications.[252]

After the Riel rebellion was suppressed trouble arose with the Turtle Mountain Indians. These Indians had been promised by Col. Gardner, U.S. Indian Inspector, immediately following the Riel Rebellion, that for 25 years they should he exempt from taxation. This was but the repetition of former promises. The Indians did not suspect that they would be called on for personal taxes. Privately Wells asked the Colonel if they would not have to pay taxes on personality, and he assured Wells that they would not. Just as soon as all fears of the Indians had been removed by the ending of the Rebellion, the County Comrs. of Roulette [Rolette] Co., Minn., [North Dakota] gave notice to all delinquents, including the Indians and half-breeds to pay taxes on personal property, including the improvements on untaxable lands. It appears that these Indians and half-breeds had been assessed, though in some way which had not attracted attention or excited opposition. The Indians refused to pay, and the sheriff began seizures, and even took live stock issued to them by the government through Mr. W. The leading Indians and mixed bloods held a secret council to determine on action & it was decided not to let Mr. W. know what they were going to do, but that they would make a rush on the county seat which was St. John. Next day after the council they gathered at a remote place in the mountains to make the attack the following morning. St. John was 3 miles south of the Canadian line and at the immediate foot of the Turtle Mountains. The line cuts off about one-third of these mountains which is in Canada. It was ten miles south of St. John to the reservation. The angry men assembled four or five miles from St. John. Some of the wiser ones came to Wells and informed him. He went out and arrived at their rendezvous early on the morning that the raid was to be made. They asked to know who had told him, but he refused to let them know. He exacted a promise from them that on submission of the question to the Federal government, if the decision should be against them, they would pay the taxes. (Insert N. 1) They readily assented to this. They had before expressed willingness to do so. Wells went to St. John and met the Comrs.

No. 1. He further told them that if they would promise to do as he requested, he would go to the town and

At this time there was a contest between the present Co. seat (St. John) which was near the northeast corner of the mountains, and Dunseitte which was at the southwest corner.

One of the Comrs. was a St. John citizen and two were Dunseitte men. Mr. Wells notified these Comrs. of the anger and plans of the Inds. and half breeds. But they had had notice, for the town was in commotion and some were preparing to leave, on his arrival. He proposed to the Comrs. to have seizures by the sheriff stopped for 3 or 4 days, till he could ride to Devil's Lake, 100 miles off, and telegraph the facts and situation to Washington and get advice, promising that he would restrain the Indians meantime. The St. John Comr.

consented but the Dunseitte members refused. Then Wells went into the town and put his proposition in writing and asked some leading citizens who had been present with him at the board meeting to certify that this paper contained the proposition which he had orally made to the Comrs. They so certified, and then all of them went together to the Comrs., and in their presence he reviewed his former proposition now in writing, and it was again refused. The St. John member of the board added his own certificate to the paper to authenticate it to that further extent.

Now he rode back to the assembled Indians, and told them that he had failed to make terms with the Comrs., and that now he should not interpose between them and the town any longer; but that he wanted from them 20 men; and after they had demanded to know why he asked for them, he told them he wanted 10 men to guard the 3 saloons, and 10 men to guard the women and children and innocent men from fright and any excesses they might attempt. The Indians promptly gave him the men; he hurried with them to the town and told the saloon-keepers to close up and go to their homes and he would guarantee that their property should not be harmed, all of which they cheerfully did. Next he told the citizens to gather at three houses so that they could be guarded; this being done he posted his guards. Then he sent a man back to the Indians to tell them to come and gather their property which the sheriff had billeted over the town. The Indians had moved up near the town and were quickly notified, and then they came with a rush and the smashing of doors and windows followed, the Indians gathering up their chairs, stoves, bedsteads, wagons, plows, horses and cows wherever they could find them. Having finished their search and recovered their effects, Wells ordered them to return to the reservation which they quietly did. In a day or two the sheriff came out to the reservation to arrest Wells, of course having no right there, but Wells did not go with him. Wells now went to Devil's Lake ~~and telegraphed the facts to Washington and in a few days received word from~~ and reported to Agent Cramsie. Wells' course was approved at Washington. The decision of the authorities there was that the Indians must pay the taxes, and they did so.

(Write to Cramsie for information and copy what Wells had said about him and this account given by Wells, so he will see the importance of his giving me data. Also write what Wells said of McLaughlin.)

A noticeable service of Cramsie to his wards was the labors he performed for them in restoring their rights to lands which had been taken from them by the settlers.

Wells removed settlers from the 2-township reservation; some left on service of notice, others he had to eject.

On Totems

The Indians worship a Supreme Being, but this worship is filtered through an intermediary which white writers call the totem, a sacred medium (apostle or prophet). To call this "medicine" is a gross error. Each male person usually (not always) has a totem. The medical doctors and the spiritual doctors and also warrior chiefs and chiefs of bands have the totem. Those who aspire to become leaders go up into some mountain to fast and pray and they repeat this till they have seen the vision and obtained a totem. Other totems are hereditary, as where the father confers his on his son or on his favorite choice. Women sometimes do, but very rarely have a totem; this is when they are doctors.

There are chiefs of bands and War chiefs. The war chief is sometimes a band chief also; as a rule these war chiefs become chief of his band in the end. They are called war chiefs because they obtain this distinction before they attain to band chieftaincy.

The Indian father and mother-in-law must not speak the name of their son- or daughter-in-law.

~~On the Cannon Ball River are rocks~~

The Sun dance was a religious worship observed by the Teton and the Yankton Sioux. The Santees had what they called the Holy dance, which was a secret order. The white man has improperly called it the Medicine dance. It was a public worship but the instructions in it were given secretly and were to be so kept. These were the only orders in the Sioux nation.

The spiritual and the medical doctors have little distinction, both employ incantations and medicines. Sometimes one relies more on his incantations; sometimes more on medicines. But the spiritual element generally has preference. It is unnecessary to distinguish them as spiritual and medical.

Minnesota War

Mr. Wells says: That the Indians always refer to the Sioux war in Minnesota as the "war over the chicken," and sometimes when they wish to minimize the cause and make it seem still more ridiculous, they call it the "war over the egg." According to their version it started in this wise: It was the product of the nagging practice. Several young men of the tribe came to a house and one asked the woman for something to eat and she refused them anything. It is understood that her manner was decided and such as to nettle them all. There were two brothers-in-law in the party, who had been nagging each other in the usual custom. One of them said to the other: "If you're so brave and resourceful shoot that chicken so that I may have something to eat." And the challenged party, rather than take the "dare," shot it. Then said he: "If you are so brave and resourceful, shoot that cow so that I may have something to eat." And then the cow was shot also. The farmer who was away returned about this time, and in [an] angry mood attempted to drive the Indians away with a pitchfork. This was resented by them and they killed the family. Realizing the gravity of what had been done they went at once to Little Crow and reached him after he had gone to bed. He got up and went to organizing his followers. He called out his Dog soldiers first. He raided the mixed bloods and forced them to take a hand. Quite a good many Indians had cut their hair and built brick houses and were imitating the white man's life. These Indians were raided, as well and compelled to imbrue their hands also in blood.

Mr. Wells says that he never knew Little Crow to be called by that name, but they always speak of him using a word signifying "His Red Nation."[253]

He tells me to ask Rev. Mr. Ross and Mr. and Mrs. William Robertson both of Allen, about all the points herein recited, as they know better than he, all three were prisoners at the time.

Little Crow had killed his own brother, or had him killed, so he could inherit the chieftainship of the tribe. Mr. Wells says he bore no good name.[254] (End of Philip Wells' narrative.)

2. The Ghost Dance and Wounded Knee

In the latter part of 1906 Ricker wrote a note in Tablet 9 to remind himself to "See Short Bull on White Clay Creek. He was the leading spirit in the troubles of 1890; propagator of Messiah craze etc." There is nothing in the Ricker collection to suggest the two men ever met.

A few weeks later Ricker talked to James Garvie about the Ghost Dance (Tablet 15). They agreed "that it is not proper and is unjust to call the Messiah movement a 'craze.' It was a religious 'movement' . . . not unlike swells of religious fervor which have swept English communities and sections and become celebrated in history."

[Tablet 17]

[Short Bull's Story]

(As taken from Short Bull by Dr. J. R. Walker, Agency Physician, Pine Ridge Reservation, 1906.)[1]

Wants to prove that he was not the cause of the trouble of 1890–91. He saw a woman. It was told that a woman gave birth to a child and this was known in heaven. This was told to him and he wanted to see the child when they heard this. This man professed to be a great man next to God.[2] Told them that he wanted to be their intermediary, and that they should dance and be together, and he would be with them. He [the Messiah] had a look. He said as many nights and days as it would take to do that he knew all about it. He said Indians like grass and flowers; and they learn, and they sing and pray. He said, Do nothing wrong. He said the people can't take anything away when they die.

Whisky is bad. Who drinks they cause murders and suicides. Across the ocean is a great church where he came from. That church belongs to me. You may go as you please. But one church, one belief, one faith. When you listen to me when I pray or teach from my church all good people will come with me.

The whole world will sing. The whole earth is now filthy and stenches. ~~(The Doctor read this word stinks)~~ These murders and suicides are that which now stinks. You say, "Father! oh Father! is that you?" All that will say, say that the Father, God, will look at you. Those that have done wrong he will shake the earth. This part of the earth will get it.

First heard of this man at Rosebud, in the year that Red Shirt's sister committed suicide. I did not see the child. I do not know where it was born. I was called by Jocko Wilson to go, and I went to see him. I went to the Rabbit Blanket Indians. I went in March. I was a long time in going. I first went to the Arapaho Agency. I do not know how long I was there. I was six days at Pocatello. I went to the Bannocks and was there nine days. Then I got on the train. I was on the train two days, and the third day in the evening I came to the fish eaters, and I was there eight days. There were many whites and Indians there. I left there on train, and on the hills above Pocatello there was an accident. Big river washed out bridge, and train upset. Came to Arapaho Agency. Came from Arapaho Agency on horseback. To my home it took fourteen days. Red Star went. At Rosebud heard that this man had sent representative to Rosebud and Pine Ridge and told them to have Short Bull come over there. He wanted a man who would be straight and would not lie. Rosebud Indians called a council and tried to pick out a man to go and they chose me. There was a paper at Rosebud that called for such a man, made by the Oglala chiefs.

I first heard that this was a holy man. Said that God's daughter gave birth to a child and we should go and see it. I do not know where. I did not see this woman. All I saw was the man and his wife.

Dance for five days. First pray and dress. The other four all dance. Dr. Walker describes Short Bull as an open, generous and kindhearted man who attends with diligence to his own business, frequenting public places only when necessity makes this necessary, and remaining quietly at home most of the time. He is one of the few real chiefs remaining. When any person for whom he has special regard comes to his house he bestirs his followers in a truly lively and commanding way to provide the most appropriate entertainment for the visitor; and in all the respects in which it could be expected of him he proves himself the real gentlemen. His face always wears a smile, telling unmistakeably that nature made him gentle and ~~truly kind~~ benevolent.

[Joseph Horn Cloud's Interview]

Horn Cloud was about sixteen years old when he witnessed the Wounded Knee massacre. His parents, two brothers, and a sister were among the fatalities.
In 1903 he invited Ricker to his home to talk about the massacre. In his letter Horn Cloud assured Ricker, "I can explain to you how this trouble commence I knew every thing's." He told Ricker, "we lost our properties and whole families and only just few people escape from that massacre." He complained that after the Ghost Dance troubles some people were reimbursed for losses they suffered, but the "childrens of Big Foot lost most properties but Government do not look at us he must be shame." He seemed to be soliciting Ricker's help when he wrote, "I wished a good man help us see about this matter."[3]

[Tablet 12]
Interview with Joseph Horn Cloud, Tuesday, October 23, 1906, at Day School No. 23.

He says: He is about 35 years old. His father's name was Horned Cloud (Joseph says that he has shortened the name Horned to Horn for convenience). Both the father and the mother of Joseph and his brothers Sherman and William and his sister Pretty Enemy were killed at the battle of Wounded Knee; and also the wife of his brother [Dewey] Beard the oldest brother.

Joseph attended Day School at Cheyenne River Agency at the school on Plum Creek; his teacher was Mrs. Helen A. Williams, wife of John Buck Williams; attended two and one-half years. When he was eight years old he attended a public school of white and Indian pupils ten miles above Pierre, S.D., one year. At this place his grandfather had a homestead, and his uncle[s], Stephen Yellow Hawk and Samuel Yellow Hawk (his Indian name was Bear Ears) had homesteads above Pierre.[4] After five years the uncles had to pay taxes. In one more year Joseph's grandfather would have had to pay taxes, but he said he was not able to stand the burden, so he sold out and went across the Missouri River to the Cheyenne River Agency and settled on the Morrow River where he died after the troubles of 1890 and where his grandmother also died after the troubles.

Big Foot's Massacre as it is always called by the Indians.[5]

In the month of August, 1890, Horned Cloud and two other families with three wagons got a pass from Capt. Hennessey and they went up to the foot of

Dog Teeth Butte, camped there on the Missouri River and hunted antelope. They returned in October.[6]

When the pass was obtained Capt. Hennessey was in camp ~~at~~ near one of Big Foot's camps ~~of his band~~. Big Foot's band proper was encamped near the forks of the Cheyenne. There were other bands of his people, scattered along the Cheyenne River. Capt. Hennessey was encamped on the River above Big Foot's camp and between it and Eagle Bear's camp or band of Big Foot's people. Big Foot was the <u>headman</u> of the Minneconjou Sioux living on that Reservation. Big Foot and Eagle Bear were about six miles apart on the river and Hennessey was camped between them. Capt. Hennessey said he came from Ft. Meade, he added, some say the Black Hills.

There were no white settlers yet on the cession to speak of; there was a cow ranch on the ~~forks of the~~ Belle Fourche River, and a few settlers on the south Cheyenne River scattered as far up as Smithville where there were a post office and a store kept by Frank Cottle who is still there in business.

There was no ghost dancing here when Horned Cloud's party went off on the hunt; but when it returned and came to Fort Cheyenne, which Hennessey's camp was called, Hennessey told them that the medicine dance, as he called it, had begun; that the Indians just before that had been dancing four days, but that the police had stopped it. When the Indians had got through their haying they began again to dance and continued this a week. The Minneconjous did not go to dancing till the Pine Ridge people came over and taught them to sing and dance. The Rosebud Indians did not take any part in starting this among the Minneconjous. There was no more dancing till they went down the Cheyenne River.

Early in November (1890) Big Foot's people went down the River to the mouth of Cherry Creek which is on the north side of the Big Cheyenne to a place of issue to draw rations. This point was about 60 miles from the Agency on the Missouri River. The Indians did the freighting of these rations from the Agency to the mouth of Cherry Creek.

After the rations were issued to them they returned to Big Foot's camp, and after a few days they closed up their houses, fences and gates to make things solid and secure, they ~~went~~ started to the Agency where Fort Bennett then was, to draw their annuities. Thinks they started Nov. 17.[7] When they got to a little store on Cheyenne River, kept by one old and two young Germans, 20 miles above Cherry Creek, they went into camp. In the night an old Indian came into the camp and told that soldiers were coming up the River; and next day two young men came in a diagonal course across from Cherry Creek to Big Foot's camp bringing news of the killing of Sitting Bull. The next day Big Foot moved his camp over the River for better grass, to a point opposite the store; at the same time, he dispatched ten of his young men to the mouth of Cherry Creek for news as to whether the report that had been brought was true. When they arrived there they found 300 of Sitting Bull's people who had fled from Standing Rock after their chieftain's tragedy. They all wanted to come to where Big Foot was, but the Minneconjous at the mouth of the Creek under Hump, who was their chief, would not permit them to move up the River.[8] Two of the ten young men returned to Big Foot and confirmed the report of Sitting Bull's death and told him of the 300 of his followers at the mouth of Cherry Creek. The remaining eight of the young men took sides with Sitting Bull's people, insisting that they should not be prevented from going to Big Foot, and there came near being a conflict between these young men and some of Hump and some of his men. But the young men had to come away with only 20 men, women and children. These were fed and given presents. The next day a number of Hump's band came up the River to Big Foot, there being some 30 wagons. That evening scouts (Indian) came to the camp and reported that soldiers were coming up the River to where Big Foot was. These scouts advised him not to attempt to go to the Agency for the annuities. Before noon, some cavalry came and Big Foot was told to go up the River to his old camp—to his old home.[9] He moved and that night camped at Narcisse Narsell's ranch under guard of the troops.[10] Before sunup the bugle sounded the call and an interpreter told them to go to Big Foot's camp. An officer counted the young men and told them to march with the soldiers. He sent the wagons on ahead preceded by a body of soldiers. Then followed ten wagons and a troop of cavalry; then ten more wagons and a like number of soldiers. The next section of wagons was headed by one driven by two old women. They were passing through a gate, two wagons abreast, when the wheels locked and the horses got entangled so that they could not proceed. The women were afraid and frightened. An officer told them to "hurry up, hurry up, be quick!" A young man named Black Coyote, a relation to the women, spoke up and said, "I am still living; I don't like to see my relations abused by a white man." He took off his coat and rushed to the officer. The interpreter Felix Bonoist [Benoit] calls out, "Hold on!" The officer, mounted, spurs his horse and rides away to the soldiers. He had been treating the Indians as though they were mere animals. He was very angry. As soon [as] this young man took off his coat all the Indians said let us go ahead to the wagons. They all mounted and rode up to the wagons in front, and then all the wagons came together in a park. The soldiers had left them for awhile. There was ice on both sides of the River; this was cut away by the Indians and both they and the soldiers went over. Now the Indians were near their old settlement. Black Coyote, a ~~son~~ nephew of Big Foot, told the officer that they would not go any farther, but would go to their old camp. The officer refused to let them stop. Then two Indians, Henry One Eye and Standing Elk rode up to him, and seizing his horse by the bits they led him to Big Foot. Then this officer said: "Let me go! I will let you go to your houses." He was released and all the Indians repaired to their camp, the soldiers going to the forks of the Cheyenne River. The Indians were not disturbed again for a long time. On December 23 Joseph and William Horn Cloud went down the river for some hay. When they were loading an Indian rode up with a sweating and foaming horse and told them to hurry and get home; that some soldiers were coming to fight. The Horn Clouds did not believe him. He asked what they were going to do with that hay. He told them there was going to be a fight; still the boys did not believe him and kept at their work and loaded up their wagon. Coming home they met their brother Frank coming to them. He told them that a white man had come and told the Indians that a lot of troops were going to come to ~~morrow~~ night or to-morrow night. Frank said that their father had sent him to tell them to hurry home. They hastened home as fast as they could with their hay. Leaving their load of hay when they got home, these two, leaving Frank with the parents and taking White Lance, another brother, the three rode over to Big Foot's, about three miles.[11] There they saw the white man that Frank had told them about, his horse still wet with sweat; he was telling the Indians that the troops would come to-night or to-morrow night, and that they should go to Pine Ridge, for there were more Indians there. But Big Foot refused. This man kept on telling them to run away. The Indians argued among themselves; some tried to persuade Big Foot to go, saying that this white man whose Christian name was John (can not give last name) and who they called Red Beard, was a friend to them and always had been, and he would not tell them anything but the truth.[12] Big Foot continued his refusal, saying that he would not leave his home. Red Beard persisted in urging them to go, telling them that he did not want to see their women and children killed. Big Foot would not yield. He said: "This is my home; this is my place; if they want to kill me—if they want to do anything to me, let them come and do as they please. I don't want to do anything wrong towards the white people." Then Red Beard spoke and said

"Red Fish," addressing one of Big Foot's men, "my friend (kola) if you want to defend yourselves you must remember your knives and your guns; do it like a man." Some of the Indians still wanted to come to the Pine Ridge Reservation. Red Beard again spoke up: "I heard the officers agree together to bring a thousand soldiers from Fort Mead to take all the men and bring them to Fort Mead as prisoners." He repeated this statement. He then said he was going to return to his ranch on the Belle Fourche by way of the soldiers' camp, and told the Indians not to tell on him. After his departure the Indians talked among themselves and some said they should go to Pine Ridge while others said they should stay at their houses. Others urged that all of them should go together to the cedars in the canyons and wait there three days, and if the soldiers did not come in that time that they should all return to their homes. ~~So they hitched up their teams and went~~ They are at this time at the mouth of Pass Creek on the south side of Cheyenne River. The creek is on the south side and flows north into the Cheyenne. This Pass Creek so called by the Indians, is by the whites called Deep Creek. At the mouth now stands the Pedro post office.

The Indians hitched up their teams and moved up the creek to the south about six miles, then bore off on the ridge toward the east about three miles. Here they stopped and held a council and decided to go to Pine Ridge. Big Foot still held out, but the sentiment of his people being against him he gave in to the overwhelming pressure. Red Cloud, No Water, Big Road, Calico, and Young Man Afraid of his Horses had been sending overtures to Big Foot to come over and join with the friendly Indians and help make peace, and they had promised if he would do this and peace was brought about, that they would give him a hundred horses. Big Foot, now seeing that opposition was of no avail, concluded to accept the offer and if a peaceable settlement of the difficulties was had, to get the horses.

They had to move ten miles to water; this brought them to a branch of the Bad River where they camped for the night. Next morning they crossed the main stream of Bad River and at noon stopped for dinner on a branch of Bad River, moving in a southwesterly course. Going six or seven miles farther, they arrived at the big wall of the bad lands on the north side of White River. The Pass was very difficult. Wagons had been ~~over it before, and men with axes and spades~~ over it before, but it was now washed out, there were great holes and gullies, but the men took axes and spades and worked a passage way so that they got down and reached the White River about sundown and crossed, the rear teams getting over after dark. This day, though the sun shone brightly, was windy, raw and cold. That night Big Foot was taken very sick with pneumonia. ~~They camped at Big Foot spring Cedar Spring, now called Big Foot Spring.~~

This was the 24th of December. They camped on the south side of the river. Next day they moved eight miles to Cedar Spring, now known as Big Foot Spring. Had to move very slow owing to Big Foot's sickness. On the 26th they moved again four miles to Red Water Creek. On the 27th they moved about noon and at supper time arrived at Medicine Root Creek about where Kyle now is. Here Big Foot said he wanted to see the chiefs and urged his people to move on. They drove five miles farther to American Horse Creek where there was a log school house, and where there is now the regulation Day School No. 17. Big Foot was unable to proceed any farther, being a very sick man. On the 28th the camp was astir early and began the march up Yellow Thunder Creek toward Porcupine Creek. By noon they had proceeded fifteen miles, and as they reached the hills skirting Porcupine on the east four Indian scouts were discovered watering their horses in the stream. A few Indians made a dash upon them and captured two, Old Hand who was a half brother to Little Bat, and another. The other two made their escape. After the capture of these scouts they all halted on the Porcupine for dinner. The Indians did not learn from their captives of the soldiers being on Wounded Knee. On the passage from White River to Porcupine, while they passed a number of houses no person was seen except Francis Mayock, a crazy Irishman who was guarding a house belonging to Condelario Benavidez. He told them all the Indians had gone to the Agency to get annuities or to do fighting.

About 2:00 o'clock P.M. they hitched up their teams and started for Wounded Knee. Having crossed the Porcupine and raised to the top of the hills on the other side they saw a cloud of dust rising and when they had descended on the other side the soldiers had also come over the hills from the west, and the two columns met here on Pine Creek, the soldiers crossing it and taking position in line of battle facing the approaching Indians who had hoisted a white flag. Four Hotchkiss cannon had been run out a few yards in front of the line of soldiers.[13] Pine Creek is a dry creek two miles east of Porcupine butte.

An officer white-haired officer with an interpreter ~~(I suppose Major Whiteside and Little Bat)~~[14] ~~asked for Big Foot, and the wagon in which he lay was pointed out. Insert No 1.~~ [Ricker's "Insert No 1" was written on the back of the page and was then crossed out.] ~~No. 1 They went up and the officer asked: "What is your name?" "My name is Big Foot." "Do you want peace or to fight?~~

(I suppose Major Whiteside and Little Bat) asked for Big Foot, and the wagon in which he lay was pointed out. They went up and the officer asked: "What is your name?" "My name is Big Foot." "Where are you going?" Big Foot answered: I am going to Pine Ridge to see the people." "Why do you go to Pine Ridge?" Big Foot replied: "I am going because they sent for me." "Do you want peace or to fight?" inquired the officer. "No," said the chief, "My great fathers were all friendly to the white people and died in peace, and I want to die the same." The officer then said, "If you are telling me the truth I want you to give me 25 guns." Big Foot answered: "I am willing to give you the 25 guns; but if I do I am afraid you will do some harm to my people. Wait till we get to the Agency and we will decide as we please. I will give you all you ask and will return to my home." Big Foot's strength was failing; he spoke slowly and in faltering accents. The officer said, "All right," and extending his arm, the two shook hands. Big Foot continuing, said: "I am going to see the Pine Ridge people to make a peace for them and the white people; and if I make a peace I will get a hundred horses for a reward."

The officer spoke to the people and said that Big Foot was in a bad place, and said that he should be put into his ambulance, at the same time motioning to some of his men to bring up the ambulance. Big Foot was then taken out of his own wagon in a blanket and removed to the officer's conveyance. The Indians and soldiers now started for Wounded Knee about five miles away, the Indians being ahead and the ambulance containing Big Foot being in the lead. This was flanked on either side by a sergeant and a soldier mounted. There were about 40 Indians on horseback; these were flanked on each side by a line of cavalry soldiers. The rest of the soldiers were in the rear of the column. On this movement from the Cheyenne the Indians had ridden either in wagons or on horseback.

It was nearly sunset when this motley procession reached the camp on Wounded Knee.

When they ~~passed~~ crossed W. K. Creek on the bridge they passed by the door of the trader's store and some of the Indians went in and bought candles, sugar, coffee, bacon, etc. The store was kept by George E. Bartlett.[15] Now they moved to the soldiers' camp. The Indians were placed just north of the ravine as shown in the map sketched by Joseph Horn Cloud. [Figure 2] The soldiers' tents were already pitched on the east side of the camp. They had been here before and had marched out that morning to intercept Big Foot. The location of Whiteside's scouts is shown by the three tents marked "Scouts." The place where the cooking was done is also in view. The tent in which Big Foot slept is just in front of the soldiers' tents. Bull Eagle lived in a house on Cemetery Hill. Down at the foot of this hill the guards were stationed during the night, and from this place the Reliefs were sent out. Horn Cloud saw for the first time the Cavalry in a light valley west of Cemetery Hill, which is shown on the map, when the Council was formed.

The Hotchkiss cannon were in front of the guards at the foot of the hill. He does not know the exact number of the guns; says there were three or four.

Colonel Forsyth came out from the Agency at night, arriving about 11 P.M. with Capt. Taylor's scouts and some wagons.

The first thing after the guard had been changed in the morning, an old Indian named Wounded Hand harangued the camp telling the people that there was going to be a council with the soldiers. Then all the young men came forward and sat down in the circle with the old men in front of where Big Foot had slept the night before. Then Big Foot was by direction of an officer brought out on a blanket and laid down near the eastern extremity of the half or three-quarters circle or council. On his left was his brother, on his right was Horned Cloud, father of Joseph Horn Cloud. Just behind Big Foot stood old man Wounded Hand. The Indians sat quietly in the circle looking at the officers. Capt. Wallace was standing just behind Horned Cloud and John Shangrau, interpreter was in the group. Capt. Wallace thinking from the costume of Joseph Horn Cloud who was in citizen clothes that perhaps he belonged to the Pine Ridge Indians asked John Shangrau who he was. Shangrau said, "You ask him; he talks English." Wallace asked Joseph his name and he replied, "Joseph Horned Cloud." "Where is your father?" continued the Captain. Joseph pointed to his father near him in the section on the east side (and north of the eastern end of the council). Horned Cloud was sitting at Big Foot's right, with a fur cap on his head. He was smoking and passing his pipe to Wounded Hand who was standing behind him. The Captain asked Joseph if he was sure that he belonged to this outfit, meaning Big Foot's band. Joseph said "Yes." An officer spoke up (it must have been Major Whiteside) and said to Big Foot, "Big Foot, I want 25 guns. Yesterday everybody had a gun. I want 25 of them."

Big Foot said, "All right." He said to the people, "Bring 25 guns. If I was able to talk I would talk for you, but I can not talk." Blood was flowing from his nose, he was stiff and weak.

The young men went to their quarters and brought out 25 guns and laid them down in the center of the circle. The officer then said, "I want five more." The young men went again and brought forward five more guns. Then the officer demanded five more, and added, "I want them all." Big Foot said: "Bring them all, boys." They answered back to Big Foot, "There are no more guns." Then the officer said, "What have you done with all the guns? I will send the soldiers to get the guns themselves." Big Foot said, "All right, let them do it." Speaking to his followers he said, "Boys, do not be mad; let them do it." The soldiers went back into the Indian camp, took sacks out of wagons and emptied them on the ground; went into tents and everywhere examining, picked up some old shot guns, knives, tomahawks, arrows and awls; and they searched the persons of the women.

Before this While this was going on the same officer said to the Indians, "I want you all to stand in a rank before the officers." There were 125 in the council, including Joseph Horn Cloud. Continuing he said, "I want the same number of soldiers to stand in front of the Indians and take their cartridges out of their guns and cock them and aim at their foreheads and pull the triggers.[16] After this you will be free. Afterwards you will go to the Agency and I will give you nine beeves." Some of the Indians were getting wild at such talk, and some said, "Now he sees that we have nothing in our hands so he talks this way." Others said, "We are not children to be talked to like this." A man cried out: "Take courage! Take courage!" Big Foot spoke up: "Yes, take courage! There are too many children and old people," meaning in these words addressed to his people, that they should be calm; because there were so many old men and women and little children that they must keep their patience and take no risk and bring on no danger.

Two or three times Big Foot was raised to a sitting posture by his brother Iron Eyes on one side and Horned Cloud on the other; he wanted to address his followers and encourage them to be patient and remain cool and do nothing to bring on trouble, but he could not sit up but a moment and had to be laid down to rest.

The ~~foolish~~ maudlin talk of the officer set all the Indians to murmuring. Capt. Wallace spoke to Joseph Horn Cloud and said, "Joseph, you better go over to the women and tell them to let the wagons go and saddle up their horses and be ready to skip, for there is going to be trouble; for that officer is half shot." Joseph started and when he came to the guards they would not let him pass, but Captain Wallace seeing this motioned to the guards to let him through, and he went on. Joseph told the women to saddle the horses and be ready to run. He went to catch his own horse which was just in the rear of this Indian camp but in front of the line of guards. They helped him to catch the horse; then he brought him in and hitched to a wagon. Then he returned to the Council. He went through the ranks of soldiers immediately in rear of the council, and then he saw the deaf man making a big cigarette out of bag paper. He was standing and three cavalry sergeants (they each had three yellow stripes or chevrons on their arms) were moving toward him from behind. They seized him before he knew they were there, two taking hold of his arms, the others trying to take the gun away from him. Before the sergeants had come up, this man who was deaf, had been holding up his gun in both hands over his head and telling the Indians that this was his own gun, that it had cost him a good deal of money, that if anybody wanted it he must pay for it, for he would not give it up without pay. As soon as this was said the three sergeants approached him from behind as above stated. Just as the struggle between him and the sergeants began someone cried: "Look out! look out!" These words were scarcely uttered when the gun went off elevated in the air at an angle of about 45 degrees and pointing eastwardly. Instantly there was a volley from the soldiers standing around the circle. These shot the men in the back.

Before this point was reached I should have said that the searching party was going around on the inside of the circle or council and taking the guns, and had got pretty well around toward the east extremity of the circle when the firing broke loose. There were a few of the warriors at this end who had not been searched and still had guns. They were near the deaf man who was gesticulating and talking about his gun.

Another omission: Just before Capt. Wallace sent Joseph to tell the women to saddle up, the Medicine Man was swinging his arms and singing ghost songs and marched around inside the circle. He was a Rosebud Indian named Good Thunder.[17] (He was wounded. Afterwards he was an Episcopal preacher on the Rosebud Reservation for awhile; then he quit & has done nothing since.)

Shakes Bird went round on the outside of the council singing ghost songs.

When the shooting began the women ran to the ravine. The shooting was in every direction. Soldiers shot into one another. ~~Indians in the circle were~~ Many of the Indians in the circle were killed. Many of them mingled with the soldiers behind them, picking up guns from dead soldiers and taking cartridge belts. They took guns they had turned over and the cartridge belts that they had turned over with them. Many Indians broke into the ravine; some ran up the ravine and to favorable positions for defense.

Beard (who is a brother of Joseph Horn Cloud, but is not called Horn Cloud, called Beard only); and William Horn Cloud, Daniel Horn Cloud, who is now called White Lance, ~~& Sherman Horn Cloud~~ and is a brother of Joseph; and George Shoot the Bear and Long Bull both cousins of Joseph; and two old men, one of whom belonged to Big Foot's band and the other to Sitting Bull's band; and a woman Helena Long Bull and a little son, these all took refuge in the pocket in the ravine, and here William Horn Cloud was killed, and here Beard killed four soldiers, one being stabbed with a knife (a sergeant) the others he shot. White Lance received three wounds in his right leg and one slight [wound] on top of his head; he was borne from here up the ravine by George Shoot the Bear and Peter Stand.

Some cannon were moved to the bank of the ravine & some were planted on Cemetery Hill.

When the firing began there was soon so much smoke enveloping the scene that nobody could be seen with distinctness. There was no wind to clear it away. It hung like a pall over the field. Through rifts in the smoke heads and feet would be visible. Women were killed in the beginning of the fight just the same as the men were killed. Women who were wounded and had babies digged hollow places in the bank and placed the little things in them for safety; some women made places for themselves and crawled into them for protection; some women were found lying dead with dead infants on their breasts; one mother lay dead; her breast covered with blood from her wound, and her little child was standing by her and nursing.

Before the burying party came out from the Agency the Indians had been over the field, especially was this true of Short Bull who belonged to the Rosebud Reservation. Short Bull who was with the hostiles came on to the field from the Agency and gathered up his relatives who were in the fight.

The soldiers shot women the same as they shot men. Beard was wounded while in the pocket first in his shoulder close to where the collar bone joins the shoulder, and the bullet ranged down his back nearly the whole length of his body; he was wounded the second time in his right leg. Men, women and children, boys and girls fled in a stream up the road and around the northeast corner of the big field and within close range of the cavalry. A great many women and boys and girls were killed along here. Some turned off into the field to get out of reach of the cavalry fire and a number were killed in this field. Joseph Horn Cloud passed up this road and went around the field and crossed over south to the canyon or ravine and went into it, and then out of it again, following the road on the north side of the field back into the fight where the cavalry was; then he soon went to a lot of horses that had collected from all quarters, some with harness, some with saddles on — all a little way northwest of the cavalry; and here he caught three horses, first one, then a second, and then a third, all of which were successively wounded; then he got two more and [with] these he went up to the hill a few hundred yards from the cavalry and northwest of the field; he heard a woman behind him call him "Brother, come and help me!" He turned back to her. She had a baby on her back. She was crying. The horses were unmanageable; they were hard on the bit and the best he could do was to circle around her in a wide circuit. At last I [he] got up to her, and he jumped off his horse and told her to get on, this horse had a saddle on, but she could not mount, as the horse kept turning; while she was trying to mount and while her foot was in the stirrup she was knocked to the ground by bullets; the infant was strapped to her back all the time; she arose and Joseph still assisting her she succeeded in getting into the saddle; Joseph threw the saddle from his own horse, which was rearing in the air, but catching by the mane he seated himself on his back, then went over to the band of horses again and caught two more; he gave one of these to Chief Dog, a policeman at the Agency who was a cousin to Joseph and wounded in the face; the other horse he gave to a Pine Ridge Indian; then Joseph came back again to the fight; this was afternoon; he came back behind the cavalry this time; when down here the cavalry moved up west to the top of the hills now Joseph the cavalry remained up there a few minutes and returned to their former position; now Joseph crossed over to the right towards the hills and to the pine ravine, going around the head of the ravine in which so many were killed and crossed and went down west and crossed Fast

Horse Creek. Joseph followed far to the right out of reach of their bullets; the cavalry came back in a few minutes and Joseph fell in behind and followed; the cavalry resumed its old position; Joseph went over to the head of the ravine or one branch of it; here he heard the Pine Ridge Indians who had come; some soldiers had advanced up the north side of the ravine and turned the head of it and got around some of the Indians who had streamed up there; these Pine Ridge Indians coming at this moment released the prisoners, as the soldiers fell back; these released Indians went with the Pine Ridge Indians back to Pine Ridge. Joseph stayed around about an hour. In the meantime he went up toward the pine hills and over to the head of the ravine; here he saw his brother Beard coming out of the ravine, he was the last to leave it, the firing all ceased and the battle was at an end. Joseph offered Beard a horse but he could not ride on account of his wounds. So he walked to Fast Horse Creek. Some Indians came. Here an Indian with a saddled horse let Beard have it, as he could ride this; then Joseph gave the Indian his horse and he was left afoot; then all three Joseph and Beard and five other Indians all went to the Holy Rosary Mission, and then off north to the hostile camp at the big white gap on the White Clay, just above the commissary. Here the Indians were exhibiting all kinds of emotions — some crying, some singing the death song, some singing the ghost song and dancing.

Here he saw the Indian woman and baby that he furnished a horse to; she gave the horse back to him; she had seven bullets through her clothing, one also passing through the wrappings around the ankles of the infant, but none of these made a single wound; the woman remained in that neighborhood a few years and then returned to the mouth of Cherry Creek on Cheyenne River, her old home, and died there of consumption.

When the Pine Ridge Indians came up and released the captives these latter ran for the ravine to avoid the shots of the soldiers, but the latter killed three, an old man, a Cheyenne woman, and a girl, and a Pine Ridge man was wounded in the right arm, his name was Yellow Hair; these were killed and wounded on top of the hills while running to reach the ravine. There were also two Indians killed near the top of the hills by some soldiers who were concealed in a hollow or ravine.

Joseph had his brother Sherman killed in the Council, also his father; and his mother and his sister Pretty Enemy were killed in the ravine back of the Indian camp; and your [his] brother William and killed in the pocket. and a little brother Tommy killed in the camp with Beard's wife and his son Tommy were killed in the camp. Joseph will send me a copy of a list he has giving the names of the killed, of the wounded, of the survivors, and of the missing Indians at W. K. His post office address is Kyle, S.D.

> Late in 1903 or in early 1904 Ricker wrote a note to himself in Tablet 44 that "Joseph Horn Cloud at Kyle, has the names of all the Indians killed at W. Knee." Early in 1907 he made the following list in Tablet 18 and attributed it to Joseph Horn Cloud.

(Copy)
Names of those killed at the Wounded Knee Massacre, Pine Ridge Agency, South Dakota, December 29, 1890.[18]

Chief Big Foot
Mrs. Big Foot
Horned Cloud
Mrs. Horned Cloud
William Horned Cloud, son
Sherman Horned Cloud, son
Pretty Enemy, niece
Mrs. Beard, daughter-in-law
Thomas Beard, grandson
Shedding Bear
Trouble-in-Front, son
Last Running
Red White Cow, daughter
Mother-in-law of Shedding Bear
High Hawk
Mrs. High Hawk
Little boy, son
Little girl, daughter
Whirl Wind Hawk
Mrs. Whirl Wind Hawk
Young lady, daughter
Young girl   "
Little girl   "
Little boy, son
Little boy, son
He Crow
Pretty Woman, daughter
Buckskin Breech Clout
~~Lodge Skin Napkin~~
Running in Lodge, son

White Feather, son
Little boy, son
Bear Woman (the oldest woman in the band)
Crazy Bear
Elk Creek
Mrs. Elk Creek
Spotted Chief, son
Red Fish
Mrs. Red Fish
Old Good Bear
Young Good Bear
Mrs. Good Bear
Little boy, son
Pretty Hawk
Mrs. Pretty Hawk
Baby Pretty Hawk
Mrs. Lap
Shoots the Right
Bad Wound, son
Bear Parts Body
Little boy, son
Brown Beaver
White Beaver Woman
Black Coyote (The one who made the trouble)
Red Water Woman
Sun In ~~Eye Ball~~ Pupil
Mrs. Sun In ~~Eye Ball~~ Pupil
Henry Three, or Pretty Bald Eagle

JOSEPH HORN CLOUD

Iron Eyes (Big Foot's brother)
Mrs. Iron Eyes
Has A Dog
Red Shirt Girl
Pretty Woman
Albert Iron Eyes
White Day
Little Boy, son
Charge At Them
Old Woman, mother
Mrs. Iron American
Mrs. Yellow Buffalo Calf
Louis Close To Home
Cast Away And Run
Bad Braves
Red Horn
Winter
Strong Fox
Mrs. Strong Fox
Little boy, son
One Feather
Little boy, son
Without Robe
Old Man Yellow Bull
Mrs. Old Man Yellow Bull
Brown Woman
Shakes The Bird
Red Eyes Horse
Shoots With Hawk's Feather (Shot with Hotchkiss see Beard's statement six inch hole in stomach)
His Mother
Ghost Horse
Little boy, son
Chief Woman
Mrs. Trouble In Love
Hat
Baby boy
Mrs. Stone Hammer
Little baby
Wolf Ears
Good Boy, son
Edward Wolf Ears
Little girl
Shoots The Bear
Kills Senaca Assiniboine
George Shoots The Bear
Mrs. Shoots The Bear
Kills Crow Indian
Little Body Bear
Mrs. Little Body Bear
Little boy, son
Baby girl
Red Eagle (This man was in the tent & was killed by the cannon)
Eagle Body, daughter
Little girl
Little Elk
Mrs. Little Elk
Black Shield's little girl
White Wolf
Red Ears Horse, sister
Old Woman, her mother
Wood Shade
Mrs. Wood Shade
~~Running Sticking Up Hairs~~; better, Running Standing Hairs
Mrs. Running Standing Hairs
Young lady, daughter
Scabbard Knife
Mrs. Scabbard Knife
He Eagle
Mrs. He Eagle
Edward He Eagle, son
Young girl, daughter
Young boy, son
Log
Mrs. Log
Really Woman, son
Brown Hoops
Little boy, son
Young girl, daughter
Mule's daughter, young lady
Red Otter Woman

THE GHOST DANCE AND WOUNDED KNEE

Black Flutes, young boy
Takes Away The Bow
Gray In Eye
Mrs. Drops Blood
Young boy, son
Little boy, son
Old Woman
Mrs. Long Bull
Young girl, daughter
Spotted Thunder
Swift Bird
Mrs. Swift Bird
Boy, son
Boy, son
Strike Scatter
Boy, son
Wolf Skin Necklace
Last Talking, old woman. She is alone. Her property, two horses, bedding & lodge
Not Go In Among, son of Hailing Bear and Her Good Medicine. Buckskin horse and saddle, rope.
Wounded Hand
Comes Out Rattling, wife
Big Voice Thunder
Mercy To Others
Long Medicine
Broken Arrow

Mrs. Broken Arrow
Young man
Young woman
Brown Turtle
Old woman, mother
Bird Wings
Not Afraid of Lodge
Bear Comes And Lies
Wears Calf's Robe
Yellow Robe
Wounded In Winter, son
Mrs. Black Hair
Bad Spotted Eagle
(a Cree Indian)
Mrs. Bad Spotted Eagle
(The above were visiting Big Foots tribe)
White American
Long Bull
Courage Bear
Mrs. Courage Bear
Fat Courage Bear
George Courage Bear
Black Hawk
She Bear, wife
Weasel Bear, daughter
(Joe Horn Cloud added Weasel Bear when we were running the list over)
180
185

List of those not killed at Wounded Knee, but who were of Big Foot's band and in the action.
List of Survivors of Big Foot's Band

Shell Necklace
Birds Afraid of Him
Sees the Elk
Made Him Long
Made A Stand
Black Zebra

Black Shield
Fast Wolf
Gray
Dewey Beard
White Lance
Joe Horn Cloud

JOSEPH HORN CLOUD

Frank Horn Cloud
Little Cloud
Bear Runs In The Woods
Good Bear
Gets On A Fight
Sinew Belly
Bull Man
One Skunk
Tattooed
Holy Comes-Medicine Comes.
(Holy & Medicine have same word in
  Dakota. Medicine is holy. The word
  medicine is now rather more
  common)
Running Hawk
You Can Eat Dog
Little Bull
Black Bugle
His War
Long Bull
Shows His Cloud
His Two Lance
Wears Fur Coat
Fat Hips
Wounded Both
Good Horse
Fast Boat
Kills In The Middle
Runs After It
Goes To War
Kills Two
Man Himself
Kills In Hurry
Shot Him Off
Scout
White Horse
Picks And Kills
He Eagle
Wind In Guts (Stomach)
Mustang Elk
White Eagle

Kills One Hundred
Hits Her On A Run
White Face Woman (the oldest in the
  band except, perhaps, Bear Woman)
Black Cow
Her Good Horse
Red Fingernail Woman
White Cow Comes Out
Iron Horn Woman
Comes Out Alive Woman
Little Girl
Hollow Horn Woman
Comes Crawling Woman
Elk Woman
Different Woman
Stops Her Horse
Hawk Woman
Smoke Woman
Good Natured Woman
Her Horse
Her First
Horse Nation
Brings It To Her
Her Elk Tooth
Liver Gall
Eagle Shape
Her Eagle
Her Yellow
Her White Horse
Her Roan
Little Eyed Woman
Ground Horn Woman (wounded &
  afterwards died)
Gray Owl Woman
Good Land Woman
Missed Not Woman
Brings Her Home
Her Cedar
Good White Cow
Kill Her White Horse
Kills Them First

207

Standing Elk	His Crow
Her Neck	Black American
Her Brown Faced Dog	Black Hair
Her Shell (~~Shawl~~) Walks	Chief Dog
She Wears Eagle	Son of Red Horn
Sees The Bear	Son of Little Body Bear
Two Lance	Enemy Afraid of Him
Young Big Foot	104 Little Wound 104

[Tablet 10]
Joe Horn Cloud told me yesterday that before Big Foot moved from Cheyenne River Agency he himself had been interpreting between the Indians and the officer who was down there in command of soldiers, after the first of July 1890, till Big Foot moved.

[Dewey Beard's Interview]

In 1906 the famous Western novelist Rex Beach published an article entitled "Wounded Knee." It was based almost entirely on a statement by Beard. Beach's contribution is evident in the long fictitious conversations as well as some questionable details. Beach, was a well known Western novelist, and probably made changes for a dramatic effect. The story did however, draw Ricker's attention to Dewey Beard.[19]

Beard was also interviewed by Dr. James Walker early in the twentieth century. The interview with Ricker was much more detailed, which may account for some notable differences in the two accounts.[20] Many years later, James H. McGregor, a retired Bureau of Indian Affairs employee, also talked to Beard but the interview was brief and added nothing to what Ricker had learned. McGregor did mention that that at the age of seventy-seven, Beard rode horses and handled a horse herd and during the summertime, with his family, sold curios to tourists at the Badlands National Park.[21]

Dewey Beard was born in 1862. Beard witnessed Custer's defeat on the Little Bighorn and was with Sitting Bull's band when they fled to Canada. Upon their return Beard lived on the Cheyenne River Reservation. After Wounded Knee he lived on the Pine Ridge Reservation until his death on November 2, 1955.[22]

Ricker thought well of Dewey Beard and wrote, he "is a good man & is one of the very few Mr. Dawson will extend credit."[23]

[Tablet 30]
Edward Truman, teacher At Day School No. 29, Pine Ridge Reservation, Feb. 20, 1907. Joseph Horn Cloud, Interpreter.[24]

Dewey Beard, 43 years of age says: That White Lance, his brother, is 38 years of age.

We, the Horned Clouds, were living on the Chey. Riv. Agency. They had no news, but one day saw some troops coming. While they were coming my father's wife had just died and I went to the soldier camp to get a pass to go to the Little Mo. Riv. to hunt. Hennessey was the officer commanding the camp. While over to the Mo. and after coming back we heard that the medicine dance had begun, and afterwards it was called the ghost dance.[25] We saw the Indians have a ghost dance; the soldiers came to see it, & we went over to see it too. We had not joined yet in it. Some 3 men from Pine Ridge Agency were visiting over there. These 3 men brought a written letter from the Red Cloud Agency, & in it were the names of Red Cloud, No Water, & Big Road & Chief Knife & several others. When it was read, it was this way: "My Dear Friend Chief Big Foot. Whenever you receive this letter I want you to come at once.[26] Whenever you come to our reservation a fire is going to be started and I want you to come and help us to put it out and make a peace. Whenever you come among us to make a peace we will give you 100 head of horses."

Big Foot said: "We have to go to the Agency and get some annuities and some blankets and quilts, & when we come back I will see if we can go to the P. R. Agency and make a peace." This was said to his people. He also returned a reply the contents of which Beard did not know. After the Council was over a few days Big F.s' people went to Ch. [Cheyenne] Riv. Agency to draw annuities. Went down the river, taking 2 days, at the 2d camp two men came to the camp, one being a nephew of Sitting Bull & was wounded in the leg; the other was a friend or neighbor, both came without blankets — had but little clothing.

They went into Big Foot's lodge. Big Foot came out and cried to his people saying that Sitting Bull was killed and his people were flying & scattering all over the country coming this way. So we were camped right across the river opposite the store, this was on the north side where the camp was, and they were going to move to the south side where the grass was good, says Joe the interpreter. Big Foot sent ten young men to visit Sitting Bull's people & told them to bring them over.

Big Foot also said that Sitting Bull's people had no food or clothing & he told these ten men to bring them over & he would feed and clothe them. I was one of the ten young men, & we went over & saw some women, & young men & women who had not much clothing on, & were keeping themselves warm by the fires; they were singing death songs, mourning, some crying for the death of Sitting Bull & the others killed. The women were on the north side of Cheyenne River and at the mouth & side of Cherry Cr. where it empties into the Cheyenne. The men were holding a council opposite & on south side of the river. We arrived at the council. The Chief Hump was the chief scout. Hump said to us: "What you come over here for?" We said: "The Chief Big Foot sent us after Sitting Bull's people. He told us we would feed & clothe them, and after that the scout could do with the S. Bull people what he pleased." (Hump was a first cousin to Horned Cloud Sr.) Hump said: "You don't have to take them up to Big Foot's camp. I will take all these people to the Agency. Big Foot's men You people want to fight, and I will bring some infantry to help you." (Joe explains that Hump was angry and supposed that the young men had come on an errand of war from their chief.) Hump would not let the 10 men take the people up the river, but had his people get their guns & bows and arrows; and he said, "Let us fix them!" Hump's people were all around and angry at the 10 young men; but the S. Bull Indians ran up and pulled Humps people back & would not let them hurt the 10 men. Hump's people were Sioux, but not a part of S. Bull's Indians; they lived on Cherry Cr. & were at this time counseling with S. Bull's people. Hump told me [Beard] to go in among S. Bull's people & shake hands by himself; as some of his relations were among them; he did not want him to take any of the 10 with him.

These 10 started toward Big Foot's camp. They overtook some of S. Bull's Inds. coming toward Big Foot's, some hid themselves from Hump's people. The 10 went right on to the camp without waiting for these fugitives. When they arrived, Big Foot asked why they did not bring S. Bull's people. They told him that Hump told them to come home without them; & he also sent word that he would send infantrymen to Big Foot to help him fight, as he sent to them an angry party. Big Foot answered, saying that his people ought to go down to the Agency to get their annuities, but now they would not go, as Hump was talking about war; so they must go back to their camp and stay there. He said Hump was making him afraid.

Big Foot was camped abt. opposite the store, when abt. daylight somebody hollered out to the people that those people that came to them (some of S. Bull's single men) had come and gone into the store to help themselves to duck &

other stuffs & goods.²⁷ The two white men running this store had got alarmed and run away without locking the building when Big Foot camped opposite. Big Foot said that he was afraid that some of his people had got some goods out of the store; that it was a wrong thing they did it; and he ordered some of his young men to search the camp. The young men searched all the lodges in B. Foot's camp, but did not find anything. While this was going on, five good saddle horses disappeared from B. F's. camp. S. Bull's people stole the horses & carried off goods from the store on them.

While we were camping on the south side of the Ch. Riv., the soldiers came to the north bank of the river; he saw mules, wagons & cavalry. The officer was called by the Indians, Three Fingers.²⁸ Three Fingers told the Indians to move up the Riv.; & that old people who had no horses to ride in the army wagons. He told them to go back to B. F.'s camp and stay there. We think that Hump had told a story to this officer abt. Big Foot & that this was the reason that the soldiers came to Big Foot's camp.²⁹ The camp went up the River. While going up the river, Beard & several others were going behind the wagons; a half-breed interpreter, Felix [Benoit] came & told them if anybody had told them to chase & kill cattle to eat not to do so. Felix said: "Tell the soldiers that I am going to kill the beeves for you." Three Fingers had told the Indians to do this in order that he could ascertain how many guns the Indians had. Felix told them that Three Fingers had done this to see how many guns they had, & then in the evening he was going to take their guns away. Three Fingers gave the Inds. 8 beeves & told the Inds. to chase and kill them, but they would not do it, & Felix did it for them. When this news was heard by Big Foot he asked why Three Fingers wanted to take the guns; he did not mean to do any harm; he did not think of war; did not want war. The soldiers were all around Big Foot's camp guarding, till the sun rose up. In the morning Big Foot told his people that the soldiers were going to move the camp up the river & to pack up & get ready to go. This was at an old herd ~~cattle camp~~ cattle ranch called Narcis Narcell (as it sounds). Felix told Big Foot that Three Fingers was a friend of his, & to march with him, & the Indians should go along with the soldiers.

Three Fingers said the young men should ride the horses & the women drive the wagons; that the column was to pass through a pole fence & gate at this ranch, and as ten wagons should go through a troop of cavalry should fall in behind; then 10 more wagons & another troop, & so on till all were distributed in this way. About 20 wagons passed, & after half an hour another 10 wagons & a troop, and so on, thus stringing the column out for several miles.

The Indians got uneasy for the safety of their people who had gone on ahead & were far away; the signs were threatening to the Indians. In passing through this gate some women got their wheels locked and choked the gate, having broken something & the children were crying for fear; and Black Coyote a full blood Ind. tried to get through the gate twice, but the interpreter Felix headed him off; the officers told them to hurry up. Then Black Coyote got angry and took his gun out of the wagon and the soldiers & interpreter ran away. As soon as Black Coyote took his gun the Inds. started and ran their horses toward the head of the column, but Black Coyote's horse was bucking & he was the last to go forward. Then the mounted young men then rushed forward passing a good many wagons. When they overtook the soldiers the latter were afraid and formed in line, as the Inds. came rushing up. The ~~troops~~ Inds. were between the river and the soldiers. The bugler blowed his bugle; the soldiers loaded their guns; and the Ind. women got into a panic from fright, supposing they were going to be killed. ~~The sergeant~~ We crossed all the wagons over the river at the crossing, and we, the Horned Clouds, were at our houses, (Dewey was married & lived close to his father) & they went into their own houses.

Just close by our house Three Fingers & some Inds. were marching along, & the soldiers were passing on ahead, & Three Fingers was on the point of going ahead too when Big Foot seized his bridle & held him back & told him that Three F. had forced him in the morning to ride with him saying he was his friend, & now he wanted Three F. to ride with him, which he did. Big Foot told the Horned Clouds to move up to his camp, which they did next day. While they were camped with B. F. somebody told me my duck (tent) was in the soldier camp & I went over to see if the tent was there. On the way I met a white man and an Indian on the road. Indian said: "You better go back home because this man wants to have a council with all these Indians." He came back with them. Somebody hollered out for all the Indians to come together, for "this white man wants to tell you something."[30] All assembled round the white man who told things which I heard myself. The white man spoke as follows:

"My dear friends: I have come over to talk with you and tell you that the officers had a council last night and they have spoke or decided this way: All the officers talk that they will catch all the Indian men tonight (not the women) and take you over to the Fort Mead & then move them on an island in the ocean in the east. If you don't want to give up the arms you can defend yourselves & do as you please." The white man said he lived there and had a lot of cattle, & he was afraid that if there was war he was going to lose all his cattle; therefore he told them truly all the soldiers said; because I am a friend to all the Indians. Then he began to tell again. "There is going to be trouble over at Pine Ridge—they have already started the trouble; and you can go over there right away if you want to save your lives. If you don't listen to me you will get into trouble; you didn't listen to me before & got into trouble. I want you to go to Pine Ridge." The Inds. called this white man Red Beard; he said he had cattle over there. Big Foot got up & said to his people & said he had recd. a letter from Pine Ridge Res. He has to go and get his annuities, & after that is done he will go. So Big Foot said he went down to the Agency to get his annuities, but they brot him back, & he had had trouble thinking about it ever since. Big F. says this night we have got to move up on one of the hills where there is wood & stay all night, for I don't want to see my women & little children scared by the soldiers, and in the morning we will come back to our camp. The people were satisfied to do this. Big F. said because the white man had told him this, his heart was bitter. Near sundown they moved up to the hill. B. F. told all the young men to stay with their horses all night on horseback, & if they saw the soldiers coming in the night, these were to fly to Big F.'s camp on the hill & let them know, so they could all move at once for Pine Ridge for safety. The young men stayed in B. F.'s camp that night & he was with them. After dark two scouts were sent up the river in the direction from which the soldiers would come to see if they were coming & to watch. They came back late at night & said it was true that the soldiers were coming but were a good way up the river yet. One young man was sent up to the hill with the news—to the camp on the hill. Dewey Beard and another were dispatched up the river to see where the soldiers were, & on their return the other young man said when we come back we have to go up to the camp on the hill. When they went up there the river was so full of ice that they stayed on the north side of the river (this was north of the Cheyenne, & Joe thinks it was what is now called the Belle Fourche River) and the soldiers were up in line on the south side. When the two returned to where the mounted young Inds. were & were told of the situation, they all went up to the camp on the hill; while the same two were left where the young Inds. had been waiting. The troops could not cross the river—it was so bad—so the two followed up to B. F.'s camp on the hill. The same two followed up the Deep Creek, called by some Pass Cr. & they met a young Ind. scout who was singing the death song, & he told these two that Big Foot had started for Pine Ridge. The two cut across the country, crossing B. F.'s trail. When we caught up to those who were far behind, these were old women and children crying and singing death songs. Beard said to the people he had overtaken that he did not like to see them suffering and mourning this way, & he would stay behind & would let them know if the soldiers were coming. He sat down on a hillside and waited & watched till near daylight. Between daylight and sunrise he started and followed up to Bad River; at this point all the people saw him and were scared, not knowing who he was, & they stopped & waited till he came up to them. The people, on his arrival, asked if the soldiers were coming & he told them that they were not—he had seen none. From there B. F. moved slowly, crossing that day a branch of Bad River, and at noon had dinner on another branch of Bad River. They struck the bad lands toward sundown that day; they passed through these and a little before sundown went down the Big Foot Pass, and at dark were at the White River.

(He forgot to say that by B. F.'s orders the people had taken their live cattle with them.)

Some of the cattle were wild, and only the gentlest were taken over that night. We never thought of fighting or war, therefore had brought our cattle along. All the people crossed the White River that night. Next morning his camp moved and that night came to a spring (now known as B. F.'s spring) just over the ridge east or northeast of Beard's present house on the Red Water Cr. B. F. had been taken with pneumonia at the White River, & he was so bad that they camped two days at this spring. While waiting at this spring, White Lance and Bad Brave, and Comes Lie Hard were dispatched back to White River to see if any soldiers were coming. Saw nobody. When B. F. came to the spring three messengers were sent forward to the Agency to give notice that B. F. was on his way to the Agency, and was very sick with pneumonia. It was further told [to] the messengers to report that B. F. came not secretly, but openly and peaceably. Next day the Inds. moved to a point on Red Water abt. one mile below Beard's present place. In the night one of the three men sent to the Agency returned to the camp, his name was Big Voice Thunder. He didn't get beyond W. K., but found soldiers camping over there.[31] Two went on to the Agency. Beard says at this point that he knows I want nothing but the truth, so he says he tells me only what he saw and heard and personally knows. Next morning the Indians saw some looking glasses shining up on the hill S. E. of them. They were going to move the camp but were waiting for those who were shining the glasses to get back into camp. Those shining the looking glasses were Bear Comes And Lie and Shaggy Feather (the latter was an Oglala who had come back from Pine Ridge with Bear Comes And Lie).

They brought news this way: That Short Bull's whole camp is going to move to the Agency the day after tomorrow & they want you to move in the same day—wanted Big Foot to hurry up to be in time; "They" means the Indians at P. Ridge Agency wanted B. F.'s company in on time, because they wanted to make peace. "They" sent word to Big Foot that cavalry was out at Wounded Knee, & for him to go around these and avoid them and come to the Agency. They sent this word by Bear Comes Lie Down (this was Shaggy Feather).

Big Foot was pretty low and it was no use to try to go round and Big Foot said he should go direct to the soldiers' camp.

About 4 o'clock P.M., after being two days on Red Water just below Beard's house, they began to move and traveled nearly or quite all night till midnight and went into camp on American Horse Cr. where the log Sch. House now is was six miles S.W. of Kyle. Just at sunrise they moved again, going up the creek, along the main road to the Agency. While on the ridge between the Medicine Root and Porcupine Creeks, they discovered a lot of scouts in front of them.[32] These retreated with great precipitation. The young Indians chased them to find out who these scouts were, and discovered that they were scouts. White Lance and others went down into a ravine and up the next hill, and on the summit met scouts coming toward them. The Indians said, "How, How!" but the white scouts did not answer them but retreated hastily. (Beard was in rear now; White Lance was in front.) The Indian Scouts chased the others down the hill and caught one and held him by the bridle rein. When he was caught he told the Indians that there was nothing wrong at all; that the soldiers were camping on Porcupine Cr.; still two of the scouts had run towards W. K. By this time the Indian column had caught up with these advance scouts. Here the Inds. stopped for dinner; when that was over they went right on. Before they got up on the ridge, some scouts Indian scouts in service of the Gov't. came in among them; there was one, High Back, [who] was in the Indian column ahead of the others, but it is not known how he got there.[33] When we got up on top of this ridge we saw some soldiers coming at the foot of Porcupine Butte, also saw some pack mules. We agreed together that we would not be afraid to go in among the soldiers—we agreed together that way. At the foot of Porcupine Butte is a dry creek or ravine; and lots of pines there; drawn up in line we found the soldiers on the east side of the creek, & in front of them were 2 Hotchkiss cannon that he saw. The Indians feared from the position and actions of the soldiers that the latter was going to fire on them; but Big Foot had told them to go right up to the soldiers calmly and confidently showing no fear;

and they did so. The soldiers aimed their guns toward the Inds.; and some of the soldiers laid down to be ready to fire. Their guns were clicking as if cartridges were being injected into barrels. All the Indians were all frightened and thought they were going to be killed. Beard dismounted by a Hotchkiss gun & shoved his hand into it because he was anxious to die. While he was doing this he heard the wagons coming. He saw Big Foot coming in a light wagon driven by Big Foot's nephew; a pole was up at the front end and a white flag was floating from it. Big Foot's wagon was driven right down in front of the line of soldiers and stopped there. Dewey was on foot at this moment. He saw an officer go up to Big Foot's wagon & he went up & listened to the officer talking.

Big Foot was lying in his wagon, his nose was bleeding all the time, the blood had run in the wagon & the officer was standing & looking at the blood. The officer opened the blanket to see Big Foot's face and spoke: "Can't you talk; aren't you able to talk?" Big Foot said, "How!" & put his hand out to shake. The officer said, "How," too. "I heard that you came out from the Cheyenne River Agency, that you came fearful as a war party; I have been looking for you; now I see you today," said the officer. The officer continued: "Now I want you to tell me where you expect you are going to."

Big Foot answered: "I am going to see my people over on the White Clay & come to the Agency."

The officer said: "I heard you were coming hostile; but now I see you today, & I am very glad to see you & you see me too." Then both shook hands.

The officer said "I am very glad to see you are peaceable. Therefore I want you to give me 25 guns."

Big Foot said: "All right; but I am afraid; if I give you the 25 guns I am afraid that you are going to do harm to my people in such a country. [Interlined here is "See next page—parenthesis."] I am willing to give you the 25 guns; but I am going to wait till we get to the Agency, and I will give you whatever you ask—the 25 guns, knives and horses."

The officer said, "I am glad you speak frankly to me; I had heard that you were hostile; but they have lied about you;" and he shook hands again with Big Foot. The officer continued: "I see you are in a hard wagon, and it is pretty hard for you in here; I want you to ride to our camp in an easier one," and he caused an ambulance to come up. Some soldiers put Big Foot into blankets and carried him & placed him in the ambulance.

(Beard says he forgot to say that when the officer demanded the 25 guns Big Foot replied that he was that kind of a man.) I am

When B. F. was put into the ambulance and they all then went over to W. K. in a friendly manner. When they arrived at W. K. soldiers were stationed who showed us where to camp in a circle. And they gave us some provisions. While the rations were being distributed, soldiers were putting up 5 tents for those who had no shelter to sleep in. Right in front of where the scouts were camped a small tent was put up large enough to hold four persons. Big Foot was put into it. During the supper & the putting of B. F. into the tent, some soldiers planted the Hotchkiss cannon on the cemetery hill & brought up ammunition for them.

When B. Foot was put into the tent a physician went to attend to him, and Little Bat was there as interpreter. After this and late in the night, some scouts (Indian) arrived. The scouts camped just over on the other side of the ravine and these called across to the B. F. Indians about some relatives they had in his camp. The scouts had a camp fire. The two lots were not allowed to pass & repass. An interpreter came into their camp & told them that soldiers were coming that night from the Agency.[34]

I will now tell you my own part in what followed—what I saw and heard. I did not sleep that night—did not lie down till morning—was afraid—could not rest or be quiet or easy. There was great uneasiness among the Indians all night; they were up most of the night—were fearful that they were to be killed—were in doubt, did not know what was to happen. The soldiers were stationed all around them, and this was a feature that added to their alarm. That night and all the day ending in that night he had no appetite, was impressed with fear and foreboding, could not & did not eat; could not help thinking of the infants & children & what might befall them, & he could not sleep or be easy. He trembled. Before the sun rose his father came from B. F's tent & says, "I will give you advice—all my sons—therefore, I have come. They say it is peace, but I am sure there is going to be fighting to-day. I have been in war all my life, and I know when my heart is growing bitter that there was going to be a fight; so I know we are going to have a fight, and I have come to tell you—all my sons, what I want you to do. If one or two Indians go to start trouble, I don't want you to go with them; don't join them. Besides this, if the white people start trouble first, then you can do what you want to—you can die among your own relations in defending them. All you, my dear sons, stand together and keep yourselves sober, & all of you, if you die at once, ~~it will be better~~ among your relations ~~It will be~~ defending them, I will be satisfied. Try to die in the front of your relations, the old folks and the little ones, & I will be satisfied if you die trying to help them. Don't get excited. When one or two under the Gov't. laws, start trouble they are arrested & taken into court & put in jail, but I don't want any of you to get into such trouble, but to stand back until all the whites assail us, and then defend our people. I have come to tell you this as advice before the trouble begins. I want you to heed my warnings."

When he was done he went to B. F's. tent. At this a man an Indian called & harangued all the men to come into a council. The haranguer said as soon as the council is through you are going right on to the Agency, & they want you to hurry up. The haranguer said that while the council was going on the women should hitch up the teams to be ready to go.

All the Inds. came to the center for the Council. Two lines of foot soldiers stood immediately around the Inds. Another two ranks of soldiers encircled the Indian camp, the last rank being mounted. There was a council. I stayed inside my lodge—did not go to the council; had a notion to start with the wagons. While I was in my tent my mother came & looked in & said, "My son, some soldiers are coming & gathering all the guns & powder, & axes & knives, & bows & arrows, & they are coming this way." When I looked out I saw soldiers coming loaded with guns, knives, axes, crowbars, war clubs, bows & arrows. I saw all this with my own eyes. I went inside & took my carbine gun & dug a little hole & laid my gun in & covered some dirt over it, & threw the quilts & blankets over to the other side of the lodge (not over the covered gun). A soldier came & looked in & told him to come to the council. Before doing so he took some cartridges and buried them outside his lodge, in front of the door, covering them with manure, so that if while at council trouble started he would know where to find ammunition. While I was going to the council with the soldier I passed my brother Joseph who was leaving the council, & I asked Joe what he was coming out of the council for, & he replied that he was going after water—that Capt. Wallace had sent him out. I went into the council & saw ten young men standing a little to one side; these had given up their guns, & belts & knives.

While I was sitting in the council my father came to me & admonished me to remember what he had said this morning. Then he asked Dewey where his other brothers were, & the latter replied, "Two of them are standing over among those ten young men." And the father added that they ought all to stay together.

Then one of the interpreters said: "This officer asked yesterday for 25 guns, but you did not give them, now he will get them, he will take them himself; so he will pick them himself, & you better give those you have in your blankets, & your knives & belts & it will be all right. When you give all the guns

& knives you will stand in one rank right along the edge of this bank (meaning the ravine), and same number of soldiers will stand in front of you and aim the guns at your foreheads, but the guns are unloaded; they will pull the trigger but the guns are not loaded." Joe explains that the Indians were to submit to this in the nature of penance, admitting thereby that in not turning over the guns the day before they had done wrong and would submit to this nonsense in order to wipe away their fault. (Forsyth must have been drunk!)[35]

The Indians did not understand soldiers' orders. They could not comprehend this foolishness. But this offended and angered them, and they reasoned among themselves and said they were human beings and not cattle to be used that way. They said they did not want to be killed like dogs. "We are people in this world."

Most of the Indians had given up their arms; there were a few standing with their guns, but the soldiers had not been to them. The knives were piled up in the center of the council; some of the young men had their guns & knives, but they had not been asked yet for them. There was a deaf Indian named Black Coyote who did not want to give up his gun; he did not understand what they were giving up their arms for; the Indians agreed among themselves that they would explain to him what the disarming meant, & then they would take his gun away from him. The Indians who had so agreed wanted to tell the officer of their plans, but the interpreter was gone just then & Horned Cloud asked where the interpreter was. The people were getting excited. Nobody said anything in answer to Horned Cloud. The people grew wild. The deaf man heard what was said about having guns pointed at their foreheads, & he said he did not want to be killed; he was a man & was raised in this world.

While the deaf man held his gun up, Beard could not hear all that was said on account of the confusion; but some soldiers came behind him and tried to take his gun from him; all the soldiers sergeants stepped back and said, "Look out! look out!" and held their guns toward the deaf man.

While the two or three sergeants came to the deaf man and were struggling with him for the possession of the gun, Dewey heard something on the west side & looked that way & saw the Indians were all excited and afraid, their faces changed as if they were wild with fear; he saw that the guns of the soldiers were pointing at the council, a part of whom were sitting down and a few were standing up. The old people had wrapped their blankets around their legs and were smoking. The struggle for the gun was short, the muzzle pointed upward toward the east & the gun was discharged. In an instant a volley followed as one shot, and the people began falling.[36] He saw everybody was rolling and kicking on the ground. He looked southeastward & he did not know what he was going to do. He has only one knife. He looked eastward & saw the soldiers were firing on the Indians & stepping backwards & firing. His thought was to rush on the soldiers and take a gun from one of them. He rushed toward them on the west to get a gun. While he was running he could see nothing for smoke; through the rifts he could see the brass buttons of the uniforms; he rushed up to a soldier whose gun rested over Dewey's shoulder & was discharged when the muzzle was near his ear, & it deafened him for awhile. Then he grabbed the gun and wrenched it away from the soldier. When he got the gun, he drew his knife and stabbed the soldier in the breast, but the knife did not enter deep, & the soldier was trying to seize Dewey by the throat and by his buckskin coat about the breast; as the soldier raised his left arm, Dewey stabbed him again, this time in the side close to the heart. When the soldier fell down he still kept struggling & tried to rise, but Dewey got astraddle of his body and held his head down & then stabbed him by the kidneys till he died. The soldier was crying loud as he could. While Dewey was on this soldier, some soldiers were shooting at him but missed him & killed soldiers on the other side. When he got up he ran right through the soldiers toward the ravine; and he was the last Indian to go to the ravine; the soldiers were shooting at him from nearly all directions, and they shot him down. He fell down on his right arm; he began to rise up, and as he did so, he saw a soldier a few yards in front of him. The soldier began snapping his gun at him, but he was excited, & probably his gun was not loaded, as it did not go off. Dewey Beard at length raised to his knees to shoot the soldier; he snapped, but he too had been in too much of a hurry & had not loaded his gun. The soldier was crying out as loud as he could. Soldiers were running all around him about this time.

Dewey tried to get to the ravine and succeeded in getting on his feet; as he was going he met a soldier coming up out of the ravine; the soldier tried to go around him but could not, and Dewey shot him in the breast & killed him. After the soldier fell he was kicking & Dewey jumped over his feet to go on. Right on the edge of the ravine on the south side were soldiers shooting at the Indians who were running down into the ravine, the soldiers' shots sounded like firecrackers and hail in a storm; a great many Indians were killed and wounded down in there. While he was going down into the ravine he was shot again, this time in one leg just above the knees; as he expresses it, "in the lap." He then sat down, got out his cartridges and shot at the soldiers right at the edge of the bank, doesn't know how many times he shot, but a good many. While shooting, a shell got stuck in his gun so he could not shoot it any more. Then he ran a little farther up the ravine. When he went to the bottom of the ravine he saw many little children lying dead in the ravine. He was now pretty weak from his wounds. Now when I saw all those little infants lying there dead in their blood his feeling that even if he eat one of the soldiers it would not appease his anger. He went farther up the ravine, and he came to an old Indian who had a gun which he was holding up, & he said to the old man, "Give me that gun, & you take this one," and they exchanged. When he got this gun he made another rush at the soldiers, accompanied by two other Indians who got killed on the flat on the ~~north~~ south side of the ravine. He now returned [to the] ravine alone. Just before he got to the edge of the ravine to go down into it, he met what at first he thought was a soldier, but it proved to be an Indian scout; the two shot at each other, but both missed his man. Just before he started down into the ravine, but after shooting at the Ind. scout, one of Big Foot's men grabbed him by his buckskin coat ~~& held him back~~ & swung himself behind Beard. The soldiers shot at the two men but missed Beard and killed the other man. The Indians all knew that Dewey was wounded, but those in the ravine wanted him to help them; and so he fought with his life to defend his own people; he took his courage to do that. I was pretty weak and now fell down. A man who was wounded by being shot through the lower jaw, had a belt of cartridges which he offered Beard and asked him to try to help them again. When he gave me the cartridges I told him I was badly wounded & pretty weak too. While I was lying on my back I looked down the ravine & saw a lot of women coming up & crying. When I saw these women, girls and little girls & boys coming up, I saw soldiers on both sides of the ravine shoot at them till they had killed every one of them. He saw a young woman among them coming & crying and calling, "Mother! Mother!" She was wounded under her chin close to her throat & the bullet had passed through a braid of her hair & carried some of it into the wound, & the bullet had entered the front side of her shoulder & passed out the back side. Her mother had been shot down behind her. Dewey was sitting up, and he called to her to come to him. When she came close to him she fell to the ground. He caught her by the dress and drew her to him & across his legs. When the women that the soldiers were shooting at got a little past him, he told this girl to follow them on the run, & she went up the ravine. He got himself up and followed up the ravine. He saw many dead men, women, & children lying in the ravine. When he went a little way up, he heard singing; going a little farther he came upon his mother who was moving slowly, being badly wounded. She had a soldier's revolver in her hand, swinging it as she went. Dewey does not know how she got it. When he caught up to her she said: "My son, pass by me; I am going to fall down now." As she went up the soldiers on both sides of the ravine shot at her and killed her; I returned fire upon them, defending my mother. When I shot at the soldiers in a northern direction, I looked back at my mother & she had already fallen down. I passed right on from my dead mother. I met a man coming down the ravine who was wounded in the knee. Now these two men were the targets for many rifles on each side of the ravine. Hundreds of bullets threw the dust & dirt around them. This wounded man had a Winchester rifle and he offered it to Beard and asked him to kill as many as he could, but Beard did not take the Winchester. A little while before this he had got rid of the disabled gun in which a shell stuck; he had given it to White Lance's partner and taken one from him; these guns were some taken from soldiers. We didn't have any guns of our own; all these guns we were using we had taken from soldiers to defend ourselves with. We take the guns not from dead soldiers, but from living ones; all of us young men took them (sic).

Afterwards, having used all the cartridges for the carbine he had, he now took the Winchester from the old man who said there were a good many cartridges inside of it. When he took this he heard more noise of shooting up the ravine. He heard someone say that White Lance was killed. Dewey was wounded so that his right arm was disabled; he placed the thumb of his right hand between his teeth and carried his Winchester on his left shoulder, and then he ran towards where he had heard that White Lance was killed. As he ran he saw lots of women and children lying along the ravine, some alive and some dead. He saw some young men just above, and these he addressed saying to them to take courage and do all they could to defend the women. I have, he said, a bad wound and am not able to defend them; I could not aim the gun, and so told the young men this way. It was now in the ravine just like a prairie fire when it reaches brush and tall grass and rages with new power; it was like hail coming down; an awful fire was concentrated on them now and nothing could be seen for the smoke. In the bottom of the ravine the bullets raised more dust than there was smoke, so that they could not see one another.

When Dewey came up into the "pit" he saw White Lance up on top of the bank, & was rolling on the ground towards the brink to get down into the ravine; he was badly wounded and at first was half dead, but later revived from his injuries. When Dewey went into the "pit" he found his brother William

Horn Cloud lying or sitting against the bank shot through the ~~lungs and breast~~ breast, breast, but yet alive; but he died that night. Just when I saw my wounded brother William, I saw White Lance slide down the bank and stand by William. Then William said to White Lance: "Shake hands with me, I am dizzy now." While they had this conversation, Dewey said: "My Dear brothers, be men and take courage. A few minutes ago, our father told us this way, and you heard it. Our father told us that all people in the world born of the same father and mother, when any great danger or tragedy comes, it is better that all of them die together than that they should die separately at different times—one by one;" meaning that it is better for all of the same family to die at one time in front of their relations, between them and the enemy; it looks better for their bones to be piled altogether in defense of their own people—better than for the family to die separately, leaving some behind to mourn for those who had died or been killed singly and alone; I think this statement has the martyr spirit—the spirit of patriotism where a family give themselves all on the altar of their country in a single desperate struggle.

White Lance and William shook hands. Then White Lance and Dewey lifted their brother up and stood him on his feet; then they placed him on White Lance's shoulder. White Lance was wounded in several places and weak from loss of blood, but he succeeded in bearing William to the bottom of the ravine. ~~William's wounded leg~~ There he was put down upon the ground, leaning against the bank (says White Lance).

Dewey says we now heard the Hotchkiss or Gatling guns shooting at us along the bank. Now there went up from these dying people a medley of death songs that would make the hardest heart weep. Each one sings a different death song if he chooses. The death song is expressive of their wish to die. It is also a requiem for the dead. It expresses that the singer is anxious to die too. At this time I am unable to do anything more; and I took a rest, telling my brothers to keep up courage. The cannon were pouring in their shots and breaking down the banks which were giving protection to the fighting Indians. The warriors had before this been shooting at the cannon on the hill and driving back the gunners. The soldiers were pretty close to the edge of the bank and these kept up a continual fire on the Indians. Even if there was no more shooting, the smoke was so thick that the wounded could not live for it; it was suffocating. The Hotchkiss had been shooting rapidly and one Indian had got killed by it. His body was penetrated in the pit of the stomach by a Hotchkiss shell, which tore a hole through his body six inches in diameter.[37] The man was insensible, but breathed for an hour when he expired. At the same time this man was shot, a young woman close to Dewey was shot through between the shoulders, the bullet came near hitting him. He heard a laugh and looked at her and she was smiling, all unconscious that she was wounded. The next moment a young man was shot down right in front of this woman. When the man fell, his bow and arrows fell all around on the ground. Dewey told some of the young men there to gather up the bow and arrows and use them. Again Dewey said to them: "Get the bow and arrows and shoot at them; the white people are afraid of arrows."

Just at this trying moment Dewey's reason and recollection seemed to resume possession of him, and the sight of this wounded young woman recalled his thoughts to his own dear wife and little boy (25 days old) and his parents, not knowing their fate. He went up the ravine in search of them. He came on to a number of women and children hovering in a little pit for shelter from the infuriated soldiers who were all around shooting at them. When he arrived there they were all wounded but were yet alive. In this same place was a young woman with a pole in hand and a black blanket on it. When she would raise it up the soldiers would whistle and yell and pour volleys into it. One woman here spoke to Beard and told him to come in among them and help them. He answered that he would stay where he was and make a fight for them; and that he did not care if he got killed, for the infants were all killed now, and he would like to die among the infants. When he was saying this the soldiers were shooting furiously. He had now regained some strength so that he could hold his gun. He was peeping out for the soldiers who were lying down on their breasts. There was one within a short distance, and him he shot and killed. Dewey now laid down again in a little hollow on his breast. When he raised up for another view of the soldiers, they were approaching; he took a shot at one and brought him down wounded, and two other soldiers took hold of the fallen man to drag him away. (After the trouble was passed, Dewey heard in the talking of the fight, some soldiers say that this wounded soldier begged them to take him back to the Indians, so they might kill him.)

Dewey laid down again in the same little hollow and reloaded his gun. The soldiers across from him were shooting at him while he was loading. While he was loading, he heard a horseman coming along the brink of the ravine—could hear the footfalls. This man as he came along, gave orders to the men which he supposed were to fire on the women in the pit for a fusillade was instantly opened on them. Dewey raised himself for a look at this horseman, and he was not sure that he had on a sword, but he had something swinging.[38] Dewey took a shot at the man and he fell from his horse. This man was the one who had driven the soldiers up close to the bank. Dewey saw him hanging down from his horse after he was shot, and the soldiers were fleeing back when they saw this officer was shot. I was wanting to see how the officer fell; so he was raising up to look, when a bullet swept close to his ear, having first struck the ground and threw dirt in his [Beard's] eyes so as to blind him. The battle was at this juncture very hot. But for being blinded by the dirt he could have now picked off a number of soldiers, as they ~~passed~~ were standing on the level ground & he was behind the bank in the hollow. A good many shots were now directed at him, and he went down and moved along the ravine, thinking he was going down, but he was going up the ravine. The sun was going down; it was pretty near sundown.[39] He saw lots of dead persons in the bottom as he passed on up the ravine. As he was going up hill in the ravine, all the cavalry were coming down the hill; they saw him and began shooting at him.[40] There was an Indian scout pretty close who shot at Dewey, and the latter shot several times at him. Dewey climbed up the hill farther in a southwesterly direction. While going he looked back down on Cemetery hill and saw something shining like a glass, and several shots were taken at him, going clear over his head and raising little clouds of dust ahead of him. While this was doing he saw five Oglala Sioux on horseback. He called to them, but they were afraid and ran away. But he kept on calling and going till they all stood still and he came up to them. He went on with them a little way and soon met his brother Joseph coming toward them on horseback. Dewey asked: "Where are you going?" Joe answered: "All my brothers and parents are dead and I have to go in and be killed too; therefore I have come back."

Dewey said: "You better come with us; don't go there; they are all killed there," and the five Oglalas joined with Beard in the same appeal. Now the Oglalas left these two brothers. Then Joe ~~told Dewey to get on~~ got off his horse and told Dewey to get on. Dewey was covered with blood. He mounted the horse and Joe walked along slowly. After a little a mounted Indian relation came up behind them. The three went together over to White Clay Cr. below the mission and into the hostile camp (above where the Commissary now is) camped there on both sides of the creek. When these arrived the Indians all flocked about them to look at them and to ~~talk with them~~ shake hands with them. They were crying and singing death songs; they did not speak with these three. When the people were done shaking hands with them, they were told that their two youngest brothers had been brought over there, and now these youngest brothers were brought to Dewey and Joe. These were Frank and Ernest. When Dewey saw these two youngest brothers, he was now more sorry than he was over at Wounded Knee. He was wondering how these two youngest ones got out of their trouble and reached White Clay. Seven of us were saved from Wounded Knee — five brothers, one sister & Dewey's little infant.

Seven of the family were lost, viz., Horned Cloud, Sr. & wife; two brothers, William & Sherman; Dewey's wife, Wears Eagle; Good or Pretty Enemy (woman who lived with the Horned Clouds & was one of the family and was a cousin of Dewey); Ernest was young and ran many miles and by over exertion and exposure, contracted consumption and died twelve years afterwards, was never well again; Dewey's little infant, Wet Feet, died afterwards in next March. This child was nursing its dead mother who was shot in the breast; it swallowed blood, & from this vomited and was never well, was always sick till it died.

When the fighting began at W. Knee, the sun was just a little above the hills.

He has never before made so complete a statement of this affair to any person. He (Dewey) says he was at this time twenty-five years old.

	hrs.	min.
First sitting	2:	15
Second "	1:	15
Third "	1	
Fourth "		:30
Fifth "	3:	30
Sixth "	3	
	11:	30

[Louis Mousseau's Interview]

> *Little is known about Louis Moussseau. He had served as a scout when the army was looking for Dull Knife after his escape from Indian Territory. Mousseau also held some position in Cody's wild west shows. Ricker wrote a brief and somewhat cryptic note about the Mousseau family.*

[Tablet 43]

M. A. Mousseau, father of Louis, has been with the Sioux 48 years & can tell much history. Is deaf. A very intelligent man, talks good English & is a full blooded Frenchman. He is father of Mrs. Little Bat. Mr. Cook told me of the account Louis Mousseau Sr. gave him of killing his first Indian. He was on the upper Missouri river. He is a French Canadian.

[Tablet 26]
Buzzard Basin. Nov. 2, 1906.
Interview of Louie Mousseau. P.O. address, Allen, S.D.
He owned the trading store at W. K. at time of the battle. He bought out William Robertson and Ephraim Bartlett, these bought out George E. Bartlett. The officers who had come out with Whiteside occupied Louie Mousseau's house behind the Commissary. He reserved the kitchen and the bedroom. They put goods into his cellar. They played cards, gambled for money and drank some. He saw these things saw Capt. Wallace gamble. He had $800 or $900 worth of goods, 4 wagon loads, just put in. When everybody was ordered into the Agency by the Agent he went in for fear of Indians. On Dec. 26, 1890, the first troops came out from the Agency to W. K., 4 companies came commanded, he thought by Capt. Wallace, as he was the one who was doing everything & giving orders around there next morning. Louie came out with these troops. After the battle he locked up his store and went into the Agency with the command. Short Bull's people were around the battle ground that night after the battle, and Louie's store was broken into and his goods destroyed and taken. He got only 2 sacks of flour, 4 sides of bacon and 4 pounds of Baking Powder. Afterwards, the Govt. paid him $407 for loss. This was all he got out of $1,200 worth in his store.

On the night of Dec. 28 after Big Foot was brought in Louie was sent into [the] Agency by Capt. Wallace who was almost white and everybody called him Captain, though he might have been Major Whiteside for all he knows. He came right back with a message from ~~Major~~ Gen. Brooke.

Forsyth came out that night with four companies that night after he had returned to W. K.

Big Foot was found this way: On the morning of Dec. 28 Little Bat came to his room early in the morning, before light ~~and told Louie~~. He wanted salt and some sardines. Louie asked him what he was doing out there, in Louie's kitchen. He was after salt and sardines. He answered that he was going out after Big Foot. He said, "You fellows have been out here a week and cannot find him, and I am going out." He went out and came back a little after sunrise and said he discovered them just as they were moving camp from Porcupine. Now one-half the soldiers in camp were sent out, the others remaining in camp. Bat and other scouts went out too. The first time Bat went alone. Louie doesn't know what took place out there. Louie says the council circle was filled clear round and the only opening was a small one at the southwest side.

Louie saw early in the game—when the disarming began—that there was going to be trouble; so he went to his house and stripped off some extra clothing so as to be free to move. Louie was at this time employed by Cressy of the Omaha Bee at $5 a day as interpreter.[41] Not till the next spring did he go into the Govt. service, when he enlisted as a scout. He approves Joseph Horn Cloud's map, except that the line of Indian tents extends too far to the north at the west end, and he says the circle was closed on the north.[42] Capt. Wallace began by saying the Great Father wanted them to give them their arms. He said that in the past when Indians gave up their guns they were not paid for them, but in this case they would be paid, that the Govt. did not want trouble—wanted only what was right and he told them to tag their guns. In a little while two old guns were brought forward—an old Spencer and a Hawkins.

As the guns were not produced he told them again that if the guns were not brought out he would have to take them by force. None were brought in response to this. He waited a little while and as no more were brought he had a bugle call and ordered the soldiers to disarm them. They went around & lifted the Indian tents right up. The women went to crying.

(He says the Hotchkiss cannon were first planted near the top of the hill. When the first soldiers went out 2 cannon were taken out, and when Forsyth came, he brought 2 more.)

One pile of guns was up at the foot of Cemetery Hill—12 in this pile, the other pile, 57 in. This was down near the council and not far from the scouts tents. An officer at the pile of 12 (and Louie was right there then) called to the one down where 57 were and asked how many he had & he answered 57, and the officer at the pile of 57 asked the other how many he had and he said 12. At this time three Indians with blankets were standing inside the circle at abt. the north & east side. Somebody went up to them (he thinks it was Captain Wallace, and a couple of orderlies and an interpreter with him.) He opened the blanket of one who had a Winchester and the Indian turned it over to him; the second one didn't have any gun that Louie saw; when he went to the third he would not give his up, but he brought it up to "arms port" and Wallace had hold of it, and they swung it first one end up & then the other, and when the muzzle was up it was discharged. Everybody went to hollering "Look out! Look out!" and there was quite a stampede. A wire fence was close by & many, both whites and Indians, went through it. The horses tied at the northeast corner of the camp to ropes when the firing began got to pitching and jumping. After this gun was discharged there was a pause of perhaps half a minute, may be not so long, two more shots were fired and he saw Wallace and the Indian fall. Then the Indians broke for the guns in the piles. Then the soldiers fired a sudden volley, that is, the dismounted cavalrymen. There was no infantry there. This dismounted cavalry must be what some speak of as infantry. He does not think that the mounted cavalry fired, their horses were jumping and charging. After this volley the firing was continuous and the field soon enveloped in smoke. ~~He says Little Bat did not cry out "Look out! Look out!" as McFarlan[43] says he did, that Bat was in the camp where upper end of the camp up~~ Little Bat was at the upper end of the camp up the ravine with a party who were disarming. There were two parties disarming at same time—both started together. After the fight was about over the cannon were moved down but were not fired after the removal. He tells about building breastworks with sacks of oats &c and says the soldiers piled some up around his store.

He tells of a woman close to the road crossing of the ravine; he and Little Bat heard some hollering (after the battle was over) down by the ravine—heard words like these, "Shoot him again!" A wounded woman [was] lying in a washout right in the road and at her feet was a little baby swathed as is their custom, and it was alive; somebody took it (he thinks was the one that went east or was the one Charley Mainvall's mother took) and it was saved;[44] a little boy about two years old was lying up against the bank half sitting as though it was yet alive, and four soldiers were standing right above it. Louie & Bat went down, drawn by what they had heard and found the woman and asked if she was hurt much & if she could get up. She did not want to be moved, and said "Those soldiers just now killed my two children (she thought both were dead) and I want to lie here and die with them." Bat went up to them and in his forcible way gave them a berating and made them go away.

He says as Horn Cloud does that the soldiers encircling the council fired toward the center at the Indians inside, and they surely shot one another.

He says it was a bungle and botch—no need of anybody being injured if it had been properly managed. He talked with Big Foot that morning and B. F. said he did not want any fight—no trouble. He said it was surprising that they should come out with cannon to meet him. He told his people to give up everything even to a jackknife, for they did not want trouble. Louie heard this. If there had been no attempt to disarm there would have been no trouble. Louie has been over all this summer (1906) on Cheyenne River Agency and the people over there say Big Foot was moving over to stay at Pine Ridge, that he had been receiving requests by Red Cloud & others to come over.

Louie says that another party of Indians belonging to Big Foot's band were following and that Standing Soldier and Red Shirt piloted them in a wide circuit to avoid W. K. and they got into the Agency the next morning after the battle and went into the friendly camp north of the Agency.[45]

Thinks 367 Indians were killed.[46]

Louie Mousseau is Chairman of the Progressive Class, but he says he does not do much in this line of work since his people are so disheartened and discouraged.

He says that the Wounded Knee massacre brought ruin to the Indians on the Pine Ridge and Rosebud Reservations. They were getting a handsome start for people in their condition. They were showing great spirit. Their hearts were lively. They were beginning to raise wheat and oats, and he says that they had done considerable threshing of wheat on sheets spread out on the ground. Three or four threshing machines were brought to the Reservation by the Govt. but the Indians had no one to show them how to use them and they smashed one up. Everybody had live stock and raised garden vegetables for their living; they kept cows, raised calves, made some butter and some had got to making "home" cheese. They had chickens, geese, turkeys, and ducks. Any one driving through the Reservation could buy nice butter when he wanted any.

Now some Indians are in starving condition. Only the other day he was over the line in Rosebud Reservation and he found people there living on parched Indian corn, and winter is just coming on. He said it made him sad.

He says that over on Cheyenne River Reservation the system is different. The Indians are advised in council what funds are to their credit and they have some voice as to how they shall be expended. They are prospering greatly. They have the blessings of freedom and are doing well. An inspector or special agent came there recently and made an independent investigation; then he cleared out the barnacles summarily and he is running the affairs temporarily. George Stover told me of this also.[47]

Louie Mousseau has been over there a year and he says there is a mighty difference between the management on Cheyenne River Res. and these two here — Pine R. and Rosebud.

Wounded Knee battle massacre set the natives back more than he can tell; they at once fell right off and have constantly declined until he dares not contemplate what the end will be. Mr. William Robertson told me the same thing about the effect of Wounded Knee.[48] The Indians have been downcast and apathetic ever since. They appeared to feel, and they have said, what is the use to make any effort; progress in civilization does not bring protection; when we get a start and show a progressive spirit and disposition the troops come and kill us off. We mourn for our dead under civilization as well as under savagery. Wherefore try to become anything according to the white man's forms? By the time we have come up to his standard of virtue there will be none of us left. Rifles decimate us, cannons devour us. We can not be food for destruction always and survive.

Mr. Robertson thinks the Indians are becoming now a little more inspired.

Mr. Louie M. says the Indians are dancing the ghost dance everywhere here under a different name. They should have been allowed to do so in 1890, they took to it with vigor because it was a new thing. Indians are proud spirited and it is poor policy to try to dominate them with force. It would have been easy to get along with them if Royer had not brought the troops, and a conciliatory disposition had been exhibited toward them.

Father Croft came out to W. K. with Forsyth the night before the battle. When Louie got up next morning in his house he found Father Croft in his bed on one side and Little Bat on the other side of him.[49]

Louie Mousseau brought out a dispatch from General Brooke the night before the battle. Probably this contained an order to disarm the Indians. Possibly when Col. Forsyth went out a little later the same night he had orders to that effect.

The Wounded Knee trouble would never have happened if men without caliber had not been in power, who were too proud to ask and take advice and learn from those who had spent their whole lives among the Indians, knew their nature and moods, and modes of thought and feeling and reasoning and the meaning of their customs. A sensible determination to be just to the Indians and to ascertain their grievances and correct them would have prevented a crime which can plead only haughty ignorance for an excuse. The needless and criminal slaughter was not all the wrong which calls down a righteous condemnation for what was done and what was not done; beyond this [the] cause of progress among the Sioux was set back at least a generation with all the consequent loss and demoralization.

Louis Mousseau complains that they have had nobody to show them on this reservation how to work; no women or field matrons to visit the homes and instruct the women how to keep house and do housework, etc. He says that over on Cheyenne River Agency the Boss Farmers get out and work like laborers in giving instruction. But here they spend their time in their offices.

Over there the civil service examination is to protect the Indian who is put right into places of trust and responsibility while the white men are kept out; here the reverse holds true, the civil service examinations keeping the Indians out while the whites do not have to pass them or they are personated by others.

[William Palmer's Interview]

[Tablet 10]

William Palmer on White River, Post-office Kyle, S.D., says the name of the Indian who fired the first shot at Wounded Knee was Blue Face who was 35 or 40 years old. He says the name of the man standing in the grave at W. K. as shown in the picture at the burying was William McWilliams.

[George Little Wound's Interview]

> Little Wound was born about 1828 near the headwaters of the South Fork of the Cheyenne River in present Wyoming. He was the son of Bull Bear and grew up in a very powerful family of the Kiyuksa Band. This band was led by Stone Knife, Little Wound's paternal grandfather.
>
> The Kiyuksa settled on the reservation in the 1870s, where Little Wound became a leading agency chief. He shared this power with Red Cloud, his father's assassin, whom he bitterly opposed throughout the remainder of his life. Little Wound died of natural causes on Little Wound Creek, Pine Ridge, during the winter of 1899. He was survived by two sons, James and George, and a daughter who had married the Oglala, Turning Hawk.[50]

[Tablet 32]

Kyle, S.D., March 1, 1907. George Little Wound, son and successor of Chief Little Wound, says there were three columns that went through the Medicine Root region during the troubles of 1890. There were the Brule hostiles which came and joined the hostiles in the Bad Lands. They camped where he now lives and destroyed property, broke into houses, "shot up" things, shot at pictures hanging in the houses, killed cattle, took provisions from cellars; and down by Kyle where the Day School buildings stand (Hunt, present teacher) they held a ghost dance. These were the Indians who committed the depredations so much heard of, and not Big Foot's band. (See Philip Wells' narrative. He fully explained the Brule invasion.) George Little Wound says that Big Foot's band did not disturb anybody or anything, committed no depredations, killed no live stock. He is confirmed by J. Horn Cloud and Dewey Beard.

There was also the column of Standing Rock Indians brought in by Standing Soldier to the Friendly camp at this Agency. Then there was Big Foot's band which came across from the White River to Porcupine Butte where it was confronted by the soldiers under Major Whiteside. These three columns may be said to have been "invaders;" for they came upon the Pine Ridge reservation from the outside.

[Ed Janis's Interview]

Edward Janis was the son of Nicholas Janis and Red Cloud's niece, Martha. The family lived in the Fort Laramie area until 1880 when they moved to Pine Ridge.[51]

[Tablet 22]

Ed Janis (son of Nick) told me at Garnett's that he helped in the burial of the dead Indians at Wounded Knee, and that One Hundred and forty-six Indians were buried in the one grave on the hill at W. K. There were three layers of bodies deposited in the grave lying across it. They were frozen and their limbs formed stiff angles. One of these dead was Flying Horse, an Oglala from the Agency, who got too close and received a deadly shot. This Flying Horse was an older brother of the minor Sitting Bull.

Wm. Garnett says that dead bodies of Indians were found in houses and other place for two months after the battle.

[William Peano's Interview]

Later in the interview Ricker mentioned that Peano was a mixed-blood who went to school at Stockville, Frontier County, Nebraska. Peano had been with Cody's Wild West Show for six years and returned to Pine Ridge just a week before the Wounded Knee massacre.

[Tablet 10]
Cane Creek, February 2, 1907

William Peano, who lives on Cane Creek, Pine Ridge Reservation, who has given me a classified list of the killed at Wounded Knee (See narrow book, "Interstate Spelling Tablet" [Tablet 22]) says:

He was at the Agency the day of the butchery at W. K. The sound of the cannon was heard at W. K. about sunrise; he will not admit, on questioning that it was much after the sun came in sight that cannon were heard.[52] Pretty soon a large body of Indians under the leader (a kind of chief, he says), Flying

Horse, started from the Agency following the ridge, for W. K. Flying Horse was killed up on the hill straight west of the battlefield at the head of a canyon. The party [of Indians] returned to the Agency, arriving about one o'clock in the afternoon. After they came, firing was opened on the Agency. The starting of the attack on the Agency was in this way:

Turning Bear, a Rosebud Indian, made an attempt to burn the Agency barn standing on a hill south of Wolf Creek, and he came down from the ridge to the base dressed in war costume but did not cross Wolf Creek, and the guard on the other or south side of the creek, an Indian policeman, spoke up and asked him the object of his approach.[53] He said he was coming to burn the barn and the Agency buildings. This guard went up to headquarters and reported. Then the Indian police came down to the brow of the hill, William Peano among the number a little later, though he was not a policeman, but he took four shots at Turning Bear. These policemen kept up a fusilade for some time. Turning Bear was not hit, though the bullets cut the earth about him lively; evidently there was no intention to hit him. But Peano says Turning Bear would have started a conflagration if he could have reached the buildings. When the firing opened on Turning Bear, the so-called hostiles commenced firing into the Agency. It lasted about an hour. The bullets that reached the center of the Agency were spent in force. No one was hurt. But later in the afternoon some soldiers went down to the sawmill on Wolf Creek (just north, rather more northeast of the Agency proper) to protect it from being burned, and one soldier was shot there by an Indian and killed. This was the only casualty of the day.

This day, Peano says, an officer wanted to shell Red Cloud's house, and if he had done so there would have been ferocious fighting. It would have turned all the Indians against the troops and Government. He says Red Cloud hearing of this report to fire on his home, fled and joined the Indians for safety. Peano says he afterwards heard also that the Indians hearing of the intention to shell Red Cloud's home, went to him and took him away with them, telling him that he was their chief; that it was his duty to be with them—and that he must go, and he did go and was with them quite a while. (See Gen. Corliss' Statement.)[54] Peano says he [Red Cloud] must have been out a month; he knows that "quite a few times," using his own words, that parties of friendly Indians went out to get him to come in. During this time that he was out, the Indians he was with camped on White Clay, below the Mission.

The "hostiles" had come in from the "stronghold" just before the W. K.

butchery (It was General—then Captain—Corliss who wanted to fire his cannon on the "hostile" camp down about Red Cloud's premises. See his statement made to me in Denver in October, 1905.⁵⁵ He did not tell me that he would have fired on Red Cloud. General Brooke refused to let him fire. He was smarting to do so, as he told me, as it was terribly galling to him to stand and take the fire from the Indians.) Peano says that the night before the butchery at W. K. he said to those around him at the Agency that there would be fighting at W. K. next day. He says the cavalry that went out under Forsyth left the Agency at 8 o'clock that night. Peano had been up to the Friendly Camp of Indians and was coming into the Agency just as this cavalry was in column on the road at the Agency about to move off for W. K. Peano, while crossing the road, overheard an officer say that he had orders to go that night and get out there before morning, and that if the Indians <u>made any break of any kind to fire on them</u>.⁵⁶

Peano says he and Antoine Herman's, and Hank Clifford's, Ben Rowland's and other families were staying at Mrs. Nettie Goings'. Peano went direct to her home and told what he had heard and told them that he knew there would be fighting at Wounded Knee on the morrow. They would not share in his forebodings. But he could not sleep any that night on account of his apprehensions; and he was the first one up in the morning expecting to hear terrible tidings. He says the soldiers in the column were very talkative; their voices and the officer's voice suggested that they had been imbibing freely.

In regard to the burying of the dead, Peano says that this burial party did not go out till the third day after the butchery; that is, January 1, 1901 1891; that it was so late in the day when they arrived at the battleground that they could do nothing—the ground was frozen—and the buriers camped in the trader's store, and the work of interring the dead was completed next day, finishing a little before sundown. The soldiers who went out were camped up at the foot of the ridge where I saw the pits—camped down on the level or creek bottom.

Peano says the true French spelling of his name is Peanox, but he does not use the X. He was with Buffalo Bill's show six years, and traveled in Europe and this country—all over both—traveled far and wide—this all before the butchery. He had been back but a week when it occurred.

There were no hostiles only those who were made such by incompetent management.

Peano says that whiskey was free at the Agency. The officers had all they could use; and the soldiers were able to get all they wanted; he heard some of them say they got it from a man named James Asay; others would not say where they got theirs.[57] A whole lot of outsiders said the same thing. He knows that a whole lot of soldiers had whiskey.

I transfer from the "narrow" book to this in order to have in compact form all that I took down from William Peano—all in one place in one book, as follows:[58]

William Peano (the true French spelling being Peanox (he drops the X) a French & Sioux half-breed was at the Agency at the time of the Wounded Knee butchery, and an officer in command of troops wanted twenty men to go out to bury the dead; and he got his number, among whom was Peano who made a record of the facts of the burial, from which I transcribe as follows:

(He was educated at Stockville, Neb., and other places and had been with Buffalo Bill's show six years, and just returned from his last trip only a week before the butchery at Wounded Knee).

There were killed of *old men* to feeble to fight *twenty-four*	24
Boys killed, 5 to 8 years old, six	6
Babies *killed* under two years of age seven	7
These were cradle-board babies; such are so carried till one year and one year and a half old; but in winter as this was they may keep them on the boards for warmth till about _ years old.	
Women *killed* of extreme old age, seven	7
All others killed, embracing men and women of vigor, and young males and females, say ten years and upwards	102
	146

All these were buried in one grave at the battleground. The burial party came out from the Agency on the third day after the battle, namely, January 1, 1891, arriving late in the day, and camping in the trader's store or old commissary that night. Next day they did the digging of the grave, collecting of the dead and the burying, and departed for the Agency when the sun was not more than an hour high.

Some dead bodies were found afterwards where wounded persons had crawled off, and some in vacant houses.

Soldiers reported seeing Indians coming when the party started for the Agency. Peano did not see these, as he was over the hill out of sight.

He says an idiot who was sitting up in a wagon chattering was killed. This is what all the Indians tell. They say he was the last killed down on the battlefield. All the Indians know he was foolish.

Big Foot was the fourth one put into the grave. He was a large man not fleshy.

[Paddy Starr's Interview]

> *Paddy Starr was forty-eight years old at the time of the interview. He lived with his wife and four children near the Pine Ridge agency. Apparently Ricker had known Starr for some time before the interview, but mistrusted him. In 1903 Ricker wrote, "Can't depend so much on him. Liable to tell anything."*[59]

[Tablet 11]

Wounded Knee. At Frank Salaway's. Tuesday, August 20, 1907

Paddy Starr says: that he was at the battle of Wounded Knee. He was standing across the ravine among the scouts; he was a scout.

Before sunrise he was up. The women had the rations that had been issued to the Indians, and they were feeling happy and singing & it seemed as though they did not suspect any evil or danger. The trouble began about sunrise. The first Paddy noticed was a single shot where quite a lot of people were standing. He looked and saw the smoke of the gun rising above this assemblage. As soon as he looked there was another shot in the same place. As soon as he heard this he saw the swords of officers waving above their heads, and the glinting of the sunbeams from the rising sun. The morning was still and voices could be heard a long way off. Then came to his ears these words: "Look out!" then more prolonged and drawled out was the repetition "Look out!"

Then broke forth the thunderous peal of guns in a volley. John Shangrau was issuing crackers to the women.[60] It seemed as though the fire was poured into these helpless creatures. All the soldiery joined in the fusilade, and the cannon rang out with fierce spirit. There were soldiers behind the scouts who were south of the ravine and about 400 yards from the headquarters & southwest from the headquarters. These soldiers fired also, and the scouts were obliged to run mounted south to escape the cross fire of the soldiers.

The fine line on Starr's map shows where the scouts fled. When they reached the X they halted, and at this point they were fired on by the soldiers, and then they moved again around behind a hill near where a Hotchkiss cannon stood. [Figure 3][61]

Firing was in all directions, it was wild and reckless; all was confusion.

After the battle was over (it did not last till noon) he and others went down along the ravine and cried to the Indians that if any were living to sit up and be saved.

He saw a few women sit up, all badly wounded. He looked into the ravine and saw men and women and children, horses and wagons piled up dead and dying.

When the firing began he saw men and women and children fleeing to the ravine, some falling as shots took effect.

He saw, after the word had been given for them to sit up and be saved, one wounded man who raised up as well as he could, bracing himself with his hands behind himself, and was shot dead by some soldiers who were coming down the ravine from above. Perhaps these soldiers had not heard the cry to sit up and be saved; nevertheless they were killing everything clean as they went.

He says there were 30 or 40 taken prisoner, mostly wounded; these were taken to the Agency.

When Paddy Starr who had the contract to bury the dead at W. K. went out to bury the dead, his party found 7 living—5 grown and two little children, infants. One of the latter was badly frozen. Thinks it lived; he handed it over to Jim Harrison, a Mexican, & told him to take it over to Red Bear's house (log house) which stood abt. 30 yards in front of the commissary. In Red Bear's house he found an old decrepit squaw sitting by the door; she was blind and deaf and was holding a baby in her arms. This old woman was the mother of Crazy Bear who was himself insane. (He says nobody went to the battlefield before his own party; I doubt this; for I think that the party that went for the wounded was ahead of him.)[62] He was two days burying the Indians. He went out with one company of the 7th Cav. (he thinks) and one wagon of working tools and two wagons of provisions for the burial party and about 30 laborers. When he went there were soldiers already out there entrenched on the ridge above the battlefield where I saw the pits.

He tells of Mary Thomas being found on the field when Zit-ka-la-nuni was found. Mary's Indian name is Niglicu win, meaning "comes out alive."[63]

He made his contract with Gen. Miles & was paid $2 for every body interred. Says 168 were put into the grave. Three women who were killed were pregnant. One boy about 10 years old, he remembers, had his left arm and shoulder and left breast torn away by a cannon shot. One woman had her entire abdomen shot away by a Hotchkiss shell. Paddy Starr having the contract to bury & a price for each body would know better than Peano how many dead were buried.[64]

[Frank Feather's Interview]

[Tablet 38]
Kyle, March 4, 1907. Wounded Knee Tragedy

Frank Feather says: The three living babies found on W. K. field by him and others next day were under one year old. There were about 100 Indians and a few white men in the visiting party. Young Bull Bear, living on Medicine Root Cr., took one of these babies; Charging Bear, living on Pass Creek took one; and some Indian took the other, these babies were first taken into the Agency before they were taken by these foster parents. These were friendly Indians who came up from the Agency—the 100 who came. They picked up also the wounded & living. An Inspector, Harry Manns [Mauns?] (he says) came out with them. This Manns was a special agent. George E. Bartlett came over with them; he and Manns were the leading white men; just a few other white men were with these, the clerk of the special agent was along also; a photographer (Trager) a little man, was along taking pictures; the additional Farmer (Clem Davis) came out also.[65]

The wounded taken up were taken to the Agency in wagons. They took in seven wounded Indians, both men and women; one of these was not wounded, he was a man, he was scared & was found in hiding on the creek & was taken in. They did not get all the wounded, for the hostile Indians were coming and the Indians at work on the field took the alarm & fled. Frank Feather remained behind on the field and was the last to leave it; he saw the hostiles and beckoned to them to come on to the field, but they did not come; they were approaching from abt. the direction of the Day School, or more from the northwest. Frank Feather was a policeman from the Agency & was ordered out by his superior with this party. This was the day that Clem Davis fled; & Frank passed his abandoned wagon when he himself went in. Dr Eastman was one of the party that visited the field that day.[66]

Frank Feather is positive that this party went out to the battlefield the next day after the fight.[67] He says the babies would not have been living if they had not done so. He says that it started in raining the night after the fight and turned to snow, and there were about three inches on the ground when they arrived on the field at noon. They had their dinner there on arrival; he took his near where Big Foot lay.

Big Foot and he were related.

The photographer was trying to get a picture of Big Foot. He set his camera, but Shot In Hand was lying dead next to it; Big Foot was lying farther back, and Feathers does not know whether Trager got a picture of Big Foot; he did not tell him which was Big Foot, and he says the photographer did not know which he was.[68]

Frank Feather was on the Little Big Horn at the time of the Custer battle. He and some other boys were on the opposite side of the river from the Indian camp, attending the pony herd. He was not in the fight. He could not give much information. He says the Indian camp was as long as from Kyle to George Little Wound's—about 3 or 4 miles.

He saw a few dead bodies. They were not mutilated. It is not to be presumed that he was herding any ponies except some belonging to his own tribe.

[Man Above's Interview]

[Tablet 12]

Oct. 25, 1906. Interview with Man Above. Joseph Horn Cloud Interpreter.

Man Above says: I was one of Capt. Taylor's Indian scouts and was at Pine Ridge Agency during the troubles.

He was sent out to Short Bulls camp—the hostile camp at the stronghold to ~~where he was~~ make a peace; ~~and when he was starting Capt. Taylor told him~~ that 50 men went with him the first time; there were 10 scouts and 40 other Indians; ~~the second~~ these all went from the Agency. When they got over there to the stronghold they stopped at Short Bull's camp. There was fighting at this time between Short Bull's men and the cowpunchers. Short Bull's men were angry at the 50 men because they came from the Agency to make a peace, and they shot their guns over the heads of the fifty men to express their indignation at their mission; and they told the fifty to go back to the Agency. This, he says was about this time of the year, the leaves were all off the trees, there were a good many soldiers at the Agency. The fifty men came back to the Agency.

Five days afterwards 20 Indian scouts and 130 other Indians went now on a second trip to Short Bull's camp on the Stronghold. This party found Short Bull's people very angry and the conditions very dangerous. Their reception was a volley over their heads, and ordered them to go back to the Agency. And they went back without accomplishing anything.

General Miles told these scouts every time to go.

Major Burke (Buffalo Bill's attaché) told the scouts that the soldiers were going to kill Big Foot's band when they could get them, because they were in the Custer battle, and Man Above told this to Capt. Taylor and the Captain said that was true; but to go ahead on their third trip to Short Bull as directed, and he gave the scouts a white flag with two points ⌖ and told them if on their return there was fighting at the Agency to hoist this flag on a pole and come right in, for they would be safe.[69] They were told by Capt. Taylor to tell Short Bull that Big Foot would be killed. They were told by Capt. Taylor to tell Short Bull that Big Foot would be killed. Big Foot's people were in the battle on the Big Horn. Joseph Horn Cloud was there as a boy. Man Above says that a survivor of the Custer Massacre told him that if they found Big Foot's band they were going to disarm them and if they got angry about it they would all be killed.

The scouts went out on the third trip—thirty in all went this time. Short Bull gave up this time. When they got back to the Agency They came back with his band, but before they reached the Agency Wounded Knee had been fought and Short Bull did not come any farther than the White Clay where he stopped.

Big Foot was shot in the head and in the body. Joseph Horn Cloud says an Indian told him so.

Man Above says: The soldiers made him work hard. The soldiers said when they came that they were going to kill Big Foot's band.

Man Above is an Oglala.

[Standing Soldier's Interview]

Ricker wrote the first paragraph of the following biographical note about Standing Soldier near the middle of the interview.

[Tablet 29]

Standing Soldier is 56 years old. He has served the government many years; under Gens. Crook and Miles and Brooke. Was a lieutenant of police 11 years at

Pine Ridge, and has been a judge of the Indian Court at Pine Ridge ten years. He has, like all his people who have served the government, done good service and been a brave and courageous man. He is said to be a good man.

Pine Ridge, Nov. 20, 1906. Interview with Standing ~~Bear~~ Soldier No. 1. ~~and Chief Red Shirt.~~

He says he was a First Sergeant of Indian Scouts under Captain Taylor during the troubles of 1890.

Just before the Battle of W. K. the scouts were camping just southwest of the hospital at the Agency, near the 7th Cavalry. While here Sitting Bull was killed.

Capt. Taylor told him that Sitting Bull's band and Big Foot's had left their Reserves and were marching this way and he thought they would come along Bear Creek, and he wanted Standing Soldier No. 1 to go and intercept them. He started next morning in charge of fifteen scouts. Red Shirt was not with him at this beginning. First night he camped on Porcupine Creek & 2nd night on the East fork of the Medicine Root. The third day he got up abt. 5 o'clock in the morning & went up on a hill & was taking in the country with a glass & saw the cattle running in every direction. He thought there might be some men around & he watched the place closely, and saw two Indians come out of a canyon & were going toward [the] northeast. They went up on a high hill & sat there awhile & then went out of sight. Standing Soldier & the scouts then went over to where the Indians had been but could not find any thing of them. From there they turned & went eastward down to Bear Creek & there they found a trail of a band of Indians going south of the main Bear Creek. They followed the trail & at the head of Corn Creek this trail turned N. W.; from there it turned north & went down to the head of Medicine Root Creek. There they first met the band of Indians. These Indians on seeing these scouts took their guns as if to fight and he saw that they were not Oglalas, and he asked them who they were. They answered that they were a part of Sitting Bull's band. These Indians told him that some of these had taken part in the fight when Sitting Bull was killed, & that the widows of those who were then killed were here among these. One of the women showed Standing Soldier where she had been shot in the shoulder at the time of the killing of Sitting Bull. After they had finished talking Standing Soldier told them that he was an Oglala and a scout and that these scouts had been sent out to meet them and that he was glad to meet them. He told them that he had no soldiers with him; that he had been sent out to meet them & that they need not be afraid & that he was going to take them to Pine Ridge Agency where they would be protected. After he got through telling them, they told him they had nothing to eat & were about starved to death; so he sent two of his scouts out to take up two cattle belonging to the Indians, & these were killed & divided up among the Indians.

These Indians did not have any tobacco, so the scouts gave them what they had. The hides of the beeves were put up on a house there.

These cattle belonged to Black Prairie Chicken, & the Govt. paid him for these cattle killed. After these Indians had had a good feast he counted the guns which numbered 28; there were 73 persons — men, women & children — they had 31 head of horses and a span of oxen. The oxen belonged to the Indians & they used them to haul the luggage of the camp.

After he had counted what the Inds. had, they gave up to him all their guns. They were perfectly willing to surrender themselves to him.[70] They stayed there that night, next day they started & reached the second branch of Medicine Root Creek. There they struck Big Foot's trail coming this way. So he sent two of his scouts ahead to tell Big Foot to wait for him till he could come up with him, and they would all come in together to General Brooke. He told his scouts to tell Big Foot that Gen. Brooke was at the Agency & that Gen. Brooke and the Agent would protect them. He sent his scouts forward in the morning, and that night Standing Soldier and his Indians camped on the third branch of the Medicine Root Creek. Early the next morning one of his scouts returned & told him that the soldiers & Big Foot's band had met opposite Porcupine Butte & that they had gone on together to W. K., and that the next morning the Indians were all killed off by the soldiers. The scout told him that the soldiers slaughtered everything that was in sight. This scout told him that one of Standing Soldiers scouts had been killed at W. K. (Harback) [High Back Bone] and that the scout interpreter had had his nose cut off in the fight (Philip Wells), and that Capt. Taylor had sent him back to tell him about these things & that the soldiers had gone to the Agency. Standing Soldier asked his scout what had become of the other two scouts whom he sent out with him, & the reply was that they both got scared & went right on to the Agency. This scout was with Capt. Taylor in the fight at W. K. He told Standing Soldier that Taylor's scouts were strung around on the outside south of the ravine, & when the firing begun the shots came among these scouts. so they advanced down into the ravine for shelter

Marshal Hand who is also present at this interview and was one of Taylor's scouts in this battle says that the fire was warm, and one-half of the scouts broke toward W. K. Creek & the other half up the ravine toward the hills, leaving Taylor standing alone; the latter when the fire got too hot advanced down into the ravine for shelter. After the battle his scout was sent back to Standing Soldier by Capt. Taylor with news of the catastrophe, and with orders from Taylor to break up the Indians' guns which he had taken. This he refused to do, saying that he would bring them in to the Agency and turn them over to Gen. Brooke. He then sent a scout back with a letter written by himself to Capt. Taylor and Philip Wells informing them that the Indians needed something to eat and were out of tobacco. Their next day's march brought them to W. K. Creek. These Indians heard the firing of guns and cannon at W. K. They were singing and crying. They were marching in the morning and sometime before noon camped on the head of the west, or third branch of Medicine Root Creek. Some of these Indians were marching on foot. These Indians thought the soldiers were fighting some other band and they were excited and afraid. He himself knew that these outnumbered his scouts, and to calm them and to prevent them from attacking his scouts he told them that it was a custom of the soldiers to salute their officers and that this was what they were doing. He thus deceived them for the sake of safety to himself & scouts and the success of his errand.

They stayed at this place where they heard the firing over night. Next morning they started and went by the head of Porcupine Creek & head of Stinking Water and arrived at the W. K. crossing about sundown. This was the upper W. K. crossing where I crossed on my way to Allen. The lower W. K. crossing is at the battleground. They came right on and after they had crossed W. K. they met Chief Red Shirt with 30 scouts bearing provisions and tobacco. After they arrived at Wolf Creek, three miles east of the Agency, he dispatched Chief Red Shirt ahead to notify Capt. Taylor and Gen. Brooke that he was coming with the Indians. When within half a mile of the Agency he told the men to turn their guns over to the women and to form themselves in line. I should here correct something that has gone before. He did not take the guns from the Indians for fear they would suspicion something wrong, but left them in their hands, though they were willing he should have them.

He formed his line with ten scouts on each flank and ten in rear & they started to enter the Agency. He stopped close to the Agency. In front of the Indians he placed himself and raised his right hand saying "God, our Father, help us that we may make peace and friendship with the Oglalas tonight." Then turning toward the Indians he said: that away back in the treaties the

STANDING SOLDIER

~~Government~~ Great Father told the Indians that they must be friendly with the white people and have no more war with them. That was why he had gone to the great trouble to go away down there to meet and bring them safely to the Agency. Then they marched right on into the Agency, stopping in front of the Agent's office, arriving towards midnight, while everybody was yet up. Here Captain Taylor came to them & he allowed nobody to come near these Indians.

(It should have been said that when Standing Soldier's scout brought word to him of the disaster at W. K. he instructed all his scouts to keep this painful information strictly to themselves and not let it be known to the Indians.)

Capt. Taylor went round and shook hands with all of the Indians. Just then a scout approached the Captain and told him that Gen. Brooke wanted to see him with two of these Indians. So he took two of the best and went over to Brooke's. When they entered Brooke's house the General asked Standing Soldier what two Indians he had with him. He told Brooke that they were members of Sitting Bull's band. Brooke asked the two Indians if they were willing to give up their guns and they said they were & that they had already delivered them to Standing Soldier. Brooke told them he was glad that they had done that & he shook hands with them & then wrote out an order to the quartermaster to issue rations to those Indians. They then went back to the Indians who gave up their arms to Captain Taylor and received rations.

Capt. Taylor encamped them where he had his scouts and they were there awhile. These Indians remained on Pine Ridge Reservation after the settlement of the troubles and are recognized as Oglalas.

The reason why he took the Indians away round the circuitous route he did was because he remembered the treaty of 1868 in which the Great Father said they should have no more fighting with the whites, and he was afraid if the Indians smelled the blood of W. K. they would break out fighting.

Standing Soldier says if he had succeeded in reaching Big Foot he should have brought his band round as he did the others and they would not have been killed.

The day he met the Indians was on the 29th of Dec. and moved to the west branch of the Medicine Root where they heard the firing.

[Here appeared the first paragraph of the biographical data that begins this interview.]

He tells how it is that the Indian scouts do the real hard work, are not recognized for it, and their white officers gain all the credit and reputation and promotion. They begin with them — in charge of them — as lieutenants or captains, and are promoted step by step till they wear stars. When as commanding officer of Indian scouts they want to find out the position of an Indian village they send the scouts forward to spy and hunt and take the risk; these come back and report to the officer who then reports to his superior and receives all the credit.

These scouts were paid $25 a month and rations, and they furnished their horses, saddles and bridles. He thinks men such as he should be paid a pension.

He and nearly all the Indian scouts belonging to Fort Robinson were over here at Pine Ridge during the capture and outbreak of the Cheyenne Indians but Lone Bear was back at the Fort.[71] After the outbreak the scouts were sent for and he got over there in time to be in the last part of the last battle. He says he came over from the Fort with the Cheyennes who were turned over to Red Cloud and there were fiftyseven in all of these, and they came over in charge of the government Indian scouts. He says there were about 18 soldiers killed in that affair.

Speaking of the capture and death of Crazy Horse he says that he was one of the scouts sent from Fort Robinson to Spotted Tail Agency to get him. When they got over to Spotted Tail they were told that Crazy Horse had said if anybody came after him he would kill him or them; so it was arranged for some of the Rosebud Indians to go out and get him, which they did; and they took him under guard to Fort Robinson. The object in taking C. Horse was to convey him to Washington to see the president, and the Agent at Red Cloud wanted the Rosebud Indians in charge to stop with him at the Agency so he could tell C. Horse the purpose for which he was being brought in and to have him left there, but they would not stop, and went on to the Fort where he was killed the same day. (I doubt whether he is correctly informed as to the object.)

An officer, (and somebody else I have forgotten) and four privates went with C. Horse into the guardhouse followed by an Oglala, Little Big Man and some of Crazy Horse's friends.[72] When inside he saw where they were taking him, and he drew his knife and began backing out. Little Big Man shouted, "Don't! don't! don't do that!" and seized him by the arms. Crazy Horse cut L. B. Man in the wrist. The soldiers were trying to keep him in with their bayonets; he got out of doors and the guard on the outside stepped up and thrust his bayonet into his side low down and pretty well around toward his back. He fell and Standing Soldier raised him up, but he was soon dead. The soldier stabbed him purposely.

Crazy Horse's body was removed by the Indians to Rosebud; from there they removed his bones to the cliff on the east side of White Horse Creek, 4 miles above Manderson and thence it is not known where they have been moved. (This account about the removal of his remains is apocryphal. It is disputed by some Indians that any Indian's remains have been put up in that cliff. I can not use the story.)[73]

Standing Soldier No. 1 is so called because there is another Standing Soldier here older than No. 1, and they are numbered to distinguish.

[Creighton Yankton's Interview]

[Tablet 29]

Interview with Creighton Yankton, an Oglala Sioux who attended school at the old Boarding School that was burned down at Pine Ridge, also school at Wabash, Indiana, a year and a half, and school at Lawrence, Kansas, and is a wheelwright by trade. This interview was at Mr. E. M. Keith's at Wounded Knee Battleground, November 18, 1906.

He says he returned from Wabash, Indiana, the next spring after the battle, and the Indians were talking much at that time about the recent troubles. I asked him to tell me what he heard them say about how the action commenced, and he stated that they told how the Indians were seated in a circle; how they were searched as well as the tents; how two Indians after the others had been searched, stood up with white sheets on and Winchesters under them, and in bitter words of contempt and reproach denounced those about them as cowards for giving up their arms; and when a soldier undertook to wrest the gun from the hands of one of these men the latter discharged its contents into the body of the sergeant who fell dead. Then the firing began.

Creighton Yankton says: He had an aunt that was wounded eight times. Her name was Big Woman; this was a name of quality as well as of capacity; for she was and is (for she is living) a big woman.

Yankton heard the Indians blame the two young men who stood up and refused to give up their guns; they said in their talk that if these two men had given up their arms they would all have been taken to the Agency and feasted, there would have been a council and an end of all trouble.

[William Denver McGaa's Interview]

William Denver McGaa was born on March 8, 1859, purportedly the first birth in Denver, Colorado. His mother was an Oglala mixed-blood and after her death McGaa took up residence at Pine Ridge. He held various jobs in the agency and later became a successful cattle rancher.[74]

Ricker lost no time in setting up an appointment with McGaa. Five days before the interview he wrote the following note.

[Tablet 39]

See W. D. McGaa, 26 miles north of Manderson and 16 miles north of Baptiste Pourrier his father-in-law. The stage runs no farther than Manderson. McGaa was with the train from Laramie which met Crook's starving army. He was Colonel Henry's scout and interpreter in the Wounded Knee operations.[75]

[Tablet 9]

Interview with Wm. Denver McGaa. At Baptiste Pourier's November 8, 1906.

He says he came to the Pine Ridge Reservation from Colorado, Fort Collins, in 1880, to live with his people. When he first came on the Reservation the Indians were getting 6,000 head of cattle and [they] were supposed to last them 7 to 9 months. They had plenty to eat—lots of meat, of sugar and coffee and flour. When the agency was over at the "Sod Agency" on the Platte, it stood about 6 or 7 miles above the mouth of Horse Creek and about 30 miles below Fort Laramie.

The buildings were built of sods.

He has seen flour, after being drawn by the Indians, dumped in great piles by the ton to get the sacks to put meat, or wild fruit or turnips into. The flour was black and poor and they did not know how to use [it] in any way; and so it was worthless to them. The bacon they received was poor and full of yellow streaks and mushy; so they would not use it, as wild game was abundant. He says he has hauled wood in and swapped with the Indians for their bacon. Says he has traded wood (which was scarce at that Agency—had to be hauled 15 or 20 miles) for an equal quantity of bacon—the load he took back was as heavy as the one he brought into the Agency.

In October, 1876, McGaa and Peter Richard had charge of 300 head of cattle, without any help, drove them from Fort Laramie to Custer City for Crook's starving army.[76] Stayed with Crook's command about a week and then carried a dispatch from Crook to Fort Robinson in two days; and from Fort Robinson they both carried dispatches to Fort Laramie.

When he came here in 1880 he took the census of the Pine Ridge Indians, and by this means he discovered that there were more Indians on the census rolls than he could account for. In issuing rations there were not so many Indians as appeared by the census; and he think[s] that the difference between what was real and what was false went into somebody's pocket.

In 1881 and 1882 he was a herder on P. Ridge. They received 6,000 head then. The cattle had to be branded. They would run 6 or 8 or a dozen head into the chute for branding. He noticed that the Boss Herder used a cold iron—one so cool that it would burn only the hair; did hair-branding; these "branded" cattle were then turned out on the range and ran till they were needed for slaughter. They were supposed to last till May—were "branded" when received about October. The brand was the Pine Ridge Agency brand—Oglala brand—FOF.[77]

There was a resident inspector who represented the Wyoming Live Stock Association and by whom he was paid a good salary. These inspectors were changed occasionally. When any stock was rounded up, if the Agency brand—FOF—did not clearly appear, as it in a great many cases did not, the inspector cut these out as belonging to outsiders. McGaa spotted lots of these cattle that he afterwards saw sold back to the government. This operation was several times repeated. Afterwards when the government had bought them times enough some of them were shipped to Chicago. "This used to be the rottenest place he ever saw, and it isn't very far from it now," he says. He thinks they are doing no better now; thinks the store keepers are doing them up; they are allowed to buy their cattle and horses at any age. The farmers will not let the mixed bloods buy from the Indians; these farmers stop them—tells the mixed bloods that it is against the rules for them to buy the cattle; at the same time the same Farmers do not prevent the store keepers from buying the same kinds of live stock.

The Indians are done up now; they are not one-half as well off as they were in 1883, 1884 and 1885. All of them had more or less live stock then; now there are scarcely any that have more than 5 or 6 head of cattle and 2 or 3 ponies; and some have not a single pony. He became chief herder in 1883 and held it a year and a half. He branded his cattle well, and this was the reason why he held his job no longer—he was let out. Says he had lots of offers to do corruptly. The excuse made for his removal was that any person who had cattle of his own could not hold a government position. He had 11 head belonging to his wife. So, rather than part with the cattle his wife had, he let his job be taken away.

McGaa was Boss Farmer at Manderson—Wounded Knee District— 9 months under Captain Brown who was agent.[78] Brown was a good Agent; he visited from house to house among the Indians; he personally looked after their interests; he examined for himself and ascertained what they were doing and what they needed; he would not let them sell cattle under three years of age; now they can be bought by favorite buyers at any age or price. The Indians can not now sell to everybody.

McGaa hired to General Brooke who was in command at the Agency, to do scouting. He went out with Col. Henry as chief guide and interpreter abt. 4 P.M. Dec. 24, 1890. At 12 o'clock that night he and Col. Henry [and] 3 or 4 of his officers reached Baptiste Pourier's stable. They traveled all night and rested their horses for two hours on Cottonwood Creek, 45 miles from the Agency. Cottonwood Creek is north of White River. They came down White Horse Creek which empties into W. K. Creek just above Manderson, thence down Wounded Knee, and crossed White River below the mouth of W. K. Cr. & went north to Harney Springs within 4 or 5 miles of the Reservation line on the north side, and north of Cottonwood Springs Creek which runs east and west. The Indians were at this time 5 or 6 miles west of Harney Springs on the Stronghold. This was the 9th (Ninth) Cavalry Colored troops. On the 27th Col. Henry sent McGaa with some scouts to the top of the Stronghold; these scouts did not show themselves to the Indians but peeked around; they discovered the last of the Indians leaving the Stronghold and going south in the direction of the Agency. On the 28th the command moved from Harney Springs down to the mouth of Fog Creek, south of Harney Springs 12 or 14 miles, and where Fog Creek empties into White River. On the 28th he and other scouts to gether went up on the Stronghold again and found that the Indians were all gone. On the 29th he led Colonel Henry and about four troops up on the Stronghold to see how strong was their position and how they had strengthened the natural surroundings. They occupied a spur pointing north and jutting out from the east half of the Stronghold; south of this position was a level plateau from 3 to 6 miles wide and 10 or 12 miles long, extending east and west. They could have been easily shelled out of the place. At the neck of their position they had breastworks across with a narrow opening sufficient to let a wagon pass through. The[y] had rifle pits also. Their idea was that the soldiers would ascend the stronghold and advance from the south, and they would defend the spur from being occupied by the soldiers. Col. Henry's command was camped south of Sheep mountain.

Mr. McGaa drew above map. [Figure 4]

White River is 8 miles south of the Stronghold. He has lived 20 years close to the spur where the Indians were entrenched.

About sundown on the 29th Colonel Henry got back to his camp at the mouth of Fog Creek. He and McGaa were riding together coming back, & he told the Colonel that they were going to get bad news; says he felt it.

Two Indians came about 9 o'clock that night and handed McGaa a letter; he gave it to the Colonel who opened it and read the news of the Wounded Knee tragedy. In half an hour the regiment was on the march for the Agency. The Colonel wanted to go by the way of the Porcupine but McGaa refused to go that way. So they moved up Wounded Knee Creek to the mouth of White Horse Creek and thence up that. On Cheyenne Creek, about two miles northeast of the Agency, one of Henry's troopers in advance of the wagon train was killed by an Indian whom the soldier took to be a soldier, as he was dressed in uniform of a soldier.

Same morning before the Ninth unsaddled the smoke was seen rising from the burning schoolhouse where the Wells' lived down near the Mission. Forsyth was down there with the 7th Cavalry. He says he didn't see much of a fight. Saw them firing a Hotchkiss pretty fast at what they thought was Indians, but he looked through the glass and saw it was a row of fence posts only. Forsyth had some men injured. Otherwise there was nothing much.

On 31st McGaa quit Gen. Brooke started out on that day and went north.

He is sure that Crazy Horse was purposely killed.

[Tablet 24]

McGaa was with the train from Laramie which met Gen. Crook's starving army. He was also with Colonel Henry who was sent out from the Agency to intercept Big Foot. He says Big Foot's Indians were coming to the Agency for protection.

[James Garvie's Interview]

[Tablet 15]

See Mr. Garvie's Statement for person to correspond with.

At Mr. E. M. Keith's, Jan. 4, 1907

James Garvie says: His mother who died in 1881 was part Sisseton and part

Wah' pa que te. His father was a white man who was killed at the Yellow Medicine Agency at about the second or third day of the Minnesota massacre, and Mr. Garvie was eight days old when the killing began at the Lower Agency on Aug. 18, 1862. It was about 30 miles between the two agencies.[79]

Mr. Garvie says there are 900 or 1,000 Ponca Indians. There are 270 of them at the junction of the Niobrara river with the Missouri & in Nebraska; have taken their allotments there and are scattered around there.[80] The rest are in Indian Territory. These Indians claim never to have been at war with the whites nor ever to have killed a white man.

Standing Bear is now living where the 270 are.[81]

Mr. Garvie says that E. A. Fry who lives at Niobrara, has published a local paper there for sometime and now publishes a magazine there.

Says he has lived there 30 or 40 years.[82]

Mr. Garvie says that the colored man Joseph Godfrey, who was in the Minnesota Massacre is living at Santee Agency about 8 miles east of Niobrara, six miles from the Reservation line.[83] The Ponca Santees have no Agency but a superintendent who takes care of the government property and draws his pay — a sinecure.

The Poncas have no actual agency — that has been abolished — but there is a Boss Farmer who issued a few rations to the old people who still draw under the treaties.

Mr. Garvie says that so great is the apprehension of Joseph Godfrey of being killed for the bloody part he had in the Minnesota Massacre, that he cannot be induced to make any statement on the subject. But Mr. G. believes that he can get him to talk. Godfrey has been shot at once. Mr. and Mrs. Garvie tell me of a Civil War veteran called Colonel Bryant who is working for the Nebraska State Historical Soc. has been trying to obtain historical facts from them.[84]

Mr. Garvie says: That Big Foot's band were carrying on the ghost dance on the Cheyenne River, some 30 miles above Fort Bennett which was a fort and Cheyenne Agency combined (the fort was the postoffice) about six miles below the mouth of the Cheyenne River. The fort is abandoned.

They were told that a company of soldiers was coming after them. Prior to this Big Foot had been notified by a policeman to move down to Fort Bennett. This he refused to do, saying that his people were doing no harm.

(Mr. Garvie gives the names of the following persons who can give very full and accurate account of the events about this time; one was Clarence Ward, an Indian missionary, whose home was and now is there; his P.O. address is either Leslie which is above him, or Callomar which is below him: the other is Edwin Phelps who was living there and is there now and since those events has been ordained a minister. His P.O. address is Cheyenne Agency S.D. Mr. Ward was living right on Cherry Creek at that time. This creek flows into Cheyenne River from the north and Mr. Ward was about 2 or 3 miles above the mouth of Cherry Creek, & Mr. Phelps was living on the south side of the Cheyenne River opposite the mouth of Cherry Creek. Mr. Garvie was at these places one year before the disturbances began. These men are both Indians. Mr. Ward doesn't speak English, but his wife is a half breed, and she and the children can talk English; but Mr. Phelps is quite well educated. When I write I should mention Mr. Garvie. Mr. Garvie says that Rev. T. L. Riggs — son of Stephen — can give me information. His address Oahe, S.D. near Pierre.)

After Big Foot had refused to go to Fort Bennett word was brought to his camp that a company of troops was coming to bring them in. On this information Big Foot moved.

(Mr. Garvie says he was not there at the time but was near Fort Pierre — was nine miles up Bad River from the fort, and was about 60 or 65 miles or 70 miles from Big Foot's camp — the journey could not be made very easily in one day. Mr. G. is not certain but is of the impression that the soldiers started to go to Big Foot's camp.)

From here on Mr. Garvie does not know specifically anything more about Big Foot's movements till the battle took place.

I have concluded that it is not proper and is unjust to call the Messiah movement a "craze." It was a religious "movement," a religious "fervor," a religious "enthusiasm;" the movement swelled to an enthusiasm and reached the height at times of religious fervor, not unlike swells of religious fervor which have swept English communities and sections and become celebrated in history.

Mr. Garvie says that the stable, thoughtful Indians of judgment who were leaders of thought and worthy to be such, did not take any stock in the Messiah story; they had no faith in it; were skeptical, doubters, scoffers, joked and laughed about it. When the time came and passed that the change of destroying the whites and restoring to the Indians their former conditions and fulfilling their hopes came and passed, these sober, calculating leaders would remark jeeringly on the failure of the deceptive scheme and ask the ardent dupes what they thought of it now that their prognostications had failed. Mr. G. says that not ten per cent of the Indians soberly, seriously believed in the movement; that he has talked only with Short Bull about it and ~~this is what he has discovered to be the true state of the case,~~ could not get any thing out of him on the subject. I suspect that as his conversations have been subsequent to the movement itself which closed with such distressing events, that many of the Indians who really believed in the new Messiah were afterwards unwilling to acknowledge their faith and participation, and would then ridicule what they had ardently embraced, and deny all responsibility for acts which were really their own. I think this is Mr. Garvie's opinion.

Mr. Garvie concurs in the designations which I have stated at the beginning of this paragraph about the "craze."

Mr. Garvie says that young people were drawn into the movement by the dancing, as this was a recreation and pleasure. This attraction swelled the numbers of those who appeared to be Messiahites. Mr. G. ridicules the idea that the leading Indians believed that the ghost shirt would turn bullets.

Mr. Garvie has written a history of Swift Bear which is now still in manuscript.[85] He wants to sell it. He says Swift Bear was made a chief by some commanding officer at Fort Robinson for an act of great humanity in saving a number of captive white soldiers from further captivity if not from a worse fate. A lot of about 30 soldiers had been killed near Fort Robinson (?) and a few were taken prisoners. These prisoners Swift Bear secretly stole away with at night and brought them to the fort. For this act of kindness he was promptly rewarded as stated.[86]

Swift Bear has always been a friend of the whites and a practical exponent of civilization. He began early (in the year 1884) to advocate ~~and to enforce his views by actual practice of the benefits~~ and to enforce his views by actual practice of the benefits the benefits of the civilized life. He took his band and settled on Ponca Creek in Gregory County, S.D., where they are now surrounded by white settlers, and are prospering with moderate success, and has ever since lived in the same place where they have all tried to imitate the white people.

Mr. Garvie happened to be the interpreter and helped to put up the school house which he was asking from the American Missionary Association, for which this Ass'n. furnished the means to erect.

Mr. Garvie thinks it was 50 or 60 years ago that the 30 soldiers were killed. I tell him it was not done at Fort Robinson; he thinks it was and says he can tell when he looks at his history of Swift Bear, which is in M S.

Mr. Garvie says that the peaceable, unoffending Winnebagoes who live now between Sioux City and Omaha, were in the heart of Minnesota in 1862 and were dispossessed entirely of their lands and homes and put down on their present reservation.⁸⁷ He thinks they have never received any compensation. Says they once asked him to take up their case and try to get something for them, but he replied that he had as much as he could do for his own people.

He says that the article published in the Omaha Bee of April 4th or the 14th, 1906, giving the "Narrative of the Santee Sioux Claim," is a concise history of the case written by himself and Lawyer Breckenridge of Omaha. Mr. G. says I will get all the facts in the documents which he will list for me on application.⁸⁸

The number of the Santees is about 1,100 and they are all in this one place on the reserve in Nebraska.⁸⁹

Mr. Garvie says he has been working on the claim of the friendly and innocent Santees; for instance the men who were forced to go on the warpath, and the innocent children and the young people who were too young to take to arms. The claim is $3,126,000.⁹⁰

The Sissetons also have a claim of over $2,000,000 which is ahead of the Santee, and it is expected it will be disposed of soon. He says that Congress has allowed the claim, and that the Court of Claims has before it the case of determining what Indians were loyal and unoffending. The Sisseton case will decide the Santee. Breckenridge has a contingent fee of 10 per cent.

[Tablet 22]

Mr. Garvie gives the following: pub. in Indianapolis pub. "Conquest of the Sioux" By C. S. or S. C. Gilman written by a friend of Mr. Garvie.⁹¹

Mr. Garvie says he wrote a biography of Artemus Ehnamani (E'hna ma ni) meaning, Walk Amongst in English. He sold it to the Bureau of Ethnology abt. 5 yrs. ago. I have it, of course. Says he sold it in 1901 after J. W. Powell was dead.⁹²

Mr. Garvie has the book issued by the Govt. in relation to the Black Hills treaty in 1876, being the minutes of the Council &c. Very scarce. Says Congressmen have failed to get it. I will try for it.

Mr. Garvie tells of the case of the Maletka (?) Indians on an Island of Matelka, Duncan or Williamson. Ask Indians Rights Assn. abt. above & see Repts. Bureau of Ethnology.⁹³

Mr. Garvie tells of a little book on the Custer battle he has which tells why Custer died as he did &c & he will send it to me if I will write & remind him.

Write Arthur Tibbetts Cannon Ball, North Dak., who is Traveling Secy.

for the International Committee of Y. M. C. A. He was a young man not old enough to fight, but rode over the Custer field after the battle. Mr. Garvie says for me to mention his name when I write to him. Both are friends.

Mr. Garvie says he wrote an article ridiculing the claims of the cattle men living between the Cheyenne and the White Rivers who put in claims for cattle killed by depredations of Big Foot's band when it came down. The aggregate of claims was $100,000. Mr. G. says he will get this for me if I will remind him in my letter to him.

[John Shangrau's Interview]

About a month before the interview Ricker met briefly with the Shangraus and wrote the following note in Tablet 3.

John Shangrau lives at Allen, S.D., and runs store and post-office. His wife said to me that she ran it. She has a delicate form, fine, Grecian features, no trace of Indian blood except the brunette, uses polished speech, is a beautiful woman, quick in conversation and entertaining.

John Shangrau was in the Wounded Knee battle, was a scout. He says nobody knows who started the fight, whether white or red fighter.

He was coming in for protection.

[Tablet 27]

Interview with John Shangrau at Allen, S.D., November 5, 1906.[94]

He says: He went from Fort Robinson in the early part of 1876 with a party of scouts, 10 altogether, ~~under command~~ in charge of Louie Richard (Reshaw); they went to Fort Laramie, thence to Fetterman where they found Gen. Crook, though his command had gone on to Sage Creek which is the headwaters of the Cheyenne River.[95] Crook started right out with these scouts who joined the other scouts at Sage Creek. There were now altogether 30 scouts with Crook. The names of the principal ones who did the tough work of the year were:

The half-breeds who were the main scouts were: Louie Richard, Louie Shangrau, Charlie Richard (cousin to Louie), Charlie Janis, Baptiste Garnier, John Provost, Mitch Shimmeno (this spelling is not right, see Mr. Mousseau's account) Baptiste Pourier, Frank Gruard, Jack Russell, John Farnham (these are all from Pine Ridge but not all halfbreeds).[96]

The command moved on. The night they got to Sage Creek the Indians shot the herder and took every hoof of their beef cattle.[97] Next morning the army moved and camped on Spring Cr. this side of Powder River, & next morning moved from there & they saw 2 Indians afoot, & the scouts charged on them, but Crook called them back. Then the army camped at the crossing of Powder River that night. About dark 5 scouts were sent on towards Crazy Woman & that night when they started he went & visited Capt. Egan & had a talk with him; & Egan said, "Shangrau what do you think of the 2 Indians that were seen this morning?"[98] He answered: "If the village is camped below us they will charge on us tonight. If there is a big camp of them they may charge early in the morning; if there are not very many they may charge tonight." He says, "Oh they are 25 or 30 miles from here now." "Don't you think it." Shangrau now went back to his tent. Just as he reached the camp fire they commenced hollering & hooting. The Indians were going up the creek firing; then they turned about & came down firing. Before they went away the soldiers began firing by volleys. When it was all over it was found that one soldier was shot through the cheek.

Frank Gruard and other scouts, 5 in all, had been sent forward at dark to avoid detection. The shooting It was a bright moonlight night. These 5 scouts were across Powder River and 6 miles in advance and about half way to Crazy Women sitting on a mountain smoking when Charlie Janis saw flashes from guns, and finally when the soldiers fired there was a great flash. The scouts knew that fighting was going on, and they returned. When they were across the river from the camp, the soldiers had a fire on each side of the road so they could examine these scouts as they came in. Next morning the army moved to Crazy Woman. There they left all the wagons and all of the wagons went back to the crossing of Powder River. From Crazy Woman they took a pack train and moved that night to Pole Creek, and from there Crook sent Louie Richard, Louie Shangrau, Frank Gruard, John Shangrau, Baptiste Garnier and Baptiste Pourier, Charley Janis, Tom Reed and Speed Stagner, scouts, forward & they camped that night on Tongue River, & next night on a little creek they called Prairie Dog Town, & next day they went to the head of Rosebud and that third day from camp they turned about and met the troops on Tongue River. They had been sent out to look for Indians but had discovered nothing. The command now turned east toward Powder River and camped on Otter Creek. They saw two mounted Indians as they were going into camp. The scouts gave them chase but could not overtake them. When they made camp Gen. Crook said to the scouts, you go and see which way they came. Louie Richard came over to John Shangrau and said to him, "Saddle up your horse, & Charley Richard, you saddle up your horse." The snow was pretty deep. And he told these scouts to take the Indians' tracks & follow them back 5 or 6 miles & see what direction they came from. They took the trail & followed back 6 miles & then came back to camp. Louie Richard asked how it was about the trail. John told him what they had done & that the trail came down the Otter Cr. all the way; so Richard told Crook. The General ordered Richard to take his ½ breed scouts & 6 companies of soldiers & follow the Indians' tracks back; so about dark they all went & traveled all night; it got so they could hardly see the tracks, then one of the scouts walked till he was tired, then another would change off & so on; abt. daylight they got on the ridge of Powder R.; the soldiers were 3 or 4 miles behind the scouts; here the latter made a fire to warm, as it was a pretty cold night. While making a fire Louie Shangrau & Frank Gruard were sent on so they could see Powder River bottom, promising to stay there till they returned. Both came back saying there was a camp, for they heard the horse bells; but they couldn't see the camp for the darkness. Frank Gruard was sent back to Crook to hurry & come up as they had discovered the camp. Meantime they sent Louie Richard & Louie Shangrau back to the River to see if they could not see the camp. Before the troops arrived these 2 scouts had returned and it was daylight. They reported a big camp. They said they counted 51 lodges. Then the troops arrived. Louie Richard told Major Reynolds about the no. of lodges & where the camp was.[99] All moved towards the camp trying to reach it before sunrise. Got within 1½ miles of the camp. The command was on the west of the Powder River & marching from west to east. The River runs north. Two Creek[s] running from west to east empty into the River. They were just little draws. The Indian camp was on the west side of Powder River & between these two draws. This was the way it was thought these draws ran, and the force was divided so one part should follow down one of them, on the inside of course, and the other down the other draw on the inside. It turned out, however to be this way: the right hand draw went down to the River, but the left hand one bore off diagonally and emptied into the right hand one about half a mile from Powder River. To the surprise of all the two divisions came together, disarranging the plan of attack which was to strike the camp simultaneously from both north and south. The command all moved down toward the river, keeping in the draw, and to the south of the camp. There was a cut bank, so that there was a first bottom on the River, and on this was the camp. The command was huddled down close in a position protected from view by a depression in the surface, and 200 yards south of the camp. While waiting in this place an Indian came out on the edge of the cut bank and began calling to the camp to wake and get up. The sun was then just up. Capt. Egan, speaking to the scouts, said, "Boys, I am going to charge into the camp. You half-breed scouts charge to the right of me and take all the horses you possibly can." To his troop he said, "You get ready." Again addressing the scouts he said: "You charge on the right hand side and take all the horses."

Instantly the charge was made. Egan's troopers dashed into the camp firing as they went. The scouts dashed forward at the same time, passing to the right of the camp and between it and the River, getting every Indian horse, about 700 head. The Indians broke for the bluffs west of the camp. They were high and steep. The soldiers destroyed the camp, burning everything. There were 51 lodges. These Indians were Oglalas.[100]

Capt. Egan lost about seven men killed, some wounded and some horses killed & others wounded.[101] Mr. Shangrau says he heard that one wounded man was given ammunition for his gun and left in the hands of the enemy. He did not see it. Says they did not see an injured Indian except an old woman who was shot in the hip. After the fighting, which lasted till about noon, and they stayed till towards evening when they left in the ordinary way. There was no hasty departure.[102] Mr. S. says he has heard several Indians who were there at this time afterwards say that when the soldiers went away they came down into the village to get whatever they could, as they were naked and suffering, they found this wounded soldier sitting up on the ground. They killed and scalped him. As the troops moved away the Indians followed them. It was cold and snowing. The command moved up the River to the mouth of Pole Creek, about ten miles from the scene of the fighting and camped. The scouts asked Reynolds who was in command, if they should not night herd the Indians' ponies. He said, "No, drive them up the River about a mile from the camp and turn them loose." Next morning it was found that over one-half had been taken back by the Indians. Louie Richard reported this to Major Reynolds. Then he wanted some scouts to go to meet Gen. Crook. Five of them, Louie Shangrau, Frank Gruard, Jack Russell, John Shangrau, and Baptiste Garnier went. They went across toward Otter Creek to meet Crook; on the way back they met 2 Indians driving 60 or 70 head of the lost horses. Frank Gruard said, "Let us stay in this hole till they pass & then go on to Crook." They did so & then went on half way to Otter Cr. Didn't see Crook, so turned back on their own trail and came to their camp of the night before. The troops had gone further up the River, though the scouts had been told that they would remain there till they returned. The scouts followed the trail of the troops, and very soon saw the tracks of the pack mules and the scouts knew that Gen. Crook had joined Reynolds, for the packers were back with him. It was snowing hard. Going two miles they saw some horses in the bottom. They went to them to get a horse for Little Bat, as his had played out. They saw Indian saddles and meat on stumps. They then knew there was a war party close by, so they caught one of the horses & Bat saddled him and then they took the horses with them. John Shangrau left the other scouts & went on ahead till he found the tracks of the Indians following the troops. He informed the scouts that he had seen the tracks of 10 warriors. So they left the horses they were driving. The timber was thick & could be scarcely passed except in the road. There were five scouts and ten Indians ahead of them. John S. suggested that they keep behind the Indians. In a little time the scouts could see where the Indians had turned off into the bottom.

This move by them was the result of discovering just ahead of them the cavalry camp. The scouts went into their camp. Gen. Crook accosted them with the remark: "Boys, I am glad you have come back. It is a shame that the Major should send you back; he might know I would be along; you might all got killed over there." That night some of the Indians charged on the camp but did no harm. This is the end of the story. The movement had consumed about seven days. The soldiers got out of grub and ate horse meat. The command marched back to the wagon train on Powder River where there was once an old fort— C. F. Smith or Reno. There was nothing remaining but some of the old houses. The command returned to Fort Fetterman where the troops cantoned. The ten scouts came back to Fort Robinson.

Wounded Knee

John Shangrau says: He and two Indian soldiers guided Major Whiteside and about six troops of the 7th Cavalry out from the Agency to W. K. John was chief of scouts at this time. On the morning of the 28th Little Bat and Hand, a half-brother of Bat and two other scouts went out early and about noon John was looking up the road towards Porcupine & he saw a mounted man coming fast, and it was Hand. He arrived & said, "We have discovered Big Foot. They are camped on Porcupine." He said that the Indians said they were going to come to the camp. John went and told Major Whiteside. He ordered the troops to saddle up right early. John said to him: "Major, Big Foot told the men that he was going to come to the camp & we may as well stay here till they come." He replied, "There are other soldiers over in there & they might shoot into them & I will go over to protect them & bring them back here." So the command went to Porcupine. Before they got there another scout came back & he reported that the Indians were moving toward W. K. So John told the Major. He answered, "We will go on and meet them." The command got up right under Porcupine Butte when they saw the Indians coming on the ridge from Porcupine. Little Bat and the other scout came back. John asked Bat how it was with those Indians. He said, "They look pretty tough. We are liable to catch it today." They came up on the hill and saw the column and stopped. John looked through a glass & saw them going forward and back & were tying up their horses tails as they do when they go to war. The soldiers then continued to advance & they to advance likewise. When they all got close together the soldiers formed in line on a little ridge, with the cannon right out in front of the soldiers. Two footmen were coming ahead of the Indians' wagons. John told the Major he was going to meet them. The Major said "All right, go on." John started toward them. When he got up to the two footmen he shook hands with them & said "Where is Big Foot?" An Indian said "He is in this wagon sick." John went up and said to Big Foot, "How, Cola" and shook hands with Big Foot. He said to Big Foot: "Partner come with me & see the commanding officer." Big Foot told his driver to drive on. The Major came up and shook hands with Big Foot. All the warriors were scattered out round. Major said: "Big Foot, I want you to come to the camp with me." "All right," said Big Foot, "I am going there." Major said to Shangrau: "John, I want the horses and guns." John answered: "Look here, Major, if you do that there is liable to be a fight here; and if there is you will kill all these women and children and the men will get away from you." "But," he says, "I have an order to do that wherever I catch them." "Well," John said, "That might be it, but we better take them to camp & then take their horses away from them and their guns." He says, "All right; you tell Big Foot to move down to camp at W. K." John told him & he replied, "All right, I am going down to camp; that is where I am going." So they all went down to the camp that day.

Next morning, the 29th, a company of Indian soldiers pulled in that morning from Pine Ridge. These were Taylor's scouts. John says they were Regular soldiers, enlisted men. (They came in in the night.) The Major sent for John & told him to tell all the Indian men to come in front of Big Foot's tent. John told them & they came and took position in a circle which was complete with an opening in the southwest side. The Major said to John to tell them he wanted their guns. John told them. Some of the Indians talking among themselves said to one another, said "You go and see Big Foot; whatever he says we will do." There were two Indians went into B. F.'s tent, & John followed them in. One of the Indians said to B. F., "The soldiers want our guns; but we came over to ask you, and whatever you say, we will do." B. F. said, "This is the third time they are going to take the guns away from me; but, I will tell; you give them some of the bad guns, but keep the good ones." John then told Big Foot: "You better give up the guns; if you give the guns, you can get guns again—you can buy guns, but if you lose a man you cannot replace him." Big Foot said: "No, we will keep the good guns." These two Indians came out & John followed. When they got back the two Indians reported what Big Foot had said, & then there were 7 or 8 poor guns given up. Then they would not give up any more. Philip Wells then came and he took Shangrau's place, & the latter was ordered with ten soldiers into the Indian camp to search for guns. This composed one of the two parties. Little Bat was also ordered with ten other soldiers to do the same thing. This was the second party. While they were searching the camp Lieutenant Preston and Charley Allen were in the camp; this was the first John saw them.[103]

Shangrau got about nine guns; Bat also got some. Shangrau started in with his party at the end of the camp toward W. K. Creek. Bat started at the other end. Meantime an Indian with a ghost shirt on, was outside the circle swinging his arms and saying ha, ha, ha. When Shangrau and Bat met, a soldier a woman came up to Shangrau & said these soldiers are taking our knives from us, and he saw a soldier with an armful of knives. Shangrau took all the knives from him & gave them to the woman & told her to give them to their owners. As soon as he gave her the knives he turned to Bat to talk to him, he heard a gun fired. He heard one of the women say: "There is a fight!" As soon as this was said he heard a volley. Bat then ran down to the ravine with Big Foot's people; they all stampeded. Shangrau went on a trot toward the cannon which were right close to the top of the hill. An Indian followed him, but was shot down before he reached John who was wondering what the Indian would do. When John got up on the hill he met a lieutenant who said to John: "Scout, we've got our revenge now."[104]

And John said, "What revenge?" "Why, don't you know, the Custer massacre?" John said: "Look here, Lieutenant, Custer had all the guns to protect himself with, but they massacred him; and here you take all the guns away from them and then massacre them; you ought to be ashamed of yourself for saying such a thing!" Shangrau now went over towards his tent to try to get his gun. As he got to his door a soldier said to him: "You better get away from there; an Indian is in there shooting." So John did not go in. A soldier ran up to the tent and ripped it down with his knife and with both hands opened it and looked in; at the same instant the Indian within shot him in the breast. Then the soldiers poured a volley into the tent and a cannon sent a shell into it. A soldier got some hay, fired it, and threw it on the tent and it was burned up. John walked down where the circle of Indians was & there they were piled up horribly and indiscriminately.

I should have said that the soldiers surrounded the Indian circle in two ranks. When John was coming out from among the dead he saw Father Croft sitting on the ground with his arms extended and his hands on the ground supporting himself. John spoke to him and said: "Father, are you shot?" He said: "Yes." "Can I help you?" "Yes." With the assistance [of] another you [he] helped [move Craft?] a little distance away. A stretcher was brought and he was taken off the field. When he was lifted on to the stretcher John saw that he was stabbed on one side of the spine between the shoulders. John said to him: "Father, you are not shot; you are stabbed." He answered: "I don't believe an Indian did that to me, I believe it was a white man." After this there was an Indian sitting up was in a pocket in the ravine shooting with deadly effect. The cannon was pitching shells over at him but failed to get him, and had to give it up. When John went over where the fight started & there he saw women and boys and girls lying dead, and some were wounded, some sitting up and some lying down (The injured men were mostly in the circle). After it was all over [they gathered ?] all the Indian and white wounded and placed them in wagons and the troops marched to the Agency arriving about 11 P.M. The next morning early

Early next morning a company of soldiers with some wagons was coming into the Agency from the mouth of W. K.; it was a troop of the 9th Cavalry following Colonel Henry in, who had reached the agency ahead, and it was escorting the wagon train of his regiment. When this troop and the train were at Cheyenne Cr. (first creek east of the Agency) they were attacked by Indians and a negro soldier was killed (this was a colored regiment). At this the scouts mounted horses and went out and some soldiers also went out. Only five Indians were seen disappearing over the hills to the north toward the Mission. The smoke of the burning Day School occupied by the Wells family was seen as soon as they got back to the Agency, and Little Bat and Louie Shangrau started right out to see. Then John Shangrau and Joe Marrivall also went out, and while they were there the 7th Cavalry came also. Then they all went down White Clay, and these scouts were on the lead going down White Clay. Going over a little ridge they went close to a little creek—a little hollow—and they saw some Indians; one hollered and said: "You scouts turn back; we want to fight the soldiers; we don't want to fight you!" The scouts turned back; Lieutenant Preston being present said, "Lets count them." Louie Shangrau said "Count nothing!" and they all pulled right back to the troops. They were in a hollow & just going up to the hill when an Indian on the ridge fired into the soldiers & shot one through the leg. Then Louie Shangrau said they want us to go up on this ridge to see if there are any Indians here & they started up again, this time toward the west; when near the top of the hill the Indian shouted to them: "Turn back, you have no ears; we want to fight the soldiers; we don't want to fight you." So they turned back. The soldiers now kept falling back for the Indians were firing from the bluff. When the soldiers got back as far as the bridge at the Mission, just southwest of there is a ridge and there were some Indians there. The soldiers went afoot up this ridge to dislodge the Indians, and just as they were nearing the crest the Indians poured a raking fire into them and killed wounded two soldiers. The soldiers retired to the foot of the ridge. Just then the 9th Cavalry arrived, and the troops now succeeded in driving the Indians away. The troops all returned after this to the Agency.

When the fight began Taylor's Indian scouts broke and ran and took shelter under the bank of W. K. creek.

About a week after the battle John Shangrau took the Indian prisoners to Fort Sheridan, Chicago, for confinement, namely, Kicking Bear and Short Bull, and some 20 more.

From there John Shangrau went to Europe with these Indians who were secured by Buffalo Bill for his Wild West from Gen. Miles.[105]

Mr. Shangrau did not hear anyone say: "Remember Custer."

[Tablet 9]

Interview with John Shangrau at Allen, S.D., Tuesday, Nov. 6, 1906.

He said: In relation to the Cheyenne Outbreak at Fort Robinson, Neb. Jan. 10, 1879.[106]

Cheyenne Outbreak

That he came to John Farnham's at Fort Robinson from Pine Ridge after the Cheyennes had broken out and had left Soldier Creek and got on the other side of the Ridge north of the Fort and west.
He was at Farnham's when Lieutenant Hardee came down and asked him if he wanted the job of going with Capt. Wessels who was at that time in command of the Fort.[107] He answered that he would act as scout if he could get five dollars a day. Hardee said if he will pay you that I will bring you a horse and saddle

& everything complete tomorrow morning. In the morning he brought two horses complete, and Shangrau and the Indian, Woman's Dress went together. They mounted and went to the Fort. They went up Soldier Creek with two companies of soldiers, Capt. Wessels in command. By evening these arrived at the camp of the troops who were out in the field; they were on a little creek which has its source west of Fort Robinson. They marched all day going west to reach this camp. Near where this camp was two creeks head; one flows south, the other north, but he does not know where it discharges. The camp was below the head of the one running in a northerly direction. He does not know the name of it. When they got there that evening John Shangrau said to the Captain that he would go up there & see how they (the Indians) are. He rode up south from the camp, and circled round where they were and he saw their track in the snow which was about 8 or 9 inches deep, going west; he came back & reported to Wessels who ordered him to take his scout, Woman's Dress, and follow the trail. He did so, the soldiers moving west at the same time at the foot of the small mountain which ranged east and west, and they were under it on the north side. Then he trailed along their course till sundown. The soldiers camped on the little creek which the Indians called, "The Crazy Man Jumped off the Bank."

John and Woman's Dress returned to the camp. Wessels asked, "What did you find?" "I was on the trail but I could see none of them. I was on the trail where it was fresh and I think they are about 5 or 6 miles from where I stopped." "Tomorrow," said the officer, "you may have seven soldiers go with you." Early in the morning he took his scout, Woman's Dress, and 7 soldiers. When he struck the trail he saw where a track came down from the north toward the Indian trail which still led west. The way the Indians dragged their meat was to put it on the hide of the animal they had slaughtered, and draw it on the snow. This was done only on snow when it slipped along easily. John called the attention of the Sergeant to this curious trail, but he did not understand it till John explained its meaning, that the Indians had been down the creek the night before & butchered a cow or steer and had come back with the meat transported in this fashion. (It is like reading hieroglyphics.) He advised the Sergeant to send a man back and report that the Indians are close by, and ask that the troops be brought close up under the bluff as a support to the scouts and escort who could, if necessary fall back to them when they should come in contact with the enemy. He sent a soldier back with a dispatch & then this party continued on the trail. John got to the head of the creek, right down into it, and he saw where they had made their fires—seven of them—and these were still alive, showing that the Cheyennes had left them but a short while previously. They discovered the remains of the breakfast, where the Indians had cooked and eaten the freshly slain meat, the bones were lying round. From there the Indians went up on to the ridge steering west. John told the Sergeant that the Indians could not have left, judging from the fires, but little over an hour earlier, and advised him to send a second courier back, saying that they are but two or three miles ahead. He sent him & the scouts went again on the trail. When John got halfway up the hill on the trail he began to feel unusual, his heart thumped and he felt stirred up. A feeling came over him as though he was going to see something when he should rise to the top of the hill — something like a presentment and the attendant excitement or emotion — "felt in in his bones." He stopped and the Sergeant came up. He told him to get ready — to fix his guns. The Sergeant replied: "Have you discovered them?" "No," said John, "but they are right close by; I know from my feeling." The Sergeant had his men load & be in readiness. John said: "Boys, if anything happens, don't run but keep together all the time." The Sergeant remarked: "We are the boys that will stay with you." John and Woman's Dress started on the trail. John from the top of the ridge looked west and saw a sharp point or promontory of a ridge, and he could distinguish the trail ascending diagonally up to the top of the ridge. John said to Woman's Dress, who is his uncle to him, "You see the point there," which was about 200 yards distant, "Uncle, it [is] like there is a rifle pit on that point; at same time you see the trail going up that hill; they might have had a rifle pit there, but may have taken that trail away and not be there now. We better go on a little farther & look again; but at same time let us be ready. If anything happens don't let us run away from each other; let us keep together." Then speaking to the Sergeant he said, "We are going again; let us keep close together," and they all started. As they were moving, all being on foot, John had his bridle rein over his arm and his gun resting across his arm, after going 70 yards right under the point, he looked up to the point and saw a red painted face looking down at him from the rifle pit, all he could see that was human was this face. Pointing to it with his finger, he said to his companion scout: "Uncle, do you see that?" At that moment the Indians above them began ~~clapping their hands and~~ discharging their guns. The Indians gave them a plunging fire at an angle of 45 degrees and a distance of 60 or 70 yards. John dropped his rein and took shelter behind a big pine tree, and shot twice at the rifle pit before he reached the tree. Woman's Dress got behind another pine tree about 20 feet from John's. He shot once or twice. John stood there a few minutes and looked back and discovered that

JOHN SHANGRAU

his horse was gone, that Woman's Dress was gone, and all the soldiers were gone—all had fled and left him alone. He reflected a few moments trying to decide what to do. He peeped around the tree at the rifle pit and saw one of the Cheyennes descending the hill toward him with gun in hand. So John concluded that the Indian was trying to get him; and so he decided to use his gun in defense, and then he would have his six-shooter left to continue the combat with. When the Cheyenne got within 30 or 40 yards John shot at the man and hit him; he whirled round and fell with his head up the hill. When he dropped John abandoned his shelter and skipped out from there. As he was running the Indians sent their bullets after him; they went glancing every way on the ledge of rock around him. He had gone perhaps 50 yards when he came upon a soldier lying dead on his face, having fallen while running from the enemy. Farther down the hill John overtook Woman's Dress and the Sergeant and the three remaining soldiers, all retreating. He found his horse standing on the side hill. Mounting him he found that the soldiers' horses had stampeded. Woman's Dress had his horse. The whole party retreated past the Indians' last camp to a place on the sidehill. John told Woman's Dress to go with the soldiers and he would go back and report to the officer. They came back slowly & John returned to the camp and reported to Capt. Wessels who went into camp on the same creek that the Indians had camped on. It was not night. Why did he not follow and attack if he wanted Indians?[108] He stayed there till next morning, which compelled this scout to do the work all over again later on.

Next morning the scouts and whole force started again, going round the point and rifle pit and approaching it this time from the west, whereas, the first time it was approached from the east. When they got in close proximity to the pit John told Wessels that he did not think the Indians were there. "They might be" the Captain replied. They went right up on the hill to the pit, but the Cheyennes were gone. They had made The soldiers found the scalp of the soldier killed below the day before, lying on a boulder up at the pit. John handed it to Wessels who thought it was a dog skin. John told him it was the scalp of his dead soldier, and he threw it away in a pet, for he was a hot-tempered man. Wessels then asked for the whereabouts of the soldier's body, which John said was lying about 100 yards down the hillside. Wessels ordered that it be taken to the camp. But the body was gone though blood stains identified the spot. The Indians had taken his clothing and thrown the body over a cliff where it was found. It was carried back on a pack mule. Next morning the force started again in pursuit and went to the stage station on the road from Laramie to Deadwood. That night troops arrived from Laramie under Major Irwin (?) Irving and camped there.[109]

The Major sent for Shangrau who responded. This officer asked him where he thought the Cheyennes were—how far off. The scout replied, "They are now two days ahead of us, but probably not more than 20 miles in advance, as they have a lot of cripples with them." He asked if the scouts could in the morning get on the trail again and follow it into the mountains. He answered, "I don't want to be killed tomorrow." "How is that?" "If I get on the trail tomorrow and get into that timber they might wait for me and shoot me down; so I would rather have a party to go along." "Then what do you think we can do?" the major inquired. He answered: "I think some of the troops should go up on the ridge and some along the foot of the hill. After we reach a certain point toward the Black Hills, we should meet there beyond at the point." Then if they are at the point He ordered this scout to take the ridge the next morning and see if the wagons could pass along the summit. He started early and found they could go with teams & he reported, and the soldiers went in two parties, one along the ridge and the other at the base of the ridge. About noon they came close to the point referred to. John said to the Major that he would go north & see if he could discover the trail going up to the point; for the troops had not been going right on the trail but a little off from it. He went 200 or 300 yards, & following it a little way he discovered that the Cheyennes had departed, going west. Shangrau told the Major that they might be at another point which he described about a mile away westwardly. The soldiers came within 400 yards of it, and the scouts and all dismounted to go up to it on foot, some leading their horses. When within 100 yards of this point the Indians made their presence known by firing into the advancing party. The Major's horse was killed. He now told Shangrau [to go] to the party at the base of the ridge. It was getting late in the evening. Shangrau offered this suggestion: That as the ridge at the top was perpendicular for 15 or more feet, he could not get down without going clear back to the station from which they had started. So he advised that they lower his mule by a rope over the precipice, then he would go down on a rope, mount and in an hour be up with the other party. The officer thought the scheme hardly practicable or safe, and ordered this scout to go the long way round. John Shangrau then mounted his mule and returned to the station. The sun was now down, and it was pretty dark and he was halfway to the other soldiers. He stood little chance of finding the camp that night; so he camped by himself right under the point from which the Cheyennes had ~~been and he had examined when with the Major~~ shot at them. He tied his mule 50 feet from where he was sitting among some big rocks. The mule kept braying all night long. John saw the fire that the Cheyennes had up on their lookout, and a little way off could be seen the fires of the party he had been with all day. He was thinking that the Cheyennes might come down from the point to him; so he listened intently all night and kept a sharp watch. At about what he supposed was midnight he heard, he thought, voices. Nothing developed and he continued his vigil till daylight. Taking his mule he rode west to find the soldiers he had been ordered to find. Half a mile away he came upon them. Riding up to Capt. Wessels' tent (the Captain had command of this party which was composed of his own soldiers), Shangrau delivered the dispatch from the Major. Looking at it, he asked the scout where the Cheyennes were. He answered: "They are right over on that point," pointing to it, which was not more than three miles distant. Wessels said: "John, the Major told me to have you take me right up to the point where those Indians are." "All right," says the scout, and they started at once. Before reaching the point, Shangrau said to the officer: "Captain, before we go any farther I am going down where I stopped last night; I heard some voices, and they may have come down." The Captain said: "All right go. Be quick!" The scout answered: "If I see any trail I will wave my hat." When he got to his last night's camp and 200 or 300 yards farther on, he came upon the trail that the Indians had made in their escape in the night. He waved his hat & the Captain halted. John reported to him that the trail pointed north. The command was put on the trail and an express was sent to Major Irving. That night Wessels camped between Hat Creek and the stage station. Shangrau went back with Lieutenant Hardee to the station and stayed overnight. In the morning the two returned to Wessels' camp. When overtaken these soldiers were already on the march along the trail. Shangrau inquired of the Captain for Woman's Dress. "It is he standing over there on the bottom where that dry creek is." Shangrau rode up to him, followed by two soldiers making four together. Woman's Dress informed him that the trail followed the bed of the creek down and nearly east, a little north. He added, pointing out the place, that there is where they butchered, and he said it was pretty fresh sign. John then said that they might be over at an opposite point down the channel, where there was timber. They moved down the channel, and when within twenty feet of them the Indians fired on them from under the sagebrush along the bank in the timber. At the first shot, Shangrau's mule was wounded and knocked down. John ran, and looking to his right saw soldiers and Woman's Dress running. At the same time he noticed that the handle of his own revolver was shot off. ~~He ran to~~ He saw one of the soldiers running on foot, which showed that his horse had been killed or disabled. John ran after him to get his gun. Just as he overtook him the soldier was shot down dead. John took his six-shooter. By this time, the party under Wessels, having heard the firing and aware that the Indians had been uncovered, had gone to the top of the ridge and were now firing down into the Cheyennes. These slipped back into their rifle pit, and John walked up to this party of soldiers who had now come down into a basin to conceal themselves.[110] The first one he met was Capt. Wessels, and he inquired for Woman's Dress. The answer was, "He is shot." "Where is he shot?" was asked. "Right through," answered the Captain. John supposed he meant that he was shot through the body, and he said: "I will go up and see him." "All right," added the Captain, "but come right back." Shangrau went to him and found that he was shot through the arm, and was with a surgeon. John saw that he was not hurt very bad, and went back to the Captain. He asked Wessels what he was going to do, if he was going after the Cheyennes. He said: "I am going to get them today!" "How are you going to do it?" The Captain explained that he would divide his men into three parties; one he would send round to come down the creek or channel. One he would send round in an opposite circuit to come up the creek or channel; and the third he would move directly towards the position of the Indians, all concentrating at this point simultaneously. The movement began in a charge from the starting place. Shangrau was with those who went directly across the flat ground towards the pit. When this party got down into this dry channel, instead of the other two parties meeting them down there, they went up on top of the higher ground so they could get a commanding position to shoot down into the Indians. Capt. Wessels commanded the party which circuited to the left and came down the channel and Lieutenant Chase commanded the one that circuited to the right and came up the channel, and an infantry officer, Lieut. Burt (?) commanded the center party.[111] The two flanking parties are on the same level with the Indians. When within fifteen yards of the Indian position, Capt. Wessels received a wound in the head, a scalp wound in the side of the head. Some soldiers in his party fell at the same fire. The Indians had exhausted their ammunition and were at the mercy of the troops now advancing in a spirited ~~charge~~ advance on the rifle pit. The soldiers were loading and firing and when they reached the pit the Indians were all dead except six women and children who were taken prisoners.[112]

The soldiers made travois on which to move their dead and wounded back to the camp. He does not remember how many there were.

John made a fire and stayed there all night with ten soldiers. The next morning a wagon was sent from the camp on the creek that the station was on but away below the station, to where Shangrau was to bring in the prisoners to the camp.

Shangrau says that Lieut. Clark had been sent sometime before to Pine Ridge for more Indian scouts.[113] He thinks that it was on this day that the officer returned with a number of them (perhaps 20) but they were too late to be put into service.

Shangrau says there was a little wounded boy among the prisoners who died on the way to Fort Robinson, but his body was taken clear through. They all returned to Fort Robinson. There John Shangrau quit scouting and came home to Pine Ridge.

Two women among these prisoners were related to Woman's Dress, and they and he came over to Pine Ridge with Shangrau.

(The End)

Arrest of Crazy Horse

John Shangaru was at Fort Robinson when the soldiers were sent out to arrest Crazy Horse. He was on the Little White Clay Creek near Red Cloud. He got wind of the move and fled to Spotted Tail Agency on the Beaver. Charley Tackett, Joe Marrivall, (father of Charley who is dead) and several Indians started out after him down on the Beaver at some point, and they got him and took him to Camp Sheridan. He was turned over to the Indians who had come from Fort Robinson in pursuit of him. They took him back.

They took him into the guard house. Little Big Man was going with them, walking by the side of Crazy Horse. He had had no part in his capture. Crazy Horse entered the first room and advanced to the second door which opened into the room where prisoners were confined. When he looked into this room he saw the irons and understood that he was to be shut up. He jumped back and a scuffle ensued between him and Little Big Man who was holding him. Crazy Horse had his knife in his hand, and the guard had his bayonet against him pushing him toward the door, when Crazy Horse surged accidentally against the bayonet and it penetrated his body. Little Big Man was cut in the hand, in the palm, and John has seen the scar, and he received this statement from Little Big Man himself.

Shangrau and Mrs. Shangrau say the Indians do not believe that Crazy Horse was purposely killed. Shangrau himself is sure he was not.

Photo 1. William Garnett was a Lakota interpreter for thirty years. RG2411.PH:1778

Photo 2. Brothers Dewey Beard, Joseph Horn Cloud, and White Lance survived the Wounded Knee massacre. Beard and Horn Cloud told their stories to Ricker. RG1227.PH: 25-4

Photo 3. *Chipps and his wife in 1907. Ricker interviewed Chipps and described him as "honorable and trustworthy."* RG1227.PH:25-2

Photo 4. One hundred forty-six bodies were interred in a mass grave at Wounded Knee. William Palmer told Ricker that one of the men standing in the grave was William McWilliams. RG2845.PH:13–12

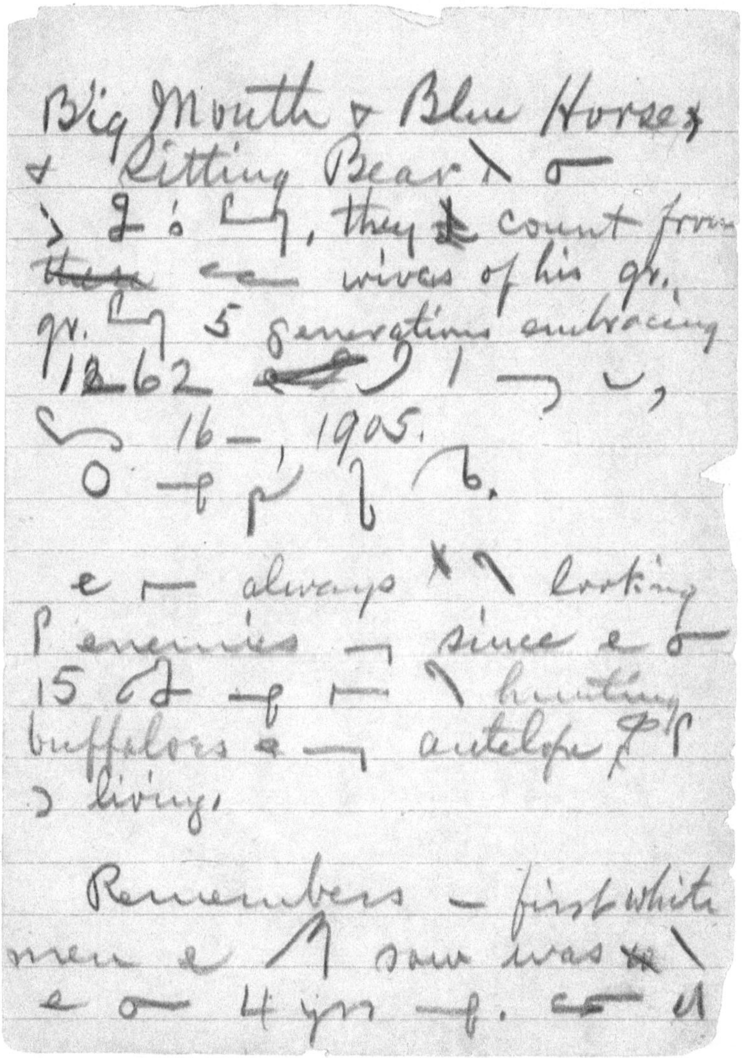

Photo 5. Occasionally Ricker mixed his arcane shorthand with his legible handwriting.

Photo 6. *American Horse and his wife.* RG2845.PH:11-6

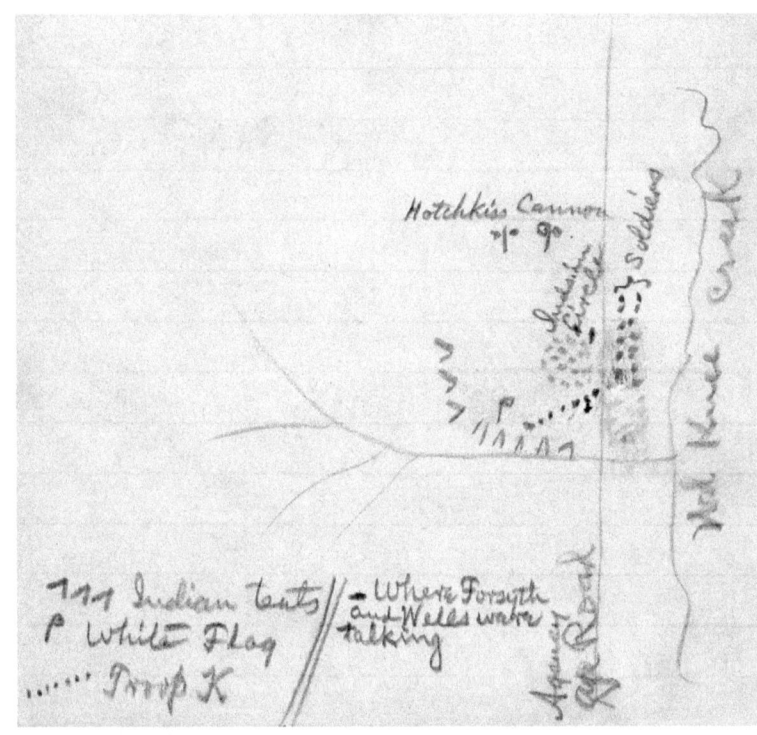

Figure 1. Phillip F. Wells's map of Wounded Knee

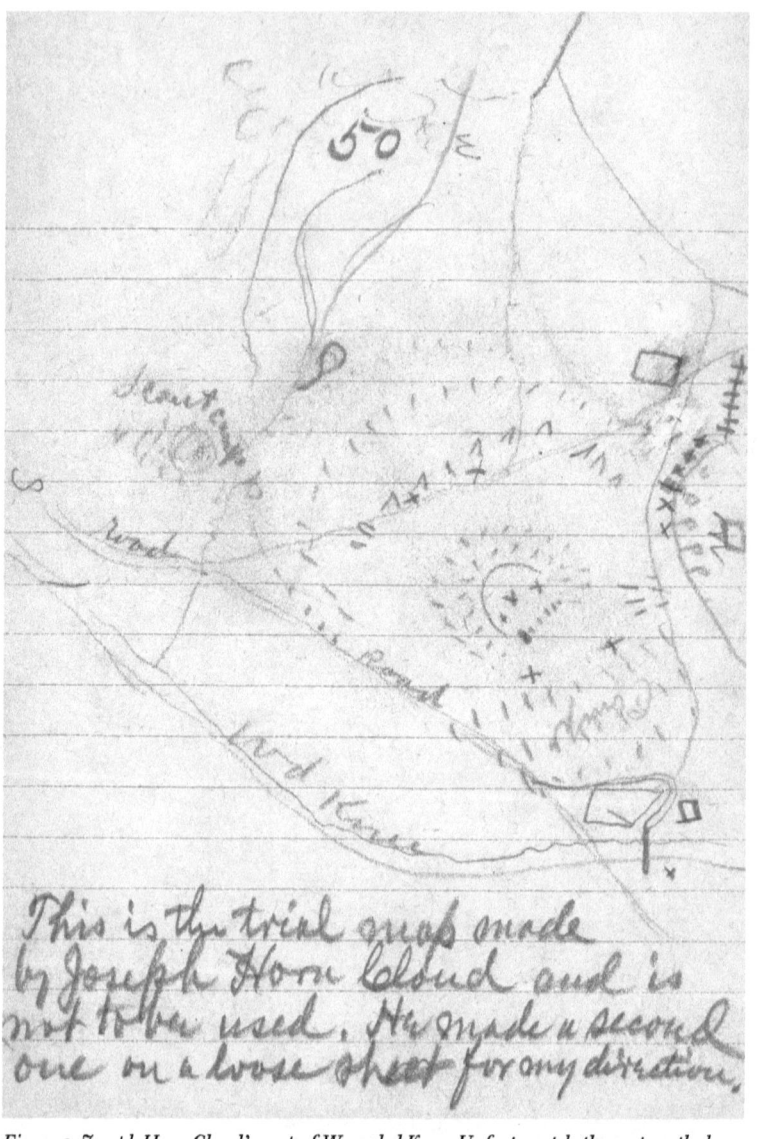

Figure 2. Joseph Horn Cloud's map of Wounded Knee. Unfortunately the map on the loose sheet was not included in the material donated to the Nebraska State Historical Society.

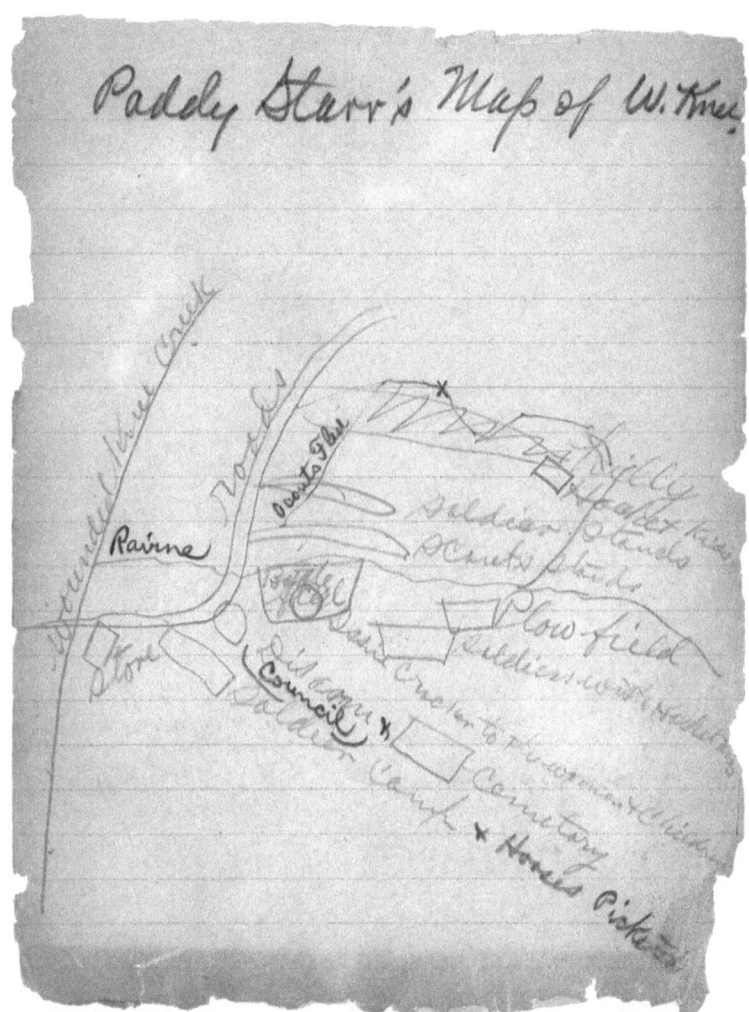

Figure 3. Paddy Starr's map of Wounded Knee

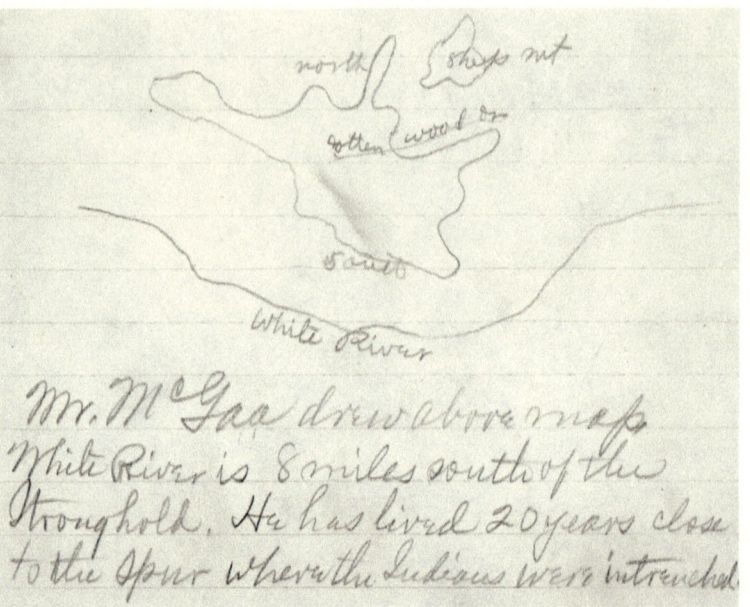

Figure 4. William D. McGaa's sketch of the Stronghold

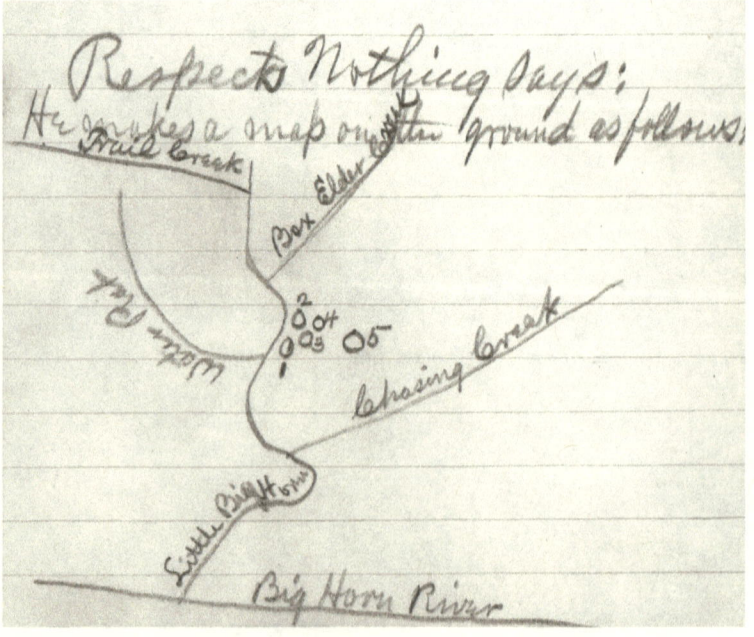

Figure 5. Respects Nothing's Little Bighorn

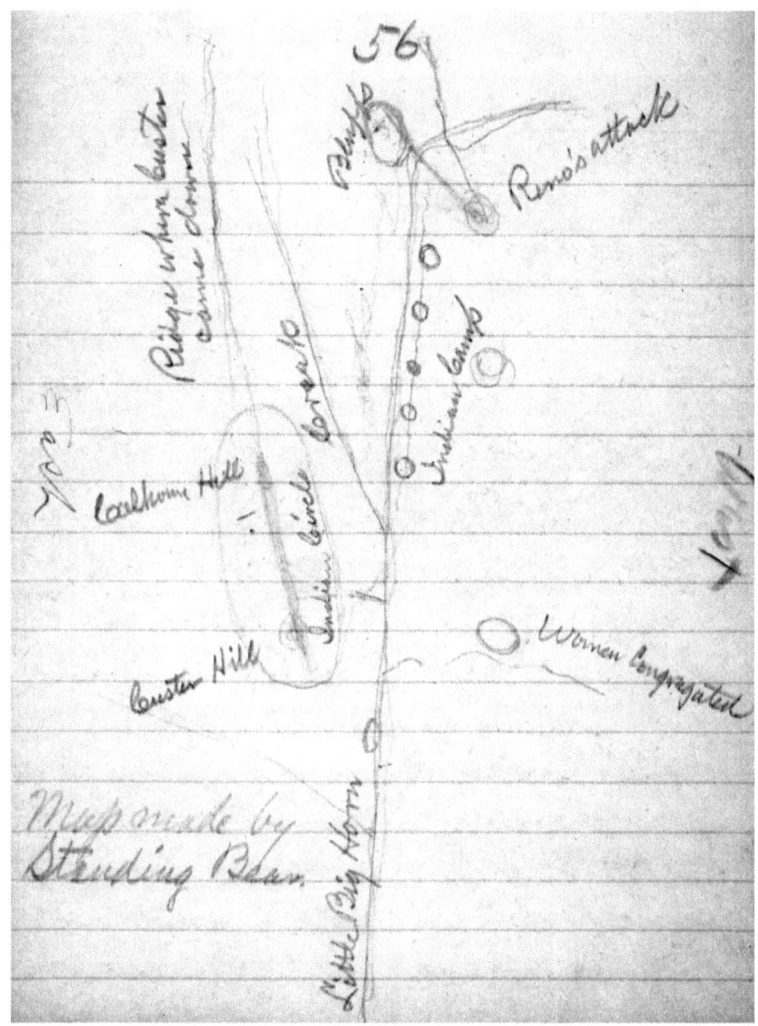

Figure 6. Standing Bear's Little Bighorn

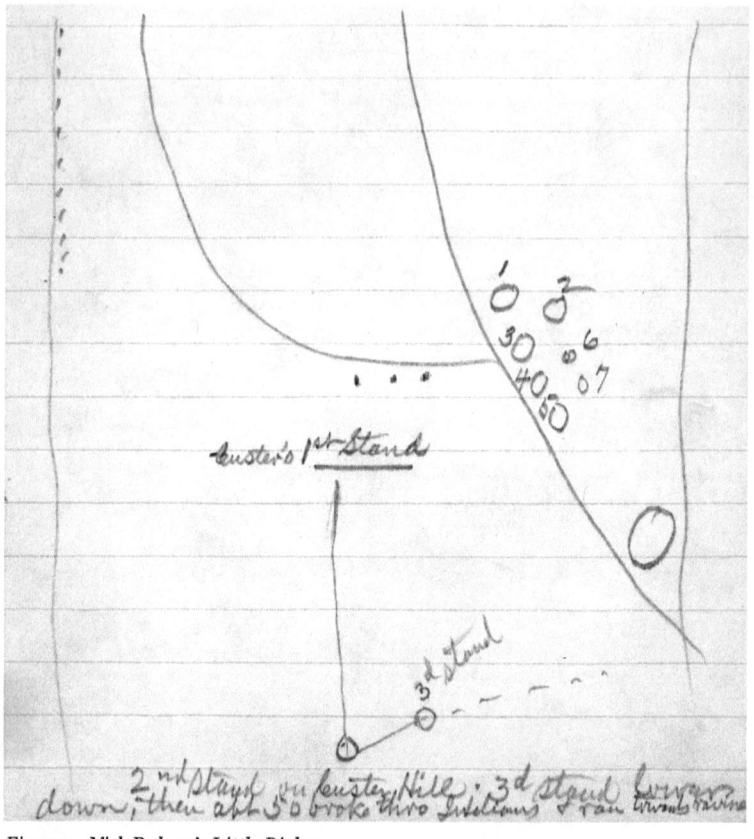

Figure 7. Nick Ruleau's Little Bighorn

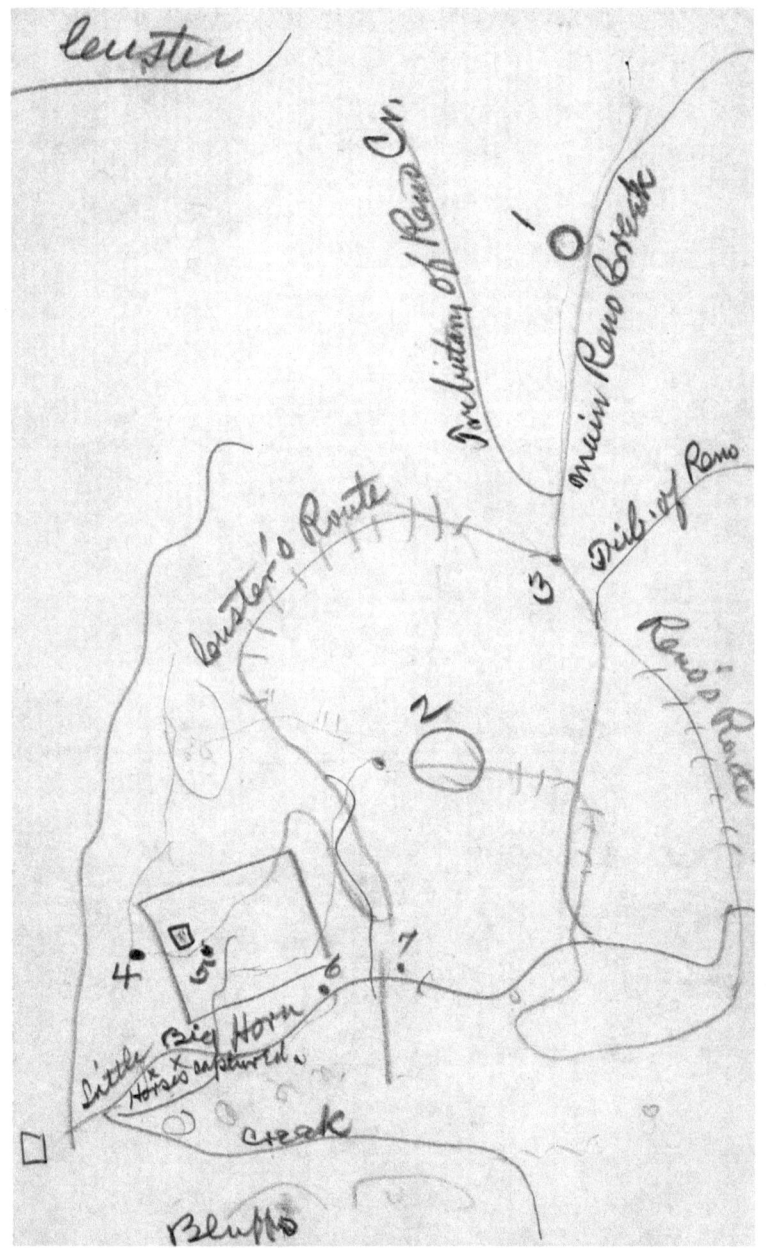

Figure 8. Two Moons' Little Bighorn

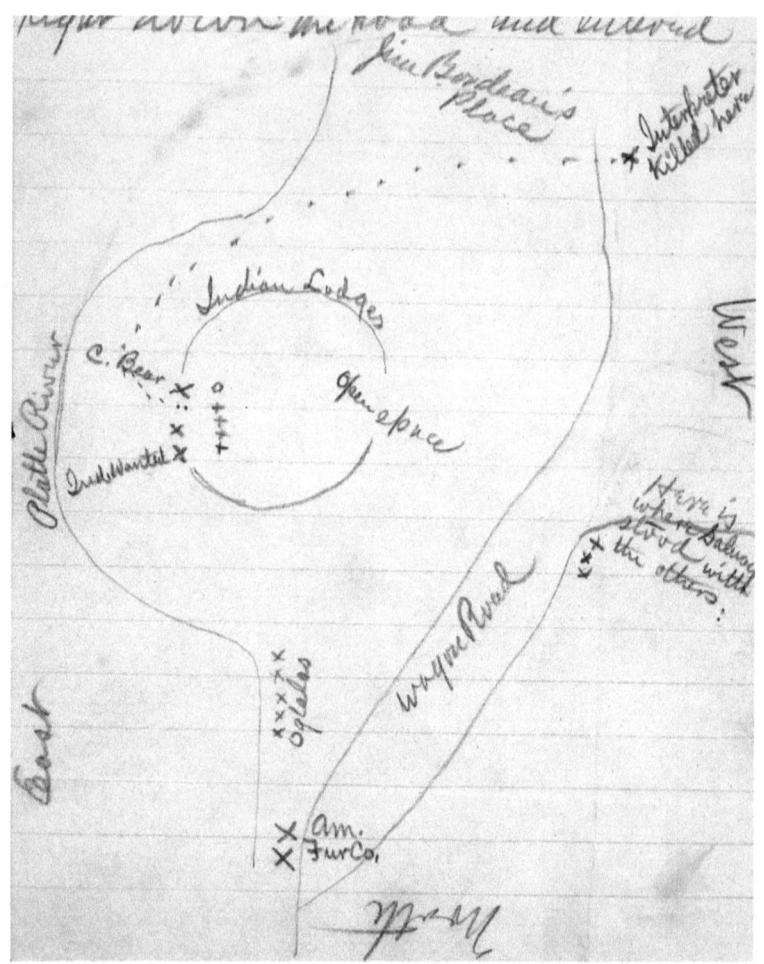

Figure 9. Frank Salaway's Grattan fight

3. The Old West—Indians and Indian Fights

[Chipps's Interview]

Chipps was born about 1836 and was a member of No Water's Oglala band. He died on January 4, 1916.

Ricker had a very good opinion of Chipps. In this interview, under the heading "Notes," he wrote, "Chipps is a good man, honorable and trustworthy, candid, truthful, and reasonable." In a letter to his wife of February 23, 1907, Ricker wrote, "He is a nice old Indian and was quite willing to tell me all he knew. He it was who was Crazy Horse's Medicine Man. He told me that he made the medicine that took Crazy Horse through all his battles without injury. He was raised with Crazy Horse."

[Tablet 18]

Thursday, February 14, 1907

Interview with Chipps, or Encouraging Bear. At his home 8 miles southeast of Kyle and 12 miles northwest of Allen. Peter Schweigerman, interpreter.

On the Subject of Crazy Horse.

Crazy Horse was born at the foot of Bear Butte, near the present Fort Mead, S.D., in the year in which the band to which he belonged, the Oglala, stole One Hundred Horses, and in the fall of the year.

He was born with light hair and was called by the Indians the lighthaired boy. His hair was always light. It did not reach to the ground as stated by Garnett, but did reach below his hips. His grandfather, Makes the Song, had a dream that Crazy Horse would be called Crazy Horse. When Crazy Horse was just 21 years old the Oglalas had a fight with the Crows and Rees, and others whose language they could not understand and in this fight he counted his coo coup in this manner: A Shoshone lay dead on the field in a position that none would approach to strike the body. Crazy Horse's horse became unmanageable and carried his rider wildly about and up within reach of the Shoshone body and Crazy Horse struck and counted coo, and from the crazy conduct of the horse the rider was ~~called~~ dubbed Crazy Horse.¹ Chipps was four years older than Crazy Horse.

Crazy Horse's father's name was Crazy Horse. Crazy Horse's mother was a Minneconjou but Chipps does not know her name.²

Crazy Horse was a man small in stature, rather light in frame and weight, light complexion. The wound by No Water for Crazy Horse taking his wife, did not change the color of his complexion; & this wound was in his face, the ball entering at the side of his nose low down on the right side and coming out at the base of the skull on the back side.³

Chipps saw No Water after he had shot Crazy Horse. Little Big Man saw Crazy Horse draw his knife when No Water entered the double lodge, and he seized and held Crazy Horse, & No Water shot him, and then took his wife.⁴

Chipps says that when we were young all we thought about was going to war with some other nation; all tried to get their names up the highest, & whoever did so was the principal man in the nation; and Crazy Horse wanted to get to the highest station.

Chipps was Medicine Man to Crazy Horse and gave him a feather, and he now has the feather; it is not the feather he was wearing when he was killed.

Bull Head at Cheyenne River Agency has the feather that Crazy Horse wore to his honor, whatever that may be. The interpreter, Peter Schweigerman, explains that when an Indian did a brave and conspicuous deed he was given a feather.⁵

Crazy Horse never wore a war bonnet. He did not paint as the Indians usually do; but he made a zigzag streak with red earth from the top of his forehead downwards and to one side of his nose at the base to the point of his chin. This was done with one finger. He striped his horse with a mould from the earth.

Chipps and Crazy Horse were raised together. The only time that they separated was when Fort Fetterman was established, Crazy Horse went north and Chipps came with the white people. Chipps was in the Fetterman massacre. The Indians who fought there were Oglalas and Minneconjous. He says 14 Indians were killed there. American Horse was there. American Horse did not lead the decoy party. Chipps says he wants to tell the truth.⁶

Crazy Horse was not accounted good for anything among the Indians but to make war; he was expected to do that; he was set apart in their minds to make war, and that was his business.

The greatest act of personal bravery on his part was when he was fighting the Shoshones; his horse was shot under him and he sprang forward to the enemy and counted coo.

Crazy Horse was held in estimation by all Indians as the greatest living warrior among the red men of the earth. He has Crazy Horse's war sack.[7]

Chipps was not at the Custer battle, but Crazy Horse told him about it. Reno did not make much of a fight. There was fighting with the Ree scouts; they made a charge and killed two Indians. Reno did not make any fight of importance.[8]

Chipps says that Crazy Horse told that there were about three thousand warriors who fought against Custer. Five Ree scouts were killed — one wore a large medal suspended from his neck. Thirty-two Indians were killed in all the fighting — 32 on the side of the hostiles. There were quite a number wounded but they lived through; I do not count strongly on this statement of casualties.[9]

He says there are two stories among the Indians — one is that Custer was killed on a hill, and the other that he was killed in a ravine. The ravine story is without particle of foundation as to Custer being killed in it or that he marched his command into it.[10]

After the Indians surrendered and got into intercourse with the whites Gall made some notable speeches and made quite a man of himself; but he was not looked upon among the Indians as a warrior at all.[11]

Grass was a peaceable man who always lived around the Agency and Chipps calls him a Loafer. He was never known to do any deed of note.[12]

At the time of the fight against the Cheyennes, Crazy Horse was camped on the Little Big Horn.

When the Indian scouts went out in the winter of 1876-7 to coax Crazy Horse to come in, he was camped on a branch of the Tongue River — the Indians called the branch Otter Creek. Chipps was the one who made the speech to Crazy Horse for these envoys. He said in substance as follows:

{11} These white men who was along told him to tell Crazy Horse: this white man who did the interpreting was Beauvias, called by the Indians Big Belly (there were lots of white men along) It was represented to Crazy Horse that they wanted a road through the country

Chipps went out with the party to coax Crazy Horse to come in. He promised he would come in the spring and Chipps and others came with him as far as Powder River & there separated from him. Chipps brought Crazy Horse Sr. in to Spotted Tail Agency.[13]

When Crazy Horse fled from his camp below Red Cloud he went to the Beaver and came to Chipps' lodge which was at the camp some three miles below Camp Sheridan. Chipps went with Crazy Horse to the Fort. No warriors chased the Indian scouts from Fort Robinson—nobody chased anybody.

When Crazy Horse arrived at the camp on Beaver Crazy Horse and Chipps accompanied by a great many, went up to Camp Sheridan. When there the officer in command asked C. H. if he wanted to go back to Red Cloud or to stay at Camp Sheridan and be confined in a cellar there until he should start on his way to see the Great Father in Washington. He told the officer he would like to keep his country, and he would go back to Red Cloud. This was all [that] was said, & next morning he started for Fort Robinson. Chipps went with him. The Brule Agent or Spotted Tail Agent (the same) (the interpreter suggests it was Major Lee) selected two Indian scouts to go back with him. When they got to Red Cloud all the Indian scouts at the bridge had their guns cocked to shoot him, but he was guarded by good boys. They went on in to the Fort & C. H. went into the house but Chipps did not go in & he does not know what was said. When C. H. came out an officer on one side held up his left hand and Little Big Man on other side held up his right hand, taking him to the guardhouse.[14] After he was taken to the guardhouse he refused to go into the cell, but he was inside the building. Chipps was inside with him—right behind him. One of the Brules were in there with C. H., and they offered to go in and be locked up and stay with him. The Brule was Turning Bear who offered to go in; he started ahead and the passage led down into the ground, but when Turning Bear saw where they were going he stopped and said it was a hard place they were going into. Crazy Horse turned back to go out of the guardhouse, and all the Indian scouts had their guns cocked to kill him if he refused to go into the guardhouse. The officer & Little Big Man both were still holding on to him. Crazy Horse made a grunt and struggled. He did not say a word. Crazy Horse got outside of the building. Chipps did not see the soldier stab C. H. with the bayonet. When the soldier jerked the bayonet from C. H.'s body he hit Chipps in the shoulder with the butt and dislocated his shoulder which is still dislocated (which I do not take great stock in).[15]

Chipps buried his body, and he is the only person who knows where it is. Crazy Horse was buried on the Beaver by the cliffs. When the Indians went down to the Missouri River his body was removed to White Clay Creek & buried; and when they returned Chipps & his brother went and took up the body to see if it had been disturbed, and finding that it had not been, they reinterred it.

The burial the first time near the cliffs was in a frame house lined with scarlet cloth.[16] His body was once buried on White Horse Creek, above Manderson, but it was moved from there to Wounded Knee where it now is. Chipps put the bones in a black blanket and laid them in a butte rock cave. There is no petrifaction—no flesh—nothing now but bones. The shot through his head by No Water shows in the skull. Crazy Horse was wounded twice—once in the head and once in calf of the leg.[17]

Crazy Horse killed in the Custer Battle 16 persons and 15 in the Reno fight. This is problematical—largely so.

Crazy Horse had one brother; and this was killed by a white man in a war with whites. He has no near relations living.[18]

Chipps is the one who made Crazy Horse's medicine for him. He is the one who gave him the medicine that he would be killed with a knife while his arm was held, as he sagely informed the author. Chipps was the one who told him not to wear a warbonnet nor to paint, except to use the streak down his countenance which represented the lightning. There is no truth in the story of the horseman coming out of the pond and telling Crazy Horse what to do.[19] We wear a feather to distinguish us for our deeds and a little stone on the left side. Chipps has these articles of medicine which belonged to Crazy Horse. They are different altogether. The medicine was the spotted eagle's heart, and it was the medicine of such persons as he gave it to; this was Crazy Horse's medicine which he rubbed on himself when he went into battle, and was his protection; and when it was used before going into action no bullet would touch him. This medicine would protect him against the knife if his arm was not held; but if it was held he would not be protected.

Chipps lives on No Flesh Creek; the next creek west is Little Wound Creek. The next west of this is American Horse Creek. No Flesh and Little Wound unite about one mile north of Kyle, and from the point of junction the stream is called Medicine Root.

[American Horse's Interview]

> American Horse was the son of Sitting Bear and succeeded his father as band leader. American Horse married a daughter of Red Cloud, whom he joined in 1871 and became one of the Oglala agency chiefs. Government officials considered American Horse a progres-

sive and invited him to Washington DC to discuss tribal affairs. American Horse also toured the country as a member of a Wild West show. He died from natural causes at his home on the Pine Ridge Reservation in 1908.[20]

Ricker wrote a brief paragraph in Tablet 33 as a preface to his interview with American Horse. This is followed by six pages of shorthand. The possibility of translating this interview seemed almost hopeless when it was evident Ricker was using an obscure and as yet unidentified system. However some numbers in this section were the same as those in Tablet 16 which contains a mixture of longhand and shorthand within the sentences. The notes in Tablet 16 suggested it was an interview, but since there were missing pages it was only a guess. After a long struggle it was possible to decipher some of the shorthand in Tablet 16. The decoded shorthand words were then superimposed on the characters in Tablet 33. Both tablets contained the American Horse interview. It seems likely that the badly worn Tablet 16 with its scribbled longhand contains the original notes. Tablet 33 is little more than a neat and clean copy. The longhand introduction in Tablet 13 begins:

Interview with American Horse
June 16, 1905, at the Agate Springs Stock Farm in Sioux County, Neb., James H. Cook proprietor, I interviewed Chief American Horse, Romero interpreter, as follows:

The six pages of shorthand follow. American Horse told Ricker he was born in 1839 near Bear Butte Creek. American Horse then said his grandfather was ninety-six years old when he died in 1886. This statement is followed by a sentence that could not be deciphered. The rest of the interview closely parallels that in Tablet 16. There are, however, brief phrases that could not be translated. These may contain details, but are certainly not long enough to describe an event. Words that could not be decoded are indicated by _.

[Tablet 16]

Big Mouth & Blue Horse & Sitting Bear who was _ _ _ _. they count from these wives of his gr. gr. grandfather 5 generations embracing 1262 _ to that _, _ 16 _ 1905. _ held _ _ _ He would always go looking for enemies and since he was 15 years old would go hunting buffaloes and antelope for his living.

Remembers the first white men he ever saw was when he was 4 yrs. old. They were in his grandfather's lodge were fur traders. He asked his grandfather how old he was when those men were there and his grandfather told him he was 4 yrs. old. That was near _ did _ _. There was an old camp there for trading. [One page of shorthand concluding with "Red Cloud, Fire Thunder"] Says some white men came from Washington when he was about 12 yrs. old, came to get _ to open _ the _. A council was held. _ was _ Many signed _ _ _ _ _ _ _ was against it _ _ was the soldier _ at the _ _ and _ _ _ a white man _ through if he could help it.

A man named Conquering Bear was the one who got permission for them to go through the country. He was one of the Sioux chiefs.[21]

2 yrs. after C. Bear got permis. to go through, he was in 3 fights; 1st fite was with the Pawnee Inds., 2d fight was with the Ute Inds.; 3d fight was with the Shoshones. A white man (an emigrant) passed close to where the Inds. were camped; this white man left camp next morning & left a lame ox & an Ind. named Straight Foretop rode along where this wh. man had camped & he killed the ox with arrows.[22] White man came back to look for ox & found him dead. He went back & told some soldiers there on the forks of the Laramie (Big & Little Laramie) Commanding officer sent 30 soldiers down to the Ind. camp with a guide & interpreter named Jules Semineau.[23] Conquering Bear was camped in a circle & the soldiers rode _ in the middle of his camp & all got off their horses. They had one big gun.[24] They trained this gun on the big lodge where this man who killed the ox was sitting. This officer called Conquering Bear & told him that he must have the man who killed the ox. Conq. Bear told him all right & went in and told the man that the officers had come for him & he must _, and he said _. He said they came over to arrest me and he went _ to come in and accept his _. Conq. Bear said to the officer that Straight Foretop wants _ to get in there and arrest him _ self. _ _ him _ Inds. were all gathering with guns on horseback and this officer said some thing when the Inds. did not understand, and then while _ shot twice wounding Conq. Bear who lived 5 days and died at the mouth of Snake Creek _ on the Running Water to a place he had been carried. Straight Foretop came around with a long gun and shot this officer down. This was about 1860 — 45 yrs ago. When Straight Foretop shot the off. he drew a butcher knife and stabbed the officer all _. The officer ordered the soldiers to shoot Conq. Bear. When this was how Straight Foretop killed the off. & then cut him. When Straight Foretop killed the off. the Inds. all fired on the soldiers. When the gun was fired? This fight was in the fall when the leaves were getting yellow. This fight was abt. 10 A.M. & as soon _ over the Inds. stampeded. The Burnsides [Burnt Thighs or Brulés] went east & Ogs went north? The Inds. came along the Running Water trail & camped.

When the Inds. camped at the mouth of Snake Cr. Conq. Bear told his people he was going to die. C. B. told his people when he signed that treaty _ this govt. offered him $50,000 a yr. for 55 yrs at 5% int.[25] This was abt. daybreak when he told his friends this and died. When Conq. Bear was dying he told them to send word to Young Man Afraid of his Horses to remember this & not to forget that he had made this treaty with the govt. & to collect the int. yearly & it was to run 55 yrs.

He told Spotted Tail & his brother Red Leaf not to get mad because he was going to _ _ to go ahead and fight the white men. He told them that when they were to _ the _ _ to remember the treaty Conq. Bear _ _.

After he was dead his brother Red Leaf's heart was bad, & he & Spotted Tail started towards Laramie & saw a stage coming towards Bordeaux Station, when it came near they charged on the stage & shot a leader in the head team & stopped them. They found 5 persons & killed them all. In the stage was a box which they opened & found gold & silver & paper money. The Indians then took everything & started back towards where they came from. As they went along the gold got too heavy & they threw it away & threw away all the silver _ a few pieces & kept some of the paper money & made cigarettes with it, a vice learned from Spaniards. The main camp at the mouth of Snake Creek had moved when Spotted Tail & Red Leaf returned, & had gone down to mouth of Chadron Creek to camp for the winter.

Massacre of Fetterman's command

List of Indian Casualties at Phil Kearney as given by Am. Horse to me;

Killed
1 Lone Bear   Oglala Sioux
2 Yellow White Man   "   "
3 Horse Looking   "   "
4 Little Bear   "   "
5 Bird head,   Arapahoe
6 Good Shield   "
7 Bear Robe, Cheyenne and Eight is wounded

American Horse says he killed the chief officer in command (who was Col. Fetterman) & he tells how he did it as follows:[26]

When Col. Fetterman and party were on wagon trail to wood camp American Horse & 9 other Oglala warriors met & attacked them. The mounted soldiers were riding in advance in column of fours, the dismounted men following closely. After firing at the troops Am. Horse & his party slowly retreated into _ rough ground over _ ridge where 2 long lines of warriors were lying in ambush; troops rushed into the trap set for them and were completely surrounded.[27] In one hour and a half every soldier was killed, also 2 civilians who were with the party. One of those civilians was a swarthy looking man that looked like a mixed blood. Those 2 men got into a pile of rocks and did a lot of shooting before they were killed. The soldiers when they discovered that they were trapped by hundreds if not thousands of Indians were badly demoralized and did poor shooting. The Indians had only 7 killed and 8 wounded. American Horse himself ran his horse at full speed directly on to Col. Fetterman knocking him down. He then jumped down upon him and killed the Colonel with his knife. One of the Inds. killed having a very brave heart succeeded in riding into the midst of the soldiers shooting right and left. After the battle the Inds. scattered the various bands going in different directions to secure game for food.

The names of the Indians killed were as _ before.

[Four lines of shorthand]

American Horse says:

Red Cloud's father's name was Red Cloud, and he has a son named Red Cloud.

When Am. Horse was abt. 8 yrs. old Red Cloud was over on the Little Big Horn scouting. The Crows were over there on the bottom. In those times they watched their horses at night. This night a boy abt. 16 yrs. old was watching the horses. Red Cloud killed the boy and took the horses, about 50 head & drove them off. Next day the Crows attacked them but beaten off followed. The Crows pushed their chief forward in advance and Red Cloud shot him. There was quite a fight and the Crows were beaten off.

The same fall these Indians (the Oglala band of Sioux) went on a raid east of here under Red Cloud and came on to the Pawnees and killed seven, Red Cloud killing 4 of them with his own hand.

At another time a Ute Ind. was crossing a stream on a wounded horse and the horse gave out and the Ute was drowning—was sinking and rising, when Red Cloud rode in on his sprightly horse and grabbed the Indian by his hair and brought him to shore when he arrived there holding on to his hair he took his knife and slashed off his scalp and let the Indian fall to the ground & he rode off with the scalp.

He says that at one time four of them (the Indians) were appointed chiefs: Himself first, Young Man Afraid, Crazy Horse, and _____ Sword (now dead) a brother to George Sword. These appointments were made 31 years ago by their people as having been great warriors. Were all app. at same time at council.

There are only 2 American Horses, and both are living, himself being one. The other lives below the battlefield on W. Knee and is a brother to Woman's Dress. He says there was never an American Horse killed. He says he got his name of "American Horse" when he was 18 yrs old (48 yrs. & _ he says). He got a big army horse and rode it in battle and killed men and from this got his name of American Horse.

When he was _ _ the council was held at Tepee Cave or Butte, near where Newcastle, Wyo. is, (in the Black Hills)

Am. Horse told us abt. the "hard winter" from which the Indians date everything; was in 1845 & he remembers it well. Snow was deep & drifts high. Buffaloes would follow along in paths. Indians follow and assail them & fatigue them and kill them on foot with arrows.

Winter of great severity.

American Horse told of the destruction of an emigrant wagon train close to where Casper now is. There were 40 wagons of an ox-train. He and Red Cloud were in this affair. They ambushed the emigrants. The train was parked and resistance was _ successfully, but the Inds. cut off 5 wagons, shooting the oxen down and their drivers; then they looted the wagons and destroyed _. One wagon was loaded with barrels of whiskey, one wagon with jugs and bottles. They knocked out a head of one barrel and taking dishes drank and many got drunk and were laid out on the ground. This was an ambuscade. The Indians formed two lines and the emigrants drove right in between these. The emigrant train was well managed for it was successfully parked, that is 35 wagons were, & this was a great success under the circumstances. In this fight 14 of the emigrants were killed.

One time Red Cloud and a small party came upon a small number of Indians in camp under an overhanging cliff. Red Cloud and his men sneaked around to the top of the cliff and Red Cloud crawled out on the ledge and peeped through a hole in the overhanging rock and saw a woman below who was dressing a skin. She happened to look up and see him, but was cautious and pretended [remainder of page is shorthand].

[Tablet 35]

Aug. 18, 1906. In my rooms at Chadron, American Horse, speaking of the Council on Chadron Creek said:

William Garnett was an interpreter with Louis Richards. Little Big Man, with some Sioux warriors, noisly, naked and painted; these were followed by Sioux and Cheyennes—all were singing and discharging their weapons. The Commissioners requested Red Cloud and Spotted Tail each to send four braves to quell the turbulence of these insolent Indians. The former sent American Horse, George Sword, Young Man Afraid of his Horses and Hollow Horn, while Spotted Tail on his part appointed Crow Dog, Black Crow, Looking Horse and Big Star.[28] They suppressed the disorder, but Little Big Man threatened to kill a commissioner and any chief that would consent to sell the Black Hills.[29]

Death of Crazy Horse

A week before the above interview American Horse, and one of his two wives, and the daughter of this wife, having come with a large number of Indians to Chadron to take cars for Cheyenne where they were to be an attraction on Pioneer Day, took dinner at my table, and American Horse gave us a description of the killing of Crazy Horse. In the struggle to escape from his captors he was held around the waist by an Indian who seized him from behind, while Little Big Man grasped his wrist and hand in which he held a knife. By turning his hand adroitly he gave Little Big Man a wound in his arm which caused him to release his hold; and thereupon making a violent effort to disengage himself he surged against a bayonet in the hands of one of the guards who was standing at a guard against infantry and swaying his piece forward and backwards. The bayonet entered his side below the ribs inflicting a mortal wound.

American Horse positively affirms that the soldier did not stab Crazy Horse intentionally. He also said that he himself during the scuffle threw his gun down on Crazy Horse to shoot him, but some Indians pressed between them and prevented him from taking his life. So passed away one of the greatest Indian warriors of the later days.

[Tablet 16]
Division of the Missouri
Chicago Ill.
Pine Ridge S.D. January 10, 1891

This to certify that American Horse is a great Sioux Chief, has been a friend of the white people and loyal to the government. He has had a good influence over his people, and his wise management and control of his people has kept them to a great extent free from excitement and separate from the hostile element.

Nelson A. Miles
Major General U.S.A.

(Copy)

Another copy of letter from R. S. Mackenzie Col. 4th Cavalry to Lt. Col. John P. Hatch Comdg. Fort Sill I. T. saying that Am. Horse is the chief of the Loafer band of Sioux & is the man who killed Sioux Jim, a member of his band who refused to be arrested by the troops, & recommends him as a very good Indian.

He tells of destroying an emigrant train at the place where Casper now is or near there

[Tablet 2A]

Copies of the Certificates held by American Horse, chief of the Loafer band of Sioux Indians, exhibited to me Monday, August 13, 1906, at my rooms in Chadron, Nebraska, in presence of one of his two wives, of his daughter Julia, whose mother was present, and Frank Goings. (Alice American Horse is the daughter of the other wife) Alice was put to school when seven years of age and was not released till she was seventeen. American Horse told me that she could not interpret between him and me because she entered school so young and was away so long that she had no knowledge of the Indian speech.

(Copy)
Camp Robinson
Oct. 22nd 1877

The bearer, American Horse is one of the principal and best chiefs of the Sioux nation. I have known him for a long time. He has done valuable service in keeping the Indians in good and peaceable order at Red Cloud Agency and can be trusted as a friend of the white man.

J. K. Mason
Major 3rd Cavy.

(Copy)
Headquarters District of Black Hills
Camp Robinson, Neb., Oct. 25, 1876.
Lt. Col. John P. Hatch,
Commanding Fort Sill I. T.

Sir:

The bearer of this letter, American Horse, a chief of the Loafer band of Sioux, is the man who killed Sioux Jim, a member of his band who refused to be arrested by the troops, for which reason I think him a very good Indian and I wish you would have him well treated when at your Post. I wish you would also have Mr. James to introduce him to the Comanche Chiefs as a friend of mine and tell them to treat him well and take him Buffalo hunting if he wishes to go.

Very Respectfully
Your obedient servant
(Sgd.) R. S. Mackenzie
Col. 4th Cavalry
Commanding District Black Hills.

P. S. American Horse thinks his sister is with the Southern Cheyennes. Please give him a line to Agent Miles, and ask him to assist him all he can as he is a very good Indian.

[Charles A. Eastman's Interview]

Dr. Eastman was raised in a traditional Native American family. He wrote a number of books including From Deep Woods to Civilization: Chapters in the Autobiography of an Indian *(Lincoln: University of Nebraska Press Bison Books, 1977).*

[Tablet 11]
Tuesday, August 20, 1907.

Dr. Charles A. Eastman said to me at Allen (I am writing this at Frank Salaway's) speaking of Hinman the interpreter, that he was a thoroughly bad man, immoral and dishonest.[30] He says he knows. The Indians caught him several times in <u>flagrante delictu</u>. Says Hinman obtained an appropriation by Congress of ten thousand dollars to remove certain of the Sioux Indians from Minnesota to Nebraska. The Indians had already moved. Hinman brought three families whom the doctor names and took the money and built mission buildings and a fine house for himself at _ _ _

These were subsequently burned down. Eastman saw the original letters of Hinman and Bishop Whipple in the Senate documents in Washington and was allowed by a friend (French) to make copies.[31] These letters were in Nos. somewhere from A to D. It requires influence to obtain access to these documents. Dr. Eastman was friendly with Gen. Miles and through the assistance of the latter he obtained the privilege of examining these papers. (Use a Senator). See Ploughed Under for statement regarding the buildings, pages 52-53.

He says that certain Indians, I think Santees, were moved by the government, men and women separately, after the Sioux massacre in Minnesota. The women were sent first down the Mississippi to St. Louis, thence up the Missouri to Ft. Thompson, and their husbands who were confined as prisoners at Davenport were afterwards transported by the same route.[32]

Sissetons. The Sissetons divided and moved, some going to Dakota and a part to Canada.

Eastman knew Inkpaduta who was in the battle of the Little Big Horn. Says he was a good man.[33]

Eastman says that Chief Joseph made himself famous among the whites because of his humanity in sparing the lives of prisoners and of women and children; that he was a good man but no uncommon commander. Says he retreated among the mountains where the army could not reach him.

Crazy Horse

Eastman thinks that Crazy Horse was a brave noble, chivalrous man, always a gentleman, quiet in demeanor, not boastful, silent, never selfseeking, a high-minded man, a pure patriot who loved his people—imbued with the spirit of the highest patriotism, and fought for his country as long as there was any hope of success. He disdained politics, all scheming and intriguing. Dr. Eastman thinks Crazy Horse had made up his mind to go to Washington, but he was not a man to count such a distinction as of such consequence as to be coveted; he shrank from notoriety and display, and sought only to be effective in war and useful to his people. He desired that his people should be satisfied to have him go to Washington, and he wanted them to express themselves to that effect. At the time of these events occurrences the Oglalas were divided into three (?) factions; the Bad Faces under Red Cloud, those under No Water, and the Cut Offs under Little Wound, and those under Crazy Horse.

Crazy Horse's popularity was steadily increasing and irritating the jealousy of the other chiefs who conspired to get him out of the way. The emissaries of Crazy Horse were dispersed throughout the Indian camps and noting the significant signs of trouble. These became aware of a conspiracy among certain of the Indians to kill him. Crazy Horse was told of what was taking place. He would not believe that there was a serious purpose of that kind. He merely said that if they wanted his life they could take it without trouble when he was off his guard and his back turned. One day a friend saw cartridges being privily distributed. Another discovered the same thing. These came to him with word of these suspicious circumstances.

Some one said he would take his sister away. I don't know what this means.

Crazy Horse said he would take his wife to her folks. The following morning he started alone with her for the camp of Touch the Cloud who was his friend, at the mouth of Beaver Creek.

Some of the younger Indians such as American Horse were treacherous to their own people; they sought to secure the favor of the military, and so were false and informing. Crazy Horse was a totally different type of man. He was brave to a fault. Dr. Eastman speaks of Mr. Colhoff telling him of a brave act of Crazy Horse in riding into Ft. Laramie in pursuit of some person. Colhoff saw this. Colhoff told me of this.

Eastman says that Woman's Dress was a liar and was serving the interests of the jealous chiefs who were conspiring against Crazy Horse. It was false that Crazy Horse was planning to compass the death of General Crook.

Eastman says that it was given out for sinister purposes that C. H. intended to kill Crook.

When word was brought to Crazy Horse by his detectives that cartridges were being issued secretly, and it was believed by the detectives that the object was to kill C. H.; he said he would take his wife to her people at the camp of Touch the Cloud at the mouth of the Beaver; and next morning he started with her alone, and another joined them. Chief Touch the Cloud was a great friend of Crazy Horse.

Those scouts sent after C. H. amounted to nothing. They got scared and retired to Camp Sheridan. The military was suspicious and fearful and this made matters worse; these fears were worked upon by the designing Indians who knew that their own schemes could be promoted by false reports.

[Mrs. Richard Stirk's Interview]

Mrs. Stirk was married to Richard C. Stirk. His interview is also in Tablet 8.

[Tablet 8]
Crazy Horse.

Mrs. Stirk gives account of the death of Crazy Horse substantially the same as others. The sister of Crazy Horse's wife told Mrs. Stirk how the killing was done. The soldier ~~stabbed him~~ bayonetted him on purpose; he had his bayonet against him to push him along, and he ran the bayonet into him. When he drew it out he wiped the blood off with Crazy Horse's blanket. Mrs. Crazy Horse was right there and saw it all. She rushed up to her husband and the Indians and all fell back to give her room. She saw all this. Mr. and Mrs. Stirk say positively that the act of the soldier was intentional. It no doubt was.

Crazy Horse's body was afterwards removed by the Indians to a place in the side of a cliff on White Horse Creek between Pine Ridge Agency and Manderson 4 miles above Manderson. The Indians tell Stirk this; he has heard the Indians when together and sitting and smoking and talking discuss this event & he is sure it is correct; Stirk says the hole in the cliff is in full view of the road on the east side of the road; he has seen it many a time, and it is about 50 feet above the bottom of the cliff. He has understood that the body was placed there with the aid of ladders.

There is a Crazy Horse related to the old chieftain, living in the third house up the W.K. creek from Baptiste Pourier's—in the only log house that has a shingled roof. Stirk thinks he can tell all about this removal.

Stirk speaking of <u>Little Big Man,</u> says the Indians always speak of him as a squaw—a woman; they say he was not a brave man; he was a bad, mischievous character, stirring up discord, trouble, but when he had fomented disturbance he stayed behind in camp and let the warriors face the difficulties he had caused.

Little Bat and Mrs. Emma Stirk's father was named Smith; he was either a Lieutenant or a Captain in the regular army. She lived with Bob Saunders whose wife took her and raised her after her mother's death when she was two years old. Her mother was a full blood Oglala Sioux.

In those days (1863) (she was then 4 years old) it was common for squaw men to buy vegetables from the traders' stores and take them out among the Indians and exchange them for furs and robes for profit. Several families together had bought a load of vegetables for this purpose. Mrs. Saunders and Mrs. Stirk's mother were sisters and her aunt with whom she was living was the only woman in the party. Little Bat was one of the party. They were all camped on the Cache la Poudre and asleep about 11 o'clock at night, horses were all loose except one which was tied up, when a lot of Oglalas,—Fire Thunder, Fast Thunder and others; these two named now live on Wounded K. Creek; they charged down on the camp without firing; Mrs. Stirk's mother & Little Bat rushed out and told them not to fire on them, saying that they were Indians (it was in winter time and snow was knee deep); the Indians replied, "All right" and said "Bring some tobacco out to us." Saunders was a white man. There were several white men in the party. Saunders put his wife and Mrs. Stirk on a horse to flee, but just at this moment an arrow struck the saddle of the horse, when Mrs. Saunders dismounted and said she would not go, but she told her husband to mount and make his escape, which he did. Mrs. Saunders thought the Indians would not harm her as she was Indian. The whites all got away, each on a horse. Mrs. Saunders now took the tobacco to the Indians. The latter demanded to know who she was and where she was from. She told them; and when this explanation was made they knew who she was, & had no purpose to do her injury, but it was well that the whites had got away. The Indians now came down to the camp where the wagon was and stayed all night. Next morning the Indians told Mrs. Saunders to make up a lot of bread for them, which she did. Then they took from the wagon what they wanted and went off carrying Mrs. Saunders and the two children — Emma and Little Bat. "Bat" was a little boy then, a few years older than Emma. They all traveled together the first day and camped at night; her aunt, Mrs. Saunders, kept crying all the time, she did not want to go, but wanted to go back. That night Mrs. Saunders begged the Indians to let her go back. Then the Indians let her and the children go — these went one direction and the Indians in another. These three traveled two days and nights alone; Emma was small & not able to walk much and Little Bat carried her on his back; they came to a stream which was not wide but was very deep & very cold; they had to strip to cross; Bat carried Emma across; when he got over he was exhausted and chilled so that he fell over helpless and insensible; Mrs. Saunders wrapped him in a Buffalo robe and put snow into his mouth to revive and resuscitate him. (When Mrs. Saunders took the tobacco to the Indians, they to have sport with her would keep saying in her presence that she was a white woman and they would kill her; and she would beg off declaring that she was an Indian. They were just teasing her with savage delight.) Mrs. Saunders was married to a Mexican and died up on the Porcupine about two years ago. She raised quite a family. "Buckskin Jack's" wife is one of her daughters.

(Mr. Stirk has hunted with Little Bat a good deal. Says Bat could follow a deer or an antelope to beat a horse; he had the greatest endurance of any man he ever saw.)

At this time that Bat was bearing Emma on his back he was lame, as the wagon had run over his foot, and she kept scolding because he was so unsteady in his gait. On this [illegible] third day after Bat had recovered so they could proceed, they came to another creek which was wooded and here they stopped to rest. A couple of horsemen appeared while they were stopping here—appeared on the ridge on opposite side of the stream. Mrs. Saunders told her wards that "There are some more Indians, and now we will be killed sure!" They then hid in the bushes, but the horsemen saw them and came to them. These two men were squaw men—one was named Geary whom Mrs. Saunders knew. They asked what she was doing there & she related what had happened. The two men took Emma with them to their camp, Geary taking her on his horse and left Mrs. Saunders and Bat. Next day about noon she and Bat reached Geary's camp, having followed the trail of the two mounted men; Mrs. Saunders knew the country and the location of Geary's camp. When they arrived at his camp her feet and Little Bat's were painfully swollen so they could hardly walk. They stayed at Geary's camp about four days when Saunders came with a wagon and took the three over to another camp, and then he went to the wagon loaded with the vegetables, but he found the potatoes all frozen. They got back to Cache la Poudre. At this time a good many Frenchmen lived on this stream.

Afterwards these Oglalas came more in contact with the whites, and came into Agency relations. The 1867 treaty came later.

[Louis Bordeaux's Interview]

> *Louis was the third child of James and Huntkalutwin "Marie" Bordeaux. He was born in 1849, probably at his father's trading post eight miles east of Fort Laramie. Louis's father was a Frenchman from Missouri and his mother was a Brulé. At the time of the interview Louis operated a ranch on the Rosebud Reservation. He died in 1917.[34] About a year before the interview, Ricker wrote a note about Bordeaux.*
>
>> See Louie Bordeaux at Rosebud who was Interpreter at Spotted Tail; knows all abt. C. Horse being brot in to that Agency. Highly recommended by Garnett Bordeaux knows through his parents all abt. killing Conquering Bear.
>
> *Ricker wrote the following sketch of Bordeaux the day after he interviewed him.*

[Tablet 11]

Louis Bordeaux, son of James Bordeaux, is (Aug. 31, 1907) 57 yrs. old. His father sent him to school from Laramie at Hamburg, Fremont County, Iowa, three years, and desired him to go to college at St. Louis, but he refused much to the disappointment of his father. Louis had a brother much younger than himself named John Bordeaux.

James Bordeaux originally owned the site of Fort Laramie where he had a trading post (I think this post belonged to the Am. Fur Co.) It was purchased by the government and the first troops sent there were commanded by an officer (Bordeaux says he was a Frenchman probably of French extraction by name of Laramie.)[35]

On questioning him about it, Louis Bordeaux says that his father, James Bordeaux, bought the Laramie trading post from the Am. Fur Co. and kept a trading post in the same place himself and afterwards sold out to the government. He has seen the original adobe buildings. Does not know the time of either sale.

James Bordeaux had a trading post on the Big Bordeaux Creek in Dawes County, Nebr. Louis Bordeaux says an Indian told him that this post was on that creek at the foot of the low hills on the north side of the Pine Ridge. He never knew where it was because his father had it before he was born. His father's headquarters were at Laramie, but this was just a winter post for one winter perhaps, and the next winter he was somewhere else with a similar post. He lived on the Bordeaux at his post one winter, possibly and probably only one. Such men or traders moved about and spent the winters trading with the Indians wherever they were encamped and hunting, and here the trading was done. Says his father also had a post on a creek which empties into the Chug in Wyoming, and this took his father's name.[36]

Says his name is Louis (pronounced according to the French Louie) Bordeaux; that when he was christened he was given a middle name, he never uses it although his children in writing use it. He did not state what it is.

He says further that Chadron has its name from Chardon mentioned in the History of the Am. Fur Co. Says the name was not Chadron; this is a corruption, but it was C-h-a-r-d-o-n, accent on last syllable, French name. This man had a post on the creek, probably for a single winter but long enough to give his name through careless speaking by English speakers to the stream as Chadron.[37]

Mr. Bordeaux says that a son of Chardon, named Louis Chardon, lives on Rosebud Reservation about twelve miles from the Agency, but he was raised and has always lived among the Indians and knows nothing about his father's life on Chadron Creek. He was too young.

Speaking of Frank Grouard, says he was a renegade. Bordeaux had seen letters of Grouard's addressed on the envelope to Frank Grouard, and on the inside addressed to him as F. M. Pratt. Grouard told Bordeaux that he had changed his name on account of some trouble, but that his true name was Pratt; that he was a Sandwich Islander, etc. Crazy Horse told Bordeaux that Grouard was with him in the northern country; that he used to kill mail carriers and bring in the mail & read the letters and tell Crazy Horse where the soldiers were, etc. Grouard spoke Indian very broken, couldn't speak as well as Big Bat. Bat talks it well. Grouard was afraid of Crazy Horse. Crazy Horse denounced Grouard to Bordeaux because he had once been a trusted man among his band & now he had used them by treacherously leaving them & turning against them.

[Tablet 11]

Louie Bordeaux. Interviewed at his home, six miles north of Georgia (Kilgore), Nebraska, on the Northwestern R.R., Friday, August 30, 1907.

Fragment of the History of Crazy Horse.

Mr. Bordeaux is of French and Indian descent, and the Sioux language is his mother tongue. He is in stature a short, thick, heavy man, of very dark complexion, the two strains of his blood showing with prominence in his color.

At the time of the Crazy Horse episode he was the official interpreter for the Spotted Tail Agency and Camp Sheridan. The Agency was three-quarters of a mile above Camp Sheridan on the Beaver Creek.

Major Burke was the officer in command of Camp Sheridan. Lieutenant Lee was the Acting Agent at Spotted Tail Agency. He was called Major because he was agent.[38]

It was in the fall of 1876 that the Indians went to the Indian Territory to view the country & decide whether to move there. These were chiefs and subchiefs, a lot of them; they went to Sidney by horseback &c.; there they went by rail as far as they could & then finished by horses &c.

Lieut. Jessie M. Lee, an army officer.

Mr. Bordeaux says that when Crazy Horse went down to Touch the Cloud's camp from his own near the Red Cloud Agency that the Indian scouts who followed him from Fort Robinson were afraid of him; that they went to Camp Sheridan with word that Crazy Horse had quitted his own camp and was in the camp below, which was Touch the Cloud's at the confluence of the Beaver and the fork of the Beaver (it was not at the mouth of the Beaver, but was in the vicinity of Conn's). These Indian scouts went into barracks at Camp Sheridan. They were careful to keep well concealed inside; but it is not true that the

Indians pursued them and they sought safety in flight and escaped to the barracks. The Indian warriors, Touch the Cloud's, numbered about 300 and were in overwhelming force against not alone [only?] the scouts from Fort Robinson but the regular garrison of troops which consisted of only two companies.

When the scouts arrived from Fort Robinson Mr. Bordeaux was up at the Agency. He was sent for. He and Major Burke and Acting Agent Lieutenant Lee and Joe Marrivaill (who was a Mexican mixed blood; I think Charley Marrivaill said he was French; ask Mary Ann) started down to the camp where Crazy Horse was.

Corrected: Before Crazy Horse started to come up to Camp Sheridan, Joe Marrivaill scout and interpreter, and mixed French and Spanish blood (Marrivaill is a French name, the Spanish probably came through the mother says Bordeaux. Marrivaill was a light man in complexion, would be called a white man) and Charley Tackett (Bordeaux says this name was not Taggart but Tackett) these two had gone down to Touch the Cloud's camp to see if they could get Crazy Horse to come up to the Post. Tackett was a Sioux mixed blood & scout & interpreter. They had been sent down after the Indian scouts had come from Fort Robinson with a letter telling of Crazy Horse's flight and asking that Crazy Horse be arrested and sent back, & offering a reward of $50 to anyone who should arrest him.[39]

White Thunder, a sub-chief and principal scout for the government, belonging at Camp Sheridan, and Black Crow, a sub-chief and right bower of Spotted Tail, had also gone down, and with these were coming back Crazy Horse, Touch the Cloud and a large number of Indians. Marrivaill and Tackett had been first met returning, and they said Crazy Horse was coming.

They were Some of these were in a four mule ambulance: namely, Major Burke and Lieut. J. M. Lee and one or two other officers.[40]

On the way down they met Crazy Horse, Touch the Cloud, White Thunder and a lot of Indians, some of them in warbonnets and fighting attitude, coming up to Camp Sheridan. Major Burke and other members of the party shook hands with Crazy Horse who was friendly, though he was not a man to talk. The party turned about and started to return. They had not gone but a little way when White Cloud Thunder approached Mr. Bordeaux and told him to tell his party to make better time and get back as soon as they could, for he was not sure but there might be trouble; he did not know what some of the Indians who were the friends of Crazy Horse and excited, might do. (Touch the Cloud's and Crazy Horse's Indians were northern Indians of the same band of Sioux.)[41]

The officers had met Crazy Horse about a mile and a half below Sheridan. The Indian camp was two miles or a little more below.

They accelerated their pace and when within a mile of the camp White Thunder told Bordeaux to hurry his party back, as stated above. Mr. Bordeaux himself kept along with the Indians until within half a mile of Camp Sheridan when he hastened forward and reached there ahead of the Indians. Crazy Horse and his followers rode into the quarters of Camp Sheridan where Major Burke and Lieutenant Lee tried to talk with him, ~~He was asked why~~ but he would say nothing. The Indians were numerous and swarming.

The officers made effort to get something out of him; they told ~~him that he must go back to Fort Robinson~~ what was required of him, that he must go back to Fort Robinson, that he would not be hurt that he should be protected etc., but he refused to speak.

Spotted Tail was present at the Post ~~and he Crazy Horse that~~ (he did not go down toward the Indian camp with Major Burke's party) and he took up the conversation with Crazy Horse, telling him that he (Crazy Horse) was under his (Spotted Tail's) control; that this was his (Spotted Tail's) Agency, and that he did not want him to come there to make trouble; that his Agency was a peaceable place and had the name of being so, and that he did not want any disturbance. He asked Crazy Horse if he would not go into the Adjutants Office and converse with the officers. He replied, "I will." These were the first words he had uttered.

One of the episodes of the excitement when this strain was at its height was the entrance into the scene of an Indian named Buffalo Chips who had a long braid of hair down his back. He came up to Crazy Horse and addressed him, saying that he was afraid to die, that he was a coward, and then to Spotted Tail he said in the same spirit of denunciation, " You are a coward!"[42] Crazy Horse said nothing. Spotted Tail answered him with a pleasant laugh. Then Buffalo Chips addressed the officers & told them to hang him (Buffalo Chips) and let Crazy Horse live a hundred years, for he was a coward; and to let Spotted Tail also live a hundred years, for he was a coward too. Chips took hold of Burke's coat when he was talking to him. Major Burke laughed and said to Chips, "We don't want to hang you; we don't want to hang anybody." The Indians were quiet but were swarming around by the hundreds, surrounding these six men, namely, Major Burke, Lieut. Lee, the military surgeon (name forgotten) Louis Bordeaux, Chief Spotted Tail and Joe Marrivaill.[43]

Then Buffalo Chips, turning to Major Burke, told him to hang him (Buffalo Chips) and to let Crazy Horse and Spotted Tail live a hundred years, as more correctly stated above.

Crazy Horse, with a few of his friends went into the Adjutant's office, and here he was asked why he had left his camp at Red Cloud. He explained that he saw a great force of soldiers and scouts coming to his camp, and he did not want trouble, so he came down to Touch the Cloud's to avoid disturbance. He said that when he came in from the north and met the officers and others on Hat Creek, he presented the pipe of peace to the Great Spirit there and said he wanted peace, he wanted no more war, and promised that he would not fight against any nation anymore, and that he wants to be at peace now; but only a day or two before this he had been called into a council at Fort Robinson with the officers, and they had asked him to go out and fight the Nez Perces; that he did not want to do that, for he remembered his promise to the Great Spirit not to fight anymore; but nevertheless he said he would go and camp beside the soldiers and fight with them till the Nez Perces were all killed.

[Here Ricker noted, "Skip to page 74," and inserted the four following paragraphs.]

(I have told Bordeaux what Billy Garnett told me, as I recollect, about Crazy Horse refusing to go against the Nez Perces & threatening to go off north to hunt. He says it may have been so, but he remembers that Billy told him that he (Billy) was not in that council; that Grouard interpreted on that occasion. Billy may be mistaken and stated to me what he learned from Grouard. I am satisfied that Crazy Horse's statement was as Bordeaux says, as reason for so thinking will appear farther on. Garnett was speaking only of what he had been told that Crazy Horse had said; he was not present when C. H. said it, but Grouard was.

Mr. Bordeaux says that Crazy Horse was slight in form, tall, very light in complexion, hair long and hung down to his hips.

Lieut. Lee was a sincere and warm friend of the Indians; had their highest good at heart; treated them upon the principle that they were men, trusted them, considered their claims and wishes and yielded to them no doubt far beyond his instructions, because he understood them and it was the better way. It was better than government by headquarters—by directions from distant headquarters.

Camp Sheridan was a four-company post, but only two companies were kept there, one of infantry and one of cavalry.)

[Here Ricker noted, "Continued from page 71½."]

It is here explained by Mr. Bordeaux that Grouard was the interpreter at that council, as Billy Garnett said when he met him coming away and Grouard told him it was too hot for him there so he left.

Bordeaux says that Grouard willfully misinterpreted Crazy Horse's words. He represented him as saying that he would not go out to fight the Nez Perces, but that he was going back to his country in the north and would take the war-path and fight the soldiers till they were all killed.

Bordeaux says Grouard was afraid of Crazy Horse after having lived among his band for years as a refugee from trouble on the Missouri where he killed a schoolmate, and had killed, as Crazy Horse told Bordeaux, mail carriers and robbed the mail and carried letters into the Indian camp and read them to Crazy Horse, the contents disclosing information as to the whereabouts and movements of the soldiers, in all of which the Indians were keenly interested.[44]

When Crazy Horse was explaining why he came down to Touch the Cloud's he also said that the Spotted Tail Agency had the reputation of being a peaceable place and he wanted to come there and have his band transferred to that Agency.[45]

Jump this ¶ in reading the narrative.

Mr. Bordeaux explains that when an Indian presents the pipe to the Great Spirit it is the holy pipe; to the wild Indian this act and vow was in the nature of an oath, as such obligations are among civilized peoples; to the Indian it is a holy, sacred act, solemn and to be kept with honor.

Mr. Bordeaux says that when the council was held at Fort Robinson and Crazy Horse was asked to go against the Nez Perces, Touch the Cloud, and High Bear who belonged to Touch the Cloud's band and was a sub-chief in it, were present at that council.[46] These two latter came to Camp Sheridan and told home. Grouard was the interpreter at the Fort Robinson council. He was sent, after the council was held, from Fort Robinson with a letter to the comdg. officer at Camp Sheridan, and Major Burke, Touch the Cloud, High Bear, Spotted Tail and other chiefs were brought into council at Sheridan. Bordeaux was present as interpreter. Here it was told by Touch the Cloud in High Bear's presence without contradiction just what Crazy Horse had said; that on Hat Creek he had promised not to go on the warpath any more etc., but now the same men who had desired to have this pledge from him were urging him to go killing men again (but this time it was to do it for them); however, he would do it; he would go and camp beside their soldiers and fight with them till all the Nez Perces were killed.

Mr. Bordeaux states that this occurred three or four days before Crazy

Horse came down to Touch the Cloud's camp. In the conference in the headquarters at Camp Sheridan Crazy Horse repeated the same thing exactly. Grouard was present in the former council and heard Bordeaux's translation of what Touch the Cloud said when telling what Crazy Horse had said, and Grouard called Bordeaux down, saying he was not correctly interpreting Touch the Cloud, accusing him of not being familiar with the northern dialect. Bordeaux told him that he could not teach him his mother tongue, and that he (Grouard) was not well enough versed in the three Sioux dialects, namely, the Teton which Bordeaux speaks & which is the prevailing speech west of the Missouri river, and the Santee which uses the d, the Yankton which uses the n, and the Teton which uses the l, etc., etc., to instruct him or to be an interpreter. Major Burke interposed and said to Grouard that Bordeaux could not be impeached, if the testimony of other interpreters of reputation could be relied on, for they all, without exception, gave him the commendation of being an accurate and brave interpreter—brave meaning that he interpreted just what a man said without change or modification. Gruard had no more to say.

In this council at Camp Sheridan Crazy Horse stated to Major Burke that he wished to have his band transferred to Spotted Tail Agency where there would be a better opportunity to live in peace, and Burke and Lee both told him to go back to Fort Robinson and have a talk with the officers there; that no harm would come to him; that he would be protected; and that they would exert their influence to have him and his band transferred. On these promises Crazy Horse consented at once that he would go back. He was going back with Touch the Cloud to his camp, and Major Burke privately told Touch the Cloud that he would hold him personally responsible for Crazy Horse; that he must not let him escape in the night. The chief said he would not let him get away.

Next morning early, Bordeaux came down from the Agency and met Crazy Horse and Touch the Cloud and a few others at the Post already there.

It should be noted here that Crazy Horse, senior, was at the camp of Touch the Cloud, having come from the north ahead of his son, and was down there. He must have gone to Fort Robinson with some of those who went that fatal day.

I have omitted in the proper place to say that when Major Burke and Lieut. Lee were riding back to the camp, returning from their trip down the creek to see Crazy Horse, as they sat in the ambulance, they were discussing the qualities of Crazy Horse as they looked back at him following behind. They agreed that he was an able young man, destined, if no ill fortune prevented, to become great among his people; that he was not trained like the old chiefs to speaking and in diplomacy; he was not spoiled by any arts to gain advantage, but was straightforward and meant what he declared and could be depended on to perform what he promised.

Touch the Cloud was an honorable and peaceable Indian, a man of good character, a very fine man, deprecated hostilities and was a peacemaker.

The night before Major Burke turned Crazy Horse over to Touch the Cloud for safe keeping.

After arriving at the camp Crazy Horse concluded that he must go back to Touch the Cloud's camp and get a saddle, he having come from his camp at Red Cloud on his horse bareback, and he was allowed to go. But Good Voice and Horned Antelope, Indian Scouts at Camp Sheridan, were sent down to watch him and not let him get away.[47] The two scouts were told if he attempted to escape to shoot his horse; if he resisted to kill him.

White Thunder was the principal scout who brought Crazy Horse up from Touch the Cloud's camp to Camp Sheridan.

Good Voice was the principal scout who was directed not to let him escape from Touch the Cloud's camp, and if necessary to shoot his horse or kill him.

Major Burke and Charley Tackett followed these; a little later Lieut. Lee, Louis Bordeaux, Swift Bear a sub-chief and Black Crow went down together in the ambulance to Touch the Cloud's camp.[48] They found Burke and Tackett around Touch the Cloud's tepee. On arrival of Lee, Burke told Lee to get Crazy Horse if he could and go right on towards Fort Robinson; in the meantime he would return to Camp Sheridan and get the Indian Scouts, so that if so obliged, they could take Crazy Horse by force.

Lieut. Lee was in a small tepee & he sent Bordeaux in to get Crazy Horse, but just at that moment Crazy Horse was invited into Touch the Cloud's tepee to have breakfast of bread, meat and coffee, and Crazy Horse asked Bordeaux to come and breakfast with him, which he did. After the repast Bordeaux asked him if he was ready now to go. Crazy Horse replied that he was; but he said, "You go on and I will come after you." Lieut. Lee said to Bordeaux "Let us go on and cross Beaver Creek, & if he doesn't come we will come back here again and wait till Major Burke comes with the scouts;" so they went on & crossed the creek & stopped. Bordeaux looked back and saw Crazy Horse coming with the two scouts before named and nine or ten of Touch the Cloud's men with him. Touch the Cloud and High Bear were in the ambulance with Lieut. Lee; these had come down with the officer from Camp Sheridan.

Lieut. Lee now proceeded slowly on the way. Crazy Horse overtook the ambulance. When these got to the Little Bordeaux Creek about fifteen miles from Camp Sheridan, scouts overtook them; when they got to about Chadron Creek more Camp Sheridan scouts overtook them, and later they were joined by more Camp Sheridan scouts till there were some sixty of these in all.

None of the Fort Robinson scouts showed up on the march to Fort Robinson, but Bordeaux says he saw some of them at the Fort after he got there.

There was no trouble on the road with Crazy Horse; but once Major Burke and Bordeaux who had had no sleep the night before, fell asleep both at the same time for a brief nap; when they waked up Crazy Horse was gone; they asked for him & were told that he had gone on ahead. Scouts were ordered to bring him back, which they did; and then he was kept in rear of the ambulance the rest of the way to the Fort.

Arriving at the Fort the occupants of the ambulance alighted and Crazy Horse dismounted. Little Big Man (who was jealous of Crazy Horse) came up, and taking him by the arm, told him, "Come along, that he was you are a coward."[49]

They all went into the Adjutant's Office. Bordeaux acted as interpreter. Lieut. Lee told Bordeaux to call Swift Bear out of the office. Lee said to Swift Bear, "I have done all I can for Crazy Horse. The Big Chief (meaning the comdg. officer at the Fort) will take care of him tonight." Swift Bear said that was all right. Lee then told Bordeaux to call out Touch the Cloud and High Bear, and he told these the same that he had Swift Bear, and in addition that the officers would take care of Crazy Horse that night and have a talk with him in the morning. Bordeaux went back into the office, and the Officer of the Day came in and took Crazy Horse by the hand and raised him up and Crazy Horse started with him, and Little Big Man stepped to his side and took him by the other arm—the left arm. They moved to the guardhouse, some Indians preceding them into the building. In moving Bordeaux Lieut. Lee and Bordeaux followed outside; Lee said to Bordeaux that Crazy Horse was turned over and they had nothing more to do with him, and cautioned Bordeaux not to get into any trouble on account of Crazy Horse, and as he said this he turned away towards the officers' quarters. Just then a tumult was heard in the guard house and the Indians came out, among them Crazy Horse and Little Big Man struggling. Bordeaux saw Little Big Man let go and then blood flow[ed] from his wound. Instantly Crazy Horse was seized by Swift Bear, Black Crow and others, friendly Indians of the Camp Sheridan scouts.

The military guard thrust Crazy Horse with his bayonet and inflicted his death wound. While this scene was in progress, the Officer of the Day was crying, "Stab the son-of-a-bitch! Stab the son-of-a-bitch!" The soldier made another thrust and grazed the door casing of the guardhouse; as he jerked back his weapon the butt of his piece struck an Indian, Chipps, Crazy Horse's medicine man, and broke his collarbone.[50] Chipps says he was the one struck and knocked down. The Officer of the Day was vigorously exerting himself to stab Crazy Horse with his sabre, but he could not reach him, as so many Indians were around the Chief.

Crazy Horse sank to the earth. Charley Roubidoux, a mixed blood scout, was near him & he told Bordeaux that he did not hear Crazy Horse say anything while the scene was transpiring.[51] Swift Bear also said Crazy Horse did not say a word; but Standing Bear said that as he was sinking he made some remark like that he was going to die.[52] He was removed into the Adjutant's Office.

Bordeaux went to the Comdg. Officer's (Col. Bradley's) office, & from there to Lieut. Clark's office, & from there he was sent to the Adjutant's Office, where Crazy Horse was lying, and he went on duty watching with the wounded man. He was relieved about twenty minutes before twelve o'clock at night.[53] Touch the Cloud and Crazy Horse's father and two doctors, Dr. McGillicuddy [being] one of them, a contract doctor, were there when Bordeaux left.[54]

Quite a while before Bordeaux's departure, Crazy Horse, Sr., said, speaking to his son: "Son, I am here." Crazy Horse, Jr., said: "Father, it is no use to depend upon me; I am going to die." The old father and Touch the Cloud both cried. Then Crazy Horse said to Bordeaux: "No white man is to blame for this; I don't blame any white man; but I blame the Indians. I don't wish to harm anybody, but one person; he has escaped from me."[55] Evidently he referred to Little Big Man. This was the last he said. Bordeaux knew he was dying. He was growing cold. Injections in his arm by the doctors revived him for a little while.[56] He was restless and turned in great pain. McGillicuddy said he could not last till midnight.

Big Bat came and relieved Bordeaux who went to headquarters for rest. In a short while Big Bat returned to headquarters, saying that Crazy Horse was dead. Lieut. Clark who had been out came in and asked: "How is my friend, Crazy Horse, getting along?" Big Bat said: "He is dead!" "Impossible that he is dead. He ought not to die." He turned to go; but painfully, unwilling to believe the cruel fact he wheeled back and asked again: "Is it true that he is dead?" Bordeaux answered, "Yes, Lieutenant, when Pourier relieved me he was dying; I know he is dead." Clark, who was a man of great humanity, could not restrain the tears as he said: "It is a shame! It is a shame! He ought not to die." He meant that he ought not to have been killed. That was the truth of the case.

Next morning his body was delivered by ambulance to his friends at Red Cloud. Next that Bordeaux saw his body was down at Camp Sheridan.

Bordeaux is very certain that Crazy Horse was killed in October, 1877.

Bordeaux says he has been told by the brother of an officer who claimed to know, that orders had been issued for Crazy Horse to be taken east and held a prisoner indefinitely.

As soon as this tragedy was committed and before Crazy Horse had breathed his last, the false word was dispatched to Camp Sheridan that he had accidentally stabbed himself.

Louis Bordeaux's Notes copied from his book in which he made them at the time of their occurrence;

"Major Lee left Brule camp with delegation of Indians for Ponca Agency for purpose of selecting camping place for the Indians for Winter." (The date, Mr. Bordeaux says was about 5th November December, 1877.)

"James Lindenberger (Lieut Lee's clerk), John Cunningham, Louis Bordeaux went back to Spotted Tail's camp on 7th of November, 1877."

"Major Lee returned with a delegation of Indians from Ponca Agency on 8th Nov. Dec. 1877."

"Left the Agency on 30th Oct. Camped on White Clay. Stayed on the 31st. Leave White Clay on 1st Nov. and camped on Wounded Knee and layed over on 2, 3 & 4. Leave Wounded on 5th and camped on Stinking Water. Agent camped 5 miles below Stinking Water. On 6th camped on 1st crossing of White River (Little White River, Bordeaux says) and camped at Agent's camp 5 miles below the crossing. Layed over on 8, 9, 10. Leave White River on 11th and camped on crossing of White River, & layed over on 12th. Camped on Sand Creek. Leave Sand Creek on 13th. Camped on 2d crossing of White River. Layed over 14th. Leave crossing of White river and camped on 1st crossing of White River and layed over on 15th. Leave 1st crossing of White River and camped on Rosebud on 16th. Leave Rosebud on 17th. Camped Rock Creek. Leave Rock Creek 18th & camped on 5 mile below Diamond Spring. Layed over on 19, 20, 21, [22?], 23, 24 & camped crossing of Turtle creek. Leave crossing of Turtle creek 25th. Camped on Turtle creek and layed over on 26, 27, 28, 29. Left Turtle Creek 30 & camped on Turtle Creek on 1st of December and camped on Forked Butte on Turtle creek. Layed over on 2, 3, 4, 5, 6, 7, 8, 9, 10. Left Turtle Creek on the 11th. Camped on Running Water. Left Running Water on 13th & camped on Running Water. Left Running Water on 14th, arrived at Agency."

Mr. Bordeaux says that when these Brule Indians were moving to the Ponca Agency they got stubborn and did not want to go any farther but undertook to stop on Turtle creek. Lieut. Lee made a speech to them. Bordeaux made notes of this speech, but a part of these notes were torn out of his book. Those remaining show that he told them that if they did not go to the Agency they would not get their annuities; if they stopped on Turtle creek they would not receive their rations; that if they did not listen to the words of the Great Father he (the Acting Agent Lieut. Lee) would be withdrawn and somebody appointed who would rob them.

This argument was effective, for the Indians went to the Agency.

Louis Bordeaux tells me that Lt. Lee has become a Major General and is writing a book on the Indians.[57] Get his address from an army register & write him.

Bordeaux told me how arms were taken from Indians and given to the Indian scouts, and by these turned back over to the owners. Write the acct. Remember what A. G. Shaw said of what took place with horses at Spotted Tail Agency.

Put down about family feud bet. Spotted Tail and Crow Dog as reason for killing the former.[58]

Bordeaux was at the attempt to make a Black Hills treaty in 1875. He can tell about the 1874 proceedings. Write to him for facts.

Nez Perces (pronounced Nez Per cês, says Bordeaux, and means "piereced noses." Nez Perces is French.

[Respects Nothing's Interview]

Respects Nothing was a Northern Oglala Lakota. The correct English translation of his name is Fears Nothing.

[Tablet 29]
Interview with Respects Nothing who was in the Custer Battle.
Frank Galligo, Interpreter. On White River at the Mouth of Grass Creek, November 9, 1906.

Respects Nothing says: Years ago there was a fight between the Crows and the Oglalas and the Crows killed an Oglala on Chasing Creek and chased their foes across the Little Big Horn and up Water Rat Creek. This they called Water

Rat because the Oglala killed there was named Water Rat. After the Custer Battle the Indians called it Custer's Camp Creek because they claimed he had a camp on it. Reno came down Trail Creek and crossed Little Big Horn at mouth of Trail Creek.

Respects Nothing says that the Indians were not camped on the Little Big Horn bottom for a distance of 5 miles; but were camped as shown on the map, as follows: [Figure 5]

1 was the camp of the Cheyennes;

2 was the camp of the Uncapapas;

3 was the camp of the Uses Bow, Itazap cho;

4 was the camp of the Minneconjous;

5 was the Oglala camp.[59]

He says all these Indians were encamped on a mile square of land, that is to say, on a section.

Respects Nothing and his wife, White Cow Robe, both tell me that Custer's advance was discovered in this way: Some Oglalas had started for the Red Cloud Agency. One of the number was slow in getting started & was behind. The others had gone forward, and he was following; he saw the dust rising from Custer's column, and also saw the soldiers; he went back and notified the Indians.[60] This was on the morning that the battle began.

Reno crossed the Little Big Horn at the mouth of Trail Creek.

When the Indian returned and gave warning of the approach of Custer there was a good deal of excitement and a rush was made for the ponies, and before the people could get out the village was attacked.

Reno crossed and came down the bottom of the River to the mouth of the Box Elder and began firing from a clump of woods at that point. The Indians left their lodges standing. The women fled down the River toward the mouth of the Chasing Creek.[61] The women did not run back to the hills. Some warriors from all the camps went up to the head of Box Elder Creek and there attacked Reno's line and drove it down into the timber.[62]

Respects Nothing had his horses down below the Indian camps and was waiting for his horses to be brought, and when they came he went right up close to the River to the point where Reno was when he had been driven into the timber, and here is where Respects Nothing began to take part. Reno fell back and recrossed the River and ascended the hills where he made his stand. He saw the pack mules come but did not see Benteen's command.[63] There were some soldiers between Reno's main body and the River retreated up the stream to the point of Reno's crossing in retreat and most of them were killed along the River before they could cross.

After Reno was up upon the bluffs he was surrounded. Some of the soldiers went down to the River to get water with their hats and the Indians fired on them and they ran back to the position on the hills.

Just as Reno reached the hills Respects Nothing heard an Indian on the north side of the River and down a little below where Reno had crossed, say that soldiers were coming down behind the ridge.[64]

On the 17th of June they fought under Crazy Horse on the Rosebud and fell back and stayed in the first camp two nights, then fell back in one day to the Little Big Horn and stayed two nights on that River before crossing, and crossed above the mouth of Trail Creek then they crossed and made camp in the Oglala camp with the other Indians. He says that all these five tribes or bands fell back to the Little Big Horn together, as all of them were in the battle together against Crook June 17th.[65]

(He says that the Indians had no expectation that the soldiers would follow. After the fight with Crook some of the Indian scouts went back to see what Crook's soldiers were doing, and they found that Crook was falling back, and so they did not expect any further fighting.)

(He saw Custer's horse which was a chestnut sorrel with stocking legs.[66] He saw Custer's clothing which was buckskin, after Custer was killed.)

(Eagle Ring was eleven years old at the time of the battle and went on the field with the old women. They stripped the dead naked and the women struck the bodies with sticks as in coup, but did not mutilate the bodies. Eagle Ring was present at this interview with Respects Nothing.)

Custer came down the ridge. Next day after the Custer battle an Indian went up on the high hill where I went up and with a field glass (probably taken from the dead on the Custer field) looked down the river and saw Terry's soldiers late in the afternoon.[67] They quit Reno and went down & confronted Terry and had a little fight there and took some horses from Terry; then they fell back to their old camp and took their lodges with them, leaving only one lodge in which they left their dead.[68] They left 20 dead on the battlefield—20 dead on the battlefield, and two others died on Wood Lice Creek.

These were all they lost altogether.[69] They fell back before Terry to Box Elder and stopped there a little while, then continued to retreat up the River to the mouth of the Wood Lice Creek abt. 15 miles, where they arrived at daylight next morning. They stayed there two days and then went up to the head of Wood Lice Creek in the mountains; stayed there two days and went across, going east, to the head of the Little Big Horn River, and were there about two days; from here they moved over to Tongue River; they ~~killed a Cheyenne Indian on turned~~ went back from the head of Little Big Horn to the Rosebud; when they were camped on the head of the Little Big Horn they killed a Cheyenne scout, and attacked a party of soldiers in which was Baptiste Pourrier and Frank Grouard, and got their horses (this must have been the Sibley scout). From the Rosebud station they went right down the river camping 2 or 3 times; then they moved to Tongue River and followed down that River, thence over to Powder River, thence went to the Cottonwood River, thence to Beaver Creek, then the next camp was on Tinder Creek, then moved to Picket Pin Butte, then to the Grand River, on the head of this Frank Grouard captured some Indians and the Indians took some horses from the soldiers.[70] From the head of Grand River the Oglalas and Cheyennes separated from the others and turned toward the Black Hills and camped on Box Elder. The three other tribes went down to the mouth of the Yellowstone and crossed the Missouri there.

The Oglalas and Cheyennes moved next to Pole Creek; at this place the two tribes split and the former went to Tongue River, and the Cheyennes followed Pole Creek up to Powder River. The Oglalas then went to the head of Rosebud, then down the Rosebud and camped on the Cheyenne Creek; they stayed around in that country the rest of the season and did some fighting with the Crows but no more with the soldiers.

Custer came down on top of the ridge northeast of Water Rat Creek. He did not come to the river or directly attempt to. He came over from that ridge to Calhoun hill where the battle began.[71] The stones in the cemetery at the southeast, or rather in the line running down toward the River from Calhoun hill is where the battle began, and it is plain to be seen that an effort was made at that point to check the advance of the Indians, and a good many soldiers fell here.[72] It should be said that the Indians attacking at this point had crossed the Little Big Horn at the mouth of Water Rat (or what Godfrey names in his map as Reno Creek).[73] The soldiers came up to Calhoun hill diagonally from the east, and the Indians came up diagonally from the River crossing to Calhoun hill. These Indians enveloped the ridge on the north side about half way and were met by Indians who had crossed the River at the lower crossing just below the corner of the cemetery and enveloped the ridge on the north side of the ridge after coming up the nose of the ridge to the northwest. Some Indians crossed the river above this lower crossing, probably at the mouth of the ravine. The soldiers were completely surrounded.[74]

The battle began about one o'clock P.M. and lasted till four o'clock P.M. The man who came back and gave notice that the soldiers were coming had a watch which was taken from some one of Crook's dead soldiers in the battle of the 17th of June on the Rosebud, and this watch showed the time to the Indians. Moreover, to test Respects Nothing, I took him outside the house and asked him to point where the sun stood when the battle was commenced by Reno, and he correctly indicated the quarter of the heavens where it would be at that time.

Custer's line was along the ridge, but it is not clear to my mind from his statement whether Custer stopped to fight before he reached his last place. But I think that he said Custer went to that point finally, and the last defenders were killed there. At any rate he said that those were all killed at Custer hill before those were down along the ravine. These latter, when the others were down, made a break through a narrow gap in the Indian line and ran toward the River trying to escape. They were on foot. The Indians followed them and killed them with war clubs of stone and wooden clubs, some of the latter having lance spears on them. In this pursuit one Indian stumbled into a low place among the soldiers and was killed by them.[75]

Respects Nothing says that the fighting with Reno was all over before Custer was engaged. Respects Nothing says that he helped drive Reno across the River, and then he galloped down to the crossing at the mouth of Water Rat or Reno Creek and crossed and went up and fought on the north side of the ridge and at Custer hill. One Indian dashed right through the soldiers at Custer hill on horseback. I have forgotten whether he said this Indian was killed, but I think he said he was killed.[76]

One soldier attempted to get away on horseback from Calhoun hill and was a long way off when he was killed by pursuing Indians.[77]

Reno could have gone to the aid of Custer if he had moved when the Indians withdrew. They went down and attacked Custer. Why should not Reno have gone down and helped in the defense? The Indians were all fighting Reno in the first battle.

Respects Nothing says the Indians took 700 guns as spoils. This must be an error.[78] Respects Nothing is an able Indian. He made a clear map on the ground floor of Frank Galligo's new house and by the aid of it gave a concise and clear description of all the events of the fighting. I think no white man could have given a better account. He confirmed exactly all those things which are known of these battles; and this fact is evidential that what he stated that is not known to the world is true. He said that he would tell me nothing but the facts as he knew them, and I am sure he did. He is an intelligent man.

[Moses Flying Hawk's Interview]

> *Flying Hawk was one of two sons of Black Fox and Iron Cedar Woman. He was born in an Oglala camp near present Rapid City, South Dakota, in 1852. He was a brother of Kicking Bear, the fanatical leader during the Ghost Dance troubles, and a nephew of the renowned Hunkpapa, Sitting Bull. Flying Hawk died at Pine Ridge, South Dakota, on December 24, 1931, the cause rumored to have been starvation.*[79]

[Tablet 13]
Near Big Bat's
Moses Flying Hawk, March 8, 1907

In interview with him he says: There at the battle of the Little Big Horn four tribes of Indians camped there as follows: There were 4 different camps; there were 3 camps of Sioux, as follows, Unkpapas, Minneconjous and Oglalas; also the Cheyennes.[80] The extreme length of the camps was about a mile and a half. (I tested his distance & he understands it well.) He says these several bands were camped in large circles; if they had been out in a straight line they would have been as far as from Mestth [?] where we are taking this down, to the White River, a distance of 3½ miles.

He says Custer came down on the second ridge ~~next to~~ from the river, and he stopped on the high hill above the Indians.[81]

About 30 Indians were killed all told.

The mutilations of the dead were among Reno's men mostly; a very few of Custer's men were mutilated, but there were so many dead that not much of this was done.

Map made by Moses Flying Hawk, marred a good deal by the pencil in explaining.[82]

All the living men on Custer Hill ran toward the river and were killed by the Indians who were on both sides of the retreating men killing them with arrows, guns and clubs. This shows that Custer & his officers who fell on Custer Hill were all killed before the soldiers ran for the river.[83] He says that Custer and his men on Custer Hill had their horses with them, but they were dismounted, and as often as the Indians killed one of Custer's men they took the horse belonging to him; if the horse attempted to escape they caught him. It was only on Custer Hill where the soldiers were surrounded.

On Calhoun Hill a part of the soldiers stood and gave battle. Custer was at this time on Custer Hill. Finally the line on Calhoun Hill was broken and the soldiers fell back toward Custer Hill, fighting as they went. A body which corresponds to Keogh's command made a stand on the northeast side of the ridge, and when the most of them were killed the others fell back toward Custer Hill fighting & falling, and the remnant joined Custer where the living remnant of his command were now surrounded.[84]

Flying Hawk with others left the pursuit of Reno after he had gone to the hills, and as the Indians had some wounded they went down into their camp with the wounded; then they crossed the river and attacked the soldiers on Calhoun Hill. There were also a lot of Indians who had followed the river down from Reno without going to their camp, and these also crossed the river and attacked Calhoun Hill.

Flying Hawk was with the leaders & could see. The Indians had crossed the river above Calhoun Hill before Custer left the second ridge. The soldiers saw the Indians down in the creek leading to the river, & then Custer came down off the second ridge and went up on to Calhoun Hill, leaving a detachment there, and he went right on over to Custer Hill and made stand there. (It is easy to see why he did this from a military point.)

The Sioux and Cheyennes were all mixed up.

Some of the Indians crossed from the place the women fled to & went across at the lower crossing west of Custer Hill, and there they caught a lot of soldiers' loose horses, and some of these Indians went up into the fight.[85]

He says Custer did not try to go down to the river by the creek, & that there was no fighting down on that creek, as others have said, (and no stones have been set there, & I think he is right).[86]

The man supposed to have been Lt. Harrington was driven back along the ridge with the rest from Calhoun Hill to Custer Hill, and on arriving there he did not stop going but went right on, & so he knows this man left the field before Custer was killed, because Custer was not yet surrounded. This man fired two shots back and was seen to fall. He got about half a mile away.[87]

Flying Hawk thinks that Reno could not get to Custer because they were watched by Indians who would have prevented them, though he does not know how many Indians there were watching.[88]

The battle began in the morning about 8 or 9 o'clock, and it ended about 1 o'clock P.M. or 2 P.M.[89]

He says that the Indians did not know that Custer was coming; but they had retired with their wounded, and when they passed the creek they saw Custer on the second ridge &c &c (??)

The fighting was good by the soldiers, especially by those under Reno.[90]

He puts the whole Indian loss, including those who died from wounds, at about 30. (?)[91]

(My own opinion about how they discovered Custer's approach is that Moses Flying Hawk is in error. Frank Feathers and others were over northeast of the river watching ponies. I did not ascertain whether any of these fled to the Indian camp and gave the alarm. But the Indians somehow got notice of the coming of the soldiers.)[92]

The marks made by Moses Flying Hawk on his map, reinforced by his statement at our interview, show that the Indians plunged across the river where the creek empties, in several places that is, in single file, one successively below the other.

He said that when Custer reached the Custer Hill he was right above the women who had collected down the river, and this is indicated by the map.

Sibley Scout

Passing from the subject of the Custer fight Moses Flying Hawk a Sioux Indian, speaking of the Sibley Scout said: That he was one of the attacking party where the scouts abandoned their horses, which party was composed of about nineteen Indians, which was augmented by reinforcements constantly arriving. A watch was kept up all night by the Indians at the point where the attack was made. He says the scouts got away by deserting their horses and ascending the mountain. Among these Indian reinforcements were some Cheyennes, one of whom was killed as stated by Big Bat. Flying Hawk rubbed his hands together as the Indians do to indicate complete destruction, saying that was what would have been the fate of the scouts if they had not sneaked away as they did, at a timely hour.

[Standing Bear's Interview]

Standing Bear was a Miniconjou Lakota who was born on Tongue River, Montana. In addition to the Ricker interview, Standing Bear also gave a brief account of the Little Bighorn battle to Wal-

ter M. Camp in 1910, and a more detailed version to John G. Neihardt in 1931.

[Tablet 13]
Manderson, March 12, 1907
Custer Battle only.

Standing Bear, a full-blood Sioux being interpreted says: There was a creek on which the Crows lived called Grease Grass Creek.[93]

An Oglala Indian went out on opposite side of L. Big Horn to look for horses and came back saying that there were white soldiers coming, & then they sent out a scout.[94]

The Indians first saw Custer about noon when he made a charge on them.

The first fighting of all the fighting was down on the river bottom and began about noon.[95]

He ~~fought~~ did not fight against Reno. Reno's bullets came right into the camp. Standing Bear was in or just back of the camp when Reno attacked it.[96]

[Figure 6. Map made by Standing Bear.]

Standing Bear says that Custer came down the ridge across the creek — the second or rear ridge from the river. He made no known attempt to reach the river to cross.[97] He went right up to Calhoun Hill and disposed his forces along the top of the ridge to Custer Hill. The men on Calhoun Hill finally gave way and fell back toward Custer Hill. Keogh made a desperate stand & he & his men were killed. The men fell back along the ridge leading their horses. No Indians crossed at the lower crossing. They all crossed at the mouth of the creek and spread out both ways around Custer completely encircling his troops and both hills.[98] Custer was first confronted and engaged by a few Indians who took position all along the south side of the ridge, and their numbers increased rapidly as the Indians came over the River and joined in the battle. There was no fighting on the creek. The soldiers made a stout defense. A good many Indian horses were killed & lying around in the big circle.[99] Twenty-four Indians were all the dead Indians he saw; does not know how many died from wounds.

No soldiers were mutilated either of Custer's or Reno's; but an Indian that was with the soldiers & killed was scalped and cut across the bowels.

The soldiers that fell back along the ridge uniting with those left alive on Custer Hill broke and ran on foot down toward the ravine and river, and were killed by Indians surrounding them, with arrows, guns and war clubs.[100]

The fight on the river bottom began about noon and Custer was finished about an hour later. It ~~did not seem as~~ seemed as though the sun was in the same place when the Custer battle was over that it was when the Reno fight started.

[Nick Ruleau's Interview]

[Tablet 29]
Interview with Nick Nicholas Ruleau at Pine Ridge, Nov. 20. 1906.

He has lived on this Reservation since 1879, and he has acted as interpreter for a good many who talked with Indians who were in the Custer battle, and in this way has obtained a good knowledge concerning that disaster. He says:

Minniconjou means "Plants along the water."

Sitting Bull's band was the Uncpapa.

He brings me a map prepared by Austin Red Hawk for him; also the names of the bands of Indians who were camped on the Little Big Horn, as follows:

Oglala Sioux, Crazy Horse chief,	350	warriors or braves
Uncpapas, Sitting Bull, chief,	1000	"
Minneconjous Buffalo Bed, chief	700	"
Uses Bow, Spotted Eagle, chief,	300	"
Cheyennes, Little Coyote "	45	" 101
Rosebuds, (Brule Sioux) Flying Chaser, chief,	80	"
Santees, Red Top, chief,	40	"
Yanctons, White Eagle, chief	abt 40	"

There were about 6,000 men, women and children in the camps. Mr. Nick Ruleau says many of these warriors — probably one-third were single men, is the reason why there were not more people in the camp as compared with the number of braves.[102]

Explanation of map: [Figure 7]

1 Uncapapas

2 Oglalas

3 Minneconjous

4 Uses Bow

5 Cheyennes

6 Yanktons

7 Santees

o This is the point to which the camps old men, women and children fled and collected.[103]

[Tablet 27]

Mr. Nick Ruleau says he has this account from Austin Red Hawk and Shot in the Face, Big Road (dead) and Iron Bull. These all agreed in statement.[104] He has talked to others who had been wounded but did not see the battle through.

Red Hawk says about three hundred were killed in the battle and two hundred died in the camps from wounds as they were moving over the country.[105]

These men said that Reno began his action about nine o'clock in the morning.[106] The Indians mounted their horses and went to where the soldiers were and found them lined up at the head of Muddy Creek.[107] The Indians waited till enough of them got together. Crazy Horse said to his followers: "Here are some of the soldiers after us again. Do your best, and let us kill them all off to-day that they may not trouble us any more. All ready! Charge!" himself leading the assault. The soldiers tried hard to hold their ground but were outnumbered; so they took to their horses and retreated. The Indians chased the soldiers across the River, killing about 40. They chased them up on the bluff or high point where the train was, and had the soldiers corralled in a small place.[108] While they had the soldiers at this point fighting one of the Indians gave notice that there were soldiers coming at the other end. So most of the Indians left Reno and went to fight the other soldiers. These latter soldiers were coming down on the ridge in three divisions. They did not come down to the river. The first division came to a point about half a mile or three-quarters of a mile from the river.[109] The Indians fell back down the river bottom through the village and crossed the Little Big Horn at the only crossing and went up on the high hill in the direction of Reno and from there assailed the leading division.[110] Crazy Horse and Gall and Knife Chief were haranging the Indians to get together so they could make another charge on the soldiers. He (Red Hawk) says when the Indians all got together they went down from this point, or hill, and met the first division of the soldiers and they fought this back to the second division; from that they drove the two divisions back to the first division.[111] All this time the soldiers fought bravely; he adds that he never saw soldiers fight like they did. He says several Indians were killed here but no soldiers were killed. The officers tried their utmost to keep the soldiers together at this point, but the horses were unmanageable; they would rear up and fall backward with their riders; some would get away. The Indians forced the troopers back to where the first stand was made on Calhoun hill and the ridge running there from towards the river.[112] At this place the soldiers stood in line and made a very good fight. The soldiers delivered volley after volley into the dense ranks of the Indians with[out] any perceptible effect on account of their great numbers. The Indians kept coming like an increasing flood which could not be checked. The soldiers were swept off their feet; they could not stay; the Indians were overwhelming. Here the troopers divided and retreated on each side of the ridge, falling back steadily to Custer Hill where another stand was made. By this time the Indians were taking the guns and cartridges of the dead soldiers and putting them to use and were more active in the struggle. Here the soldiers made a desperate fight. What was left of them retreated to the (what he calls) the third stand. These were surrounded and the Indians rushed on to the soldiers. Some of the soldiers broke through the Indians and ran for the ravine but were all killed without getting into it.[113] From where they made the third stand a soldier broke away from the Indians and got away. When quite a distance from the Indians and the Indians had given up the chase, they saw him fall off his horse. They went over to him and found that he had a bullet wound in his right temple. The Indians don't know whether he shot himself or he was shot by someone, but they believe he shot himself as they saw nobody near him.[114] It was about noon when they annihilated Custer and his men.[115] After the battle was over the Indians stripped the dead bodies of clothing and took their arms and ammunition. The Indians did not scalp any of Custer's men; but they did scalp all of Reno's men who were killed. Reno had some Indian scouts with him, some of whom were wounded and were alive; the Indians said that these Indians wanted to die—that was what they were scouting with the soldiers for; so they killed them and scalped them.[116]

After the annihilation of Custer's men the Indians all went back to Reno and besieged him all the afternoon, and all night and all the next day till about sundown.

Red Hawk says the women did not take any hand in the battle and did not mutilate any of the dead.[117]

About sundown the next day they saw some soldiers coming up the river; so the Indians stopped fighting Reno and moved away that night.[118] If they had fought Reno another day or two they would have wiped his command out. If the Indians did not kill Reno's men they all would have died of thirst. Reno made a desperate fight. He managed to keep the Indians from rushing his position.[119]

About a month after the battle some thirty Indians, including Red Hawk, went back to the battle field and were looking over it. At the mouth of the ravine they found eight dead soldiers lying with their uniforms on and their guns and ammunition and everything by them. Red Hawk said they could not

THE OLD WEST—INDIANS AND INDIAN FIGHTS

understand how these soldiers were killed down there.[120] They did not, out of respect for their superstition that if they take anything from any person who has been dead a long time that his spirit will haunt them, remove any of the things which belonged to these 8 dead soldiers.

Sitting Bull took no part in the battle. Gall, Crazy Horse and Knife Chief were the leading chiefs in command. Knife Chief and Crazy Horse were Oglalas. Gall was an Uncapapa. Red Hawk says Rain-in-the-Face was not in the battle; he was away and did not get back till sometime after the battle.[121]

The chiefs in this battle ranked as follows: Crazy Horse had command of all the Indians. Gall was next in precedence; and Knife Chief third.

The latter received a bullet through both arms and his body breaking both arms. He lives on the Porcupine abt. 8 miles below the village (near Day School 13).[122]

[Tablet 27]

Nicholas Ruleau says that "we" call Respects Nothing also Fear Nothing, & that he is called by this name quite as much as by the first. Nick Ruleau of Pine Ridge Agency, Nov. 20, 1906 says: He has heard a good many Indians tell about their part in the Fetterman massacre. They say they killed an even hundred foot soldiers. They further say that the Indian loss was 150 killed, and that enough more died of wounds to bring the loss up to two hundred.

[Iron Hawk's Interview]

> Iron Hawk was a Hunkpapa Lakota born in Montana in 1862. Iron Hawk gave a longer account of the Little Bighorn battle, which was published in DeMallie, The Sixth Grandfather, 190–93. Ricker may have been aware of a reluctance on the part of Iron Hawk to talk about the battle. Earlier in the year Ricker made a note to "See Spotted Elk who lives close to Iron Hawk. Spotted Elk is the pussy Indian chief who used to be in Chadron about 1887. Garnett says he may be able to get Iron Hawk to open out to me." Peter Shangrau may have served as the interpreter for this interview.[123]

[Tablet 25]

Chadron, May 12, 1907.

Iron Hawk says God gave us a spirit to work, to sleep, to talk, to do all good things in our generations. He knows that his life is from God; that he lives in Him, that it has been so from his birth. He says this is his own idea — his own mind. He has known from the first, his birth, that he was to be a friend to every body and everything—to all animals of their kind, as well as to all human beings. He knows every day and night that he is going to have one friend to talk to him in friendship. He has no bad heart toward anybody. He lived that way when he had a strong mind to think. This is Sunday but one of my friends wants me to talk with him. I am 73 yrs. old now. I know that my mind is not strong enough. I am raised to know everything—to have knowledge of everything. (There is one thing he has forgotten; he will now tell it to be put in connection with what he has said.) God made this world and in this world he has soldiers—Indian soldiers—and he is one of these soldiers; in different tribes there are distinct powers or governments, just as among white people, there are independent states and governments. He is one of the Indians called the Seven Star Soldiers—one of the highest soldiers among the Indians. He does not persecute any person; he is active in doing good for his people by trying to keep them out of trouble and in defending them. (He says the soldiers of the Seven Stars among the Indians are those who have highest authority, as Generals and Major Generals.) He was living away up North—in Montana—there were peaceable Indians staying with the whites and through them he heard that the whites wanted the Rocky Mts. & the Black Hills. He was opposed to parting with these and would not listen to any proposition looking to their surrender, and had nothing to do with the giving up of them. The word came up from Fort Laramie as to what the Gov't. wanted and he did not like it (This was the time of the 1876 treaty). He heard this treaty was made at Laramie. He was living on Powder River with some Cheyennes and a few Oglalas. He was living on the game which they hunted; this particular time of which he speaks was in the spring when they were hunting. In the early morning—about when the sun was rising—he heard there were some soldiers surrounding them, & they began to shoot. The fighting lasted all day long—till the sun was down. The Indians left their tepees and their horses, and fled on foot, north to the Big Horse River Blue Earth a stream, at the point of it, and escaped. The soldiers destroyed their camp.[124] The Indians found a vast number of other Indians camped on the Blue Earth, a small stream. These Indians in great numbers consisted of many different tribes. They all fell back together from the Blue Earth to the Little Big Horn where the Crows now are. They did not know that Custer was anywhere about (He explained that in the passage from the Blue Earth to the Little Big Horn, they camped several times, crossing the Powder River and camping on it; & crossed the Tongue.) While in camp here two Indian messengers, who lived on the Standing Rock Agency, arrived from Fort

Yates and delivered the intelligence that Custer, whom the Indians called Long Hair, — *Pehin Hanska* — had cut his hair and donned a suit of buckskin, & was coming west to fight them; and these messengers warned the Indians to keep scouts on the lookout for his approach. The Indians then broke their camp and fell back to the Little Big Horn, crossing the Tongue and the Rosebud. (Iron Hawk was not with Crazy Horse in the battle of June 17, 1876) (Horse Runs Ahead, was present at this interview. He was in the Crook battle June 17, & was wounded in the heel, so he did not fight in the Custer battle but was there.) Iron Hawk continues: the Indian tribes who fought Custer were Ogalas, Cheyennes, Rosebud or Brule, Minneconjous, Uncpapa, Santee, a few Araphoes and Sans Arcs or No Bows (Itazi Pco, pronounced, Etah z Pcho). The Indians were camped on the Little Big Horn two nights before the Custer battle which began on the third day in the morning.[125] The battle began early, about 8 or 9 o'clock judging from the position of the sun as shown by Iron Hawk.

Two young men were going back on the Indian trail toward the east looking for ~~horses~~ ponies and they discovered the troops coming. One of these boys was killed. The other returned to the camp and gave the alarm and the camp was thrown into the utmost confusion.[126] The Uncpapas were in the upper camp up the river. Soon the soldiers were seen in line of battle with three flags displayed, their staffs being planted in the ground, and then the firing began.[127] The soldiers could not be seen but the smoke of their fire was plain. They were in the point of the timber. The troops did not get into the camp among the tepees. They did not advance beyond the timber; their first firing was from the point of timber. He says the soldiers were in the timber but a short time. Iron Hawk was busy from the start arousing the warriors to duty and hurrying them to mount their horses in readiness to defend the camp. These braves were collecting on the flank of the soldiers close to the high bank which borders the river bottom on the west.[128] Presently Crazy Horse having collected his warriors, made a dash for the soldiers in the timber and ran into them; when the warriors assembling close to the bank saw this movement and heard the yells of Crazy Horse's men, they also advanced furiously with great yelling coming down on the flank.[129] The soldiers broke and ran in retreat, the Indians using war clubs as the principal weapon, a few using bows and arrows, most of the execution being by knocking the troopers from their horses; the Indians rushing right in among them. The Uncapapas were the first Indians reached when Reno began his attack. Iron Hawk says the Indians were so thick that Reno's men would have been run over and could not have lasted but a short time if they had stood their ground in the woods.

All the Indians said another lot of soldiers are moving down on the other side of the ridge.[130] They all made a rush and got across the river. At one end of the attacking Indians was Sitting Bull & at the other end was Crazy Horse (He is not sure abt. Sitting Bull but thinks he was in the fight. Says there were so many Indians that there was no telling about many things.) About 19 Indians were killed. Others were wounded, but how many he does not know, but these lived. The soldiers were stripped but not mutilated.

Thinks Sitting Bull was at one end of the attacking Indians, Crazy Horse at one end and Iron Hawk was on the side between the ridge and the river in the attack on Custer.[131] They surrounded Custer. Says Custer's men in the beginning shot straight, but later they shot like drunken men, firing into the ground, into the air, wildly in every way. Where Custer fell there were abt. 20 on horseback and about 30 on foot.[132] The Indians pressed and crowded right in around them on Custer Hill; one broke through on horse back, and got away. Indians followed. Iron Hawk told them to let him go & tell the story; he outstripped them, but he dismounted after riding about three-quarters of a mile, and shot himself in the forehead. He would have escaped.[133] When Custer was retreating towards Custer Hill Indians followed along picking up guns & revolvers & ammunition and went to using these instead of clubs and bows and arrows. From Custer Hill a lot of soldiers broke and ran towards the river when the Indians pressed in on them, & they were killed in trying to escape.[134] Two men on this hill wore buckskin suits; another wore such suit at the other end, which means Calhoun Hill.[135]

Iron Hawk was wounded in the battle, shot through the body; he showed me the wound, bullet passing through from one side below the ribs and slanting upwards went nearly through but did not come out on the other side.

He did not go over the field after the battle. He knew Rain-in-the-Face & he says he was in the fight. He says the whole nation was in the fight; he seems to argue from this that Rain-in-the-Face was there.

He does not know positively, I think.

Iron Hawk has a silver medal with the image of Pres. Grant on one side and these words "United States of America. Liberty, Justice and Equality. Let us have Peace." On the reverse side is the open Holy Bible a globe with the words on opposite sides of the globe "Atlantic Ocean" Pacific Ocean," a stump, plow, rake, hoe, shovel, axe, and these words & figures "On Earth Peace, Good Will

Toward Men. 1871." This medal is abt. 2½ inches in diameter and some ⁵⁄₁₆ of an inch thick.

Iron Hawk says the Indians crossed the river any where to confront Custer. The first Indians to reach Custer were about one hundred.[136]

He says Custer did not get anywhere near the river; his nearest approach was about a mile off. It must have been about three-fourths of a mile at least.[137]

He remembers that Keogh and his men were killed near the little ravine.[138] Iron Hawk was on the field between the ridge and the river.

The forgoing interview was on Sunday May 12th in the tent of Archie Sword, son of the brother of Captain George Sword, at Chadron. Archie Sword is a son-in-law of Iron Hawk. He is a freight handler at the depot. Iron Hawk's description of the Custer Battle was in the sign language graphic in the extreme. He is a large powerful man, features strong and typical, pleasing face, grave demeanor which give way to great animation when he reaches interesting discourse.

Iron Hawk says that the sun was at the meridian when the Custer battle was all over. He looked at the sun when all were killed. Iron Hawk's language in expressing the time was that the sun was "in the middle" of the sky when he looked up. When the fighting began under Reno, Iron Hawk's gestures indicated that it was 8 or 9 o'clock.

[Frank S. Shively's Interview]

[Tablet 7]

Frank S. Shively, Assistant Clerk at Crow Agency, Montana, says he is 33 years old, was educated at Carlisle, left there in 1898, after having been there 8 years. He says that the Crows are very different from other tribes; are more secretive than most of the others, they have their lodges and councils and the secret work and private communications therein are sacred and not to be divulged, and it is impossible to tell, I may say, how much the lives of these people are governed, the character builded,[139] and the fortunes determined by the unspoken laws of these close orders. These people communicate very little. It will be noticed that in writings concerning the internal history of the Indians that what is known and reported of the Crows is sketchy and fragmentary as compared with what can be and has been obtained as to other tribes.

The painting of the face is symbolical; the coloring is not put on without design but is used to decorate according to understood principles of expression, and may be read with intelligence, the meanings varying with the devices; so, when a feather is worn in the hair the slant of it may tell of the position which the wearer holds, and that he is filling it as he understands it should be.

He tells me that he traced Ab-sar'-o-kee back fifty years and could not learn its origin. The old Agency which was moved from where it used to be something like 100 miles above here to this place was called Ab-sar'o-kee. The Crows pronounced it Ab-sare'-o-ke.

Mr. Shively was a clerk at this [Lapwai] agency. The agent was S. G. Fisher, an honest agent who went there a rich man and went away, resigned, as a poor man. Mr. Shively heard Agent Fisher talk to Chief Joseph in his office in the presence of several persons. Agent Fisher was Chief of Scouts for Gen. Howard on the Nez Percé campaign. Fisher told Joseph that he was going to tear him to pieces, that he was a chief, Fisher knew, but he had the credit of other men; that Looking Glass and White Bird Chiefs were the real leaders; they planned the campaign and directed the operations and to them was due the credit of the success as far as there was any success. Mr. Martin was present and heard this.

Mr. Fisher is at Grangeville, Idaho.[140]

Mr. Shively mentioned this subject to a Crow Indian who came into the office and was one of a party of Crows who met Chief Joseph's band when it crossed the mountains, and Mr. S. said that this Indian said that chiefs White Bird and Looking Glass were the brains of the movement for escape. Joseph had been to school when young and had learned to read and write and he in fact was the interpreter and clerk for these two chiefs, and little else.

Mr. Shively says that Chief Joseph assented to what Mr. Fisher said as relating to himself and White Bird and Looking Glass. Fisher asked him if it was not true and he said it was.

[Tablet 7]

His father's father is said to have been a Dunkard preacher. His father was a soldier in an Indiana regiment, or Ohio Reg't. After the war he came out as a soldier into the west and was stationed at Fort Ellis. He married a Crow woman in 1872; the son was born, 1873, and he [the father] was killed by the Sioux in June, 1874. Mr. Shively wants to find out whether the Shiveleys in Indiana are his relations. The Crow Scouts with Custer's column were White Man Runs Him (the spokesman) Custer had six Crow Scouts, Curly was one, Goes Ahead, Hairy Moccasin, White Swan and Half Yellow Face.[141] Three came with Custer

On Aug. 29th or 30th Curly was at the Agency and told Mr. Shively that he and White Man Runs him and Goes Ahead and Hairy Moccasin were together with Custer awhile at first but Curly left the others early; the other three came with Custer to the River; when Custer found out that he could not cross, he spoke to them (the three remaining ones) through the interpreter and told them they could go, that he got them to do scouting but not fighting, that they were now going to do fighting and that was for the soldiers to do. They went back to Reno but had to fight their way against Sioux. On their way back when they reached the ridge separating Custer and Reno they looked back to see Custer's troops and saw the gray horses of the soldiers in the center of the ring of Indians, slowly retreating up the ridge—up the stretch from the River up to the Calhoun Hill and the battle ridge. Curly says he was on the sharp point where Shively and I mounted, and he came down back along the ridge so that he saw Custer come down Medicine Tail Creek (Godfrey calls it Reno Cr.) and hugged up close under the black bluff up the river. Curley fell back, found Reno was on the bluffs; he avoided Reno and continued toward the creek that Reno went down on and crossed the River, he passed Benteen who was coming in towards Reno, but he kept away from Benteen and swung round by Custer butte and went to the Custer Lookout; from there he made his way down to the mouth of the Little Big Horn.[142]

He was 3 or 4 days behind time reaching there. The other Crow Scouts did not stay with Reno but circled round and on the morning of the 26th saw the boat and the soldiers at a little below the junction of the Little Big Horn and the Big Horn, the soldiers marching along in touch with the boat. White Man Runs Him told Shively that Barney Bravo was the interpreter, who interpretted between the three scouts and Terry just below the mouth of the Little Big Horn, telling of the disaster to Custer. Mr. Shively says Barney Bravo is living on Crow Reservation and he will interview him in relation to his part in the matter and write me.

What Bloody Knife was Chief of the Arikare Scouts and Half Yellow Face was Chief of the Crow scouts, & Godfrey says Girard was in command of all the scouts. Bloody Knife said to Custer after seeing the whole Indian village from Custer Lookout, "I am going home to-day, not in the way we came but in the spirit—going home to my people." He was killed with Custer. This was told to Shively by either by Goes Ahead or White Man Runs Him.

It seems that Reno fought in forenoon and Custer in afternoon.

The Indian and the Priest

The Indian came to Shively and asked why some of the white people come in long black robes & crosses worshiping in fancy houses where they have lights

& pretty pictures, while others come dressed in ordinary civilian clothes but with a book teaching us to worship God & his Son, while black robed people teach us to worship God and His Son and a woman. Just about this moment the Catholic priest came up (this was at Crow Agency) and asked the Indian, an old man, to join him in this worship. The Indian said "No; I do not wish to worship anything that I do not know." The priest replied, "Then we will teach you to know those things." "Teach me right here in the open air" the Indian said. The priest said, "We have the most wonderful religion ever taught to mankind." Then [the] Indian asked for proof of that, saying, "I have one better than yours." The priest said, "We have a book to prove that." The Indian says "that is no proof, white man made that book." The priest asked for the Indian's proof of his religion. The Indian said, "There is the grass, the trees, the eagle, the buffalo, the thunder—the being that made power behind those things is my God." The priest was non-plussed. The Indian now slapped Shively on the arm in a questioning way and said: "you have been to school & have been taught by white people & I suppose they taught you their religion. But do you believe in your mother's God and mine?" Shively said: "I do." The old Indian shook his hand and said: "Then you have not forgotten your mother's and my God?" Shively answered: "I have not." Then he said: "Then you don't believe the white man's teaching of their religion to you?" Shively replied: "Yes I do believe it." He leaned back as though slapped in the face. "How can you believe your mother's and my God and also that of the white peoples?" Shively explained to him that his God—the power behind all those things in nature mentioned by him which he worshipped, is the same God that existed for him as well as the whites and all mankind & every thing were made by Him. "Then," he said, "I can see now and I can go to that church with that understanding, and the priest can worship in his own way and I in mine."

[Two Moons Interview]

Two Moons was born in western Wyoming in 1842, the son of Carries the Otter, an Arikara captive married into the Northern Cheyenne tribe.[143]

[Tablet A]
Interview of Two Moons and of General Creel cost 300 ^{00}.[144]
New Capitol Hotel, Washington City, Monday, March 3, 1913.

Interview of Chief Two Moons of Lame Deer, Montana. Henry Leads, of Lower Brule, (Sioux) South Dakota, interpreting.

Two Moons says he and his Cheyennes were in the battle of Tongue River on March 17, 1876. There were 200 Sioux warriors there under Crazy Horse. There were more Cheyennes than Sioux, but he does not remember how many. There were no Indians but Cheyennes & Sioux at the battle of Tongue River.[145]

Battle of the Rosebud June 17, 1876.

There were no Indians but Cheyenne and Sioux in the battle of the Rosebud. Sitting Bull was not at the battle of either Tongue River or the Rosebud. He says they fought Gen. Crook at Rosebud. Three <u>Cheyennes were killed here at Rosebud</u>. He says there must have been between 20 and 30 Indians killed at the battle of the Little Big Horn. There were seven (7) Cheyennes killed. Two Moons told me the first time I met him at the New Capitol Hotel, that when the Indians started in to attack Custer, word came to him that the women were leaving the camp and leaving their clothing behind; and that he went back and directed them to remove all of such things with them.

At the same time he stated that he and his Cheyennes helped to drive Reno across the river, and when that was done ~~they went back down the river and~~ left a guard to keep Reno on the ridge, and then they went back down the river to the attack on Custer.

At another time he told me that it was a Cheyenne woman who discovered the approach of Custer and gave the alarm that the soldiers were coming.

He has told me repeatedly that Custer <u>did</u> <u>not</u> cross the Little Big Horn.

He said that when the fight was deadliest and the soldiers were surrounded, a man stood upon the ridge waving his sword in view of the several Troops which occupied various positions. This was probably Custer himself.[146]

The White Horse Troop fought with signal desperation. If the others had not given up, but had fought with equal stubbornness of the White Horse Troop, Custer would have driven the Indians from the field.

The Indians knocked soldiers from their horses with their tomahawks.

March 4, 1913. Willis T. Rowland Two Moons' own Interpreter, Lame Deer, Montana.

When he came back from driving Reno across river to attack Custer he set the women to moving the goods with them. All at once a man cried out "some more soldiers coming! There are more soldiers now than up above."

When he reached the women he told the women to go and pack up and be ready to move.

When Custer came in he marched as though he was going to cross the river at the point above the reservation. When he got within a few yards of the Little

Horn, shots from the Inds. on the opposite side turned him; so that his course was thrown about ½ a mile away from the river. [A crude map shows only a rectangle and four wavy lines one of which is labeled "creek."]

When Custer got up on top where the stones are the troops dismounted and they tried to lead the horses down into the gulch.

The Gray Horse Company was the only Troop that held their horses. Each man held his own. Not a shot was fired while this was going on. They were making preparations.

After Two Moons got back from showing the women what to do, to the battlefield, he rode up & down in front of his men and told them to get ready to charge.

On that creek where Custer came down there were a few Sioux only who had joined the Cheyennes on that north side of the river; they were all Cheyennes except these few Sioux.

After he got his men all ready he ordered his men to charge. They charged right up the sloping ground & hill on the soldiers who stood where the first line of stones is. The soldier fire was so heavy that the Cheyennes had to fall back. He then ordered a second charge with same result. Immediately he ordered a third charge which was made; the Indians did not stop this time but drove the soldiers. This did not last long; it was about all of the fight; after this it was merely a slaughter.

Two Moons now swept to the right and north of the ridge. There was a White Horse, a Bay Horse Troop and a Black Horse troop. The Gray Horse is what he has called the White Horse. The horses in the gulch were now turned loose by the soldiers & they fled toward the river. Some were caught tied together; some jumped into the river before the Indians got them but the Inds. got them all.

He says the fight didn't last from beginning to end did not last more than 2½ hours.

The young people of the Ind. camp must have robbed the dead of clothing, for next day they appeared up the river above the camp mounted on captured horses, dressed in soldier clothing, which led the Inds. to think other troops were coming, which alarmed the camp until it was discovered who these mounted persons were.

Orders were given to starve Reno out; but after Custer was destroyed Ind. scouts were sent below & Terry's soldiers were seen coming, so that next morning the camp packed up and the soldiers Indians withdrew.

Wednesday Evening, Feb. 5, 1913.

The Cheyennes crossed the Little Big Horn at the mouth of the creek above the Reservation. The Sioux crossed at the crossing below the Reservation.

Two Moons says this is the fifth time he has given his account of the Battle of the Big Horn; four times Rowland's father, Wm Rowland was the interpreter and now Willis T. Rowland, the son is interpreting.

[Figure 8]

1. This circle shows where the dead daughter of a Sioux chief was placed away in a tepee, a day or two before Custer came along; and when he arrived his scouts burned the tepee.

2. This is where Reno made his stand on the hill.

3. This is the place, about 3 miles from the Little Horn, where Custer halted and separated his forces & sent Reno by the route marked above Reno Creek

4 & 5. A man in buckskin was shot at 4 & he staggered to 5 & fell. The Inds. have always kept this a secret for fear that the whites would try to punish. It must have been Custer.

W. T. Rowland who sat on the field with his uncle Roan Bear who was a brother to his mother & spoke good English, (now dead) who was in the battle, says his uncle told him that the Gray Horse Troop stood at the monument with their horses, but finally had to let them go, being surrounded and hard pressed.

Roland [Rowland] says a Troop was deployed on the ridge where the first fighting took place; another Troop was deployed at right angles, thus: [Here appears a line labeled "first line." Below is a diagonal line labeled "second troop."]

The second line advanced north over the ridge and were killed.

~~The Sioux~~ When the Custer column was discovered word was sent up to those pressing Reno, and were told to leave a guard to hold Reno, and to come down and help against Custer. The Sioux crossed at the lower place and waited in the breaks concealed west of the monument. When the Sioux began firing the Cheyennes swung around north of the ridge to avoid Sioux bullets. The Sioux conquerors found so much whisky on the horses that many of them got full.

On the map made by Rowland at 6 and 7 were the two ~~Indians~~ Cheyenne guards posted, and No. 6 fired the first shot at the advancing Custer column. Rowland gave me the names of these guards, but I did not put them down.

Rowland told me of an outpost of Indians some twenty miles out from the Little Big Horn river, who discovered the approach of Custer.

Rowland further stated that the man seen by the Indians among Custer's men, who was dressed in the buckskin suit, had short hair; and as the Indians knew Custer as Long Hair, they did not think the man with the buckskin suit was the General.

The fact is, that Custer went out from Fort Lincoln on this expedition with his hair cut—another circumstance suggesting that the man in buckskin was in reality Gen. Custer.

[Henry Twist's Interview]

[Tablet 18]
Kyle, S.D. Feb.19, 1907

Henry Twist or Yellow Horse says: At the time of the Black Hills Agreement he belonged to the Cheyenne River Agency. He says the Comrs. who came over there. "Charging" (a chief) asked the Comrs. if they would give each Indian two pounds of beef a day and clothe the Indians as long as one remained, if they would sign the agreement, and the Comrs. said they would.

~~Chief Flying Bird asked the Comrs if they would pay~~ The Comrs. told the Indians that the Great Father had sent them there to buy the Black Hills and to pay them whatever they asked. ~~White Swan~~ Chief Flying Bird asked if they would pay the Indians this as long as there was a hill standing—till they were all leveled down. They said they would. Then White Swan got up and told the chairman of the commission if what he had said was true to touch the pen which this Indian had picked up and handed to him.

The Chairman touched the pen. This the only thing that Yellow Horse saw that he remembers.

[Charles Turning Hawk's Interview]

Ricker wrote the following under the heading "Notes" in Tablet 18.

Charles Turning Hawk is a full blooded Sioux Indian trader at Kyle, S.D. He is president of the Oglala Council. An intelligent and able man. Can not speak English. Has made some study of the Dakota & being a trader has acquired some knowledge of his native tongue & can make calculations in that dialect. He is one of the best subjects of the later generation for a sketch and portrait.
[Tablet 18]

Charles Turning Hawk Trader at Kyle (Feb. 19, 1907) Says:

When the Com. first came out in 1876 [1875] to make the Black Hills Agreement, the Indians had a meeting among themselves. They expected the commission out to treat for the Hills. The Oglala Sioux had this meeting at the

Lone Tree. Chief Red Dog got up and told them that if they did not sell the Hills the whites would take them from them without paying for them. Red Dog told them to let the Hills go into the hands of the Great Father to hold them till some of our children could read and write; that these would figure the value of the Black Hills with the Great Father & sell [them] to the Govt. That the Inds. would figure with the Govt. & let it pay the Inds. to the seventh generation.

After Red Dog had made this speech, Red Cloud and Spotted Tail agreed to it & told Red Dog to tell this to the Comrs. & if the Comrs. agreed to that they would sign; and then the Fox (which was a society called Fox, composed of the Dog Soldiers) agreed that if anyone signed before the Comrs. agreed to this that he should be killed. (The Oglala Inds. call the Dog Soldiers Fox Soldiers. The whites call them Dog Soldiers.)

After the chiefs had sanctioned the resolution of the Fox Soldiers, Red Dog made the speech to the Comrs. & told them that the Inds. wanted pay for the Black Hills for seven generations.

Soon after Red Dog finished his speech Charles Turning Hawk left. They all had orders to go back to their camp except 12 of the Fox Soldiers. These Fox Soldiers were to protect both white men and Indians at the council. C. Turning Hawk was at that time 20 yrs. old and he heard this, & he has always thought that the Gov't. owes for the Black Hills. The Inds. received for the Black Hills nothing; but the Agents always tell them that the Govt. is feeding them under the Black Hills Agreement.

They claim that they were to be fed 30 yrs. under the treaty of 1868; that this expired in 1898; and that they have been fed under the Hills agreement only since 1898.

[George Sword's Interview]

> George Sword was born in 1847. In spite of a traditional upbringing, he decided to cooperate with the whites after assessing their numerical superiority on a trip to Washington DC in 1870. He was appointed captain of the Pine Ridge police in 1879, and later served as a judge. Sword joined the Episcopal Church. He died at his home on Pine Ridge on October 17, 1910.[147]
>
> Also known as Hunts the Enemy, Owns Sword was the son of the Oglala Brave Bear, of the Bad Face Band. Sword later took the Christian name of George. He was an exceptionally brave and intelligent individual whose leadership abilities led to his election to the office of Shirt Wearer in the late 1860s. The fact that his uncle

was Chief Red Cloud may have contributed to Sword's political aspirations and success. Sword twice visited Washington as a member of Oglala delegations, and perhaps as a result of these visits, he became a "progressive" leader at an early age, realizing that acceptance of the ways of the whites was inevitable. An emissary for the U.S. military, Sword was instrumental in the negotiations in 1877 that led to the surrender of the renowned Crazy Horse. Three years later, he accepted the position of captain of the Pine Ridge Indian Police, and in this capacity he faithfully served the U.S. government for many years. His devotion to his office and Indian Agent Valentine McGillycuddy led at times to friction with Chief Red Cloud, especially during the Ghost Dance troubles of the late 1880s. On a humanitarian note, Sword adopted a little girl who was found alive on the frozen battlefield of Wounded Knee in 1890.[148]

A year prior to the interview Ricker wrote two notes about George Sword in Tablet 39.

See Capt. Sword N. W. of Agency; in his band over there are Skirt, Brown Eyes, Bear Stops Looks Back, & another who were in the Custer battle. Capt. Sword denies that he was in the Custer battle. Was at W. K. Knows of Indian battles of early times.

[Tablet 16]

Captain George Sword Interviewed at his home adjoining Day School No. 3, Pine Ridge Reservation, April 29, 1907.

Certain certificates in his possession, one by Rev. Wm. J. Cleveland of Pine Ridge, and another by Hon. Eben W. Martin of Deadwood, state that Captain Sword has a fine record of service under the Government as chief justice in the court of Indian Judges, as Captain of Indian Police and as First Sergeant of U. S. scouts during the campaigns of 1876-7. In 1877 he went to the hostile camp during January, and induced Crazy Horse to come on to the Reservation. In the spring following the Custer fight he accompanied Gen. Sheridan and Gen. Crook from Fort Robinson to the battlefield. He was one of those who arrested the Cheyennes when they returned in 1878 from the Indian Territory. He was captain of Indian police fourteen years, and assisted the army during the troubles of 1890-1, at which time he was Major of police. Afterwards he received the honorable distinction from the Interior Department of "Representative" of the Indians at large at Washington. In recognition of his services and influence, the Government built him a neat frame house in 1880 — a two-story building — which was leveled by fire in 1882. On the recommendation of the Agent at Pine Ridge, the Department contributed $400.00 (four hundred dollars) toward replacing and refurnishing his house. In the fire he lost nearly all his goods, papers and valuable collection, tools, etc., the estimated loss being $1,281.00.

The certificate under the hand of Mr. W. J. Cleveland shows that this fire occurred January 10, 1905; while the statement in a letter from C. F. Larrabee, Acting Commissioner of Indian Affairs, under date of March 29, 1907, makes it appear that the fire was in 1882.[149] He tells me that the fire caught from the stove. It was burned when his family was away, and white people surmise that "an enemy" did it. He now shows me from his record it was in January, 1905, that he was burned out.

~~Sixteen (16)~~ Fourteen (14) years he has been a Helper in the Episcopal Church. He showed me a certificate under the hand of Rt. Rev. W. H. Hare, Missionary Bishop of South Dakota, dated May 22, 1893, showing yearly renewals by this bishop down to May, 1899, and two later renewals by Rev. W. J. Cleveland, continuing his incumbency down to Sept., 1904.

Captain Sword informs me that on ~~December 1876~~ January 1, 1877, he, with thirty Indians ~~scouts~~ left Fort Robinson in deep snow and marched to the Big Horn Mountains in Montana carrying a big bag of tobacco as a present to Crazy Horse, with an invitation to this chief to come in to the Agency and live on the Reservation. Capt. Sword says that none of this delegation went as scouts, but as volunteer Indians carrying the olive branch of peace and good will. He states that the Commissioner of Indian Affairs wrote to Gen. Crook to dispatch these Indians on this peace mission. He adds that besides the thirty men and himself three or four women went in the party. Crazy Horse agreed to come to the Agency. He distinctly states that no other Indians went on this mission. After his return with the information that Crazy Horse would come down from the north, Red Cloud and Spotted Tail, each with a multitude of followers, went to visit this formidable chief in his mountain fastness and supplement Sword's work with their own powerful influence.[150] Crazy Horse returned with these two chiefs. Sword says that he came in good faith, to have permanent peace with the whites—to stop bloodshed on both sides.

Capt. George Sword sang several hymns in Lakota while I was busy writing down the foregoing about him. He showed me the history of his ancestors year by year since and including the year 1793, neatly kept in his son's handwriting in a substantial book used only for that purpose. Capt. Sword showed me the record of his own birth in 1847.

He showed me four wounds, three having been given him by Crow Indians and one by a white man.

Capt. Sword was at the battle of Fort Phil Kearny in 1866. He says there were seven Oglalas killed and two Cheyennes making nine Indians killed in the Fetterman massacre.

Capt. Sword tells me that his brother was a chief, and after the death of the brother he became the chief.

Capt. Sword has lent me a picture of himself, McGillicuddy, Billy Garnett, Lieut. Standing Soldier and Young Man Afraid of His Horses. He wants me to get a very large bust picture made at Chadron from his own in this picture.

Send Sword the name of photographer.

Captain George Sword says he was in the Wagon Box Fight.

Peter Shangrau, interpreter.

Sword says the wagon boxes were not on the ground but on the wagons [running gear?] with the wagon sheets on the bows and the soldiers had holes and dirt thrown up, and they shot from under the wagons. Says the Indians charged three or four times, but not to exceed four times. There were a lot of Indians, about three hundred; they charged right up on the wagons.

They left one Indian who was killed right up close to the wagons, his name he can give in Lakota as follows Ji pa la meaning to sting like a wasp. He knew of only two others who were killed, one was Lone Man, and the name of the other he does not know.[151]

He has no knowledge of any soldiers coming out from Fort Phil Kearny to reinforce the besieged. He says the wood choppers had a wagon off to themselves and some men were in this and they fled from the wagon and he thinks there were two of these killed.

He says there was no person in command of the Indians, these were young men thirsting for the fray. In those days they were not looking up to chiefs. The custom was for someone to make a feast and this gave him the privilege to act as leader. He could announce at the feast that he wished to make fight or make a foray for horses, and the braves went with him. Of course the most daring and ambitious ones would try to outstrip him; but he was on his mettle to make a brave showing; if he failed he won nothing [but] ridicule. The braves, for lack of a regular chief or leader, kept their eyes on those having repute for great bravery, and when these were seen to dash into action the others followed, and when the bravest turned back they were followed by the others again. On this occasion of the Wagon Box Fight the big braves were all there; among these Red Cloud,

Crazy Horse, and Fast Thunder, the latter considered the bravest in this fight, as he went nearer the wagons than any other man. George Sword himself and his brother Sword (George at this time was called Chase the Animal, but on the death of his brother who was the chief, George became chief and took the name of Sword. At the time of this fight the father of these brothers was an old man remaining behind, was not in the fight.) He does not know that American Horse was in the Wagon Box Fight. Red Cloud was at the Fetterman Massacre, but he does not know that he was commanding, for in those days braves did about as stated above.[152] Capt. Sword says his father died April 1, 1874. The Wagon Box Fight was fought by the Oglalas with a few Minneconjous mingled in.

[Frank Salaway's Interview]

In January 1907, W. R. Jones told Ricker that Salaway was "an honest and truthful man, nothing tricky about him."[153]

[Tablet 48]
Tuesday, August 20, 1907.
Frank Salaway. At His Home 8 Miles N. E. of Allen, South Dakota.

My first recollection is when my father who was an employee of the Hudson's Bay Company went to the depot to unload furs and robes and to load up with goods for the return. They were at the place called by the company Fort Northwest (nor'west, he calls it).

My uncle with whom I lived when my father made the trip down the St. Lawrence never to return, told me that I was born in what is the present State of Idaho about half way between Fort Hall and the "Fort Nor'west" while journeying to the latter place.

My father was a French Canadian, commonly called Kanuck French.

My mother was a half breed, but I do not know what was her nationality. Her father was a Frenchman. My very first recollection was of this grandfather. He was a noted bear hunter. One day I saw a horse and travois come to the house; this travois had bows covered with red cloth to keep the sun from the occupant. It was in the autumn and towards the close of day. This was my grandfather who had been on a hunt. Some men lifted him off the travois and brought him into the house and placed him on a bed. I remember also his wife (my grandmother) who had come along with the travois. She was a squaw. My grandfather killed the bear, a white one, and the hide was brought along at this time. My grandfather told the story of his encounter with and victory over the beast. ~~but I was too young to remember the particulars~~ It is enough to say that he was so injured on this occasion that he never went hunting again. He and my grandmother were traveling through the spruce pine woods, which cover a large part of that level and undulating country consisting of prairie and timber marked by stretches of even surface and ridges. My grandfather discovered a bear lying in a low place or hole at the roots of a large tree. The bear was asleep. My grandfather and grandmother were traveling with a travois. My grandfather said he was going to get that bear. He stole up to the place where bruin was asleep, but way above him on the rim of the hole. He had a new flintlock gun which had never failed fire. He placed the muzzle to the bear's ear but the piece did not go off. He snapped six times and each time failed. The bear awoke. He tried to reach my grandfather but he could not get ~~out of the hole he was~~ to my grandfather. The tree was a fallen one, the roots were upturned and the bear was lying in the depression; my grandfather had climbed up on the roots. My G. F. jumped down on the side where there was a clump of willows. The bear took after him. Twice my g. f. turned and snapped his treacherous gun at the animal without the gun being discharged. He kept running and dodging to avoid the bear till he was getting tired. At last he knew the bear was going to overtake him. Then he threw his gun away and grappled with his antagonist. He seized the bear by the ear with his left hand and the bear took his left wrist in his mouth and tore the flesh. In the struggle which followed my g. f. came down on his back and the bear on top astride of his body. My g. f. was a tall and powerful man. The bear stood over him looking down into his face without offering to hurt him. This was the situation sometime. In the meantime the bear licked him in the face. My grandmother was standing off by herself with the horse and travois frightened half to death. She walked round in great excitement, and the bear divided his attention between her and the victim beneath him. She finally told my g. f. not to hurt the bear; if he did not perhaps the bear would go away and leave him unharmed. My g. f. had a long hunting knife with double edge in the scabbard on his belt. He had not, in his excitement, thought of this before. But my g. m's caution reminded [The narrative ends abruptly.] [Tablet 27]

Interview with Frank Salaway at his home 8 miles northeast of Allen S.D., beginning Saturday, November 3, 1906.

Mr. Salaway says he can neither read nor write. He was born somewhere in Idaho, place not known, in the year 1828, of French and Indian parents. His father was a Canadian Frenchman and his mother an Indian woman, but he does not know to what tribe she belonged. There were two brothers, no sisters. His brother was three years older than he. I think he never met him after the brother was "cached" as he described his disappearance.

Death of Crazy Horse

Mr. Salaway was at Fort Robinson when Crazy Horse was killed. He is sure that the killing was deliberate and intentional. He is satisfied of that from what he heard the soldier say. Little Big Man, who was a cousin of Crazy Horse, went out after him. When Crazy Horse discovered that he was in the guard house he became furious, and reaching down to his leggings he drew a butcher knife to stab Little Big Man who seized him before he could give a blow. The guard standing at the door ran Crazy Horse through with his bayonet which entered his side and pierced his kidneys.

Killing of Conquering Bear and Massacre of soldiers near Fort Laramie in 1854.[154]

During emigration times it was a common thing for the travelers to turn out and leave behind any cattle that became footsore and could not travel. If the owner could get a trifle for the abandoned stock he thought himself lucky. Sometimes five or six such animals would be found together.

The case about to be related was where a Mormon passing along had to drop a cow behind. An Indian seeing the cow butchered her. The Mormon saw the butchered cow and reported it to the commanding officer at the Fort.[155] The officer sent for Chief Conquering Bear, Chief of the Brulé Sioux. (The Brulés were camped close to Jim Bordeau's trading post about ten miles below the fort, and the Oglalas were camped nearer the Am. Fur Company's post which was five miles ~~above~~ below the Fort. At this time there were two chiefs of the Oglalas, Old Man Afraid of His Horses, and Old Man Bad Wound. Both these chiefs were pretty good ones and good men. Neither was much at war, they were more on-lookers.

Conquering Bear went up to the fort as requested; and he was told that he must bring the man who shot the cow. (She was lame, poor and nearly dead, and it was fall of the year.) The chief answered the lieutenant that he did not think the Indian had done any harm owing to the circumstances and the custom of the time and place. But he further said he did not want trouble, and told the officer to send the owner of the cow to his camp and he would give him his choice of a horse out of his own herd of horses of sixty odd head. That he said was the best he could do. The lieutenant then said, "I want you to bring that man in here." The chief replied: "That man does not belong to my band. He is a Sioux but he belongs to the Minneconjou band."[156] The lieutenant said that was immaterial; he wanted him to bring that man. Conquering Bear [said,] "If you want him why don't you go up there and arrest him? That is what your soldiers are here for. He has no friends there, only 2 or 3 men. You must be careful in taking him; he is high-tempered and hard to manage and might give trouble. That is all I have He does not belong to me. This is all I have got to say. My band is not going to help you." The lieutenant answered "You will see my soldiers there tomorrow by 10 o'clock." "All right" says Conquering Bear, "I'll show you his lodge; I'll show you the man." He went back.

When Conquering Bear passed down through the Oglala camp he told them what the lieutenant was going to do, and people around the Fur Company post talked about it as a matter of fresh news and commented on the foolish purpose and the great labor over the worthless old cow, and that the proposed move was likely to make trouble with the Indians. Sure enough next morning the soldiers came down the hill—all infantry, the officer and interpreter mounted. They had a piece of light artillery which a pair of mules had the honor of drawing to the seat [of] maudlin war. You could tell that the lieutenant and the interpreter were drunk. The name of the latter was (Ousless Aye—it is too much for me; Mr. S. cannot is unlettered and cannot spell it; he says it is French; I think it is _____).[157]

The command stopped quite awhile in front of Am. Fur Co's store and the interpreter was drunk and talking wildly and flourishing his pistol and threatening to give the Indians a new set of ears (some sense); some of the Oglalas and some of the leading employees belonging to the store tried to reason with the whiskey-primed interpreter and persuade him not to carry out the declared purpose; and the lieutenant was quiet and had little to say. Mr. Salaway says that he was talking to one of the infantrymen, who was a Frenchman, and this man says they are drunk and we will all get killed; that it is a piece of foolishness anyhow.

The troops started on the way down to the Brulé camp. Some of the Oglalas followed, saying through a young warrior who had some influence, that they would go down, as they could see there was bound to be trouble, and exert themselves to keep the Brulés from coming up to the Fur Co's store; and they went on and there was a continuous string going until a good many Oglalas were finally down there. These took position on one side of the camp, down near to the river (Platte); while Mr. Salaway and five or six others including

Charley Garrow (the spelling may not be right) all of whom posted themselves on an eminence on the opposite side of the village, so they had a good view, and they had a spy glass in the party.[158] The village was quiet and very few of the inhabitants stirring about. A few horses were tethered within the camp which was nearly a complete circle. On the river side was Conquering Bear's lodge, between which and the two small lodges next up the river was a small space, and in one of these two was the Indian wanted. The command marched right down the road and entered the Brulé camp through the open space in the circle of lodges. The wagon road was a quarter of a mile from the camp. The circle was nearly as far from the Platte River as from the wagon road. Conquering Bear's Lodge is shown on the map by an X. [Figure 9] The two other crosses north of his were two small lodges, in the second of which from his was the Indian wanted. Between these two lodges and his was a space, not very large the two dots • • in this space are the lieutenant and the interpreter. Conquering Bear's lodge faced east and the officer and interpreter were in rear of the opening to his lodge. This figure or o is the cannon trained on his lodge. These marks † † † † are the soldiers in single rank.

After the positions were taken (the officer and interpreter were on horseback) the men on the eminence with the spy glass, including Mr. Salaway, saw Conquering Bear come out of his lodge and walk up to the officer and could see him pointing to the two lodges, in the farthest of which the Indian was. There were three of his friends with him in there. For the conversation between the officer and Conquering Bear Mr. Salaway was indebted to an Indian afterwards who heard it. Conquering Bear pointed to the Indian's lodge and told the lieutenant that he was in there with three of his friends; that he was a firm man and might make trouble. The officer directed the chief to get him out, that he must arrest him. Conquering Bear then replied: "If you want me to get that man I will take him; but you must wait till I get my arms." He then turned to enter his lodge to arm himself, and just as he was in the opening the officer cried "Fire!" and the guns volleyed and the cannon thundered. Conquering Bear fell with nine bullet wounds in his body, but he lived nine days, long enough to know how completely this wanton assault upon his life had been avenged. (He died on the Running Water. See the first statement of American Horse taken in June, 1905 at Mr. Cook's. The treaty that Am. Horse says Conquering Bear told his people about, Mr. S. says was the Horse Creek treaty of 1851. Horse Creek is below Laramie and on south side of the Platte. These Indians, both, Brulés and Oglalas—their presence in the neighborhood of Laramie at this time was on account of their expectancy of the annual distribution provided for by this treaty; they were waiting for Major [J. W.] Whitfield to arrive and distribute the goods which were already on the ground stored in the Am. Fur Co's house. Mr. S. says that the Indians had sold or leased to the government for 50 years the right of way for a road five (5) miles wide—5 miles wide—on each side of the Platte River.)

The soldiers did not get a chance to fire their weapons again. The Indians poured out of their lodges and surrounded the unfortunate soldiers. The Indians were mostly armed with bows and arrows but a few had guns. In ten minutes not a soldier was left alive. Nearly all fell where they stood. One soldier got up close to the wagon road where the command had marched into the camp, and fell there. The interpreter who bestrode a fine horse he had borrowed for the occasion, broke in the direction of the river but circled to the right passing the Jim Bordeaux trading house on a smaller circuit and crossed the wagon road below the camp, but an Indian who had been out hunting antelope was returning in ignorance of what was going on except that he could hear the tumult, was coming towards the fleeing man, when another who was giving him chase made a signal to him to shoot the other; he fired and brought down the interpreter's horse. The enemy was on him in a moment and his body was filled with arrows. Not a man escaped.

When the Oglalas saw how the Brulé band had been treated, and it looked at first as though the interpreter was likely to escape, a few of them started in pursuit of him to assist their friends.

This fighting took place a little before noon.

The Brulés at once took down their lodges and crossed the Platte and moved to Rawhide Creek eight miles away. The Oglalas moved off with them. ~~Next morning an Indian arrived early and gave notice to John Dee Mr. salaway and Edward Glode that~~ Next morning, the Indians, Brulés and Oglalas, came to take their annuity goods which were stored in one of the houses of the American Fur Company. John Dee was the manager of the Company and Charles Garow [Gareau] was the clerk. There was some stampeding among the people. A number went to the island in the river just below the mouth of the Laramie (about two miles) Gareau fled to Green River, Utah, and left his wife and child behind who went to the Fort. He was gone a month. Excitement was high. Some of the squaw men ran away and their wives went off with their tribes. It was a year before all those who became separated by their fears were reunited.

~~The men came over in an imposing procession~~ Mr. Salaway was courting his present wife. Her brother did not want her to remain behind, and she departed with the tribe, but returned the next year (1855) and he married her. He says there was no law then governing the marriage relation; that a man could take a woman and keep her as long as he wished and let her go at will.

The men came over in an imposing procession and forced open the building containing their annuity goods, and helped themselves. Then they recrossed the river and went back to camp. But ~~next morning~~ on the third morning it was seen that the Indians were not through with their operations. An Indian came early to Mr. Salaway and Edward Glode and told them that the warriors would return that day and take what goods they wanted from the store belonging to the Am. Fur Company, and advised them all to keep away and give them no trouble. Everybody was careful to acquiesce in this warning. Along about sunrise the first of these promised visitors appeared. As they gathered before the store, Red Leaf, brother of Conquering Bear, mounted the steps and harangued (Red Leaf was the one who was taken prisoner with Red Cloud and stripped of his horses by Gen. Crook) the warriors, telling them that Conquering Bear was yet alive, and that he had always been friendly to the whites and the Am. Fur Co. had often befriended him, and it was his wish that they would not break the door of the Fur Co's store but that they should leave their goods untouched. The words of Red Leaf communicating the noble desires of his dying brother fell on deaf ears. By the time he was done speaking a mob of his people pressed around him and defied all restraint, the latch gave way, the door flew open, the men jammed in and got what they wanted. They left most of the provisions and all the whiskey, the latter manifestly by oversight, as it was discovered in the middle of the floor buried by loose papers, and its presence in the house being up to that time a secret withheld from the employees who now had good occasion to regale themselves. The Indians had all departed by ten o'clock and peace reigned without jar for ~~nearly about two week~~ about ten days. Then, as soon as Conquering Bear had died on the ninth day after the battle, Spotted Tail, Red Leaf, Young Conquering Bear and Long Chin returned to execute the usual custom of killing a white man as an act of revenge when one of their people is killed. These men encountered the mail stage at Cold Spring, 35 miles below Fort Laramie, and making an attack, killed the driver on the seat and the assistant who was riding beside the six mules in the team and carrying the blacksnake whip. The only passenger was a man named Kinkaid who had come from Salt Lake and had with [him] a large sum of gold. He was wounded in the leg but escaped while the captors were appropriating his gold. Not acquainted with the value of this money, one of the number has since given away the secret that when anybody gave one of them anything to eat, following the Indian custom of returning a present for a gift, they would hand back a piece of this coin, a twenty dollar piece or a fifty dollar coin.

Now the Indians scattered to the Missouri River and to northern places and remained away until the following spring of 1855.

Mr. Salaway was working for Joe ~~Bisnett~~ Bissonnette in the fall of 1855, and the news [came] of the battle of Ash Hollow, and ~~Bisnett~~ Bissonnette was uneasy about a train of 18 wagons of goods which was coming up for him, and he feared that it was in the vicinity of the battle; and he sent Mr. Salaway off to take charge of it or bring information about it; and he also bore a dispatch from the fort to Gen. Harney. He was at the battlefield soon after the fight.[159] He says there were not many Indians killed; Gen. Harney had given orders not to shoot women and as men as well as women, wore blankets, many if not most of these escaped on account of their costume. There were some Indian prisoners and these were left behind under guard for want of transportation and were mostly ~~young men or~~ boys and girls.

General Harney came on up to Fort Laramie and this was the time he went over to Fort Pierre as described by Mr. Mousseau, so Mr. S. says.

Mr. S. relates an instance of gross barbarity committed by soldiers. Mrs. Magloire A. Mousseau at that time was the wife of another man. She was shot through one leg. She had ~~a child~~ an infant child which was put up as a target and shot at by some of the soldiers who killed it. This was related to Mr. S. by the interpreter of General Harney. (Mrs. Mousseau's husband abandoned her.)

These were the Brulés who fought Harney at Ash Hollow. Little Tonda [Thunder] was the chief at this time. He was a chief when Conquering Bear was a chief; they had two.[160]

It was after the massacre and sacking of the Am. Fur Co's store on the Platte in 1854 — about a month after — that Mr. Salaway made his journey from Laramie to Fort Pierre, 300 miles in 3 days and nights; he traveled day and night on foot, stopping when sleepy and lying down for a nap, then going on again. He went to try to get some of the company's goods over from Pierre. He stayed there seven days and then came back in the same length of time.

Battle of Horse Creek in 1865[161]

About May, 1865, a lot of Brulé Sioux and Oglalas were encamped around Jim Bordeaux's. Big Mouth was an Oglala and down there.[162] He was a captain of Indian police and was around Bordeau's—was in employ of Govt.—had about 20 soldiers—he had a Brulé for lieutenant, who belonged to the Corn band.

Early one morning Two Face appeared on the opposite side of the Platte, and some of them on this side made a raft and sent it over and brought him over and the white woman he had with him that he was bringing to deliver.[163]

James Beauvais of St. Louis, had at this time the ranch which had once belonged to the Am. Fur Co. At this time General Moonlight commanded Fort Laramie, and Colonel Jarrow was Indian Agent and made his headquarters at Beauvais'. He was not a military man—at any rate not now. Big Mouth is a brother-in-law of Mr. Salaway.[164]

The woman who crossed with Two Face was attired at Jim Bordeau's in white woman's clothes by Mrs. Jack Harmon who gave her a dress and other needful clothing. She came in bare legged and otherwise costumed like an Indian woman. Then she and Two Face were taken up to Fort Laramie by Big Mouth who returned and said that Two Face had been put into the guardhouse. Big Mouth told Mr. Salaway that he went to Col. Jarrow (who was a Frenchman) and then Jarrow went with him to Beauvais, and finally both went along with him when he took Two Face and the white woman to the Fort. There was a conference up there and it was settled that Two Face should be held in the guard house and that Big Mouth be sent out to bring in the rest of Two Face's party.

Blackfoot who was a sub chief was the head of this party of ~~seven~~ six lodges.[165] Big Mouth took ten Indian police and went into the village after dark. He told his mission but all the time kept a watch on Blackfoot, not knowing just what he might do. They started pretty early next day for the Fort. After crossing the river at the fort and leaving the women, the men were taken to the guardhouse and ironed with ball and chain. The women were given the lodges and taken down to Bordeau's. About a week after, these men were given a trial, the white woman appeared against them. She testified that she and her little child was captured about 35 miles below Fort Kearny on the Little Blue; that they took her to the Arkansas river and her little child; there they dragged the child to death and the whole village ravished her, and then they were going to kill her.[166] The Cheyennes were her captors. Two Face bought her, paying three horses for her, and was going to keep her for sensual use. He was coming back accompanied by this Blackfoot band. Then Blackfoot bought her from Two Face. When they got ready to bring her back they all went into the river with her swimming, and all ravished her.

About two days after this, Two Face and Blackfoot were hung.¹⁶⁷ Soon after, all the Indians, Big Mouth and all, were moved down to the South Platte at the California Crossing.¹⁶⁸ Colonel Jarrow was to go down with them and take charge of them after their arrival. All the mountaineers around there were engaged to remove the Indians. On a given day they were collecting at Bordeau's. Beauvais ~~was moving some stuff to the Fort~~ was leaving for the states for goods and was going to do some wagoning back.

Gen. Moonlight was commanding at the fort. He sent Captain Fouts with a hundred or more men down to begin the march.¹⁶⁹ The white woman and Capt. Fouts' wife and daughter and Jim Bordeau were going. Mr. Salaway went on foot. Beauvais was driving 50 steers, and had 21 wagons with six yoke of cattle to each. They were the big Murphy wagons that loaded with 9,000 [pounds]. Bordeau had his teams, a lot of loose cattle and ponies and his family. Mr. Salaway drove six yoke of cattle for him. Some of the mountaineers had loose horses also. Four Indian prisoners were along with ball and chain. Over these was a guard. When they pulled out the mountaineers kept with the Indians. Generally the wagons went ahead. The prisoners were behind with the rear guard. A short drive was made the first day, camp being made down on the Platte.¹⁷⁰ The second day the march was a short one. The Indian boys had since the start been playing among themselves with their ponies, racing and having a good time, as is their habit when they move from place to place. Mr. S. heard Capt. Fouts give an order to the interpreter to have this sport stopped. In the evening of the second day after the camp had been made the leading persons were together, including the chiefs and headmen of the Indians, and Mr. S. Capt. Fouts asked the interpreter if he gave the Indians his order to stop running their ponies. The interpreter replied that he had. No respect, it should be noted, had been given to this. So the Captain told the interpreter to tell the chiefs present that if there was any more racing during the march he would tie the offenders to a wagon wheel and give each 25 lashes. Mr. S. noticed the chiefs and headmen who were sitting in a row, pass significant looks and winks to one another. It was evident to any who could read between the lines that something was brewing. ~~That night~~ The third day a short march only was made. It was the night of the third day that what I have detailed about the orders above to the chiefs took place. In the night of the third day the arrangements were completed by the leaders among the Indians. They had the crossing on the Platte picked out by their young men. Word was passed round. Early in the morning of the fourth day the advance guard with the prisoners started. The wagons began to pull out. No move was made by the Indians to take down their tents. Still the train kept pulling out. When Mr. S. had gone nearly a mile he looked back several times and the Indian tents were yet up. The camp was made the night before on both sides of Horse Creek; the soldiers had passed over and the Indians did not cross, but went into camp on the west or north side. This camp was about half a mile up Horse Creek from the Platte. ~~Mr. S. stopped when he got over the creek & went up about ½ mile beyond. About this time the~~ The rear guard had crossed the night before and camped with the prisoners over the Horse Creek. ~~Captain Fouts~~ The train had got well along on the road. The plan was to reach Scott's Bluffs that night, about 20 miles distant. Capt. Fouts hurried back to the Indian camp to hurry the Indians up. Two shots were heard. Capt. Fouts was shot dead.[171] At that instant the three Indian prisoners who had complained the night before of the hardship of walking and carrying their balls and chains were promised horses. The other Indian prisoner was lame with swelled leg and he had been riding in the wagon which the rear guard had for tents, etc. The three prisoners now had their horses. On the instant that the firing commenced on the ~~east~~ west or north side of Horse Creek in the Indian camp, these three prisoners mounted their horses and broke to reach the Indian camp. The guards called to them to come back, one spoke to Calico and said, "Come back!" Some of the Indians who of course were mounted came dashing up towards the prisoners to help them in their escape, it being a preconceived plan known by prisoners as well as the Indian leaders in camp, to secure them and get them away.[172] Between these rescuers and the guards a fight took place and five guards were killed right there. One of the guards followed into the Indian camp and fell there. These were all the killed—six soldiers and Captain Fouts—seven in all and two white persons were wounded.[173] The tents at once came down and the Indians began to cross to the island thence over the Platte into the woods beyond and out of sight.

Consternation had spread through the train. Men were hurrying their preparations for defense. The wagons were parked some two miles beyond the Creek, and breast-works were being made and the people collected inside. A few were in panic. There was a Captain Shuman with the soldiers.[174] There were some regular soldiers and a part of the command were going east—probably to Fort Kearny or Omaha to be mustered out. About 80 soldiers (say a company) were sent back with wagons to gather up the dead. The crossing place where the Indians were going over was shut off from view from the trains people by a swelling rise of ground going up in a wide sweep from both ways.

The command A single Indian showed himself on this gentle elevation. The command advanced to the crest and halted in line. The Indians were mostly across the Platte, but a rear guard of warriors were under the bank superintending the passage of the last of their people. These could not be seen by the troops drawn up above the slope. Presently a mounted warrior came up from the river and rode out boldly toward the soldiers; soon another, and then another till seven were on the plateau deploying at extreme distances but still beyond range of the soldiers' guns. They advanced. All at once there was a fusilade from the ridge, and the solders had emptied all their pieces. Turning, they beat a hasty and inglorious retreat for the wagons. The seven mounted Indians were now going as if to a picnic party. They gave immediate chase, yelling and firing and swinging blankets parapharnalia till the pursued believed that the hosts of darkness were at their heels. When the Indians had had sport enough they went back. (It makes one think of somebody saying "Boo!" and every body else running for dear life.) The dead were all buried near where the wagons were corralled, except Capt. Fouts, whose body was taken on. The expedition returned to Fort Laramie. Bordeau returned, Beauvais and the soldiers whose time was expiring and some others with stock and teams continued the eastward journey. An express hurried back to Fort Laramie to convey to General Moonlight the news of the serious end of the movement. The General with a command of cavalry started northeasterly to head off the escaping Indians. Unfortunately for his plans he came upon their trail and fell in behind them at the head of Deadman Creek some fifteen miles south of where Fort Robinson now is. He followed down this stream nearly to the mouth and halted to graze and refresh his mounts. The Indians had reached Soldier Creek a few miles to the northeast and were in camp. But as usual they were alert. Their scouts were on the hills skirting the Deadman valley. These discovered Moonlight's approach and word went to the Indian camp. The women and noncombatants were sent on the way with the camp belongings, while the warriors headed for the pass in the hills where the creek issues forth. Moonlight and his troopers were at present ease and in fancied security. Their horses were divested of all their trappings and grazing upon the rich grass at full freedom. Suddenly the Indian scouts darted from the tops of the flanking hills, and with shots and yells and the waving of fabrics blankets as was their method when stampeding a drove, they frightened the cavalry horses into a furious run out into the open country valley of the White River where they were received by the waiting warriors who had come back from Soldier Creek, and were driven away.

341

The Indians hurried off to the Black Hills, leaving Moonlight and his troopers afoot. They had to send to Fort Laramie for transportation.[175]

[Tablet 28]

Interview with Frank Salaway. 8 miles east of Allen, S.D. Sunday November 4, 1906.

I note a few things in this tablet from Mr. Salaway on certain subjects on which I interviewed Mr. Mosseau.[176] Mr. Salaway has little knowledge of dates; as he is unlettered he never gave any thought to the element of time. But he fixes some dates by association. He says:

He saw California Joe killed. He declares that California Joe was a bad man, that it was he who killed _____ Richard (Reshaw) [John Sr.] on the upper Running Water. He gives all the particulars of the search for Richard, tracks, blood-spots, finding of his wagon overturned in the Running Water River with things in it, and circumstances pointing to California Joe, etc. Mr. S. says that Joe reported that Tom Newcomb had done the deed. This was the reason that Newcomb killed him. Farnham told me that Newcomb had threatened to kill him, and further said that Newcomb was a young fellow who was light-headed and wanted to make fame for himself by taking the life of a man like California Joe who had a reputation. Mr. S. says that Newcomb had made the threat to take Joe's life. Newcomb worked for Mr. S. a ~~long time; I think he said two years~~ year after this occurred.[177]

Joe was coming out of the dugout (which has been described by others) He advanced three or four steps from the door when Newcomb came up past the corner not exactly parallel with the building but diagonally from the opposite corner, and he said to Joe: "Here I am; hunt your hole!"

Joe had his revolver strapped on but did not offer to use it; he turned when Newcomb said this and started to go back into the dugout. Newcomb shot him down. A good many people were around there then.[178]

Mr. S. says Newcomb was a pretty good fellow; a good worker; he worked for Mr. S. a year after this killing was done. Newcomb had said he would kill California Joe on sight for reporting that he had killed Richard (Reshaw).

Chadron. Mr. Salaway does not know what his first name was, nor does he know positively where his house stood, but his impression is that it was up near the hills. Thinks he was not there long; says that it was the way the transients had, when winter was nigh was to set about and build a cabin for winter, and when warm weather came to go on and leave it for good. His idea is that Chadron's residence was of this character. He was spoken of as a good man. This confirms Mousseau. Mr. S. knew Chardon of Missouri River fame. He says his name was bad. This supports Chittenden's History of the Am. Fur Trade. He always heard the French speak of the creek as "La Fourché Chadron"— the creek of Chadron—The creek of Chadron, as Mr. S. explained it.

Bordeaux: He knew Jim Bordeau well. Jim had a trading house on the Bordeaux about a quarter below Nelson's house—where the road to Spotted Tail Agency crossed and took up over the hill. This was a stopping place for Bordeau. This man was a signer of the treaty of 1868.

Bisnett had a place where Peter B. Nelson succeeded him at the Nelson House.[179]

Boucher was a later character who was up on the Little Bordeaux somewhere.

Mr. Salaway tells of changed conditions on P. Ridge the same as the others. He deprecates the system and particularly the ring. He says what is needed is citizenship, so that the oppressed and aggrieved may take advantage of laws as white men do; so they may have some protection; the situation is anomalous when one class of men have a code of laws and another class have a different one, or properly none at all, and are the despised victims of robbers who are in the service for their private interests alone.

He says the Day Schools are worthless; the children learn nothing. The Indians' money is thrown away. When an Indian learns and is qualified there is no employment for him or her. His own daughter became a typewriter and was given a place in Agent Brown's office. When he went out she went out and was kept out of a job till she got married, and now her fingers have forgotten their cunning.

The Indians have a good deal of money and the study of their masters is how to spend it; so the road system and the ditching business have been discovered and day's work are supplied with more ill than good to the employed.

Stock isn't raised anymore. It is no use to try to keep any. If you have a few cows or steers and they get over the ridge out of sight that is the last seen of them. The Indians are hungry. They must eat. They can not be blamed for eating. Don't look for the cattle.

Mr. Salaway does not attribute the discouragement of the Indians to the Wounded Knee affair. He says it commenced prior to that.

Mr. Salaway says he was one of the parties who made the treaty of 1868 at Laramie. Red Cloud was emphatic in his disapproval of the terms to which the others were willing to submit, and he withdrew. Big Mouth, an able and fluent man, was left to fix things. Gen. Sherman informed the Indians that some kind of a treaty must be made. That the government wanted the Indians to keep away from the neighborhood of Laramie—to keep back from the emigrant trail etc. The Indians said to them that they better make the treaty with the mountaineers; for so long as these should come to Laramie the Indians would do so. Then it was that Mr. Salaway, Jim Bordeau and a Mr. Charles Garrow or Yarrow or Gary were appointed to represent the half breeds, and Bisnett to represent the mountaineers.

The Indians came over to Whitestone [Whetstone], S.D. Big Mouth was killed by Spotted Tail and his men because of his friendship for the whites. [Tablet 26]

Near Allen, S.D., Nov. 4, 1906. Frank Salaway.

Mr. S. says that he was Assistant Farmer at Whitestone, S.D., on the Missouri. As I understand it, it was after or about 1868. The Farmer over him rode up to the Agency on a good horse and a man was with him. They went inside. After awhile the man came out alone, mounted the horse and went off. Later the Agent asked S. where that horse was. He was government property. S. said that man took him. "What did you let him go for?" "He was not in my charge; I had nothing to do with him" said S. The agent replied that he ought to have a care for the stock. Then he added: "There are some cattle gone too." S. said "I know where they are." "You do? Where are they?" "I know," he says, "and I can get them if you give me authority, and I can get the horse too. I know where he is." "Get them," the Agent rejoined. And Mr. Salaway went and took the cattle out of another man's herd and recovered 83 head, some of them large work cattle. The Farmer remarked to him afterwards: "What did you do that for? There was good steak in them!"

[Red Cloud and Clarence Three Stars's Interviews]

> Red Cloud was born in 1821 on Blue Water Creek in western Nebraska. He would become the dominant leader of the Bad Face band of the Oglalas. His resistance against the establishment of forts on the Bozeman Trail in 1866–68 became known as Red Cloud's War. Red Cloud died in 1909, and was buried in the Holy Rosary Mission cemetery at Pine Ridge. On the last page of Tablet 18, Ricker wrote, "Red Cloud's Indian name is: Magpiya Luta."
>
> At the time of the interview Clarence Three Stars taught school on the Pine Ridge Reservation. He was Red Cloud's interpreter when the old chief made his last trip to Washington DC in 1897.[180]

[Tablet 25]
Interview with Chief Red Cloud at Pine Ridge (in his home) November 24 1906. Aged 86. Clarence Three Stars, Interpreter;

According to our understanding the south line of the Reservation was to be along the Niobrara River clear to the mouth, under the treaty of 1868. It has been a puzzle to me and to the Indian people how the line came to be where it has been put. They always settle questions by the treaty, and the treaty does not mention. The agreement when made was that the line was to run from the head waters of the Niobrara to the mouth.

The first treaty that I heard of was the treaty of 1851; at that time the south line of our great Sioux Reservation was the Platte River.

Under these two treaties the first line of our great Sioux Reservation was the Platte River, and the next one was the Niobrara River.

As the line is to-day we never knew how it came so to be because it is not mentioned in the treaty of 1868. The treaty does not say that we shall cede the part between the Platte River and the present line for a given sum, and we do not understand how we lost it.

The treaties of 1876 and 1888 provide that all the land not within the boundaries fixed by these treaties for our Reservation belongs to the government.

In the agreement of 1876 the boundary line of the great Sioux Reservation was never fully explained to us. They told us the line was to start at the old temporary Whetstone Agency on the Missouri River, and from there ~~to run straight due west~~ to run parallel with the Niobrara River and twelve miles north of it, ~~striking somewhere near Crow Butte, and from there to run to the head waters of the Cheyenne River, and then follow this stream to its mouth~~ striking somewhere near Crow Butte, and from there right on west to the old line of the Reservation as previously established; thence to the line now between the two Dakotas, striking what the Indians call Great River but called by the whites Grand River, thence down the Missouri River to the place of beginning. The Indians did not understand the white man's way of bounding tracts; they cannot understand except by landmarks like hills and streams. They did not intend to sell the Black Hills, and they were not mentioned in the agreement or in any treaty as being sold to the government. I told the commissioners in the council of 1876 that I would not sell the Black Hills unless they gave me money enough to last seven generations. The commissioners did not accept this, and so we made up our minds that the Hills were not sold; but a few years afterwards we discovered that the Hills were outside the line that the government recognized as the boundary of the Sioux Reservation. The interpreters at that council were not good, and I believe they made the mistake of interpreting my proposition for money for seven generations to seven millions. The commissioners thought this was too much and so we stopped counciling with them. We never sold the Black Hills to the government.

I have been in Washington about twenty times.[181] ~~It seemed~~ I understood that the white people went all the time into the Hills; it seemed that they wanted the Hills; and the Great Grand Father (this is what they call the Great Father) sent commissioners out to talk with us about the Black Hills. The first thing they said was that the Great Father wanted to borrow the Hills for fifteen years for so much a year, but I do not remember the amount. But we did not at that time even think of loaning the Hills, and we quit counciling with them and they went home. This was in 1875. Then they came out again in 1876 and they wanted to buy the Hills.

The reason we say we never sold the Hills to the government is that the value between the Hills and the other land is different and so great that we never had in contemplation the sale of the Hills which were of such great value, at so insignificant a price.

After I made my talk in the council Spotted Tail stood up and said that as long as the earth remains as it is we will not let anybody have the Black Hills. This is all that was said or done in 1875.

I tell you freely the things I plainly remember. There are other things not now so clear in my mind and these I do not try to speak. I try hard to remember what you want to know.

There were some battles fought after the treaty of 1851. I remember the one where 100 soldiers were killed and where 30 were killed. I have no hesitation to tell you all I can recall about the fighting that was done. The Indians were right; they were defending themselves and their country, as they had the right to do.

In answer to my question why the Indians speak of the Fetterman Massacre as the fight where a Hundred were Killed when there were but 81 killed, he replied that when they saw the soldiers coming they counted them alive and made out one hundred. They did not count them after they had fallen.

Asked as to the number of Indians slain, he replied that he did not know; he did not know of more than about ten; there might have been others who died of wounds, it was hard to know their own loss, because when the battle was ended the Indians broke into their several bands and dispersed.

When the Thirty soldiers were killed was the time when Conquering Bear was assassinated by the drunken lieutenant's orders. I declined to have Red Cloud make any statements about this fight, as I already have a full account by an eye witness.[182]

Clarence Three Stars relates that the name of the drunken ~~lieutenant~~ interpreter but for whose insolence this miserable tragedy would not have taken place was named Wyuse (the spelling is uncertain).[183] The Indian who killed the cow over which the trouble arose was Clarence Three Stars' grandfather, and he was named High Forehead. He was head warrior at the time. The story, as Clarence learned it from his father and from Red Cloud and others, differs in a few particulars from what I have already taken down. He says that the soldiers came once to Conquering Bear and demanded the Indian who had killed the cow and the Chief said he did not know who had done it but would try to find out. Next day the soldiers came back and Conquering Bear said he had not found out yet who had killed the cow; whereupon the interpreter misrepresented him by saying that he refused to give the man up. Thereupon Conquering Bear was shot down in cold blood, and the exasperated Indians wiped out the entire command.

Clarence Three Stars says that the Indians rule of pitching a camp was in a circle, with an opening to the east. Whenever a camp broke up and the Indians separated with the intention of joining again, the agreement was according to a stated number of moons which was registered upon the pipe stem by a notch for each moon as it passed and to meet on some creek agreed on.

Clarence Three Stars says that it was in 1896 when Red Cloud and American Horse and Red Star and himself went to Washington, and that it was in this Washington interview that Red Cloud stated that he was 76 years old.[184] That makes him now 86 years old. At this present interview I found him in better appearance than I did when I met him in his home three years ago. He is stone blind and quite deaf.

He quietly told my interpreter, Clarence Three Stars, that he usually charged visitors something, and when they wanted to take his picture his price was $5; but as I was from Chadron, a home man, he would not ask me anything.

He went on to tell us that he had received a letter from an officer at Fort Robinson saying that as he [was] very old and feeble that he is liable to die any time; and that people wished his consent to be buried at that post and have a handsome monument erected. He returned answer that members of his family and some of his grandchildren are buried at Pine Ridge, and it was his desire to lie beside them; therefore he was constrained to decline the proposition.

Red Cloud in answer to my question whether American Horse was in the Fetterman Massacre said he could not remember whether he was in the battle or not, but he knew that he was in the camp.

He could not remember where he was camped when the horses were taken from him and Red Leaf. His son, Jack Red Cloud, having just come in and hearing the question and answer, interposed that he was there when that event occurred and remembered where the camp was. He said it was on the second one west of Chadron—on the Deadhorse—at the place where the road crosses and there is a high white cut bank. Red Leaf's camp was a mile farther up the stream.

Red Cloud could not remember the Wagon Box Fight at all.

He could not understand anything about La Bonte.[185]

Clarence Three Stars Says: That the young men went out north and were active in the campaigns.

That the name Oglala is properly applicable to Red Cloud's band who were loafers and hangers-on at the posts and agencies. These formed but a very small part of the large body of Indian population now called Oglala; that is to say, by extension the word covers now, instead of a few, a good many.

Clarence Three Stars says that there are 23 bands on Pine Ridge Reservation; one Gopher, one Rabbit, etc. One band he named is on White Clay below Day School No. _ where he is teaching (~~about a~~ one mile below the Mission). Each band has a chief. He said he would furnish me the list.[186] I want the locality of each band, and origin of name of each. For instance the Rabbit band got the name from the circumstance that those dwelling together in a settlement at a particular time, probably pressed for game for food, lived by hunting rabbits.

Three Stars says that the name of Bad Faces was not applied to Red Cloud's band because of a bad moral quality, but it came about in this way: On a certain hard winter when the snow was deep and game scarce Red Cloud's followers were grossly indolent and would make no effort to hunt buffaloes and to supply their wants, but hung around the lodges of the more enterprising and subsisted off the others. Their faces hung down long and looked unhappy and this caused these people to be called Bad Faces because their faces looked bad.

Three Stars says that Red cloud was not elected a chief, but he was a head warrior, and because of his devotion to the cause of his people from the standpoint of patriotism, his ability to do and his courage and self-assertion in acting for them he came to be recognized on account of his force of character and the need of it in their behalf, as their chieftain. The government also in the same way, by a sort of natural selection, recognized him as a chief.

Three Stars says that the chiefs did not possess all power. The several bands had each a chief and over all was a chief of the tribe; but even this chief did not exert at times the supreme power. In the council, which was the legislative body, the chiefs and head men or leading warriors sat down and smoked the pipe. I do not know whether it was invariable, but I think it was usual for the tribal chief first to break the silence when a matter was under deliberation, and after he had spoken, others, as they were moved, arose and addressed the council. When all had been heard or signified their unwillingness to speak, the chief took the voice of each separately on the question and as the majority voted the question was decided. The result was the law, and the head warrior was the executor of the law; and he went about putting this into effect; he was the executive instrument of the council which was the law-making body and the highest authority; therefore it was that the headman was the mouthpiece of the tribe or nation, the exponent of its special authority wielding all power which even the chief could not modify.

In the headman was concentrated the whole power to execute the orders of the council. When it came to directing or deciding in a case which had not been acted on in council, (I think) the chief had the power to make the prompt decision for the time.

Red Cloud was a headman, and his bravery, promptness and efficiency in this office led his people to treat him at length as a chief. He was not an orator; his speeches were usually brief; he was emphatically a man of action, and this distinguishing trait, together with the possession of prudence in his management of tribal matters showing his great care and thought for his people and their welfare, endeared him to them, and while there were always some who were reluctant to acknowledge him, and perhaps did not adore him, yet they admitted his superior qualities and would listen and turn to him [in] moments of extremity. For many years, in spite of all divisions and jealousies, this man has been greatly endeared to the Oglalas, and they are proud of his fame.

Three Stars says, speaking of what Mr. Deon says about Indians striking Red Cloud in the face with quirts, that my explanation is the correct one, that he did not notice this because he was too superior to be incensed or moved by trifles—that the superior mind cannot be reached by those manifestations of spite and littleness which mark the inferior mind.[187] His nature can not demean itself by bestowing notice on the selfish and contemptible.

Moreover, I will add, that the larger mind invariably draws the fire of malice malicious shaft from the mean intellect poor spirit and infertile intellect.

Three Stars informs me that the joint photograph of Young Man Afraid of His Horses and of Little Wound which he has lent me were taken in the City of Washington in the year 1891 when the Sioux delegation was there. Three Stars says he was present when the picture was taken.

The affair on Lightning Creek Wyoming.[188] The following is a copy of a letter written by Clarence Three Stars and published in "The Red Man and Helper" of December 11, 1903, a Carlisle school publication.

"A Carlisle Ex-Student's Account of the Wyoming Pale-face Uprising.

The following letter is from a most reliable ex-student and tells its own story. Note that he calls this affair "A paleface uprising," which is what it was:

Pine Ridge Agency, S.D. Nov. 30th, 1903.
Mr. Edgar A. Allen Carlisle, Pa.

Dear Sir:

Your letter under date of November 24th in reference to the paleface uprising of Wyoming is received. In reply will state as follows: The following are former pupils of Carlisle who were in the trouble. Charles Red Hawk (Smith) and wife, William Brown and wife, all of whom were of good reputation and were doing well under the circumstances they were in.

William Brown has a cattle ranch on the eastern part of Pine Ridge reservation, on Pass Creek, and Charles Red Hawk has been for several years assistant farmer, and he was in charge of 50 or 75 Indians who are working on dams and roads, and was respected, by the people.

Williams and Charles were out in Wyoming on a pleasure trip. They know the game laws of Wyoming, as they have been there before and they have acquaintances there. Among them was Mr. Miller, the sheriff who was killed in the fight.[189] William Brown was here Nov. 25th to see me, and told me the whole story. He told me that when he was examined at the Agency he did not tell all he knew because he was scared at the time, but now he tells me all of it.

He said that sheriff Miller and posse came to the camp Oct. 30th and said he had a warrant to arrest the Indians and take them to New Castle. William told him that he had not committed any crime or violated any law, but that he was willing to go and face what it was.

Red Hawk said that the sheriff could search the wagons and see if they had anything in their possession to show that they had violated the game law or whatever it was that the sheriff wanted. He, Red Hawk, also told him that the teams were all tired and could not very well go back with him in haste.

At this time the sheriff told them that they might go on straight to the reservation and it would be all right, and Red Hawk said they were going home quietly and peaceably, and there was no reason why they should be molested.

After this conversation they went away and the party of Indians camped on Warm Creek.

The next morning they broke camp early and started on the road following the creek down. During all this time they were in a large pasture, so when they came to a gate a little boy and a young man who were in the lead went to the gate to open it, and just as they opened the gate a party of white men rushed forward from behind a hill near by and took their stand in the hollow of a dry creek; and just as the boy and the young man turned back the whites fired upon them killing the boy and his horse, while the other one escaped.[190]

And after this the whites kept firing into the wagon train where the women and children were, as the men were on horseback.

When Red Hawk heard the firing of the guns he rushed forward just as fast as he could to where his wife was. She was in the third wagon from the lead wagon.

The other men, namely, He Crow, Black Kettle, Lost Bear, Gray Bear, Black Feather and William Brown came to where Charlie was and inquired of each other as to what course they would take.[191]

They all agreed to defend themselves, as there was no other way at that moment.

After this consultation all ran to their wagons to get their guns.

Charlie was shot down while he was getting his gun out from the wagon, the bullet entering above the knees on both legs, breaking the bones, and he fell under the wagon. His wife was in the wagon.

She was shot through the breast, and she is now in a critical condition and may die. (She recovered and lives on White Clay.)

At this time the other men came to where Charlie was, and saw that he was shot and helpless and the whites still firing into the wagons at intervals.

Then all said, "We must shoot too, in self-defense."

So they all took a stand behind the trunks of trees. At this moment Miller and Faulkner became bold and came out of the hole and aimed at the Indians, but both were shot down in the twinkling of an eye, as these Indians are sharp shooters.[192]

After this the whites were kept at bay but the Indians did this in self-defense.

If it had been a general fight the whites would never have escaped — not a single one of them.

All the Indians concerned are wishing that a general and impartial investigation be made, and the cause leading to the trouble be placed properly in the eye of the public.

Charlie never shot a single fire. Even if he had it would have been in self-defense, but he was shot down while he was in a friendly spirit, as he was always.

Charlie while lying under the wagon helpless called out to the whites they must not shoot the women, but they paid no attention to him, and his wife was shot as before stated.

The whites never warned the Indians as they should have done, but lay in a hole like a snake, although snakes warn people, but these snakes would not.

The number of Indians reported killed in certain papers from here was correct.

After hearing the whole story my opinion is that the whites were the aggressors without any just cause. They no doubt wished to rob them of their wagons, buggies, harness and valuables. Whites have done this before, and after they robbed them stated that the Indians had violated game laws, and they were arrested and fined.

Charlie Red Hawk and William Brown were not leaders in the trouble, but just because they could talk English they were the ones mentioned conspicuously and blamed for the trouble.

They did their best to avoid a serious crisis, but the whites were under the influence of mysterious water and were acting mysteriously and killed innocent persons, and the Indians killed two in self-defense.

The whites were in the hollow all night, and next morning a party of Indian women who hid themselves in the woods came out and were going where the whites were to get some things from the wagons which they had left behind, and when they came within a short distance the whites raised their guns and a girl of the party of woman called out, saying: "You cowards, you have killed some innocent persons; you could kill us, too, if you wish," and she was going right to where they were; and when she got there the men put down their guns and cried like babies, and the girl went around and shook hands with the men.

The girl is alive and she can and will tell this story often in camp among her friends.

I have described more of William's and Charlie's position in the fight than other matters, and have written in haste. I could give more of the causes leading to the trouble, but the part I have described is the information important to you.

Yours Truly

Clarence Three Stars.

Copy of Petition twice presented to the Secretary of the Interior. It bore date when presented the first time, March 9, 1896, and when presented the second time, May 1, 1897. Clarence Three Stars was one of the delegate at one time.

Washington, D. C. May 1st, 1897.

To the Secretary of the Interior,

Sir:

As the duly elected delegates of the Sioux Indians residing on Pine Ridge Reservation in South Dakota, we have the honor to submit the following resolutions adopted in said council held on Wounded Knee February 13th, 1897.

pt. 1st. We, the undersigned adult males of the Ogallala Indians on Pine Ridge Agency respectfully and earnestly petition and request the Secretary of the Interior to cause this our prayer to be brought before the President, to the end that he may obtain from Congress the enactment of such laws as will secure to us the right to hold our land in common by us as a people for stock grazing purposes only. Experience teaches us that we cannot prosper by farming, as our land is not suitable for that occupation; that by following stock raising we will in time become civilized, enlightened, thrifty, self-governing and independent citizens; that we are not in favor of land in severalty, knowing that this is not the best thing for us in our march toward the white man's standard and intelligent citizenship.

As to matters set forth in petition No. 1, we desire to state that the experience of the white man and Indians have clearly shown that while our country is a fine cattle country it is totally unfit for farming purposes. It is a well known fact that a cattle range should be free from fencing as possible and all waters should be of easy access. The White river flows along our northern line, and all the creeks on our reservation flow from the south to the north into the White River. Between these streams the land is high and rolling, and in some places [are] breaks of timber that offer shelter for our cattle during winter storms. If the water is left so that our cattle can reach it easily, then they will scatter but little, but if the water is cut off they will drift off a long ways, and by that means get lost to us. It is for this reason that we ask at your hands that our reservation shall be held in common and a free range for our cattle. We feel well satisfied that you will not allot to all of us until a majority of the tribe want to take it in that way. But what we fear is that some of them might select to take land in severalty and that you will allow them to do so.

By reading our Agent's report for this year you can see that there are six thousand three hundred and eighty-one (6,381) Indians on our reservation.[193] One hundred could take 640 acres each and by that means get all our water and leave the rest with no water for their cattle. This we want you to protect us against. We want a free range, free water and an opportunity to learn our people to be self-sustaining or rely on their efforts to become men in every sense of the word. We know that there are 8 or 10 men on our reservation who have been agitating the taking of land in severalty, and we are fully satisfied that they have been doing this to curry favor with the government officials at the expense and detriment of all the Indians. Their acts do not agree with their work in the past, for with all the years that the government has been trying to make farmers of the Indians, these men have shown no desire to farm and have not done any more in this line than the rest of the Indians. At the present time these men agree with us, but we fear that some outside influence may in the future induce these men to ask for their land in severalty, and this our tribe is opposed to.

To show how this will work we can say, that after an Indian gets his 640 acres, then he would want to lease it to some white men, who after leasing the land would bring their cattle there and by that means get their cattle on our reservation to the ruin of the cattle business of the Indians. We know that there are white men who would be willing and are standing ready to do this way and this very thing. Under the law when an Indian takes his land in severalty he becomes a citizen and that means the right to have free whiskey the same as the white man, and therefore every piece of land taken in severalty means a whisky government, and we know the evil result of whisky among white people, and we ask what would be the result among the Indian?

We ask that you consider this point carefully.

About Mixed Bloods and Half Breeds: Experience in the past has shown that our safest guides along the white man's path has been our kinsmen of the mixed bloods. They are of our blood and live with us and are fast receiving education and fitted to fill any position on the reservation; and the Indian mother has the same love and affection for their mixed blood children as has the Indian woman for her Indian child, and it is the desire of our people that they have the same rights on our reservation as the full bloods under the treaty of 1868; all whites who had intermarried with our women were incorporated in our tribe. Their children have been raised to expect a home on our reservation, and it is extremely hard that when they arrive at man's age that they can be ordered from their home and people and sent away without a trial or hearing among strangers without a dollar in their pocket. We want them to be under the same charge of the agent and the Government as the full bloods, subject to the same laws and regulations, no more, no less.

We know of no mixed blood who was ever ordered off on account of his bad moral effect on the Indians, but were ordered off for standing up for the Indian rights under the laws and treaty, and writing letters at the solicitation of the Indians who thought that they had been wronged. This we want stopped. If a mixed blood violates the law, let him be tried and punished by the courts of the country. If this is not done, and a mixed blood can be ordered off without trial then he becomes intimidated and afraid to advise his Indian kin in any manner.

We therefore, as directed by our people, respectfully ask that your Department issue such orders as may be necessary to put our mixed bloods on the same footing as our full bloods.

Very respectfully, ~~Little Wound~~ Chairman ~~Kicking Bear~~ Delegate ~~George Fire Thunder~~ Delegate ~~Philip F. Wells Delegate & Sec.~~

[Tablet 17]

Clarence Three Stars says:

Little Wound was wounded when 15 years old, which gave him his name. The ~~Oglalas~~ Cutoffs went out to fight the Crows down on the Platte River. Little Wound was left with the horses of the ~~Oglalas~~ Cutoffs and in their absence some Crows stole up and got the horses away; he ran to his camp where he had a horse; they were using only arrows then; he gave chase & had a running fight with them & received a flesh wound in the thigh. The war party which went into the Crow camp took the Crow horses and were on their way back to camp [when] they met the Crows going off with their own horses, and the two parties had a fight. Little Wound had before these parties met, retaken his horses. In the fight the Crow horses got away & went back to the Crow camp. Neither party got any horses. Next day the Crows attacked the ~~Oglalas~~ Cutoffs camp and the Sioux had to retreat.

[Alfred N. Coe's Interview]

[Tablet fragment, Box 19]

Rev. Alfred N. Coe, a Yankton Sioux was born at Vermilion, S.D. in the spring of 1867 of a half breed mother and a white father named Charles Coe who died when this son was two years old. The mother lived until he was eleven. At the age of 14 he began working for the government in a flouring mill at Yankton. When ten or eleven years old he began attendance at a Presbyterian day school, and from that time pursued studies in a desultory way. He attended an academy at Scotland, S.D. and a Presbyterian College at Pierre, and in 1894 entered the Presbyterian Theological Seminary at Omaha where he was graduated in 1897. While in college at Pierre he was employed by the government as Indian interpreter and in this manner supported himself while getting his education. During vacations he was employed with surveying parties and as assistant issue clerk. Following his graduation from the Theological Seminary he ~~began preaching~~ was ordained by the Dakota Presbytery and began preaching at Fort Totten, N.D. among the Devil's Lake Indians in 1897. He has held appointments since at Yankton Agency, Crow Creek S.D., Fort Belknap, Montana, and Pine Ridge, having come to the latter place in November, 1902. He was the first to push the theory at Pine Ridge that the Indians should be taught self-support.

He never attended a govt. school but is self educated — had to struggle.

He is the only one at present who holds degree of B.D. (bachelor of divinity) among the Dakota Sioux. (There has been one before him who was an Episcopal, but he is dead.)

Mr. Coe was the official Interpreter on the trial of Two Sticks and his fellow criminals in 1893 for the murder of some cowboys on Mule Creek, & he interpreted the sentence of death to Two Sticks. The cause of this murder was revenge for W. Knee & superstition. Two Sticks was hung & his companions imprisoned.

Rev. Alfred N. Coe's statement taken April 20, 1904, E. S. R.[194] Taken in shorthand & extended by Lee Cord of Chadron for E. S. R. April 21, 1904.

My name is Alfred N. Coe and I was born in Vermillion, Clay County, Territory of Dakota in 1867. My parents' names were Charles and Josette Coe. My mother's father's name was Henry Aungie who had two sons and six daughters of whom one was my mother. Mrs. Aungie, my grandmother was the daughter of Colonel Robert Dixon who was an officer in the British Army during the war of 1812 afterwards became a citizen of our country and was connected with the Hudson Bay Company at Ft. Snelling and his Son-in-law, Henry Aungie was a sergeant in the United States Army. Colonel Dixon's oldest daughter, Ellen Dixon my grandmother's sister witnessed the marriage of Jefferson Davis to the daughter of General Zacariah Taylor. After Colonel Dixon's death his family resided in Minnesota. Then the Aungies were connected with the American Fur Company at Ft. Vermillion and Ft. Pierre and Ft. George in the Territory of Dakota. After I was eight years old most of my relatives moved onto the Yankton Indian reservation in Dakota Territory to what is now Greenwood, S.D. where I spent a number of years in a Presbyterian day school. My Indian blood is accounted for by the fact that Mrs. Dixon, my great grandmother was a full blood Sioux Indian from which I have inherited the Indian Blood. After my school days at Greenwood, S.D., I spent some time at the Normal Training School, Santee Agency, Nebr. under the Reverend A. L. Riggs and later on I spent two years at the Presbyterian Academy at Scotland, S.D. I then spent nearly five years at the Pierre College under the late Doctor Blackburn, the Pierre College and the Presbyterian Academy now being combined in one under the term of Huron College. Before attending the Pierre College, however, I discovered that it to be necessary for me to obtain outside work in order to pay my expenses through the Pierre College and accepted employment as an interpreter in the United States Court and in that way earned the necessary means to give me what schooling I did obtain at the Pierre College and it was during my employment as official interpreter in the United States District Court at Deadwood that the notorious Two Sticks case from Pine Ridge was brought to trial under the Honorable E. S. Dundee of Omaha, Judge Presiding. In the fall of 1894 I entered the Presbyterian Theological Seminary at Omaha, Nebr. and graduated with my class in April 1897 and was ordained by the Dakota Presbytery at Flandreau, S.D. May 2nd, 1897 and since that time I have preached at Devil's Lake Agency in North Dakota _____ Agency S.D., Crow Creek, S.D., Ft. Belknap, Montana and Pine Ridge, S.D. Father died when I as but a child and my mother when I was eleven years old and I have accordingly and to fight against poverty, ill health and race prejudice.

Relative to the trial of this notorious Two Sticks Case, it may be of interest to know that Two Sticks was from Rose Bud Agency and drifted over to the Pine Ridge Agency where his oldest son was killed during the Wounded Knee Battle. Two Sticks is known among the Indians as a man of notorious character and has caused trouble often and through one of his troublesome disposition; he was so crippled that he had to depend on two sticks to move about from which he got the name of Two Sticks. You are to understand, therefore, that Two Sticks is not the real name of that Indian, and it was developed on the trial of that famous Two Sticks Murder Case that since the Wounded Knee trouble he would advise his sons and followers to uphold vengeance for the sake of his oldest son who was killed in the battle while in the state of humbleness, and as Two Sticks was a follower and a believer of the false Messiah craze that every time he goes into the sweat house and goes through his heathen custom that he claims the Great Spirit had commanded him to take up vengeance and kill white men. That on the Night of February 3rd, 1893 he and his two sons and two other young men went up to the Humphrey & Stenger ranch—Humphrey & Stenger, it will be remembered, at that time had the beef contract for the Pine Ridge Agency from the Government, near the mouth of Mule Creek on White River on the Pine Ridge Reservation, South Dakota and murdered two of the cow-boys on the ranch and two boys who were looking for stray horses from Nebraska. Of course, it was at night and away from other people that it would seem hard to get the facts but as an <u>Indian's greatest difficulty is to keep secrets</u>, that they boasted afterwards of their deed and said that the white men were bigger cowards than children and that before they fired their guns the white men run under the bed in the house and the fact that one of the men was shot in the back part of the thigh goes in a measure to prove that the white man at that time did attempt to get away instead of attempting to make a fight.

The sweat house is made in this way: Willow poles are bent and crossed & the ends stuck into the ground. Over these a sheet is spread. Stones are heated outside and carried inside and placed in a heap and water is then thrown over them. The person strips and while he is receiving his vapor bath he receives his messages from the Great Spirit.

Two Sticks was troublesome and in some difficulty on the Rosebud Reservation with his own people he was injured in a fray and so crippled that afterwards he went about on two sticks which gave him this name.

[Jacob White Eye's Interview]

[Tablet 10]
Kyle, S.D., Feb. 26, '07

Jacob White Eye, clerk for J. L. Dawson, Indian trader, says: That about 1891 or 1892 the Agent issued an order saying it was from the Comr. of Indian Affairs, requiring all Indians not more than fifty years of age to cut their hair, the penalty being that they could not draw rations or be employed to work on the reservation improvements, like making roads or building dams. The children, when they entered school, likewise had their hair cut off. Thinks this was an order from Comr. Jones.[195]

[Eagle Elk's Interview]

The son of Long Whirlwind and Pretty Feather Woman, the Oglala named Eagle Elk was born in the fall of 1851, near the confluence of the White and Missouri rivers. Although born of a Yankton Nakota mother, he grew up among his father's people, the Oyukhpe Oglalas

(People Who Lay Down Their Packs), a powerful band of the Smoke People (Northern Oglalas) who moved into the Powder River region in the late 1850s. Eagle Elk was a member of the Hoksi Hakakta, or Last Child Society, an unusual military lodge whose forty members consisted of the last born males of selected families. Under the leadership of Eagle Elk's older cousin, the renowned Crazy Horse, this lodge achieved a reputation of fearlessness, many of its young men serving as his bodyguard. In addition to the customary confrontations with enemy tribes, Eagle Elk participated in many of the fights with the whites, among them the Fetterman battle of 1866, and the Little Bighorn battle a decade later. In 1871 Eagle Elk married a Sans Arc woman, and after the surrender of the Sioux, his family settled down in the Wounded Knee District on Pine Ridge Agency. Some sixty years later, from November 27 through December 1, 1944, Eagle Elk granted an interview to Dr. John G. Neihardt. This material became the basis for Neihardt's work, When the Tree Flowered: An Authentic Tale of the Old Sioux World *(New York, 1951), in which its fictionalized narrator, Eagle Voice, told of his life.*[196]

[Tablet 4]

At this point Eagle Elk entered and I asked him to tell me how the management had affected the Indians in Pass Creek District. He said that ~~when the alloting agent came to have them take their lands they were~~ the Day Schools were begun out here in 1894. For several years before, the Indians had lived here and built round them fairly good homes—very good for the Indians—and they had fenced little fields and were raising pigs and chickens, while their cattle ranged outside and grew into good beeves which were marketed in Omaha and were considered among the best product of the Reservation. In 1894 the authorities were taken with an active desire to build Day Schools in Pass Creek, and these were erected in places remote from the settlements already planted. The result was that the families had to remove into the vicinity of the schools to keep their children in attendance and the attendance was compulsory. This broke up the homes and scattered the improvements. Several of these schools had to be moved afterwards or abandoned, because of their out-of-the-way situation. This caused the removal of the Indians a second time and the breaking up of the old homes again and the making of new ones. About 1903 the allotment of lands was begun, and hope revived among these people that a brilliant dawn had arrived. Some made selections for allotments in their present locations while others took theirs where they had last lived before they moved to keep up with the traveling school houses. About this time the "internal improvement" rage was started, and then the Indians after putting their crops in in the spring, were taken away from their homes long distances off to work on the roads and ditches for $1.25 a day. As they remained all the season they were obliged to take their families along. The day laborer had to support all these upon high provisions paid for from low wages. When he went home in the fall his income had been exhausted, and his crop had perished for want of care or been broken into by the range stock and destroyed. The consequence was that he had to subsist through the winter on his little herd. This bitter training by civilization has now (Oct. 1906) been going on three years. This process of civilizing is steadily diminishing the cattle, and these, it may confidently be asserted in ante-bellum phrase, are "in course of ultimate extinction."

The original houses spoken of here were made by the Indians under the tutelage of a white man, R. P. Whitfield, Farmer of Pass Creek District. This man took the most lively interest in the welfare and progress of these people. He was always in the field among them, carefully directing their tentative operations, giving them ~~the best~~ good advice, showing them in all things, and answering to their satisfaction ~~and ultimate good all~~ the various questions they asked. The Indians regretted his removal when the administration changed from Cleveland to Harrison. He was the only farmer who ever came to their homes to instruct them. He organized among them the co-operation system which white farmers are so accustomed to and known as "changing work."

[Little Wolf's Interview]

[Tablet A]

Interview of Little Wolf a Chief of the Cheyennes at New Capitol Hotel in Washington. Wednesday, March 5, 1913. He says that when the Northern Cheyennes went south they started from Fort Keogh in Montana and went under Capt. Ewers to some post on the Yellowstone to one just above Standing Rock Agency, Fort Yates, stayed there three or four months then came to a soldier camp where Fort Mead afterwards was built.[197] This was in 1878.

This was Little Chief's band that went down and on the way met Dull Knife's band coming up; they met on a creek they call Coal Creek (don't know what the whites call it) it is north of the south Platte River. Little Chief's band continued going south, while Dull Knife came on north. There were several chiefs in Little Chiefs band, Little Wolf being one. They went on to Wolf Creek at the mouth of Beaver in Oklahoma.

Little Chief went down to visit the Northern Cheyennes in Indian Territory and to bring them back north. This interview is to be followed by Gen. Creel's which is in another tablet. [Tablet B] Both relate to same thing. Hereto attached.

Willis T. Rowland, son of Wm Rowland, has been an interpreter and scout for 25 years (this is March 5, 1913). Says his father was an interpreter and chief scout for 40 years, served under Gen. Crook; he served under Dr. McGillicudy at Pine Ridge and worked for others. He died at Lame Deer, in December '96. He cannot remember the date so well as the woman who first gave it to me. He was 79 years old. He joined the Cheyennes when he was 17 years old, & always lived on the frontier. He used to interpret for the Cheyennes, Sioux and Arapahoes. He was a great interpreter. He came to Washington as interpreter with Little Wolf about 1870 or 1871, the greatest Cheyenne Chief the Cheyennes ever had. Greatest commander, greatest warrior & governor, and so reputed among the Cheyennes. He died about 20 years ago 81 years of age.

[Peter Shangrau's Interview]

[Tablet 16]

Peter Shangrau Interviewed at Captain George Sword's on Janis Creek, near Day School No. 3, Pine Ridge Reservation, S.D., April 30, 1907.

The Ute Hegira of 1906.[198]

He says he was invited by a telegram from Colonel Auger at Fort Robinson to report to him which he did on or about the 27th October, 1906; but was sent at once to Gillette, Wy., where he reported to Major Gresham on the morning of the 28th[199] (Pete S. lives at the foot of Slim Buttes about 25 miles north of Chadron.) He went as a scout. About 1 o'clock P.M. the troops and horses and equipage arrived by rail at a corral stockyards on the B. & M. some 40 or 50 miles above Gillette, and there disembarkation took place. At sunset the column started, only troops and pack mules going, and marched four or five miles to the Powder River, and then moved down the river what the whites Indians call Lodge Pole Creek and what the whites call Clear Creek; thence they went down this stream five or six miles to the confluence with the Big Powder River, and then they moved down this River ten or fifteen miles and there camped at 1 or 2 o'clock A.M. The troops laid here all day at a cow ranch concealed in the brush. That evening at six the command saddled up and resumed the course down the river, progressing 25 miles that night. (He thinks there were five troops.) (Captain Carter P. Johnson was there in command of the scouts, but he did not have his Troop with him.)[200]

Next morning about 4 o'clock an ambulance arrived bearing Frank Goings, Pine Ridge Agency Interpreter, and American Horse. The troops rested at this place all day at a post-office. Two scouts, Bill Roney and H. J. Christensen, white men who had been secured at Gillette for scouts, and who had gone direct from the railroad to find the Utes, came in about 7 o'clock P.M. and reported that they had located the Utes on a prong of the Little Powder River, at the head thereof, and that they were there at noon that day. Another scout was sent off to ascertain if the Utes were in the same position as when seen by the two who had reported, with orders to intercept the command which was to move back up the Big Powder River a mile to a prong of this stream, thence south up that stream on which this scout was to find and intercept the troops. Having moved some twenty miles the scout encountered the column and reported that the Utes had moved that evening towards the head of Three Bar Creek. So the command had to turn and go back to the camp of the night before and thence fifteen miles farther down the Big Powder to a cow ranch. The troops were camped back in the hills a half a mile from the river. Arrived abt. 3 or 4 o'clock A.M. Stayed there all day and the next night. Next day Peter Shangrau, Frank Goings, Woman's Dress and American Horse and the two white scouts who went out from Gillette, started out and found an old man who was wolf-trapping, and from him they learned that the Utes were camped, as he thought, on the right hand prong of the Three Bar Creek. The scouts, using field glasses, could see the smoke rising from the Ute camp. The two white men would not go farther but stayed with the wolf-trapper, while the other scouts went on. When they were within a mile of the Ute camp they saw a Ute come down a hill behind themselves. Woman's Dress and American Horse were singing. The latter stopped to wait for the Ute to come up. The two shook hands when they met.[201] The other scouts had continued to advance toward the camp. After these two had met, another Ute joined the advance scouts. He had a changed countenance manifesting alarm. Within five minutes American Horse and the Ute overtook the main body of scouts and all shook hands. The other Ute now rode on ahead and gave the usual Indian sign of riding his horse backward & forward in front & at right angles to the line of advance, and whooped and shouted to attract the attention of the camp. The other Ute also sounded the alarm. The scouts saw the Utes immediately running for their horses and noticed great commotion in the camp. The scouts went forward a quarter of a mile when they were met by fifteen or twenty mounted Utes, and these and the scouts all went together to the camp. The Ute who came up to American Horse could talk a little English. Shangrau inquired for a Ute with whom he was acquainted & who comes to Pine Ridge every year, and the Ute said he was an uncle to the man who was named Ma su ke (Marshuska) and Shangrau asked to be conducted to his tepee. This was done and Shangrau unsaddled his horse and turned him loose. Frank Goings, Woman's Dress and American Horse disapproved this act on the part of Shangrau, but he told them not to be afraid of the Utes, for if they manifested any such feeling it would be worse for them all. Then all of them turned their horses loose. Then old American Horse said "We came up here to talk—to make a good talk to you people." He said "the Great Father sent me here with his boys. We came up on a train. We got off over at the railroad over at Powder River; and we borrowed these horses from a cow ranch."

When he said this, a Ute chief spoke up and asked if any soldiers came up with these scouts, and Am. Horse replied, "No; we came up on the train from the Agency." Woman's Dress broke in at this point with the remark that the scouts had all come up on the train and had borrowed these horses from a cow man. The Utes were collected and engaged in discussion among themselves. After a while they began talking with the scouts and saying to them that they must have come up with some soldiers, as they could see that some of the scouts were riding government horses (branded) and were using Gov't. saddles. At this point Shangrau told them that there were soldiers over on the Big Powder; that they had been sent out to prevent a clash between some Sioux who had gone into Wyoming to hunt, and it was feared there would be trouble between them and the white people who had appealed to the Great Father to send troops to prevent conflict. Then he told about the fighting in 1903 on Lightning Creek, and that it was that experience which led the Gov't. to send these soldiers out to look after the Sioux and avoid a recurrence of that affair. He added that the troops intended no harm to the Utes—had not come to fight them.

The Utes expressed themselves as willing to go

American Horse now became engaged with them and told them that a telegram came to his Agency from the Gr. Father telling him to come out and meet these Utes & take them to any place they wanted to go if they selected one of six which he named as follows: Pine Ridge our reservation (that is Pine Ridge), Spring Creek (wherever that may be), Cherry Creek, on Cheyenne Agency close to Missouri River, Fort Robinson, Fort Mead, and White Rock which was their own Reservation from which they had drawn out. After American Horse had told them this they were all willing to go to Cherry Creek. Am. Horse then said that the white people would do one thing—that all the Indian people have now got experience and have learned what the whites will do, and that now we Indians have to do what they require. Some of the Utes then asked him what it was the whites would do, & he said that when the Indians make any kind of a treaty with them they must sign a paper. He told them he wanted them to sign a paper saying they would go to Cherry Creek; that the Great Spirit would see them do this & witness their pledge; & that then they must keep the pledge by going, and so avoiding any trouble with the white people. Frank Goings wrote a paper and about six only signed it by touching the pen. Pete does not know why more did not sign; says they were yet a good deal excited and wild.

After the paper was signed the scouts were ready to return to their camp. Pete told Am. Horse that he must stay with the Utes till the return of the scouts and the officers the next day. It had been arranged with the Utes that they would come back with the military officers next day and meet the Indians. Am. Horse consented to remain overnight. It was about 3 P.M. when the three scouts—Pete Shangrau and Woman's Dress and Frank Goings started back to the soldiers' camp which was 10 or 12 miles distant in a northwesterly or a more nearly western direction. They got back after dark and reported. It was arranged to go in the morning. About 7 A.M. these scouts & Captain Carter P. Johnson and Colonel Lodges (Colonel from Fort Mead), also a white scout, and a colored and a white soldier for horse-holders for the Captain and the Colonel [started out].[202]

About 10 o'clock this party arrived in the vicinity of the Ute camp on (thinks) Three Bar Creek. When within four or five miles of the Utes they met American Horse. He reported that everything was all right at the Indian camp. Capt. Johnson now told the scouts to go on ahead while the rest of the party would follow leisurely. (Johnson was in command of the scouts.) Johnson told these scouts to proceed in advance and to get a few of the Utes—ten or a dozen—and bring them out to meet these officers about a mile from the camp. Am. Horse did not want to go with the scouts, but wished to stay with the officers, claiming that he was tired. Johnson told him they could go slow, but that he must return with the scouts, & he did so. After the scouts had separated from the rest, Am. Horse told the other scouts that something was going on in the camp, but he did not know what it was; there was a good deal of talking among the Utes which he could not understand. The scouts got right up to the camp where they met about 40 mounted Utes who came out to meet them. All the scouts halted and began talking with the Utes, except Shangrau who went right on into the camp. He looked through the lodges and found that all the bedding and utensils had been taken away—the lodges were empty. The Utes were still in camp, that is mostly women and children, while a lot of mounted Utes were off at distances on the hills riding round. This occupied but a few minutes until the Colonel & his party appeared on the hill about a mile from camp, where they stopped and waited for the scouts to bring the Indian delegation. All these Utes—abt. 40—wanted to go out to meet the officers, but as this was contrary to the instructions the scouts had received, Shangrau rode off to Johnson and told him what the Utes desired. Johnson consented, but the Colonel asked Shangrau for his opinion about letting all of them advance, and he said it would be all right, and then the Colonel said let them come, and Shangrau motioned for all of them to come. They and the scouts came up and the Captain and the Colonel shook hands with the Indians. A council took place but there was but little talking. Johnson told them that what Am. Horse had told them was all right. The Colonel told them that he & his party had come over to see them, & that to-morrow he wanted them to come over half way & meet him and have a big talk. That was agreed to. Then Johnson et al. returned to the soldier camp. A council was arranged for next day when the same person[s] who were out the day before, ~~went were joined~~ except Am. Horse who pretended to be sick, were joined by some white scouts, making ten altogether. Started about 7 o'clock & arriving at the big hill where it had been agreed they should meet, these stopped and waited for the Utes. The Indians—abt. 50 or 60, including women on horseback, came up.

On this morning when the scouts met the great crowd, the other scouts stopped and engaged in shaking hands and talking, while Shangrau rode down into the camp. He found that the women were all gone and everything was gone in way of bedding & utensils & the canvas was mostly all taken off and the lodge poles were left standing. The women & children could be seen on the hills where they had fires to keep them warm, for it was cold, it being in November.

At the council the Utes said they would go, but objected to going with the soldiers, & said they would go by themselves. The Colonel said to Capt. Johnson that he could not allow this, as he was ordered to bring them in. The Indians did not want the soldiers at all. They suggested that they would be willing to go with twenty soldiers who might act as an escort to show them the way to Fort Mead. It had already been settled that the Indians would go to Cherry

Creek if satisfactory arrangements could be made with the government and the Indians on the Cheyenne Reservation. Capt. Johnson had said to them that they should camp at Fort Mead and he would take a number of them and go to Washington and see the Great Father. Then came the hitch over going with the soldiers. When the Indians said they would go by themselves the Colonel and the Captain talked the question over. The Colonel's objections to acceding to the wishes of the Indians was that he was under orders to control them, and he could not allow them too much latitude, for if he was to do so and trouble arose, he would be held responsible. He and Johnson at length planned to have the escort of 20 soldiers and Woman's Dress and Shangrau march with the Indians, while the troops should be kept eight or ten or twelve miles in advance, so that couriers and dispatches could keep the main body and the Indians in constant touch. The officers realized that pacific measures alone could prevent fighting; so, having concocted this plan by which they could make the situation secure and still not excite or antagonize the Indians, the latter were informed of this and told that it would be necessary for the soldiers to move within this distance to the end that they supply the Indians with rations. This was reasonable and at once agreed to. The march to Fort Mead occupied some twenty days.[203] The Indians moved very slowly; their horses were poor; they were in destitute condition; the weather was cold; they were half famished; and whenever they decided to camp they could not be urged or persuaded to go on, but stopped doggedly.

Capt. Johnson went to Washington with some of the Utes and had conferences with President Roosevelt.[204]

When the scouts visited the Ute camp the second time Shangrau used his arts of persuasion with the Indians to prevent them from fighting. He reasoned with some of them — told them their horses were poor and useless, that the Indians would find it hard to live; that winter was at hand; that they could not vanquish the whites; if they were to kill all the soldiers it would not be the end, but only the beginning of trouble, for as many more would come again and again until the Indians were worn out and conquered or destroyed. He said to them that the scouts had not come to hurt them, neither had the soldiers; that the scouts did not want to fight that they had families and homes and wanted to go back to them; that if the Utes wanted and intended to fight just to say so and the scouts would go back to their reservation. This had great influence with the Indians. They were also told that the soldiers would treat them well and that it would be all right if they went along with the troops.

[Maggie Palmer's Interview]

[Tablet 1]

Mrs. Maggie Palmer Interviewed at the home of the Palmers on White River between the mouths of Jones Creek and Big Hollow Creek (the next below this is Clifford Creek) January 9, 1907.

See Mrs. Janis, widow of Antoine, on Agency.[205]

Her father, Joseph Antoine Janis was born in St. Louis (she thinks; ask Big Bat; he knows) does not know when born or exact age. He died April 10, 1889 (?) and is buried at Pine Ridge.[206] Bill Garnett says he died in 1890.

Mr. Janis came to Fort Laramie and lived among the Indians. He traded with them. He had three brothers, William, who lived out west with the other brothers a good many years, and returned to St. Charles and died there; and Ridget who went to California in the gold excitement and both he and his wife died there; and Nicholas who died at the home of his son-in-law, Ben Tibbitts. He was a quiet, sober man who never drank intoxicating liquors; was a man of solid qualities and possessed valuable frontier information. John Palmer, husband of Mrs. Maggie Palmer, died December 26, 1903, aged 73.

Kyle, S.D. is the P.O. of the Palmers.

[Mrs. Nicholas Janis's Interview]

[Tablet 8]

Mrs. Nicholas Janis.

Says: Her husband, Nick Janis was called by the Indians, "Tall White Man." He was very large of stature, stood six feet in his stockings, and weighed 230 pounds. She was married to Mr. Janis at Fort Laramie when he was 24 years old. He was born in 18 Sep the year 1825, in St. Joe, Missouri, and died at the home of his son-in-law, Ben Tibbitts in September, 1901.[207] He had swelling joints when he died—probably rheumatism. He was French descent. His folks don't know whether he had any other blood. But I am pretty sure he had some white. They say he had no Indian blood.

He started out in the employ of the American Fur Company and traversed all the country in which it operated. He traded for Jim Bordeau; he took goods out from Bordeau's store and traded for robes & skins. He traded one winter for Bordeau; his wife was out with him; they were with what was called the Cut-off, which was Little Wound's band which sloughed off from the main band and hence was called "Cutoff." The Cutoff was on the Rawhide and Platte streams. After that winter's work for Bordeau Janis & wife went off among the Cheyennes who were further south. He has been on all the rivers in south of the Platte. He worked for Bullock who was a former trader at Laramie. He also traded for a man named Gay. He was on the Connor expedition. He operated all through the north. He was all through Utah and that country. He was a noted hunter. The last trip he made his party got 120 buffaloes. He and his family lived on the Missouri River a long time. They moved over there on the Missouri when Mrs. Tibbitts was 17 years old. They lived there 3 years Mrs. Tibbitts says. She was the oldest child. She is now about 50 years old. Nick had nine children. Nick Janis had a remarkable memory of dates and circumstances, and it is greatly to be regretted that his life was not written.

He was guide for Gen. Connor's expedition. They took a lot of prisoners — Cheyennes and Arapahoes — and brought them back. He was with the troops a good deal. A commission came out from Washington and he gathered the Indian Chiefs and took them down to the Missouri river. He took chiefs to Washington several times. He was official interpreter. (See treaties where his name is signed. Ask Big Bat about him.[208]

One time when he was trading among the Crow Indians and was getting robes; Nick was ahead with his wife, and in the night he felt the buffalo robe being pulled off and supposed the Crows were stealing it. It turned out to be a wolf (lupus) taking it away.

One time Nick & his wife and Emily (Mrs. Tibbitts) were out hunting buffaloes. Nick got a lot of meat this time and loaded it on his wife's mule. Emily was riding on the mule too. Nick rode a mule a lot. Mrs. Janis' mule got scared and ran away with Mrs. Janis who carried Emily, a little infant, in her arms, and with baby, meat and all. The mule ran and bucked them off into a sand bank and threw Emily into a bunch of prickly pears and filled her hands with thorns and her mouth with sand.

[Mrs. Julia Bradford's Interview]

[Tablet 8]

Henry Clay Clifford.

Interview with Mrs. Julia Bradford daughter of Henry (Hank) C. Clifford [who] was born in 1837 in the state of Indiana, and died at his home on the north side of White River, 20 miles northwest of Kyle, S.D., in January, 1906, at the age of 69 years and is buried at Kyle. His parents moved to Missouri (to Chillicothe) when he was a boy. About 1860 he came He began freighting from Nebraska City to Fort Kearny about 1860 or prior to that; this is what brought him to this country. He married into the Sioux about 1865 or 1867. He had seven children. He hunted with W. F. Cody a good deal. He followed hunting for and collecting fossils for 20 years.[209] He traveled some in the eastern states exhibiting and selling these fossils. I remember his going to Chicago with a lot of curios which he packed & boxed in Chadron. For a time he traveled (about a year) with Cody's Wild West show. At one time (one winter) he was away in the show business on his own account. He was gone three years at one time running a medicine show with the Kickapoo Indians. In the later years of his life he was in the stock business on the Pine Ridge Agency, and before this was raising stock on the Running Water at what was the Hough ranch afterwards. He did irrigating there also. He conducted experiments with forage plants from seeds furnished by the Gov't., and was the first to introduce alfalfa raising in the section of country where he lived. See Buffalo Bill's Book for some account of Clifford.[210] Hank Clifford had a brother Mortimer who was a freighter. Married a half-blood Sioux and lived for many years in Frontier County, Neb., at Stockville. He helped organize the county and develop it. Was always in the stock business. Hunted buffaloes for sometime; but as soon as he could returned to civilization and engaged in stock raising. Was younger than Hank & was born in Missouri. He is mentioned in Cody's book. He can have no special place in my books.

Hank Clifford was a good writer and contributed articles to the press.

[Mrs. Nettie Elizabeth Goings's Interview]

[Tablet 13]

Pine Ridge March 13, 1907.

Mrs. Nettie Elizabeth Goings says: She and Frank Grouard are children of the same father by different mothers. The brother of Frank Gruard's mother was named Black Lodge Pole. The name of her father & Frank's was John Brazeau. He was a French Creole. He was from St. Louis & worked for the American Fur Company. He came up and settled at Fort Pierre some twenty years; he and Papineau were companions & chums, & he was an associate of the Picottes. She says Frank got into some trouble on the Missouri & went off among the Indians. Mr. Brazeau was related to the Chouteaus and Pecots (Picottes).

Mrs. Goings is the mother of Frank Goings, Agency interpreter at P. Ridge.

She says that Frank [Grouard] and three other boys were in school and the four got into difficulty & she speaks of says that there was something said about a killing but she was young & does not know just how it was etc!! He got on a boat going up the river & the father boarded the same boat to bring him back, but did not succeed in doing so. His right Christian name was Walter—full name Walter Brazeau. His Indian name was Grabber.

Mrs. Goings Indian name is Money. Her father had money & she may have used money in a way to draw to herself that name. She does not doubt that he may have been in the family of Parley Platt [Pratt?] in Salt Lake; she says that he told her that he lived in the family of some white man away off north or west, and he showed her the picture of the man. She says her family were acq. with the Pratts in St. Louis.

Choteau Pratt was killed at the Lower Brule Agency on the Missouri.

[William Girton's Interview]

[Tablet 18]

Kyle, S.D., Feb. 27, '07

William Girton, Assistant Farmer at Medicine Root, a full blood Sioux Indian, who was a pupil 5 yrs. at Carlisle, was enlisted by Capt. Pratt & served 3 yrs. in the U.S. Army at Fort Douglas, Utah; has been Captain of Police at Pine Ridge, is serving his 2d term as Asst. Farmer at Med. Root, & altogether has been in Gov't. service 12 yrs., says:

That the father of Bull Bear was Bull Hoop. He was chief of the whole Sioux Nation. Bull Bear was a great chief, the celebrated and stedfast friend of the white man; that the Red Cloud element were wild and warlike Indians and jealous of the popularity and power of Bull Bear, and hated him for his friendship for the whites; so it was arranged to put him out of way, and to this end he was made drunk and while in this condition was stabbed by one of Red Cloud's adherents. He does not know that Red Cloud did the deed, but he evidently thinks he knew of the plan and was consenting to it. He says there were those who wanted Bull Bear out of the way so they might receive promotion, & he seems to squint at Red Cloud.[211]

[William Young's Interview]

[Tablet 28]

William Young who is a quarter blood Indian says that the Indians do not posses much sense of gratitude.

And if you give them anything they expect and want more, and the more you give the more they ask for. A great many persons have told me the same things in respect to them.

William Young tells me that his father, who was a Frenchman, (and his mother half French and Indian) was burning charcoal at the Rosebud Agency when it was first established, when a Sioux Indian came along and asked for something to eat. He said he had not eaten anything that day nor anything the day before. His father, Henry Young, could not quit his attention to the coal burning, but he gave the Indian [something?] to eat, showed him where the coffee and other eatables were, and he helped himself. When he was through eating he got on his pony and rode up behind Mr. Young and shot him in the back with a steel-pointed arrow. Mr. Young was twenty miles from the Agency and was alone. He walked to the Agency. When the arrow was pulled out the steel remained in his body. A doctor opened his side but could not get the arrow. Mr. Young carried that arrowhead in his body over twenty years before he died.

William Young is the young man who piloted me to Salaways' and Mousseau's.

[Mrs. Charles C. Clifford's Interview]

[Tablet 10]

Deer Springs, S.D., Feb. 4, 1904 [1907].

At the home of Charles C. Clifford. I arrived here from William Garnett's and William Peano's the 2d instant.

Mrs. Clifford related some facts to me to-day which belong to the account given by Mrs. Richard Stirk of the distresses through which herself and her aunt and Little Bat passed near the Cache la Poudre. Mrs. Stirk and Mrs. Clifford are cousins according to the white man's system of relationship, and it was Mrs. Clifford's mother who was the aunt that carried Mrs. Stirk on her back. Mrs. Jack Russel and Mrs. Clifford are full sisters. Mrs. Clifford says:

That her father, Bob Saunders and his wife Mary (her father and mother) (In Dakota the mother's name was Wi ta sna un) were going with others somewhere with goods. Saunders had been married before to a white woman and had a child. This woman died ten days after the child was born. They were attacked as described by Mrs. Stirk. Saunders supposed his wife was killed in the attack, and she supposed that he had been killed. Mrs. Saunders fled with the two. She was big with child and it was hard for her to travel. She was taken on

~~horseback with and carried with one of the captors. One of the captors. The captors decided that they could not take their captive along after they had~~

There was an Indian among the captors who wanted Mrs. Saunders for his wife and began to call her his wife. She was a pretty woman whose hair came down nearly to her knees. The other captors felt that they could not carry this party along farther; they had trailed along with them as an encumbrance a whole day; so they told their companion who wanted her for his wife, that he would have to hunt some game to feed her. He told them to remain in camp with her till he returned with meat, and he started off. As soon as he was gone the other captors broke camp and told Mrs. Saunders to take Emma (This was the name of Mrs. Stirk when a girl; Mrs. Clifford does not know what other name she had) and Baptiste Garnier and flee. These Indians had put up this device of getting their companion off hunting in order to rid themselves of the woman and children. She now went with her serious charge as one free. They traveled day and night. It was late in the fall and there were streams to be crossed which were not frozen sufficiently to bear up and they had to wade in ice-cold water. It was snowing. The snow became knee deep to the woman. Emma was two or three years old and large and heavy. Her mother was dead and Mrs. Saunders was raising her. She strapped the girl to her back with a rope. Being herself heavy with child at the time, this was a laborious burden, as she waded through the snow and endured the cold. Emma was transferred to the boy's back occasionally to give her respite and to save her strength. But when he carried her the shawl did not stay on her well and she grew very cold, and then the woman would have to take [her]. The boy bore his part with the courage which distinguished him afterwards as a man. ~~But on the second~~ This forlorn party hurried with all the strength they had to make good their escape from the one Indian who had gone out to hunt; but their progress was slow, the best they could do. On the second day Bat was so hungry that he was ravenous. They had two large hounds which they prized, but Bat said he was starving and he suggested that they kill one of the dogs. They had no gun to shoot him, and he was too strong for them to kill with a knife; so it was decided to end his life by strangulation.

They put a noose around his neck and then began to choke him. His pitiful cries brought his friend to his aid. The other dog now assailed the woman and the boy furiously to save his companion. He leaped at them and rent their clothing and probably would have torn their flesh had not the perishing dog ceased his outcries as the tightening rope stopped his breathing. When he was dead a piece was cut from his ham. Bat had a few matches in his pocket and built a fire. The meat was held in the blaze awhile. It did not cook very well, but Bat waited as long as he could and then he began on it and devoured it as one famished, the blood meantime running down the sides of his mouth. It was three or four days that they were out. At last they came in sight of a light. It was a mile off. Mrs. Saunders nearly fell with despair and exhaustion when she relaxed the tension which was sustaining her. When she arrived she was among her friends. As they removed her moccasins the skin came with them. She was frozen to her knees, and it was a long time before she was a well woman, her life barely being saved. She lived to be the mother of thirteen children, ten of whom grew to manhood and womanhood. She died on Pine Ridge Reservation May 18, 1905. Buried at Holy Rosary Mission.

I omitted to state that among those of the captors who bade these people go and save themselves was one who knew Mrs. Sanborn [Saunders] and claimed some relationship with her, and he did not want the Indian who began to claim her as his wife to have her.

[Amos Ross's Interview]

[Tablet 26]
Allen, S.D., Nov. 7, 1906.
Interview with Rev. Amos Ross, Episcopal Minister who says: He is a Santee Sioux. The Agency of his tribe is in Knox Co. Neb. Niobrara is only 12 miles from the Agency. On Dec. 7, 1880, Mr. Ross came to the Pine Ridge and began work at Wounded Knee, near where the battleground is. He at first worked half a day in the school and the rest of his labor was missionary. He has been here ever since. When the missionary work grew he dropped school teaching; did not intend to teach when he came, but seeing the need for instruction he at first undertook it for awhile. He has taken direct personal interest in the personal welfare of the Indians, helping then in numerous ways, teaching them how to plow and put seeds in the ground and to care for stock. When he came here he belonged to the order of Deacon; when in 1892 he was advanced to the Priest order in the church the Reservation was divided by Bishop Hare and all that part of the Reservation east of the Porcupine was put under his charge as missionary. Mr. Ross is the only Episcopal Indian minister that has come in from the outside and been on the Reservation. After awhile the Presbyterians came in and they have had their native missionaries. All the churches on the Reservation have native resident Indians as helpers called catechist whose duty is to conduct the Sunday services under direction of the clergyman, to prepare

candidates for baptism to visit the sick, and if able to do so, to preach. These catechists have been selected from among the most suitable of the Indians who belong on the Reservation. Mr. Ross says he knows of no native tribe that has shown such proficiency in advancement as the Sioux. The Santees and Cheyenne River Agency Indians and the Standing Rock Indians have had the gospel and other advantages much longer. When Mr. R. began here they all wore the blanket, and it was very slow and uphill work, but now in 26 years none wear blankets but only a few of the oldest ones.

Appendix A

Forts

The number following each fort is the page number from Francis Paul Prucha, A Guide to the Military Posts of the United States *(Madison: State Historical Society of Wisconsin, 1964).*

Fort Abraham Lincoln, 55. Established June 14, 1872; abandoned November 19, 1891. Across the Missouri River from Bismarck, North Dakota.

Fort Bennett, 60. Established May 17, 1870; abandoned November 17, 1891. Right bank of Missouri River, east of Mission Ridge, South Dakota.

Fort Buford, 63. Established June 13, 1866; abandoned 1895. Right bank of Missouri River, above the mouth of the Yellowstone River.

Fort C. F. Smith, 64. Established August 12, 1866; abandoned July 29, 1868. Right bank of Big Horn River, about thirty-five miles south of Hardin, Montana.

Fort Douglas, 72. Established October 26, 1862; abandoned, no date. Three miles east of Salt Lake City, Utah.

Fort Ellis, 73. Established August 27, 1867; abandoned August 31, 1886. Left bank of East Gallatin River, east of Bozeman, Montana.

Fort Fetterman, 74. Established July 19, 1867; abandoned May 20, 1882. Right bank of North Platte River, five miles northwest of Douglas, Wyoming.

Fort Hall, 77. Established May 27, 1870; abandoned May 1, 1883. Present Fort Hall, Idaho, north of Pocatello.

Fort Kearny, 82. Established 1848 as Fort Childs, designated Fort Kearny January 31, 1849; abandoned May 17, 1871. Right bank of Platte River, southeast of Kearney, Nebraska.

Fort Keogh, 82. Established August 28, 1876; abandoned November 8, 1877. Right bank of Yellowstone River at Miles City, Montana.

Fort Laramie, 84. Established 1834 as a trading post, then purchased by the army on June 26, 1849; abandoned except for small guard, March 2, 1890. Near Torrington, Wyoming.

Fort Lincoln. See Fort Abraham Lincoln.

APPENDIX A

Fort Meade, 91. Established August 28, 1878. Right bank of Bear Butte Creek, near Sturgis, South Dakota.

Fort Mitchell, 92. Established 1864; abandoned 1867. Right bank of North Platte River, west of Gering, Nebraska.

Fort Pierre, 97. Established from a trading post July 7, 1855; abandoned May 16, 1857. Right bank of Missouri River, northwest of Pierre, South Dakota.

Fort Phil Kearny, 97. Established July 13, 1866; abandoned July 31, 1868. Right bank of Piney Fork of Powder River, twelve miles northwest of Buffalo, Wyoming.

Fort Randall, 100. Established June 26, 1856; abandoned December 6, 1892. Right bank of Missouri River, opposite Pickstown, South Dakota.

Fort Reno, 101. Established August 28, 1865; abandoned August 18, 1868. Right bank of Powder River, thirty-eight miles north of Midwest, Wyoming.

Fort Riley, 102. Established May 17, 1853. Ten miles northeast of Junction City, Kansas.

Fort Robinson, 102. Established March 8, 1874; abandoned 1948. Three miles west of Crawford, Nebraska.

Camp Sheridan. Established March 1874; abandoned 1881. On Beaver Creek north of Hays Springs, Nebraska. In the summer of 1875 moved upstream half a mile.

Fort Sidney, 107. Established December 13, 1867; abandoned June 1, 1894. In Sidney, Nebraska.

Fort Sill, 107-8. Established March 4, 1869. Right bank of Cache Creek, opposite Medicine Park, Oklahoma.

Fort Snelling, 108. Established August 1819 on Mississippi River at Minneapolis, Minnesota.

Fort Sully, 110. Established September 1863; abandoned November 30, 1894. Left bank of Missouri River, ten miles below Pierre, South Dakota.

Fort Totten, 112. Established July 17, 1867; abandoned November 18, 1890. South shore of Devil's Lake, North Dakota.

Fort Yates, 118. Established December 23, 1874. Right bank of Missouri River at present Fort Yates, North Dakota.

Appendix B

Agencies

Sources include the Annual Reports of the Commissioner of Indian Affairs, *Olson,* Red Cloud and the Sioux Problem, *and Hyde,* Spotted Tail's Folk.

Cheyenne River Agency. The Cheyenne River Agency for the Miniconjous, and some Sans Arcs and Blackfeet, was created in 1868. It was not until 1870 that construction began at a site on the Missouri River below the mouth of the Cheyenne River. The agency was later moved downstream to a location on the right bank of the Missouri due west of present Agar, South Dakota.

Crow Creek Agency. The agency was opened in 1863, near present Fort Thompson, South Dakota. It was occupied briefly by the Santees and Winnebagos who had been removed from Minnesota after the uprising in 1862. Later, Lower Yanctonais, Two Kettles, and a minority of other Dakota bands settled there.

Flandreau Agency. In March 1869 a group of Santees left the Crow Creek Reservation and moved north to the vicinity of present Flandreau, South Dakota. By 1876 they had filed for eighty-five homesteads. Missionary John P. Williamson joined them and was named agent in 1874. Flandreau was not a reservation.

Grand River Agency. See Standing Rock Agency.

Lower Brule Agency. The Lower Brulés were assigned to the Crow Creek Agency. In 1868 a subagency was built on the west side of the Missouri River about fifteen miles above the mouth of the White River. The agency was moved a short distance on two occasions in the 1870s. In 1875 it became an independent agency. In 1894 the agency was moved upstream to a point east of the present town of Lower Brule, South Dakota.

Pine Ridge Agency. The Pine Ridge Agency opened in October 1878. It was not as far from the Missouri River as the Oglalas would have liked, but it was close to their old homeland. The agency was located at present Pine Ridge, South Dakota.

Ponca Agency. Construction at the first agency began in 1859. It was about three miles northeast of present Verdel, Nebraska, and overlooked the Missouri River to the north. In the summer of 1867, the agency was moved to the north side of the Niobrara River southeast of present Lynch, Nebraska. In 1877 the Poncas began the move to Oklahoma. That winter it served as the agency for the Brulés (Spotted Tail Agency No. 2).

Red Cloud Agency No. 1. Construction began in the late summer of 1871. It was often called the Sod Agency although there were both log and sod buildings. Agents dealt with most of the Oglala Lakotas, Northern Cheyennes, and Arapahos, plus a few Brulés. The agency was located on the left bank of the North Platte River about six miles southeast of present Torrington, Wyoming.

Red Cloud Agency No. 2. In August 1873 the Sod Agency was moved to a new site, despite opposition on the part of some of the Lakotas. Red Cloud No. 2 was on the south side of the White River, about three miles southwest of present Crawford, Nebraska.

Red Cloud Agency No. 3. In an attempt to reduce shipping costs, the Indian office relocated the agency to the Missouri River in the fall of 1877. The Oglalas opposed the new site above the mouth of Yellow Medicine Creek, today's Medicine Creek. After a year the agency was moved to Pine Ridge.

Rosebud Creek Agency. Construction of the Rosebud Agency began in the fall of 1878. The agency continues today at Rosebud, South Dakota.

Sod Agency. See Red Cloud No. 1.

Spotted Tail Agency. Officials complained about the excessive cost of hauling annuities overland from steamboats on the Missouri River to the agency on Beaver Creek. The agency was moved in the fall of 1877 to the abandoned Ponca Agency near present Verdel, Nebraska. The Brulés opposed the move to the Missouri. In the spring the agency was moved again to present Rosebud, South Dakota.

Standing Rock Agency. The Grand River Agency was established in 1868 near present Fort Yates, North Dakota. It was moved twice before being established permanently near the mouth of the Grand River. It was for the Hunkpapas, Blackfeet Lakotas, and Upper and Lower Yanktonais.

Whetstone Agency No. 1. The first Whetstone Agency was established in August of 1868. It was on the west side of the Missouri River north of Whetstone Creek and east of present Burke, South Dakota. Whetstone was for the Brulés, the majority of whom visited the agency Only to receive their annuities. Approximately one thousand people lived permanently in the vicinity. Nearly all of the Indians assigned to the agency wanted an agency farther west and the Indian office consented. Abandonment of the agency began on June 1, 1871.

Whetstone Agency No. 2. The second Whetstone Agency was on White Clay Creek, about four miles northeast of Crawford, Nebraska. Construction of the agency buildings began in late June 1871. The Indian office had been trying to persuade the Lakotas to become farmers, but Agent J. M. Washburn judged the soil in the vicinity barren and recommended another move.

Whetstone Agency No. 3. The next Whetstone Agency was established late in 1872, near the mouth of Beaver Creek in the northeast corner of Dawes County, Nebraska.

The Brulés found the location satisfactory, but the Indian office thought the location "unfavorable" and "unhealthy." As a result the buildings that were erected were only temporary. In August 1874 a special commission arrived to select a new location and persuaded the Brulés that a move would be advantageous.

Whetstone Agency No. 4. The agency was moved about ten miles to the southeast and reestablished near the head of West Beaver Creek. On January 1, 1875, the name was changed to Spotted Tail Agency, although the old title, Whetstone, continued to be used frequently. The agency was occupied until 1877 (see Spotted Tail Agency).

Yankton Agency. Construction began in 1859 near present Lake Andes, South Dakota.

Yellow Medicine Creek Agency. See Red Cloud Agency No. 3.

Notes

Introduction

1. Tablet 41, Eli S. Ricker Collection, RG8, Nebraska State Historical Society, Lincoln (hereafter Ricker's notebooks will be cited as tablet and number).
2. Brownfield is about thirty-five miles northwest of Portland, Maine. Declaration for Pension, May 15, 1912, Eli S. Ricker Pension File, Civil War and later Pension Application Files, Records of the Veterans Administration, Record Group 15, National Archives and Records Administration (NARA).

    Unless otherwise noted biographical data is from three sources. Brief biographical sketches were published in H. W. Beckwith, *History of Iroquois County* (Chicago: H. H. Hill and Co., 1880; reprint, Evansville IN: Unigraphic Inc., 1979), 459-61, and Albert Watkins, *History of Nebraska* (Lincoln: Western Publishing and Engraving Co., 1913), 555-58. The Ricker collection includes numerous letters written by Ricker to members of his family. This source provided significant details about his life. Unless otherwise noted, quotations attributed to Ricker are from this source.
3. J. N. Reece, *Report of the Adjutant General of the State of Illinois* (Springfield: Phillips Brothers Printers, 1901), 5: 614-15. Ricker's letters from the Carolinas have been published.

    Edward G. Longacre, "We Left a Black Track in South Carolina: Letters of Corporal Eli S. Ricker, 1865," *South Carolina Historical Magazine* 82 (1981): 210-24.
4. Ricker wrote that Corp. William Loft was killed on March 16 and Corp. William Olson was killed on March 24. The adjutant general's report listed the fatalities, but noted that Olson died of his wounds on March 26. Reece, *Report of the Adjutant General of the State of Illinois*, 5:610. Fifty-one enlisted men were killed in the 102d Illinois regiment during the war. Another sixty-eight died of disease. Frederick H. Dyer, *A Compendium of the War of the Rebellion* (Des Moines IA: Dyer Publishing Co., 1908), 1090.

    Ricker was mustered out in Washington DC on June 6. Declaration for Pension, May 15, 1912, Ricker pension file.
5. Mary's uncle may have been D. M. Smith, who was a Union soldier correspond-

ing with Ricker. The tone of Smith's letters in the Ricker collection suggest he was older than Ricker.
6. Declaration for Pension, Mar. 12, 1915, Ricker pension file.
7. Years later Ricker's son Leslie recalled having "many hired help" on the farm. Leslie Ricker to Dear Relatives of the Round Table, Aug. 31, 1930, Ricker Coll. Ricker was also a justice of the peace at Loda in 1875. Summons notice, Box 28, Ricker Coll.
8. Declaration for Pension, May 15, 1912, Ricker pension file.
9. Ibid; Leslie Ricker to Dear Relatives, Aug. 31, 1930. Their children were Albion Harmon, born April 11, 1868; Mary Catherine (married Charles Nichols), born November 29, 1869; Sarah Evelyn (married Ferbrache), born November 19, 1871; Leslie D., born July 30, 1873; and Jessie Irene (married Klingaman), born September 4, 1879. Declaration for Pension, May 15, 1912, Ricker pension file. Mary was nicknamed Kate and Sarah was Sade.
10. *Chadron Democrat,* Nov. 7, 1889.
11. Election notice, April 6, 1886, Box 24, Ricker Coll.; *Chadron Democrat,* Nov. 11, 1886; J. E. Cobbey, ed., *Consolidated Statutes of Nebraska, 1891* (Lincoln: State Journal Co., 1891), 284-85.
12. *Chadron Democrat,* Nov. 15 and 17, 1887; *Dawes County Journal,* Nov. 29, 1895. When Ricker ran as a Populist he won his race by 145 votes out of a total of 1,487. *Dawes County Journal,* Nov. 5, 1897; *Crawford Tribune,* Nov. 17, 1899.
13. *Chadron Times,* Feb. 25, 1904. Ricker chose to purchase land although government land was available for homesteads when he arrived in Chadron. Leslie Ricker to A. E. Sheldon, June 27, 1926, Ricker Coll.
14. *Chadron Times,* Feb. 25, 1904. The ad read, "For Sale Gray Cliff Ranch of nearly 1,000 acres, one of the best home places in Dawes County. Fenced, running water, complete in every respect. This place will be sold at a bargain on easy terms if sold at once. E. S. and L. D. Ricker, Chadron, Neb." L. D. Ricker is the son, Leslie. He owned land adjacent to his father's ranch. Leslie Ricker to A. E. Sheldon, June 27, 1926; *Chadron Times,* Feb. 23, 1905. The Rickers lived at 638 Gunnison Avenue, Grand Junction. W. A. Balloo to Ricker, Sept. 24, 1905, Ricker Coll. Later they moved to 640 North 7th Street.
15. Tablet 22. This was probably written early in 1907. Leslie Ricker to A. E. Sheldon, June 27, 1926. The Lincoln, *Nebraska State Journal,* Nov. 7, 1926, reported that the interest arose "about 1900."
16. *Chadron Times,* June 11, 1903.
17. Ibid., July 30, Nov. 12, 1903. W. Fletcher Johnson's *Life of Sitting Bull,* published in 1891, was an early example generally in this vein. It carried comments by Dr. Charles A. Eastman and Elaine Goodale. They were both sympathetic to the Indians' plight, but they were careful not to express excessively radical views. For example, Goodale was quoted as saying, "The killing of women and children was in part unavoidable, owing to the confusion." Then, in the same breath, she added,

the killing "was in many cases deliberate and intentional." W. Fletcher Johnson, *Life of Sitting Bull and the History of the Indian War of 1890–91* (Philadelphia: Edgewood Publishing Co., 1891), 457.

Other events in 1903 may have stirred Ricker's interest. On May 28 a monument was erected at Wounded Knee beside the mass grave of many of the Indians killed there. Ricker did not mention the event in his newspaper, but he must have been aware of it. A big crowd attended the dedication of the large, expensive stone obelisk. At least one other local newspaper carried a report on the event. The monument was purchased for $350 from Kimball Brothers of Lincoln, Nebraska. *Rushville Standard*, May 22, 1903. At some later time Ricker obtained a photo of the monument. Ricker Coll., RG1227.PH.20–16.

18. *Chadron Times*, Nov. 5, 12, 19, Dec. 3, 1903. Ricker's competitors in the *Chadron Journal* limited their coverage of the incident to a few lines. *Chadron Journal*, Nov. 6, 1903. Ricker copied a letter by Clarence Three Stars, which described the incident (Tablet 25). Also see "Sheriffs Battle Indians on Lightning Creek," *The Wyoming Pioneer* 1 (1941): 190–201. Leslie D. Ricker to A. E. Sheldon, June 27, 1926.

19. The Bartlett interview is in Box 19, Ricker Coll. Allen's first account of Wounded Knee is Tablet C dated December 23, 1903. At that time Allen was living on his ranch about six miles southwest of Martin, South Dakota. Charles W. Allen, *From Fort Laramie to Wounded Knee: In the West That Was*, ed. Richard E. Jensen (Lincoln: University of Nebraska Press, 1997), xix.

20. Leslie D. Ricker to A. E. Sheldon, June 27, 1926.

21. The letter was mailed from Kyle on February 23, 1907, and addressed to Mrs. Mary M. Ricker, 640 N. 7th Street, Grand Junction, Colorado. On the envelope someone, perhaps Leslie Ricker, had written "Letters written while traveling over Pine Ridge Indian Agency."

22. He used the letterhead for at least three years. Ricker to Leslie, et al. Feb. 7, 1910.

23. Tablet 22.

24. Ibid.

25. "About Face," Ricker Coll.

26. Tablet 22.

27. Addison E. Sheldon, "Life of Red Cloud," MSS, Nebraska State Historical Society, 1932.

28. Hamblin's title in the Office of Indian Affairs was assistant historian. Box 28, Ricker Coll.

29. No salutation, from Grandma, July 31, 1911; Leslie Ricker to Dear Relatives, Aug. 31, 1930; Index to Correspondence Files 22691, Feb. 29, 1912, Records of the Bureau of Indian Affairs, Record Group 75, NARA. Ibid., 86034, Aug. 12, 1912; Ricker to Leslie, Margaret, and Agnes, Aug. 10, 1912.

30. Leslie Ricker to Dear Friend (A. E. Sheldon), Feb. 13, 1927, Ricker donor file 1227, Nebraska State Historical Society, Lincoln (hereafter cited as donor file).

31. Mother to Leslie, May 21, 1919, Ricker Coll.
32. Ibid. The house was at 1132 Ouray Ave.
33. Ricker began receiving $24 a month in 1913. This was increased to $30 in 1918. Act of May 11, 1912, Declaration for Pension, Ricker Pension File; A. H. Ricker to Sheldon, July 15, 1926, donor file.
34. Application for Reimbursement, July 21, 1926, Ricker Pension File. Later Ricker mentioned, "I have been all used up for six or eight weeks." Ricker to Dear Leslie, Apr. 29, 1926. Death certificate, June 15, 1926; Ricker Pension File; Addison E. Sheldon, "A Memorial to the Sioux Nation," Nebraska History 21 (1940): 283-84. The Grand Junction *Daily Sentinel*, May 17, 1926, listed the cause of death simply as heart failure.
35. Beckwith, History of Iroquois County, 461; Leslie Ricker to Dear Relatives, Aug. 31, 1930. Ricker attended the Methodist Church when he arrived in Chadron. Box 24, Ricker Coll.; *Chadron Times*, Feb. 16, 1905; W. H. Korns to Ricker, Feb. 23, 1905. It is evident from his letters that Ricker was a regular reader of *Science and Health*, a magazine published by the Church of Christ, Scientist.
36. Beckwith, *History of Iroquois County*, 461; *Chadron Democrat*, Nov. 4, 1886; *Dawes County Journal*, Nov. 5, 1897.
37. Unfortunately, Mary Ricker's letter has been lost.
38. A. E. Sheldon to A. H. Ricker, June 24, 1926; A. H. Ricker to Sheldon, June 4, Sept. 24, 1926, donor file. Albion was living in Hollywood, California, at the time of his father's death. He spent the summer in Grand Junction attending to his father's affairs. Ricker was nearly penniless when he died and Albion submitted a request for burial expenses to the veterans' bureau. Albion ignored the extensive library when he attested that his father had no cash, insurance, personal property, or real estate. Affidavit Supporting Burial Claim, July 14, 1926, Ricker pension file.
39. A. H. Ricker to Sheldon, July 15, 1926; Sheldon to A. H. Ricker, Sept. 21, 1926; A. H. Ricker to Sheldon, Sept. 24, 1926.
40. Sheldon to A. H. Ricker, June 24, 1926.
41. A. H. Ricker to Sheldon, Sept. 24, 1926; Report of Annual Meeting, Jan. 11, 1927, RG014, Nebraska State Historical Society, Lincoln.
42. George Bartlett's interview was on Nov. 30, 1903. Box 19, Ricker Coll.
43. *Nebraska State Journal*, Nov. 7, 1926.
44. Tablet 16.
45. Tablet A.
46. Tablet 5.
47. Tablet 2.
48. Tablet 10.

1. The Garnett and Wells Interviews

1. William Garnett's father was Richard B. Garnett, a Virginian, who entered West Point in 1836. Lieutenant Garnett was the commanding officer of Fort Laramie

from 1852 to 1854. During this time he took an Oglala woman named Looks At Him as his common-law wife and she bore him a son, William. When the Civil War broke out Garnett joined the Confederate army with the rank of brigadier general. He was killed on July 3, 1863, during Pickett's charge in the Battle of Gettysburg. Donald F. Danker, "The Violent Deaths of Yellow Bear and John Richard Jr.," *Nebraska History* 63 (1982): 137.

Ricker wrote about a brief conversation he had with Antoine Herman in 1907 (Tablet 13): "Antoine Herman, of Kyle, told me that his father who lived at Laramie in those early days, told him that it was a question whether Garnett, or a sergeant or a certain private was the sire of Billy Garnett."

2. On June 26, 1849, the adobe trading post originally built by Sublette and Campbell and known by various names but most often as Fort Laramie, was sold to the U.S. government. Construction of log and timber buildings adjacent to the old structures began the following year. Remi Nadeau, *Fort Laramie and the Sioux Indians* (Englewood Cliffs NJ: Prentice-Hall Inc., 1967), 64-65.

3. In 1845 Col. Stephen Watts Kearny commanded an army expedition that went as far west as South Pass. Dwight L. Clarke, *Stephen Watts Kearny: Soldier of the West* (Norman: University of Oklahoma Press, 1961), 25.

Nicholas Janis was born in 1827. In 1845 he and his brother "Antoine" began trading with the Lakotas and spending much of their time in the vicinity of Fort Laramie. Nicholas married Martha, Red Cloud's niece. In the 1870s he and his wife operated a ranch east of the fort, which they sold in 1880. They then moved to Pine Ridge to be with Martha's people. Nicholas died in 1902. Janet Lecompte, "Antoine Janis," *The Mountain Men and the Fur Trade of the Far West*, ed. LeRoy R. Hafen 10 vols. (Glendale CA: Arthur H. Clark Co., 1971) 8: 196-201.

4. Peter John DeSmet, a young Catholic priest, helped found a mission to the Potawatomis in 1838 near present Council Bluffs, Iowa. Two years later he made his first ascent of the Platte River on his way to Flathead country. Father DeSmet traveled widely in the Far West spreading the word of his God until 1870. John K. Killoren, S. J., *"Come, Black Robe": DeSmet and the Indian Tragedy* (Norman: University of Oklahoma Press, 1994), 47, 339.

5. Ricker interviewed Ben Tibbitts in 1906 (Tablet 8). Tibbitts said he came west after the Civil War.

6. Most Plains tribes assembled in September and signed the treaty recognizing "the right of the United States government to establish roads, military and other posts" in Indian country. Equally as important was the attempt to prevent intertribal warfare and attacks on whites. Charles J. Kappler, ed., *Indian Affairs, Laws and Treaties* (Washington DC: GPO, 1904), 594-96. It was estimated that ten thousand Indians attended.

7. Todd Randall was a trader who had married a Brulé woman in the 1860s. He also occasionally served as a subagent. George E. Hyde, *Spotted Tail's Folk: A History of the Brulé Sioux* (Norman: University of Oklahoma Press, 1961), 145, 189.

8. Conquering Bear was killed in the Grattan fight near Fort Laramie on August 18, 1854. Donald F. Danker, "A High Price to Pay for a Lame Cow," *Kansas History* 10 (1987): 114.
9. Born about 1835, Young Man Afraid of His Horses was the son of Old Man Afraid of His Horses (1802–87) who was known among the Oglalas as "Our Brave Man," and who really was not afraid of anything. Old Man was the leader of the Hunkpatilla band, which later took the name Payabya band, meaning that they camped near the head of the circle, that is, near the eastern entrance. In 1868 Young Man succeeded his father and was elected as Shirt Wearer, one of six so chosen to lead the Oglala tribe. Young Man married the daughter of Henry Chatillion, and later married an Oglala full-blood. In 1877 Young Man enlisted as a U.S. Indian scout with the rank of sergeant. Termed a progressive Oglala, he died of heart failure near Newcastle, Wyoming, in 1893, while en route to the Crow Agency in Montana. Richard G. Hardorff, *The Surrender and Death of Crazy Horse* (Spokane: Arthur H. Clark Co., 1998), 39 n. 23. Also see Joseph G. Agonito, "Young Man Afraid of His Horses: The Reservation Years," *Nebraska History* 79 (1998): 116–32.
10. By this treaty, which was signed in late April, the Lakotas surrendered their claim to all land except a reservation encompassing roughly the western half of the Dakotas, eastern Montana, and northeastern Wyoming. They also promised to cease intertribal warfare. In payment the government promised to provide food, clothing and agricultural equipment, and instructors to show the Lakotas how to become farmers. Of more immediate importance to the Indians was the government's promise to remove the military posts in Montana and northern Wyoming. Kappler, *Indian Affairs*, 998–1007.
11. George Sword's interview is in Tablet 16. American Horse's interview is in Tablets 16, 33, and 35.
12. George W. Colhoff's interview is in Tablets 17 and 25. Red Cloud arrived at Fort Laramie from the Powder River country nearly six months after the Fort Laramie treaty was signed. Presents left there by the treaty commissioners were given to him after he signed. James C. Olson, *Red Cloud and the Sioux Problem* (Lincoln: University of Nebraska Press Bison Books, 1975), 79–81.
13. Article Six mentions "any individual belonging to said tribes of Indians, or legally incorporated with them." Kappler, *Indian Affairs*, 999.
14. For Red Cloud's account of these events see R. Eli Paul, ed. *Autobiography of Red Cloud: War Leader of the Oglalas* (Helena: Montana Historical Society Press, 1997), 64–70. Bull Bear was killed in November 1841. Robert W. Larson, *Red Cloud: Warrior-Statesman of the Lakota Sioux* (Norman: University of Oklahoma Press, 1997), 58.
15. Born in 1823, Spotted Tail was the head chief of the Brulé Lakotas. He was an unusually intelligent man, who was respected by both Indians and whites alike. Having experienced the superiority of the whites at an early age, Spotted Tail

guided his people in a dignified way on the difficult path of social reform until 1881, when an assassin's bullet ended his life. Hardorff note, *Death of Crazy Horse*, 49 n. 50.

Big Mouth, a Loafer band chief, lived with his followers near the Whetstone Agency. He was jealous of Spotted Tail's growing influence in the tribe and hoped to rise above him in the Lakota hierarchy. Agent D. C. Poole confirmed that alcohol was involved and that Spotted Tail had been warned of Big Mouth's intentions. The killing occurred in the early morning hours of October 27, 1869. D. C. Poole, *Among the Sioux of Dakota: Eighteen Months' Experience as an Indian Agent, 1869-70* (St. Paul: Minnesota Historical Society Press, 1988), 82-83, 93. Hyde described Big Mouth as "jovial and fat." He became a chief after Smoke died in 1864. Hyde, *Spotted Tail's Folk*, 100.

16. During the winter of 1880-81 "whiskey ranches" were established just south of the reservation border only about two miles from the Pine Ridge Agency. Agent Valentine McGillycuddy set up two police substations in an attempt to halt the illegal traffic, but this effort was not entirely successful. As a result a parcel of land five miles wide (north-south) and ten miles long was temporarily added to the reservation. The agency was then seven miles from the border and the agent reported, "we have had little or no trouble" with the whiskey peddlers. V. T. McGillycuddy, "Pine Ridge Agency, Dakota," *Annual Report of the Commissioner of Indian Affairs* (Washington DC: GPO, 1881), 45 (hereafter, Annual Report of the Commissioner); McGillycuddy, "Pine Ridge Agency, Dakota," *Annual Report of the Commissioner*, 1882, 35. This Nebraska extension had been removed from the public domain by executive order. In 1904 President Theodore Roosevelt restored the extension to the public domain. *Annual Report of the Department of the Interior* (Washington DC: GPO, 1905), 530.

17. John E. Smith was a brigadier general in the Civil War. In 1874 he was a colonel, Fourteenth Infantry, in command of Fort Laramie. Thomas R. Buecker, *Fort Robinson and the American West 1874-1899* (Lincoln: Nebraska State Historical Society, 1999), 6.

Born in 1848, Kicking Bear was the son of Old Black Fox, an Oglala chief, and Iron Cedar Woman, a sister of Chief Sitting Bull. Although an Oglala by birth, Kicking Bear became a Miniconjou band chief through his marriage to Woodpecker Woman, a niece of the Miniconjou leader Big Foot. Kicking Bear was a close ally of his cousin Crazy Horse, both having an inveterate hatred for the whites. According to Garnett, Kicking Bear ambushed and killed Frank S. Appleton, chief clerk at Red Cloud Agency, on February 9, 1874, to avenge the death of a Lakota relative who was slain by white men along the Platte. However, his main rise to notoriety came through his leading part in the Ghost Dance troubles of 1890. Kicking Bear died near Manderson, Pine Ridge, in 1904. Hardorff note, *Death of Crazy Horse*, 43 n. 35.

18. Frank Appleton was the son of Amos Appleton who had been hired to build the

Red Cloud Agency No. 2. Buecker, *Fort Robinson and the American West*, 213 n. 22. The agent was John J. Saville, a physician nominated by the Episcopal Church. He served as agent to the Oglalas from July 1873 through December 1875. Olson, *Red Cloud and the Sioux Problem*, 158, 216.
19. B. F. Walters was the agency trader. Buecker, *Fort Robinson and the American West*, 6.
20. John Farnham is mentioned in several tablets. Frequently Ricker would begin a sentence with "Farnham said" or "Farnham told me," but the Farnham interview in Tablet 12 consists of only two sentences. It is likely there is a missing tablet.
21. Whalen's interview in Tablet 13 discusses the agencies.
22. Baptiste Pourier told Ricker (Tablet 15) that a soldier caught Richard "in a house where a loose woman held forth" and ordered him to leave, whereupon Richard told the soldier he would get even with him for the insult. The murdered man was Corp. Francis Conrad, Fourth Infantry. The incident occurred on September 9, 1869. Hiram Kelly, Richard's partner, also said Richard was intoxicated. Bryan Jones, "John Richard, Jr., and the Killing at Fetterman," *Annals of Wyoming* 43 (1971): 243.
23. Jules Ecoffey began trading with the Lakota about 1854 and was good friends with Red Cloud. George E. Hyde, *Red Cloud's Folk, A History of the Oglala Sioux Indians* (Norman: University of Oklahoma Press, 1937), 196. Ecoffey and his partner, Adolph Cuny, operated a large cattle ranch and a road ranche near Fort Laramie. Paul L. Hedren, *Fort Laramie in 1876* (Lincoln: University of Nebraska Press, 1988), 45–46.
24. Although Richard had been indicted, Baptiste Pourier said President Grant promised to pardon Richard in return for his assistance in bringing the chiefs to Washington. The president's promise apparently convinced authorities in Wyoming Territory that there was no need for a trial. Richard accompanied the chiefs to Washington, but his role in their decision to go remains cloudy. Olson, *Red Cloud and the Sioux Problem*, 93. Approximately thirty Lakotas made the trip to Washington and spent more than a month there. John E. Smith, "Misc. No. 121," *Annual Report of the Commissioner*, 1870, 324.
25. Red Leaf was a chief of a Brulé band and a brother of Conquering Bear. Jesse M. Lee, "Spotted Tail Agency, Nebraska," *Annual Report of the Commissioner*, 1877, 67.
26. Col. Ranald Mackenzie, Fourth Cavalry, arrived at Camp Robinson on August 13, 1876, to begin disarming the Oglalas. He was in command of the camp from March 14 to May 26, 1877. Red Cloud's and Red Leaf's followers were camped on Chadron Creek about thirty miles northeast of the fort. Gen. George Crook issued the order to bring the Indians back to the agency, where they could be watched. Buecker, *Fort Robinson and the American West*, 85, 88, 198; Jerome A. Greene, "The Surrounding of Red Cloud and Red Leaf, 1876: A Preemptive Maneuver of the Great Sioux War," *Nebraska History* 82 (2001): 69–75.

27. Red Dog was the leader of the Obyuhpe Band, which Lakota verb means "to throw down," translated by George Hyde as "where they lay down or throw down their packs." This was one of the oldest and strongest groups among the Northern Oglalas. Red Dog was married to a sister of Red Cloud and maintained close association with the Bad Face band. Contemporary sources describe Red Dog as an orator, rather heavy set and with an intelligent face. His family was the keeper of the band's winter count, which record was later maintained by Cloud Shield, Red Dog's son. Hardorff note, *Death of Crazy Horse*, 39 n. 22.
28. Julia Bradford talked about her father, Henry Clay Clifford, in an interview with Ricker (Tablet 8).
29. The troops set out on October 22. Col. Ranald S. Mackenzie commanded the operation and his men went to Red Cloud's camp. Maj. George A. Gordon, Fifth Cavalry, commanded half of the brigade and went to Red Leaf's camp. Charles M. Robinson III, *Bad Hand: A Biography of General Ranald S. Mackenzie* (Austin, Tex.: State House Press, 1993), 203–4; Greene, "The Surrounding of Red Cloud and Red Leaf," 72.
30. Brothers Frank and Luther North became acquainted with the Pawnees in the late 1850s, and by 1861 Frank was working as a clerk and interpreter for a trader on the reservation in present Nance County, Nebraska. Troops of Pawnee scouts were organized on seven separate occasions for periods of up to a few months. If other tribes were represented they were a small minority. In addition to scouting, Pawnees fought beside the soldiers against the Lakotas, Cheyennes, and other old enemies. Frank commanded the scouts on all their sorties except the first, when he was second in command. Donald F. Danker, "The North Brothers and the Pawnee Scouts," *Nebraska History* 42 (1961): 161–79. For the 1876 campaign Frank enlisted one hundred Pawnees at their reservation in Indian Territory. They had been living there only about a year after being expelled from their old home in Nebraska. There was one Ponca in the troop, who had married a Pawnee woman. Donald F. Danker, ed., *Man of the Plains: Recollections of Luther North, 1856–1882* (Lincoln: University of Nebraska Press, 1961), 200.
31. The Pawnee Scouts rounded up 722 horses, which were later sold. Only about seventy or eighty guns were found. Women, children, and the elderly rode, but the warriors were forced to walk. Olson, *Red Cloud and the Sioux Problem*, 233.
32. George W. Manypenny led the seven-member commission that arrived at the Red Cloud Agency on September 6, 1876. The primary goal was to convince the Lakotas to surrender the Black Hills and all lands west of the 103rd meridian. The agencies were also to be moved either to the Missouri River or Indian Territory. Ibid., 224. Red Cloud told the commission that he wanted some younger men to visit Indian Territory so it is unlikely that he went. Spotted Tail and several others did investigate the southern reservations, but they did not like the country and were opposed to moving there. Ibid., 226, 231.

33. Baptiste "Big Bat" Pourier was interviewed on January 6, 1907 (Tablets 13 and 15). Frank Grouard's "pedigree" is discussed later in the interview.

After graduating from West Point, George Crook was assigned to the Fourth Infantry on July 1, 1852. By 1873 he had risen to the rank of brigadier general. Crook died on March 21, 1890. Charles M. Robinson III, *General Crook and the Western Frontier* (Norman: University of Oklahoma Press, 2001).

34. E. A. Howard, a civilian, had served as the agent at the Spotted Tail Agency for three years prior to the army's takeover in August 1876. Lee, "Spotted Tail Agency, Nebraska," *Annual Report of the Commissioner*, 1877, 65.

35. Dr. J. W. Daniels assumed the duties of agent at the old Sod Agency (Red Cloud No. 1) on the Platte River early in 1871. He served until August 1873. Olson, *Red Cloud and the Sioux Problem*, 145, 159. Agent J. J. Saville also called him an Indian Inspector. Saville, "Red Cloud Agency, Dakota," *Annual Report of the Commissioner*, 1874, 251.

36. Several army officers served as agents at this time. Garnett is probably referring to Lt. Jesse M. Lee, Ninth Infantry, who began his duties at the Spotted Tail Agency on March 3, 1877. He served until July 1, 1878. William J. Pollock, "Rosebud (formerly Spotted Tail) Agency, Dakota," *Annual Report of the Commissioner*, 1878, 38.

37. Howard was named agent for the Poncas in Indian Territory early in 1877. E. A. Howard, "Office of the Ponca Indian Agency Indian Territory," *Annual Report of the Commissioner*, 1877, 96.

38. Crook deposed Red Cloud and made Spotted Tail head chief in October 1876. Harry H. Anderson, "Indian Peace-Talkers and the Conclusion of the Sioux War of 1876," *Nebraska History* 44 (1963): 240.

39. Army officers served as acting agents prior to the arrival of James Irwin in June 1877. James Irwin, "Red Cloud Agency, Nebraska," *Annual Report of the Commissioner*, 1877, 62. Lt. Oscar Elting was the agent in the summer of 1876. Buecker, *Fort Robinson and the American West*, 85.

40. The commission, headed by William B. Allison, opened discussions with the Lakotas on September 20, 1875. The commissioners heard rumors that the Indians might ask as much as $50 million for the Black Hills. Olson, *Red Cloud and the Sioux Problem*, 208.

41. Capt. John G. Bourke met Three Bears, a Lakota, in 1876, and described him as "young in years but mature in thought." He also noted that Three Bears "made no pretensions as a speaker." In battle Three Bears depended upon "stealthy movements and crafty combinations" for success. Bourke met the Arapaho, Sharp Nose, at the same time and thought he would make a "lion-like attack" in battle. According to Bourke there were nearly four hundred Lakota, Arapaho, Shoshone, and Bannock scouts. John G. Bourke, *Mackenzie's Last Fight with the Cheyennes: A Winter Campaign in Wyoming and Montana* (Governor's Island, New York: Mili-

tary Service Institution, 1890; reprint, Bellevue, Nebr.: Old Army Press, 1970), 4, 12.

42. William Rowland was the Cheyenne interpreter. He married a Cheyenne woman in 1850, and remained with the tribe. George Bird Grinnell, *The Fighting Cheyennes* (Norman: University of Oklahoma Press, 1956), 360. Ricker wrote the following in Tablet 22:

> William Young Rowland was a native of Kentucky. Left home when 12 years old. Got in with the American Fur Company. It is said he went to Salt Lake in 1847 with an expedition. Mrs. Nellie Rowland, relict [widow] of Ben Rowland, Kyle, S.D. has photos of William Rowland's father and mother. I have seen them. The above is from Willis Rowland, son of Ben Rowland. James Rowland of Kirby, Montana, can give history of his father William Rowland. Ask for a sketch of Bill Rowland as interpreter for Arapahos & Cheyenne and his fine sign talking. Mr. Jones says he was one of the greatest sign talkers.

Ricker wrote a brief note about Louis Shangrau in Tablet 22: "Mrs. Louie Shangrau says, Jan. 22, 1907, that her husband died here at his home on Cane Creek, S.D., in January, 1899, aged over 50. She was a daughter of Nick Janis; name Louise." In Tablet 22, Ricker mentioned, "Louie Richard's widow's name is Mrs. Jennie Richard Merriman, lives on Lake Creek 5 miles from Mrs. Ellis Brown."

43. Ricker wrote the following note in Tablet 22: "Daylight's son, Richard Daylight was at 'Bat's' and he speaks good English. He says the Wind River Indians are Snakes or Shoshones. The Indians call them Snakes and the Whites call them Shoshones. He says these are a different tribe from the Crows." Tom Cosgrove commanded the Shoshone scouts. Bourke, *Mackenzie's Last Fight*, 9.

44. Addison E. Sheldon was director of fieldwork and then superintendent of the archives at the Nebraska State Historical Society from 1901 to 1911. Anne Polk Diffendal, "A Centennial History of the Nebraska State Historical Society, 1878–1978," *Nebraska History* 59 (1978): 333, 340.

45. In 1877 Agent James Irwin estimated there were eleven hundred Arapahoes under Black Coal at the Red Cloud Agency No. 2. Irwin, "Red Cloud Agency, Nebraska," *Annual Report of the Commissioner*, 1877, 63.

46. Garnett and other informants discussed at length the slaying of Crazy Horse.

The Indian delegates met with Rutherford B. Hayes on September 26, 1877. They discussed moving the agencies to the Missouri River, but all were opposed. The president told them it was too late to change the various agreements to send their annuities up the Missouri. He promised that in the spring new arrangements could be made to send the goods to a site of the Indians' choosing. Olson, *Red Cloud and the Sioux Problem*, 248–51.

47. Married to Sans Arc Woman, Yellow Bear was one of the principal Oglala chiefs of the Oyuhpe band. In 1877 he enlisted in the U.S. Indian Scouts with the rank of corporal and the same year visited Washington DC as a member of the Oglala delegation to see the President. Hardorff note, *Death of Crazy Horse*, 40 n. 26. This

Yellow Bear was not the one killed by John Richard. Employed by James Irwin as his personal interpreter, Leon Palladay was born of French parents in St. Louis about 1830. His experience with the Lakotas dates from 1845, when he was employed by the American Fur Company at Fort John, the forerunner of Fort Laramie. Ibid., 41 n. 31.

In an 1879 court deposition Palladay said he "talked the Sioux language" since he was twelve years old. Bayard H. Paine, "An Indian Depredation Claim that Proved A Boomerang," *Nebraska History Magazine* 15 (1934): 54.

48. Magloire Mousseau told Ricker that Richard and his nephew were killed by the Cheyennes (Tablet 28). W. R. Jones said Richard and a man named Palladay were killed by the Cheyennes (Tablet 2).

49. Hollow Horn Bear's interview is in Richard G. Hardorff, *Lakota Recollections of the Custer Fight: New Sources of Indian-Military History* (Lincoln: University of Nebraska Press, 1997), 176–86.

Spotted Tail returned to the agency on April 6, 1877, "after an absence of over fifty days." He had convinced Roman Nose, Touch the Cloud, Red Bear, High Bear, and more than nine hundred of their followers to come to the agency. They arrived on April 14. Lee, "Spotted Tail Agency, Nebraska," *Annual Report of the Commissioner*, 1877, 66. Garnett used the term "Sitting Bull Indians" to refer to any of the Indians who were reluctant to come to the agency. Sitting Bull was a Hunkpapa leader.

50. A graduate of West Point, 2d Lt. William Philo Clark was assigned to the Second Cavalry on June 15, 1868. He was promoted to first lieutenant on July 10, 1869, and served as regimental adjutant until July 1876. On January 25, 1881, he was promoted to captain, which rank he held until his death on September 22, 1884. Upon the transfer of reservation management from the Indian Bureau to the War Department in 1876, Clark was assigned to Camp Robinson as the military agent and placed in charge of the U.S. Indian Scouts. He was a confidant to Gen. George Crook, commander of the Department of the Platte, with whom he was in constant communication regarding the volatile state of affairs at Red Cloud Agency. After the ill-fated removal of the Lakotas to the Missouri River late in 1877, Clark was relieved from his assignment and returned to Company K, Second Cavalry, for field service. Known to the Indians as White Hat, Clark was an expert in sign communication. As a result, he was directed in 1881 by Gen. William T. Sherman to compile a manual for use by army officers. Clark had barely finished his research in 1884 when he suddenly died. His work was published the following year under the title, *The Indian Sign Language* (Philadelphia: L. R. Hamersly Co., 1885). Hardorff note, *Death of Crazy Horse*, 30 n. 8.

Dr. James Irwin served as the Oglala Indian agent from July 1, 1877, through December 1878. He resigned over philosophical differences with the commissioner of Indian affairs and with the Indian Bureau stemming from the mismanagement of the department. Hardorff note, *Death of Crazy Horse*, 41 n. 30.

51. José Merrivale and Frank C. Boucher accompanied Spotted Tail and 250 Brulé headmen from the agency on February 13, 1877, to search for Crazy Horse. Spotted Tail convinced many Lakotas to surrender at the agency, but he did not find Crazy Horse. It was April before Crazy Horse concluded his cause was hopeless and set out for the agency. Kingsley M. Bray, "Crazy Horse and the End of the Great Sioux War," *Nebraska History* 79 (1998): 106, 112.
52. Col. Ranald S. Mackenzie's force of 750 cavalrymen and 350 Pawnee Scouts attacked Dull Knife's village of two hundred lodges on November 25, 1876. It was a rout and nearly all of the Cheyennes' tepees, supplies, and horses were captured. Six soldiers were killed and twenty-five were wounded. The attack occurred on the Red or North Fork of the Powder River. Jerome A. Greene, *Yellowstone Command: Colonel Nelson A. Miles and the Great Sioux War, 1876–1877* (Lincoln: University of Nebraska Press, 1991), 147–48.
53. Gen. George Crook's army fought the Lakotas at Slim Buttes on September 9, 1876. Jerome A. Greene, *Slim Buttes, 1876: An Episode of the Great Sioux War* (Norman: University of Oklahoma Press, 1982), 61.
54. In September 1876 a commission treated for the sale of the Black Hills with the Sioux chiefs who were not fighting the army. The commissioners succeeded, in part, because they ignored Article Twelve of the Treaty of 1868 calling for the signatures of three-fourths of the adult males before any sale of land was allowed. Olson, *Red Cloud and the Sioux Problem*, 229. On the trip to Washington in 1896 Philip Wells learned that only 223 or 224 adult males signed the treaty. Philip H. Wells, "Ninety-six Years Among the Indians of the Northwest—Adventures and Reminiscences of an Indian Scout and Interpreter in the Dakotas," *North Dakota History* 15 (1948): 274.
55. Washakie was chief of the Eastern Shoshones for fifty years until his death in 1900. Grace Raymond Hebard, *Washakie: Chief of the Shoshones* (Lincoln: University of Nebraska Press Bison Books, 1995), 283. Although Ricker frequently mentioned the new Fort Reno it was never "described." The same can be said of the Snake or Shoshone scouts.
56. Previously Garnett said Sharp Nose was the Arapaho sergeant.
57. Grinnell called the Cheyenne simply Beaver Dam and said he was captured on November 22. Grinnell, *The Fighting Cheyennes*, 362. According to Bourke the Cheyenne was captured on November 17 or 18 by a party of scouts while they were on patrol. Bourke, *Mackenzie's Last Fight*, 11.
58. Ricker made some notes about Bush in Tablet 39 that were based on an article in *The Light* for January 1905. Ricker wrote, "It is stated that he has been Policeman at the Agency since Sept. 1, 1879. He was conspicuous for bravery in the Two Sticks trouble at the Bad Lands and along the Cheyenne river in 1894. Besides these points, interview him abt. the Black hills Treaty and the Red Cloud Agency, abt. both of which he is well informed." If Ricker interviewed Bush the notes have been lost.

59. Sitting Bear arrived on the morning of November 23. Mackenzie decided to attack this camp rather than continue the search for Crazy Horse's camp. Bourke, *Mackenzie's Last Fight*, 13.
60. Ricker interviewed William L. Judkins, who had served under Crook in 1876-77. Box 19, Ricker Coll.
61. Known among the Lakotas as Plenty Wolves, Yankton Charley was a Dakota who had married into the Oglala tribe. In 1877 Plenty Wolves was enlisted as a U.S. Indian Scout and appears to have been quite popular with the military personnel at Camp Robinson. For his account of the killing of Crazy Horse, see Helen H. Blish, *A Pictographic History of the Oglala Sioux* (Lincoln: University of Nebraska Press, 1967), 401-2. Hardorff note, *Death of Crazy Horse*, 54 n. 57.
62. In Tablet 10 Ricker wrote the following note about Samuel Last Horse: "He it was who in the Cheyenne battle with No Neck was one of the advance scouts and could not get away till Garnett and Bat advanced and released them."
63. Lt. John A. McKinney, Fourth Cavalry, with Company M was advancing when a small party of Cheyennes hiding in a gully opened fire. McKinney was killed and six of his men were wounded. Bourke, *MacKenzie's Last Fight*, 23.
64. In 1878 the Cheyennes under Little Wolf and Dull Knife escaped from the reservation in Indian Territory to return to their homeland in the north. They separated on the North Platte River and Dull Knife's band was soon captured and taken to Camp Robinson. Little Wolf's band wintered in the Nebraska Sandhills and in the spring continued their trek northward into Montana. They surrendered to the army near Fort Keogh in March. Grinnell, *The Fighting Cheyennes*, 402-13.
65. David Y. Mears's interview is in Tablet 24. He was born in Pennsylvania in 1833. From 1874 to 1879 he was transportation manager for General Crook on his Indian campaigns. Mears then settled near Fort Niobrara and then at Chadron, Nebraska, where he served as the town's first mayor. David Y. Mears, "Campaigning Agains Crazy Horse," *Proceedings and Collections of the Nebraska State Historical Society* 10 (1907): 68-77.
66. The necklace is illustrated in Bourke's *Mackenzie's Last Fight*, 45.
67. It was later determined that forty Cheyennes lost their lives. Ibid., 27-28.
68. 68. John B. Sanborn was a brigadier general in the Civil War. Francis B. Heitman, *Historical Register and Dictionary of the United States Army* (Washington DC: GPO, 1903), 858. He served on the commission investigating the Fetterman debacle and was a member of the Indian Peace Commission of 1867. Sanborn could be described as pro-Indian. Olson, *Red Cloud and the Sioux Problem*, 53, 59.
69. Patrick E. Connor enlisted in the army in 1839, and was mustered out in April 1866 with the rank of brevet major-general. Early in 1865 he took command of the District of the Plains. He had overall command of expeditions to the Powder and Tongue rivers during the winter of 1865-66 that Keeps The Battle was referring to. Brigham D. Madsen, *Glory Hunter: A Biography of Patrick Edward Connor* (Salt Lake City: University of Utah Press, 1990).

70. White Thunder was the leader of the Brulé Loafer band. He had an excellent reputation as a brave and honest man, who was regarded as a progressive leader during the reservation years. Elderly Brulés credit him with the slaying of Capt. W. D. Fouts on Horse Creek in 1865. In 1884 White Thunder and his old father were assassinated by Young Spotted Tail after an incident involving the stealing of White Thunder's young wife. Hardorff note, *Death of Crazy Horse*, 98 n. 5.

Later Ricker learned that Taggart's name was Charles Tackett. He was married to Red Road, the daughter of Spotted Tail. Susan Bordeaux Bettelyoun and Josephine Waggoner, *With My Own Eyes: A Lakota Woman Tells Her People's History*, ed. Emily Levine (Lincoln: University of Nebraska Press Bison Books, 1999), 130.

In 1891 Capt. F. A. Whitney described Charles Tackett as "the Rosebud Guide and interpreter." He went on to say that Tackett "has lived with the Rosebud Indians for years, knows them thoroughly, and is intelligent and trustworthy." Whitney to asst. adj. gen., Jan. 9, 1891, Entry 2546, Box 127, Records of the U.S. Army Continental Commands, Record Group 393, NARA.

71. Although Sword said he left about January 1 (Tablet 16) Olson concluded that the mission to Crazy Horse began late in the month as Garrett says. Olson, *Red Cloud and the Sioux Problem*, 237 n. 90.

72. Spotted Tail left about the middle of February 1877. Lee, "Spotted Tail Agency, Nebraska," *Annual Report of the Commissioner*, 1877, 66.

73. J. Wesley Rosenquest joined the army in 1871 and was promoted to second lieutenant in the cavalry in 1876. He left the military in 1877. Heitman, *Historical Register*, 846.

74. Short Buffalo recalled that He Dog gave Lieutenant Clark a shirt, horse, and saddle, and Crazy Horse gave Red Cloud a shirt. Eleanor Hinman, "Oglala Sources on the Life of Crazy Horse," *Nebraska History* 57 (1976): 40.

75. Crazy Horse and his followers, numbering about eleven hundred, arrived at Camp Robinson on May 6, 1877. General Crook met with them on May 25 to discuss the location of their agency and a trip to Washington to visit the President. Irwin, "Red Cloud Agency, Nebraska," *Annual Report of the Commissioner*, 1877, 63; Olson, *Red Cloud and the Sioux Problem*, 240. At first Crazy Horse wanted to go, but an increasing divisiveness within his band and with white officials finally led to his refusal. Crazy Horse's increasing defiance fueled rumors of an outbreak. The army finally decided that he must be arrested and sent to Chicago until conditions became more secure. Four hundred cavalrymen, three hundred Sioux, and four hundred Arapahos set out to capture him on September 4 and he was killed the next day. Buecker, *Fort Robinson and the American West*, 103–16.

76. Robert O. Pugh was a native of England who married a Lakota woman (Tablet 12). Ricker interviewed him on several occasions.

77. In the 1870s Two Strike was a chief of the Brulés. Lee, "Spotted Tail Agency, Ne-

braska," *Annual Report of the Commissioner,* 1877, 67. He was born in 1821 and died in 1914. Hyde, *Spotted Tail's Folk,* 31.

78. Obviously the several following paragraphs are Ricker's interjection and not part of Garnett's interview. Ricker had more to say about Crazy Horse in Tablet 22. Some of the information undoubtedly came from informants who knew the Oglala warrior, but Ricker did not mention a source:

>In personal appearance Crazy Horse was slightly below medium size and his weight was not above 140 pounds. His face was thin, and after he became a man and received a bullet for a private revenge through his head from side to side his color deepened, though when young his complexion was fair and his hair light and long, touching the ground when combed out. His positive qualities made him feared as well as respected by his people; but not a voice can be heard to speak against his name. His idiocracies [idiosyncrasies?] were so much a part of himself that they were never laid aside, but were as unbending as all his clearly defined habits. Smoking the same pipe with other persons, the tobacco must not be packed down in the bowl with a stick as was the almost universal custom; it must be pressed down with the thumb by all the smokers quaffing the pipe or he would not touch it (see elsewhere abt. his not painting etc). His aversion to mourning as the Indians do was shown when his only brother, brave as himself, died by the bullet of an enemy, he smothered his emotion, if any he had, and said he would give expression to his feelings by severing his long hair from his head. Cold, calculating, unemotional, nothing could set aside his purpose. Swift to strike, his blows fell like hail. Independent, headstrong, self-reliant, they called him "Crazy" Horse. If there was any other origin to which his name can be ascribed, it has not been learned by the author. (See elsewhere for his faith that he would not die by a bullet.) (Get his "medicine" from Garnett.) Little Big Man was his evil genius. Twice he held him when he was over a yawning grave. Acting according to Indian standards, he possessed himself of another Indian's wife. The Indian stalked into his tent to kill him. Little Big Man knowing that Crazy Horse would take his assailant's life seized the former and held him while the other improved his chance to send a bullet through his head. When Crazy Horse perished Little Big Man interfered again. George Colhoff who has no high opinion of Indian courage, says the only instance he ever saw of it was when Crazy Horse chased _____ right into Fort Laramie all alone.

In the interview with George Colhoff, Ricker mentioned only that "Crazy Horse ran some men into Laramie." The interview is in Tablet 17.

79. The reference is to Helen "Nellie" Laravie. Born along the South Platte about 1860, she was one of four daughters of Joseph Laravie, a French trader, and a Southern Cheyenne woman. Among her mother's people, Helen Laravie was known as Chi-Chi. In 1878 she settled among Lip's Wajaje band near Eagle Nest Butte on Pine Ridge and was known among the Lakotas as Ista Gli Win, "Brown Eyes Woman." Hardorff note, *Death of Crazy Horse,* 26 n. 1.

80. A member of Big Road's band, Black Elk participated in the Fetterman battle on

December 21, 1866, during which his right leg was crushed, the injury making him a cripple for life. Black Elk's father, named Black Elk also, was a brother of Makes the Song, who was the paternal grandfather of Crazy Horse. Black Elk was married to White Cow Sees, and upon his death at Pine Ridge in 1889 she married Good Thunder, a brother of the deceased. Hardorff note, *Death of Crazy Horse,* 29 n. 6.

Capt. William J. Fetterman and about eighty troops were lured into an ambush by Crazy Horse and annihilated near Fort Phil Kearny. Larson, *Red Cloud: Warrior-Statesman of the Lakota Sioux,* 100–101.

81. Born along the Cache La Poudre in Colorado, John Provost was the son of "Old Man Provost" and a Lakota woman. In 1879 John Provost was employed as interpreter at Red Cloud Agency when his brother, Charley Provost, committed suicide after a dispute with Agent Valentine McGillycuddy. John Provost avenged his brother's death by wantonly slaying Bernard Clementi, for which he served five years in the Detroit House of Corrections. Hardorff note, *Death of Crazy Horse,* 29 n. 7.

82. Captain Jack and his Modocs had fled from their reservation in Oregon. Fighting broke out when an attempt was made to arrest him in November 1871. For the next seven months the army pursued Captain Jack across the lava beds on the Oregon-California border and fought several skirmishes. On April 11, 1873, Jack and his lieutenants met with a peace commission and following a prearranged plan, killed Gen. E. R. S. Canby and Methodist minister Eleazar Thomas. The Modoc band was forced to surrender and those involved in the killings were tried for their crimes. Jack and three others were executed on October 3, 1873. Keith A. Murray, *The Modocs and Their War* (Norman: University of Oklahoma Press, 1959).

83. As a result of state pressure to occupy ceded Indian lands, the Nez Perce Indians were ordered by the U.S. Army to leave the Wallowa Valley in Oregon and settle on a reservation by April 1, 1877. This removal policy resulted in an armed confrontation on June 17, 1877, during which the U.S. troops were decisively defeated. Fearing indiscriminate reprisals by the whites, Chief Joseph's Nez Perce decided to seek sanctuary in Canada and began an epic trek of some thirteen hundred miles, which carried them across the Bitterroot Mountains, through Yellowstone Park, and into present Montana. During this remarkable retreat, the Indians fought six battles in four months and inflicted heavy casualties on their white adversaries. However, the end was inevitable, and as a result of the extreme suffering of the young and the elderly, Chief Joseph finally surrendered on October 5, 1877, in the Bear Paw Mountains of Montana, only a short distance from the Canadian border. Hardorff note, *Death of Crazy Horse,* 31 n. 10.

84. Known to the Indians as Cut Foot, Frank D. Yates was a partner in the Yates Trading Company located at Red Cloud Agency. He was a brother of Capt. George F. Yates, Seventh Cavalry, who was slain with Custer's battalion at the Little Bighorn, June 25, 1876. Frank Yates and his father-in-law, Capt. W. H. Brown, also

operated the first passenger, mail, and express stagecoach from Cheyenne north to Custer City in January 1876. Hardorff note, *Death of Crazy Horse*, 33 n. 13.

85. Born in 1846 Woman's Dress was the son of the Oglala Bad Face, and was a paternal grandson of Chief Smoke, in whose camp both Crazy Horse and Red Cloud grew up. Woman's Dress was a brother of Keeps the Battle, both related to the renowned Northern Oglala, Iron Hawk. Apparently they had come from one family, but being orphaned at an early age they were raised by different relatives. Woman's Dress was also related to Louis Shangrau and Baptiste Pourier through marriage. In 1877 Woman's Dress enlisted in the U.S. Indian Scouts and was later transferred to the Pine Ridge Indian Police. His service record includes some twenty reenlistments, each for a period of six months, for which he received rations and $40 per month. Some traditional Oglalas described Woman's Dress's character as that of "a two-edged sword against his own people." Later in life he became a lonely, embittered man who complained that he had been "thrown away," discarded not only by his own people, but also by the whites, who never gave him the recognition that he so rightfully deserved. Woman's Dress died on Wounded Knee Creek, Pine Ridge, January 9, 1921. Hardorff note, *Death of Crazy Horse*, 33, n. 14. In Tablet 43 Ricker mentioned, "old Woman's Dress is an old timer but not so bright intellectually."

86. Luther Prentice Bradley was appointed lieutenant colonel of the Fifty-First Illinois Infantry on November 6, 1861. After the Civil War ended he accepted a commission as lieutenant colonel in the Twenty-Seventh U.S. Infantry. In 1869 Colonel Bradley was transferred to the Ninth Infantry. He was the commanding officer at Fort Robinson from May to November 1877. Buecker, *Fort Robinson and the American West*, 97, 198.

87. Born about 1821, Blue Horse was known to the whites as a progressive Oglala. He was a member of the U.S. Indian Scouts and resided in the Wakpamni District on Pine Ridge. Hardorff note, *Death of Crazy Horse*, 40 n. 27.

Dr. Eastman talked to Blue Horse in 1890 and called him the "chief emeritus" of the Loafer band. Blue Horse said he had always been a friend to the white man and that he was one of the first to scout for the army. He also was one of the first Indians to go to Europe with Buffalo Bill Cody. Charles A. Eastman, *From Deep Woods to Civilization: Chapters in the Autobiography of an Indian* (Lincoln: University of Nebraska Press Bison Books, 1977), 78.

Three Bears was an Oglala band chief. In 1876 he enlisted in the U.S. Indian Scouts with the rank of sergeant and in the same year visited Washington DC, as a member of the Oglala delegation. Hardorff note, *Death of Crazy Horse*, 40 n. 28.

88. Garnett was interviewed by Hugh Scott in 1920. The information he provided is similar to that in the Ricker interview except Garnett told Scott about a plot to kill Crazy Horse:

> So I went back to Fort Robinson and I told General Crook and Lieutenant Clark that the Indians were coming—those that they wanted—and they came there in about one-half hour after I got there. They plotted how to get

ahold of this man, Crazy Horse. It was told there about his trying to do away with Crook. Those friendly Indians were surprised to hear that they were going to get away with Crook as they didn't know anything about it. So it was planned that every one of those Indian chiefs was going to pick out four brave men of their respective bands, and that night those picked men were going to the Crazy Horse village (Crazy Horse's people did not mix with the others; they had a separate village of their own) and kill Crazy Horse. The man who actually killed him was going to get $300.00. There was a horse Lieutenant Clark had, and he was also going to get that horse. Now this was a kind of private council in General Bradley's apartments, but he was not there, he was at his office. Those present were General Crook, Lieutenant Clark, Frank Gruard, Baptiste Pourier and myself, and the rest were all Indians, Red Cloud, Little Wound, Red Dog, Young Man Afraid of His Horse, No Flesh, Yellow Bear, High Wolf, Slow Bull, Black Bear, American Horse, Three Bears, Blue Horse and No Water. These are all Oglalas.

Carroll Friswold and Robert A. Clark, eds., *The Killing of Chief Crazy Horse* (Glendale CA: Arthur H. Clark Co., 1976), 79.

The Garnett interview with Scott then continued in much the same vein as that with Ricker. In 1930 Red Feather told Eleanor Hinman that Crook had promised to give $100 and a sorrel horse to anyone who killed Crazy Horse. Hinman, "Oglala Sources," 27.

89. Captions for a series of pictographs, now lost, portray He Dog as a close friend of Crazy Horse and an advocate for peace. Hardorff, *Death of Crazy Horse*, 131-50.

90. Julius Wilmot Mason obtained a commission as second lieutenant in the Second Cavalry on April 26, 1861, and was promoted to first lieutenant on June 1, 1861. Having been transferred to the Fifth Cavalry on August 3, 1861, he was promoted to captain on December 6, 1862, and was transferred on July 1, 1876, to become a major in the Third Cavalry. In 1863 Mason received brevets of major and lieutenant colonel for gallant and meritorious service in the battles of Beverly Ford and Brandy Station, both in Virginia. He died on December 19, 1882. On September 2, 1877, Mason and Companies D, E, and G, Third Cavalry, arrived at Camp Robinson from Fort Laramie to strengthen the garrison. Hardorff note, *Death of Crazy Horse*, 42 n. 33.

91. The name of this full-blood wife was Black Shawl Woman. Born in an Oglala camp about 1843, she was the daughter of Old Red Feather, whose family maintained close kinship ties with Big Road's band, Itesica. In 1871 Black Shawl Woman became the second wife of Crazy Horse. This marriage resulted in the birth of their only child, a daughter named They are Afraid of Her, who died in 1873 as a result of frail health. Black Shawl died in 1927, at age eighty-four, apparently victim of the influenza that swept the reservations in the 1920s. For an account of Crazy Horse's death witnessed by Black Shawl's brother, see the Red Feather Interview in Hinman, "Oglala Sources," 24-30. Hardorff note, *Death of Crazy Horse*, 43 n. 34.

92. Young Black Fox was the half brother of Kicking Bear and Flying Hawk. On Sep-

tember 4, 1877, Young Black Fox commanded Crazy Horse's warriors in his absence. The courage displayed by Black Fox on that occasion earned him the respect of both Indians and whites alike. In the same year Young Black Fox sought sanctuary in Canada, but he was killed on his return to the United States in 1881 by Indians of an enemy tribe. Hardorff note, *Death of Crazy Horse*, 44 n. 36.

93. Col. Henry E. Maynadier was stationed at Fort Laramie in 1866. In that year a commission headed by Edward B. Taylor met with Lakota leaders in June to discuss safe passage on the Bozeman Trail. John S. Gray, *Custer's Last Campaign: Mitch Boyer and the Little Bighorn Reconstructed* (Lincoln: University of Nebraska Press, 1991), 36–37.

While escorting several Oglala and Brulé bands to Fort Kearny to be held as prisoners, Capt. W. D. Fouts and four enlisted men of the Seventh Iowa Volunteer Cavalry were slain near the junction of Horse Creek and the North Platte River in June 1865. According to the Oglala Thunder Bear, Captain Fouts was killed by Charging Shield and Foam. Hardorff note, *Death of Crazy Horse*, 45 n. 38.

94. One of two sons of Black Fox and Iron Cedar Woman, Flying Hawk was born in an Oglala camp near present Rapid City, South Dakota, in 1852. He was a brother of Kicking Bear and a nephew of the Hunkpapa Sitting Bull. Flying Hawk was also related to Crazy Horse, who was his cousin. Flying Hawk married two sisters, White Day and Goes Out Looking, of whom the latter bore him a son named Felix. Flying Hawk died at Pine Ridge on December 24, 1931, the cause rumored to have been starvation. Hardorff note, *Death of Crazy Horse*, 45 n. 39.

Second Lt. Henry Moore Harrington was a member of C Company, Seventh Cavalry, and participated in the battle of the Little Bighorn on June 25, 1876. After the engagement, survivors were unable to identify his remains and Harrington was declared MIA and presumed killed. His whereabouts on June 25 have been the subject of continued speculation. Hardorff note, *Death of Crazy Horse*, 46 n. 40.

95. Agent Hugh D. Gallagher included a eulogy of No Flesh in his annual report dated August 27, 1889. Gallagher, "Report of Pine Ridge Agency," *Annual Report of the Commissioner*, 1889, 153:

> The death of this prominent Sioux chief, which occurred a few weeks ago merits more than a passing notice. No Flesh in early life was a scout under General Crook, and is credited by that officer with having saved his life, by warning him against attending a council with Crazy Horse and his band, where his assassination had been plotted. The deep interest manifested by No Flesh in the education of Indian youth was of great assistance to the agent, being, as it was, of a practical character. Children that had escaped from school might evade the vigilant eye of the police but No Flesh would invariably find them and return them back to School. He asked the Sioux commissioners to permit his name to head the list in approval of the bill presented by them. This privilege was granted him and he was proud of it.
>
> Knowing he was going to die he sent for me near midnight, and asked me to remember him kindly to the Great Father, and to see that he was buried

with honors fitting a person of his rank, and above all, have the American flag spread over his coffin. His instructions were carried out to the letter, and the body now rests in the neat little cemetery at the agency.

No Water was the leader of the Hoka Yuta (Badger Eaters), a band of the Itesica Oglalas. No Water was married to Black Buffalo Woman, a daughter of Red Cloud's brother, and had a family of three children. The oldest child was a son also named No Water, who was still living at Pine Ridge in 1930. Born about 1863, Young No Water is chiefly remembered for his failed assassination attempt on the life of Indian Agent Valentine T. McGillycuddy in 1880.

Hardorff note, *Death of Crazy Horse*, 46 n. 42.

96. The son of Crippled Warbonnet, Lone Horn was born into a distinguished family whose ancestors were hereditary leaders of the Miniconjous. His brother was a Shirt Wearer, who was painted by George Catlin in 1832. Upon the latter's death in 1836, Lone Horn took his brother's name and became the patriarch councilor of the tribe. Lone Horn had four sons who each became leaders of Miniconjou bands. Their names were Frog, Roman Nose, Touch the Cloud (1837-1905), and Spotted Elk, the latter better known as Big Foot (1826-90). Richard G. Hardorff, *The Oglala Lakota Crazy Horse: A Preliminary Genealogical Study and an Annotated Listing of Primary Sources* (Mattituck NJ: J. M. Carroll and Co., 1985), 27-28.

97. Touch the Cloud became a Miniconjou band leader upon his father's death in 1875. Evidence suggests that Touch the Cloud was related to Rattle Blanket Woman, the mother of Crazy Horse, who may have been his paternal aunt. Upon his surrender in 1877, Touch the Cloud enlisted in the U.S. Indian Scouts with the rank of sergeant. He died on the Cheyenne River Reservation on September 5, 1905. Hardorff note, *Death of Crazy Horse*, 48 n. 44.

98. Known to the early French as Sans Arcs, this tribe was one of the seven groups that make up the Teton Sioux. In the Lakota language, the Sans Arcs were known as the Itazipco Oyate, which means "No Bows" or "Without Bows." The name is said to have origin when a Sans Arc band was defeated east of the Missouri River after discarding their bows on the advice of a bardache. Hardorff note, *Death of Crazy Horse*, 50 n. 51.

99. Red Bear was a band chief who surrendered in March 1877. He enlisted with the rank of sergeant and led the Sans Arc contingent of U.S. Indian Scouts. Hardorff note, *Death of Crazy Horse*, 50 n. 52.

100. Upon his surrender in 1877, Little Wolf enlisted as a U.S. Indian Scout along with his brother, Lone Bear. They had kinship ties with the Oglala Bad Face band, and may have been cousins of Woman's Dress, although the Oglala, He Dog, told Hinman that they were brothers. However, other sources contradict He Dog's statement, the contradiction perhaps resulting from a mistranslation of Lakota kinship terminology, which identifies the male children of one's paternal uncle as brothers also. Hardorff note, *Death of Crazy Horse*, 34 n. 15.

101. Lone Bear was a Northern Oglala born about 1847. Upon his surrender in 1877, he

enlisted as a U.S. Indian Scout and was later transferred to the Pine Ridge Indian Police. In this capacity he served the white authorities for more than twenty years. It was said of him that he had fought in the Little Bighorn battle of 1876, and that he had cut off the tongue of one of Reno's wounded troopers, keeping the grisly memento the remainder of his life. Hardorff note, *Death of Crazy Horse*, 34 n. 16.

102. The Bad Face band was one of seven bands that made up the Oglala tribe. They were known among the Lakotas as the Itesica, which is derived from *ite*, which means "face," and *sica*, which means "bad." According to Hyde, *Red Cloud's Folk*, 305, the name Bad Face was applied to Smoke's nephew, Spotted Bear, and later to the whole camp, as a result of domestic quarreling between the latter and his wife. However, William K. Powers, *Oglala Religion* (Lincoln: University of Nebraska Press, 1977), 31, states the name was derived from their manner of painting their faces for war. Hardorff note, *Death of Crazy Horse*, 34 n. 7.

103. Although Ricker dismisses this whole matter as a fabrication, Woman's Dress's statement merits serious consideration because of corroborating sources. According to Lieutenant Clark, one of his enlisted Indian Scouts commenced a liaison with an Oglala girl who lived in the lodge next to Crazy Horse so as to be able to monitor the chief's intentions. Clark did not disclose the name of the scout, but He Dog reveals that both Lone Bear and Woman's Dress spied at Crazy Horse's lodge. Hardorff note, *Death of Crazy Horse*, 37 n. 19.

104. On March 2, 1889, President Grover Cleveland signed a Sioux Bill that provided for division of the Sioux reservation, allotments in severalty, and cession of surplus lands. Purchasers were to pay $1.25 per acre for three years, $0.75 for the next two years, and $0.50 thereafter; the government was to provide for surveys and pay for them; benefits with respect to education and farming were not to be charged to land sales; a $3 million trust fund was to be established; and Indians from the Red Cloud and Red Leaf bands were to be paid $40 a head for horses taken from them in 1876.

During June 1889 a special commission consisting of former Governor Charles Foster of Ohio, Senator William Warner of Missouri, and Maj. Gen. George Crook, was able to persuade the Lakotas to accept the land agreement and thus obtained the required signatures necessary for its approval. As a result of the land sale, South Dakota became a state on November 2, 1889, and on February 10, 1890, Congress passed a homesteading bill for the region between the White River and Cheyenne River, the land rush commencing on February 12. Hardorff note, *Death of Crazy Horse*, 38 n. 20.

105. F. M. Conn was occasionally mentioned in the Chadron Times in the early 1900s.
106. Bordeaux's interview with biographical data is in Tablet 11.
107. The Ricker collection contains a crude sketch map titled "Made by Garnett to illustrate locations of buildings when Crazy Horse was killed" (Box 28, folder 91). Buildings, represented by rectangles, are arranged around an open area. Two "Barracks" are on the east side and two more are on the west side. On the south side is the "Guardhouse" and "Adjt's office." In front of the guardhouse is a rectangle

divided into ten sections, labeled "Artillery Parked." In the northwest corner is a building labeled "Lt. Clark's." Four other rectangles are not labeled.

108. Also known as Charging Bear, Little Big Man was a member of Big Road's (Wide Trail) Oglala band of Bad Faces, which surrendered at Camp Robinson in 1877. Having enlisted as a U.S. Indian Scout, Little Big Man was transferred to the Pine Ridge Indian Police in 1879 in recognition of his valuable service to the military. He was a close ally of Crazy Horse and was said to have been his cousin. A son of Little Big Man, named Bad Whirlwind, and a daughter were living at Standing Rock Agency as late as the 1920s. Hardorff note, *Death of Crazy Horse*, 28 n. 4.

109. Ricker wrote the following note about the Corn Band in Tablet 22, verso page 15.

> The Corn band was a band similar to the Loafers, as they seemed to be of peaceable instincts and partial to the whites, but they hanged round the Spotted Tail Agency. Swift Bear was their chief. He held, with others, on to Crazy Horse after Little Big Man was shaken off.

110. Ricker wrote the following note about the Corn band in Tablet 22:

> The Corn band was a band similar to the Loafers, as they seemed to be of peaceable instincts and partial to the whites, but they hanged round the Spotted Tail Agency. Swift Bear was their chief. He held, with others, on to Crazy Horse after Little Big Man was shaken off.

111. American Horse's description is in Tablet 35.

112. Ricker may have seen the articles in the *Crawford Tribune* (April 17 and June 16, 1903) that identified the soldier as Pvt. William Gentles. Recent scholarship casts doubt on this identification and other candidates are possible. Ephriam D. Dickson III, "Crazy Horse: Who Really Wielded the Bayonet that Killed the Oglala Leader," *Greasy Grass* 12 (1996): 2-10.

113. Dr. Valentine T. McGillycuddy was hired as a contract surgeon at Camp Robinson in 1877. On March 5, 1879, he began his duties as the new agent at Pine Ridge. He served in this capacity until May 18, 1886. McGillycuddy, "Pine Ridge Agency, Dakota," *Annual Report of the Commissioner*, 1879, 37-40; James M. Bell, "Pine Ridge Agency, Dakota," *Annual Report of the Commissioner*, 1886, 76-77.

114. Born about 1811, Worm was one of three children of the Oglala, Makes the Song. Both he and his father were known by the name Crazy Horse, which was a family name passed on from one generation to another. Worm's sister was Rattling Stone Woman, born about 1815, who later married One Horse. Little is known about Worm's brother. Apparently, he was slain in 1844 during a raid on the Crow Indians. Worm married the Minneconjou, Rattle Blanket Woman, from which union a daughter was born about 1838, followed by a son in 1840, the latter being the renowned Crazy Horse who was killed at Camp Robinson in 1877. Upon his wife's suicide about 1844, Worm married two sisters of Spotted Tail, one of whom gave him a son named Little Hawk. This son was killed along the Platte River in 1870. After the death of Crazy Horse in 1877, Worm settled among the Brulés on the Rosebud Reservation where he passed away in 1881. See Ricker's interview with

Chipps (Tablet 18, page 1). *Rapid City Journal,* November 29, 1986; Hardorff, *The Oglala Lakota Crazy Horse,* 28-35. Hardorff note, *Death of Crazy Horse,* 56.

115. In 1920 Garnett told the story of the killing of Crazy Horse to Hugh Scott and James McLaughlin. Although shorter, it was similar to the Ricker account. Hardorff, *Death of Crazy Horse,* 75-100.

116. The identity of this individual has not been established. However, most scholars believe this was Little Hawk, a half brother of Worm, although Bull Head, Ashes, and Spotted Crow are also said to have been uncles of Crazy Horse. Hardorff note, *Death of Crazy Horse,* 57 n. 60.

117. The lumber for this pen was provided by Lt. Jesse M. Lee, military Indian agent to the Brulés who erected the structure on September 12, 1877, to prevent cattle from disturbing Crazy Horse's remains. Sepulchered in a red blanket, the body had been placed on a scaffold on September 8, on a hill overlooking Camp Sheridan. Hardorff note, *Death of Crazy Horse,* 58 n. 61.

118. Capt. Peter D. Vroom was a career soldier, who joined the army in 1862 and served for forty-one years. Heitman, *Historical Register,* 990.

119. Lame Deer's Miniconjou band was camped on a tributary of the Rosebud when they were discovered by Gen. Nelson A. Miles's scouts. On the morning of May 7, 1877, Lt. Edward Casey led a charge through the village sweeping away the Indians' horses. Miles followed with the rest of the command and for a time it seemed the Miniconjous would surrender peacefully, but fighting broke out and Lame Deer was one of the first fatalities. The Indians scattered and Miles ended the action later in the day. G. W. Baird, A Report to the Citizens Concerning Certain Late Disturbances on the Western Frontier (Ashland: Lewis Osborne, 1972), 42-44.

120. No Water's wife, Black Buffalo Woman, eloped with Crazy Horse. When No Water found them he shot Crazy Horse in the face. Black Buffalo Woman returned to her husband. He Dog, a close friend of Crazy Horse, told the story to Eleanor Hinman, but did not mention Little Big Man nor did John Colhoff, who was present at the interview. Hinman, "Oglala Sources," 13, 16-18.

121. Second Lt. George A. Dodd, Third Cavalry, entered the military academy in 1872. Heitman, *Historical Register,* 376.

122. Ezra A. Hayt was appointed commissioner on September 17, 1877. Fraud and other problems at several agencies led to three government investigations of the commissioner and on January 29, 1880, he was removed from office. Roy W. Meyer, "Ezra A. Hayt," *The Commissioners of Indian Affairs,* 1824-1977, ed. Robert M. Kvasnicka and Herman Viola (Lincoln: University of Nebraska Press, 1979): 155-66. Hayt visited the Lakotas in July 1878. Olson, *Red Cloud and the Sioux Problem,* 260.

123. Lt. Emmet Crawford, Third Cavalry, came with the soldiers that founded Camp Robinson. He was killed in 1886 by Mexican nationals while in pursuit of Apache renegades in northern Mexico. Buecker, *Fort Robinson and the American West,* 21, 44.

NOTES TO PAGES 80-83

124. During the summer of 1864 Indians attacked isolated white settlements in Kansas and Nebraska. On November 29 troops under Col. John M. Chivington attacked Black Kettle's Cheyennes in a village on Sand Creek. Chivington estimated that between four and five hundred Indians were killed. Black Kettle was one of the chiefs who had been trying to negotiate a peaceful settlement to the war. At the time of the attack an American flag and a white flag were being flown over the village. Grinnell, *The Fighting Cheyennes*, 169-74.

125. Hugh D. Gallagher arrived at Pine Ridge in October 1887 to take up his duties as agent. Gallagher, "Pine Ridge Agency, Dakota," *Annual Report of the Commissioner*, 1887, 40. When Agent Daniel Royer was appointed to the post in 1890 Gallagher made his home in Chadron. *Chadron Democrat*, Oct. 23, 1890. Ricker often addresses Gallagher with the honorary rank of colonel. William Henry Clapp was the Pine Ridge agent from 1896 to early 1900. Allen, *From Fort Laramie to Wounded Knee*, 256 n. 13.

126. Red Cloud demanded a meeting with the President to discuss real and imagined problems in dealing with Agent Saville. Government officials saw the meeting as an opportunity to open negotiations for the relinquishment of the Black Hills. The delegates had their first meeting with President Grant on May 19, 1875, and discussions with other government officials continued for a month. Virtually nothing was accomplished. Robert M. Utley, *The Last Days of the Sioux Nation* (New Haven: Yale University Press, 1963), 176-98. Ricker wrote a note in Tablet 17 about the negotiations for the hills: "Nov. 24, 1906. Wm. Provost says: That the following old-timers who were here say that the Indians never sold the Black Hills namely: Ben Tibbitts, Hank Clifford (dead) Nick Janis (dead) Ben Claymore, Merriman, John Palmer (dead)."

127. W. H. Bingham began his duties as agent on August 16, 1872. W. H. Bingham, "Cheyenne River Indian Agency, Dakota," *Annual Report of the Commissioner*, 1874, 231.

128. Charges that Saville was "guilty of gross frauds upon the Indians in his charge" were brought by a commission appointed by Secretary of the Interior Columbus Delano. The subsequent investigation was inconclusive, but Saville resigned nonetheless. Olson, *Red Cloud and the Sioux Problem*, 216 n. 9. James S. Hastings succeeded Saville on December 3, 1875. Hastings, "Red Cloud Agency, Nebraska," *Annual Report of the Commissioner*, 1876, 33.

129. In 1875 the commissioner of Indian affairs asked geologist Walter P. Jenney to go to the Black Hills and prove or disprove the rumors of gold there. Jenney spent nearly five months in the hills and concluded gold was present "in paying quantities." Col. Richard I. Dodge, commanding six companies of cavalry and two of infantry, provided an escort. When he arrived Jenney discovered "hundreds" of miners illegally trespassing in the Black Hills. Walter P. Jenney, "Report of Geological Survey of the Black Hills," *Annual Report of the Commissioner*, 1875, 181-83.

130. Olson found no evidence that government officials ever told Red Cloud or Spotted

Tail that they were going to discuss the sale of the hills, but disagreed that the discussion was "sprung on them." Olson pointed out that the chiefs' request to go to Washington listed their desire to discuss the sale of the hills. He concluded that the Indians' pretense of being "all at sea" was "clearly an act of calculated obfuscation." Olson, *Red Cloud and the Sioux Problem*, 177.

131. Congress appropriated the amount in 1875, but the Lakotas wanted $50,000. The secretary of the interior promised he would try to persuade Congress to provide that amount. This failure angered the Indians and Commissioner Smith grumbled, "The Indian mind seems incapable of discriminating between a promise to present a claim to Congress and a promise to pay the amount of the claim. J. Q. Smith, "Report of the Commissioner of Indian Affairs," *Annual Report of the Commissioner*, 1876, xvi.

132. Edward P. Smith, a Congregational minister, served as an Indian agent before being named commissioner on March 12, 1873. The investigation in 1875 into the quality of the annuities issued at the Red Cloud Agency led to fierce personal attacks on Smith in the press. Then, near the end of the year, he faced another investigation into his accounting for Indian funds, but avoided the confrontation by submitting his resignation on December 11. Richard C. Crawford, "Edward Parmelee Smith," *The Commissioners of Indian Affairs*, 141–47.

133. The Oglala Sitting Bull led a delegation to Crazy Horse's camp and succeeded in persuading some of the moderates to go the cantonment at the mouth of the Tongue River and talk with Miles about a peace treaty. On December 16, 1876, the advance column of this party neared the cantonment and was attacked by Miles's Crow scouts; five were killed including Sitting Bull. Crazy Horse saw the attack as further proof that the whites wanted to continue the war. Anderson, "Indian Peace-Talkers and the Conclusion of the Sioux War of 1876," 236.

134. J. W. Daniels was Sisseton agent prior to coming to the Sod Agency. Daniels, "Sisseton Agency, Dakota," *Annual Report of the Commissioner*, 1871, 530. Lt. John W. Wham was the agent. Olson, *Red Cloud and the Sioux Problem*, 132. He was honorably discharged from the army at his request on January 1, 1871. He returned to the army as paymaster from March 1877 until his retirement in 1901. Heitman, *Historical Register*, 1022.

135. Senator William B. Allison of Iowa was chairman of the commission composed of Brig. Gen. A. H. Terry, Congressman Abram Comingo, G. P. Beauvais, W. H. Ashby, A. G. Lawrence, and S. D. Hinman. A number of newspaper reporters and perhaps curiosity seekers also attended. The commissioners arrived at Red Cloud Agency on September 4, 1875. Many of the Lakotas were opposed to selling the Black Hills but those who did wanted millions of dollars. Spotted Bear thought $70 million would be sufficient. The commissioners' counter offer of $6 million was rejected. W. B. Allison, et al., "Report of the Commission Appointed to Treat with the Sioux Indians for the Relinquishment of the Black Hills," *Annual Report of the Commissioner*, 1875, 186.

136. The Oglalas and the Brulés spent two weeks arguing about where the meeting would take place. It was finally decided to meet eight miles down the White River, east of the Red Cloud Agency. Ibid., 186.
137. Spotted Tail's remarks may have been summarized in the commission's report. His main theme was a request for enough money so the interest would support the Lakotas forever. Ibid., 188.
138. Ricker's long interview with Philip Wells is in Tablets 3, 4, and 5.
139. Little Big Man was either trying to start a riot or intimidate the commissioners. John G. Bourke, *On the Border with Crook* (Lincoln: University of Nebraska Press Bison Books, 1971), 243; Olson, *Red Cloud and the Sioux Problem*, 204-5.
140. Fifty-three Lakota leaders signed the agreement in June 1875. J. W. Daniels, "Agreement Between the United States and the Sioux for the Relinquishment of Hunting Rights in Nebraska," *Annual Report of the Commissioner*, 1875, 179. Rev. Samuel D. Hinman was in Yankton, South Dakota, about this time. He was an interpreter for the Allison Commission and arranged meetings with the Lakota. Grant K. Anderson, "Samuel D. Hinman and the Opening of the Black Hills," *Nebraska History* 60 (1979): 520-42.
141. Agent Howard mentioned that a mail carrier was murdered in May 1876, and two white men got into a drunken brawl at the agency and one was killed. Howard, "Spotted Tail Agency, Nebraska," *Annual Report of the Commissioner*, 1876, 35.
142. George W. Manypenny served on the commission. Vroom was not a member. Olson, *Red Cloud and the Sioux Problem*, 224. Ricker wrote the following in Tablet 22:

> Garnett says he saw Mannypenny in Washington in 1877, and again in 1885. At the latter date Mannypenny was in the Indian office giving bystanders a gust of wind about how he was out here in 1876 and sent out for Crazy Horse and brought him in and then the soldiers killed him. Garnett contradicted him, stated the facts and stopped his wind gust. Garnett told him he was not there, & then Mannypenny said well, he sent out his man. Wm. Garnett told him that he himself interpreted at Red Cloud Agency for the 1876 treaty and that Hinman who was present made the treaty show that Hinman was the interpreter.

143. The agent at Crow Creek was in charge of the Lower Brulés until 1875, when Congress approved an independent agency. Henry F. Livingston, "Crow Creek Agency, Dakota Territory, *Annual Report of the Commissioner*, 1875, 238.
144. The commission consisted of Newton Edmunds, former governor of Dakota, Peter Shannon, a Dakota lawyer, and James H. Teller of Ohio. Samuel D. Hinman was again listed as an interpreter. They arrived at Pine Ridge on October 22, 1882. Olson, *Red Cloud and the Sioux Problem*, 287-88.
145. This was probably Newton Edmunds, who was chairman of the commission and had negotiated treaties in the past. Ibid., 287. The proposed reservations would not be joined. The western boundaries of Standing Rock and Cheyenne River were

moved eastward about thirty miles. Except for the small Lower Brule and Crow Creek reservations, all the land between the White and Cheyenne rivers would be open to white settlement.

146. Secretary of the Interior Henry M. Teller approved the commission's request that they get only the signatures of the chiefs and headmen. Ibid.

147. These government employees were hired to teach the Indians how to cultivate the land. Several farmers were stationed at various locations at each agency in 1885. William A. Swan, "Cheyenne River Agency, Dakota Territory," *Annual Report of the Commissioner*, 1884, 20.

148. Garnett's claim that he saw small children signing the treaty is puzzling. Hinman was unsuccessful in getting signatures and only made a list of those who seemed to support the treaty. Olson, *Red Cloud and the Sioux Problem*, 291.

149. William Welsh served as chairman of the Board of Indian Commissioners, a watchdog committee appointed by President Grant in 1869 to guard against fraud in the purchase of supplies for Indian reservations. William's nephew, Herbert, was a founder of the Indian Rights Association. William T. Hagan, *The Indian Rights Association: The Herbert Welsh Years, 1882-1904* (Tucson: University of Arizona Press, 1985), 4.

The Indian Rights Association was formed in 1882. Its goal was "to secure the civilization of the two hundred and ninety thousand Indians of the United States (inclusive of the thirty thousand natives of Alaska), and to prepare the way for their absorption into the common life of our own [white] people." In the 1880s the association had a membership of more than three hundred and an annual budget from donations in excess of $4,000. *Indian Rights Association: Second Annual Report of the Executive Committee* (Philadelphia: n.p., 1885), 5. The association quickly became the foremost Indian reform group.

150. The first meeting was on September 1, 1883. Olson, *Red Cloud and the Sioux Problem*, 291.

151. Senator Henry Dawes introduced the Sioux bill, which became law on March 2, 1889. It called for the reduction of the Great Sioux Reservation into five smaller reservations, opening the rest to white settlement. "An Act to Divide a Portion of the Reservation of the Sioux Nation," *Annual Report of the Commissioner*, 1889, 449-58.

152. Capt. Richard H. Pratt was the superintendent of a school for Indians at Carlisle, Pennsylvania. Episcopal missionary William J. Cleveland and his wife began their ministry at the Spotted Tail Agency in 1875. E. A. Howard, "Spotted Tail Agency, Nebraska," *Annual Report of the Commissioner*, 1875, 254.

153. Charles Foster, former governor of Ohio, Senator William Warner of Missouri, and Gen. George Crook arrived on the Rosebud Reservation in June 1889. Olson, *Red Cloud and the Sioux Problem*, 313.

154. Short Bull and Kicking Bear were prominent members of a delegation that went to Nevada to visit Wovoka, the initiator of the Ghost Dance. Richard E. Jensen,

R. Eli Paul, and John E. Carter, *Eyewitness at Wounded Knee* (Lincoln: University of Nebraska Press, 1991), 3.

155. Ricker interviewed Elbert Mead (Tablet 24), who received the contract to move the thirty bodies from the Pine Ridge cemetery and transfer them to Fort Riley, Kansas. The bodies were exhumed on August 8 and 9, 1906, under contract with the chief quartermaster at Omaha.

156. Ricker wrote the following note in Tablet 22. He then crossed it with a large X:
> Have Garnet repeat the story of W.K. as told by Sergt Dorsney of the 7th Cav. when he took Garnett & Bob Pugh over the W.K. field. And the Wells episode. He says Dorsney used to come down from abt. Spearfish; he lives up there somewhere. R. O. Pugh can tell.

157. James W. Forsyth entered the military academy in 1851. He served in the Union army in the Civil War and in 1886 took command of the Seventh Cavalry. He retired in 1897 with the rank of major general. Heitman, Historical Register, 430. Forsyth was the senior officer at Wounded Knee. Jensen, Paul, and Carter, *Eyewitness at Wounded Knee*, 35.

158. The Bureau of Indian Affairs in mid-1889 tried to install American Horse as chief of all the Lakotas. Olson, *Red Cloud and the Sioux Problem*, 318.

159. On July 7, 1876, Lt. Frederick W. Sibley, Second Cavalry, and a detachment of twenty-five troopers and four civilians encountered a force of Cheyennes near the headwaters of the Little Bighorn, which nearly succeeded in capturing the entire command. After a short fight, Sibley abandoned his horses and escaped on foot. The only casualty was a Cheyenne named Tall Bear, better known by his Sioux name, White Antelope. Hardorff note, *Lakota Recollections*, 29 n. 15.

160. This may be Fanny Kelly, who was captured by an Oglala band in 1864. Fanny Kelly, *Narrative of My Captivity Among the Sioux Indians*, ed. Clark and Mary Lee Spence (Chicago: Donnelly, Gossette & Loyd, 1880; reprint, R. R. Donnelley and Sons Co., 1990). Another possibility is Elizabeth, wife of Hiram B. "Hi" Kelly. Jones, "John Richard, Jr. and the Killing at Fetterman," 238.

161. Many Lakotas adopted the so-called Ghost Dance religion in 1890. Adherents believed that whites would disappear, their ancestors would come back to life, and they would live in a land of plenty.

162. These three short paragraphs appear to be another of the Ricker asides he inserted in the middle of interviews.
According to Charles E. Hanson, Jr., Francis C. Boucher occupied the former Bordeaux trading post on Bordeaux Creek about 1872, and sold guns and ammunition to Indians until August 1876, when soldiers from Fort Robinson confiscated a large quantity of ammunition and put Boucher out of business. Charles E. Hanson, Jr. and Veronica Sue Walters, "The Early Fur Trade in Northwestern Nebraska," *Nebraska History* 57 (1976): 311.

163. Standing Soldier's interview is in Tablet 29.

164. Unfortunately, Ricker did not record what Wells said about the officer. The next

page of the tablet was blank. Joseph Horn Cloud and Dewey Beard report this incident.

165. Dripper was probably Andrew Dripps. He had a trading post above the sod agency in 1860. He was about seventy years old at that time. Harvey L. Carter, "Andrew Drips," *The Mountain Men and the Fur Trade of the Far West*, ed. LeRoy R. Hafen (Glendale, Calif.: Arthur H. Clark Co., 1971), 8: 143–56.

166. James Bordeaux had worked for the American Fur Company at Fort Laramie. When it was sold to the government in 1849 he opened his own trading post. Charles E. Hanson, Jr., "James Bordeaux," *The Museum of the Fur Trade Quarterly* 2 (1966): 6.

167. In the 1870s William G. Bullock operated a cattle ranch on the Laramie River a few miles above the fort. Hedren, *Fort Laramie in 1876*, 46.

168. Cornelius "Lame Johnny" Donahue was arrested in 1879 for robbing a stagecoach in the Black Hills. A police officer was taking him to a Deadwood jail when they were accosted by a masked gunman. The officer was allowed to proceed unharmed. The next day Lame Johnny's body was found hanging from a tree, the victim of a vigilante. Jesse Brown and A. M. Willard, *The Black Hills Trails* (Rapid City SD: Rapid City Journal Co., 1924), 298–301.

169. Born on September 20, 1853, Frank Grouard was captured by Lakotas in 1869 and stayed among them for six years. However, after a domestic quarrel with his Oglala inlaws, Grouard left the Lakota camps and drifted into Red Cloud agency in 1875, destitute and dressed only in a loincloth. He was hired by Gen. George Crook's staff as a scout and rendered valuable services throughout the Indian wars of 1876 and 1877. Upon Crook's recommendation, Grouard obtained permanent employment as a scout and interpreter with the government at $150 per month. According to William Garnett, Grouard had been married to two or three women, but he did not have children with any of them. Mari Sandoz claimed his second wife was Sally Garnett, the sister of William Garnett. Sally eventually left Grouard and went to Pine Ridge where she married Charles Twiss, the mixed-blood son of a former Indian agent. It should be noted further that Sally Garnett was actually known as Sally Bouyer and that she was a half sister of William, she having been born from the second marriage of Garnett's mother. Apparently, Sally's marriage to Twiss did not last either, because William Garnett stated that she had married Philip White. Grouard's third wife was Eulalie Garnier, the sister of Baptiste Garnier, who was known on the frontier as Little Bat. Nicknamed LaLie she had been married to John Hunton, a roadhouse operator on the Chugwater in Wyoming. She had left him about 1886 and had married Grouard but this marriage failed, too, and she eventually settled on Pine Ridge with someone else. In later years Grouard left his government job at Fort McKinney, Wyoming, and went to Pine Ridge to live with the Oglalas. However, he did not stay long. Frank Goings, a native judge on the Court of Indian Offenses, recalled that the last time Frank Grouard visited the reservation was in 1902. Grouard wanted his name entered

on the agency rolls to be eligible for a land allotment, a scheme he tried to accomplish through the help of Standing Soldier, an elderly Oglala. However, during the bribing process, Standing Soldier became dangerously intoxicated, and Grouard fearing arrest, fled the reservation and was never seen again. He went to Missouri, and on August 20, 1905, he suddenly died in the town of St. Joseph, where he lies buried in a forgotten grave in Ashland Cemetery.

History has not been kind to Frank Grouard. Scholars are still debating whether he was a mixed-blood Lakota or a Mulatto who lied about his ancestry. Grouard himself consistently repeated he was born in Tahiti, on the Isle of Taiarapu. Hardorff note, *Death of Crazy Horse*, 30–31 n. 9.

170. Mrs. Nettie Goings told Ricker (Tablet 13) that Grouard was her half-brother and their father was John Brazeau. Letters in the Walter Camp Collection would seem to support Grouard's contention that he was born in Tahiti. Richard G. Hardorff, "The Frank Grouard Genealogy," *Custer and His Times: Book Two*, ed. John M. Carroll (Ft. Worth TX: Little Bighorn Associates, Inc., 1984), 123–33.

171. Frank Grouard did not explain the reason for the killing, but said it "caused a whole lot of trouble It took two days to quiet this trouble down." Joe DeBarthe, *Life and Adventures of Frank Grouard*, Edgar I. Stewart, ed. (Norman: University of Oklahoma Press, 1958), 87.

172. Garnett's story of Yellow Bear and John Richard was published by Danker, "The Violent Deaths of Yellow Bear and John Richard Jr.," 137–51.

173. Col. John E. Smith escorted Red Cloud and twenty other Lakota leaders from Fort Laramie on May 26, 1870, to Washington DC. G. W. Bullock was the interpreter and post sutler. Olson, *Red Cloud and the Sioux Problem*, 96–97.

174. The term *melt* is a colloquial synonym for spleen. Yellow Bear belonged to the Oglalas' Spleen band. Fredrick Webb Hodge, ed., *Handbook of American Indians*, Smithsonian Institution, Bureau of American Ethnology, Bulletin 30 (Washington DC: GPO, 1907), 691.

175. Richard left the Fort Fetterman area with the Lakotas in September 1869, and was gone for ten months. On October 29 two soldiers were killed about fifteen miles from the fort while they were hunting. There were no other homicides during this time. Jones, "John Richard, Jr. and the Killing at Fetterman," 246.

176. In her vivid account of the last Sun Dance, Julia McGillycuddy also notes that it was held in Nebraska. She also pointed out that the agent's ban was not total, but that an abbreviated ceremony must be held in private. Julia B. McGillycuddy, *McGillycuddy, Agent: A Biography of Dr. Valentine T. McGillycuddy* (Stanford CA: Stanford University Press, 1941), 168.

177. The flagpole incident occurred on October 23, 1874. J. J. Saville to E. P. Smith, Oct. 24, 1874, and W. Jordan to G. D. Ruggles, Oct. 29, 1874, Letters Received by the Office of Indian Affairs, Red Cloud Agency (National Archives Microfilm Publication M234, roll 718), Records of the Bureau of Indian Affairs, Record Group 75, NARA (hereafter cited as Red Cloud Agency letters).

178. Capt. William H. Jordan, Ninth Infantry, was in command at Camp Robinson from July 12, 1874 to October 24, 1876. Buecker, *Fort Robinson and the American West*, 198.
179. Spider was an Oglala headman and a half brother to Red Cloud. Bray, "Crazy Horse and the End of the Great Sioux War," 100.
180. In 1880 Agent McGillycuddy salvaged a flagpole from the abandoned Camp Sheridan a few miles away and placed it at the agency. McGillycuddy, "Pine Ridge Agency, Dakota," *Annual Report of the Commissioner*, 1881, 50.
181. James S. Hastings began his duties as agent at Red Cloud on December 3, 1875. He was replaced by Lt. C. A. Johnson, who served until July 1, 1877, when he was replaced by James Irwin. Hastings, "Red Cloud Agency, Nebraska," *Annual Report of the Commissioner*, 1876, 33; Irwin, "Red Cloud Agency, Nebraska," *Annual Report of the Commissioner*, 1877, 62. Lt. Oscar Elting was the agent in the summer of 1876. Buecker, *Fort Robinson and the American West*, 85.
182. Ricker wrote the following note in Tablet 10: "George Running Horse lives 1½ mile from Kyle, up towards Allen. He was in the Tall Bull fight on south Platte where Tall Bull was killed. Many Indians live on Medicine Root Cr. who were in that fight and fight between Sioux & Pawnees in 1873."
183. Maj. Eugene A. Carr, Fifth Cavalry, commanded the Republican River Expedition in the summer of 1869. The command included the Pawnee Scouts under Maj. Frank J. North. William F. Cody was chief of scouts for the cavalry. On July 11 the command routed the Cheyennes under Tall Bull near Summit Springs. James T. King, *War Eagle: A Life of General Eugene A. Carr* (Lincoln: University of Nebraska Press, 1963), 101, 113.
184. Frank North probably killed Tall Bull, but William Cody also claimed credit.
185. On August 5, 1873, an estimated one thousand Oglala and Brulé warriors attacked about 350 Pawnee men, women, and children on a small tributary of the Republican River since called Massacre Canyon. Paul D. Riley, "The Battle of Massacre Canyon," *Nebraska History* 54 (1973): 221-49.
186. Philip Wells died January 2, 1947. Donald F. Danker, "The Wounded Knee Interviews of Eli S. Ricker," *Nebraska History* 62 (1981): 242 n. 58.
187. James "Bully" Wells served in the army for fifteen years and came to Minnesota in 1819, when Fort Snelling was founded. In the mid-1830s he opened a trading post about twenty miles up the Minnesota River and in 1853 he moved to the vicinity of Faribault. He was a member of the territorial legislature in 1849 and 1851. Upham wrote that Wells was "murdered mysteriously in 1863." Warren Upham, "Minnesota Geographic Names," *Collections of the Minnesota Historical Society* 17 (1920): 211, 464. Alexander Faribault was the son of a fur trader and began trading with the Indians in 1826 in the vicinity of Faribault, Minnesota, which was named for him. Ibid., 462.
188. Rev. Archer B. Ffennell was murdered in 1876, "by two Indians with a real or imagined grievance." At the time Ffennell was a missionary at St. John's Mission on the

Cheyenne River Reservation. M. A. DeWolfe Howe, *The Life and Labors of Bishop Hare: Apostle to the Sioux* (New York: Sturgis and Walton Co., 1913), 132-33. In 1872 Rev. William Hobart Hare was elected to the post of Missionary Bishop of Niobrara. The Niobrara district included present North and South Dakota west of the Missouri River. Ibid., 29-30.

189. Brave Bear and three accomplices murdered three Métis in northeastern North Dakota in July 1874. He and The Only One were captured at the Devil's Lake Agency in March 1876, or possibly 1877. The Only One was killed and Brave Bear was imprisoned but escaped. He murdered another man before he was captured again, tried for this crime, and executed in 1882. Louis L. Pfaller, O.S.B., "The Brave Bear Murder Case," *North Dakota History* 36 (1969): 133, 139.

190. The Hunkpapa Sitting Bull and his followers had fled to Canada. Sitting Bull, on board the General Sherman, arrived at Fort Yates on August 1, 1881. Robert M. Utley, *The Lance and the Shield: The Life and Times of Sitting Bull* (New York: Henry Holt and Co., 1993), 238.

191. The Drexel or Holy Rosary Mission was founded in 1888 by Father John Jutz. Utley, *The Last Days of the Sioux Nation*, 137. The "affair" was a brief skirmish between Lakota warriors and the soldiers shortly after the Wounded Knee massacre.

192. Four cowboys were killed on the night of February 2-3, 1893, at the Humphrey and Stenger ranch about thirty miles northwest of the agency. Acting agent Capt. George LeRoy Brown sent the agency police to arrest the accused and in the ensuing gunfight Two Sticks was wounded and two of his accomplices were killed. *Chadron Citizen*, Feb. 9, 1893. Ricker's interview with Alfred N. Coe deals with the Two Sticks case (Tablet 39).

193. Holley's book is a hodgepodge of northern Plains history mingled with data on the native inhabitants, whose customs Holley speculates "strongly indicate a Jewish origin...yet there are also many indications of a Persian origin." Frances Chamberlain Holley, *Once Their Home, or Our Legacy from the Dahkotahs* (Chicago: Donohue and Henneberry, 1892), 224. Her account of the arrest is generally similar to the scholarly offering by Rev. Louis Pfaller, "The Brave Bear Murder Case," 127.

194. James McLaughlin was the agent at Devil's Lake from 1876 until 1881, when he transferred to Standing Rock. Louis L. Pfaller, O. S. B., *James McLaughlin: The Man with an Indian Heart* (New York: Vantage Press, 1978), 46, 61. Sitting Bull and his Hunkpapa followers were imprisoned at Fort Randall from mid-September 1881 to mid-May 1883 after their return from Canada. Utley, *The Lance and the Shield*, 241, 248.

195. Maj. Marcus A. Reno commanded companies A, G, and M of the Seventh Cavalry. His unit was the first to fire upon the Indians about three o'clock in the afternoon. Gray, *Custer's Last Campaign*, 245, 272.

196. Born near the forks of the Cheyenne River in 1836, Rain in the Face was one of two Hunkpapa sons born of his father's second marriage. Rain's younger brother was Shave Head, a first sergeant in the Standing Rock Indian Police, who was

killed in the line of duty during the arrest of Sitting Bull in 1890. Of Rain's four half brothers, Iron Horn had risen in social standing and was the chief of a minor Hunkpapa band. In 1873 Rain was implicated in the killings of two civilians along the Yellowstone. He was arrested by Capt. Thomas W. Custer late in 1875, and brought to Fort Lincoln, from where he escaped early in 1876, swearing vengeance on the Custers. There are conflicting reports whether Rain actually participated in the Little Bighorn battle; however, the extreme mutilation of Tom Custer's body gave rise to immediate speculation about Rain's involvement. His reputation as Custer's slayer was firmly cemented by the writings of Elizabeth Custer and Longfellow's poem, "The Revenge of Rain in the Face." He died at his home at Standing Rock Agency, North Dakota, on September 14, 1905. Hardorff note, *Lakota Recollections,* 48 n. 26.

197. The so-called Minnesota War or Sioux Uprising started on August 17, 1862, when five white people were killed. The fighting escalated and scores of whites and Indians were killed before peace was restored. Gary Clayton Anderson, *Little Crow: Spokesman for the Sioux* (St. Paul: Minnesota Historical Society Press, 1986), 130.

198. Maj. Gen. Nelson A. Miles was the commanding general of the Division of the Missouri, which included the Lakota reservations. Utley, *The Last Days of the Sioux Nation,* 104. He arrived at the Pine Ridge Agency two days after the Wounded Knee massacre. He was convinced that Colonel Forsyth had placed his troops so they shot one another at Wounded Knee and that the soldiers killed women and children. Forsyth was relieved of his command on January 4, 1891, when Miles convened a court of inquiry to determine whether the "disposition made of the troops was judicious" and whether "any non-combatants were unnecessarily injured or destroyed." The case was ruled in favor of Forsyth. *Reports and Correspondence Relating to the Army Investigation of the Battle of Wounded Knee and the Sioux Campaign of 1890–91* (National Archives Microfilm publication M983, roll 148), Records of the Office of the Adjutant General, Record Group 94 (hereafter cited as *Reports, Campaign of 1890–91*).

199. The First Infantry arrived at Fort Niobrara on December 9 from Benicia Barracks in California. Jensen, Paul, and Carter, *Eyewitness at Wounded Knee,* 35. There is no evidence that Miles ordered one of the officers to examine the Wounded Knee site.

Ricker wrote "Caution here" across this part of the paragraph.

200. Written diagonally across this part of the paragraph is "He wants little said about this. Simply say he was informed on good authority."

201. Rev. Charles Smith Cook was a Yankton Sioux educated at Trinity College and Seabury Divinity School. He was an Episcopalian missionary stationed on the reservation. Eastman, *From Deep Woods to Civilization,* 85.

202. Maj. Jacob F. Kent and Capt. Frank D. Baldwin headed the investigation of the events at Wounded Knee. Utley, *The Last Days of the Sioux Nation,* 245. Statements by Wells, other Indians, and army officers are in *Reports, Campaign of 1890–*

91, 651–758. Nearly all of Ricker's copies are identical to the statements in this publication. A more polished version of Wells's statement is in Wells, "Ninety-six Years Among the Indians." This article also includes a biography of Wells.
203. Big Foot or Spotted Elk was a respected Miniconjou chief. His love of traditional ways led him and his many followers to embrace the Ghost Dance.
204. This paragraph was not in *Reports, Campaign of 1890–91*.
205. Maj. Samuel M. Whitside of the Seventh Cavalry had served for more than thirty years in the military. Heitman, Historical Register, 1031. He was in command of Troops A, B, I, and K of the Seventh Cavalry with a platoon of the First Artillery. On December 26 the soldiers camped on the site of the Wounded Knee massacre. J. Forsyth to assistant adjutant general, Dec. 31, 1890, *Reports, Campaign of 1890–91*.
206. John W. Cramsie wrote that Wells had been "more or less identified" with the Sisseton, Cuthead, and Wahpeton Sioux around Devil's Lake since 1867. Cramsie, "Devil's Lake Agency, Dakota," *Annual Report of the Commissioner*, 1887, 27.
207. This letter was published with only minor differences in punctuation in Wells, "Ninety-six Years Among the Indians," 289.
208. Lt. Charles W. Taylor entered West Point in 1874. After graduation he was assigned to the Ninth Cavalry. Heitman, Historical Register, 694. He commanded the Oglala and Cheyenne scouts at Pine Ridge. These were regular army troops as opposed to civilian scouts.
209. Unfortunately a copy of the document was not in the Ricker collection.
210. Daniel M. Browning served as commissioner from April 1893 until May 1897. His biographer was of the opinion that Browning "did not make a significant contribution as commissioner." William T. Hagan, "Daniel M. Browning," *The Commissioners of Indian Affairs*, 205–9.
211. Little Wound's father was Bull Bear, who was killed in 1841. Perhaps the 1844 date was wrong or he referred to an uncle, who would be called a father.
212. Joseph Antoine Janis began roaming the West about 1841, and became a trader and at times a Sioux interpreter. In 1859 he and his Oglala wife and family settled on the Cache la Poudre and soon a thriving community grew up there. In 1878 they moved to Pine Ridge, where he died in 1890. Lecompte, "Antoine Janis," 196–201.
213. The last battle between the Pawnees and their enemies, the Oglala, and Brulés occurred on August 5, 1873. The Pawnees, numbering about 350 men, women, and children, were on a buffalo hunt when they were attacked by an overwhelming number of Lakotas and forced to retreat into Massacre Canyon. Estimates of the number killed varied, but a few days later an army patrol counted fifty-six slain Pawnees. Antoine Janis was with the Oglalas and talked to Little Wound before the battle. Little Wound said he had orders not to attack the Pawnees on their reservation, but wondered if Janis knew of any rule against an attack so far from the reservation. Janis admitted he knew of no such rule. Janis mentioned that the Oglalas had taken three women and four girls prisoner, while Stephen F. Estes,

who traveled with the Brulés, counted a woman, two girls, and a boy taken prisoner. Both men expected the immediate return of the prisoners, but there was no mention of sending them back on "good" horses. The only mention of horses was an estimate that "more than 100" Pawnee horses were killed. "Indian Office Documents on Sioux-Pawnee Battle," *Nebraska History Magazine* 16 (1935): 147–55.

In 1907 Ricker had a brief conversation with Mrs. Charles Turning Hawk (Tablet 38). He wrote the following note:

> Mrs. Charles Turning Hawk, daughter of Chief little Wound says: Chief Little Wound died in August (George Little Wound can give the year.) He is buried in the Catholic Cemetery at Kyle. Moses Red Kettle says he thinks Chief Little Wound died about six years ago. (This is 1907.)

214. After the worst fighting was over Capt. Henry Jackson was sent with Troop C to gather stray horses some distance from the Wounded Knee council site. The troop was fired upon by an estimated 100 to 130 Indians, who had ridden out from the agency. Jackson testified that he fell back "about 400 yards to a good position and held them off." When Troops E and G came to the rescue the Indians broke off the encounter. Testimony of Capt. Henry Jackson, Jan. 7, 1891, *Reports, Campaign of 1890–91*, 686–89.

215. The Ghost Dancers or "hostiles" congregated on an easily defended butte or mesa, which was dubbed "The Stronghold." The army was powerless to evict them without risking heavy casualties on both sides.

Jack Red Cloud was the son of the famous chief. He was a Ghost Dance leader with a camp on White Clay Creek. Young Red Cloud moved with relative freedom between the believer and nonbeliever camps in an effort to maintain peaceful relationships. Jensen, Paul, and Carter, *Eyewitness at Wounded Knee*, 13.

Father John Jutz, S.J., was in charge of the Drexel or Holy Rosary Catholic Mission. Jutz was assigned to the Rosebud Reservation in 1886, and then to Pine Ridge three years later. Sister Mary Clement Fitzgerald, "Bishop Marty and His Sioux Missions," *South Dakota Historical Collections* 20 (1940): 540, 548.

Father Jutz and Jack Red Cloud talked to the Ghost Dance leaders at the Stronghold on December 4. On the second trip Father Jutz persuaded some of the leaders to come to the agency for a talk with Brig. Gen. John R. Brooke. John Shangrau returned with the delegation and it was through his efforts that most of the Ghost Dancers returned to the agency about a week later. Utley, *The Last Days of the Sioux Nation*, 137, 142.

216. The "Messiah" was Wovoka, whose visions were the basis of the Ghost Dance.

Walker River Indian Reservation is in western Nevada. The name of the reservation and that of Dr. James R. Walker is coincidental.

217. The purifying sweat bath was an old element of Lakota religion. Men and women holding hands in a dance was introduced with the Ghost Dance. L. W. Colby, with the help of George Sword and Pine Ridge teacher Emma Sickels, recorded thirty-one Ghost Dance songs, including eleven attributed to Big Foot's band. L. W.

Colby, "Wanagi Olowan Kin: The Ghost Songs of the Dakotas," *Proceedings and Collections of the Nebraska State Historical Society* 1 (1895): 142-49.

218. The Sun Dance was at the heart of the Lakotas' traditional religion and it included self-torture, both considered by the Office of Indian Affairs as sufficient reasons to ban the ceremony. James Owen Dorsey, "A Study of Siouan Cults," *Eleventh Annual Report of the Bureau of American Ethnology* (Washington DC: GPO, 1894); James R. Walker, "The Sun Dance and Other Ceremonies of the Oglala Division of the Teton Dakota," *Anthropological Papers* 16, American Museum of Natural History (Washington DC: GPO, 1917).

The Lakotas had borrowed the so-called Omaha dance from the Omaha tribe in the distant past. Originally it was a ceremony to protect participants from their enemies' weapons. As years passed the ceremony was misused and its power was lost until the Omaha dance became merely a social event. Clark Wissler, "Societies and Ceremonial Associations in the Oglala Division of the Teton-Dakota," *Anthropological Papers* 11, American Museum of Natural History (Washington DC: GPO, 1912), 49.

219. Agent Hugh D. Gallagher's first report about the Ghost Dance was filed on June 14, 1890. He thought it would soon die out. H. Gallagher to T. J. Morgan, June 14, 1890, Frame 3, Special Case No. 188, Ghost Dance 1890-91, Records of the Bureau of Indian Affairs, Record Group 75, NARA.

220. Early in September Agent Gallagher and twenty-five policemen attempted to break up a Ghost Dance on the Pine Ridge Reservation. They were turned away by armed dancers. E. B. Reynolds to T. J. Morgan, Sept. 23, 1890, Frame 32, Ibid.

221. Dr. Valentine T. McGillycuddy began his duties as Pine Ridge agent on March 10, 1879. He was replaced by Capt. James M. Bell, Seventh Cavalry, in May 1886, largely as the result of opposition by the Democratic party. H. D. Gallagher replaced the captain on October 1. Utley, *The Last Days of the Sioux Nation*, 265, 304, 307.

222. Thomas J. Morgan, a Baptist minister and educator, was appointed commissioner of Indian affairs on June 10, 1889. He firmly believed the only solution to the "Indian problem" lay in the eradication of the native culture and its replacement with white Americans' ideals. Francis Paul Prucha, "Thomas Jefferson Morgan," *The Commissioners of Indian Affairs*, 193-203.

223. Pro-Indian whites frequently mentioned starvation as a cause for the Lakotas' discontent and the spread of the Ghost Dance. It had the advantage of being an easily understood and logical reason, especially when the recent reduction in the government-supplied rations was mentioned. In spite of the reduction, more than a pound of usable meat and a variety of other foodstuffs were provided per person per day. Richard E. Jensen, "Notes on the Lakota Ghost Dance," paper read before the Thirty-third Annual Missouri Valley History Conference, Omaha, Mar. 8, 1990.

Red Cloud carried the food shortage theme to extremes when he claimed that 217 people had died of starvation on the Pine Ridge Reservation in a year. Thomas A. Bland, *A Brief History of the Late Military Invasion of the Home of the Sioux* (Washington DC: National Indian Defense Association, 1891), 20.

224. Daniel F. Royer, an Alpena, South Dakota, dentist, was appointed agent for the Pine Ridge Reservation and arrived there in late September 1890. His paramount concern was the suppression of the Ghost Dance, but it was soon apparent he did not have the temperament for such an undertaking. In a letter to Thomas J. Morgan, commissioner of Indian affairs, he wrote: "I have been carefully investigating the matter [of the Ghost Dance] and I find I have an elephant on my hands." D. F. Royer to T. J. Morgan, Oct. 12, 1890, Executive Documents of the Senate of the United States, 51st Cong., 2d sess., 1891-92, S. Doc. 9: 5 (Washington DC: GPO, 1892). By the end of the month he was insisting that military intervention was necessary not only to suppress the new religion, but to protect whites from an outbreak. He believed a war was inevitable and his actions proved to be a self-fulfilling prophecy. Years later Royer moved to California and by 1927 was "in trouble for using too much morphine." Friswold and Clark, *The Killing of Chief Crazy Horse*, 127.

225. Capt. Richard H. Pratt, superintendent of the school for Indians at Carlisle, Pennsylvania, headed a commission to persuade the Lakotas to sell about nine million acres of the reservation considered surplus after the Indians received their 160-acre allotments in severalty. Wells listed the change in the reservation boundaries as one of the events that contributed to the acceptance of the Ghost Dance. Wells, "Ninety-Six Years Among the Indians," 283.

226. It has been reported that either sixty-one or sixty-seven delegates went to Washington. Utley, *The Last Days of the Sioux Nation*, 47; Olson, *Red Cloud and the Sioux Problem*, 310. The Indian delegates and their agents went to Washington in October and spent a week in futile discussions. Gallagher, "Report of Pine Ridge Agency," *Annual Report of the Commissioner*, 1889, 157.

227. After the Lakotas' adamant refusal to sell land in 1888, the government raised the offer of $.50 to $1.25 an acre for land sold during the first three years. It was presumed this would be the best land. A downward sliding scale covered land sold in later years. Heads of families would receive 320 instead of the original offer of 160 acres. There were other concessions as well. The 1889 law was approved on March 2 and published in *Annual Report of the Commissioner*, 1889, 449-58. The boundary was moved as Wells explains.

The commission concluded its efforts at Pine Ridge on June 28. Red Cloud and his people opposed the offer, while American Horse and No Flesh favored it. Ibid., 157.

228. Agent L. F. Spencer at Rosebud explained that two thousand Indians from the reservation would be transferred to Pine Ridge. He claimed they "do not take

kindly to the change" because they were Brulés and wanted to remain with their kinfolk. Pine Ridge was populated primarily by Oglalas and some Cheyennes. Spencer, "Report of Rosebud Agency," *Annual Report of the Commissioner,* 1889, 159.

229. Troops began arriving at Pine Ridge on November 20, 1890, to quell the Ghost Dance. Utley, *The Last Days of the Sioux Nation,* 113.
230. Brig. Gen. John R. Brooke had overall command of the soldiers on the reservations. Brooke had served in the Civil War. He retired in 1902 with the rank of major general. Heitman, *Historical Register,* 248.
231. Gilbert E. Bailey was a geologist as well as a reporter for the *Chicago Inter-Ocean.* George R. Kolbenschlag, *A Whirlwind Passes: News Correspondents and the Sioux Disturbances of 1890–1891* (Vermillion: University of South Dakota Press, 1990), xi, 92.
232. Sitting Bull was the Hunkpapa leader from the Standing Rock Reservation. He was killed on December 15, 1890, when the reservation police attempted to arrest him for his part in the Ghost Dance. Seven civilians and six Indian policemen were also killed in the shootout. Utley, *The Lance and the Shield.*
233. Eugene A. Carr was a colonel in the Sixth Cavalry in 1890, but was later promoted to the rank of brigadier general. For a complete biography, see King, *War Eagle.*
234. Ricker interviewed Craven in October 1906 (Tablet 3).
235. George D. Wallace entered the military academy in 1868. He was under Major Reno's command in the Little Bighorn battle. *Harper's Weekly,* Jan. 17, 1901. He was the commanding officer of Troop K of the Seventh Cavalry when he was killed at Wounded Knee. Utley, *The Last Days of the Sioux Nation,* 194. The manner of his death was the subject of considerable speculation by Ricker's interviewees. The army concluded he received four bullet wounds to the body and was bludgeoned with a hatchet to the head. Nelson A. Miles, *Annual Report of the Secretary of War* (Washington DC: GPO, 1891), 154. Captain Corliss, who was at the agency, was told that Wallace was wounded and then killed with a tomahawk wielded by a woman. Corliss interview in the *Denver Post,* Nov. 15, 1903. John Mackintosh, "Lakota Bullet Ends Wallace's Life—14 Years after Little Bighorn," *Greasy Grass* 16 (2000): 21–30 provides a brief biography.
236. Father Francis M. J. Craft, S.J., was longtime missionary to the Lakotas. He accompanied Forsyth's command to Wounded Knee on the evening of December 28. He said he went there "to see if I could be of any service . . . by going among the Indians and reassuring them." Statement of Rev. Francis J. M. Craft, *Reports, Campaign of 1890–91.* The photograph of Father Craft may be one by George Trager dated January 1, 1891. Jensen, Paul, and Carter, *Eyewitness at Wounded Knee,* 136, photograph 94.
237. Lt. James D. Mann died on January 15, 1891. He was assigned to the Seventh Cavalry in 1877, four years after entering West Point. Heitman, *Historical Register,* 687.

238. William H. Forbes took over as agent on May 4, 1871. Forbes, "Fort Totten Agency, Dakota Territory" *Annual Report of the Commissioner,* 1872, 534. McLaughlin was hired as a blacksmith in 1871. Construction of the first school began in the summer of 1873. Forbes died on July 20, 1875. He was succeeded by Paul Beckwith despite strong support for McLaughlin. McLaughlin took over as agent on July 3, 1876. He was transferred Standing Rock in September 1881. Pfaller, *James McLaughlin,* 5, 18, 27–28, 38, 60.

239. Cramsie took office on September 4, 1881. John W. Cramsie, "Devil's Lake Agency," *Annual Report of the Commissioner,* 1882, 20. He was McLaughlin's brother-in-law. Pfaller, *James McLaughlin,* 60.

240. Lt. Edward W. Casey graduated from West Point in 1873, and his first assignment was at Fort Sully. He was stationed at Fort Keogh early in 1890 when his proposal to organize a troop of Indian scouts with full military status was approved. Cheyenne scouts were enlisted that spring and in December they were on the Pine Ridge Reservation. Casey's men had been in regular contact with the so-called "hostiles" entrenched at the Stronghold after the Wounded Knee massacre. Casey thought he might be able to get them to surrender so on January 7 he set out for The Stronghold. On the way he met a small party of hostiles who seemed friendly but warned him to go back to the agency. Casey turned to leave and Plenty Horses shot the officer in the back of the head and killed him. Katherine M. Weist, "Ned Casey and His Cheyenne Scouts: A Noble Experiment in an Atmosphere of Tension," *Montana, the Magazine of Western History* 27 (1977): 26–39.

241. Casey recruited the scouts at the Tongue River Reservation. Jensen, Paul, and Carter, *Eyewitness at Wounded Knee,* 86. Ricker acquired a typed copy of Casey's letter (below) listing his scouts. Box 28, Ricker Coll.

> TROOP OF U.S. SCOUTS.
> Fort Keogh, Mont. November 14, 1890.
> Post Adjutant Fort Keogh
> Sir:
> I have the honor to make the following report concerning Indian Scouts and their families, as called for by communications herewith returned. The Indians at this post were enlisted by authority of the Hon. The Secretary of War, by endorsement, dated War Department April 7, 1890, upon a letter of mine to the Major General Comd'g. the Army dated Washington D.C. March 18, 1890. The number of persons constituting the families of scouts, including women and all children is 158. See list appended hereto. All Scouts enlisted up to this date are from that portion of the Cheyenne tribe located at the Lame Deer Agency Montana. I would state that I am authorized to enlist 100 men, and that I expect ultimately to take a portion from the Cheyenne located at Pine Ridge Dakota. At present my Troop numbers 58 men. As the number of persons constituting families, will probably increase as enlistments continue, I would request that necessary provision be made for issue of rations, to such increase, as from time to time may occur. If any re-

NOTE TO PAGE 170

ports as to numbers present should be required from me from time to time, I ask for instructions concerning the same. If it should be practicable to make this issue from the Post Commissary, it would put the matter upon its simplest basis.

Very respectfully
Your obedient servant
E. W. Casey
1st Lieut. 22nd Infantry Comd'g. Scouts

					Children		
Name of Scout		Women	No. of women	Under 5 yrs.	Between 5 and 10	Between 10 and 20	Total children
1 Willis Trowland	Serg.	Wife	1				
2 High Walking	Corp.	2 wives and mother in law	3	1	1	1	3
3 Stump Horn	"	Wife mother and sister	3	3	1	2	6
4 Wolf Voice	"	Wife and sister	2	1			1
5 Bear Black	"	Wife and mother	2	1			1
6 Big Backs	Pvt	Wife	1				
7 Big Crow	"	Wife and sister	2	2			2
8 Bear Man	"	Wife	1		1		1
9 Big Left Hand	"	Wife and mother	2				
10 Black Crane	"	Wife mother sister mother in law	4	1			1
11 Black Medicine	"	Wife	1				
12 Buffalo Horn	"	Wife	1	1			1
13 Bull Head	"	Wife	1	2	1	1	4
14 Bull Sheep	"	Wife	1	1	1	3	5
15 Elk River	"	Wife	1			1	1
16 Flying	"	Wife	1	1			1
17 Fire Wolf	"	Wife	1		1	1	2
18 Fisher	"	Wife	1	3		1	4
19 Hawk	"	Mother	1	2	1	4	7

NOTE TO PAGE 170

20	Hairy Hand	"	Wife and mother in law	2			
21	Issues	"	Wife and mother in law	2			2
22	King Fisher	"	Wife	1	1		1
23	Lazy Man	"	Wife	1	1		1
24	Little Dog	"	Mother	1		1	1	2
25	Little Eagle	"	Mother	1			
26	Little Wolf	"	Wife	1			
27	Looks Behind	"	Wife	1	2	2	4
28	Lone Wolf	"	Wife sister	2	2		1	3
29	Medicine Wolf	"	Wife and mother in law	2	1	1	1	3
30	Pine	"	Wife	1	2		2
31	Red Robe	"	Wife	1			1	1
32	Ridge Walker	"	Wife	1			
33	Rising Sun	"	Wives	2	1		1
34	Rock Roads	"	Wife	1	1		1
35	Scalp Cane	"	Wife	1			1	1
36	Shoulder Blade	"	Wife and sister	2	1		1
37	Sioux	"	Wife and mother in law				
38	Sweet Medicine	"	Wife and mother	2			
39	Teeth	"	Wife and mother	2	1	1	2
40	Walking Horse	"	Wife	1	1	1	2
41	Weasel Bear	"	Wife	1	1	1	2
42	White Beard	"	Wife	1		1	1
43	White Moon	"	2 Wives	2	2	1	3
44	White Powder	"	Wife and mother in law	2	2	1	3
45	Wild Hog	"	Mother	1			2	2
46	William Summers	"	Wife	1			
47	Wolf Name	"	Wife	1	1	1	2
48	Yellow Hair	"	Wife and				

			mother in law	2		1		1
49	Yellow Robe	"	Wife	1				
50	Zachariah T. Rowland		Mother	1		1	2	3
	Grand Total			72	38	21	27	86

Unmarried
51 Charles Means
52 Crane
53 Dumb
54 David Smoking Bear
55 Lame Bear
56 Red Turtle
57 Powder Face
58 Whirlwind

242. Plenty Horses told the court he shot Casey so his Brulé countrymen would consider him a warrior. Utley, *The Last Days of the Sioux Nation*, 266.
243. Francis Ellington Leupp served as commissioner from January 1905 to June 1909. He was more tolerant of Indian customs than most of his contemporaries, but like most he believed assimilation was necessary for the survival of the Indians. Donald L. Parman, "Francis Ellington Leupp," *The Commissioners of Indian Affairs*, 221-32.
244. In the biographical sketch of Wells that Ricker wrote earlier, he said that Wells was head farmer at Standing Rock in 1882.
245. The description of the route is obviously garbled. The Pretty Stone Buttes are near the headwaters of the Cannonball River. Perhaps Wells went up the Cannonball, crossed to the Grand, descended it, and then went north to the agency.
246. The discovery of gold in the Black Hills brought a flood of prospectors, but the Treaty of 1868 declared that the Lakotas' land was off limits to whites. The route Wells chose was heavily patrolled by the army to intercept the intruders. Olson, *Red Cloud and the Sioux Problem*, 171.
247. In September 1875 the Allison Commission tried to buy the Black Hills but the Lakotas refused to sell. After these negotiations failed the army withdrew its patrols, but the order to evict whites remained in effect. Ibid., 201, 214.
248. French explorers first met with the Santees in 1660 and by the 1680s French traders and missionaries were visiting them regularly. In 1805 Lt. Zebulon M. Pike was the first "big knife" to visit the Santees. Roy W. Meyer, *History of the Santee Sioux: United States Indian Policy on Trial* (Lincoln: University of Nebraska Press, 1967), 1, 9, 24.
249. According to Red Cloud the Koya band held a council about 1842 for the purpose of changing the band name:

Several names were proposed, and there was much discussion, but at last an old man, seeing a little garter snake wriggling through the grass, caught it up and holding it by the head and tail bit it in two in the middle, exclaiming, "This shall be our name, 'Ki-ya-ksa,' meaning literally "bitten in two." The general translation, however, is incorrectly "cut off."
Paul, *Autobiography of Red Cloud*, 70.

250. Ricker wrote the following in Tablet 22 without giving a source:
The Loafer band was a waiting body of Indians which lived around Fort Laramie, noted for its friendly disposition toward white people. When the Indians started down and the fight came off at Horse Creek, these Loafers also went along, but they returned the next year. Big Mouth was the chief at fort Laramie. He was the father of Mrs. John Farnham. The Loafer band was one band till 1868. Not many Indians besides the Loafers moved down to Whetstone; on their way back they split, a part adhering to Red Cloud and part to Spotted Tail. The Whetstone movement contemplated but one Agency for all. When abt. five yrs. afterwards the two Agencies of Red Cloud & Spotted Tail were made, one band of Loafers adhered to one Agency & the other band to the other Agency.

251. In 1869 the Hudson's Bay Company's governing power was transferred to Canada. Métis and Indians from the Red River settlements felt their rights would be threatened. Louis Riel led an attempt to establish an independent government. When Canadian troops arrived in the Red River valley the rebellion collapsed in 1870. George F. G. Stanley, *The Birth of Western Canada: A History of the Riel Rebellions* (Toronto: University of Toronto Press, 1960).

252. Henry J. Nowlan entered the military in 1863. Major Nowlan died in 1898. Heitman, *Historical Register*, 753.

253. Many Santees in Minnesota bore a grudge against neighboring white settlers and the government for the unfair treatment they had received. On August 17, 1862, five whites were murdered by four Santees in Meeker County. The Santee realized the whites would seek revenge and argued that it was time to evict the newcomers. Santee warriors, under the grudging leadership of Little Crow, attacked the settlements killing many whites. Col. Henry Sibley arrived with 1,500 troops and put an end to the rebellion. Four hundred Santees were sentenced to be hanged, but President Lincoln pardoned all but thirty-eight. Clair Jacobson, *Whitestone Hill: The Indians and the Battle* (LaCrosse WI: Pine Tree Publishing, 1991), 67-68.

254. Chief Big Thunder died in the fall of 1845. When Little Crow claimed the chieftainship his half brothers, one of whom wanted to be the chief, threatened to shoot him. Little Crow dared him to do so and he did, severely wounding him. Tribal members viewed Little Crow's actions as courageous and gave him their support. Tribal elders sanctioned the execution of the half brothers. Anderson, *Little Crow*, 43-44.

2. The Ghost Dance and Wounded Knee

1. James R. Walker practiced medicine on the reservation from 1896 to 1914. In 1902 he began gathering ethnographic data for the American Museum of Natural History. James R. Walker, *Lakota Society*, ed. Raymond J. DeMallie (Lincoln: University of Nebraska Press, 1982), ix–x.
2. Short Bull was referring to Wovoka, the Paiute shaman, who lived near Walker Lake in western Nevada. Wovoka's vision in January 1889 was the genesis for the Ghost Dance religion. Paul Bailey, *Wovoka, The Indian Messiah* (Los Angeles: Westernlore Press, 1957).
3. Danker, "The Wounded Knee Interviews of Eli S. Ricker," 235; Horn Cloud to Ricker, Dec. 23, 1903, Box 2, Ricker Coll.

    A year after the interview Ricker scribbled the curious remark that "Joe Horn Cloud is a liar" (Tablet 18). This statement must not have had anything to do with the interview. Certainly Horn Cloud's account contains nothing that could be labeled a lie.
4. The Dawes Act of 1887 provided that Indians could homestead. The U.S. General Land Office tract books, which include homesteads and attempted homesteads, indicate that a community of Indians had homesteaded near the site described by Horn Cloud, which was in Range 81, Township 3. The homesteaders' names are spelled in the Dakota language. The federal land office records consulted are tract books housed in the National Archives annex. In an interview made on August 6, 1977, Lawrence Riggs, 311 East Prospect, Pierre, South Dakota, indicated that his grandfather, T. L. Riggs, a Congregational missionary, was instrumental in aiding some of his Indian charges to homestead near his Oahe Mission on the Peoria Bottoms of the Missouri River, a site now covered by the Oahe Reservoir. It is possible that Horn Cloud referred to this group. Danker, "Wounded Knee Interviews," 239–40 n. 36.
5. Ricker made the following comments about battles and massacres in Tablet 22:

    The Indians sneer at the whiteman's conventional reference to the Custer massacre and the battle of Wounded Knee. They ridicule the lack of impartiality of the whites in speaking of the two events—when the whites got the worst of it it was a massacre; when the Indians got the worst of it it was a battle. The Indians understand that on the Little Big Horn they were defending themselves—their village—their property—their lives—their women and children. They understand that at W.K. they were attacked, wantonly, cruelly, brutally, and that what little fighting they did was in self-defense. The affair at W.K. was a drunken slaughter—of white soldiers and innocent Indians—for which white men were responsible—solely responsible. A little reason and patience & forebearance would have avoided the murderous clash.
6. In the spring of 1890 Capt. Argalus G. Henissee, in command of three compa-

nies of infantry, established a temporary camp in the forks of the Cheyenne River just west of the Cheyenne River Reservation. There was concern that the Indians, angered over a recent edict to sell reservation land, might abuse whites in the area. The camp was later manned by three troops of the Eighth Cavalry and one company of the Third Infantry. Utley, *The Last Days of the Sioux Nation*, 80, 132.

Henissee joined the army in 1861 and served in the infantry until transferred to the Eighth Cavalry in 1870. He retired in 1902 with the rank of colonel. Heitman, *Historical Register*, 523.

7. In the next interview Dewey Beard told Ricker they left on December 17, 1890.
8. Hump had been a devoted Ghost Dancer, but in early December he recanted. Jensen, Paul, and Carter, *Eyewitness at Wounded Knee*, 13. In his interview, Dewey Beard discussed the animosity Hump had for Big Foot, but the cause was not explained.
9. On December 21 Lt. Col. Edwin V. Sumner, Eighth Cavalry, arrived with three troops of cavalry and two of infantry. Utley, *The Last Days of the Sioux Nation*, 179.
10. Narcisse Narcelle was the mixed-blood agency farmer. He opposed the Ghost Dance. Ibid., 131.
11. At the end of Tablet 18 Ricker wrote, "White Lance is a wolf."
12. Red Beard was John Dunn, a rancher on the Belle Fourche or northern fork of the Cheyenne River. Utley, *The Last Days of the Sioux Nation*, 183. In mid-September Dunn and twelve others signed a petition requesting the military to protect them from the Ghost Dancers. John Dunn, et al., Sept. 26, 1890, Sen. Doc. 9: 4. Dunn did urge Big Foot's people to go to Pine Ridge. Dunn's statement of Jan. 17, 1891, is in *Report of the Secretary of War; Being Part of the Message and Documents Communicated to the Two Houses of Congress at the Beginning of the First Session of the Fifty-Second Congress* (Washington DC: GPO, 1892), 235–36.
13. A Hotchkiss gun was a mobile, breech-loading cannon that fired an explosive shell 3.2 inches in diameter. Four of these light cannons were brought to Wounded Knee. There were no Gatling guns. Jensen, Paul, and Carter, *Eyewitness at Wounded Knee*, 128.
14. Baptiste "Little Bat" Garnier was born in 1854, the son of a white man and a Lakota woman. He served as a scout for the army on several occasions. In about 1880 he moved to the Fort Robinson vicinity. E. A. Brininstool, *Fighting Indian Warriors* (Harrisburg PA: Stackpole Co., 1953), 271–79.

Ricker wrote the following note in Tablet 22:

Little Bat. ~~By Garnett~~ Was foully murdered in a cowardly manner when unarmed, by a bartender (or keeper) named J. D. Haguewood, in a saloon in Crawford, Neb., (date) The murderer had a trial in the Dawes County District Court at the _____ term, (year) and was acquitted by a "Dawes County jury," a term of local reproach for years, earned by the panels in that county for failure to convict the killers who flourished there without any wholesome check from the law.

15. Ricker's interview with Bartlett is in Tablets 44 and 45. Louie Mousseau told Ricker that he owned the store in 1890 (Tablet 26). He purchased it from William Robertson and Ephraim Bartlett, who in turn bought out George E. Bartlett.
16. As improbable as it seems, Dewey Beard described a similar situation in his interview. He also told James R. Walker that the interpreter, Philip Wells, said, "When the soldiers have all your guns, you Indians will all march past them and they will hold out their guns towards you." Walker, *Lakota Society*, 164.
17. Good Thunder was interviewed by Walter Camp in 1912 and admitted he was a Ghost Dancer, but minimized his role at Wounded Knee. Walter Mason Camp, Interview with Good Thunder, July 12 and 13, 1912, Camp MSS, Box 6, Lilly Library, Indiana University, Bloomington, Indiana.
18. For an attempt to compile a complete list see Richard E. Jensen, "Big Foot's Followers at Wounded Knee," *Nebraska History* 71 (1990): 194-212.
19. Rex E. Beach, "Wounded Knee," *Appleton's Booklovers Magazine* 7 (1906): 731-36.
20. Walker, *Lakota Society*, 157-68.
21. James H. McGregor, *The Wounded Knee Massacre, From the Viewpoint of the Sioux* (Baltimore: Wirth Brothers 1940), 103.
22. Danker, "Wounded Knee Interviews," 240 n. 47; *Sheridan County Star*, Rushville, Nebraska, Nov. 3, 1955.
23. Tablet 18. Dawson was a storekeeper at Pine Ridge.
24. Ricker talked briefly to Edward Truman and made the following note in Tablet 10: "Below Kyle, Day School No. 29, Feb. 16, 1907. Edward Truman, Teacher, says that Joseph Horn Cloud initiated the movement for the monument at Wounded Knee and it was due to his exertion that it was erected. He should have this signed credit."
25. Whites in the area were also hearing about the dance. On May 8, 1890, the *Chadron Democrat* carried a short, tentative article about a messiah appearing to Indians in Montana. It seems to have aroused the curiosity of editor Charles Allen. A week later he published a description of the Ghost Dance religion based upon information supplied by informants from Pine Ridge. Allen, *From Fort Laramie to Wounded Knee*, 158-59.
26. Beard uses Pine Ridge Agency and Red Cloud Agency interchangeably. He is referring to the Pine Ridge Agency that opened in October 1878.
27. Duck refers here to cotton cloth.
28. Lt. Col. Edwin V. Sumner, or Three Fingers, was in command of the camp at the forks of the Cheyenne River. He went in search of Big Foot with orders to arrest him. They met on December 21 and Big Foot convinced the colonel that he would turn himself in at Fort Bennett. Jensen, Paul, and Carter, *Eyewitness at Wounded Knee*, 17.

Sumner had been a cavalry officer since joining the army in 1861. He retired in 1899. Heitman, *Historical Register*, 936.
29. Beard was probably correct. Hump had been meeting with an old army friend,

Capt. Ezra P. Ewers, who convinced the chief to renounce the Ghost Dance. Jensen, Paul, and Carter, *Eyewitness at Wounded Knee*, 17.
30. The white man was John Dunn or Red Beard. See n. 12.
31. The soldiers were discovered on December 26. Utley, *The Last Days of the Sioux Nation*, 193.
32. They were probably Baptiste "Little Bat" Garnier, Old Hand, and two others. They were taken to Big Foot, who sent Old Hand and one other to tell the army that Big Foot was going to surrender. Ibid., 194. Later Ricker or Beard erroneously calls them "white scouts."
33. High Back Bone, a scout, was killed at Wounded Knee. Jensen, Paul, and Carter, *Eyewitness at Wounded Knee*, 127.
34. The reinforcements included four troops of the Seventh Cavalry and a troop of Oglala scouts, all under Col. James W. Forsyth. Ibid., 35.
35. Ricker's outrage is evident by his note with an exclamation point about Forsyth being drunk. Rex Beach must have been told the same thing by Beard. In the "Wounded Knee" article in *Appleton's Booklovers Magazine*, the episode is reported as follows:

> At this point, Philip Wells spoke saying, "When the soldiers have taken your rifles, you must march past in a line and they will hold out their guns to you." He meant by this that they would hold their weapons in front of them, as soldiers do sometimes; but we thought they would take aim at us.

Either Beach edited an incredible statement to make it credible or Beard told the same story twice. Wells does not mention the episode. Danker note, "Wounded Knee Interviews" 242 n. 55.
36. Beard told James R. Walker a slightly different story. He said that Black Coyote, who either he or the interpreter called Black Fox, refused to surrender his rifle, but Beard did not mention a struggle. Beard said he heard the first shots and then Black Coyote fired toward the sound of the gunfire. Walker, *Lakota Society*, 165. When Ricker interviewed William Palmer (Tablet 10) he was told the man's name was Blue Face.
37. He was identified as Shoots With Hawk's Feather in Horn Cloud's list of fatalities.
38. This unexpected detail about a sword seems to suggest that Ricker asked Beard if the horseman was an officer. If so, Beard's clever reply leaves the question open to whatever interpretation one wanted. Four officers were wounded, but their location at the time is not known.
39. Reports by the army suggest the fighting ended about noon or a little later. Forsyth to Brooke, Dec. 29, 1890, 1:30 P.M., *Reports, Campaign of 1890–91*. Eyewitness Charles Allen concurred. Allen, *From Fort Laramie to Wounded Knee*, 208–9.
40. Lt. Sedgwick Rice led a platoon down the ravine. Utley, *The Last Days of the Sioux Nation*, 222.
41. Charles "Will" Cressey dispatched accounts to the Omaha Bee before and after

the slaughter at Wounded Knee. Many of these were written to sell newspapers rather than report the truth. Kolbenschlag, *A Whirlwind Passes*.
42. Mousseau's crude map of Wounded Knee appeared on the first page of the interview. It has not been reproduced.
43. Peter McFarland was a civilian teamster who hauled supplies for the Seventh Cavalry and accompanied the soldiers to Wounded Knee. Ricker interviewed him on April 18, 1905 (Tablet 31).
44. The "one that went east" was probably Marguerite Elizabeth "Lost Bird" Colby. Leonard Colby, commander of the Nebraska National Guard, adopted the baby. Renée Sansom Flood, *Lost Bird of Wounded Knee: Spirit of the Lakota* (New York: Charles Scribner's Sons, 1995), 86, 116.
45. In Tablet 10 Ricker wrote, "Samuel Last Horse who saw the W. K. battle ground and reported to Standing Soldier who was taking the Standing Rock Indians into the Agency." Ricker wrote another note in Tablet 39:

> Pine Ridge. See Standing Soldier No. 2, 2 miles north of Agency. He was a scout and piloted the Standing Rock Indians around by Porcupine Creek after W.K. battle and to avoid their seeing the field, and brought them in close to the Sand Hills and camped them in the camp of Friendlies south of Agency. See Red Shirt at Agency who was with Standing Soldier. These were sent out [to] head off and guide these Indians.

46. Mousseau's estimate is higher than most, but not unrealistic. Jensen, "Big Foot's Followers at Wounded Knee," 198.
47. Ricker's interview with George Stover is in Tablet 26.
48. Robertson's interview is in Tablets 12 and 28, but either Ricker did not write about Wounded Knee or his comments have been lost.
49. Ricker wrote to Father Francis Craft questioning him about the Wounded Knee massacre. Craft replied that he did not have time to provide the answers "as they should be carefully prepared, if mentioned at all." He was adamant in his defense of the soldiers. He claimed that it was the Indians' misdirected gunfire that killed the women and children and that the Indians fired, "without provocation, upon the troops." Craft to Ricker, Jan. 16, 1907, Box 2, Ricker Coll.
50. Hardorff note, *Death of Crazy Horse*, 39–40.
51. Lecompte, "Antoine Janis," 196–201.
52. On the day of the massacre Forsyth wrote the "hot fight" lasted "from about 9:15 until 9:45" in the morning. Forsyth to Brooke, Dec. 29, 1890, *Reports, Campaign of 1890–91*.
53. Turning Bear was considered a chief by many of the Brulés. He was a Ghost Dancer. Utley, *The Last Days of the Sioux Nation*, 82, 137.
54. Capt. Augustus W. Corliss commanded a company of the Eighth Infantry acting as an artillery unit guarding the agency. Jensen, Paul, and Carter, *Eyewitness at Wounded Knee*, 81. His interview is in Tablet 24.

Red Cloud went to the Badlands with the fleeing Ghost Dancers. On January 9, 1891, he returned to the agency. There he said he had been kidnapped by Short Bull's Brulés, who threatened to kill him if he tried to escape. Bland, *A Brief History of the Late Military Invasion of the Home of the Sioux*, 22.

55. When the army arrived at Pine Ridge, it issued orders calling upon the Lakotas to assemble near the agency. Most of the Ghost Dancers refused and these "hostiles" gathered first near the mouth of White Clay Creek. Later they congregated in the Badlands at a place called the Stronghold. Utley, *The Last Days of the Sioux Nation*, 121-22.

56. When Maj. Samuel M. Whitside set out to capture Big Foot his orders included the remark, "If he fights, destroy him." F. W. Roe to Whitside, Dec. 27, 1890, *Reports, Campaign of 1890-91*.

57. James Asay operated a trading post at the Pine Ridge Agency. *Chadron Democrat*, July 4, 1899. A month later his trader's license was revoked for selling whiskey on the reservation. C. G. Penney to commissioner, Sept. 19, 1893; T. J. Morgan to F. E. Pierce, Jan. 31, 1891, Letters Sent to the Office of Indian Affairs from the Pine Ridge Agency (National Archives Microfilm Publication M1282, roll 21), Records of the Bureau of Indian Affairs, Record Group 75, NARA (hereafter cited as Pine Ridge Agency Letters).

58. Tablet 22 is the narrow notebook. It measured three and a quarter by nine inches.

59. Danker note, "Wounded Knee Interviews" 243 n. 66; Ricker Tablet 44.

60. Shangrau's interview is in Tablets 9 and 27.

61. Starr's map was a loose, unnumbered sheet in Tablet 48.

62. In Tablet 22 Ricker wrote, "See Apple, Indian name Owl Ring, 3 miles east of Allen. He it was [with] a party of Indians who visited the W. K. Battlefield and gathered up the living children next day." If Ricker visited Apple he left no record of the meeting.

63. Ricker's Zit-ka-la-nuni was Lost Bird, the baby girl adopted by General Colby. Mary Thomas or Comes Out Alive spent her life on Pine Ridge. Flood, *Lost Bird*, 250.

64. Historians have sided with Peano's count of 146. Jensen, Paul, and Carter, *Eyewitness at Wounded Knee*, 116.

65. George Trager accompanied the burial detail on January 1 and took several photographs. Ibid., 49. Ricker wrote a note about the photographs in Tablet 39:

> Locke, the Photographer, has Indian Pictures. Probably has one of the "Ghost Dance." Ask him if he knows where Jim Meadows is. Meadows had a lot of negatives taken of the Indians and of ghost dancing before the W.K. fight. When A. H. Baumann sold his Rushville gallery to Meadows he let him have these negatives. Meadows was burned out at Lead several years ago. Baumann took these views. He has been in business in Rushville, Gordon, Buffalo, Wyo., and Crawford.

C. J. "Clem" Davis resigned as farmer at the Wounded Knee district in 1892, and moved to Chadron, Nebraska, with his family. *Chadron Citizen*, Feb. 18, 1892.

66. Dr. Charles A. Eastman began practicing medicine at Pine Ridge on October 1, 1890. Eastman was a Santee mixed-blood who spent his youth as a traditional Dakota. His initiation into the white world is described in his autobiography, *From Deep Woods to Civilization.*
67. Feather combined incidents that occurred on December 30, when a rescue party went to Wounded Knee, and January 1, when the burial party was there. W. A. Birdsall confirmed that Clem Davis was with the rescue party (Tablet 25).
68. Birdsall was with the burial party and identified the photograph as that of Big Foot (Tablet 25). In Tablet 44 Ricker wrote, "Ask Charley Eason for the W. Knee plates. He bot Trager out. Guy Sawyer had the photos. Joe Ford, Gus Trager & W. H. Hayward were the Northwestern Co."
69. John M. Burke served as Cody's press agent and general manager of the Wild West shows. His title was honorary. Don Russell, *The Lives and Legends of Buffalo Bill* (Norman: University of Oklahoma Press, 1960), 202.
70. William Garnett (Tablet 1) told Ricker that scout Crazy Thunder was the one who convinced the Indians to surrender.
71. Lone Bear was born about 1847. He was in the Little Bighorn battle. After the Oglalas surrendered, he enlisted in the U.S. Indian Scouts and later in the Pine Ridge police, where he served for more than twenty years. Hardorff, *Lakota Recollections,* 153 n. 1.
72. Capt. James Kennington was the officer of the day. Buecker, *Fort Robinson and the American West,* 115–16.
73. Three months later Chipps told Ricker much the same story about the burial near a cliff along Beaver Creek (Tablet 18). Richard Stirk told a similar story (Tablet 8). In Tablet 9 Ricker mentioned C. F. Coffee who "knows who has Crazy Horse's bones." There is no other mention of Coffee in the Ricker collection. Agent James Irwin met some of Spotted Tail's people early in November 1877, in the vicinity of the mouth of Wounded Knee Creek. They had broken away from the main column bound for the new agency on the Missouri River. They had Crazy Horse's remains with them. Irwin, "Red Cloud Agency, Dakota," *Annual Report of the Commissioner,* 1878, 37.

Crazy Horse's body was first taken to the Spotted Tail Agency vicinity for burial. Lt. Jesse Lee at Camp Sheridan ordered the construction of a board enclosure around Crazy Horse's coffin-scaffold. See Chapter One, n. 117.
74. *Empire Magazine,* June 29, 1980; Ann Woodbury Hafen, "William W. McGaa," *The Mountain Men and the Fur Trade of the Far West,* ed. LeRoy R. Hafen, 10 vols. (Glendale CA: Arthur H. Clark Co., 1971) 8: 232.
75. Maj. Guy V. Henry, Ninth Cavalry, entered the miliary academy in 1856, and was a brigadier general when he retired in 1898. He died a year later. Heitman, *Historical Register,* 523.
76. Gen. George Crook, with an army of nearly twenty-five hundred men had been scouring the northern Plains in search of "hostile" Sioux during the summer of

1876. The troops were in present-day North Dakota and already short on rations when the general decided to proceed to the Black Hills to protect the settlements there. On this march it became necessary to butcher some of their horses to survive. Greene, *Slim Buttes*, 88.

77. In Tablet 22 Ricker included a drawing of the brand: ⌐◯⌐ . The Wyoming Livestock Association required the brand to be named, so it was called "FOF."

78. Capt. George LeRoy Brown, Eleventh Infantry, served from late in 1891 until 1893. *Annual Report of the Commissioner*, 1891, 1892, and 1893.

79. His father was probably Stuart B. Garvie, a trader. *Annual Report of the Commissioner*, 1891, 92. The Yellow Medicine or Upper Sioux Agency was south of present-day Granite Falls, Minnesota. The Lower Sioux Agency was east of Redwood Falls, Minnesota. It was also called the Redwood Agency. Ibid., 120.

80. In 1906 there were 570 Southern Poncas in Oklahoma and 263 Northern Poncas around the mouth of the Niobrara River in present day Knox County, Nebraska. James H. Howard, *The Ponca Tribe* (Lincoln: University of Nebraska Press Bison Books, 1995), 10.

81. In 1858 the Poncas accepted a reservation that is roughly today's Boyd County, Nebraska. Their Lakota allies viewed this as a capitulation to the whites and began to attack the Poncas. Then in 1868 the Ponca reservation was included in land set side for the Lakotas. Nine years later the Poncas were forced against their wishes to move to an Oklahoma reservation. In 1878 Chief Standing Bear's son died and the chief decided to bury the young man on the old reservation. The army was ordered to arrest this small group because they were considered escapees from their reservation. They succeeded in reaching Nebraska, where white sympathizers arranged to bring Standing Bear's case to trial. The judge ruled that because an Indian was a person he was entitled to the protections offered under the U.S. Constitution. Standing Bear's followers formed the nucleus of the so-called Northern Poncas. Ibid., 33–39.

82. Edwin A. Fry published the *Niobrara Pioneer* from 1874 to 1905 at Niobrara, Nebraska, and then the *Wonderland Magazine*. He probably would have been a good informant because of his experience as a Pine Ridge trader and a witness to the last Sun Dance. Addison E. Sheldon, "Niobrara Journalist Death," *Nebraska History Magazine* 17 (1936): 139.

83. Joseph Godfrey was one of the 303 Indians convicted and sentenced to death for their part in the 1862 uprising in Minnesota. He provided so much evidence to convict his former comrades that his sentence was commuted after three years in prison. He died in 1909 on his farm near Niobrara. Meyer, *History of the Santee Sioux*, 127.

84. Jay Amos Barrett was the librarian from about 1893 to 1907.

85. Swift Bear was the leader of the Brulé Corn band. He was a progressive leader and, being the brother-in law of James Bordeaux, was well liked by the whites for his

friendly disposition. Swift Bear was known among the Lakotas for his ability to breed fast horses. He died in 1909. Hardorff note, *Death of Crazy Horse*, 54 n. 56.
86. This account has similarities to the Grattan fight near Fort Laramie, which occurred fifty-three years before the interview. Thirty soldiers were killed, but there were no prisoners. Swift Bear went to the aid of a wounded soldier, although the man died the following day. Lloyd E. McCann, "The Grattan Massacre," *Nebraska History* 37 (1956): 20.
87. After the Sioux Uprising in 1862 white residents in Minnesota demanded that all Indians be removed from the state. It made no difference that few if any Winnebagos participated. In the summer of 1863, nearly two thousand Winnebagos were shipped to Crow Creek on the Missouri. There was no game in the area, the Indian office was unable to provide much food, and the Winnebagos nearly starved during the winter. Many made their way south to the Omaha Reservation, where they were well received, but the problem of subsistence was still serious. In 1865 the Omahas agreed to transfer part of their reservation to the newcomers. Edmund J. Danziger, Jr., "The Crow Creek Experiment: An Aftermath of the Sioux War of 1862," *North Dakota History* 37 (1970): 105-23.
88. C. F. Breckenridge practiced law in Omaha, Nebraska, from about 1873 until his death in 1911. His son, R. W., was also a lawyer. *Omaha Daily News*, Oct. 12, 1911. The article in the *Omaha Bee* could not be found.
89. Although the Santees did not participate in the Sioux Uprising, they fell victim to the wrath of white Minnesotans. Louis L. Pfaller, O.S.B., "The Peace Mission of 1863-1864," *North Dakota History* 37 (1970): 310. Like the Winnebagos the Santees were also exiled to Crow Creek. After numerous bureaucratic snafus the Santees were moved to a reservation near the mouth of the Niobrara River in 1866. Roy W. Meyer, "The Establishment of the Santee Reservation, 1866-1869" *Nebraska History* 45 (1964): 59-97.
90. In 1924 the Santees were awarded approximately $348,000. Meyer, *History of the Santee Sioux*, 302.
91. This slender book discusses missionary work in South Dakota in the 1890s. The author thanked "Rev. James Garvie, for courtesies shown me." Samuel C. Gilman, *Conquest of the Sioux* (Indianapolis: Carlon and Hollenbeck, 1897), 11.
92. John Wesley Powell, director of the Bureau of American Ethnology, died in 1902.
93. The reference is to Metlakatla, a Tsimshian Indian town in British Columbia, and to the Rev. William Duncan, missionary of the Church of England. In 1887 some controversy caused Duncan to move the mission to Annette Island, Alaska, and most of the Tsimshians followed. Hodge, *Handbook of American Indians*, 850-51.
94. Shangrau goes on to describe General Crook's expedition to the Powder River in March 1876. Frank Grouard was also a scout on the expedition and his recollection of it is in DeBarthe, *Life and Adventures of Frank Grouard*.
95. Louis Richard had three brothers, Charles, Peter, and John Jr. John Richard Sr. married Mary Gardiner, a mixed-blood Oglala, in 1844. He was a trader in the Fort

Laramie area. John Dishon McDermott, "John Baptiste Richard," *The Mountain Men and the Fur Trade of the Far West* ed. LeRoy R. Hafen, 10 vols. (Glendale, Calif.: Arthur H. Clark Co., 1965), 2: 293.

The entire command left Fetterman on March 1, 1876. J. W. Vaughn, *The Reynolds Campaign on Powder River* (Norman: University of Oklahoma Press, 1961), 42-43.

Shangrau's head of the Cheyenne River is Lightning Creek.

96. Ricker interviewed John "Buckskin Jack" Russell on November 13, 1906 (Tablet 8). John Farnham's brief interview is in Ricker's Tablet 12.
97. The herder was wounded on the night of March 1-2. Bourke, *On the Border with Crook*, 256.
98. Capt. James Egan, Second Cavalry, entered the army as a private in 1856. He retired in 1879. Heitman, *Historical Register*, 399.
99. Col. Joseph J. Reynolds, Third Cavalry, entered West Point in 1839. He retired in 1877. Ibid., 824. He was in command of the troops attacking the village. Vaughn, *The Reynolds Campaign*, 60.
100. Frank Grouard said this was Crazy Horse's village. DeBarthe, *Life and Adventures of Frank Grouard*, 98. Ricker interviewed Two Moons, who told him there were two hundred warriors there under Crazy Horse, but a greater number of Cheyennes were in the camp (Tablet A). J. W. Vaughn concluded it was a Cheyenne village "with some lodges of visiting Sioux," but that it was "unlikely that Crazy Horse was present." Vaughn, *The Reynolds Campaign*, 123.
101. Six men were wounded and four were killed during the campaign. Ibid., 212.
102. Bourke disagreed. He stated, "We fell back at such a rate that our dead were left in the hands of the Indians." Bourke, *On the Border with Crook*, 279. Robert E. Strahorn, a reporter for the *Rocky Mountain News*, witnessed the battle. In his report he had high praise for the scouts. Robert E. Strahorn, "The Battle of Powder River, March 17, 1876," *Battles and Skirmishes of the Great Sioux War, 1876-1877*, ed. Jerome A. Greene (Norman: University of Oklahoma Press, 1993), 3-19.
103. Charles Allen was the editor of the *Chadron Democrat*. His autobiography, *From Fort Laramie to Wounded Knee*, contains one of the best eyewitness accounts of the Wounded Knee disaster. Allen's inteview is in Volume Two.
104. The officer near the cannons would probably have been either Capt. Allyn Capron, First Artillery, or Lt. Harry L. Hawthorne, First Artillery. Utley, *The Last Days of the Sioux Nation*, 201.
105. Twenty-seven Ghost Dancers were taken to Chicago on January 26, 1891, where they were to be held for six months. Buffalo Bill Cody used his considerable influence to secure their release and took them on a yearlong tour of Europe with his Wild West show. Jensen, Paul, and Carter, *Eyewitness at Wounded Knee*, 171.
106. In September 1878 three hundred Cheyennes under Dull Knife and Little Wolf fled from virtual incarceration on a reservation in Indian Territory in a daring attempt to return to their homeland in Montana. Dull Knife's group of about 150 was

NOTES TO PAGES 264-274

captured by the army and imprisoned in a soldiers' barracks at Camp Robinson while the government tried to decide what to do with them. On January 9, 1879, they made a desperate dash for freedom. Buecker, *Fort Robinson and the American West*, 127-41.

107. Lt. Francis H. Hardie entered the military academy in 1872, and was later assigned to the Third Cavalry. Heitman, *Historical Register*, 499.

Henry W. Wessels began his military career as a cadet in the naval academy in 1862, and then enlisted in the Union Army during the Civil War. By 1879 he had risen to the rank of captain and was assigned to the Third Cavalry. Ibid., 1019. Wessels took command of Camp Robinson on December 5, 1878. Buecker, *Fort Robinson and the American West*, 198.

108. It was probably Ricker who posed this question. Men in Wessels's command, as well as his superiors, also questioned the captain's cautious approach. Ibid., 143.

109. Maj. Andrew W. Evans, Third Cavalry, arrived at the station from Fort Laramie on January 19 and took command. Wessells's men were reinforced by two troops of the Third Cavalry under Capt. John B. Johnson. Ibid., 144.

110. This episode occurred on January 22, 1879, along Antelope Creek. Ibid., 145.

111. Lt. George F. Chase, Third Cavalry, entered West Point in 1867. Heitman, *Historical Register*, 297. Ricker's question mark is appropriate. The infantry officer was Lt. John Baxter, Jr., Company K, Ninth Infantry. He was on detached service with the Third Cavalry headquarters from September 21, 1878, to February 24, 1879. Personal communication from Thomas R. Buecker, March 8, 2000.

112. Three enlisted men were killed and four were wounded. Thirty-two Cheyennes were in the pit. Seventeen men, four women, and two children were killed. Buecker, *Fort Robinson and the American West*, 146. In Tablet 39 Ricker wrote, "Cheyennes made last stand on Antelope creek on or near Section 1-34-56."

113. Shangrau's memory failed again. The officer who went for more scouts was Lt. George A. Dodd, Troop L, Third Cavalry. He left Fort Robinson on January 18, 1879, for Pine Ridge. The scouts he recruited were mustered in on January 20. Personal communication from Thomas R. Buecker, March 8, 2000.

3. The Old West—Indians and Indian Fights

1. This episode would have taken place in 1861. However, He Dog, who thought Crazy Horse was born in 1838, stated that the latter was given his name when he was about eighteen years old after a fight with Arapahoes (Gros Ventres?), who made a stand on a high hill covered with big rocks, near a river. This incident may have taken place in 1857, when Lakota winter counts recorded that a war party of Oglalas and Miniconjous killed ten enemies on Captive Hill, at the head of the Moreau River, near present Spearfish, South Dakota. This same incident of tribal warfare, and the prominence displayed by Crazy Horse and his cousin, Kicking Bear, is mentioned in the Thunder Tail Narrative, Holy Rosary Mission Files, Marquette University. Chipps's statement may explain the cause of the name change,

but not the origin of the name because both Worm and Makes the Song had been known as Crazy Horse. Hardorff note, *Death of Crazy Horse*, 74-75 n. 2.

2. The name of Crazy Horse's mother was Rattle Blanket Woman. Born about 1815, she was a Miniconjou by birth and probably was related to the powerful Lone Horn family, whose name frequents the Miniconjou winter counts. Evidence suggests she committed suicide about 1844 due to severe mental depression caused by the death of a relative. Hardorff note, *Death of Crazy Horse*, 75 n. 3.

3. This shooting took place on Powder River during the summer of 1870, two days after No Water's wife, Black Buffalo Woman, left her husband for Crazy Horse. The assault was accomplished with a handgun. Striking the face near the nostrils, the bullet glanced off the underlying bone structure and deflected through the fleshy layer of the gum and the cheek, fracturing the upper jaw before exiting at the neck near the base of the skull. Although Chipps stated that the ball entered the right side of Crazy Horse's face, other contemporary sources strongly suggest it was the opposite side. According to He Dog, the bullet struck the jawbone just below the left nostril. This location is confirmed by George W. Oaks, a teamster, who saw Crazy Horse at Camp Robinson several times and commented that he "had quite a scar on his left cheek." William J. Bordeaux, son of Louis Bordeaux, also corroborated the location of the scar on the left cheek through information received from Crazy Horse's sister, Mrs. Joe Clown, and other contemporaries. The final corroborating evidence is provided by an unidentified reporter for the *New York Sun*, who met Crazy Horse in May of 1877, and who wrote that the "bullet wound through his left cheek . . . disfigured his face and gives to the mouth a drawn and somewhat fierce or brutal expression." Hardorff note, *Death of Crazy Horse*, 75 n. 4.

4. The best description of this incident is given by He Dog in Hinman, "Oglala Sources," 12, 15-18. A few months after the shooting Black Buffalo Woman gave birth to a light-haired little girl, rumored to have been Crazy Horse's daughter. Hardorff note, *Death of Crazy Horse*, 76 n. 5.

5. Bull Head was a Miniconjou band leader and a maternal uncle of Crazy Horse. To count coup was principally the touching of an armed enemy during a combat situation, the display of contempt being heralded by the Plains Indians as one of the most glorious acts of warfare. Hardorff note, *Death of Crazy Horse*, 75 n. 6.

6. The Fetterman fight took place on December 21, 1866, near Fort Phil Kearny, Wyoming Territory, during which a combined force of Oglalas, Miniconjous, and Cheyennes decoyed and killed Capt. William J. Fetterman and his command of seventy-eight soldiers and two civilians. Hardorff note, *Death of Crazy Horse*, 77 n. 8.

7. This war sack was actually a medicine bundle, stored in a bag made from tanned animal skin, and which contained the claws and dried heart of the spotted eagle. These objects, imbued with protective powers, were part of a powerful medicine

bundle given to Crazy Horse by Chipps after the No Water shooting in 1870. Hardorff note, *Death of Crazy Horse*, 77 n. 10.

8. On June 25, 1876, Maj. Marcus A. Reno and three companies of the Seventh Cavalry led an abortive attack on the Indian village at the Little Bighorn. Reno's conduct, like that of his superior, Gen. George A. Custer, has been the subject of considerable controversy. Consisting of some twenty-five warriors, Custer's auxiliary force of Arikara (Ree) Indians may have been responsible for the deaths of as many as four Lakotas and two Cheyennes. During Reno's charge the Rees killed Swift Bear and White Bull, both Hunkpapa Lakotas. Hardorff note, *Death of Crazy Horse*, 78, n. 11.

9. Ricker is premature in his criticism because Chipps's casualty count is corroborated by numerous independent sources. Hardorff note, *Death of Crazy Horse*, 78 n. 12.

10. Custer's body was found six feet southwest of the present commemorative monument on Custer Hill. However, a stone placed by the War Department in 1890 to identify Custer's kill site is actually some fifty feet from the correct location. Hardorff note, *Death of Crazy Horse*, 78 n. 13.

11. Gall, also known as Man Who Goes in the Middle, was born in a Hunkpapa Lakota camp on the banks of the Grand River, South Dakota, in 1840. Throughout his non-reservation life he proved himself a fierce opponent to the white aggressors. In November 1867 the military issued orders for his arrest, and while resisting capture near abandoned Fort Berthold, he was bayonetted entirely through the body from both front and rear and was left for dead. Miraculously, he recovered enough from the shock of his wounds to make his escape before daylight, walking twenty miles in severe winter weather to the house of a relative. Gall survived this ordeal, and it was said that out of vengeance he killed and scalped seven whites, among whom was Lt. Eban Crosby on October 14, 1871. During Reno's attack on the Hunkpapa lodges, Gall's two wives and three children were killed. To avenge his family, he mutilated a number of Custer's soldiers, and fearing reprisals, he took his band to Canada. He surrendered to the U.S. military at Poplar Creek, Montana, in the winter of 1880. His conduct on the reservation was exemplary, and he later became a justice of the Indian Police Court at Standing Rock Agency. Gall died on December 5, 1893, from an overdose of weight-reduction medication. He lies buried at Wakpala, South Dakota. Hardorff note, *Lakota Recollections*, 42 n. 14.

12. Grass was an Oglala band chief and a signer of the Fort Laramie Treaty of 1868. A note in the Camp manuscripts reveals that Grass once was wounded and captured by soldiers near Platte Bridge. Expecting to be killed, he was instead taken to the post hospital and restored to health. Grass vowed never to fight the whites again. He and his band settled near the Oglala agency and became known as *Wagluhe Oyate*, people who loafed around the forts. Grass is not to be confused with John Grass, who was a Blackfoot Lakota. Hardorff note, *Death of Crazy Horse*, 79 n. 15.

13. Leading a small camp of Oglalas, the elder Crazy Horse traveled with his wife's

Miniconjou relatives, Touch the Cloud and Roman Nose, to Camp Sheridan, Nebraska, where he and some 256 lodges of Northern Lakota bands surrendered to Gen. George Crook on April 14, 1877. Hardorff note, *Death of Crazy Horse*, 79 n. 16.

14. This was Capt. James Kennington, Fourteenth Infantry, who served as officer-of-the-day on September 5, 1877. Hardorff note, *Death of Crazy Horse*, 80 n. 17.

15. Chipps's statement is corroborated by Louis Bordeaux, who told Ricker that the butt of the guard's rifle struck Chipps's shoulder and broke the latter's collar bone. Bordeaux interview, Tablet 11. Hardorff note, *Death of Crazy Horse*, 81 n. 18.

16. Reference is made to the cliff burial near Camp Sheridan, where on September 6 relatives sepulchered the remains of Crazy Horse in a coffin draped with red blankets, on a three-feet-high scaffold. Hardorff note, *Death of Crazy Horse*, 81 n. 19.

17. A *New York Tribune* reporter confirmed the existence of two bullet wounds, one of which was in Crazy Horse's face, resulting in an "ugly scar." However, in an interview with Walter Camp, Chipps revealed that Crazy Horse had bullet scars not only on his leg, but also on his arm. The plurality of injuries is confirmed by Red Feather, who commented that Crazy Horse was wounded twice when he began his fighting career, which statement excludes the No Water wound which was sustained much later. According to Crazy Horse's cousin Eagle Elk, the arm wound was sustained during a fight with Pawnees when Crazy Horse was a very young boy. The second scar resulted from a gunshot wound received in a fight with Utes when a bullet struck Crazy Horse in his left calf. The latter information was obtained from Owns Horn, a Miniconjou cousin of Crazy Horse. Hardorff note, *Death of Crazy Horse*, 17 n. 20.

18. The name of Crazy Horse's half brother was Little Hawk. Born about 1846 he was the only child conceived of Worm's second marriage with two Brulé women, the sisters of Spotted Tail. Lakota elders claimed that Little Hawk exhibited traits that eventually would have made him a greater man than Crazy Horse, if not for his rashness. He was slain in combat in 1870 while Crazy Horse was convalescing from the No Water shooting. Hardorff note, *Death of Crazy Horse*, 82 n. 21.

19. For another vision by Crazy Horse involving water, see the Flying Hawk Interview in M. I. McCreight, *Firewater and Forked Tongues* (Pasadena: Trail's End, 1947), 138–39, in which a reference to straws of grass tends to corroborate Garnett's statement.

In spite of Chipps's denial, the water spirit did give certain instructions to Crazy Horse which, if adhered to, would apparently prevent his death. However, it was the nearly-fatal shooting by No Water in 1870 that led to Chipps's eagle Wotawe which made Crazy Horse bulletproof. Hardorff note, *Death of Crazy Horse*, 82 n. 22.

20. Hardorff, *Death of Crazy Horse*, 65; Elbert D. Belish, "American Horse (Wasechun-Tashunka): The Man Who Killed Fetterman," *Annals of Wyoming* 63 (1991): 54–67.

21. There was opposition to the Horse Creek treaty of 1851. The primary concern was the clause that allowed the government to build roads and military posts in Indian country. The treaty also stipulated that a "head chief" must be chosen to speak for the entire tribe. Kappler, *Indian Affairs*, 594-95. The idea of a single leader was contrary to Lakota custom. Frank Salaway (Tablet 27) told Ricker that Conquering Bear, a Brulé, was chosen.
22. Straight Foretop was a Miniconjou. His name was usually translated High Forehead. McCann, "The Grattan Massacre," 6.
23. Semineau may have been present, but Lucien Auguste was the official interpreter. Ibid., 8.
24. On August 19, 1854, Lt. John L. Grattan led twenty-nine soldiers into the Lakota camp. They had two light cannons. Ibid., 8-9.
25. The 1851 treaty signed at Horse Creek gave the tribe $50,000 a year for ten years. If the President approved, the term could be extended to fifteen years. Interest was not mentioned. Kappler, *Indian Affairs*, 595.
26. See nn. 6, 20.
27. The name of the ridge was in shorthand. Belish called it Lodge Trail Ridge. Belish, "American Horse," 56.
28. Black Crow was the leader of a Brulé band. He was an ambitious man who had married Spotted Tail's daughter, and who was later implicated in the 1881 assassination of his father-in-law. Hardorff note, *Death of Crazy Horse* 98 n. 6.
29. American Horse was referring to the 1875 Allison Commission that came to discuss the sale of the Black Hills. The council was held near Red Cloud Agency, and not on Chadron Creek.
30. Some of Samuel D. Hinman's contemporaries praised him for his defense of the Santees who were imprisoned after the 1862 uprising in Minnesota. Meyer, *History of the Santee Sioux*, 136-38.
31. Henry B. Whipple was consecrated Episcopal bishop of Minnesota in 1859. Ibid., 138.
32. Prisoners were incarcerated at Mankato, Minnesota, and at Fort Snelling. The men and women at Mankato were moved to Camp McClellan near Davenport, Iowa, in April 1863. A month later a group from Fort Snelling, consisting mostly of women and children, was transported by boat down the Mississippi River and up the Missouri. A second group went by boat as far as Hannibal, Missouri, and crossed the state by rail in boxcars. The two groups were reunited at St. Joseph and continued upriver to Crow Creek. Ibid., 143-46.
33. Eastman's assessment of Inkpaduta is surprising. The latter was part of a small band that had been expelled from the tribe for the murder of the chief. In 1857 Inkpaduta's people attacked a white settlement in northwestern Iowa, killing thirty-four settlers. Although the army and its Indian associates pursued Inkpaduta he was never captured. Ibid., 97-100.
34. William J. Bordeaux, *Custer's Conqueror* (Sioux Falls SD: Smith and Co., 1969), 77.

35. James Bordeaux began working for the American Fur Company in 1830 in the upper Missouri country. In 1841 the company built Fort John or Laramie, an adobe trading post on the Laramie River where Bordeaux was stationed. Bordeaux remained there until June 1849 when the fort was sold to the government. He then began operating his own trading post about eight miles down the North Platte River. The Lakotas robbed this store after the Grattan defeat in 1854 and he sold the building to John Richard. John Dishon McDermott, "James Bordeaux," *The Mountain Men and the Fur Trade of the Far West,* ed. LeRoy R. Hafen, 10 vols. (Glendale CA: Arthur H. Clark Co., 1968), 5: 65-80.

   A trapper named LaRamee was killed about 1820 along the river that would bear his name. John Dishon McDermott, "J. LaRamee," *The Mountain Men and the Fur Trade of the Far West,* ed. LeRoy R. Hafen, 10 vols. (Glendale CA: Arthur H. Clark Co., 1968), 6: 223-25.

   The first officer to command the army Fort Laramie was Maj. Winslow F. Sanderson.

36. Bordeaux stayed along the North Platte River until 1868, when he moved to Bordeaux Creek. He remained in the general area until his death in 1878. McDermott, "James Bordeaux," 65-80.

37. Chadron Creek was named for Louis B. Chartran. He had a trading post near present Chadron, Nebraska, in the early 1840s. Charles E. Hanson, Jr., "The Chadron Creek Trading Post," *The Museum of the Fur Trade Quarterly* 12 (1976): 6, 18.

38. Capt. Daniel W. Burke, Fourteenth Infantry, commanded Camp Sheridan. The garrison consisted of C Company, Fourteenth Infantry, and M Company, Third Cavalry, an aggregate of seven commissioned officers and 106 enlisted men. Hardorff note, *Death of Crazy Horse,* 96 n. 1.

   Jesse M. Lee had served in the Civil War and would continue his military career into the twentieth century. In regard to his service in 1877, records reveal that on May 14 Lee commenced to serve a special assignment as acting Indian agent at Spotted Tail Agency. His account of the killing of Crazy Horse may be found in the *Journal of the Military Service Institution of the United States* (May-June 1914): 323-40. This same article, along with a few extractions of Lee's diary and his wife's recollections of the slaying, was later published by E. A. Brininstool in *Crazy Horse, The Invincible Oglala Sioux Chief* (Los Angeles: Wetzel Publishing Co., 1949). After reading Lee's writings, one cannot escape the impression that Lee felt personally responsible for Crazy Horse's death. Hardorff note, *Death of Crazy Horse,* 96-97 n. 2.

39. The reward was $200, quite large when compared with an enlisted soldier's annual pay of $150. Hardorff note, *Death of Crazy Horse,* 98 n. 4.

40. In addition to Captain Burke and Lieutenant Lee, only one other officer was present, Dr. Egon A. Koerper, assistant surgeon, U.S.A., attached to Camp Sheridan. Hardorff note, *Death of Crazy Horse,* 98 n. 7.

41. The Northern Indians were of different Lakota bands: Touch the Cloud led the

Miniconjous, while Crazy Horse led the Oglalas. Hardorff note, *Death of Crazy Horse*, 100 n. 8.

42. According to Lieutenant Lee, Buffalo Chips had stated: "Crazy Horse is brave, but he feels too weak to die today. Kill me—Kill me!" In this version, neither Spotted Tail nor Crazy Horse was called a coward by Buffalo Chips, which is a preposterous accusation in view of their fearless reputations. Hardorff note, *Death of Crazy Horse*, 101 n. 9. Ricker identified Buffalo Chips as Charley White in Tablet 13.

43. The surgeon was Dr. Egon A. Koerper. See n. 40.

44. A similar charge was made by Money, an Oglala woman better known to the whites as Nettie Goings. She, like others, maintained that Grouard's last name was Brazeau, or Prazost, an erroneous identification disproven by historical evidence. Hardorff note, *Death of Crazy Horse*, 102 n. 11. See Goings interview in this chapter.

45. Blaming Red Cloud and his agency Oglalas for the slaying of his son, Worm refused to live among them any longer and instead settled among the Brulés on the Rosebud Reservation in 1878. Worm died there in 1881. Although little is known of his descendants, one of them, Black Bull, his grandson, later became a member of the Rosebud Indian Police. Hardorff note, *Death of Crazy Horse*, 103 n. 12.

46. High Bear, also known as Tall Bear, was the leader of a small band of Northern Sans Arcs. He was a close ally of the Miniconjou, Touch the Cloud, with whom he enlisted in the U.S. Indian Scouts in 1877. High Bear died at the Cheyenne River Agency in 1910. Hardorff note, *Death of Crazy Horse*, 104 n. 12.

47. Good Voice was the leader of a band of *Wajaje* Brulés and a member of the Brulé delegation that visited Washington in 1877. He enlisted in the U.S. Indian Scouts in 1877 and later became one of the first on the reservation to adopt the white man's dress. Hardorff note, *Death of Crazy Horse*, 107 n. 14.

48. Swift Bear was an uncle of Louis Bordeaux whose mother, christianized Marie, was Swift Bear's sister. Hardorff note, *Death of Crazy Horse*, 107 n. 15.

49. Bordeaux's recollection of Little Big Man's alleged statement has to be viewed with skepticism. According to Red Feather, who was Crazy Horse's brother-in-law, Little Big Man's words were advisory and conciliatory "We'll do whatever White Hat [Lieutenant Clark] says," promising Crazy Horse "to stay by him all the time." Red Feather's statement is corroborated by Garnett, who recalled that Little Big Man assured Crazy Horse, "wherever he was taken to, he would go with him and stand by him." Further evidence that Louis's recollection of this incident erred may be found in his embellished account in Bordeaux, *Custer's Conqueror*, 87–88. Hardorff note, *Death of Crazy Horse*, 109 n. 16.

50. This statement is confirmed by Lt. John G. Bourke, who obtained the information from Little Big Man in 1881. However, according to Pvt. George W. McAnulty, Ninth Infantry, the bayonet thrust did not miss Crazy Horse but "went clear through his body and pinned him against the log building!" Hardorff note, *Death of Crazy Horse*, 110 n. 18.

51. Charles Robidoux was a mixed-blood of French and Brulé parentage. One of his

relatives, Louis Robidoux, lived at the Jordan Trading Post at the Brulé agency, where he was employed as the official interpreter around the turn of the century. Hardorff note, *Death of Crazy Horse*, 110 n. 19.

52. This was probably the Brulé Standing Bear, a member of the Wears Salt Band which was led by Lip. Standing Bear was a mixed-blood who operated a store on the Rosebud Reservation in the early 1880s. He died on Pass Creek in 1898. Standing Bear was the father of Henry Standing Bear. Standing Bear's recollection is corroborated by William Garnett, who recalled that Crazy Horse's words were, "You've got me hurt now" [Tablet 1], while He Dog remembered the words as, "They have stabbed me." He Dog recalled further that Crazy Horse was moaning, but that it was more from anger than from pain. Woman's Dress, who also was a witness to the stabbing, added that Crazy Horse, when he was lying on the ground and was suffering from his wound, kept repeating the words, "Father, I want to see you." Hardorff note, *Death of Crazy Horse*, 111 n. 20.

53. Since Crazy Horse died at 11:40 P.M., Bordeaux must have left the adjutant's office prior to that time. Hardorff note, *Death of Crazy Horse*, 111 n. 21.

54. The second doctor was Capt. Charles E. Munn, U.S. Medical Department, who was the post surgeon at Camp Robinson. Hardorff note, *Death of Crazy Horse*, 111 n. 22.

55. Although Bordeaux provided the translation, the words spoken by Crazy Horse were actually addressed to Lt. Jesse M. Lee, who had been asked to come to the adjutant's office by Touch the Cloud, the uncle of Crazy Horse. Since Bordeaux was Lee's interpreter, both men probably went to the adjutant's office together, arriving about 10 P.M. Hardorff note, *Death of Crazy Horse*, 111 n. 23.

56. Crazy Horse's vital signs began to weaken about 10 P.M. When Dr. McGillycuddy attempted to revive him by giving him some brandy, Worm objected, stating in sign language that the liquor would only make his son's "brain whirl." McGillycuddy then administered several hypodermics of morphine to Crazy Horse, which seemed to ease the pain, but which did not prevent his death, which followed shortly thereafter. This sudden death, occurring after the injections, aroused Worm's suspicion that his son was poisoned. Hardorff note, *Death of Crazy Horse*, 112 n. 24.

57. Lee was promoted to brigadier general on June 17, 1902. Heitman, *Historical Register*, 624. He did not finish his book but did write about the death of Crazy Horse. Jesse M. Lee, "Story of Jesse M. Lee." *Nebraska History Magazine* 12 (1929): 5–32.

58. Crow Dog killed Spotted Tail on August 5, 1881. Hyde, *Spotted Tail's Folk*, 299. He was tried in Deadwood and condemned to be hung. The verdict was appealed to the U.S. Supreme Court and the tribunal declared that Deadwood did not have jurisdiction in reservation matters and ordered Crow Dog's release. V. T. McGillycuddy, "Pine Ridge Agency, Dakota," *Annual Report of the Commissioner*, 1884, 41. Unfortunately Ricker did not "put down" details of the family feud. For a recent analysis of the incident see Sidney L. Harring, *Crow Dog's Case: American*

Indian Sovereignty, Tribal Law, and United States Law in the Ninteenth Century (Cambridge: Cambridge University Press, 1994), 100-41.

59. Water Rat Creek, or Muskrat Creek, is the Lakota name for present Medicine Tail Coulee, so named by the Crow Indians who inhabit this region. Respects Nothing has located the Miniconjou camp too far inland. The Miniconjous themselves recall that their camp was situated across from Medicine Tail Ford, which in the early days was significantly known as the Minneconjou Ford. The correct English translation of "Itazapcho" is not Uses the Bow Band, but rather No Bows Band, the name by which the early French identified this subdivision of the Lakotas. Hardorff note, *Lakota Recollections*, 25 n. 2.

60. This may have been the Oglala Lakota Black Bear. Questioned in 1911 about this matter, Black Bear still seemed afraid to talk about his involvement in events that had taken place some thirty-five years earlier. Hardorff note, *Lakota Recollections*, 26 n. 3.

61. Trail Creek is the Lakota identification of present Reno Creek, named after Maj. Marcus A. Reno, who led companies A, M, and G of the Seventh Cavalry in an abortive attack on the southern end of the Indian village. Box Elder Creek is the Lakota name for the present Shoulder Blade Creek. Chasing Creek is probably the Lakota name for present Squaw Creek. Hardorff note, *Lakota Recollections*, 26 nn. 4, 5, 6.

62. Quick to see a strategic vantage point, Lakotas from all bands collected on the bluffs just south of the mouth of Box Elder (Shoulder Blade Creek). Eventually they charged and pressured Reno's left flank, forcing his command to seek shelter in the dry riverbed along the edge of the woods. Hardorff note, *Lakota Recollections*, 26 n. 7.

63. Capt. Frederick W. Benteen commanded Companies D, H, and K of the Seventh Cavalry. Hardorff note, *Lakota Recollections*, 27 n. 8.

64. This was Gen. George A. Custer's battalion, consisting of Companies I, L, and C under command of Capt. Myles W. Keogh, and Companies E and F commanded by Capt. George Yates. Apparently, Custer's battalion was then descending Cedar Coulee. Hardorff note, *Lakota Recollections*, 27 n. 9.

65. Reference is to the battle of the Rosebud, June 17, 1876, when a united force of Sioux and Cheyennes fought a victory over units of the Second and Third Cavalry and Fourth and Ninth Infantry, the whole commanded by Gen. George Crook. In view of the length of this battle and the ammunition expended, it seems almost incredible that the casualty count amounted to only nine troopers and about six Indians. Hardorff note, *Lakota Recollections*, 28 n. 10.

66. On June 25, 1876, Custer rode Vic, abbreviated from Victory, a sorrel horse with four white feet and a blaze on his face. Hardorff note, *Lakota Recollections*, 28 n. 11.

67. Gen. Alfred H. Terry, who commanded the Department of Dakota and accompanied the Montana Column. Hardorff note, *Lakota Recollections*, 28 n. 12.

68. Military eyewitnesses discovered two lodges standing on the benchland opposite

the mouth of present Deep Ravine. One lodge revealed the remains of five warriors, while the other contained only three. Hardorff note, *Lakota Recollections,* 28 n. 13.

69. Respects Nothing's total of twenty killed has reference to the body count of slain Lakotas only. On Wood Louse Creek, known to the Crow Indians as Little Fat Creek, the Miniconjou, Three Bears, and the Oglala, Black White Man, died from the trauma of their wounds. Hardorff note, *Lakota Recollections,* 29 n. 14.

70. On September 10, 1876, Capt. Anson Mills and two battalions of the Third Cavalry captured a Miniconjou village of thirty-six lodges near Slim Buttes, present South Dakota. The casualty total consisted of one trooper, one civilian, and six Lakotas, among whom was the Miniconjou leader Iron Shield. Hardorff note, *Lakota Recollections,* 30 n. 16.

71. The "ridge northeast of Water Rat" is most likely the present Luce Ridge, which is situated along the north bank of Medicine Tail Coulee. This ridge curves at its eastern end into Nye-Cartwright Ridge, about a mile east of the river, which then runs westward to Calhoun Hill. Luce Ridge was named after Capt. Edward S. Luce, Little Bighorn Battlefield superintendent from 1940 through 1956, who discovered a concentration of military artifacts at this location. Nye-Cartwright Ridge was named after Ralph G. Cartwright, a schoolteacher in Lead, South Dakota, and Lt. Col. Edward L. Nye, whose interest in the Little Bighorn battle led to the discovery of hundreds of casings on the latter ridge. Hardorff note, *Lakota Recollections,* 31 n. 17.

72. Reference is to the western terminus of Calhoun Hill, known to the Lakotas as Greasy Grass Hill, which contained the bodies of some twenty slain troopers and two non-commissioned officers, the latter of C Company. Numerous military and Indian artifacts have been found along and near this ridge. Calhoun Hill was named after Lt. James Calhoun, L Company, Seventh Cavalry, who was slain with his men at this location. Hardorff note, *Lakota Recollections,* 31 n. 18.

73. Edward S. Godfrey's article, "Custer's Last Battle," was published in the *Century Magazine* in January 1892. It included the map. For a more recent republication see Edward S. Godfrey, *Custer's Last Battle,* ed. Eugene McAuliffe (Omaha NE: n.p., 1952).

74. Just below (downstream) of the northwest corner of the present boundary fence lies a river crossing that leads to a natural passageway around and to the northeast of Custer Hill. Upstream from this lower crossing was yet another ford, sometimes called Cheyenne Ford, which lies directly opposite the mouth of Deep Ravine, the latter not to be confused with Deep Coulee, which runs along the south side of Calhoun Hill. Hardorff note, *Lakota Recollections,* 32 n. 20.

75. The "low place" is the present Deep Ravine in which the bodies of twenty-eight of Custer's men were discovered by military survivors two days after the battle. Respects Nothing makes clear that the battle ended with the killing of these men. The Indian killed at this location was the Cheyenne Noisy Walking, known to the

Lakotas as Left Hand. He was the son of the prominent Cheyenne White Bull, whose nickname was Ice. Hardorff note, *Lakota Recollections*, 32 n. 21.

76. This act of valor was performed by Bearded Man, a Southern Cheyenne chief of the Elk Society, known to his own people as Lame White Man. He was killed just south of Custer Hill and, being mistaken for a Ree Indian Scout, was scalped and otherwise mutilated by the Miniconjou Little Crow. The alleged location where Lame White Man was slain was marked under the direction of his grandson, John Stands in Timber, by a wooden cross placed by the National Park Service on the river side of the blacktop on Custer Ridge. Hardorff note, *Lakota Recollections*, 33 n. 22.

77. Nearly every Indian eyewitness makes reference to this or other attempted escapes, the end result being inevitably the same in that the soldier either committed suicide or was shot in the back. Hardorff note, *Lakota Recollections*, 33 n. 23.

78. Inasmuch as the total casualties of both Custer's and Reno's battles amounted to some 260 men, the maximum number of revolvers, carbines, and rifles could not have been much more than 520 pieces. Yet, some Indian accounts are persistent in their tally of 700. Hardorff note, *Lakota Recollections*, 34 n. 24.

79. For another account of the Little Bighorn battle by Flying Hawk, see McCreight, *Firewater and Forked Tongues*, 111–16. Hardorff note, *Lakota Recollections*, 49 n. 1.

80. Known to the whites as Sioux, these warlike peoples were divided into three distinct entities, each with their own peculiar dialect. They identified themselves as the Teton Lakotas, the Santee Dakotas, and the Yankton and Yanktonai Nakotas. Of the Sioux gathered at the Little Bighorn, the Tetons were most numerous, their population being represented by the seven groups that make up the Lakotas. From their own statements, we know that the Hunkpapa, Miniconjou, and Oglala camps were the largest. The Blackfeet, Brulés, Two Kettles, and Sans Arcs were represented in much smaller numbers, and their lodges, with the exception of the Sans Arcs, were fused with the larger camps. To illustrate the difference in dialect, consider Sioux spelling of Chief Red Top's name, which was known among the Santees as Inkpa Duta, and among the Tetons as Inkpa Luta. Hardorff note, *Lakota Recollections*, 50 n. 2.

81. The "second ridge" is probably the elevated area just east of the present blacktop near Medicine Tail Ford. Viewing this location from the west bank of the river, one sees across the stream a line of perpendicular bluffs that rise some fifteen feet above the river's floodplain. The top of the bluffs is fairly level and forms the tableland through which the present blacktop makes a large loop. East of this road, the land rises sharply, its elevation giving the appearance of being the second ridge back from the river. This latter elevation contains the marker erected for Sgt. James Butler of L Company. Hardorff note, *Lakota Recollections*, 50 n. 3.

82. The map is nothing more than seemingly scribbled lines with a note "Indian women congregated" at one end.

83. On June 27 military survivors found the remains of twenty-eight individuals on

the bottom of a ravine, some four hundred yards southwest of Custer Hill. Flying Hawk makes clear that these were the remains of troopers who had failed to gain the safety of the timber along the river at the end of the battle. His narrative refutes the existence of the so-called "south line," a theory that suggests the deployment of E Company at the head of this ravine at the beginning of the battle. This theory, widely though incorrectly accepted by scholars and historians alike, was advanced by Charles Kuhlman and expounded in his *Legend into History* (Fort Collins CO: Old Army Press, 1977), 181–89; for a counter view of this invalid theory see Hardorff, *Markers, Artifacts, and Indian Testimony: Preliminary Findings on the Custer Battle* (Short Hills NJ: Don Horn Publications, 1985), 54–63. For further refutation, see the Weston interviews with Two Eagles, Lone Bear, Lights, Hollow Horn Bear, and Julia Face in Hardorff, *Lakota Recollections*, 141–94. Hardorff note, *Lakota Recollections*, 51 n. 4.

84. In his account to McCreight, *Firewater and Forked Tongues*, 113, Flying Hawk recalled that upon the destruction of Keogh's troop, the remnant fell back to make yet another stand on Custer Ridge, some distance south of the present monument site. It was probably at this location that the Cheyenne Lame White Man was killed. From this location the survivors withdrew to join the troopers already on Custer Hill. Hardorff note, *Lakota Recollections*, 51 n. 5.

85. The noncombatants were congregated near present Squaw Creek. The lower crossing was at the mouth of Deep Ravine, and since the Cheyennes were camped near this crossing, it has been identified by some scholars as the Cheyenne Ford. After having defended their camp circle, many of the Hunkpapas arrived late at Custer's battlefield. These Hunkpapas crossed at the Cheyenne Ford and ascended the tableland near the foot of Deep Ravine. Hardorff note, *Lakota Recollections*, 52 n. 6.

86. Flying Hawk's reference to Custer being on "the second ridge" suggests strongly that troops may have come within three hundred yards of the river as measured from the elevation. This conclusion is supported by Flying Hawk's kinsman, He Dog, who told Walter Camp in 1910 that Custer's command was scattered along and parallel with the river, and only some 600 feet from it. Hardorff note, *Lakota Recollections*, 52 n. 7.

87. Listed as missing in action, the whereabouts of Lt. Henry M. Harrington continues to be a subject of speculation which often unjustly results in implied charges of desertion and cowardice. Hardorff note, *Lakota Recollections*, 52 n. 8.

Ricker wrote the following in Tablet 22: See Flying Hawk at mouth of W.K. He was in the Custer battle and pursued Lt. Harrington & saw him shoot himself & says it was accidental as he was beating his horse with his revolver.

88. Examination of the evidence reveals that the Indians withdrew from Reno's front upon the commencement of the fight on Custer ridge. Many scholars have contributed Reno's inactivity on the bluffs to his timidness, indecisiveness, and lack of general leadership abilities. When subordinates no longer could restrain their

impatience with Reno's delay, a move was made in Custer's direction by Capt. Thomas B. Weir and subsequently by Capt. Frederick H. Benteen, the latter ignoring Reno's frantic trumpet signals to abort this move. Hardorff note, *Lakota Recollections*, 53 n. 9.

89. Flying Hawk confirms the statements made by Respects Nothing and also by Ruleau's informants, who all indicated that only three hours passed between the opening of the valley fight and the end of the battle. Hardorff note, *Lakota Recollections*, 53 n. 10.

90. This opinion is not shared by a majority of Indian sources, who compare Reno's retreat to a wild buffalo stampede with the Indians doing the chasing. The behavior displayed by the troopers seemed to have elicited a number of insulting remarks from the Indians. Of interest also is an interview with the Hunkpapa Lakota Little Knife, who stated that Reno's retreating soldiers fired wildly over their shoulders, killing some of their own comrades, and that some of the troopers became unhorsed and confronted the Indians with their hands raised in an appeal for pity. Hardorff note, *Lakota Recollections*, 53 n. 11.

91. For a listing of Indian casualties, see the White Bull interview in Hardorff, *Lakota Recollections*, 107-28.

92. Ricker's conclusion is supported by the Miniconjou Standing Bear, who crossed the river to Medicine Tail Coulee to collect his family's ponies. Before he did so, he ascended the elevation now known as Weir Point, from where he saw the advance of both Reno's and Custer's troops. Hardorff note, *Lakota Recollections*, 54 n. 13.

93. Ricker made the following notation on the inside back cover of Tablet 8: "See Standing Bear at Manderson who was in Custer fight & has painted pictures of the fight. He married a German woman." Some of Standing Bear's artwork was published in John G. Neihardt, *Black Elk Speaks: Being the Life Story of a Holy Man of the Oglala Sioux* (Lincoln: University of Nebraska Press, 1979).

94. This is another reference to the young Lakota named Deeds, who accompanied his relative, Brown Back, to the head of Reno Creek in search of a stray pony. Near the divide they became aware of the presence of Custer's troops, and although they both fled the location immediately, only Brown Back reached the village to sound the alarm. After the battle, the slain body of Deeds was found in the brush near the mouth of Reno Creek. There exists a mass of conflicting evidence regarding the true identity and band affiliation of these two individuals, and also regarding the location and circumstances of Deeds's death. Hardorff note, *Lakota Recollections*, 58 n. 2.

95. The first fighting has reference to the feeble attack by Maj. Marcus A. Reno on the southern end of the great village, about 3 P.M. Chicago time. Hardorff note, *Lakota Recollections*, 58 n. 3.

96. Although Standing Bear's interview with Walter Camp gives the impression that he was present in the Oglala camp, his statement to Ricker makes clear he was

among the Miniconjou lodges just downstream (north) of the Hunkpapas. Hardorff note, *Lakota Recollections*, 59 n. 4.

97. Mentioned in several other accounts, the "second" or "rear" ridge is the elevation just east of the present blacktop that loops past Medicine Tail Ford on the east bank of the river. His statement that Custer did not attempt to reach the ford is contradicted by his opposite assertion three years later. He then emphasized to Walter Camp that Custer's soldiers had advanced nearly to the river, when increased Indian resistance finally succeeded in forcing them back. Hardorff note, *Lakota Recollections*, 59 n. 5.

98. Although Medicine Tail Ford was the principal crossing used, quite a number of the Hunkpapas used the Cheyenne Ford; see Raymond J. DeMallie, *The Sixth Grandfather: Black Elk's Teachings Given to John G. Neihardt* (Lincoln: University of Nebraska Press, 1984), 190, which contains Iron Hawk's statement that "the Hunkpapas gathered at the foot of the gulch on the east side of the Little Big Horn that leads up to the Custer hill." Obviously, Iron Hawk described the mouth of Deep Ravine because it was from this location that he observed the stampede of the gray horses and the futile escape attempt of the last of Custer's men. Hardorff note, *Lakota Recollections*, 59 n. 6.

99. The accuracy of Standing Bear's statement is in doubt because Captain Frederick W. Benteen attested to having counted only two dead ponies, while Capt. Thomas M. Dougall saw five or six. Hardorff note, *Lakota Recollections*, 59 n. 7.

100. Standing Bear's recollection seems clear and concise about the sequence of events that led to the deaths of Custer's men found in Deep Ravine. Reliving this last phase of the battle, he told John Neihardt that these soldiers "went into the side of a hill into a draw and there was tall grass in here. We were right on top of the soldiers and there was no use in hiding from us. Then I saw an Indian rush at the men and then the Indians killed every soldier including some of our own Indians who had gone ahead of the rest. When we killed the last man, we could hear the women coming over and it was just a sight with men and horses mixed up together—horses on top of men and men on top of horses." DeMallie, *The Sixth Grandfather*, 186-87. The Little Bighorn battle chapter in the latter publication contains the literal translations of Neihardt's interviews with three elderly Lakotas in 1931. Their statements are rich in detail and reveal much information not available in the reworded and abridged previous publication, *Black Elk Speaks*. Hardorff note, *Lakota Recollections*, 60 n. 9.

101. The estimate of 45 Cheyenne warriors appears to be much too low. The Cheyenne, Wooden Leg, estimated the number of his people at the Little Bighorn at 1600, while his kinsmen Tall Bull and White Bull told Walter Camp that their encampment consisted of 200 lodges and 3000 people. Hardorff note, *Lakota Recollections*, 39.

102. Ruleau's population figure of six thousand is about half the estimated total of most witnesses. However, when compared with recent studies, his total appears to be

in line. John S. Gray, *Centennial Campaign: The Sioux War of 1876* (Fort Collins CO: Old Army Press, 1976), 357. Dr. Gray deduced the total Indian population at the Little Bighorn at one thousand lodges, containing 7,120 persons, including 1,780 adult males. Robert A. Marshall, "How Many Indians Were There?" *The Research Review* (June 1977): 8, estimated a ceiling of 795 lodges and a corresponding population of 5,056 people. Hardorff note, *Lakota Recollections*, 39 n. 4.

103. The location of the Oglala circle seems incorrect. The Oglalas, and most other Lakotas, indicate their camp was on the flat just southwest of the encampment. Hardorff note, *Lakota Recollections*, 39 n. 5.

104. Big Road, more accurately translated as Wide Road, was a chief of a Bad Face band of Northern Oglalas. He was an intelligent, but unreconstructed man who preferred exile in Canada in 1877 rather than reservation life on one of the Missouri agencies. For an account of his stay in Canada with Sitting Bull, see Stanley Huntley's interview with the hostile Sioux in the *Chicago Daily Tribune* of July 5, 1879. The other three Lakotas have not been positively identified. Hardorff note, *Lakota Recollections*, 40 n. 6.

105. In view of the casualty totals obtained from other eyewitnesses, Ruleau's hearsay numbers are too exaggerated to merit serious consideration. See the casualty count in the White Bull interview. Hardorff note, *Lakota Recollections*, 40 n. 7.

106. At the inquiry in 1879, Lt. George Wallace, the official itinerist, made clear that his watch readings did not represent local sun time, but rather Chicago time, which was the official time maintained at Fort Abraham Lincoln. Lt. Edward S. Godfrey made clear that the watches of the officers had not been changed since leaving Fort Lincoln. Thus, as a result of the watch readings submitted by Lieutenant Wallace, scholars have come to a general agreement that Reno's valley battle commenced about 3 P.M., Chicago time. However, it should be noted that the difference between Chicago time and the far west (San Francisco time) was then calculated to be some two and a quarter hours, which follows that the valley fight started at about one o'clock far western time. Because the watch recovered at the Rosebud battlefield may have carried San Francisco time, it does not seem impossible that it was still operative a week later when, according to Respects Nothing, it was read by one of the agency or mixed-blood Indians. Hardorff note, *Lakota Recollections*, 40 n. 8.

107. Muddy Creek is probably yet another name for Shoulder Blade Creek. It probably refers to the mouth of this creek, which sheltered many of the Indians early in Reno's valley fight. See J. W. Vaughn, *Indian Fights* (Norman: University of Oklahoma Press, 1966), 145-66, which gives a survey of Shoulderblade, its drainage area, and the positions of Reno's skirmish lines. Hardorff note, *Lakota Recollections*, 40 n. 9.

108. The pack train and its escort did not arrive until an hour after Reno had gained the bluffs. Ruleau is correct as to his number of forty slain of Reno's command, which breaks down as follows: three officers, thirty-two enlisted men, three Ree Indian scouts, and two civilians. Hardorff note, *Lakota Recollections*, 41 n. 11.

109. One of the most debated issues of the Little Bighorn battle centers around the question of whether Custer attempted to cross the river. Was an attempt made to cross at Medicine Tail Ford before his command was forced back toward Calhoun Hill? Or was it never near the ford, but instead did his command travel straight from Cedar Coulee to Calhoun Hill? The early Cheyenne statements suggest Custer indeed reached the river and had quite a spirited engagement there. However, the later Cheyenne accounts refute any combat at the crossing. Instead, these sources assert that Custer went directly to Calhoun Hill, and that his closest position to the stream was held by troopers at that location. The same bewildering contradiction holds true for the Sioux accounts, which are equally divided on this issue. However, modern field research now has established that soldiers were deployed near the ford and also on Luce Ridge, the heights situated along the north bank of Medicine Tail Coulee, about one mile east of the river. A reconstruction of the combat scenario suggests that the troops near the crossing were withdrawn to Calhoun Hill before those on Luce Ridge followed. This latter movement was observed by the recent Indian reinforcements coming from the Reno fight, which might explain why these warriors categorically denied any combat at the ford. Of course, we have to be careful with our conception of "at" and "near," which does not necessarily have to mean at the river's edge. Ruleau's statement, although hearsay and perhaps subjected to personal impressions, offers the first indication of three divisions prior to Custer's movement to Calhoun Hill. His further statement that Custer came within half a mile of the river corroborates the growing evidence that troopers were deployed simultaneously on the flat near the river and also on Luce Ridge. Hardorff note, *Lakota Recollections*, 41 n. 12.

110. The high hill can only be the cluster of three knobs now known as Weir Point, from where Capt. Thomas B. Weir of Benteen's command in vain scanned Custer's battlefield more than an hour later. Hardorff note, *Lakota Recollections*, 42 n. 13.

111. This statement, associated with the three dots on the map, seems to suggest the troops nearest the river were forced eastward onto a second unit, the whole then withdrawing to the balance of Custer's command. A similar observation was made by Curly, a surviving Crow Indian scout with Custer's battalion, who stated that Custer came down a coulee to its mouth; that the column was "stretched up this deep coulee and away back on side of ridge;" that the Indians' fire then forced the head of the column to retreat to a ridge northeast, where they reunited with the main command. Very little information is available on Knife Chief. Apparently, he was a prominent Oglala Lakota and a ranked member of a soldier lodge. During the Ghost Dance troubles of the 1890s, he was an active militant, commanding a band of 150 dancers. Hardorff note, *Lakota Recollections*, 42 n. 14.

112. Many years after the battle, the location just north of Luce Ridge yielded the remains of four troopers and three horses. These casualties may have occurred during Custer's march to Calhoun Hill, or, more likely, they may have been individuals

attempting to escape from Calhoun Hill toward Reno's command. Hardorff note, *Lakota Recollections,* 43 n. 15.

113. The second stand, perhaps better known as Keogh's Stand, was a desperate fight that took place on the east slope of Custer Ridge and which involved I Company and survivors from companies C and L. The third stand was on Custer Hill, from where some forty men fled down the ravine toward the river. Ruleau is in error stating these men were slain along the edge of the ravine because some twenty-eight bodies were found on the bottom of the washout. This statement is a good indication of Ruleau's mental editing, he having gained this impression after viewing the faulty marker locations of these men. Hardorff note, *Lakota Recollections,* 45 n. 18.

114. This is yet another trooper who attempted to escape. This individual is not to be confused with the soldier observed by Fears Nothing who made the attempted escape from Calhoun Hill. Hardorff note, *Lakota Recollections,* 45 n. 19.

115. Of interest here is not the absolute time itself, but rather the opportunity it affords to figure the length of time expired since the opening of the valley fight, which Ruleau was told started at nine o'clock in the morning. Converting this into Chicago time (military time), we learn that Reno's battle commenced at 3 P.M., and that Custer's battle ended at 6 P.M. Hardorff note, *Lakota Recollections,* 45 n. 20.

116. Those slain on Custer Hill were farthest away from the village and seemed to have been spared the scalping and extreme disfiguration observed on the field nearer the village. The names of the three slain Rees were Bloody Knife, Bobtail Bull, and Little Soldier. Particular vengeance was directed toward Bloody Knife, who was part Hunkpapa Lakota, his body having been decapitated and the head placed on a pole and carried in triumph around the village. Positive identification of the remains of Bobtail Bull and Little Soldier was made impossible due to the obliteration of the facial features by the Sioux. Bobtail Bull was a brother of the Cheyenne Plenty Crows, the latter having been taken captive by the Cheyennes and raised since a young boy. Hardorff note, *Lakota Recollections,* 46 n. 21.

117. Sioux and Cheyennes reported the presence of several women who participated in the assault on Custer's force. One of these was the Hunkpapa Moving Robe Woman, who avenged the death of her younger brother by slaying several of Custer's troopers. Hardorff note, *Lakota Recollections,* 46 n. 22.

118. This was Gen. Alfred H. Terry's force of units from the Second Cavalry and Seventh Infantry. The Indian withdrawal was over the benchland south of Shoulder Blade toward the Big Horn Mountain, late in the afternoon of June 26. Hardorff note, *Lakota Recollections,* 46 n. 23.

119. If anyone emerges as a hero from the Little Bighorn battle, then it was Capt. Frederick W. Benteen, whose exemplary determination prevented the Indians from carrying Reno's entrenchments. His conduct was given indirect praise in the findings of the Reno court of inquiry, which concluded that subordinates in some instances did more for the safety of the command by brilliant displays of courage than did Major Reno. On June 26 water was obtained by a number of volunteers,

who later received the Medal of Honor. A total of twenty-four were issued to the survivors of the Seventh Cavalry, the greatest number ever awarded for a single armed confrontation. Hardorff note, *Lakota Recollections*, 47 n. 24.

120. It is unfortunate that Ruleau was not asked to be more specific as to in which ravine these soldiers had been found. After the battle, rumors were persistent that a number of Custer's troopers had escaped from the battlefield, only to be trapped and slain in a ravine some distance to the east. However, Ruleau's statement may have reference to present Deep Ravine and its branches, which contained the bodies of over thirty men. So overwhelming was the stench coming from these decomposing corpses on the bottom that the burials of these men were accomplished by breaking off large clumps of dirt from the edge of the ravine and dropping these onto the bodies below. Many of the men involved in this task took to vomiting, and it stands to reason that some of the bodies at this site may never have received any dirt coverage at all. Hardorff note, *Lakota Recollections*, 47 n. 25.

121. Although only a minor chief among the Hunkpaps, Gall's reputation and status among the whites received a considerable boost from his frank interview given on the tenth anniversary of the Custer Battle. Gall explained that his savage behavior during the battle resulted from the killing of his family during Reno's attack. Other Indian sources fail to mention casualties among the noncombatants, but contemporary newspapers disclose the discovery of several slain women and children near the point of Reno's assault. Gall's status was elevated further by the Indian agent at Standing Rock, who was determined to eradicate the political strength of Sitting Bull. Hardorff note, *Lakota Recollections*, 47 n. 26.

122. The wounding of Knife Chief is confirmed by his son, Thomas Steals Horses. Apparently Knife Chief was shot near Reno's line in the valley, and being severely wounded, he remained lying on the battlefield until relatives were able to remove him on a pony travois. Hardorff note, *Lakota Recollections*, 48 n. 27.

123. Hardorff, *Lakota Recollections*, 63.

124. Squadrons from the Second and Third Cavalry under Col. Joseph J. Reynolds attacked the camp on March 17, 1876. Vaughn, *The Reynolds Campaign*, 60.

125. Iron Hawk makes clear that the great village on the Little Bighorn was erected on June 23, which date was positively confirmed by the Oglala, Knife, who courted his wife in the valley on the same day, and eloped with her on June 24, the time and romantic interlude firmly implanted on his memory. Some sources suggest the village may not have been established until June 24, which contradiction is perhaps due to the fact that on the latter date several small bands joined the great encampment. Hardorff note, *Lakota Recollections*, 64 n. 5.

126. A clear reference to Deeds and his slaying. Hardorff note, *Lakota Recollections*, 64 n. 3.

127. This was Major Reno's command of Companies A, M, and G, which deployed in skirmish order across the valley near the present Garryowen bend. Hardorff note, *Lakota Recollections*, 64 n. 4.

128. Iron Hawk's party had collected below the high bank of the dry river channel just north (downstream) of Reno's position in the woods. Eventually, these Indians filtered into the brush behind Reno's line and may have fired the volley that killed several of Reno's men. Hardorff note, *Lakota Recollections,* 64 n. 5.

129. Arriving late at the valley fight, Crazy Horse's presence gave renewed vigor to the Indian attack that drove Reno's disorganized command from the valley floor. According to Standing Bear, the valor displayed by Crazy Horse during this phase of the battle was spoken of by all the people. Hardorff note, *Lakota Recollections,* 65 n. 6.

130. The "other lot of soldiers" was Custer's command of five companies. Hardorff note, *Lakota Recollections,* 65 n. 7.

131. Iron Hawk was positioned near the forks of Deep Ravine, southwest of Custer Hill, where he participated in the final stages of the battle. Hardorff note, *Lakota Recollections,* 66 n. 9.

132. A body count of the slain on Custer Hill revealed the remains of ten individuals on the crest, while some thirty-two bodies were found on its southwestern slope. Initially as many as ninety troopers may have occupied this elevation. See, for example, the account by the Cheyenne Two Moons, who stated that near the end of the battle some forty-five men left the hill in an attempt to reach the woods along the river. The crest of Custer Hill was a nearly level place some thirty feet in diameter. Six sorrel horses had been slain around its perimeter, the color identifying them as belonging to Company C. Custer was found near the southwestern edge of the elevation, behind a horse, his right leg across the body of a soldier, while his back was slumped against the bodies of two others. The latter were identified as probably Sgt. John Vickory, the regimental color bearer, who lay with his face up. The second body was identified as that of Chief Trumpeter Henry Voss, who lay across Vickory's head, Voss's face being down. Vickory had his right arm cut off at the shoulder. Some twenty feet back from Custer, toward the east side of this level place, lay the extremely mutilated body of Capt. Tom Custer. He was lying on his face, the skull broken and flattened from repeated blows to the head. Lt. William W. Cooke, his thighs slashed and one of his black whiskers scalped, was found between two horses, close to Tom Custer. The fourth officer on the crest was Lt. Algernon E. Smith, his body having been riddled with arrows. Of the remaining four enlistees, the names of only two are known—Pvts. John Parker and Edward C. Driscoll, both of Company I, whose bodies lay near the eastern edge of the elevation. Hardorff note, *Lakota Recollections,* 66 n. 10.

133. Yet another reference to an attempted escape, this one occurring near the end of the battle, from Custer Hill. Although the evidence is at variance, this individual may have been Corp. John Foley of C Company, whose body was found on a little elevation along Medicine Tail Coulee, some three hundred yards east from the river. Hardorff note, *Lakota Recollections,* 67 n. 10.

134. For a graphic description of this final phase of the battle, see Iron Hawk's frank

interview in DeMallie, *The Sixth Grandfather,* 191-92, which contains his vivid recollections of the killings in and around Deep Ravine. Hardorff note, *Lakota Recollections,* 67 n. 12.

135. Having learned the identity of their white adversaries several weeks later, many Indians formed the conclusion that Custer must have been one of the buckskin-clad men slain on the hill. One Indian, Standing Bear, had taken a buckskin jacket from one of the dead men, which he gave to his mother, and for many years they supposed it was Custer's jacket. This garment was kept hidden until his mother finally cut it up and disposed of it for fear of being caught with incriminating evidence. The Indians' conception of a Custer fully clad in buckskin has been perpetuated through the renditions of many artists. This visualization seemed to have gained acceptance among a number of scholars. However, a careful scrutiny of the present evidence seems to suggest the opposite to be true. Custer may have worn a buckskin outfit on June 25, but so did both of his slain brothers, while at least five other officers who fell with him may also have worn buckskin jackets. A melancholy reflection by Custer's longtime orderly John Burkman, reveals an image of Custer wearing a white hat, fringed buckskin coat, and a red tie while galloping away at noon, June 25. But sequential evidence about Custer's apparel seems to suggest a different picture. One source is provided by the Ree Scout, Soldier, who told Walter Camp that Custer took off his buckskin coat and tied it behind his saddle. There can be no doubt that this observation was made hours after Burkman's because it occurred near the lower forks of Reno Creek. The validity of Soldier's statement receives a boost from Lt. Charles A. DeRudio, who attested to having seen both Custer and Lieutenant Cook near Reno Hill, the identification made possible through their clothing—a blue shirt and buckskin pants—the only officers to wear such a combination. Moreover, Peter Thompson, a survivor of Company C, gained his last view of Custer north of Reno Hill, and he described Custer as an alert man, dressed in a shirt, buckskin pants tucked in his boots, and buckskin jacket fastened to the rear of his saddle. Although Thompson embellished considerably on his recollections, the essence of this observation does not involve a self-serving matter. We may therefore conclude from these corroborating sources that the clothing pillaged from Custer's body consisted of a blue shirt and fringed buckskin pants, and that the man fully clad in buckskin was either Boston Custer or his brother, Capt. Tom Custer. Hardorff note, *Lakota Recollections,* 67 n. 13.

136. The initial force that blocked Custer's progress at Medicine Tail Ford consisted of some ten to twenty Indians, four of whom were Cheyennes. Hardorff note, *Lakota Recollections,* 68 n. 14.

137. Although this statement is supported by others, notably the Hunkpapa Gall, there is opposing and more convincing evidence that some of Custer's men came close enough to the river to fire into and over the teepees on the other side. Hardorff note, *Lakota Recollections,* 69 n. 15.

138. As a result of rank seniority, Capt. Miles W. Keogh commanded Companies I, L,

and C in the Little Bighorn battle. On June 27 the remains of Captain Keogh and his immediate command—principally I Company and a few men from L and C—were discovered on the eastern slope of Custer Ridge, near the head of a narrow ravine. Keogh's remains were found in an old buffalo wallow. Across his breast lay the body of his trumpeter, John W. Patton, while near him were found Sgts. James Bustard and Frank E. Varden, both of Company I. Keogh's body did not reveal any mutilation. Contemporary observers concluded that he had been crippled by a gunshot wound that extensively fractured his left knee and leg. Death came later as his trumpeter and noncommissioned staff chose to remain with him to the end. Hardorff note, *Lakota Recollections*, 69 n. 16.

139. Ricker's page ended here. At the top of the next page he wrote "Absarokee Ab-sar'-o-kee."

140. Stanton G. Fisher wrote about the 1877 campaign against the Nez Perce in his book, "Chief of Scouts to General Howard during the Nez Perce Campaign," *Contributions to the Historical Society of Montana* (Helena: State Publishing Co., 1896). Brig. Gen. Oliver O. Howard, commanding the Military Department of the Columbia, led the campaign against the Nez Perce. Whites considered Chief Joseph the dominant leader in Nez Perce War of 1877, but White Bird played a greater role in planning the campaign. Looking Glass emerged as a principal military leader. Jerome A. Greene, *Nez Perce Summer, 1877: The U.S. Army and the Nee-Me-Poo Crisis* (Helena: Montana Historical Society Press, 2000).

141. Ricker did not provide a source for the following note he wrote early in 1907 in Tablet 22: "The Crow Scouts with Custer were: Curly, white Swan, goes Ahead, Wool Moccasin and Yellow Face. White Swan died 2 or 3 years ago and Yellow Face died a little over 20 yrs. ago. Daylight who was visiting at Pourier's left Crow Agency January 3, and he saw Curly the day of his departure. Curly cannot talk English but can use & understand a few simple words. He has had two daughters; the older married and died. The other is a little girl and is now in school at the Crow Agency. White Swan was badly wounded, shot in the wrist and several times in the body. Daylight is a kind of leading man on the Crow Reservation. He was one of Crook's Crow Scouts whom 'Bat' went after, 70 of them; and he was in the battle of the Rosebud."

142. The Crow scout Curley was born about 1856. He was a scout for the Seventh Cavalry from June to September 1876. Curley eluded Custer's fate by posing as an attacking Lakota just long enough to escape. He carried the news of the defeat to officers on the steamboat Far West. Kenneth Hammer, ed., *Custer in '76: Walter Camp's Notes on the Custer Fight* (Provo, Utah: Brigham Young University Press, 1976), 158–59.

143. Hardorff note, *Lakota Recollections*, 129 n. 1.

144. Ricker's interview with Brig. Gen. Heber M. Creel is in Tablet B. Creel entered the military academy in 1873. He served in both the both the Seventh and Eighth

cavalry before resigning in 1882. Heitman, *Historical Register,* 338. Ricker's cryptic note "cost 30000" cannot be explained.

145. The Tongue River fight was on June 9, 1876, while the one on the Powder River was on March 17, 1876. Strahorn, "The Battle of Powder River, March 17, 1876," 3; Reuben Briggs Davenport, "The Skirmish at Tongue River Heights, June 9, 18t6," *Battles and Skirmishes of the Great Sioux War, 1876-1877,* ed. Jerome A. Greene (Norman: University of Oklahoma Press, 1993), 20.

146. Ricker's informants were divided on the sword issue. Charles Clifford (Tablet 10) agreed with Two Moons, but his opinion was based on what other Indians told him. F. E. Server said "there not being a sabre in the command" (Tablet 7). Lt. Edward S. Godfrey was at the Little Bighorn and later wrote about it. He was explicit in his comment, "No one, not even the officer of the day, carried the saber." Godfrey, *Custer's Last Battle,* 8.

147. Joshua Garrett-Davis, "Dakota Images: George Sword," *South Dakota History* 29 (1999): 262.

148. Hardorff note, *Lakota Recollections,* 69 n. 17.

149. Charles F. Larrabee served as acting commissioner during the numerous absences of Commissioner Francis Leupp. Parman, "Francis Ellington Leupp," 224.

150. Sword was still in the north when about 250 men led by Spotted Tail left Camp Sheridan. Greene, *Yellowstone Command,* 188.

151. Estimates by whites of Indians killed or wounded ranges as high as eleven hundred. Grace Raymond Hebard and E. A. Brininstool, *The Bozeman Trail* (Glendale CA: Arthur H. Clark Co., 1960), 2: 70.

152. Philip Wells recounted his brief discussion of the Fetterman fight with Red Cloud. Wells, "Ninety-six Years Among the Indians," 191-92.

153. Ricker Tablet 2, 147 verso.

154. For detailed coverage of this episode see Donald F. Danker, "A High Price to Pay for a Lame Cow," 111-17. Salaway's account has been described as "remarkable for both its faithfulness to facts established in the Investigations following the battle and for corroboration which it gives to other documentary accounts." McCann, "The Grattan Massacre," 3.

155. Lt. Hugh B. Fleming was the post commander. The incident was reported on August 18, 1854. Danker, "A High Price to Pay for a Lame Cow," 112.

156. High Forehead was the Miniconjou who slaughtered the cow. Ibid.

157. Lt. John L. Grattan led twenty-nine soldiers. The interpreter was Lucien Auguste. Ibid., 113. In his interview with Clarence Three Stars (Tablet 25) Ricker noted the interpreter's name was "Wyuse (the spelling is uncertain)."

158. Charles Gareau was the interpreter at Fort John, P. Chouteau, Jr. and Company's trading post near Fort Laramie. McCann, "The Grattan Massacre," 5 n. 6.

159. Joseph Bissonnette had been a trader with the Lakotas, principally the Brulés, since the 1840s. Hyde, *Spotted Tail's Folk,* 43. Ricker made the following note on Bissonnette in Tablet 17: "One of the sons of Joseph Bissonnette who died at

Pine Ridge Agency and was buried on W. K. Cr. below Manderson, on his homestead there. Herbert Bissonnette, tells me that the family lived on the Bordeaux Cr. where Sol. Hartsell lives; and that they moved away from there in 1879 because American Horse and other Indians carried on too thriving a business stealing their horses. Jim Bordeaux lived on the creek above them, he says a mile and a half or two miles—up on 'that flat,' which was probably on the McMillan land or in that vicinity. It must not be forgotten that the Indian idea of miles is not very accurate. Joseph Bissonnette was a full-blood Frenchman. He was not a son-in-law of Mousseau. He was an official interpreter."

160. Little Thunder and his band of about four hundred Brulés were camped along Blue Water Creek opposite Ash Hollow. On September 3, 1855, they were attacked by Gen. William Harney in command of nearly seven hundred troops. Danker, "A High Price to Pay for a Lame Cow," 117.

161. Companies of the Seventh Iowa Volunteer Cavalry were sent to protect the Platte River Road. Capt. William D. Fouts, in command of about 140 troops, left Fort Laramie escorting a Lakota band estimated at 1,500 to Julesburg, Colorado. On the morning of June 14, 1865, Fouts rode into the Indians' camp on Horse Creek to urge them to continue the march. It is not known what happened next except that Fouts was shot and killed. Upon hearing the gunfire, Capt. John Wilcox and part of the troops rode to the camp to investigate and in a brief encounter three or four privates were killed. The army then retreated, claiming to have killed between twenty and thirty Indians. Later Fouts's commanding officer admitted that the incident must have been the result of "some unwarranted provocation given on the part of Captain Fouts." Albert Watkins, "Fort Mitchell Cemetery," *Nebraska History and Record of Pioneer Days* 1 (1918): 3.

162. Big Mouth was chief of the so-called Laramie Loafers band. Nadeau, *Fort Laramie and the Sioux Indians*, 207.

163. Two Face was a Lakota subchief. Ibid. The white woman was Lucinda Eubanks, the wife of William Eubanks, Jr. They lived with their children near the present town of Oak in southeastern Nebraska. On August 8, 1864, the Cheyennes attacked their home and other road ranches along the Oregon Trail. Mr. Eubanks was killed and Mrs. Eubanks, her baby boy, her four-year-old daughter Isabelle, and a neighbor, Laura Roper, were captured. Laura and Isabelle were sold to an Arapaho band, which released them to the army in September at a council in western Kansas. Sometime that winter Mrs. Eubanks and the boy were sold to Two Face. He surrendered the captives about the middle of May 1865. Leroy W. Hagerty, "Indian Raids Along the Platte and Little Blue Rivers, 1864-1865," *Nebraska History* 28 (1947): 247-50. Mrs. Eubanks's statement taken after her release described her captivity. Sol Lewis, *The Sand Creek Massacre: A Documentary History* (New York: Sol Lewis, 1973), iii. Fanny Kelly was captured by an Oglala band in May 1864 and released in December. Her husband, Josiah, had offered a re-

ward for her release and Mrs. Kelly believed Two Face turned over Mrs. Eubanks in the hope of getting the reward. Kelly, *Narrative of My Captivity*, 263.

James F. Varley used slightly different sources to summarize these events resulting in some difference in details. James F. Varley, *Brigham and the Brigadier: General Patrick Connor and His California Volunteers in Utah and Along the Oregon Trail* (Tucson: Westernlore Press, 1989), 211–12.

164. Geminien P. Beauvais opened a road ranche five miles east of Fort Laramie in 1853. His Indian name was Big Belly. Charles E. Hanson, Jr., "Geminien P. Beauvais," *The Mountain Men and the Fur Trade of the Far West*, ed. Leroy R. Hafen, 10 vols. (Glendale CA: Arthur H. Clark Co., 1969), 7: 38, 42. Col. Thomas O. Moonlight assumed command of Fort Laramie in March 1865. Vital Jarrot was appointed agent for the Upper Platte in April 1865. Nadeau, *Fort Laramie and the Sioux Indians*, 176, 201.

165. Later Ricker was told that the subchief's name was Blackfeet (Tablet 25). It is rendered Blackfoot in Nadeau, *Fort Laramie and the Sioux Indians*, 178.

166. If the Eubanks's child was dragged he survived and was still living in the 1940s. Hagerty, "Indian Raids Along the Platte and Little Blue Rivers," 251.

167. They were hung on May 26, 1865. Nadeau, *Fort Laramie and the Sioux Indians*, 178. Ricker wrote a note about the condemned men in Tablet 25: "Thunder Bear who is a judge of the Pine Ridge Indians Court was a nephew of Black Shield who was hung at Laramie. I have been told that his name was Calico, but Thunder Bear denies this. Thunder Bear says the woman (was it Mrs. Kelly?) was taken captive by the Cheyennes, and by these was sexually outraged, and that some Oglalas bought her and brought her in to the fort with the purpose of effecting peace, and that the two who came were hung."

168. Moonlight realized the Lakotas around the fort might seek revenge after the executions so he ordered them to be taken to Fort Kearny, away from the influence of Spotted Tail and other warring chiefs. Nadeau, *Fort Laramie and the Sioux Indians*, 179. However, George Hyde wrote that Maj. Gen. G. M. Dodge, who was preparing for an expedition against the hostiles in the Powder River country, gave the order to send the Indians to Fort Kearny. He Considered them hostile and an embarrassment. Hyde, *Spotted Tail's Folk*, 102. James F. Varley concluded that the military believed these Lakotas friendly and wanted them moved to Fort Kearny away from the negative influence of the Cheyennes. Varley, *Brigham and the Brigadier*, 219.

169. See note 160. For another eyewitness account of this march see Susan Bordeaux Bettelyoun and Josephine Waggoner, *With My Own Eyes*, 88–90.

170. They left on June 11, 1865, and camped that night at Bordeaux's trading post. John J. Pattison, "With the U. S. Army along the Oregon Trail," *Nebraska History* 15 (1934): 85.

171. On the reverse of the page Ricker wrote "The name of the captain who was killed at Horse Creek was Fouts — Captain Fouts. Charley Allison was the interpreter for

Capt. Fouts." Ricker was mistaken. The interpreter was Charley Elliston. Nadeau, *Fort Laramie and the Sioux Indians,* 179.

Ricker interviewed A. G. Shaw a year later and they briefly discussed the Horse Creek fight. Shaw thought that Salaway knew of a plot to kill Fouts and Ricker agreed noting, "I thought so when Salaway gave me his account" (Tablet 11).

172. On the reverse of the page Ricker noted, "Calico, White Face, and One Side were the three Indian prisoners mounted. The one prisoner in the wagon was kept there as he could not run away."

Ricker penned a reminder in Tablet 39 to "See Calico, below Agency, 2nd neighbor to Mrs. Bat, halfway from her to the Mission. It was his father and brother who were hung at Laramie in Wakefield affair."

173. In his diary Pattison recorded the deaths of Fouts and Pvts. Phillip Alder, Edward McMahen, and Richard Groger. Four soldiers were wounded. John J. Pattison, "With the U. S. Army along the Oregon Trail," 85. Hyde reported that Fouts and four men were killed and seven were wounded. Hyde, *Spotted Tail's Folk,* 105.

174. Capt. J. S. Shuman of the Eleventh Ohio Volunteer Cavalry commanded Fort Mitchell. Merrill J. Mattes, *The Great Platte River Road* (Lincoln: Nebraska State Historical Society, 1969), 474.

175. The soldiers' horses were picketed, but the Indians were still able to capture part of the herd. Nadeau, *Fort Laramie and the Sioux Indians,* 186. Hyde believed the horses were loose. Hyde, *Spotted Tail's Folk,* 105.

176. The interview with Magloire Mousseau is in Tablet 28.

177. Moses E. "California Joe" Milner had wandered throughout most of the West and served as an army scout. In November 1875 John Richard Sr. and Alfred Palladay were murdered along the upper Niobrara River. California Joe was implicated, but it was soon concluded that the perpetrators were Cheyenne Indians. Joe E. Milner and Earle R. Forrest, *California Joe: Noted Scout and Indian Fighter* (Lincoln: University of Nebraska Press, 1987).

178. If the dugout or the general event was "described by others," Ricker failed to record it in his notebooks.

California Joe was killed at Fort Robinson on October 29, 1876. V. T. McGillycuddy was there and wrote about the incident nearly a half-century later. Dr. McGillycuddy said the men met in a saloon and seemed to have settled their differences. Later in the day Newcomb found California Joe near a corral and shot him with a rifle. Ibid., 281-82.

179. Bisnet is Joseph Bissonette, Jr. Peter B. Nelson homesteaded near Chadron, Nebraska, in 1878. Later he moved to Chadron and opened an opera house. *Hay Springs News,* Dec. 31, 1937. Hanson, Charles E., Jr. "Reconstruction of the Bordeaux Trading Post." *Nebraska History* 53 (1972): 141.

180. Larson, Red Cloud: Warrior-Statesman of the Lakota Sioux.

181. Olson discusses ten trips. Olson, *Red Cloud and the Sioux Problem,* 375.

182. Frank Salaway described the incident in his interview in Tablet 27. American Horse's account is in Tablet 16.
183. Charles Eastman met Three Stars in 1890 and described him as a friend and a "Christian chief." Eastman, *From Deep Woods to Civilization*, 121. The drunken interpreter was Lucien Auguste. McCann, "The Grattan Massacre," 11.
184. Three Stars probably meant 1897. It was Red Cloud's last trip to the capital. Olson, *Red Cloud and the Sioux Problem*, 337.
185. Magloire Mousseau told Ricker (Tablet 28) that Red Cloud and LeBonte were friends, however, Red Cloud's men killed the trapper.
186. If he furnished the list it has been lost.
187. Ricker's interview with Sam Deon is in Tablets 17 and 25.
188. In the early winter of 1903 about twenty-five Indians from Pine Ridge were in eastern Wyoming hunting small game. They were accused of breaking the state's hunting laws, as well as slaughtering settlers' cattle. When a sheriff's posse was sent to arrest them a gunfight erupted, resulting in several deaths. Ricker recorded other accounts by Roy Lemons (Tablet 31) and Hugh Houghton (Box 19, Ricker Coll.). It seems the incident affected Ricker, who published four lengthy articles about it in the *Chadron Times* (Nov. 5, 12, 19, and Dec. 3, 1903). By comparison his competitors in the *Chadron Journal* limited their coverage to one article of only a few lines on Nov. 6, 1903. More than twenty years later Ricker's son Leslie recalled these events and wrote that his father went to Wyoming to obtain the "inside facts." Leslie D. Ricker to A. E. Sheldon, June 27, 1926. Ricker Coll.
189. Ricker was told the Indians were on a trip to the Black Hills to collect "berries, roots, herbs, etc." and had "drifted over into Wyoming." He was assured this party was aware of Wyoming's hunting laws. *Chadron Times*, Dec. 3, 1903. William Miller was sheriff of Weston County, Wyoming. "Sheriffs Battle Indians on Lightning Creek." 191.
190. In the version published in "Sheriffs Battle Indians on Lightning Creek," Chief Eagle Feather threw a handful of dirt in the air as a signal to commence firing and Sheriff Miller was the first to be shot. There is no mention of the killing of the boy and his horse.
191. "Sheriffs Battle Indians on Lightning Creek" listed Black Kettle as a fatality. He and Eagle Feather were the only Indians mentioned by name.
192. Deputy Sheriff Louis Falkenberg was the other white fatality. Ibid.
193. The report was H. W. Clapp, "Report of Pine Ridge Agency," *Annual Report of the Commissioner*, 1896, 292.
194. Two pages were typed. However, the first sentence and last two paragraphs are in Ricker's hand. Box 19.
195. Thomas J. Morgan was commissioner in 1891 and 1892. William A. Jones was commissioner from 1897 to 1904. Kvasnicka and Viola, *The Commissioners of Indian Affairs*, vii.
196. Hardorff note, *Lakota Recollections*, 99 n. 1.

197. Capt. Ezra P. Ewers, Fifth Infantry, fought against Crazy Horse on the Tongue River in 1877. He retired from the army in 1891. Heitman, *Historical Register*, 411.
198. In 1906 there was a large exodus from the Ute reservation in response to the division of the land into family allotments. David D. Laudenschlager, "The Utes in South Dakota, 1906-1908," *South Dakota History* 9 (1979): 235-36.
199. Jacob A. Augur entered the military academy in 1865. In 1906 he was a colonel in the Tenth Cavalry. Heitman, *Historical Register*, 175. John Gresham was a major in the Sixth Cavalry at the time. He received a Medal of Honor for his role in the Wounded Knee massacre. Ibid., 477.
200. Johnson gave Ricker a typewritten statement concerning the 1879 Cheyenne outbreak at Fort Robinson (Box 26, Ricker Coll.). At that time he was a sergeant. He enlisted in the army in 1876 and had attained the rank of captain in 1899. Heitman, *Historical Register*, 574.
201. The Ute was a member of Appah's band, which numbered about three hundred. This meeting was on October 22. Laudenschlager, "The Utes in South Dakota," 238.
202. Lt. Col. Alexander P. Rodgers was stationed at Fort Meade. Ibid., 239.
203. They arrived at the fort on November 20. Ibid.
204. The Ute delegation met the President in January. Ibid., 241. This Ute party would live on the Cheyenne River Reservation until 1908, when they returned to their old home in Utah. Ibid., 246.
205. Mary Janis was a member of the Red Cloud family. They met when Antoine was a trader in the Fort Laramie vicinity. Lecompte, "Antoine Janis," 197.
206. Joseph Antoine was born on March 6, 1824, and died on April 10, 1890. Ibid., 201.
207. Nicholas Janis came west in 1845, and traded with the Oglalas in the Fort Laramie vicinity. He married Martha, Red Cloud's niece. In the 1870s he operated a ranch east of the fort. Janet Lecompte concluded that he was born in St. Charles, Missouri, on October 12, 1827, and died on September 13, 1902. Ibid., 196-97, 201.
208. Janis served as a guide on Connor's 1865 expedition to the Powder River country. Fred B. Rogers, *Soldiers of the Overland: Being Some Accounts of the Services of General Patrick Edward Connor* (San Francisco: The Grabhorne Press, 1938), 172, 204.
209. On at least one occasion Clifford exhibited his fossils in a saloon in Chadron and charged fifty cents to view the bones. *Chadron Democrat*, Aug. 15, June 20, 1889.
210. Probably William F. Cody, *The Adventures of Buffalo Bill* (New York: Boblin Sales Co., 1904).
211. Red Cloud shot and killed the Oglala chief Bull Bear in 1841. Alcohol was involved. Hyde, *Spotted Tail's Folk*, 99.

Bibliography

Agonito, Joseph G. "Young Man Afraid of His Horses: The Reservation Years." *Nebraska History* 79 (1998): 116-32.
Allen, Charles W. *From Fort Laramie to Wounded Knee: In the West that Was.* Ed. Richard E. Jensen. Lincoln: University of Nebraska Press, 1997.
Allison, William B., et. al. "Report of the Commission Appointed to Treat with the Sioux Indians for the Relinquishment of the Black Hills." *Annual Report of the Commissioner of Indian Affairs.* Washington DC: GPO (1875), 184-200.
"An Act to Divide a Portion of the Reservation of the Sioux Nation." *Annual Report of the Commissioner of Indian Affairs.* Washington DC: GPO (1889), 449-58.
Anderson, Gary Clayton. *Little Crow: Spokesman for the Sioux.* St. Paul: Minnesota Historical Society Press, 1986.
Anderson, Grant K. "Samuel D. Hinman and the Opening of the Black Hills." *Nebraska History* 60 (1979): 520-42.
Anderson, Harry H. "Indian Peace-Talkers and the Conclusion of the Sioux War of 1876." *Nebraska History* 44 (1963): 233-54.
Andreas, A. T. *History of the State of Nebraska.* Chicago: Western Historical Company, 1882. Reprint, Evansville IN: Unigraphic Inc., 1975.
Annual Report of the Department of the Interior. Washington DC: GPO, 1905.
Bailey, Paul. *Wovoka, The Indian Messiah.* Los Angeles: Westernlore Press, 1957.
Baird, G. W. *A Report to the Citizens Concerning Certain Late Disturbances on the Western Frontier.* Ashland CA: Lewis Osborne, 1972.
Beach, Rex E. "Wounded Knee." *Appleton's Booklovers Magazine* 7 (1906): 732-36.
Beckwith, H. W. *History of Iroquois County.* Chicago: H. H. Hill and Co., 1880. Reprint, Evansville IN: Unigraphic Inc., 1979.
Belish, Elbert D. "American Horse (Wasechun-Tashunka): The Man Who Killed Fetterman." *Annals of Wyoming* 63 (1991): 54-67.
Bell, James M. "Pine Ridge Agency, Dakota." *Annual Report of the Commissioner of Indian Affairs.* Washington DC: GPO (1886): 76-77.
Bettelyoun, Susan Bordeaux and Josephine Waggoner. *With My Own Eyes: A Lakota Woman Tells Her People's History.* Ed. Emily Leavine. Lincoln: University of Nebraska Press, 1999.

Bingham, H. W. "Cheyenne River Indian Agency." *Annual Report of the Commissioner of Indian Affairs*. Washington DC: GPO (1874): 231–33.

Bland, Thomas A. *A Brief History of the Late Military Invasion of the Home of the Sioux*. Washington DC: National Indian Defense Association, 1891.

Blish, Helen H. *A Pictographic History of the Oglala Sioux*. Lincoln: University of Nebraska Press, 1967.

Bordeaux, William J. *Custer's Conqueror*. Sioux Falls SD: Smith and Co., 1969.

Bourke, John G. *Mackenzie's Last Fight with the Cheyennes: A Winter Campaign in Wyoming and Montana*. Governor's Island NY: Military Service Institution, 1890. Reprint, Bellevue NE: Old Army Press, 1970.

———. *On the Border with Crook*. Lincoln: University of Nebraska Press, 1971.

Bray, Kingsley M. "Crazy Horse and the End of the Great Sioux War." *Nebraska History* 79 (1998): 94–115.

Brininstool, E. A. *Crazy Horse, The Invincible Oglala Sioux Chief*. Los Angeles: Wetzel Publishing Co., 1949.

———. *Fighting Indian Warriors*. Harrisburg PA: Stackpole Co., 1953.

Brown, Jesse, and A. M. Willard. *The Black Hills Trails*. Rapid City SD: Rapid City Journal Co., 1924.

Buecker, Thomas R. *Fort Robinson and the American West, 1874–1899*. Lincoln: Nebraska State Historical Society, 1999.

Carter, Harvey L. "Andrew Dripps." *The Mountain Men and the Fur Trade of the Far West*. Ed. Leroy R. Hafen. Vol. 8. Glendale CA: Arthur H. Clark Co. (1971): 143–56.

———. "Big Bat Pourier's Version of the Sibley Scout." *Nebraska History* 66 (1985): 129–43.

Clapp, W. H. "Report of Pine Ridge Agency." *Annual Report of the Commissioner of Indian Affairs*. Washington DC: GPO (1896), 291–95.

Clark, William P. *The Indian Sign Language*. Philadelphia: L. R. Hamersly Co., 1885.

Clarke, Dwight L. *Stephen Watts Kearny: Soldier of the West*. Norman: University of Oklahoma Press, 1961.

Cobbey, J. E., ed. *Consolidated Statutes of Nebraska, 1891*. Lincoln: State Journal Co., 1891.

Cody, William F. *The Adventures of Buffalo Bill*. New York: Boblin Sales Co., 1904.

Colby, L. W. "Wanagi Olowan Kin: The Ghost Songs of the Dakotas." *Proceedings and Collections of the Nebraska State Historical Society* 1 (1895): 131–50.

Cramsie, John W. "Devils Lake Agency." *Annual Report of the Commissioner of Indian Affairs*. Washington DC: GPO (1882), 20–22.

———. "Devil's Lake Agency." *Annual Report of the Commissioner of Indian Affairs*. Washington DC: GPO (1887), 26–29.

Crawford, Richard C. "Edward Parmelee Smith." *The Commissioners of Indian Affairs, 1824–1977*. Ed. Robert M. Kvasnicka and Herman Viola. Lincoln: University of Nebraska Press (1979), 141–47.

BIBLIOGRAPHY

Daniels, J. W. "Sisseton Agency, Dakota." *Annual Report of the Commissioner of Indian Affairs.* Washington DC: GPO (1871), 530-33.

———. "Agreement Between the United States and the Sioux for the Relinquishment of Hunting Rights in Nebraska." *Annual Report of the Commissioner of Indian Affairs.* Washington DC: GPO (1875), 179-80.

Danker, Donald F., ed. *Man of the Plains: Recollections of Luther North, 1856-1882.* Lincoln: University of Nebraska Press, 1961.

———. "The North Brothers and the Pawnee Scouts." *Nebraska History* 42 (1961): 161-79.

———. "The Wounded Knee Interviews of Eli S. Ricker." *Nebraska History* 62 (1981): 151-243.

———. "The Violent Deaths of Yellow Bear and John Richard Jr." *Nebraska History* 63 (1982): 137-51.

———. "A High Price to Pay for a Lame Cow." *Kansas History* 10 (1987): 111-17.

Danzinger, Edmund J., Jr. "The Crow Creek Experiment: An Aftermath of the Sioux War of 1862." *North Dakota History* 37 (1970): 105-23.

Davenport, Reuben Briggs. "The Skirmish at Tongue River Heights, June 9, 1876." *Battles and Skirmishes of the Great Sioux War, 1876-1877.* Ed. Jerome A. Greene. Norman: University of Oklahoma Press, 1993.

DeBarthe, Joe. *Life and Adventures of Frank Grouard.* Ed. Edgar I. Stewart. Norman: University of Oklahoma Press, 1958.

DeMallie, Raymond J. *The Sixth Grandfather: Black Elk's Teachings Given to John G. Neihardt.* Lincoln: University of Nebraska Press, 1984.

Dickson, Ephriam D., III. "Crazy Horse: Who Really Wielded the Bayonet that Killed the Oglala Leader." *Greasy Grass* 12 (1996): 2-10.

Diffendal, Anne Polk. "A Centennial History of the Nebraska State Historical Society, 1878-1978." *Nebraska History* 59 (1978): 311-437.

Dorsey, James Owen. "A Study of Siouan Cults." *Eleventh Annual Report of the Bureau of American Ethnology.* Washington DC: GPO, 1894.

Dyer, Frederick H. *A Compendium of the War of the Rebellion.* Des Moines IA: Dyer Publishing Co., 1908.

Eastman, Charles A. *From Deep Woods to Civilization: Chapters in the Autobiography of an Indian.* Lincoln: University of Nebraska Press, 1977.

Executive Documents of the Senate of the United States, 51st Cong., 2d sess., 1891-92. Doc. 9. Washington DC: GPO, 1892.

Fisher, S. G. "Chief of Scouts to General Howard during the Nez Perce Campaign." *Contributions to the Historical Society of Montana.* Helena: State Publishing Co., 1896.

Fitzgerald, Sister Mary Clement. "Bishop Marty and His Sioux Missions." *South Dakota Historical Collections* 20 (1940): 522-88.

Flood, Renée Sansom. *Lost Bird of Wounded Knee: Spirit of the Lakota.* New York: Charles Scribner's Sons, 1995.

Forbes, William. "Fort Totten Agency, Dakota Territory." *Annual Report of the Commissioner of Indian Affairs*. Washington DC: GPO, 1872.

Friswold, Carroll, and Robert A. Clark, eds. *The Killing of Chief Crazy Horse*. Glendale CA: Arthur H. Clark Co., 1976.

Gallagher, Hugh D. "Report of Pine Ridge Agency." *Annual Report of the Commissioner of Indian Affairs*. Washington DC: GPO (1887), 40-42.

———. "Report of Pine Ridge Agency." *Annual Report of the Commissioner of Indian Affairs*. Washington DC: GPO, 1889.

Garrett-Davis, Joshua. "Dakota Images: George Sword." *South Dakota History* 29 (1999): 262-63.

Gilman, Samuel C. *Conquest of the Sioux*. Indianapolis: Carlon and Hollenbeck, 1897.

Godfrey, Edward S. *Custer's Last Battle*. Ed. Eugene McAuliffe. Omaha NE: n.p., 1952.

Gray, John S. *Centennial Campaign: The Sioux War of 1876*. Fort Collins CO: Old Army Press, 1976.

———. *Custer's Last Campaign: Mitch Boyer and the Little Big Horn Reconstructed*. Lincoln: University of Nebraska Press, 1991.

Greene, Jerome A. *Slim Buttes, 1876: An Episode of the Great Sioux War*. Norman: University of Oklahoma Press, 1982.

———. *Yellowstone Command: Colonel Nelson A. Miles and the Great Sioux War, 1876-1877*. Lincoln: University of Nebraska Press, 1991.

———. *Nez Perce Summer, 1877: The U.S. Army and the Nee-Me-Poo Crisis*. Helena: Montana Historical Society Press, 2000.

———. "The Surrounding of Red Cloud and Red Leaf, 1876: A Preemptive Maneuver of the Great Sioux War." *Nebraska History* 82 (2001): 69-75.

Grinnell, George Bird. *The Fighting Cheyennes*. Norman: University of Oklahoma Press, 1956.

Hafen, Ann W. "William W. McGaa." *The Mountain Men and the Fur Trade of the Far West*. Ed. Leroy R. Hafen. Vol. 8. Glendale CA: Arthur H. Clark Co. (1971), 229-34.

Hagan, William T. "Daniel M. Browning." *The Commissioners of Indian Affairs, 1824-1977*. Eds. Robert M. Kvasnicka and Herman Viola. Lincoln: University of Nebraska Press (1979), 205-9.

———. *The Indian Rights Association: The Herbert Welsh Years, 1882-1904*. Tucson: University of Arizona Press, 1985.

Hagerty, Leroy W. "Indian Raids Along the Platte and Little Blue Rivers, 1864-1865." *Nebraska History* 28 (1947): 239-60.

Hammer, Kenneth, ed. *Custer in '76: Walter Camp's Notes on the Custer Fight*. Provo UT: Brigham Young University Press, 1976.

Hanson, Charles E., Jr. "James Bordeaux." *The Museum of the Fur Trade Quarterly* 2 (1966): 2-12.

———. "Geminien P. Beauvis." *The Mountain Men and the Fur Trade of the Far West*. Ed. Leroy R. Hafen. Vol. 7. Glendale CA: Arthur H. Clark Co. (1969), 34-43.

———. "Reconstruction of the Bordeaux Trading Post." *Nebraska History* 53 (1972): 137-66.

———. "The Chadron Creek Trading Post." *The Museum of the Fur Trade Quarterly* 12 (1976): 1-20.

Hanson, Charles E., Jr., and Veronica Sue Walters. "The Early Fur Trade in Northwestern Nebraska." *Nebraska History* 57 (1976): 291-314.

Hardorff, Richard G. "The Frank Grouard Genealogy." *Custer and His Times: Book Two.* Ed. John M. Carroll. Fort Worth TX: Little Bighorn Associates Inc. (1984): 123-33.

———. *Markers, Artifacts and Indian Testimony: Preliminary Findings on the Custer Battle.* Short Hills NJ: Don Horn Publications, 1985.

———. *The Oglala Lakota Crazy Horse: A Preliminary Genealogical Study and an Annotated Listing of Primary Sources.* Mattituck NJ: J. M. Carroll and Co., 1985.

———. *Lakota Recollections of the Custer Fight: New Sources of Indian-Military History.* Lincoln: University of Nebraska Press, 1997.

———. *The Surrender and Death of Crazy Horse.* Spokane: Arthur H. Clark Co., 1998.

Harring, Sidney L. *Crow Dog's Case: American Indian Sovereignty, Tribal Law, and United States Law in the Nineteenth Century.* Cambridge: Cambridge University Press, 1994.

Hastings, James S. "Red Cloud Agency, Nebraska." *Annual Report of the Commissioner of Indian Affairs.* Washington DCI GPO (1876), 33.

Hebard, Grace Raymond. *Washakie: Chief of the Shoshones.* Lincoln: University of Nebraska Press, 1995.

Hebard, Grace Raymond, and E. A. Brininstool. *The Bozeman Trail.* 2 vols. Glendale CA: Arthur H. Clark Co., 1960.

Hedren, Paul L. *Fort Laramie in 1876: Chronicle of a Frontier Post at War.* Lincoln: University of Nebraska Press, 1988.

Heitman, Francis B. *Historical Register and Dictionary of the United States Army.* Washington DC: GPO, 1903.

Hinman, Eleanor H. "Oglala Sources on the Life of Crazy Horse." *Nebraska History* 57 (1976): 1-51.

Hodge, Frederick Webb, ed. *Handbook of American Indians.* Smithsonian Institution, Bureau of American Ethnology. Bulletin 30. Washington DC: GPO, 1907.

Holley, Frances Chamberlain. *Once Their Home, or Our Legacy from the Dahkotahs.* Chicago: Donohue and Henneberry, 1892.

Howard, E. A. "Spotted Tail Agency, Nebraska." *Annual Report of the Commissioner of Indian Affairs.* Washington DC: GPO (1875), 253-55.

———. "Spotted Tail Agency, Nebraska." *Annual Report of the Commissioner of Indian Affairs.* Washington DC: GPO (1876), 33-36.

———. "Office of the Ponca Indian Agency, Indian Territory." *Annual Report of the Commissioner of Indian Affairs.* Washington DC: GPO (1877), 96-102.

Howard, James H. *The Ponca Tribe.* Lincoln: University of Nebraska Press, 1995.

Howe, M. A. DeWolfe. *The Life and Labors of Bishop Hare: Apostle to the Sioux*. New York: Sturgis and Walton Co., 1913.

Hyde, George E. *Red Cloud's Folk, A History of the Oglala Sioux Indians*. Norman: University of Oklahoma Press, 1937.

———. *Spotted Tail's Folk: A History of the Brulé Sioux*. Norman: University of Oklahoma Press, 1961.

———. "Indian Office Documents on Sioux-Pawnee Battle." *Nebraska History* 16 (1935): 147-55.

Indian Rights Association: Second Annual Report of the Executive Committee. Philadelphia: n.p., 1885.

Irwin, James. "Red Cloud Agency, Nebraska." *Annual Report of the Commissioner of Indian Affairs*. Washington DC: GPO (1877), 62-63.

———. "Red Cloud Agency, Dakota." *Annual Report of the Commissioner of Indian Affairs*. Washington DC: GPO (1878), 36-37.

Jacobson, Clair. *Whitestone Hill: The Indians and the Battle*. LaCrosse WI: Pine Tree Publishing, 1991.

Jenney, Walter P. "Report of Geological Survey of the Black Hills." *Annual Report of the Commissioner of Indian Affairs*. Washington DC: GPO (1875), 181-83.

Jensen, Richard E. "Big Foot's Followers at Wounded Knee." *Nebraska History* 71 (1990): 194-212.

Jensen, Richard E., R. Eli Paul, and John E. Carter. *Eyewitness at Wounded Knee*. Lincoln: University of Nebraska Press, 1991.

Jones, Bryan. "John Richard, Jr., and the Killing at Fetterman." *Annals of Wyoming* 43 (1971): 237-57.

Kappler, Charles J., ed. *Indian Affairs Laws and Treaties*. Washington DC: GPO, 1904.

Kelly, Fanny. *Narrative of My Captivity Among the Sioux Indians*. Chicago: Donnelly, Gossette & Loyd, 1880. Reprint edited by Clark and Mary Lee Spence. Chicago: Lakeside Press, 1990.

Killoren, John K., S.J. *"Come, Black Robe": DeSmet and the Indian Tragedy*. Norman: University of Oklahoma Press, 1994.

King, James T. *War Eagle: A Life of General Eugene A. Carr*. Lincoln: University of Nebraska Press, 1963.

Kolbenschlag, George R. *A Whirlwind Passes: News Correspondents and the Sioux Disturbances of 1890-1891*. Vermillion: University of South Dakota Press, 1990.

Kuhlman, Charles. *Legend into History*. Fort Collins CO: Old Army Press, 1977.

Kvasnicka, Robert M. and Herman Viola, eds. *The Commissioners of Indian Affairs, 1824-1977*. Lincoln: University of Nebraska Press, 1979.

Larson, Robert W. *Red Cloud: Warrior-Statesman of the Lakota Sioux*. Norman: University of Oklahoma Press, 1997.

Laudenschlager, David D. "The Utes in South Dakota, 1906-1908." *South Dakota History* 9 (1979): 233-47.

BIBLIOGRAPHY

LeCompte, Janet. "Antoine Janis." *The Mountain Men and the Fur Trade of the Far West*. Ed. Leroy R. Hafen. Vol. 8. Glendale CA: Arthur H. Clark Co. (1971): 196-201.

Lee, Jesse M. "Spotted Tail Agency, Nebraska." *Annual Report of the Commissioner of Indian Affairs*. Washington DC: GPO (1877), 65-71.

———. "Crazy Horse." *Journal of the Military Service Institution of the United States* (May-June, 1914): 323-40.

———. "Story of Jesse M. Lee." *Nebraska History* 12 (1929): 5-32.

Lewis, Sol. *The Sand Creek Massacre: A Documentary History*. New York: Sol Lewis, 1973.

Livingston, Henry F. "Crow Creek Agency, Dakota Territory." *Annual Report of the Commissioner of Indian Affairs*. Washington DC: GPO (1875), 238-39.

Longacre, Edward G. "We Left a Black Track in South Carolina: Letters of Corporal Eli S. Ricker, 1865." *South Carolina Historical Magazine* 82 (1981): 210-24.

Mackintosh, John. "Lakota Bullet Ends Wallace's Life—14 Years after Little Bighorn." *Greasy Grass* 16 (2000): 21-30.

Madsen, Brigham D. *Glory Hunter: A Biography of Patrick Edward Connor*. Salt Lake City: University of Utah Press, 1990.

Marshall, Robert A. "How Many Indians Were There?" *The Research Review* (June 1977): 8-17.

Mattes, Merrill J. *The Great Platte River Road*. Lincoln: Nebraska State Historical Society, 1969.

McCann, Lloyd E. "The Grattan Massacre." *Nebraska History* 37 (1956): 1-26.

McCreight, M. I. *Firewater and Forked Tongues*. Pasadena: Trail's End, 1947.

McDermott John Dishon. "John Baptiste Richard." *The Mountain Men and the Fur Trade of the Far West*. Ed. Leroy R. Hafen. Vol. 2. Glendale CA: Arthur H. Clark Co. (1965), 289-303.

———. "James Bordeaux." *The Mountain Men and the Fur Trade of the Far West*. Ed. Leroy R. Hafen. Vol. 5. Glendale CA: Arthur H. Clark Co. (1968), 65-80.

———. "J. LaRamee." *The Mountain Men and the Fur Trade of the Far West*. Ed. Leroy R. Hafen. Vol. 6. Glendale CA: Arthur H. Clark Co. (1968), 223-25.

McGillycuddy, Julia B. *McGillycuddy Agent: A Biography of Dr. Valentine T. McGillycuddy*. Stanford CA: Stanford University Press, 1941.

McGillycuddy, V. T. "Pine Ridge Agency, Dakota." *Annual Report of the Commissioner of Indian Affairs*. Washington DC: GPO (1879), 37-40.

———. "Pine Ridge Agency, Dakota." *Annual Report of the Commissioner of Indian Affairs*. Washington DC: GPO (1881), 44-50.

———. "Pine Ridge Agency, Dakota." *Annual Report of the Commissioner of Indian Affairs—1882*. Washington DC: GPO (1882), 35-39.

———. "Pine Ridge Agency, Dakota." *Annual Report of the Commissioner of Indian Affairs*. Washington DC: GPO (1884), 36-42.

McGregor, James H. *The Wounded Knee Massacre From the Viewpoint of the Sioux*. Baltimore: Wirth Brothers, 1940.

Mears, David T. "Campaigning Against Crazy Horse." *Proceedings and Collections of the Nebraska State Historical Society* 10 (1907): 68–77.
Meyer, Roy W. "The Establishment of the Santee Reservation 1866–1869." *Nebraska History* 45 (1964): 59–97.
———. *History of the Santee Sioux: United States Indian Policy on Trial.* Lincoln: University of Nebraska Press, 1967.
———. "Ezra A. Hayt." *The Commissioners of Indian Affairs, 1824–1977.* Ed. Robert M. Kvasnicka and Herman Viola. Lincoln: University of Nebraska Press (1979): 155–66.
Miles, Nelson A. *Annual Report of the Secretary of War.* Washington DC: GPO, 1891.
Milner, Joe E., and Earle R. Forrest. *California Joe: Noted Scout and Indian Fighter.* Lincoln: University of Nebraska Press, 1987.
Murray, Keith A. *The Modocs and Their War.* Norman: University of Oklahoma Press, 1959.
Nadeau, Remi. *Fort Laramie and the Sioux Indians.* Englewood Cliffs NJ: Prentice-Hall Inc., 1967.
Neihardt, John G. *When the Tree Flowered: An Authentic Tale of the Old Sioux World.* New York: Macmillian Co. 1951.
———. *Black Elk Speaks: Being the Life Story of a Holy Man of the Oglala Sioux.* Lincoln: University of Nebraska Press, 1979.
Olson, James C. *Red Cloud and the Sioux Problem.* Lincoln: University of Nebraska Press, 1975.
Paine, Bayard H. "An Indian Depredation Claim that Proved A Boomerang." *Nebraska History* 15 (1934): 45–55.
Parman, Donald L. "Francis Ellington Leupp." Pp. 221–31 in *The Commissioners of Indian Affairs, 1824–1977.* Ed. Robert M. Kvasnicka and Herman Viola. Lincoln: University of Nebraska Press, 1979.
Pattison, John J. "With the U. S. Army along the Oregon Trail." *Nebraska History* 15 (1934): 79–93.
Paul, R. Eli, ed. *Autobiography of Red Cloud: War Leader of the Oglalas.* Helena: Montana Historical Society Press, 1997.
Pfaller, Louis L., O.S.B. "The Brave Bear Murder Case." *North Dakota History* 36 (1969): 121–39.
———. "The Peace Mission of 1863–1864." *North Dakota History* 37 (1970): 293–313.
———. *James McLaughlin: The Man with an Indian Heart.* New York: Vantage Press, 1978.
Pollock, William J. "Rosebud (formerly Spotted Tail) Agency, Dakota." *Annual Report of the Commissioner of Indian Affairs.* Washington DC: GPO (1878), 38–40.
Poole, D. C. *Among the Sioux of Dakota: Eighteen Months' Experience as an Indian Agent, 1869–70.* St. Paul: Minnesota Historical Society Press, 1988.
Powers, William K. *Oglala Religion.* Lincoln: University of Nebraska Press, 1977.
Prucha, Francis Paul. "Thomas Jefferson Morgan." *The Commissioners of Indian Af-*

fairs, 1824–1977. Eds. Robert M. Kvasnicka and Herman Viola. Lincoln: University of Nebraska Press (1979), 193–203.

———. *A Guide to the Military Posts of the United States.* Madison: State Historical Society of Wisconsin, 1964.

Reece, J. N. *Report of the Adjutant General of the State of Illinois.* 5 Springfield: Phillips Brothers Printers, 1901.

Report of the Secretary of War; Being Part of the Message and Documents Communicated to the Two Houses of Congress at the Beginning of the First Session of the Fifty-Second Congress. Washington DC: GPO, 1892.

Riley, Paul D. "The Battle of Massacre Canyon." *Nebraska History* 54 (1973): 221–49.

Robinson, Charles M., III. *Bad Hand: A Biography of General Ranald S. Mackenzie.* Austin TX: State House Press, 1993.

———. *General Crook and the Western Frontier.* Norman: University of Oklahoma Press, 2001.

Rogers, Fred B. *The Soldiers of the Overland: Being Some Account of the Services of General Patrick Edward Connor.* San Francisco: The Grabhorne Press, 1938.

Russell, Don. *The Lives and Legends of Buffalo Bill.* Norman: University of Oklahoma Press, 1960.

Saville, J. J. "Red Cloud Agency, Dakota." *Annual Report of the Commissioner of Indian Affairs.* Washington DC: GPO (1874), 251 52.

———. "Red Cloud Agency, Nebraska." *Annual Report of the Commissioner of Indian Affairs.* Washington DC: GPO, 1875.

Sheldon, Addison E. "Niobrara Journalist Death." *Nebraska History* 17 (1936): 139.

"Sheriffs Battle Indians on Lightning Creek." *The Wyoming Pioneer* 1 (1941): 190–201.

Smith, John E. "Misc. No. 121." *Annual Report of the Commissioner of Indian Affairs.* Washington DC: GPO (1870), 324–26.

Smith, J. Q. "Report of the Commissioner of Indian Affairs." *Annual Report of the Commissioner of Indian Affairs.* Washington DC: GPO (1876), v–xxv.

Spencer, L. F. "Report of Rosebud Agency." *Fifty-eighth Annual Report of the Commissioner of Indian Affairs.* Washington DC: GPO (1889), 158–61.

Stanley, George F. G. *The Birth of Western Canada: A History of the Riel Rebellions.* Toronto: University of Toronto Press, 1960.

Strahorn, Robert E. "The Battle of Powder River, March 17, 1876." *Battles and Skirmishes of the Great Sioux War, 1876–1877.* Ed. Jerome A. Greene. Norman: University of Oklahoma Press, 1993.

Swan, William A. "Cheyenne River Agency, Dakota Territory." *Annual Report of the Commissioner of Indian Affairs.* Washington DC: GPO (1884), 20–23.

Upham, Warren. "Minnesota Geographic Names." *Collections of the Minnesota Historical Society* 17 (1920): 1–735.

Utley, Robert M. *The Last Days of the Sioux Nation.* New Haven: Yale University Press, 1963.

———. *The Lance and the Shield: The Life and Times of Sitting Bull*. New York: Henry Holt and Co., 1993.
Varley, James F. *Brigham and the Brigadier: General Patrick Connor and His California Volunteers in Utah and Along the Oregon Trail*. Tucson: Westernlore Press, 1989.
Vaughn, J. W. *The Reynolds Campaign on Powder River*. Norman: University of Oklahoma Press, 1961.
———. *Indian Fights*. Norman: University of Oklahoma Press, 1966.
Walker, James R. "The Sun Dance and Other Ceremonies of the Oglala Division of the Teton Dakota." *Anthropological Papers* 16, American Museum of Natural History. Washington DC, 1917.
———. *Lakota Society*. Ed. Raymond J. DeMallie. Lincoln: University of Nebraska Press, 1982.
Watkins, Albert. *History of Nebraska*. Lincoln: Western Publishing and Engraving Co., 1913.
———. "Fort Mitchell Cemetery." *Nebraska History and Record of Pioneer Days* 1 (Dec. 1918): 2-3.
Weist, Katherine M. "Ned Casey and His Cheyenne Scouts: A Noble Experiment in an Atmosphere of Tension." *Montana the Magazine of Western History* 27 (1977): 26-39.
Wells, Phillip H. "Ninety-six Years Among the Indians of the Northwest—Adventures and Reminiscences of an Indian Scout and Interpreter in the Dakotas." *North Dakota History* 15 (1948): 85-133, 169-215, 265-312.
Wissler, Clark. "Societies and Ceremonial Associations in the Oglala Division of the Teton-Dakota." *Anthropological Papers* 11. American Museum of Natural History. Washington DC: GPO, 1912.

Manuscripts and Government Records

Good Thunder Interview, July 12 and 13, 1912. Camp, Walter Mason MSS. Lilly Library, Indiana University, Bloomington.
Hinman, Eleanor H. Collection. Nebraska State Historical Society, Lincoln.
Jensen, Richard E. "Notes on the Lakota Ghost Dance." Paper read before the Thirty-third Annual Missouri Valley History Conference, Omaha, Mar. 8, 1990.
National Archives and Records Administration. Eli S. Ricker Pension File. Civil War and later Pension Application Files. Records of the Veterans Administration. Record Group 15.
———. Letters Sent to the Office of Indian Affairs from the Pine Ridge Agency. Microcopy 1282, roll 21. Records of the Bureau of Indian Affairs. Record Group 75.
———. Letters Received by the Office of Indian Affairs. Red Cloud Agency. Microcopy 234, roll 718. Records of the Bureau of Indian Affairs. Record Group 75.
———. Special Case No. 188. Ghost Dance 1890-91. Records of the Bureau of Indian Affairs. Records of the Bureau of Indian Affairs. Record Group 75.

BIBLIOGRAPHY

———. Index to Correspondence Files. Feb. 29, 1912. Records of the Bureau of Indian Affairs. Record Group 75.

———. *Reports and Correspondence Relating to the Army Investigation of the Battle of Wounded Knee and to the Sioux Campaign of 1890-91.* Microcopy 983, roll 148. Records of the Office of the Adjutant General. Record Group 94.

———. Records of the U.S. Army Continental Commands. Record Group 393.

Report of Annual Meeting, Jan. 11, 1927. Nebraska State Historical Society, Lincoln.

Ricker, Eli S. Collection. MS 8. Nebraska State Historical Society, Lincoln.

Sheldon, Addison E. "Life of Red Cloud." MSS. Nebraska State Historical Society, 1932.

Newspapers and Magazines

Appleton's Booklovers Magazine
Billings (MT) Gazette
Chicago Daily Tribune
Chicago Inter-Ocean
Chicago Times
Chadron (NE) Advocate
Chadron Democrat
Chadron Journal
Chadron Times
Crawford (NE) Tribune
Dawes County (NE) Journal
Denver Post
Denver Rocky Mountain News
Empire Magazine
Grand Junction (CO) Daily Sentinel

Greencastle (IN) Banner
Harper's Weekly
Hay Springs (NE) News
Holdrege (NE) Daily Citizen
Lincoln Nebraska State Journal
New York Sun
New York Tribune
Omaha Bee
Omaha Daily News
Omaha World Herald
Rushville (NE) Standard
Sheridan County (NE) Star
Stanton (NE) Picket
St. Paul (MN) Pioneer Press
Washington (DC) Evening Star

Index

Abel, Annie Heloise, xviii
Adams, Alex, 19, 78, 132
African Americans, 103, 250, 252
alcohol consumption, 6, 8, 94, 100, 105-6, 168, 189, 219, 235-36, 282, 317, 333, 336, 347, 354, 370, 387 n. 16
Allen, Charles W., xvi, 262, 434 n. 103
Allen, Edgar A., 350
Allen (SD), 188, 227, 244, 256, 264, 273, 285, 330-31, 342, 344, 373
American Fur Company, 291, 332, 333, 335-37, 356, 367, 369
American Horse (Teton Sioux), 4, 17, 47, 57, 62-64, 71-72, 77, 82-83, 86, 96-98, 133, 215, 274, 287, 330, 334, 347-48, 362-65; interview with, 277-85; name origin, 282; wife of, 284
American Horse, Alice (Teton Sioux), 284
American Horse, Julia (Teton Sioux), 284
American Horse Creek, 277
American Missionary Association, 254
annuities, 9, 75, 87, 90, 94, 173, 192, 237, 245, 249, 252; decrease of, 150
antelope, 278
Apache Campaign, 74
Apple, Moss, 116
Appleton, Amos, 387 n. 18
Appleton, Frank, 7, 387 n. 17, 387 n. 18
Arapaho, 14, 16-17, 20, 22-23, 25-27, 36, 42, 44, 54, 63, 81, 99, 105, 280, 409
Arapaho Agency, 190
Arapaho Scouts, 15-16, 26, 44
Arickaree Creek, 81
Arikara, 273
Arikara Scouts, 275, 320
Arkansas John, 97
Arkansas River, 338
Asay, James, 236, 430 n. 57

Ash Creek, 10-11, 57
Ash Hollow: battle of, 337
Augur, Jacob A., 361, 461 n. 199
Auguste, Lucien, 347
Aungie, Henry, 356; wife of, 356

Bad Brave (Teton Sioux), 205, 214
Bad Face Band, Oglala, 66, 98, 286, 326, 344, 348, 402 n. 102; name origin, 348, 402 n. 102
Bad River, 195, 214, 253
Bad Spotted Eagle (Cree), 206; wife of, 206
Bad Whirlwind (Teton Sioux), 403 n. 108
Bad Wound (Teton Sioux), 204
Bailey, Gilbert E., 153, 419 n. 231
Bannocks, 190
Bare Bad Hair (French trader), 101
Barrett, Jay Amos, 252, 432 n. 84
Bartlett, Ephraim, 227
Bartlett, George E., xvi, 198, 227, 239
battles, sham, 55
Baxter, John, Jr., 270, 435 n. 111
Bay Horse Troop, 323
Beach, Rex, 208
Bear, John (Teton Sioux), 97
Bear Brains (Teton Sioux), 115
Bear Butte, 273
Bear Butte Creek, 278, 408
Bear Comes and Lie(s) (Teton Sioux), 206, 214; aka Bear Comes Lie Down, 215
Bear Creek, 151, 242
Beard (Teton Sioux): wife of, 204
Beard, Dewey (Teton Sioux), 191, 201-2, 206, 232; interview with, 208-26
Beard, Thomas (Teton Sioux), 204
Bear Ears (Teton Sioux), 191
Bear Parts Body (Teton Sioux), 204
Bear Robe (Cheyenne), 280

Bear Runs in the Woods (Teton Sioux), 207
bears, 145
Bear Stops Looks Back (Teton Sioux), 327
Bear Woman (Teton Sioux), 204, 207
Beauvais, Ben, 101
Beauvais, Geminien P., 338, 458 n. 164; aka Big Belly, 275
Beaver Creek, 7, 68, 73, 276, 287, 292, 298, 305, 408, 410
beef issues, 9, 75-78, 85, 88, 120, 185
Bell, Jason M., 149
Bell (Major), 149
Belle Fourche River, 39, 40-41, 44, 192, 195, 213
Benavidez, Condelario, 196
Benoit, Felix, 193
Benteen, Frederick W., 303, 320, 443 n. 63
Big Belly, 275; aka Geminien P. Beauvais, 338, 458 n. 164
Big Bordeaux Creek, 97
Big Foot (Teton Sioux), xv, 127-32, 134-35, 142, 153-54, 156, 158-59, 191-201, 204, 206, 208-17, 221, 227, 229, 230, 232-33, 237, 240-43, 245, 251-53, 256, 260-62, 401 n. 96; brother-in-law of, 159; photograph of, 240; wife of, 204
Big Foot Spring, 196
Big Hollow Creek, 367
Big Horn Mountains, 328
Big Horn River, 320
Big Knives (name for American soldiers), 178
Big Laramie River, 1
Big Mouth (Teton Sioux), 5, 6, 278, 337-39, 343-44, 387 n. 15
Big Road (Teton Sioux), 16, 52, 195, 209, 312, 449 n. 104
Big Sioux River, 122
Big Star (Teton Sioux), 283
Big Thunder (Santee), 424 n. 254
Big Voice Thunder (Teton Sioux), 206, 214
Big Woman (Teton Sioux), 247
Bingham, W. H., 82, 405 n. 127
Bird Head (Arapaho), 280
Birds Afraid of Him (Teton Sioux), 206
Bird Wings (Teton Sioux), 206
Bismarck (ND), 176
Bisnet, Joe. *See* Bissonette, Joseph
Bissonette, Joseph, 101, 337, 344, 456 n. 159, 459 n. 176

Bites in Two Band, Oglala: name origin of, 181
Bitter Cottonwood Creek, 101
Black American (Teton Sioux), 208
Black Bear (Cheyenne), 50
Black Bear (Teton Sioux), 77, 82
Black Beard Treaty, 40
Black Buffalo Woman (Teton Sioux), 274, 404 n. 120, 436 n. 2
Black Bugle (Teton Sioux), 207
Blackburn (Doctor), 357
Black Coal (Arapaho), 17
Black Cow (Teton Sioux), 207
Black Coyote (Teton Sioux), 193-94, 204, 212, 219
Black Crow (Teton Sioux), 283, 293, 298-99, 439 n. 28
Black Elk (Teton Sioux), 59-60, 396 n. 80; son-in-law of, 60
Black Feather (Teton Sioux), 351
Blackfeet Sioux, 410, 445 n. 80
Black Flutes (Teton Sioux), 206
Blackfoot (Teton Sioux), 338-39
Black Fox (Teton Sioux), 63-64, 75, 307, 400 n. 94
Black Hair (Teton Sioux), 208; wife of, 206
Black Hawk (Teton Sioux), 206
Black Hills, 10, 17, 40-41, 65, 81-86, 88, 103, 121, 126, 139, 177, 192, 255, 268, 282-85, 302, 305, 315, 325-26, 342, 345-46; gold miners in, 405 n. 129
Black Hills Treaty, 14, 139, 255, 302, 325, 393 n. 54, 406 n. 135
Black Horse Troop, 323
Black Kettle (Teton Sioux), 80, 351
Black Lodge Pole (Teton Sioux), 369; attacked at Sand Creek, 405 n. 124
Black Moccasin (Cheyenne), 54
Black Pipe Creek, 78, 81, 92, 94, 151
Black Prairie Chicken (Teton Sioux), 243
Black Shawl Woman (Teton Sioux), 399 n. 91
Black Shield (Teton Sioux), 206; daughter of, 205
Black Zebra (Teton Sioux), 206
Bloody Knife (Arikara), 320
Blue Earth Creek, 315
Blue Face (Teton Sioux), 232
Blue Horse (Teton Sioux), 62, 77, 85, 96, 278, 398 n. 87
Bonoist, Felix, 193

INDEX

Bordeaux, James, 101, 290-91, 332, 335, 337-39, 343-44, 367, 410 n. 166, 440 n. 35
Bordeaux, John, 291
Bordeaux, Louis, 69, 72-73, 82, 84-85, 97, 103; interview with, 290-302
Bordeaux, Marie, 290
Bordeaux Creek, xiv, 291, 299
Bordeaux Station, 279
Boucher, Frank C., 17, 98, 343
Boucher Creek, 97-98
Bourke, John G., 37, 42
Bouyer, Sally, 410 n. 169
Box Elder Creek, 44, 303
Bozeman Trail, 344
Bradford, Julia, vi; interview with, 368-69
Bradley, Luther Prentice, 61-62, 71, 300, 398 n. 86
Brave Bear (Teton Sioux), 122-23, 326, 413 n. 189
Bravo, Barney, 320
Brazeau, John, 369
Brazeau, Walter, 370
Breckenridge, C. F., 255, 433 n. 88
Brings Her Home (Teton Sioux), 207
Brings It to Her (Teton Sioux), 207
Broken Arm (Teton Sioux), 170
Broken Arrow (Teton Sioux), 206; wife of, 206
Brooke, John R., 152, 227, 241, 243-45, 250-51, 419 n. 230
Brown, Donald, 149
Brown, George LeRoy, 122, 250, 343
Brown, W. H., 397 n. 84
Brown, William (Teton Sioux), 350-52
Brown Beaver (Teton Sioux), 204
Brown Eyes (Teton Sioux), 327
Brown Eyes Woman (Teton Sioux), 396 n. 79
Brown Hoops (Teton Sioux), 205
Browning, Daniel M., 140, 415 n. 210
Brown Turtle (Teton Sioux), 206
Brown Woman (Teton Sioux), 205
Brule Agency, 102
Brulé Sioux, 6, 74, 86, 89, 115, 143, 145, 181, 232, 276, 279, 301-2, 311, 316, 333-35, 445 n. 80
Bryant (Colonel). *See* Barrett, Jay Amos
Buckskin Breech Clout (Teton Sioux), 204
Buckskin Jack. *See* Russell, Jack
buffalo, 52, 143-45, 321; as food, 182
Buffalo Bed (Teton Sioux), 311

Buffalo Chips (aka Charles White), 294
Buffalo Robes, 33, 37, 51, 107, 109, 368
Bull Bear (Teton Sioux), 6, 239, 370; son of, 6, 232
Bull Eagle (Teton Sioux), 82, 198
Bull Head (Teton Sioux), 274, 436 n. 5
Bull Hoop (Teton Sioux), 370
Bull Man (Teton Sioux), 207
Bullock, William G., 101, 104, 368
Burke, Daniel W., 292-94, 296-99, 440 n. 38
Burke, John M., 241, 431 n. 69
Burt (Lieutenant). *See* Baxter, John, Jr.
Bush, Joe, 25, 54, 393 n. 58
buttes, 10, 20, 39, 151, 176, 192, 305, 361
Buzzard Basin, 227

Cache la Poudre River, 81, 288, 290, 371
Calhoun Hill, 308, 320
Calico (Teton Sioux), 195, 340
California Crossing, 339
California Joe. *See* Milner, Moses E.
Callhoun Hill, 305-6, 312
Cameron (Lieutenant), 106
Camp Robinson, 104, 114, 116, 284
Camp Sheridan, 7, 10, 32, 49, 65, 68-69, 79-80, 264, 271, 276, 287, 292-99, 301, 408
Camp Sheridan Trail, 10
Canada, 46, 64, 102, 148, 185, 208, 286
Canby, E. R. S., 66, 397 n. 82
Cane Creek, 1, 120, 233
Cannon Ball River: buffalo hunt on, 176
Captain Jack (Modoc), 397 n. 82
captive-women stories, 338, 372, 457 n. 163
Carlisle Indian School, 151, 318, 350, 370; graduate of, 170
Carr, Eugene A., 120, 154, 412 n. 183, 419 n. 233
Carries the Otter (Arikara/Cheyenne), 321
Carson, George, 19
Casecellor (Mr.), 100
Casey, Edward W., 170, 420 n. 240, 420 n. 241
Casper (WY), 284
Cast Away and Run (Teton Sioux), 205
Catholics, 102, 149-50, 153, 160, 321; Eli Ricker's sentiment against, xxii
cavalry, 154, 198, 202-3, 229, 235, 341. *See also* Second Cavalry; Third Cavalry; Fourth Cavalry; Fifth Cavalry; Seventh Cavalry; Eighth Cavalry; Ninth Cavalry

477

Cedar Spring, 196
Cedar Woman (Teton Sioux), 400 n. 94
Chadron (NE), xiii–xv, xxii, 79, 283–84, 291, 314, 318, 329, 342, 347–48, 356, 361, 369
Chadron Creek, 9, 11, 20, 21, 56–57, 81–82, 97–98, 177, 280, 291, 299, 343; council on, 283; name origin of, 291
Chadron Democrat, xvi
Chadron Times, xiv–xv, xvii, xxi
Chardon, Louis, 291
Charge at Them (Teton Sioux), 205
Charging (Teton Sioux), 325
Charging Bear (Teton Sioux), 34, 54, 239, 403 n. 108
Chase, George F., 270, 435 n. 111
Chase the Animal (aka George Sword and Hunts the Enemy), 330
Chasing Creek (Reno Creek), 302–3
Cherry Creek, 81, 192–93, 203, 210, 253, 363–64, 366
Cheyenne, 6, 12, 15, 18–19, 22, 26, 28, 31–33, 35, 37–38, 42–43, 49–51, 54, 57, 61, 63, 79–82, 97, 99, 104, 120, 154, 246, 264, 266–68, 270, 275, 280, 283, 285, 303, 305, 308–9, 311, 315–16, 322–24, 327, 329, 338, 360, 361, 368, 409
Cheyenne Agency, 65, 75
Cheyenne Charley (aka Little Buckshot of the Prairie), 80, 81
Cheyenne Creek, 251, 263, 305
Cheyenne Outbreak, 264, 435 n. 106
Cheyenne Reservation, 66, 366
Cheyenne River, 3, 88, 132, 135, 192, 194–95, 203, 209–11, 232, 252–53, 256, 345, 409
Cheyenne River Agency, 74–75, 82–83, 85, 90, 102, 128, 176, 179, 182, 191, 208–9, 216, 229, 231, 252, 274, 325, 374, 377
Cheyenne River Reservation, 74, 143, 145, 154, 208, 230
Cheyenne Scouts, 44, 48, 170, 305
Chief Dog (Teton Sioux), 62, 202, 208
Chief Joseph (Nez Perce), 286, 319, 397 n. 82, 397 n. 83
chiefs: definition of, 187; roles of, 349
Chief Woman (Teton Sioux), 205
Clementi, Bernard, 397 n. 81
Chippewa, 184; language, 139
Chipps (Teton Sioux), 74, 300; interview with, 273–77
Christensen, H. J., 362

Christian Science, xxi
Chug Water River, 104
Chuzon (Mr.): trading post of, 100
Civil Service Commission, 168, 174
Civil War, xi
Clapp, William Henry, 82, 139, 140
Clark, A. M., xiv–xv
Clark (Mr.), 10–11, 87
Clark, William Philo, 17, 26–27, 32–33, 42, 44–47, 49, 51, 53–55, 60–64, 67–69, 71–76, 104, 271, 300–301, 392 n. 50
Claws (Teton Sioux), 82
Cleveland, Grover (president), 148–49, 360, 402 n. 104
Cleveland, William J., 92, 327–28
Clifford, Charles C., 371; interview with wife of, 371–73
Clifford, Henry C., 118, 235, 368, 369; ranch of, 10
Clifford, Mortimer, 369
Clifford Creek, 367
Close to Home (Teton Sioux), 205
Coal Creek, 360
coal mines, 39
Cody, William F., 369; and attaché John F. Burke, 241; book by, 369; wild west shows of, 20, 226, 233, 235–36, 264, 369
Coe, Alfred N. (Yankton): interview with, 355–58
Coe, Charles, 355–56
Coe, Josette (Yankton), 356
Cogill, Tom, 19
Colby, Marguerite E. *See* Lost Bird
Colhoff, George, 5, 102, 287
Collins, John S., 101
Comanches, 285
Comes Crawling Woman (Teton Sioux), 207
Comes Out Alive (Teton Sioux) (aka Mary Thomas), 239, 430 n. 63
Comes Out Alive Woman (Teton Sioux), 207
Comes Out Rattling (Teton Sioux): wife of, 206
Conn, Frank M., 68, 73, 402 n. 105
Connor, Patrick E., 42, 368, 394 n. 69
Conquering Bear (Teton Sioux), 2, 29, 76, 82, 114–15, 279, 290, 332–34, 336, 346–47
Conrad, Francis, 388 n. 22
Cook, Charles Smith, 127, 131–32, 135–36, 414 n. 201
Cook, James H., 278

478

Cooney, Adolph, 9, 104–5
Cord, Lee, 356
Corliss, Augustus W., 234–35, 429 n. 54
Corn Band, Teton Sioux, 403 n. 109, 403 n. 110
Corn Creek, 242
Cottle, Frank, 192
Cottonwood River, 305
coup, 36, 172, 273–74
Courage Bear (Teton Sioux), 206; wife of, 206
Courage Bear, George (Teton Sioux), 206
Covington (NE), 177
Coxville (SD), 96
Craft, Francis M. J., 160, 231, 263, 419 n. 236, 429 n. 49
Cramsie, John W., 137, 169–70, 184, 186
Craven, Gus, 154
Crawford, Emmet, 79, 114–15, 404 n. 123
Crazy Bear (Teton Sioux), 204, 238; mother of, 238
Crazy Horse (Teton Sioux), v, xxiv, 4, 16–17, 23, 25, 35, 43, 45–47, 49, 50–53, 55, 57–76, 85, 87, 97, 101, 117–18, 246–47, 251, 271, 273–77, 282–83, 286–88, 292–301, 304, 311–12, 314, 316–17, 322, 327–28, 330, 332, 359, 387 n. 17, 396 n. 78, 398 n. 88, 400 n. 114; arrest of, 271; as scout, 49, 246; brother of, 277, 438 n. 18; burial of, 276–77, 404 n. 117; camp of, 23, 24, 26, 34, 45, 47, 49, 51, 54, 61, 63; death of, 58, 66–67, 70–71, 73, 246, 272, 276, 283, 288, 300, 332; father of, 72–73, 97, 274, 297, 300; mother of, 274, 401 n. 97, 436 n. 2; named for, 288; naming of, 274; sister-in-law of, 287; spied on by scouts, 402 n. 103; tactics of, 65, 118; vision of, 117; wife of, 288, 399 n. 91, 404 n. 120, 436 n. 3; wounding of by No Water, 274, 436 n. 3
"Crazy Man Jumped Off the Bank" Creek, 265
Crazy Thunder (Teton Sioux), 99, 100
Crazy Woman Creek, 1, 25, 35, 38–39, 257
Creel, Herbert M., 321, 361, 445 n. 144
Cressey, Charles H., 228, 428 n. 41
Cripple Warbonnet (Teton Sioux): son of, 401 n. 96
Crook Commission, 92
Crook, George, 12–26, 34–35, 37–47, 49–54, 61–62, 66–68, 77, 81–82, 89, 92–94, 241, 248–49, 251, 256–60, 287, 304, 306, 316, 322, 327, 328, 336, 361, 390 n. 33
Crook Treaty (1889), 68, 92, 98
Crosby (Mr.), 15
Crow, 39, 84, 273, 281, 302, 305, 310, 315, 318–19, 355, 368; language, 139
Crow Agency, 321
Crow Butte, 10
Crow Creek (SD), 356
Crow Creek Agency, 89, 102, 377
Crow Creek Reservation, 179
Crow Dog (Teton Sioux), 82, 283, 302, 442 n. 58
Crow Scouts, 319–20, 455 n. 141
Cunningham, John, 301
Curly (Crow), 319–20, 455 n. 142
Custer, George Armstrong, 22, 32, 34, 38, 55, 64, 66, 97, 102, 118, 126, 208, 240–41, 248, 255–56, 275, 277, 302–11, 313, 315–20, 322–25, 327; revenge for, 262, 264
Custer Hill, 306–10, 313, 317
Cut Foot: aka Frank D. Yates, 397 n. 84
Cutoff Band, Oglala, 6, 63, 83, 86, 89, 102, 286, 355, 367; name origin of, 6, 423–24 n. 249

Dakota Conflict of 1862, 169, 187, 252, 255, 424 n. 253
dances, 28, 40, 50, 54, 107–8, 113, 145–46, 171, 175
Daniels, J. W., 12–13, 84, 390 n. 35, 406 n. 134
Dartenberger (Mr.), 94
Davenport (IA), 286
Davis, Clem, 239
Davis, Jefferson, 356
Dawes, Henry, 92, 408 n. 151
Dawes County (NE), 291
Dawson, J. L., 208, 358
Day (Teton Sioux), 77
Daylight, Richard, 391 n. 43
day schools, 90, 145, 160–61, 191, 196, 209, 232, 239, 263, 314, 327, 343, 348, 359, 361
Deadhorse Creek, 348
Deadman Creek, 16, 87, 341
Dee, John, 19, 335
Deep Creek, 195, 213. *See also* Pass Creek
Deer Creek, 101
Deere, John, 19, 75
Democratic Party, xxi, 149
Deon, Peter A. (aka Sam Deon), 349

479

INDEX

Deon, Sam. *See* Deon, Peter A.
De Smet, Pierre-Jean, 2
Diamond Spring, 301
Different Woman (Teton Sioux), 207
diseases, 3, 18
Dixon, Ellen, 356–57
Dixon, Robert, 356
Dodd, George A., 404 n. 121
dogs: as food, 4, 54, 372
Dog Soldiers, 123–25, 152, 177, 188, 326
Dog Teeth Butte, 192
Donahue, Cornelius, 410 n. 168; aka Lame Johnnie, 101
Don't Eat the Badger Band, Oglala, 181
Dorsney (Sergeant), 94, 95
dreams, 145, 187
Drexel Mission. *See* Holy Rosary Mission
drinking. *See* alcohol consumption
Dripper. *See* Dripps, Andrew
Dripper's Ranch. *See* Dripps, Andrew
Dripps, Andrew, 100
Drops Blood (Teton Sioux): wife of, 206
Drum Carrier (Teton Sioux), 116
Dull Knife (Cheyenne), 32, 81, 226, 360, 394 n. 64; family of, 36; son of, 35–36
Duncan, William, 255
Dundee, Elmer S., 357
Dunn, John, 194, 426 n. 12; aka Red Beard, 195, 213, 426 n. 12

Eagle Bear (Teton Sioux), 192
Eagle Body (Teton Sioux), 205
Eagle Elk (Teton Sioux), 167, 172; interview with, 358–60
Eagle Horse (Teton Sioux), 97
Eagle Nest Butte, 151
Eagle Ring (Teton Sioux), 304
eagles, 171
Eagle Shape (Teton Sioux), 207
Eastman, Charles A., 240, 431 n. 66; interview with, 285–87
Ecoffey, Jules, 9, 104, 105, 388 n. 23
Egan, James, 75, 105, 112, 257, 259, 434 n. 98
Ehnamani, Artemus, 255
Eighth Cavalry, 193
Eldon. *See* Elting, Oscar
Elk Creek (Teton Sioux), 204; wife of, 204
Elk Woman (Teton Sioux), 207
Elting, Oscar, 14, 118–19
Encouraging Bear (Teton Sioux), 273

enemies: Sioux concept of, 175
Enemy Afraid of Him (Teton Sioux), 208
Etahzepah Cho Band, Sans Arc: word origin of, 182
Eubanks, Lucinda, 457 n. 163
Eubanks, William, Jr., 457 n. 163
Evans, Andrew W., 268, 435 n. 109
Ewers, Ezra P., 360, 461 n. 197
Extravagance Clan, 181

Face (Teton Sioux), 82
face painting, 318
Falkenberg, Louis, 460 n. 192
Fargo (ND), 176
Faribault, Alexander, 121, 126
Faribault (MN): name origin of, 121
Farnham, John, 8, 256, 264, 388 n. 18; wife of, 5
Fast Boat (Teton Sioux), 207
Fast Horse (Teton Sioux), 147
Fast Horse Creek, 203
Fast Thunder (Teton Sioux), 20, 29–31, 43, 82, 151, 330
Fast Wolf (Teton Sioux), 206
Fat Courage Bear (Teton Sioux), 206
Fat Hips (Teton Sioux), 207
Fauts (Captain). *See* Fouts, W. D.
Fears Nothing (Teton Sioux), 314; aka Respects Nothing, 302
Feather, Frank (Teton Sioux), 309; interview with, 239–40
Feather on the Head (Teton Sioux), 20
feathers: wearing of, 319
Feeler, William, 82
Fennell (Reverend). *See* Ffennell, Archer B.
Fetterman, Judd, 280
Fetterman, William J., 397 n. 80
Fetterman Fight of 1866, 59, 314, 329–30, 346, 348, 359
Few Tails (Teton Sioux), 45
Ffennell, Archer B., 122, 412 n. 188
Fifth Cavalry, 10
Fire Eater (Cheyenne), 81–82
Fire Thunder (Teton Sioux), 279, 288
Fire Thunder, George (Teton Sioux), 94, 139, 355
First Infantry, 127
Fisher, Stanton G., 319
Flagpole Incident at Red Cloud Agency, 88, 114

Flandreau (SD), 357, 409
Flandreau Agency, 377
Flatbottle Band, Oglala, 181
Flatfoot Band, Oglala, 181
Floyd River, 126
Flying Bird (Teton Sioux), 325
Flying Chaser (Teton Sioux), 311
Flying Hawk, Moses (Teton Sioux), 64, 97, 399 n. 92, 400 n. 94; interview with, 307-9
Flying Horse (Teton Sioux), 142, 233-34
Fog Creek, 250-51
foodways, 4, 53, 57, 105, 329, 372
Forbes, William, 169
Forsyth, James W., 95, 126-30, 138, 142, 155-57, 159-60, 198, 219, 227-28, 231, 235, 251, 409 n. 157
Fort Abraham Lincoln, 325, 375
Fort Bennett, 192, 252-53, 375
Fort Buford, 122, 375
Fort C. F. Smith, 25, 260, 375
Fort Cheyenne, 192
Fort Douglas, 370, 375
Fort Ellis, 319
Fort Fetterman, 8, 18-20, 22, 32, 44, 49-50, 101, 106-7, 256, 260, 274, 280-81, 375
Fort George, 356
Fort Hall, 330, 375
Fort Kearny, 338, 340, 369, 375
Fort Keogh, 54, 75, 81, 84, 88, 99, 104, 360, 375
Fort Laramie, 1-3, 5-7, 9, 15, 18, 40, 50, 64, 85, 101, 103-4, 106, 126, 233, 248-49, 256, 287, 290-91, 315, 332, 336-38, 341-42, 367, 375
Fort Lincoln. *See* Fort Abraham Lincoln
Fort Meade, 75, 79, 192, 195, 212, 273, 360, 363-66, 376
Fort Mitchell, 376
Fort Northwest, 330
Fort Phil Kearny, 280, 376; battle of 1866, 329
Fort Pierre, 1, 103, 253, 337, 356, 369, 376
Fort Randall, 177, 376
Fort Reno, 15, 22, 25, 34, 38-39, 50, 260, 376
Fort Riley, 137, 376
Fort Robinson, 9, 13, 15-16, 18-19, 22-23, 25, 32, 39, 43-45, 47, 49, 51, 60-61, 69, 80, 87, 96-97, 115, 118, 246, 249, 254, 256, 260, 264-65, 271, 276, 292-99, 327-28, 332, 341, 347, 361, 363, 376
Fort Sheridan. *See* Camp Sheridan

Fort Sidney, 376
Fort Sill, 284, 376
Fort Snelling, 356, 376
Fort Sully, 376
Fort Thompson, 286
Fort Totten, 122, 169, 170, 356, 376
Fort Vermillion, 356
Fort Yates, 61, 75, 96, 99, 122, 124, 136, 169, 176, 316, 360, 376
Foster, Charles, 92
Fourth Cavalry, 10, 15, 26, 44, 47, 284-85
Fouts, W. D., 64, 104, 339-40, 400 n. 93
Fox (Teton Sioux), 135. *See also* (aka) Wells, Philips
Fox Soldiers, 326
French language: influence on Indian speech, 183
Friday (Teton Sioux), 17, 292
Frog (Teton Sioux), 132, 134-35, 401 n. 96
Fry, Edwin A., 252, 432 n. 82
fry bread, 105
fur trade, xvii, 122, 278, 330, 343
Gall (Teton Sioux) (aka Man Who Goes in the Middle), 275, 314, 437 n. 11
Gallagher, H. D., 81, 98, 122, 136, 146-50, 170, 405 n. 125
Galligo, Frank, 302, 306
Gallino, David, 103
Gardner (Colonel), 184
Gareau, Charles, 334-35, 344, 456 n. 158
Garnett, Richard B., 1
Garnett, Sally, 410 n. 169
Garnett, William, xxiv, 233, 283, 295-96, 329, 371, 384-85 n. 1; interview with, 1-121
Garnier, Baptiste, 154, 196-97, 217, 226-27, 229, 231, 256, 260-63, 288-90, 371-72, 410 n. 169, 426 n. 14
Garnier, Eulalie, 410 n. 169
Garrow, Charles. *See* Gareau, Charles
Garvie, James, 189; interview with, 251-56
gatling guns, 63, 223
Gay (Mr.), 368
Geary (Mr.), 290
Georgia (NE), 292
Gets on a Fight (Teton Sioux), 207
Gettysburg (Civil War battle), 1
Ghost Dance, xv, 98, 128, 131, 134-35, 143-46, 152, 173-74, 189, 191-92, 201, 209, 213, 231-32, 252, 307, 327, 417 n. 223, 427 n. 25

481

Ghost Horse (Teton Sioux), 205
ghost shirts, 143-45, 254, 262
Gilman, Samuel C., 255
Girton, William: interview with, 370
Glode, Edward, 335-36
Godfrey, Joseph, 252, 432 n. 83
Goes Ahead (Crow), 319-20
Goes Out Looking (Teton Sioux), 400 n. 94
Goes to War (Teton Sioux), 207
Goings, Frank, 284, 362-64, 369; mother of, 94
Goings, Nettie Elizabeth: interview with, 369-70
Good, James W., xxiii
Good Bear (Teton Sioux), 207; older, 204; wife of, 204; younger, 204
Good Boy (Teton Sioux), 205
Good Horse (Teton Sioux), 207
Good Land Woman (Teton Sioux), 207
Good Natured Woman (Teton Sioux), 207
Good Shield (Arapaho), 280
Good Singer (Teton Sioux) (aka Little Wound), 140
Good Thunder (Teton Sioux), 201
Good Voice (Teton Sioux), 82, 298, 441 n. 47
Good White Cow (Teton Sioux), 207
Goolay, Henry, 98
Gordon, George A., 10, 11
government commissions, 12-14, 21, 40, 85-88, 90, 92-93, 103, 122, 139, 151, 168, 174, 325, 368, 410
government distributions. *See* annuities
Grabber (Teton Sioux), 370
Grand Prairie Seminary and Commercial College, xiii
Grand River, 176, 305, 345
Grand River Agency, 377
Grant, Ulysses S. (president), 9, 65, 82-84, 88, 105
Grass (Teton Sioux), 275, 437 n. 12
Gray (Teton Sioux), 206
Gray Bear (Teton Sioux), 351
Gray Cliff Ranch, xiv
Gray Eyes (Teton Sioux), 116
Gray Horse Troop, 323-24
Gray in Eye (Teton Sioux), 206
Gray Owl Woman (Teton Sioux), 207
Grease Grass Creek, 310. *See also* Little Bighorn
Great River, 345

Great Sioux Reservation, 345; partition of, 93
Green River (UT), 335
Greenwood (SD), 357
Gregory County (SD), 254
Gresham, John, 361
Grindstone Butte, 3
Grindstone Creek, 3
Grouard, Frank, 12-14, 19, 21, 42, 44, 51, 54, 60, 62, 72-73, 97, 102-3, 154, 256-59, 292, 295, 297, 305, 369, 410 n. 169
Ground Horn Woman (Teton Sioux), 207
Gruard, Frank. *See* Grouard, Frank

Haight (Commissioner of Indian Affairs). *See* Hayt, Ezra A.
Hailing Bear (Teton Sioux), 206
Hairy Moccasin (Crow), 319
Half Diamond E Ranch, 9
Half Yellow Face (Crow), 319-20
Hamblin, Howard M., xviii
Hamburg (IA), 291
Hand, Marshal, 243
Hardee (Lieutenant). *See* Hardie, Francis H.
Hardie, Francis H., 264, 269, 435 n. 107
Hare, William Hobart, 122, 328, 373, 413 n. 188
Harmon, Jack: wife of, 338
Harney, William S., 337
Harney Springs, 250
Harrington, Henry Moore, 64, 308, 400 n. 94
Harrison, Jim, 238
Harrison, William Henry (president), 149
Has a Dog (Teton Sioux), 205
Hastings, James S., 98, 118-19, 412 n. 181
Hat Creek, 45, 47, 269, 295-96
Hat Creek Stagecoach Station, 45, 47
Hawk Woman (Teton Sioux), 207
Hawkins rifles, 228
Hayes, Rutherford B. (president), 16-18, 22, 74, 76
Hay Minne Choka Ha Band, Santee: name origin of, 180
Hayt, Ezra A., 76, 404 n. 122
He Crow (Teton Sioux), 204, 351
He Dog (Teton Sioux), 16, 52, 62, 82
He Eagle (Teton Sioux), 205, 207; wife of, 205
He Eagle, Edward (Teton Sioux), 205
Help Them (Teton Sioux), 135-36
Henissee, Argalus G., 191-92, 209, 425 n. 6

482

Hennessey, Argalus G. *See* Henissee, Argalus G.
Henry, Guy V., 248, 250-51, 263, 431 n. 75
Her Brown Faced Dog (Teton Sioux), 208
Her Cedar (Teton Sioux), 207
Her Eagle (Teton Sioux), 207
Her Elk Tooth (Teton Sioux), 207
Her First (Teton Sioux), 207
Her Good Horse (Teton Sioux), 207
Her Good Medicine (Teton Sioux), 206
Her Horse (Teton Sioux), 207
Herman, Antoine, 235
Her Neck (Teton Sioux), 208
Her Roan (Teton Sioux), 207
Her Shell Walks (Teton Sioux), 208
Her White Horse (Teton Sioux), 207
Her Yellow (Teton Sioux), 207
High Back Bone (Teton Sioux), 215, 243
High Bear (Teton Sioux), 296, 298-99; aka Tall Bear, 441 n. 46
High Forehead (Teton Sioux), 279, 347, 439 n. 22
High Hawk (Teton Sioux), 204; wife of, 204
High Lance (Teton Sioux), 82
High Star (Teton Sioux), 83, 86
High Wolf (Teton Sioux), 77
Hinman, Samuel D., 86, 88-92, 285
His Crow (Teton Sioux), 208
His Red Nation (Santee) (aka Little Crow), 188, 424 n. 254
His Two Lance (Teton Sioux), 207
His War (Teton Sioux), 207
Hits Her on a Run (Teton Sioux), 207
Hoksi Hakakta (Last Child Society), 359
Holley, Francis Chamberlain, 123
Hollow Horn Bear (Teton Sioux), 17
Hollow Horn Woman (Teton Sioux), 207
Holy Comes-Medicine Comes (Teton Sioux), 207
Holy Road, 52
Holy Rosary Mission, 90, 105, 143, 152-53, 160, 162, 203, 344, 373, 413 n. 191; as Drexel Mission, 122, 138, 142, 160, 174
Horn Cloud, Daniel (Teton Sioux), 201
Horn Cloud, Frank (Teton Sioux), 194, 207
Horn Cloud, Joseph (Teton Sioux), 209, 228, 232, 240-41; interview with, 191-208
Horn Cloud, Sherman (Teton Sioux), 203
Horn Cloud, William (Teton Sioux), 194, 201, 223

Horned Antelope (Teton Sioux), 298
Horned Cloud (Teton Sioux), 191-92, 198, 200, 204, 209-10, 212, 219, 226; wife of, 204
Horse Creek, 2, 64, 104, 248, 334, 340; battle of 1865, 337; treaty of 1851, 2, 334, 439 n. 21
Horse Looking (Teton Sioux), 280
Horse Nation (Teton Sioux), 207
Horse Runs Ahead (Teton Sioux), 316
horse stealing, 56, 101, 108, 117
Horseshoe Creek, 101
Hose-Yanka (Teton Sioux), 132
Hotchkiss cannon, 130, 142, 158, 196, 198, 205, 215-17, 223, 228, 238-39, 251, 426 n. 13
Hough Ranch, 369
Houghton, Fred J., xiv
Howard, E. A., 12-13, 82, 390 n. 34
Howard, Oliver O., 319
Hudson's Bay Company, 330, 356
Hump (Teton Sioux), 193
Humphrey & Stenger Ranch, 358
Hunkpapa Agency, 102
Hunkpapa Sioux, 74, 182, 303, 311, 316, 410, 445 n. 80; name origin of, 182
Hunt (teacher at Kyle SD), 232
Hunter, John, 1, 410 n. 169
hunting, xvi; antelope, 192, 278, 289, 335; bear, 330, 331; buffalo, 124, 176, 278, 282, 285, 348, 368, 369; deer, 289; rabbit, 348
Huntkalutwin (Teton Sioux), 290
Hunts the Enemy (Teton Sioux): aka Chase the Animal; Sword, George, 45, 326
Huron College, 357

Indian Rights Association, 86, 91-92, 255
Indian scouts. *See* scouts
Indian Territory, 12-13, 15-16, 18-19, 32, 46, 52, 54, 57, 79-80, 87, 89, 226, 252, 292, 327, 361
infantry. *See* First Infantry; One Hundred Second Illinois Volunteer Infantry
Inkpaduta (Santee), 286
interpreters, xxiv, 1, 2, 8-9, 11, 14-15, 17-19, 23, 26-27, 30, 32, 42-47, 50, 59, 62, 69, 75-77, 82-85, 89-90, 92, 94-95, 103, 120, 122-23, 127-28, 132, 138-40, 147, 151, 164, 170, 173, 182, 193, 196, 198, 209, 211-12, 217-19, 228, 240, 243, 248, 250, 254, 273-

483

interpreters (*continued*)
 74, 276, 278-79, 283-85, 290, 292-93, 295-97, 299, 311, 314, 319, 320, 324, 329, 333-35, 337-39, 344, 346-47, 356-57, 361, 368-69
intoxicaton. *See* alcohol consumption
Iron American (Teton Sioux); wife of, 205
Iron Bear (Teton Sioux), 25
Iron Bull (Teton Sioux), 312
Iron Cedar Woman (Teton Sioux), 307, 387 n. 17
Iron Crow (Teton Sioux), 16, 52
Iron Eyes (Teton Sioux), 200, 205; wife of, 205
Iron Eyes, Albert (Teton Sioux), 205
Iron Hawk (Teton Sioux), 52-53, 398 n. 85; interview with, 314-18
Iron Horn (Teton Sioux), 414 n. 197
Iron Horn Woman (Teton Sioux), 207
Iron Horse (Teton Sioux), 82
Irwin, James, 17, 62, 74, 76, 392 n. 50
Irwin (Major). *See* Evans, Andrew W.
Isnakiyapi (Teton Sioux), 123
Ista Gli Win (Teton Sioux), 396 n. 79
Itazap Cho Sioux, 303
Itazi Pco Sioux, 316

James (Mr.), 285
Janis Creek, 361
Janis, Antoine, 17, 104, 141
Janis, Charlie, 256-57
Janis, Dave, 106, 112
Janis, Edward: interview with, 233
Janis, Emily, 2, 106
Janis, Joseph Antoine, 367, 415 n. 212
Janis, Martha, 233, 461 n. 207
Janis, Mary, 461 n. 205
Janis, Nicholas (Tall White Man), 2, 82, 98, 103, 106, 113, 367-68, 385 n. 3, 461 n. 207; interview with wife of, 367-68
Janis, Peter, 104-6
Jarrot, Vital, 338-39
Jarrow, V. *See* Jarrot, Vital
Jarvis, Mitch, 19
Jenney, Walter P., 83, 405 n. 129
Ji Pa A (Teton Sioux), 329
Johnson, Carter P., 362, 364-66
Johnson, Lengthy, 101
Jones, William A., 104, 358
Jones, W. R., 330

Jones Creek, 367
Jordan, William H., 114, 118-19, 412 n. 178
Judkins, William L., 26
Jutz, John, 142-43, 152-53, 161-62, 416 n. 215

Kearny, Stephen Watts, 2
Keeps the Battle (Teton Sioux), 20, 42-43, 398 n. 85
Keith, E. M., 247
Kelly, Elizabeth (Mrs. Hiram; Fanny [?]), 97
Kelly, Fanny (Elizabeth [?]), 97, 409 n. 160, 457 n. 163
Kelly, Hiram, 388 n. 22
Kennington, James, 438 n. 14
Kent, J. Ford, 131, 135-36
Kent, Jacob F., 127
Keogh, Miles W., 84, 308, 310, 318, 408
Key Yah K'csar Band, Oglala; name origin of, 181
Kickapoo, 369
Kicking Bear (Teton Sioux), 7, 8, 63-64, 94, 139, 143, 145, 264, 307, 355, 387 n. 17, 399 n. 92; brother of, 400 n. 94
Kilgore (NE), 292
Kill Her White Horse (Teton Sioux), 207
Kills a Hundred (Teton Sioux), 26
Kills Crow Indian (Teton Sioux), 205
Kills in Hurry (Teton Sioux), 207
Kills in the Middle (Teton Sioux), 207
Kills One Hundred (Teton Sioux), 207
Kills Senaca Assiniboine (Teton Sioux), 205
Kills Them First (Teton Sioux), 207
Kinkaid (Mr.), 336
Kinkaid, Moses P., xiv
Kiyuksa Lakota, 232
Knife (Teton Sioux), 209
Knife Chief (Teton Sioux), 312, 314
Koerper, Egon A., 294
Kyle (SD), 196, 204, 232, 239, 325, 358, 370

La Bonte Creek, 101, 348
Lame Deer, 75, 361
Lamedeer (WY), 104
Lame Johnnie. *See* Donahue, Cornelius
Lance Creek, 3, 6
land allotment, 90, 93-94, 123, 175, 252, 353, 359-60; reaction to, 353
Lap (Teton Sioux); wife of, 204
Laparelle Creek, 101
Lapwai Agency, 319

484

INDEX

Laramie-Black Hills Trail, 47
Laramie River, 104, 279
Laravie, Helen "Nellie," 396 n. 79
Larrabee, C. F., 328
Last Child Society, 359
Last Horse, Samuel (Teton Sioux), 31, 100, 394 n. 62
Last Running (Teton Sioux), 204
Last Talking (Teton Sioux), 206
Lawrence (KS), 247
Lawson (Captain), 74
Leads, Henry, 321
Lee, Jesse M., 69, 276, 292-95, 297-99, 301-2, 356, 390 n. 36, 440 n. 38
LeGard (Doctor), 37
Leupp, Francis Ellington, 172, 423 n. 243
Lightning Creek Incident, xvi, 350, 363
Lindenberger, James, 301
liquor. *See* alcohol consumption
Little Battle (Teton Sioux), 26, 54
Little Bear (Teton Sioux), 280
Little Bighorn, xvii, 125-26, 240, 275, 281, 286, 302-5, 307, 311-12, 315-16, 320, 322, 324, 359; battle site, 45
Little Bighorn River, 320
Little Big Man (Teton Sioux), 16, 59, 63, 69-71, 73-79, 86, 101, 113, 246, 271, 272, 274, 276, 283, 288, 299-300, 332, 403 n. 108
Little Blue River, 338
Little Body Bear (Teton Sioux), 205; son of, 208; wife of, 205
Little Buckshot of the Prairie (aka Cheyenne Charley), 80-81
Little Bull (Teton Sioux), 22, 54, 207
Little Chief (Cheyenne), 360-61
Little Cloud (Teton Sioux), 207
Little Coyote (Cheyenne), 311
Little Crow (Santee) (aka His Red Nation), 188, 424 n. 254
Little Elk (Teton Sioux), 205; wife of, 205
Little Eyed Woman (Teton Sioux), 207
Little Hawk (Teton Sioux), 52, 403 n. 114, 438 n. 18
Little Shell Band, Chippewa, 184
Little White River, 77-79, 113, 301
Little Wolf (Cheyenne), 32, 36, 51, 81; interview with, 360-61
Little Wolf (Teton Sioux), 66-67, 401 n. 100
Little Wound (Teton Sioux), 6, 10, 17, 62-63, 77, 82-83, 86, 94, 132-33, 138-41, 143, 181, 208, 232, 277, 286, 350, 355, 367, 415 n. 213; aka Good Singer, 140
Little Wound, George (Teton Sioux), 240; interview with, 232-33
Little Wound, James (Teton Sioux), 232
Little Wound Creek, 232, 277
Liver Gall (Teton Sioux), 207
Loafer Band, Oglala, 5, 20, 90-91, 96, 181, 275, 284-85, 424 n. 250
Lodges (Colonel), 364
Loft, William, 381 n. 4
Log (Teton Sioux), 205; wife of, 205
Lone Bear (Teton Sioux), 25, 54, 66-67, 80-82, 84, 246, 280, 401 n. 100, 401 n. 101
Lone Cottonwood River, 122
Lone Horn (Teton Sioux), 65, 74, 82-84, 401 n. 96
Lone Man (Teton Sioux), 329
Lone Tree, 14, 85-86, 89, 326
Lone Wolf (Cheyenne), 394 n. 64
Long Bull (Teton Sioux), 201, 206-7; wife of, 206
Long Bull, Helena (Teton Sioux), 201
Long Knife; aka William Rowland, 24
Long Lake Treaty, 40
Long Mandan (Teton Sioux), 82
Long Medicine (Teton Sioux), 206
Long Whirlwind (Teton Sioux), 358
Looking Cloud (Teton Sioux), 95
Looking Glass (Nez Perce), 319
Looking Horse (Teton Sioux), 283
Looks at Him, 385 n. 1
Lost Bear (Teton Sioux), 351
Lost Bird (Teton Sioux) (Marguerite E. Colby), 229; aka Zit Ka La Nuni, 239, 429 n. 44, 430 n. 63
Low Dog (Teton Sioux), 75
Lower Brule Agency, 89, 102, 178, 370, 377
Lusk (WY), 4

Mackenzie, Ranald S., 1, 9-11, 13, 18-19, 21-22, 25-38, 44-45, 54, 96, 104, 284-85, 388 n. 26
Made a Stand (Teton Sioux), 206
Made Him Long (Teton Sioux), 206
Magpiya Luta (Teton Sioux). *See* (aka) Red Cloud
Makes the Song (Teton Sioux), 273, 397 n. 80, 403 n. 114

485

Man Above (Teton Sioux): interview with, 240–41
Man Afraid of His Horses (Teton Sioux). *See* Old Man Afraid of His Horses
Manaydier Treaty, 64
Man Himself (Teton Sioux), 207
Mann, James D., 163, 419 n. 237
Manns, Harry, 239
Man That Owns a Sword (Teton Sioux), 4
Man Who Goes in the Middle. *See* (aka) Gall
Man Who Wears the Human Necklace (Cheyenne), 51
Many Beaver Dam (Cheyenne), 23–24
Manypenny, George W., 389 n. 32, 409 n. 142; commission, 12, 87
Manypenny Treaty, 87–88
Marrivaill, Charley. *See* Merrivale, Charley
Marrivall, Joe. *See* Merrivale, Jose
Marshuska (Ute), 363
Martin, Eben W., 327
Martin (Mr.), 319
Mason, J. K., 284
Mason, Julius Wilmot, 63, 399 n. 90
Massacre Canyon, 121, 415 n. 213
Mauns, Harry, 239
Maynadier, Henry E., 400 n. 93
Mayock, Francis, 196
McCormick (Mr.), 101
McFarland, Peter, 429 n. 43
McGaa, William Denver: interview with, 248–51
McGillycuddy, Valentine T., xxv, 72, 91–92, 113, 148–49, 300, 327, 329, 403 n. 113, 417 n. 221
McGregor, James H., 208
McKenney. *See* McKinney, John A.
McKinney, John A., 31, 32, 39, 394 n. 63
McLaughlin, James, 124, 137, 145, 154, 169, 176, 413 n. 194
McWilliams, William, 232
Mears, David Y., 34, 394 n. 65
Medicine Dance (Ghost Dance), 192
medicine man: at Wounded Knee, 128–29, 134–35, 155; for Crazy Horse, 273–74, 300; Good Thunder as, 201; role in a Sun Dance, 58
Medicine Root Creek, 121, 153–54, 196, 242–45
Medicine Root District, 90, 121–22, 150, 153–54, 173, 196, 215, 232, 239, 242–43, 277, 370
medicine shows, 369
Medicine Tail Creek, 320
Melt Band, Oglala (aka Spleen Band), 105
Mercy to Others (Teton Sioux), 206
Merrivale, Charley, 271, 293; mother of, 229
Merrivale, Jose, 17, 263, 271, 293–94
Messiah, 64, 143–44, 148, 189, 254, 416 n. 216
Messiah Movement, 143, 150, 189–90, 253–54, 357
Methodist Church, xxi
Métis, 184
Middleton, Doc, 101
Miles (Agent), 285
Miles, Nelson A., 126–27, 159, 239, 241, 264, 284–85, 330, 414 n. 198
Miller, William, 350
Milner, Moses E.: aka California Joe, 342, 459 n. 177
Milwaukee Railroad, 1
Miniconjou Agency, 102
Miniconjou Sioux, 65–66, 74–75, 83, 143, 182, 192–93, 274, 303, 307, 311, 316, 330, 333, 445 n. 80; name origin, 311; word origin of, 182
Minnesota, 126
Minnesota War, 1862. *See* Dakota Conflict of 1862
Missed Not Woman (Teton Sioux), 207
missionaries, 253–54; Catholic, 160; Episcopal, 122, 135–36, 373; Protestant, 160
Missouri River, 5, 8, 12, 14, 16, 18–19, 40, 46, 52, 73–76, 78–79, 81, 83, 87, 99, 103, 138, 151, 191–92, 209, 252, 276, 283, 286, 296–97, 305, 337, 343–45, 363, 368–70
Modoc, 60
Money (Teton Sioux), 370
Moonlight, Thomas O., 338–39, 341
Morgan, Thomas J., 149, 417 n. 222
Mormons, 2, 332
Morrow River, 191
Mousseau, Louis: interview with, 226–32
Mousseau, Magloire A., 226, 256, 337; wife of, 337
Muddy Creek, 312
Mule (Teton Sioux): daughter of, 205
Mule Creek, 356, 358

INDEX

Muskrat Creek: aka Water Rat Creek, 302-3, 305
Mustang Elk (Teton Sioux), 207

Narcelle, Narcissee, 426 n. 10; ranch of, 193
Narsell, Narcisse. *See* Narcelle, Narcissee
Nebraska State Historical Society, xxii-xxiii, xxvi, 252
Necklace of Human Fingers, 37, 50-51
Neihardt, John G., 310, 359
Nelson, Peter B., 343, 459 n. 179
Newcastle (WY), 282, 350
Newcomb, Tom, 342
New Ulm Massacre, 1862. *See* Dakota Conflict of 1862
Nez Perce, 60-61, 295-96, 319, 397 n. 83; name origin, 302
Night Dance, 50
Niglicu Win (Teton Sioux), 239
Nine Mile Ranch, 101
Nines, George, 113
Ninth Cavalry, 163, 250-51, 263-64
Niobrara River, 10, 17, 19, 88, 252, 279, 302, 334, 342, 345, 369
No Bows. *See* Sans Arc Sioux
No Fat (Teton Sioux), 82
No Flesh (Teton Sioux), 65, 113, 400 n. 95
No Flesh Creek, 277
Nolan, Henry J., 184
Nolan, Paddy, 8
No Neck (Teton Sioux), 31, 54, 154
North, Frank, 10, 26, 103, 389 n. 30
North, Luther H., 10, 389 n. 30
Northern Cheyenne Agency, 177
Not Afraid of Lodge (Teton Sioux), 206
Not Go in Among (Teton Sioux), 209
No Water (Teton Sioux), 65, 75-76, 132, 195, 209, 273-74, 277, 286; wife of, 404 n. 120, 436 n. 3
Nowlan, Henry J., 424 n. 252; son of, 206

O'Bierne (Mr.), 79
O'Burn (Mr.), 79
Obyuhpe Band, Teton Sioux, 389 n. 27
Oglala Agency, 102
Oglala Scouts, 22
Oglala Sioux, 3, 5-6, 22, 29, 52, 54, 59, 61, 63-64, 66, 74, 76, 78-79, 81-82, 85-86, 92, 98-99, 102, 113, 131, 135, 141, 190, 214, 225, 233, 241-42, 244-49, 259, 273-74,
277, 280-81, 286, 288, 290, 302-5, 307, 310-11, 314-15, 325-27, 329-30, 332-37, 344, 348-49, 355, 358-59, 445 n. 80; name origin, 180
Ojibwa. *See* Chippewa
Old Black Fox, 387 n. 17
Old Hand (Teton Sioux), 196
Old Man Afraid of His Horses (Teton Sioux), 2, 19, 105, 332, 386 n. 9; name origin, 3
Old Man Bad Wound (Teton Sioux), 332
Old Man Yellow Bull (Teton Sioux), 205; wife of, 205
Old Red Feather (Teton Sioux), 399 n. 91
Old Woman (Teton Sioux), 205
Old Woman's Creek: name origin, 3
Olson, William, 381 n. 4
Omaha, 104, 140
Omaha Bee, 228, 255
Omaha Dance, 145, 171, 175
Omaha (NE), 356, 359
One Eye, Henry, 194
One Feather (Teton Sioux), 205
One Horse (Teton Sioux), 403 n. 114
One Hundred Second Illinois Volunteer Infantry, xi
One Skunk (Teton Sioux), 207
origin stories, 180
Osage, 10, 104
Osage Scouts, 10
Otoe, 10, 104
Otoe Scouts, 10
Otter Creek, 257, 259, 275
owls, 171-72
Owns Sword (Teton Sioux), 326

Paddock (Major), 19
Painted Horse (Teton Sioux), 22, 34
Palladay, Alfred, 17
Palladay, Leon, 17, 62, 83, 392 n. 47
Palmer, John, 367
Palmer, John (Mrs.). *See* Palmer, Maggie
Palmer, Maggie: interview with, 367
Palmer, William, v; interview with, 232
Papineau, William, 369
Pass Creek, 76, 78, 81, 92, 94, 145, 151, 167, 195, 213, 239, 350; aka Deep Creek, 195
Pass Creek District, 359-60
Pass Creek Indians, 151-52, 167, 172
Patton Creek, 113
Pawnee, 10-11, 21, 23, 25-26, 36, 38, 44,

487

Pawnee (*continued*)
103-4, 120-21, 140-41, 279, 281; and last battle with the Teton Sioux, 415 n. 213
Pawnee Scouts, 10, 16, 21, 26, 38, 44, 103-4, 120, 389 n. 30
Peano, William, 239, 371; interview with, 233-37
Pedro (SD), 195
Pembina River, 184
Penny, Charles G., 149-50
Peno, William, xxiv
Peoples' Independent Party, xiv
Phelps, Edwin, 253
photography, 239-40, 329, 347, 350, 430 n. 65
Picket Pin Butte, 305
Picks and Kills (Teton Sioux), 207
Pierre College, 357
Pierre (SD), 356
Pine Ridge Agency, 6, 82, 102, 127, 132, 134-37, 152, 154, 173, 197, 204, 209, 240, 243, 249, 288, 314, 350, 353, 357-59, 362, 369, 377
Pine Ridge Reservation, xv, 20, 26, 90, 134, 145, 149, 151, 189, 190, 311; conditions on, 343; Nebraska extension, 6-8, 91, 113, 387 n. 16
Platt, Parley, 370
Platte River, 2, 6, 40, 74, 79, 100, 105, 120, 334-35, 345, 355, 360; as linguistic division, 183
Plenty Horses (Teton Sioux), 170
Plenty Wolf. *See* Plenty Wolves
Plenty Wolves (Teton Sioux): aka Yankton Charley, 71, 394 n. 61
Ploughed Under, 286
Plum Creek, 191
Pocatello (ID), 190
Pole Creek, 257, 259, 305, 361
Ponca, 107, 252
Ponca Agency, 301-2, 377, 432 n. 81
Ponca Creek, 254
Ponca Reservation, 19
Poplar River Reservation, 179
Porcupine Butte, 261
Porcupine Creek, xvii, 196, 215, 242, 244, 260, 289
Porcupine Tail Creek, 131
Pourier, Baptiste, 1, 12-15, 19, 27, 29-33, 37, 42, 44, 51, 54, 60, 62, 67, 72-73, 97, 102, 104, 112, 154, 248, 250, 256-57, 288-90,

292, 300, 305, 307, 309, 367-68, 372, 398 n. 85; son-in-law of, 248
Powder River, 1, 5, 15, 22, 28, 39-40, 50, 54, 256-58, 260, 275, 305, 315, 359, 361-63
Powell, Dan, 19
Powell, John Wesley, 255, 433 n. 92
Pratt, Choteau, 370
Pratt, F. M., 292
Pratt, Richard Henry, 92, 151, 370, 408 n. 153, 418 n. 225
Pratt Commission, 151
Prazo (Prazost): aka Frank Grouard, 103
Presbyterian Academy, 357
Presbyterian Theological Seminary, 356
Presbyterians, 357; college of, 356; day school of, 355, 356
Preston, Guy, 158, 160, 262, 264
Pretty Bald Eagle (Teton Sioux), 204
Pretty Enemy (Teton Sioux), 191, 203-4, 226
Pretty Feather Woman (Teton Sioux), 358
Pretty Hawk (Teton Sioux), 204; infant of, 204; wife of, 204
Pretty Stone Buttes, 176
Pretty Woman (Teton Sioux), 204-5
Price and Jenks Ranch, 9, 56
Provost, Charley, 397 n. 81
Provost, John, 60, 256, 397 n. 81
Pugh, Robert O., 56, 94, 99, 395 n. 76
Pumpkin Buttes, 39

Quick Bear (Teton Sioux), 11

Rabbit Blanket Indians, 190
Racer (Teton Sioux), 114-15
railroads, 1, 90
Rain in the Face (Teton Sioux), 126, 314, 317, 413 n. 196
ranches, 10, 101, 104, 193, 369
Randall, Todd, 2, 83
ration issues. *See* annuities
Rattle Blanket Woman (Teton Sioux), 274, 401 n. 97, 403 n. 114, 436 n. 2
Rattling Ribs (Teton Sioux), 82
Rattling Stone Woman (Teton Sioux), 403 n. 114
Rawhide Creek, 6, 335
Really Woman (Teton Sioux), 205
Red Bear (Teton Sioux), 66, 195, 213, 238, 401 n. 99
Red Beard. *See* Dunn, John

488

INDEX

Red Cloud (Teton Sioux), 5, 6, 9-10, 12-14, 16-17, 19-21, 39-40, 45-48, 53, 57, 59-60, 62, 76-77, 79-80, 83-86, 88, 91, 98, 131-33, 152, 195, 229, 232, 235, 246, 279, 281-83, 286, 326-30, 336, 343, 347-49, 370, 409-10; band of, 66, 181, 348; brother of, 115; brother-in-law of, 115; camp of, 10, 11; daughter of, 277; delegation to Washington, 8, 9, 82-84, 104, 106, 405 n. 126, 405-6 n. 130; father of, 281; house of, 49, 234; interview with, 344-55; aka Magpiya Luta, 344; nephew of, 16; niece of, 233; son-in-law of, 107
Red Cloud, Jack (Teton Sioux), 46, 84, 142, 152, 170, 348, 416 n. 215
Red Cloud Agency, 7-9, 12-14, 20-22, 25, 35, 41, 43, 51-52, 59, 69, 71, 73-74, 79, 81-83, 85, 87-88, 97, 101, 103-4, 118, 209, 246, 276, 284, 292, 295, 298, 301, 303, 378
Red Cloud Butte, 54
Red Dog (Teton Sioux), 9, 26, 53, 62, 77, 85, 326, 389 n. 27
Red Eagle (Teton Sioux), 205
Red Ears Horse (Teton Sioux), 205
Red Eyes Horse (Teton Sioux), 205
Red Fingernail Woman (Teton Sioux), 207
Red Fish (Teton Sioux), 195, 204; wife of, 204
Red Hawk (Teton Sioux), 312-14
Red Hawk, Austin (Teton Sioux), 311-12
Red Hawk, Charles (Teton Sioux), 350, 352
Red Horn (Teton Sioux), 205; son of, 208
Red Horse (Teton Sioux), 22, 23
Red Leaf (Teton Sioux), 9-12, 21, 79, 98, 114-15, 279, 336, 348, 388 n. 25
Red Man and Helper, 350
Red Otter Woman (Teton Sioux), 205
Red River, 184
Red Shirt (Teton Sioux), 20, 22-24, 27, 34, 38, 54, 82, 91, 230, 242, 244; sister of, 190
Red Shirt Girl (Teton Sioux), 205
Red Star (Teton Sioux), 143, 190, 347
Red Top (Santee), 311
Red Water Creek, 196, 214
Red Water Woman (Teton Sioux), 204
Red White Cow (Teton Sioux), 204
Ree. *See* Arikara
Reed, Tom, 257
Reichart, Peter, 170
religion, 321

Reno, Marcus A., 15, 23, 39, 118, 125-26, 275, 277, 303-13, 316-18, 320, 322-24, 413 n. 195
Reno Creek, 305-6, 320, 324. *See also* Chasing Creek
Republican Party, xxi, 148-49
Republican River, 6, 40, 74, 81, 83, 86, 88, 102, 121
Respects Nothing (Teton Sioux), 302; aka Fears Nothing, 314; interview with, 302-7
Reynolds (Mr.), 101
Reynolds, Joseph J., 258-60, 434 n. 99
Richard, Charlie, 256
Richard, Joe, 85
Richard, John, Jr., 8, 104-9, 388 n. 22, 388 n. 24; brother-in-law of, 112
Richard, John, Sr., 17, 101
Richard, Louis, 9, 15, 19, 22, 39, 41, 44-45, 49, 82, 115-16, 256-59, 283, 433 n. 95
Richard, Peter, 248
Ricker, Albion, xv, xxiii
Ricker, Bradford W., xi
Ricker, Catherine Harmon, xi
Ricker, Eli S.: anti-Catholic sentiment of, xxii; comments on battles and massacres, 425 n. 5; marriage of, xiii
Ricker, Leslie, xiv-xvi, xx-xxi
Ricker, Margaret, xxi
Ricker, Mary, xix-xxi
Ricker Universal Cooker, xx
Riel Rebellion, 184
Riggs, A. L., 357
Riggs, T. L., 253
Ring Thunder (Teton Sioux), 82
Roan Bear (Teton Sioux), 324
Robertson, William, 227, 230; wife of, 188
Rock Creek, 301
Rocky Mountains, 2, 315
Rodgers, Alexander P., 461 n. 202
Rogers, Dave, 87
Roman Nose (Teton Sioux), 401 n. 96
Romero (Mr.), 278
Roney, Bill, 362
Roosevelt, Theodore (president), 366
Roper, Laura, 457 n. 163
Rosebud: battle of, 46, 84, 97, 322
Rosebud Agency, 102
Rosebud Creek Agency, 378
Rosebud Reservation, 90, 151, 190
Rosenquest, J. Wesley, 47, 395 n. 73

489

Ross, Amos (Santee), 174, 188; interview with, 373-74
Roubidoux, Charles, 300, 441 n. 51
Rowland, Ben, 92, 235
Rowland, William, xxiv, 23, 42, 104, 361, 391 n. 42; aka Long Knife, 24
Rowland, Willis T., 322, 324, 361
Royer, Daniel F, 98, 150, 152, 231, 418 n. 224
Ruleau, Nicholas: interview with, 311-14
Running Hawk (Teton Sioux), 207
Running in Lodge (Teton Sioux), 204
Running Standing Hairs (Teton Sioux): wife of, 205
Running Water. *See* Niobrara River
Runs After It (Teton Sioux), 207
Russell, Jack, 256, 259; wife of, 289

Sabine Creek, 1
Sage Creek, 19, 22, 256
Salaway, Frank, 103, 237, 285, 330-31, 337, 342, 344; interview with, 330-44
Salt Lake City (UT), 370
Sanborn, John B., 40, 139, 394 n. 68
Sand Creek, 301, 405 n. 124
Sans, 66, 74, 182, 316, 409
Sans Arc Sioux, 303, 401 n. 98, 445 n. 80
Santee Agency, 252, 357
Santee Sioux, 85, 94, 102, 179-80, 187, 252, 255, 285-86, 297, 311, 356, 373-74, 409, 445 n. 80; family relationships, 179; land claims, 255; name origins of, 178
Santee Uprising. *See* Dakota Conflict of 1862
Satterly, Ed, 75
Saunders, Bob, 288-89, 371; wife of, 288-90, 372
Saville, John J., 7, 59, 82-83, 87-88, 114-15, 118-20, 387 n. 17, 405 n. 128
Scabbard Knife (Teton Sioux), 205; wife of, 205
Scalp Dance, 28, 40, 50, 107, 108
scalping, 36, 107, 175, 259, 267, 281, 310, 313
Schweigerman, Peter, 273, 274
Scott's Bluff, 100, 340
Scout (Teton Sioux), 207
scouts, 10, 12-16, 18-54, 59-63, 65, 68-71, 73-78, 80-81, 89, 96-97, 99-100, 104, 120, 122, 127, 131, 138, 142, 153-55, 158, 170, 193, 196, 198, 213, 215, 217, 227-28, 237-38, 240-46, 250, 256-61, 263-68, 271, 275-76, 287, 292-93, 295, 298-99, 302, 304-5, 309, 313, 316, 319-20, 323-24, 327-28, 341, 362-66, 420-23 n. 241; organization of, 49. *See also* Sibley Scouts; Taylor's Scouts
Scraper (Teton Sioux), 28-31
Second Cavalry, 75, 105, 107
Sees The Bear (Teton Sioux), 208
Sees the Elk (Teton Sioux), 206
Sells the Pistol (Teton Sioux), 143, 145
Selwyn (Agent), 98
Semineau, Jules, 279
Seven Star Soldiers, 315
Seventh Cavalry, xv, 137-38, 149, 158, 162-63, 184, 242, 251, 260, 263
Shaggy Feather (Teton Sioux), 214-15
Shakes Bird (Teton Sioux), 201
Shakes the Bird (Teton Sioux), 205
Shangrau, John, 154, 198, 237; interview with, 256-72; wife of, 256
Shangrau, Louis, 15, 19, 22, 33, 36, 39, 41, 44-45, 49, 104-7, 110-12, 256-59, 263-64, 391 n. 42, 398 n. 85
Shangrau, Peter, 314, 329; interview with, 361-66
Shannon, Peter, 89, 92
Sharp Nose (Arapaho), 15, 17, 20, 21, 26-27, 42, 44, 390 n. 41
Sharp's carbines, 49
Sharp's rifles, 15
Shave Head (Teton Sioux), 413 n. 196
Shaw, A. G., 302
She Bear (Teton Sioux), 206
Shedding Bear (Teton Sioux), 204; mother-in-law of, 204
Sheep Mountain, 152, 251
Sheldon, Addison E., xv, xviii, xxii-xxiii, 16, 24
Shell Boy (Teton Sioux), 63
Shell Necklace (Teton Sioux), 206
Sheridan, Philip H., 45, 54, 327
Sherman, William T., 54
Shimmeno, Mitch, 256
Shively, Frank S.: interview with, 318-21
Shoot the Bear, George (Teton Sioux), 201
Shoot the Leaf Band, Santee: name origins, 180
Shoots the Bear (Teton Sioux), 205: wife of, 205
Shoots the Bear, George (Teton Sioux), 205
Shoots the Right (Teton Sioux), 204

Shoots with Hawk's Feather (Teton Sioux), 205
Short Bull (Teton Sioux), 94, 143, 145, 201-2, 215, 227, 240-41, 254, 264; camp of, 240; interview with, 189-90
Shoshone, 15-16, 22, 26, 28, 33-34, 36-39, 50-51, 54, 140, 273, 275, 279
Shoshone Scouts, 22, 26
Shot Him Off (Teton Sioux), 207
Shot in Hand (Teton Sioux), 240
Shot in the Face (Teton Sioux), 312
Shoulder (Teton Sioux), 82
Shows His Cloud (Teton Sioux), 207
Shuman, J. S., 340, 459 n. 174
Sibley, Frederick W., 409 n. 159
Sibley Scouts, 97, 305, 309
Sicangu Sioux, 181
Sidney and Black Hills Trail, 10
Sidney (NE), 10, 12, 62, 292, 408
sign language, 104, 318
Sinew Belly (Teton Sioux), 207
Sioux Bill of 1889, 402 n. 104
Sioux City (IA), 177
Sioux Jim, 96-97, 284-85
Sioux language, 297
Sioux Reservation: allotments and land cessions, 420 n. 104
Sioux Scouts, 15-16, 22, 39
Sioux Uprising. *See* Dakota Conflict of 1862
Sisseton Sioux, 102, 255, 286
Sisters of Saint Francis, 162
Sitting Bear (Teton Sioux), 25-26, 277-78
Sitting Bull (Hunkpapa), 17, 23-25, 43, 46, 52, 57, 60, 64, 74, 85, 87, 99, 103, 122, 124, 145, 153, 169, 176, 193, 201, 208-10, 242, 245, 307, 311, 314, 317, 322, 419 n. 232; nephew of, 400 n. 94; sister of, 387 n. 17
Sitting Bull (Oglala), 82, 84-85, 87-88, 104, 116, 233, 406 n. 133
Six Feather (Teton Sioux), 22
Skirt (Teton Sioux), 327
Skunk Head (Teton Sioux), 26-27
Slade Gang, 101
Sleeping Bear (Teton Sioux), 170
Slim Buttes, 20, 361; battle of, 20, 444 n. 70
Slow Bear (Teton Sioux), 107, 109
Slow Bull (Teton Sioux), 62, 77, 85
smallpox, 3
Smith (Mr.): father of Baptiste Garnier and Emma Stirk, 288

Smith, D. M., 381 n. 5
Smith, Edward P., 406 n. 132
Smith, John E., 7, 104, 120
Smith, Mary A., xii
Smith, Raymond, 94
Smoke Woman (Teton Sioux), 207
Snake. *See* Shoshone
Snake Creek, 279
Socialist Party, xxi
Sod Agency, 6, 8, 36, 84-85, 87, 100, 104-5, 248, 378
Soreback Band, Oglala, 181
Spanish language: influence on Indian speech, 183
Spencer rifles, 116, 228
Spider (Teton Sioux), 115, 412 n. 179
spiritual beliefs, 187
Spleen Band, Oglala (aka Melt Band), 105
Spotted Chief (Teton Sioux), 204
Spotted Eagle (Teton Sioux), 311
Spotted Elk (Teton Sioux), 314, 401 n. 96
Spotted Tail (Teton Sioux), 6-8, 12-14, 17-19, 32, 44, 46, 57, 60, 66, 68-69, 73-74, 76, 78, 80, 82-83, 85-86, 89, 102-3, 116, 118, 246, 271, 275-76, 279, 283, 290, 292, 294-96, 301-2, 326, 328, 336, 343-44, 346, 386 n. 15, 442 n. 58
Spotted Tail Agency, 7, 8, 12-13, 17, 19, 21, 32, 41, 43, 46, 73, 76, 79, 87, 103, 246, 271, 275, 292, 296, 297, 302, 343, 378
Spotted Thunder (Teton Sioux), 206
Spring Creek, 256, 363
squaw: discussed as derogatory term, 183
stagecoach stations, 10, 45, 47-48, 267, 269, 279
Stagner, Speed, 257
Stand, Peter (Teton Sioux), 201
Standing Bear (Ponca), 252
Standing Bear (Teton Sioux), 98, 300, 442 n. 52; interview with, 309-11; daughter of, 98
Standing Elk (Teton Sioux), 194, 208
Standing Rock Agency, 52, 85, 90, 92, 102, 122, 124, 136, 153, 169, 176, 179, 182, 315, 360, 378
Standing Rock Reservation, 145
Standing Soldier (Teton Sioux), 99-100, 153-54, 230, 233, 329, 411 n. 169; interview with, 241-47
Starr, Paddy: interview with, 237-39

St. Charles (MO), 113, 367
Stevenson, Ed, 19, 74, 78
Stinking Water Creek, 244, 301
Stirk, Emma, 371-72; interview with, 287-90
Stirk, (Mrs.) Richard. *See* Stirk, Emma
Stirk, Richard C., 102, 287-88
St. John (MN), 185
St. Louis (MO), 286, 367, 369-70
Stockville (NE), 233
Stone Hammer (Teton Sioux): wife of, 205
Stone Knife (Teton Sioux), 232
Stops Her Horse (Teton Sioux), 207
Stover, George, 230
St. Paul and Milwaukee Railroad, 90
Straight Foretop (Teton Sioux). *See* High Forehead
Strike Scatter (Teton Sioux), 206
Strong Fox (Teton Sioux), 205; wife of, 205
Stronghold, vi, 51, 152, 234, 240, 250-51
Sumner, Edwin V., 154; aka Three Fingers, 211-12, 426 n. 9, 427 n. 28
Sun Dance, 54-58, 113, 187, 417 n. 218
Sun in Pupil (Teton Sioux), 204; wife of, 204
sweat lodge: construction of, 358
Swift Bear (Teton Sioux), 70-71, 82, 254, 298-300, 432 n. 85
Swift Bird (Teton Sioux), 206; wife of, 206
Sword (brother of George Sword), 282
Sword, Archie (Teton Sioux), 318
Sword, George (Teton Sioux) (aka Chase the Animal; Hunts the Enemy), xxiv, 45, 54, 90-92, 115, 282-83, 318, 361; brother of, 4; interview with, 326-30

Tackett, Charles, 45, 69, 271, 293, 298, 395 n. 70
Taggart, Charles. *See* Tackett, Charles
Takes Away the Bow (Teton Sioux), 206
Tall Bear (aka High Bear), 441 n. 46
Tall Bull (Teton Sioux), 120, 412 n. 184, 441 n. 46
Tall White Man. *See* Janis, Nicholas
Tattooed (Teton Sioux), 207
taxation of Indians, 185
Taylor, Charles W., 138, 142, 153-55, 158, 160, 198, 240-45, 261, 264, 356, 415 n. 208
Taylor's Scouts, 138, 142, 153-55, 158, 160, 198, 240, 242-44
teepees: description of, 107
Tepee Cave, 282

Terry, Alfred H., 304, 323, 443 n. 67
Teton: word origin of, 179
Teton Sioux, xv, 1-4, 10, 12, 14-17, 22-23, 25-26, 28-29, 34-36, 38-40, 42, 44-45, 49, 51-52, 59, 66, 81, 88, 96, 102, 104, 118, 120-23, 126, 137, 140-41, 143, 154, 175, 178, 181-82, 187, 226, 231, 255, 279, 284, 286, 292, 308-9, 319, 322, 324-25, 346, 350, 353, 355, 357, 359, 363, 369-71, 374, 445 n. 80; language, 182; structure of bands, 178
Thick Ears: aka William Garnett, 100
Third Cavalry, 63
Thomas (Reverend), 66
Thomas, Eleazar, 397 n. 82
Thomas, Mary (aka Comes Out Alive), 239, 430 n. 63
Thompson (Mr.), 75
Three Bar Creek, 362, 364
Three Bears (Teton Sioux), 15, 17, 20-21, 29, 32-33, 42, 62, 77, 82, 96, 115, 390 n. 41, 398 n. 87
Three Fingers: aka Edwin V. Sumner, 211-12
Three Stars: aka George Crook, 24, 53, 92
Three Stars, Clarence (Teton Sioux), 83, 86; interview with, 344-55
Three, Henry (Teton Sioux), 204
Three-Mile Ranch, 104
Thunder Bear (Teton Sioux), 94, 139, 147
Tibbetts, Arthur, 255
Tibbitts, Ben, 19, 74, 77, 103, 116, 367; wife of, 2
Tibbitts, Emily, 2
Tinder Creek, 305
tobacco, 45, 47, 243, 244, 289, 328
Tongue River, 154, 177, 257, 275, 305, 309, 322
totems, 187
Touch the Cloud (Teton Sioux), 65-66, 68-69, 74-76, 287, 292-93, 295-300, 401 n. 96, 401 n. 97; camp of, 68
trading posts, 100-101
Trager, George E. (photographer): 239-40, 430 n. 65
Trail Creek, 303-4
trails, 2, 39, 44, 279, 341, 344
treaties and agreements: of 1851, 2, 74, 102, 279, 334-35, 345-46; of 1867, 290; of 1868, 3-5, 14, 39-40, 87, 139, 177, 245, 326, 343, 345, 354; of 1875, 302; of 1876, 13, 16, 19,

21, 59, 87, 89, 112, 177, 255, 315, 325, 345; of 1889, 68, 82, 89, 92–93, 98, 150–51; proposed with Utes, 364
treaty making: failure of, 123, 132
Trouble in Front (Teton Sioux), 204
Trouble in Love (Teton Sioux): wife of, 205
Truman, Edward, 209
Trunk Butte, 57
Tsimshian, 255
Turning Bear (Teton Sioux), 234, 276, 429 n. 53
Turning Hawk (Teton Sioux), 232
Turning Hawk, Charles (Teton Sioux): interview with, 325–26
Turtle Creek, 301–2
Turtle Mountain Reservation, 122, 137, 148, 184–85
Tut, John, 101
Twiss, Charles, 410 n. 169
Twiss, Thomas S., 2
Twist, Henry: interview with, 325
Twist, Jim, 31
Two Face (Teton Sioux), 338–39, 457 n. 163
Two Kettle Sioux, 182, 409; word origin of, 182
Two Lance (Teton Sioux), 208
Two Moons (Cheyenne): interview with, 321–25
Two Sticks (Teton Sioux), 122, 356–58

United States Department of the Interior, 13, 119, 176
United States Department of War, 13, 119
Universalist Church, xxi
Uses Bow Sioux, 311
Ute, 142, 279, 281, 361–66

visions, 145, 187
voyageurs, 178
Vroom, Peter D., 74, 87, 404 n. 118

Wabash (IN), 247
Wagon Box Fight, 329–30, 348
wagon trains, 251, 260; attacks on, 263, 282, 351
Wahpa-kuta Band, Santee: name origin, 180
Wahpeton Santee: name origins of, 180
Wahpeton (ND): name origin of, 180
wah-she-tschun: name in Lakota for Caucasians, 178

wah she tschunik: word in Lakota for the French, 178
Wajaje Sioux, 29, 77, 114–15
Walker, James R., 143, 189, 208, 425 n. 1
Walker Lake, 143
Wallace, George D., 158, 198, 200, 218, 227–28, 419 n. 235
Walters, B. F., 8
Ward, Clarence, 101, 252–53
Warm Creek, 3, 351
Warner (Senator), 92
War over the Chicken, 187. *See also* Dakota Conflict of 1862
Warrior Society, 171
Washakie (Shoshone), 22, 39
Washington DC: Crazy Horse delegation to, 246, 276, 286; delegation to, 6, 9, 16–17, 19, 22, 46–47, 53, 59, 65, 71, 74, 82–84, 86, 89, 92, 94, 104, 106, 115, 139–40, 143, 151, 278, 326–27, 344, 347, 350, 361, 366, 368; Red Cloud delegation to, 8, 9, 346
Water Rat Creek, 305; aka Muskrat Creek, 302; name origin, 302
water rights, 354
Wears Calf's Robe (Teton Sioux), 206
Wears Eagle (Teton Sioux), 208, 226
Wears Fur Coat (Teton Sioux), 207
Weasel Bear (Teton Sioux), 206
Welch, Herbert. *See* Welsh, Herbert
Wells, Aaron, 121
Wells, Bully. *See* Wells, James
Wells, James, 121–22, 126, 412 n. 187
Wells, Philip, xxiv, 86, 92, 94, 100, 130, 232, 243–44, 262, 355; interview with, 121–88; letter to Francis E. Leupp, 172; wife of, 161–62; wounding of, 95. *See also* Fox
Wells, Wallace, 121
Welsh, Herbert, 91–92
Welsh, William, 91
Wessels, Henry W., 264–65, 267–70, 435 n. 107
West Point: graduate of, 1, 127
Wet Feet (Teton Sioux), 226
Whalen, Jack, 8, 20
Wham, John W., 84–85, 98, 406 n. 134
Whetstone Agency, 5–6, 103, 106, 345, 378–79
Whipple, Henry B., 285, 439 n. 31
Whirl Wind Hawk (Teton Sioux), 204; wife of, 204

493

whiskey. *See* alcohol consumption
White, Charles (aka Buffalo Chips), 294
White American (Teton Sioux), 206
White Beaver Woman (Teton Sioux), 204
White Bird (Teton Sioux), 77, 87, 90, 319
White Clay Creek, 7, 8, 61, 79-80, 91, 107, 146, 170, 189, 203, 225, 234, 271, 276, 301
White Cow Comes Out (Teton Sioux), 207
White Cow Robe (Teton Sioux), 303
White Cow Sees (Teton Sioux), 397 n. 80
White Day (Teton Sioux), 205, 400 n. 94
White Deer (Teton Sioux), 160
White Eagle (Teton Sioux), 207
White Eagle (Yankton), 311
White Eye, Jacob (Teton Sioux): interview with, 358
White Face (Teton Sioux), 22
White Face Woman (Teton Sioux), 207
White Feather (Teton Sioux), 204
White Horse (Teton Sioux), 207
White Horse Creek, 247, 250-51, 277, 288
White Horse Troop, 77, 322
White Lance (Teton Sioux), 194, 201, 206, 209, 214-15, 222-23
White Man Runs Him (Crow), 319-20
White River, 1, 7-8, 10, 16, 19, 63-64, 75-79, 81, 86-87, 89, 113, 123, 151, 153-54, 170, 195-96, 214, 232-33, 250-51, 256, 301, 302, 307, 341, 353, 358, 367, 368, 409
White Swan (Teton Sioux), 325
White Tail (Teton Sioux), 17, 82
White Thunder (Teton Sioux), 45, 293-94, 298, 395 n. 70
White Wolf (Teton Sioux), 205
Whitfield, J. W., 335
Whitfield, R. P., 360
Whitside, Samuel M., 128-29, 154, 158-59, 196-99, 227, 233, 260, 415 n. 205
wild west shows, 20, 226, 233, 235-36, 264, 278, 369
Williams, Helen A., 191
Williams, John Buck; wife of, 191
Williamson, John P., 409
Wilson, Jocko, 190
Winchester rifles, 87, 105, 107, 109, 132, 222, 228, 247
Wind in Guts (Teton Sioux), 207
Winnebago, 10, 104, 254, 409, 433 n. 87; land claims, 255
Winnebago Scouts, 10

Winter (Teton Sioux), 205
Wi Ta Sna Un (Santee), 371
Without Robe (Teton Sioux), 205
Wolf Creek, 79-80, 97, 113, 142, 153-54, 162, 234-44, 361
Wolf Ears (Teton Sioux), 205
Wolf Ears, Edward (Teton Sioux), 205
Wolf Skin Necklace (Teton Sioux), 206
wolves, 4, 98
Woman's Dress (Teton Sioux), 20, 61-62, 66-68, 154, 265-67, 269-71, 282, 287, 362-64, 366, 398 n. 85, 401 n. 100
Women's Society Dance, 145
Wood Lice Creek, 304-5
Woodpecker Woman, 387 n. 17
Wood Shade (Teton Sioux), 205
word and name origins, 3, 6, 121, 178-83, 282, 291, 302, 311, 348
Worm (Teton Sioux), 403 n. 114, 438 n. 18
Wounded Both (Teton Sioux), 207
Wounded Hand (Teton Sioux), 198, 206
Wounded in Winter (Teton Sioux); son of, 206
Wounded Knee, vi, xv-xvii, xxiv, 19, 64, 73, 94, 99-100, 122, 126-27, 131, 133, 135-36, 138, 142, 152-55, 159-60, 162-63, 170, 174, 189, 191, 196-98, 204, 206, 208, 213-15, 217, 226-27, 230-39, 241-45, 247-48, 250-51, 256, 260-64, 277, 327, 343, 353, 357, 359, 373; article by Rex Beach, 208
Wounded Knee Creek, 20, 250, 301
Wounded Knee Monument, 427 n. 24
Wounded Knee Survivors, 206
Wounded Knee Victims, 204
Wovoka (Paiute), 416 n. 216, 425 n. 2
Wyoming, 54, 232, 249, 291, 321, 350, 363
Wyoming Incident, xvi, 350
Wyoming Live Stock Association, 249

Yankton, Creighton (Teton Sioux): interview with, 247
Yankton Agency, 102, 356, 379
Yankton Charley (Teton Sioux), 27, 73, 394 n. 61; aka Plenty Wolves, 71
Yankton Reservation, 356
Yankton Sioux, 102, 179, 187, 297, 311, 355, 445 n. 80; word origin of, 179
Yanktonai Sioux, 179, 409-10, 445 n. 80
Yates, Frank D., 61, 75, 96; aka Cut Foot, 397 n. 84

INDEX

Yates, George F.: brother of, 397 n. 84
Yellow Bear (Teton Sioux), 17, 62, 104-9, 112, 391 n. 47; mother of, 106; sister of, 106
Yellow Buffalo Calf (Teton Sioux): wife of, 205
Yellow Bull (Teton Sioux), 205
Yellow Face. *See* Half Yellow Face
Yellow Hair (Teton Sioux), 203
Yellow Hawk, Samuel (Teton Sioux), 191
Yellow Hawk, Stephen (Teton Sioux), 191
Yellow Horse (Teton Sioux), 325
Yellow Medicine Creek, 19, 76, 409
Yellow Medicine Creek Agency, 19, 252, 379
Yellow Robe (Teton Sioux), 206
Yellowstone River, 305, 360

Yellow Thunder Creek, 196
Yellow White Man (Teton Sioux), 280
You Can Eat Dog (Teton Sioux), 207
Young Bad Wound (Teton Sioux), 82; wife of, 82
Young Black Fox (Teton Sioux), 399 n. 92
Young Lady (Teton Sioux), 205
Young Man Afraid of His Horses (Teton Sioux), 3-4, 12, 16, 19, 52, 76-77, 82, 86, 115, 131-32, 146-47, 195, 279, 282-83, 329, 350, 386 n. 9
Young Men's Christian Association, 256
Young, William: interview with, 370-71

Zit Ka La Nuni (Teton Sioux). *See* Lost Bird

www.ingramcontent.com/pod-product-compliance
Lightning Source LLC
Chambersburg PA
CBHW030513230426
43665CB00010B/605